3. 69 1976

808.8

W9-BSQ-376

A St NICHOLAS ANTHOLOGY

A St. NICHOLAS ANTHOLOGY

THE EARLY YEARS

SELECTED AND EDITED BY
BURTON C. FRYE

FOREWORD BY
DR. RICHARD L. DARLING

MEREDITH PRESS / *New York*

SBN: 696-77906-4
Library of Congress Catalog Card Number: 73-91010
Manufactured in the United States of America for Meredith Press

The editor wishes to thank the staff of the New York Public Library for their assistance in his research activities.

CONTENTS

FOREWORD

THE JULY, 1873, issue of *Scribner's Monthly, an Illustrated Magazine for the People* (after October, 1881, *The Century Illustrated Monthly Magazine*) included an unsigned article, "Children's Magazines," which outlined the qualities of a good magazine for the young.[1] The author declared that "the child's magazine needs to be stronger, truer, bolder, more uncompromising" than that for adults.

> *Its cheer must be the cheer of the bird-song, not of condescending editorial babble. If it mean freshness and heartiness, and life and joy, and its words are simply, directly, and musically put together, it will trill its own way. We must not help it overmuch. In all except skillful handling of methods, we must be as little children if we would enter into this kingdom.*

This was the manifesto of Mary Mapes Dodge for *St. Nicholas: Scribner's Illustrated Magazine for Girls and Boys*, the first issue of which appeared the following November. The magazine was to have "no old, lame jokes." It would have "no sermonizing either, no wearisome spinning out of facts, nor rattling of the dry bones of history." Mrs. Dodge did not propose to exclude instruction and moral teaching, but it could not be didactic. Nor did she propose to exclude the reality of harsh and cruel facts. But when they appeared, they "must march forward boldly, say what they have to say, and go." The illustrations had to be good and real. Above all, she felt that "a child's magazine is its pleasure ground," that it must be "strong, warm, beautiful and true."

For more than thirty-two years, Mrs. Dodge, faithful to her own precepts, produced a magazine without peer. With superb taste and consummate editorial skill, she made *St. Nicholas* the world's best children's magazine and influenced the development of American children's literature in the years of its flowering. Already a successful author of children's books, *Irvington Stories* (1864) and *Hans Brinker; or, The Silver Skates* (1865), acquainted with distinguished men who had frequented her father's home, and editor of a juvenile section for the periodical *Hearth and Home*, she attracted contributions from the great and near great authors of her day. With the able editorial assistance, in the early years, of Frank R. Stockton, Mrs. Dodge created a magazine circulated to every corner of the country, and wherever English was read. From the children of the entire land, and from remote places, poured thousands of letters of gratitude, and youthful contributions to the pages of *St. Nicholas*.

The thirty-two years of Mrs. Dodge's editorship were the greatest of its years. This is the period covered in this anthology. Louisa May Alcott, Susan Coolidge, Frances Hodgson Burnett, Lucretia P. Hale, Robert Louis Stevenson, Rudyard Kipling, Sidney Lanier, and Howard Pyle are only a few of the illustrious authors and illustrators who appeared in the eagerly awaited monthly issues and the thick red annuals *St. Nicholas* brought each year at Christmastime. In ad-

---

[1] "Children's Magazines," *Scribner's Monthly*, III (July, 1873) 352-354.

dition to the best of stories and poems, the magazine provided for girls and boys songs, art and music appreciation, biography, science and natural history, and the various exciting departments. Mrs. Dodge herself conducted "Jack-in-the-Pulpit." Each issue included a "Young Contributor's Department" where many a famous writer of later days first saw his creations in print. The younger children found their fare in "For Very Little Folks." Each month brought riddles, puzzles, recipes, and directions for making a host of useful things. The frontispiece was always a handsome picture, giving promise of more within. Young readers turned eagerly to "The Letter Box" to find their own letters to *St. Nicholas.*

After Mrs. Dodge's death, in 1905, the magazine she had created and made great enjoyed a long twilight and then slowly declined, though it was not until 1939 that it finally stopped. It is the Mary Mapes Dodge years, however, that most writers have in mind when they rhapsodize about *St. Nicholas.* They represent the most sustained contribution of quality thus far in American children's literature.

There have been earlier anthologies from the pages of *St. Nicholas.* No follower of that worthy, though recently downgraded, saint will agree completely with any other that a selection from his magazine is just right. Each has his favorite story or poem whose absence from an anthology he will lament. Yet it would be ungracious to protest the absence of this or that when a whole feast has been selected.

Burton Frye has ranged through the years of *St. Nicholas,* gathering a selection of its treasures for each season from various volumes. He has organized them in four parts, Fall, Winter, Spring, and Summer, with a goodly measure of memorable work in each. Most of the best contributors are here, sometimes with their best-known stories, such as Kipling with "How the Camel Got His Hump," or Lucretia P. Hale, with one of her *Peterkin Papers.* Louisa May Alcott is represented by "An Old-Fashioned Thanksgiving," an almost forgotten story with much of the warmth and humor of her *Little Women.* Mr. Frye has chosen pictures, verse, including some of Mrs. Dodge's own, signed simply M.M.D., songs, articles, and selections from the departments. His choices from The St. Nicholas League include youthful poems of Edna St. Vincent Millay, Stephen Vincent Benet, and William Rose Benet.

The selection is a generous one, but *St. Nicholas'* thousands of pages contain many more delightful pieces. Perhaps we can hope that a subsequent volume will bring us additional delights.

Richard L. Darling

A St NICHOLAS ANTHOLOGY
FALL

CONTENTS

HOW THE CAMEL GOT HIS HUMP
By Rudyard Kipling

January, 1898

ow this is the second tale, and it tells how the camel got his big hump. In the beginning of years, when the world was so new and all, and the animals were just beginning to work for Man, there was a Camel, and he lived in the middle of a Howling Desert because he did not want to work. So he ate sticks and thorns and tamarisk and milkweed and prickles, most 'scruciating idle; and when anybody spoke to him he said, "Humph!"—just "Humph!" and no more.

Presently the Horse came to him one Monday morning, with a saddle on his back and a bit in his mouth, and said: "Camel, O Camel, come out and trot like the rest of us."

"Humph!" said the Camel; and the Horse went away and told the Man.

Presently the Dog came to him, with a stick in his mouth, and said: "Camel, O Camel, come and fetch and carry like the rest of us."

"Humph!" said the Camel; and the Dog went away and told the Man.

Presently the Ox came to him, with a yoke on his neck, and said: "Camel, O Camel, come and plow like the rest of us."

"Humph!" said the Camel; and the Ox went away and told the Man.

At the end of the day the Man called the Horse and the Dog and the Ox together, and said: "Three, O Three, I'm very sorry for you, with the world so new and all; but that Humph-thing in the desert can't work or he would have been here by now, so I am going to leave him alone, and you must work double time to make up for it."

That made the Three very angry, with the world so new and all, and they held a palaver on the edge of the desert; and the Camel came chewing milkweed *most* 'scruciating idle, and laughed at them. Then he said, "Humph!" and went away again.

Presently there came along the Djinn in charge of All Deserts, rolling in a cloud of dust (Djinns always travel that way because it is Magic), and he stopped to palaver with the Three.

"Djinn of All Deserts," said the Horse, "*is* it right for any one to be idle, with the world so new and all?"

"Certainly not," said the Djinn.

"Well," said the Horse, "there's a thing in the middle of your desert with a long neck and long legs, and he hasn't done a stroke of work since Monday morning. He won't trot."

"Whew!" said the Djinn, whistling, "that's my camel, for all the gold in Arabia! What does he say about it?"

"He says 'Humph!'" said the Dog; "and he won't fetch and carry."

"Did he say anything else?"

"Only 'Humph'; and he won't plow," said the Ox.

"Very good," said the Djinn. "I'll humph him if you will kindly wait a minute."

The Djinn rolled himself up in his dust-cloak, and took a bearing across the Desert, and found the Camel most 'scruciatingly idle, looking at his own reflection in a pool of water.

"Come hither, my tall friend," said the Djinn. "What's this I hear of your doing no work, with the world so new and all?"

"Humph!" said the Camel.

The Djinn sat down, with his chin in his hand, and began to think a Great Magic, while the Camel looked at his reflection in the pool of water.

"You've given the Three extra work ever since Monday morning, all on account of your 'scruciating idleness," said the Djinn. "Have you anything to say for yourself?"

"Humph!" said the Camel.

"You'll say that once too often," said the Djinn, and he went on thinking Magics, with his chin in his hand.

And the Camel said it again; but no sooner had he said it than he saw his back, that he was so proud of, puffing up and puffing up into a great big lollopping humph.

"Do you see that?" said the Djinn. "That's your very own humph that you've brought upon your very own self by not working. Today is Thursday, and you've done no work since Monday, when the work began. Now you are going to work."

"How can I," said the Camel, "with this humph on my back?"

"That's made a-purpose," said the Djinn, "all because you missed those three days. You will be able to work now for three days without eating, because you can live on your humph; and don't you ever say I never did anything for you. Come out of the desert and go to the Three, and behave. Humph yourself!"

And the Camel humphed himself, humph and all, and went away to join the Three. And from that day to this the Camel always wears a humph (they call it "hump" now, not to hurt his feelings); but he has never yet caught up with the three days that he missed at the beginning of the world, and he has never yet learned to behave.

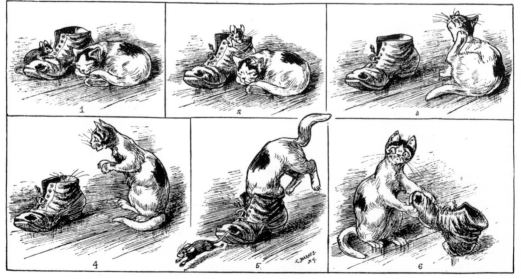

THE MISCHIEVOUS MOUSE AND THE ANGRY CAT.

AN OLD-FASHIONED THANKSGIVING

By Louisa May Alcott

November, 1881

SIXTY years ago, up among the New Hampshire hills, lived Farmer Bassett, with a houseful of sturdy sons and daughters growing up about him. They were poor in money, but rich in land and love, for the wide acres of wood, corn, and pasture land fed, warmed, and clothed the flock, while mutual patience, affection, and courage made the old farm-house a very happy home.

November had come; the crops were in, and barn, buttery, and bin were overflowing with the harvest that rewarded the summer's hard work. The big kitchen was a jolly place just now, for in the great fireplace roared a cheerful fire; on the walls hung garlands of dried apples, onions, and corn; up aloft from the beams shone crook-necked squashes, juicy hams, and dried venison—for in those days deer still haunted the deep forests, and hunters flourished. Savory smells were in the air; on the crane hung steaming kettles, and down among the red embers copper saucepans simmered, all suggestive of some approaching feast.

A white-headed baby lay in the old blue cradle that had rocked six other babies, now and then lifting his head to look out, like a round, full moon, then subsided to kick and crow contentedly, and suck the rosy apple he had no teeth to bite. Two small boys sat on the wooden settle shelling corn for popping, and picking out the biggest nuts from the goodly store their own hands had gathered in October. Four young girls stood at the long dresser, busily chopping meat, pounding spice, and slicing apples; and the tongues of Tilly, Prue, Roxy, and Rhody went as fast as their hands. Farmer Bassett, and Eph, the oldest boy, were "chorin' 'round" outside, for Thanksgiving was at hand, and all must be in order for that time-honored day.

To and fro, from table to hearth, bustled buxom Mrs. Bassett, flushed and floury, but busy and blithe as the queen bee of this busy little hive should be.

"I do like to begin seasonable and have things to my mind. Thanksgivin' dinners can't be drove, and it does take a sight of victuals to fill all these hungry stomicks," said the good woman, as she gave a vigorous stir to the great kettle of cider apple-sauce, and cast a glance of housewifely pride at the fine array of pies set forth on the buttery shelves.

"Only one more day and then it will be the time to eat. I didn't take but one bowl of hasty pudding this morning, so I shall have plenty of room when the nice things come," confided Seth to Sol, as he cracked a large hazel-nut as easily as a squirrel.

"No need of my starvin' beforehand. *I always* have room enough, and I'd like to have Thanksgiving every day," answered Solomon, gloating like a young ogre over the little pig that lay near by, ready for roasting.

"Sakes alive, I don't, boys! It's a marcy it don't come but once a year. I should be worn to a thread-paper with all this extra work atop of my winter weavin' and spinnin'," laughed their mother, as she plunged her plump arms into the long bread-trough and began to knead the dough as if a famine were at hand.

Tilly, the oldest girl, a red-cheeked, black-eyed lass of fourteen, was grinding briskly at the mortar, for spices were costly, and not a grain must be wasted. Prue kept time with the chopper, and the twins sliced away at the apples till their little brown arms ached, for all knew how to work, and did so now with a will.

"I think it's real fun to have Thanksgiving at home. I'm sorry Gran'ma is sick, so we can't go there as usual, but I like to mess 'round here, don't you, girls?" asked Tilly, pausing to take a sniff at the spicy pestle.

"It will be kind of lonesome with only our own folks." "I like to see all the cousins and aunts, and have games, and sing," cried the twins, who were regular little romps, and could run, swim, coast, and shout as well as their brothers.

"I don't care a mite for all that. It will be so nice to eat dinner together, warm and comfortable at home," said quiet Prue, who loved her own cozy nooks like a cat.

"Come, girls, fly 'round and get your chores done, so we can clear away for dinner jest as soon as I clap my bread into the oven," called Mrs. Bassett presently, as she rounded off the last loaf of brown bread which was to feed the hungry mouths that seldom tasted any other.

"Here's a man comin' up the hill lively!" "Guess it's Gad Hopkins. Pa told him to bring a dezzen oranges, if they warn't too high!" shouted Sol and Seth, running to the door, while the girls smacked their lips at the thought of this rare treat, and Baby threw his apple overboard, as if getting ready for a new cargo.

But all were doomed to disappointment, for it was not Gad, with the much-desired fruit. It was a stranger, who threw himself off his horse and hurried up to Mr. Bassett in the yard, with some brief message that made the farmer drop his ax and look so sober that his wife guessed at once some bad news had come; and crying, "Mother's wuss! I know she is!" out ran the good

woman, forgetful of the flour on her arms and the oven waiting for its most important batch.

The man said old Mr. Chadwick, down to Keene, stopped him as he passed, and told him to tell Mrs. Bassett her mother was failin' fast, and she'd better come to-day. He knew no more, and having delivered his errand he rode away, saying it looked like snow and he must be jogging, or he wouldn't get home till night.

"We must go right off, Eldad. Hitch up, and I'll be ready in less'n no time," said Mrs. Bassett, wasting not a minute in tears and lamentations, but pulling off her apron as she went in, with her head in a sad jumble of bread, anxiety, turkey, sorrow, haste, and cider apple-sauce.

A few words told the story, and the children left their work to help her get ready, mingling their grief for "Gran'ma" with regrets for the lost dinner.

"I'm dreadful sorry, dears, but it can't be helped. I couldn't cook nor eat no way now, and if that blessed woman gets better sudden, as she has before, we'll have cause for thanksgivin', and I'll give you a dinner you won't forget in a hurry," said Mrs. Bassett, as she tied on her brown silk pumpkin-hood, with a sob for the good old mother who had made it for her.

Not a child complained after that, but ran about helpfully, bringing moccasins, heating the footstone, and getting ready for a long drive, because Gran'ma lived twenty miles away, and there were no railroads in those parts to whisk people to and fro like magic. By the time the old yellow sleigh was at the door, the bread was in the oven, and Mrs. Bassett was waiting, with her camlet cloak on, and the baby done up like a small bale of blankets.

"Now, Eph, you must look after the cattle like a man, and keep up the fires, for there's a storm brewin', and neither the children nor dumb critters must suffer," said Mr. Bassett, as he turned up the collar of his rough coat and put on his blue mittens, while the old mare shook her bells as if she preferred a trip to Keene to hauling wood all day.

"Tilly, put extry comfortables on the beds to-night, the wind is so searchin' up chamber. Have the baked beans and Injun-puddin' for dinner, and whatever you do, don't let the boys git at the mince-pies, or you'll have them down sick. I shall come back the minute I can leave Mother. Pa will come to-morrer anyway, so keep snug and be good. I depend on you, my darter; use your jedgment, and don't let nothin' happen while Mother's away."

"Yes'm, yes'm—good-bye, good-bye!" called the children, as Mrs. Bassett was packed into the sleigh and driven away, leaving a stream of directions behind her.

Eph, the sixteen-year-old boy, immediately put on his biggest boots, assumed a sober, responsible manner, and surveyed his little responsibilities with a paternal air, drolly like his father's. Tilly tied on her mother's bunch of keys, rolled up the sleeves of her homespun gown, and began to order about the younger girls. They soon forgot poor Granny, and found it great fun to keep house all alone, for Mother seldom left home, but ruled her family in the good old-fashioned way. There were no servants, for the little daughters were Mrs. Bassett's only maids, and the stout boys helped their father, all working happily together with no wages but love; learning in the best manner the use of the heads and hands with which they were to make their own way in the world.

The few flakes that caused the farmer to predict bad weather soon increased to a regular snowstorm, with gusts of wind, for up among the hills winter came early and

lingered long. But the children were busy, gay, and warm in-doors, and never minded the rising gale nor the whirling white storm outside.

Tilly got them a good dinner, and when it was over the two elder girls went to their spinning, for in the kitchen stood the big and little wheels, and baskets of wool-rolls, ready to be twisted into yarn for the winter's knitting, and each day brought its stint of work to the daughters, who hoped to be as thrifty as their mother.

Eph kept up a glorious fire, and superintended the small boys, who popped corn and whittled boats on the hearth; while Roxy and Rhody dressed corn-cob dolls in the settle corner, and Bose, the brindled mastiff, lay on the braided mat, luxuriously warming his old legs. Thus employed, they made a pretty picture, these rosy boys and girls, in their homespun suits, with the rustic toys or tasks which most children nowadays would find very poor or tiresome.

Tilly and Prue sang, as they stepped to and fro, drawing out the smoothly twisted threads to the musical hum of the great spinning-wheels. The little girls chattered like magpies over their dolls and the new bed-spread they were planning to make, all white dimity stars on a blue calico ground, as a Christmas present to Ma. The boys roared at Eph's jokes, and had rough and tumble games over Bose, who didn't mind them in the least; and so the afternoon wore pleasantly away.

At sunset the boys went out to feed the cattle, bring in heaps of wood, and lock up for the night, as the lonely farm-house seldom had visitors after dark. The girls got the simple supper of brown bread and milk, baked apples, and a doughnut all 'round as a treat. Then they sat before the fire, the sisters knitting, the brothers with books or games, for Eph loved reading, and Sol and

Seth never failed to play a few games of Morris with barley corns, on the little board they had made themselves at one corner of the dresser.

"Read out a piece," said Tilly from Mother's chair, where she sat in state, finishing off the sixth woolen sock she had knit that month.

"It's the old history book, but here's a bit you may like, since it's about our folks," answered Eph, turning the yellow page to look at a picture of two quaintly dressed children in some ancient castle.

"Yes, read that. I always like to hear about the Lady Matildy I was named for, and Lord Bassett, Pa's great-great-great-grandpa. He's only a farmer now, but it's nice to know we were somebody two or three hundred years ago," said Tilly, bridling and tossing her curly head as she fancied the Lady Matilda might have done.

"Don't read the queer words, 'cause we don't understand 'em. Tell it," commanded Roxy, from the cradle, where she was drowsily cuddled with Rhody.

"Well, a long time ago, when Charles the First was in prison, Lord Bassett was a true friend to him," began Eph, plunging into his story without delay. "The lord had some papers that would have hung a lot of people if the king's enemies got hold of 'em, so when he heard one day, all of a sudden, that soldiers were at the castle-gate to carry him off, he had just time to call his girl to him, and say: 'I may be going to my death, but I won't betray my master. There is no time to burn the papers, and I can not take them with me; they are hidden in the old leathern chair where I sit. No one knows this but you, and you must guard them till I come or send you a safe messenger to take them away. Promise me to be brave and silent, and I can go without fear.' You see, he wasn't afraid to die, but he *was* to seem a traitor. Lady Matildy promised solemnly, and the words were hardly out

of her mouth when the men came in, and her father was carried away a prisoner and sent off to the Tower."

"But she didn't cry; she just called her brother, and sat down in that chair, with her head leaning back on those papers, like a queen, and waited while the soldiers hunted the house over for 'em: wasn't that a smart girl?" cried Tilly, beaming with pride, for she was named for this ancestress, and knew the story by heart.

"I reckon she was scared, though, when the men came swearin' in and asked her if she knew anything about it. The boy did his part then, for *he* didn't know, and fired up and stood before his sister; and he says, says he, as bold as a lion: 'If my lord had told us where the papers be, we would die before we would betray him. But we are children and know nothing, and it is cowardly of you to try to fight us with oaths and drawn swords!' "

As Eph quoted from the book, Seth planted himself before Tilly, with the long poker in his hand, saying, as he flourished it valiantly:

"Why didn't the boy take his father's sword and lay about him? I would, if any one was ha'sh to Tilly."

"You bantam! he was only a bit of a boy, and couldn't do anything. Sit down and hear the rest of it," commanded Tilly, with a pat on the yellow head, and a private resolve that Seth should have the largest piece of pie at dinner next day, as reward for his chivalry.

"Well, the men went off after turning the castle out of window, but they said they should come again; so faithful Matildy was full of trouble, and hardly dared to leave the room where the chair stood. All day she sat there, and at night her sleep was so full of fear about it, that she often got up and went to see that all was safe. The servants thought the fright had hurt her wits, and let her be, but Rupert, the boy, stood by her and never was afraid of her queer ways. She was 'a pious maid,' the book says, and often spent the long evenings reading the Bible, with her brother by her, all alone in the great room, with no one to help her bear her secret, and no good news of her father. At last, word came that the king was dead and his friends banished out of England. Then the poor children were in a sad plight, for they had no mother, and the servants all ran away, leaving only one faithful old man to help them."

"But the father did come?" cried Roxy, eagerly.

"You'll see," continued Eph, half telling, half reading.

"Matilda was sure he would, so she sat on in the big chair, guarding the papers, and no one could get her away, till one day a man came with her father's ring and told her to give up the secret. She knew the ring, but would not tell until she had asked many questions, so as to be very sure, and while the man answered all about her father and the king, she looked at him sharply. Then she stood up and said, in a tremble, for there was something strange about the man: 'Sir, I doubt you in spite of the ring, and I will not answer till you pull off the false beard you wear, that I may see your face and know if you are my father's friend or foe.' Off came the disguise, and Matilda found it was my lord himself, come to take them with him out of England. He was very proud of that faithful girl, I guess, for the old chair still stands in the castle, and the name keeps in the family, Pa says, even over here, where some of the Bassetts came along with the Pilgrims."

"Our Tilly would have been as brave, I know, and she looks like the old picter down to Gran'ma's, don't she, Eph?" cried Prue, who admired her bold, bright sister very much.

"Well, I think you'd do the settin' part best, Prue, you are so patient. Till would fight like a wild cat, but she can't hold her tongue worth a cent," answered Eph; whereat Tilly pulled his hair, and the story ended with a general frolic.

When the moon-faced clock behind the door struck nine, Tilly tucked up the children under the "extry comfortables," and having kissed them all around, as Mother did, crept into her own nest, never minding the little drifts of snow that sifted in upon her coverlet between the shingles of the roof, nor the storm that raged without.

As if he felt the need of unusual vigilance, old Bose lay down on the mat before the door, and pussy had the warm hearth all to herself. If any late wanderer had looked in at midnight, he would have seen the fire blazing up again, and in the cheerful glow the old cat blinking her yellow eyes, as she sat bolt upright beside the spinning-wheel, like some sort of household goblin, guarding the children while they slept.

When they woke, like early birds, it still snowed, but up the little Bassetts jumped, broke the ice in their jugs, and went down with cheeks glowing like winter apples, after a brisk scrub and scramble into their clothes. Eph was off to the barn, and Tilly soon had a great kettle of mush ready, which, with milk warm from the cows made a wholesome breakfast for the seven hearty children.

"Now about dinner," said the young housekeeper, as the pewter spoons stopped clattering, and the earthen bowls stood empty.

"Ma said, have what we liked, but she didn't expect us to have a real Thanksgiving dinner, because she won't be here to cook it, and we don't know how," began Prue, doubtfully.

"I can roast a turkey and make a pudding as well as anybody, I guess. The pies are all ready, and if we can't boil vegetables and so on, we don't deserve any dinner," cried Tilly, burning to distinguish herself, and bound to enjoy to the utmost her brief authority.

"Yes, yes!" cried all the boys, "let's have a dinner anyway; Ma won't care, and the good victuals will spoil if they ain't eaten right up."

"Pa is coming to-night, so we won't have dinner till late; that will be real genteel and give us plenty of time," added Tilly, suddenly realizing the novelty of the task she had undertaken.

"Did you ever roast a turkey?" asked Roxy, with an air of deep interest.

"Should you darst to try?" said Rhody, in an awe-stricken tone.

"You will see what I can do. Ma said I was to use my judgment about things, and I'm going to. All you children have got to do is to keep out of the way, and let Prue and me work. Eph, I wish you'd put a fire in the best room, so the little ones can play in there. We shall want the settin'-room for the table, and I won't have them pickin' 'round when we get things fixed," commanded Tilly, bound to make her short reign a brilliant one.

"I don't know about that. Ma didn't tell us to," began cautious Eph who felt that this invasion of the sacred best parlor was a daring step.

"Don't we always do it Sundays and Thanksgivings? Wouldn't Ma wish the children kept safe and warm anyhow? Can I get up a nice dinner with four rascals under my feet all the time? Come, now, if you want roast turkey and onions, plum-puddin' and mince-pie, you'll have to do as I tell you, and be lively about it."

Tilly spoke with such spirit, and her suggestion was so irresistible, that Eph gave in, and, laughing good-naturedly, tramped away to heat up the best room, devoutly hoping that nothing serious would happen to punish such audacity.

The young folks delightedly trooped away to destroy the order of that prim apartment with housekeeping under the black horse-hair sofa, "horseback-riders" on the arms of the best rocking-chair, and an Indian war-dance all over the well-waxed furniture. Eph, finding the society of peaceful sheep and cows more to his mind than that of two excited sisters, lingered over his chores in the barn as long as possible, and left the girls in peace.

Now Tilly and Prue were in their glory, and as soon as the breakfast-things were out of the way, they prepared for a grand cooking-time. They were handy girls, though they had never heard of a cooking-school, never touched a piano, and knew nothing of embroidery beyond the samplers which hung framed in the parlor; one ornamented with a pink mourner under a blue weeping-willow, the other with this pleasing verse, each word being done in a different color, which gave the effect of a distracted rainbow:

This sampler neat was worked by me,
In my twelfth year, Prudence B.

Both rolled up their sleeves, put on their largest aprons, and got out all the spoons, dishes, pots, and pans they could find, "so as to have everything handy," Prue said.

"Now, sister, we'll have dinner at five; Pa will be here by that time, if he is coming to-night, and be so surprised to find us all ready, for he won't have had any very nice victuals if Gran'ma is so sick," said Tilly, importantly. "I shall give the children a piece at noon" (Tilly meant luncheon); "doughnuts and cheese, with apple-pie and cider, will please 'em. There's beans for Eph; he likes cold pork, so we won't stop to warm it up, for there's lots to do, and I don't mind saying to you I'm dreadful dubersome about the turkey."

"It's all ready but the stuffing, and roasting is as easy as can be. I can baste first-rate. Ma always likes to have me, I'm so patient and stiddy, she says," answered Prue, for the responsibility of this great undertaking did not rest upon her, so she took a cheerful view of things.

"I know, but it's the stuffin' that troubles me," said Tilly, rubbing her round elbows as she eyed the immense fowl laid out on a platter before her. "I don't know how much I want, nor what sort of yarbs to put in, and he's so awful big, I'm kind of afraid of him."

"I ain't! I fed him all summer, and he never gobbled at *me*. I feel real mean to be thinking of gobbling him, poor old chap," laughed Prue, patting her departed pet with an air of mingled affection and appetite.

"Well, I'll get the puddin' off my mind fust, for it ought to bile all day. Put the big kettle on, and see that the spit is clean, while I get ready."

Prue obediently tugged away at the crane, with its black hooks, from which hung the iron tea-kettle and three-legged pot; then she settled the long spit in the grooves made for it in the tall andirons, and put the dripping-pan underneath, for in those days meat was roasted as it should be, not baked in ovens.

Meantime Tilly attacked the plum-pudding. She felt pretty sure of coming out right, here, for she had seen her mother do it so many times, it looked very easy. So in went suet and fruit; all sorts of spice, to be sure she got the right ones, and brandy instead of wine. But she forgot both sugar and salt, and tied it in the cloth so tightly that it had no room to swell, so it would come out as heavy as lead and as hard as a

cannon-ball, if the bag did not burst and spoil it all. Happily unconscious of these mistakes, Tilly popped it into the pot, and proudly watched it bobbing about before she put the cover on and left it to its fate.

"I can't remember what flavorin' Ma puts in," she said, when she had got her bread well soaked for the stuffing. "Sage and onions and applesauce go with goose, but I can't feel sure of anything but pepper and salt for a turkey."

"Ma puts in some kind of mint, I know, but I forget whether it is spearmint, peppermint, or pennyroyal," answered Prue, in a tone of doubt, but trying to show her knowledge of "yarbs," or, at least, of their names.

"Seems to me it's sweet marjoram or summer savory. I guess we'll put both in, and then we are sure to be right. The best is up garret; you run and get some, while I mash the bread," commanded Tilly, diving into the mess.

Away trotted Prue, but in her haste she got catnip and wormwood, for the garret was darkish, and Prue's little nose was so full of the smell of the onions she had been peeling, that everything smelt of them. Eager to be of use, she pounded up the herbs and scattered the mixture with a liberal hand into the bowl.

"It doesn't smell just right, but I suppose it will when it is cooked," said Tilly, as she filled the empty stomach, that seemed aching for food, and sewed it up with the blue yarn, which happened to be handy. She forgot to tie down his legs and wings, but she set him by till his hour came, well satisfied with her work.

"Shall we roast the little pig, too? I think he'd look nice with a necklace of sausages, as Ma fixed him at Christmas," asked Prue, elated with their success.

"I couldn't do it. I loved that little pig,

and cried when he was killed. I should feel as if I was roasting the baby," answered Tilly, glancing toward the buttery where piggy hung, looking so pink and pretty it certainly did seem cruel to eat him.

It took a long time to get all the vegetables ready, for, as the cellar was full, the girls thought they would have every sort. Eph helped, and by noon all was ready for cooking, and the cranberry-sauce, a good deal scorched, was cooking in the lean-to.

Luncheon was a lively meal, and doughnuts and cheese vanished in such quantities that Tilly feared no one would have an appetite for her sumptuous dinner. The boys assured her they would be starving by five o'clock, and Sol mourned bitterly over the little pig that was not to be served up.

"Now you all go and coast, while Prue and I set the table and get out the best chiny," said Tilly, bent on having her dinner look well, no matter what its other failings might be.

Out came the rough sleds, on went the round hoods, old hats, red cloaks, and moccasins, and away trudged the four younger Bassetts, to disport themselves in the snow, and try the ice down by the old mill, where the great wheel turned and splashed so merrily in the summer-time.

Eph took his fiddle and scraped away to his heart's content in the parlor, while the girls, after a short rest, set the table and made all ready to dish up the dinner when that exciting moment came. It was not at all the sort of table we see now, but would look very plain and countrified to us, with its green-handled knives, and two-pronged steel forks; its red-and-white china, and pewter platters, scoured till they shone, with mugs and spoons to match, and a brown jug for the cider. The cloth was coarse, but white as snow, and the little maids had seen the blue-eyed flax grow, out of which their mother wove the linen; they had watched and watched while it bleached

in the green meadow. They had no napkins and little silver; but the best tankard and Ma's few wedding-spoons were set forth in state. Nuts and apples at the corners gave an air, and the place of honor was left in the middle for the oranges yet to come.

"Don't it look beautiful?" said Prue, when they paused to admire the general effect.

"Pretty nice, I think. I wish Ma could see how well we can do it," began Tilly, when a loud howling startled both girls, and sent them flying to the window. The short afternoon had passed so quickly that twilight had come before they knew it, and now, as they looked out through the gathering dusk, they saw four small black figures tearing up the road, to come bursting in, all screaming at once: "The bear, the bear! Eph, get the gun! He's coming, he's coming!"

Eph had dropped his fiddle, and got down his gun before the girls could calm the children enough to tell their story, which they did in a somewhat incoherent manner. "Down in the holler, coastin', we heard a growl," began Sol, with his eyes as big as saucers. "I see him fust lookin' over the wall," roared Seth, eager to get his share of honor.

"Awful big and shaggy," quavered Roxy, clinging to Tilly, while Rhody hid in Prue's skirts, and piped out: "His great paws kept clawing at us, and I was so scared my legs would hardly go."

"We ran away as fast as we could go, and he came growlin' after us. He's awful hungry, and he'll eat every one of us if he gets in," continued Sol, looking about him for a safe retreat.

"Oh, Eph, don't let him eat us," cried both little girls, flying upstairs to hide under their mother's bed, as their surest shelter.

"No danger of that, you little geese. I'll shoot him as soon as he comes. Get out of the way, boys," and Eph raised the window to get good aim.

"There he is! Fire away, and don't miss!" cried Seth, hastily following Sol, who had climbed to the top of the dresser as a good perch from which to view the approaching fray.

Prue retired to the hearth as if bent on dying at her post rather than desert the turkey, now "browning beautiful," as she expressed it. But Tilly boldly stood at the open window, ready to lend a hand if the enemy proved too much for Eph.

All had seen bears, but none had ever come so near before, and even brave Eph felt that the big brown beast slowly trotting up the door-yard was an unusually formidable specimen. He was growling horribly, and stopped now and then as if to rest and shake himself.

"Get the ax, Tilly, and if I should miss, stand ready to keep him off while I load again," said Eph, anxious to kill his first bear in style and alone; a girl's help didn't count.

Tilly flew for the ax, and was at her brother's side by the time the bear was near enough to be dangerous. He stood on his hind legs, and seemed to sniff with relish the savory odors that poured out of the window.

"Fire, Eph!" cried Tilly, firmly.

"Wait till he rears again. I'll get a better shot then," answered the boy, while Prue covered her ears to shut out the bang, and the small boys cheered from their dusty refuge up among the pumpkins.

But a very singular thing happened next, and all who saw it stood amazed, for suddenly Tilly threw down the ax, flung open the door, and ran straight into the arms of the bear, who stood erect to receive her, while his growlings changed to a loud "Haw, haw!" that startled the children more than the report of a gun.

"It's Gad Hopkins, tryin' to fool us!" cried Eph, much disgusted at the loss of his prey, for these hardy boys loved to hunt, and prided themselves on the number of wild animals and birds they could shoot in a year.

"Oh, Gad, how could you scare us so?" laughed Tilly, still held fast in one shaggy arm of the bear, while the other drew a dozen oranges from some deep pocket in the buffalo-skin coat, and fired them into the kitchen with such good aim that Eph ducked, Prue screamed, and Sol and Seth came down much quicker than they went up.

"Wal, you see I got upsot over yonder, and the old horse went home while I was floundering in a drift, so I tied on the buffalers to tote 'em easy, and come along till I see the children playin' in the holler. I jest meant to give 'em a little scare, but they run like partridges, and I kep' up the joke to see how Eph would like this sort of company," and Gad haw-hawed again.

"You'd have had a warm welcome if we hadn't found you out. I'd have put a bullet through you in a jiffy, old chap," said Eph, coming out to shake hands with the young giant, who was only a year or two older than himself.

"Come in and set up to dinner with us. Prue and I have done it all ourselves, and Pa will be along soon, I reckon," cried Tilly, trying to escape.

"Couldn't, no ways. My folks will think I'm dead ef I don't get along home, sence the horse and sleigh have gone ahead empty. I've done my arrant and had my joke; now I want my pay, Tilly," and Gad took a hearty kiss from the rosy cheeks of his "little sweetheart," as he called her. His own cheeks tingled with the smart slap she gave him as she ran away, calling out that she hated bears and would bring her ax next time.

"I ain't afeared—your sharp eyes found me out; and ef you run into a bear's arms you must expect a hug," answered Gad, as he pushed back the robe and settled his fur cap more becomingly.

"I should have known you in a minute if I hadn't been asleep when the girls squalled. You did it well, though, and I advise you not to try it again in a hurry, or you'll get shot," said Eph, as they parted, he rather crestfallen and Gad in high glee.

"My sakes alive—the turkey is all burnt one side, and the kettles have biled over so the pies I put to warm are all ashes!" scolded Tilly, as the flurry subsided and she remembered her dinner.

"Well, I can't help it. I couldn't think of victuals when I expected to be eaten alive myself, could I?" pleaded poor Prue, who had tumbled into the cradle when the rain of oranges began.

Tilly laughed, and all the rest joined in, so good-humor was restored, and the spirits of the younger ones were revived by sucks from the one orange which passed from hand to hand with great rapidity while the older girls dished up the dinner. They were just struggling to get the pudding out of the cloth when Roxy called out: "Here's Pa!"

"There's folks with him," added Rhody.

"Lots of 'em! I see two big sleighs chock full," shouted Seth, peering through the dusk.

"It looks like a semintary. Guess Gran-'ma's dead and come up to be buried here," said Sol, in a solemn tone. This startling suggestion made Tilly, Prue, and Eph hasten to look out, full of dismay at such an ending of their festival.

"If that is a funeral, the mourners are uncommonly jolly," said Eph, dryly, as merry voices and loud laughter broke the white silence without.

"I see Aunt Cinthy, and Cousin Hetty —and there's Mose and Amos. I do declare, Pa's bringin' 'em all home to have some fun here," cried Prue, as she recognized one familiar face after another.

"Oh, my patience! Ain't I glad I got dinner, and don't I hope it will turn out good!" exclaimed Tilly, while the twins pranced with delight, and the small boys roared:

"Hooray for Pa! Hooray for Thanksgivin'!"

The cheer was answered heartily, and in came Father, Mother, Baby, aunts, and cousins, all in great spirits, and all much surprised to find such a festive welcome awaiting them.

"Ain't Gran'ma dead at all?" asked Sol, in the midst of the kissing and handshaking.

"Bless your heart, no! It was all a mistake of old Mr. Chadwick's. He's as deaf as an adder, and when Mrs. Brooks told him Mother was mendin' fast, and she wanted me to come down to-day, certain sure, he got the message all wrong, and give it to the fust person passin' in such a way as to scare me 'most to death, and send us down in a hurry. Mother was sittin' up as chirk as you please, and dreadful sorry you didn't all come."

"So, to keep the house quiet for her, and give you a taste of the fun, your Pa fetched us all up to spend the evenin', and we are goin' to have a jolly time on't, to jedge by the looks of things," said Aunt Cinthy, briskly finishing the tale when Mrs. Bassett paused for want of breath.

"What in the world put it into your head we was comin', and set you to gittin' up such a supper?" asked Mr. Bassett, looking about him, well pleased and much surprised at the plentiful table.

Tilly modestly began to tell, but the others broke in and sang her praises in a sort of chorus, in which bears, pigs, pies, and oranges were oddly mixed. Great satisfaction was expressed by all, and Tilly and Prue were so elated by the commendation of Ma and the aunts, that they set forth their dinner, sure everything was perfect.

But when the eating began, which it did the moment wraps were off, then their pride got a fall; for the first person who tasted the stuffing (it was big Cousin Mose, and that made it harder to bear) nearly choked over the bitter morsel.

"Tilly Bassett, whatever made you put wormwood and catnip in your stuffin'?" demanded Ma, trying not to be severe, for all the rest were laughing, and Tilly looked ready to cry.

"I did it," said Prue, nobly taking all the blame, which caused Pa to kiss her on the spot, and declare that it didn't do a mite of harm, for the turkey was all right.

"I never see onions cooked better. All the vegetables is well done, and the dinner a credit to you, my dears," declared Aunt Cinthy, with her mouth full of the fragrant vegetable she praised.

The pudding was an utter failure in spite of the blazing brandy in which it lay—as hard and heavy as one of the stone balls on Squire Dunkin's great gate. It was speedily whisked out of sight, and all fell upon the pies, which were perfect. But Tilly and Prue were much depressed, and didn't recover their spirits till dinner was over and the evening fun well under way.

"Blind-man's bluff," "Hunt the slipper," "Come, Philander," and other lively games soon set every one bubbling over with jollity, and when Eph struck up "Money Musk" on his fiddle, old and young fell into their places for a dance. All down the long kitchen they stood, Mr. and Mrs. Bassett at the top, the twins at the bottom, and then away they went, heeling and toeing, cutting pigeon-wings, and taking their steps in a way that would convulse modern children with their new-fangled romps called dancing. Mose and Tilly covered themselves with glory by the vigor with which they kept it up, till fat Aunt Cinthy fell into a chair, breathlessly declaring that a very little of such exercise was enough for a woman of her "heft."

Apples and cider, chat and singing, finished the evening, and after a grand kissing all round, the guests drove away in the clear moonlight which came out to cheer their long drive.

When the jingle of the last bell had died away, Mr. Bassett said soberly, as they stood together on the hearth: "Children, we have special cause to be thankful that the sorrow we expected was changed into joy, so we'll read a chapter 'fore we go to bed, and give thanks where thanks is due."

Then Tilly set out the light-stand with the big Bible on it, and a candle on each side, and all sat quietly in the fire-light, smiling as they listened with happy hearts to the sweet old words that fit all times and seasons so beautifully.

When the good-nights were over, and the children in bed, Prue put her arm round Tilly and whispered tenderly, for she felt her shake, and was sure she was crying:

"Don't mind about the old stuffin' and puddin', deary—nobody cared, and Ma said we really did do surprisin' well for such young girls."

The laughter Tilly was trying to smother broke out then, and was so infectious, Prue could not help joining her, even before she knew the cause of the merriment.

"I was mad about the mistakes, but don't care enough to cry. I'm laughing to think how Gad fooled Eph and I found him out. I thought Mose and Amos would have died over it, when I told them, it was so funny," explained Tilly, when she got her breath.

"I was so scared that when the first orange hit me, I thought it was a bullet, and scrabbled into the cradle as fast as I could.

It was real mean to frighten the little ones so," laughed Prue, as Tilly gave a growl.

Here a smart rap on the wall of the next room caused a sudden lull in the fun, and Mrs. Bassett's voice was heard, saying warningly, "Girls, go to sleep immediate, or you'll wake the baby."

"Yes'm," answered two meek voices, and after a few irrepressible giggles, silence reigned, broken only by an occasional snore from the boys, or the soft scurry of mice in the buttery, taking their part in this old-fashioned Thanksgiving.

"A HAPPY THANKSGIVING TO YOU!"

GRIZEL COCHRANE'S RIDE

By Elia W. Peattie

February, 1887

IN the midsummer of 1685, the hearts of the people of old Edinburgh were filled with trouble and excitement. King Charles the Second, of England, was dead, and his brother, the Duke of York, reigned in his stead to the dissatisfaction of a great number of the people.

The hopes of this class lay with the young Duke of Monmouth, the ambitious and disinherited son of Charles the Second, who, on account of the King's displeasure, had been living for some time at foreign courts. On hearing of the accession of his uncle, the Duke of York, to the throne, Monmouth yielded to the plans of the English and Scottish lords who favored his own pretensions, and prepared to invade England with a small but enthusiastic force of men.

The Duke of Argyle, the noblest lord of Scotland, who also was an exile, undertook to conduct the invasion at the north, while Monmouth should enter England at the west, gather the yeomanry about him and form a triumphant conjunction with Argyle in London, and force the "usurper," as

they called King James the Second, from his throne.

Both landings were duly made. The power of Monmouth's name and rank rallied to his banner at first a large number of adherents; but their defeat at Sedgemoor put an end to his invasion. And the Duke of Argyle, a few days after his landing in Scotland, was met by a superior force of the King's troops. Retreating into a morass, his soldiers were scattered and dispersed. Many of his officers deserted him in a panic of fear. The brave old nobleman himself was taken prisoner, and beheaded at Edinburgh, while all the people secretly mourned. He died without betraying his friends, though the relentless King of England threatened to compel him to do so, by the torture of the thumbscrew and the rack.

Many of his officers and followers underwent the same fate; and among those imprisoned to await execution was a certain nobleman, Sir John Cochrane, who had been made famous by other political intrigues. His friends used all the influence

17

that their high position accorded them to procure his pardon, but without success; and the unfortunate baronet, a moody and impulsive man by nature, felt that there was no escape from the terrible destiny, and prepared to meet it in a manner worthy of a follower of the brave old duke. But he had one friend on whose help he had not counted.

In an upper chamber of an irregular, many-storied mansion far down the Canongate, Grizel Cochrane, the imprisoned man's daughter, sat through the dread hours waiting to learn her father's sentence. There was too little doubt as to what it would be. The King and his generals meant to make merciless examples of the leaders of the rebellion. Even the royal blood that flowed in the veins of Monmouth had not saved his head from the block. This proud prince, fleeing from the defeat of Sedgemoor, had been found hiding in a ditch, covered over with the ferns that flourished at the bottom. Grizel wept as she thought of the young duke's horrible fate. She remembered when she had last seen him about the court at Holland, where she had shared her father's exile. Gay, generous, and handsome, he seemed a creature born to live and rule. What a contrast was the abject, weeping coward covered with mud and slime, who had been carried in triumph to the grim Tower of London to meet his doom! The girl had been taught to believe in Monmouth's rights, and she walked the floor trembling with shame and impatience as she thought of his bitter defeat. She walked to the little dormer window and leaned out to look at the gray castle, far up the street, with its dull and lichen-covered walls. She knew that her father looked down from the barred windows of one of the upper apartments accorded to prisoners of state. She wondered if a thought of his little daughter crept in his mind amid his

ruined hopes. The grim castle frowning at her from its rocky height filled her with dread; and shuddering, she turned from it toward the street below to let her eyes follow absently the passers-by. They whispered together as they passed the house, and when now and then some person caught a glimpse of her face in the ivy-sheltered window, she only met a look of commiseration. No one offered her a happy greeting.

"They all think him doomed," she cried to herself. "No one hath the grace to feign hope." Bitter tears filled her eyes, until suddenly through the mist she was conscious that some one below was lifting a plumed hat to her. It was a stately gentleman with a girdled vest and gorgeous coat and jeweled sword-hilt.

"Mistress Cochrane," said he, in that hushed voice we use when we wish to direct a remark to one person, which no one else shall overhear, "I have that to tell thee which is most important."

"Is it secret?" asked Grizel, in the same guarded tone that he had used.

"Yes," he replied, without looking up, and continuing slowly in his walk, as if he had merely exchanged a morning salutation.

"Then," she returned hastily, "I will tell Mother; and we will meet thee in the twilight, at the side door under the balcony." She continued to look from the window, and the man sauntered on as if he had no care in the world but to keep the scarlet heels of his shoes from the dust. After a time Grizel arose, changed her loose robe for a more ceremonious dress, bound her brown braids into a prim gilded net, and descended into the drawing-room.

Her mother sat in mournful state at the end of the lofty apartment. About her were two ladies and several gentlemen, all conversing in low tones such as they might use, Grizel thought to herself, if her father were

"SOME ONE BELOW WAS LIFTING A PLUMED HAT TO HER."

dead in the house. They all stopped talking as she entered, and looked at her in surprise. In those days it was thought very improper and forward for a young girl to enter a drawing-room uninvited, if guests were present. Grizel's eyes fell before the embarrassing scrutiny, and she dropped a timid courtesy, lifting her green silken skirts daintily, like a high-born little maiden, as she was. Lady Cochrane made a dignified apology to her guests and then turned to Grizel.

"Well, my daughter?" she said, questioningly.

"I pray thy pardon, Mother," said Grizel, in a trembling voice, speaking low, that only her mother might hear; "but within a few moments Sir Thomas Hanford will be secretly below the balcony, with news for us."

The lady half rose from her seat, trembling.

"Is he commissioned by the governor?" she asked.

"I can not tell," said the little girl; but here her voice broke, and regardless of the strangers, she flung herself into her mother's lap, weeping: "I am sure it is bad news of Father!" Lady Cochrane wound her arm about her daughter's waist, and, with a gesture of apology, led her from the room. Half an hour later she re-entered it hurriedly, followed by Grizel, who sank unnoticed in the deep embrasure of a window, and shivered there behind the heavy folds of the velvet hangings.

"I have just received terrible intelligence, my friends," announced Lady Cochrane, standing, tall and pale, in the midst of her guests. "The governor has been informally notified that the next post from London will bring Sir John's sentence. He is to be hanged at the Cross." There was a perfect silence in the dim room; then one of the ladies broke into loud sobbing, and a gentleman led Lady Cochrane to a chair, while the others talked apart in earnest whispers.

"Who brought the information?" asked one of the gentlemen, at length. "Is there not hope that it is a false report?"

"I am not at liberty," said Lady Cochrane, "to tell who brought me this terrible news; but it was a friend of the governor, from whom I would not have expected a service. Oh, is it too late," she cried, rising from her chair and pacing the room, "to make another attempt at intercession? Surely something can be done!"

The gentleman who had stood by her chair—a gray-headed, sober-visaged man—returned answer:

"Do not count on any remedy now, dear Lady Cochrane. I know this new King. He will be relentless toward any one who has questioned his right to reign. Besides, the post has already left London several days, and will doubtless be here by to-morrow noon."

"I am sure," said a gentleman who had not yet spoken, "that if we had a few days more he might be saved. They say King James will do anything for money, and the wars have emptied his treasury. Might we not delay the post?" he suggested, in a low voice.

"No," said the gray-headed gentleman; "that is utterly impossible."

Grizel, shivering behind the curtain, listened with eager ears. Then she saw her mother throw herself into the arms of one of the ladies and break into ungoverned sobs. The poor girl could stand no more, but glided from the room unnoticed and crept up to her dark chamber, where she sat, repeating aimlessly to herself the words that by chance had fixed themselves strongest in her memory: "Delay the post—delay the post!"

The moon arose and shone in through the panes, making a wavering mosaic on the floor as it glimmered through the wind-blown ivy at the window. Like a flash, definite resolution sprang into Grizel's mind. If, by delaying the post, time for intercession with the King could be gained, and her father's life so saved, then the post *must* be delayed! But how? She had heard the gentleman say that it would be impossible. She knew that the postboy went heavily armed, to guard against the highwaymen who frequented the roads in search of plunder. This made her think of the wild stories of masked men who sprung from some secluded spot upon the postboys, and carried off the letters and money with which they were intrusted.

Suddenly she bounded from her seat, stood still a moment with her hands pressed to her head, ran from her room, and up the stairs which led to the servants' sleeping apartments. She listened at a door, and then, satisfied that the room was empty, entered, and went straight to the oaken wardrobe. By the light of the moon she selected a jacket and a pair of trousers. She looked about her for a hat and found one hanging on a peg near the window; then she searched for some time before she found a pair of boots. They were worn and coated with mud.

"They are all the better," she said to herself, and hurried on tiptoe down the corridor. She went next to the anteroom of her father's chamber. It was full of fond associations, and the hot tears sprang up into her eyes as she looked about it. She took up a brace of pistols, examined them awkwardly, her hands trembling under their weight as she found at once to her delight and her terror that they were loaded. Then she hurried with them to her room.

Half an hour later, the butler saw a figure which he took to be that of Allen, the stable-boy, creeping down the back stairs, boots in hand.

"Whaur noo, me laddie?" he asked. "It's gey late for ye to gang oot the nicht."

"I hae forgot to bar the stable door," re-plied Grizel in a low and trembling voice, imitating as well as she could the broad dialect of the boy.

"Hech!" said the butler. "I ne'er hear ye mak sae little hammer in a' yer days."

She fled on. The great kitchen was deserted. She gathered up all the keys from their pegs by the door, let herself quietly out, and sped across the yard to the stable. With trembling hands she fitted first one key and then another to the door until she found the right one. Once inside the stable, she stood irresolute. She patted Bay Bess, her own little pony.

"Thou wouldst never do, Bess," she said. "Thou art such a lazy little creature." The round, fat carriage-horses stood there. "You are just holiday horses, too," said Grizel to them, "and would be winded after an hour of the work I want you for to-night." But in the shadow of the high stall stood Black Ronald, Sir John Cochrane's great, dark battle-horse, that riderless, covered with dust and foam, had dashed down the Canongate after the terrible rout of Argyle in the bogs of Levenside, while all the people stood and stared at the familiar steed, carrying, as he did, the first silent message of disaster. Him Grizel unfastened and led out.

"Thou art a true hero," she said, rubbing his nose with the experienced touch of a horsewoman; "and I'll give thee a chance to-night to show that thou art as loyal as ever." Her hands were cold with excitement, but she managed to buckle the saddle and bridle upon him, while the huge animal stood in restless expectancy, anxious to be gone. She drew on the boots without any trouble, and slipped the pistols into the holsters.

"I believe thou knowest what I would have of thee," said Grizel as she led the horse out into the yard and on toward the gateway. Frightened, as he half circled about her in his impatience, she undid the fastening of the great gates, but her strength was not sufficient to swing them open.

"Ronald," she said in despair, "I can not open the gates!" Ronald turned his head about and looked at her with his beautiful eyes. He seemed to be trying to say, "I can."

"All right," said Grizel, as if he had spoken. She mounted the black steed, laughed nervously as she climbed into the saddle. "Now," she said, "go on!" The horse made a dash at the gates, burst them open, and leaped out into the road. He curveted about for a moment, his hoofs striking fire from the cobble-stones. Then Grizel turned his head down the Canongate, away from the castle. She knew the point at which she intended to leave the city, and toward that point she headed Black Ronald. The horse seemed to know he was doing his old master a service, as he took his monstrous strides forward. Only once did Grizel look backward, and then a little shudder, half terror, half remorse, struck her, for she saw her home ablaze with light, and heard cries of excitement borne faintly to her on the rushing night wind. They had discovered her flight. Once she thought she heard hoof-beats behind her, but she knew she could not be overtaken.

Through the streets, now narrow, now broad, now straight, now crooked, dashed Black Ronald and his mistress. Once he nearly ran down a drowsy watchman who stood nodding at a sharp corner, but horse and rider were three hundred yards away before the frightened guardian regained his composure and sprang his discordant rattle.

Now the houses grew scarcer, and presently the battlements of the town wall loomed up ahead, and Grizel's heart sank, for there were lights in the road. She heard shouts, and knew she was to be challenged.

She firmly set her teeth, said a little prayer, and leaned far forward upon Black Ronald's neck. The horse gave a snort of defiance, shied violently away from a soldier who stood by the way, and then went through the gateway like a shot. Grizel clung tightly to her saddle-bow, and urged her steed on. On, on they went down the firm roadway lined on either side by rows of noble oaks—on, on, out into the country-side, where the sweet odor of the heather arose gracious and fragrant to the trembling girl. There was little chance of her taking a wrong path. The road over which the postboy came was the King's highway, always kept in a state of repair.

She gave herself no time to notice the green upland farms, or the stately residences which stood out on either hand in the moonlight. She concentrated her strength and mind on urging her horse forward. She was too excited to form a definite plan, and her only clear idea was to meet the postboy before daylight, for she knew it would not be safe to trust too much to her disguise. Now and then a feeling of terror flashed over her, and she turned sick with dread; but her firm purpose upheld her.

It was almost four in the morning, and the wind was blowing chill from the sea, when she entered the rolling woodlands about the Tweed. Grizel was shivering with the cold, and was so tired that she with difficulty kept her place in the saddle.

"We can not hold out much longer, Ronald," she said; "and if we fail, we can never hold up our heads again." Ronald, the sure-footed, stumbled and nearly fell. "It is no use," sighed Grizel; "we must rest." She dismounted, but it was some moments before her tired limbs could obey her will. Beside the roadway was a ditch filled with running water, and Grizel managed to lead Ronald down the incline to its brink, and let him drink. She scooped up a little in her hand and moistened her tongue; then, realizing that Ronald must not be allowed to stand still, she, with great difficulty, mounted upon his back again, and, heartsick, fearful, yet not daring to turn back, coaxed him gently forward.

The moon had set long before this, and in the misty east the sky began to blanch with the first gleam of morning. Suddenly, around the curve of the road where it leaves the banks of the Tweed, came a dark object. Grizel's heart leaped wildly. Thirty seconds later she saw that it was indeed a horseman. He broke into a song:

> "The Lord o' Argyle cam' wi' plumes
>   and wi' spears,
> And Monmouth he landed wi' gay
>   cavaliers!
> The pibroch has caa'd every tartan
>   thegither,
> B' thoosans their footsteps a' pressin' the
>   heather;
> Th' North and the Sooth sent their
>   bravest ones out,
> But a joust wi' Kirke's Lambs put them
>   all to the rout."

By this time, the horseman was so close that Grizel could distinguish objects hanging upon the horse in front of the rider. They were the mailbags! For the first time she realized her weakness and saw how unlikely it was that she would be able to cope with an armed man. The blood rushed to her head, and a courage that was the inspiration of the moment took possession of her. She struck Black Ronald a lash with her whip.

"Go!" she said to him shrilly, while her heartbeats hammered in her ears, "Go!"

The astonished and excited horse leaped down the road. As she met the postboy, she drew Black Ronald, with a sudden strength that was born of the danger, back upon his haunches. His huge body blocked the way.

"Dismount!" she cried to the other rider. Her voice was hoarse from fright, and sounded strangely in her own ears. But a wild courage nerved her, and the hand that drew and held the pistol was as firm as a man's. Black Ronald was rearing wildly, and in grasping the reins tighter, her other hand mechanically altered its position about the pistol.

She had not meant to fire, she had only thought to aim and threaten, but suddenly there was a flash of light in the gray atmosphere, a dull reverberation, and to the girl's horrified amazement she saw the horse in front of her stagger and fall heavily to the ground. The rider, thrown from his saddle, was pinned to the earth by his horse and stunned by the fall. Dizzy with pain and confused by the rapidity of the assault, he made no effort to draw his weapon.

The mail-bags had swung by their own momentum quite clear of the horse in its fall, and now lay loosely over its back, joined by the heavy strap.

It was a painful task for the exhausted girl to dismount, but she did so, and, lifting the cumbersome leathern bags, she threw them over Black Ronald's neck. It was yet more painful for her tender heart to leave the poor fellow she had injured lying in so pitiable a condition, but her father's life was in danger, and that, to her, was of more moment than the postboy's hurts.

"Heaven forgive me," she said, bending over him. "I pray this may not be his death!" She clambered over the fallen horse and mounted Ronald, who was calm again. Then she turned his head toward Edinboro' Town and hurriedly urged him forward. But as she sped away from the scene of the encounter, she kept looking back, with an

"GRIZEL SAW THE HORSE IN FRONT OF HER FALL HEAVILY TO THE GROUND."

awe-struck face, to the fallen postboy. In the excitement of the meeting and in her one great resolve to obtain her father's death-warrant, she had lost all thought of the risks she ran or of the injuries she might inflict; and it was with unspeakable relief, therefore, that she at last saw the postboy struggle to his feet, and stand gazing after her. "Thank Heaven, he is not killed!" she exclaimed again and again, as she now joyfully pressed Ronald into a gallop. Throughout the homeward journey, Grizel made it a point to urge him to greater speed when nearing a farmhouse, so that there would be less risk of discovery. Once or twice she was accosted by laborers in the field, and once by the driver of a cart, but their remarks were lost upon the wind as the faithful Ronald thundered on. She did not feel the need of sleep, for she had forgotten it in all her excitement, but she was greatly exhausted and suffering from the effects of her rough ride.

Soon the smoke in the distance showed Grizel that her native town lay an hour's journey ahead. She set her teeth and said an encouraging word to the horse. He seemed to understand, for he redoubled his energies. Now the roofs became visible, and now, grim and sullen, the turrets of the castle loomed up. Grizel felt a great lump in her throat as she thought of her father in his lonely despair.

She turned Ronald from the road again and cut through a clump of elms. She came out in a few minutes and rode more slowly toward a smaller gate than the one by which she had left the city. A stout soldier looked at her carelessly and then turned to his tankard of ale, after he had noticed the mail-bags. Grizel turned into a crooked, narrow street lined on each side with toppling, frowning buildings. She drew rein before a humble house, and slipped wearily from her saddle and knocked at the door.

An old woman opened the heavy oaken door and Grizel fell into her arms.

"The bags—the mail," she gasped, and fainted. When she recovered consciousness, she found herself on a low, rough bed. The old woman was bending over her.

"Losh keep me!" said the dame. "I did na ken ye! Ma puir bairnie! Hoo cam' ye by these?" and she pointed to the clothes of Allen.

"The bags?" said Grizel, sitting bolt upright—

"Are under the hearth," said the old woman.

"And Ronald?" continued Grizel.

"Is in the byre wi' the coos," said the other with a knowing leer. "Not a soul kens it. Ne'er a body saw ye come."

Breathlessly Grizel explained all to her old nurse, and then sprung off the bed. At her request the old dame locked the door and brought her the bags. By the aid of a sharp knife the pair slashed open the leathern covering, and the inclosed packets fell upon the floor. With trembling hands Grizel fumbled them all over, tossing one after another impatiently aside as she read the addresses. At last she came upon a large one addressed to the governor. With beating heart she hesitated a moment, and then tore the packet open with shaking fingers. She easily read the bold handwriting. Suddenly everything swam before her, and again she nearly fell into her companion's arms.

It was too true. What she read was a formal warrant of the King, signed by his majesty, and stamped and sealed with red wax. It ordered the governor to hang Sir John Cochrane of Ochiltree at the Cross in Edinburgh at ten o'clock in the morning, on the third day of the following week. She clutched the paper and hid it in her dress.

The disposition of the rest of the mail was soon decided upon. The old lady's son Jock—a wild fellow—was to put the sacks on the back of a donkey and turn it loose outside the gates, at his earliest opportunity. And then Grizel, clad in some rough garments the old lady procured, slipped out of the house, and painfully made her way toward the Canongate.

It was four o'clock in the afternoon when she reached her home. The porter at the gate could scarcely be made to understand that the uncouth figure before him was his young mistress. But a moment later her mother was embracing her, with tears of joy.

All the male friends of Sir John were hastily summoned, and Grizel related her adventure, and displayed the death-warrant of her father. The hated document was consigned to the flames, a consultation was held, and that night three of the gentlemen left for London.

The next day, the donkey and the mail-sacks were found by a sentry, and some little excitement was occasioned; but when the postboy came in later, and related how he had been attacked by six stalwart rob-bers, and how he had slain two of them and was then overpowered and forced to surrender the bags, all wonderment was set at rest.

The Cochrane family passed a week of great anxiety, but when it was ended, the three friends returned from London with joyful news. The King had listened to their petition, and had ordered the removal of Sir John to the Tower of London, until his case could be reconsidered. So to London Sir John went; and after a time the payment of five thousand pounds to some of the King's advisers secured an absolute pardon. His lands, which had been confiscated, were restored to him; and on his arrival at his Scottish home, he was warmly welcomed by a great concourse of his friends. He thanked them in a speech, taking care, however, not to tell who was so greatly instrumental in making his liberation possible. But we may be sure that he was secretly proud of the pluck and devotion of his daughter Grizel.

YE END OF MISTRESS COCHRANE'S RIDE

THE SEARCH FOR JEAN BAPTISTE

By Mary Austin

September, 1903

I

ONE bred to the hills and the care of dumb, helpless things must in the end, whatever else befalls, come back to them. That is the comfort they give him for their care and the revenge they have of their helplessness. If this were not so Gabriel Lausanne would never have found Jean Baptiste. Babette, who was the mother of Jean Baptiste and the wife of Gabriel, understood this also, and so came to her last sickness in more comfort of mind than would have been otherwise possible; for it was understood between them that when he had buried her, Gabriel was to go to America to find Jean Baptiste.

He had been a good son to them in his youth and good to look upon: a little short of stature,—no taller, in fact, than Babette, who was a head shorter than Gabriel—but broad in the shoulders and strong in the thighs beyond belief. But the strength of his thews and sinews had been Jean Baptiste's undoing. About the time he came to the age of a man and the fullness of his strength, he began to think too much of himself and his cleverness in breaking other people's collar-bones by pitching them over his shoulder.

The towns drew him; the hills had no power to hold. He left minding the sheep; he sought jolly companions, and went boisterously about with them from inn door to inn door. Finally the fame of his wrestling spread until there were few men in the province dared try a fall with him. From bragging he went to broiling, and at last fell into such grievous trouble that there was nothing for it but to slip away to America between the night and the morning.

Then Gabriel and Babette, who had not thought before to take stock of their years, began to understand that they were old, and at the time when they had looked to see children's children about their knees, Babette had slipped away to find the little ones who died before Jean Baptiste was born, and Gabriel was beginning his search for Jean Baptiste, the well beloved.

America is a wide land, but the places in it where men fare forth to the hills with sheep are known and limited; and when he had inquired where these were, there, because of the faith he had, went Gabriel Lausanne. He came, in the course of a year, to the shepherd world that lies within the Sierra Nevada and its outlying spurs. For it is known that the shepherds of the Sierras are strange, Frenchmen, Basques mostly, and a few Mexicans, but never an English-speaking one, from the Temblor Hills to the Minaretts.

Things went hardly with Gabriel at first, for he was new to the land and bewildered by its bigness; but once he had gotten a place to help at lambing-time his work was assured, for there was little he did not know about lambs. And finally he was given charge of a flock, and went wandering with it into the high glacier meadows, learning the haps and seasons of the hills. He got to know the trails and the landmark peaks, what meadows were free and what could be rented for a song, the trail of bear and wildcat, the chances of snow in August, and all shepherd's lore. He knew the brands of sheep as a man knows the faces of his neighbors, and from the signs of the trails how they fared that were ahead of him, and how to prosper his own.

All this time he had not left off inquiring for Jean Baptiste, though the manner in which he should do this gave much trouble of mind to Gabriel Lausanne. He thought it reasonable to suppose that Jean Baptiste had not kept his own name, lest the old wrong should find him out by means of it. And if it should come to his ears that inquiries were made concerning him, he might be more careful to hide himself, suspecting an enemy. In the end Gabriel had to content himself asking every man he met for news of his son, whom he loved dearly and would find.

"Jean Baptiste, your father loves you," he wrote upon the rocks; "Jean Baptiste, your father loves you," he cut painstakingly upon the blazed trunks of pines; and "Jean Baptiste!" he whispered nightly to the wide-open stars when he lay with his flocks wintering on the sunward slopes of the Little Antelope.

II

So the years went over him, and his heart warmed toward the big new land where any meadow might hold his son, or any coyote-scaring fire might be Jean Baptiste's.

By as many shepherds as he met Gabriel Lausanne was respected for his knowledge of ailing sheep, and laughed at for his simple heart, but as yet he had not come up with the shepherds of Los Alamos. The Los Alamos grant covered thousands of acres of good pasturelands, but they counted their flocks and herds by tens of thousands, and reached out as far as they could or dared into the free forest-lands and the glacier meadows set between.

They sent out large flocks, strong and well shepherded; and what they could not get by the fair right of first comers, they took by force and wile. They wrested the best feeding-grounds from small shepherds by the sheer force of numbers, and when they met with bands strong and adventurous as their own, the shepherds cracked one another's heads merrily with their long staves, and the pasture went to the men with the thickest skulls.

They were bold rogues, those shepherds of Los Alamos. They would head their flocks away from the line of the Forest Reserve, under the ranger's eye, and as soon as his head was turned cut back to the forbidden pastures, and out again before he could come up with them.

They turned streams out of their courses, and left uncovered fires behind them to run unchecked in the wood, for the sake of the new feed that grew up in the burned districts. For them the forest existed only to feed sheep, and Los Alamos sheep at that.

There are shepherds in the Sierras who from long association grow into a considerable knowledge of woodcraft and have respect for the big trees, but not the shepherds of Los Alamos. No doubt there was much mischief charged to them which was not properly their own, but in any event they had never been loved, and were even dreaded because of that one of them who was called "The Mule."

Every shepherd has two names—the one he signs to his contract and the one he is known by. The Mule, so called because of a certain manner of surly silence and the exceeding breadth and strength of his back, had been picked up by Le Berge, the head shepherd, at a shearing, poorly clad and wholly at the end of his means. There was that in his look and the way in which he handled a sheep that made it plain that he had been born to it; and when he had plucked up a man who annoyed him and pitched him over his shoulder, Le Berge loved him as a brother. He hired him forthwith, though he had to discharge another man to make place for him. And now it was said that whoever came in the way of the shepherds of Los Alamos must try a fall with The Mule for the right of the feeding-grounds; and the fame of his wrestling was such that timid shepherds kept well away from his trail.

III

GABRIEL LAUSANNE, keeping to the small meadows and treeless hills, had not yet fallen in with the flocks of Los Alamos. The fifth year of his shepherding there was no rain at all on the inland ranges. The foot-hill pastures failed early, and by the middle of July the flocks were all driven to the feeding-grounds of the high Sierras.

Gabriel came early to Manache, a chain of grassy, gentian-flowered plats strung on the thread of a snow-fed brook, large and open, and much frequented by shepherds. In Manache, if one waits long enough, one gets to know all the flocks and every shepherd ranging between Tahoe and Temblors. Gabriel, a little wearied at heart, purposed to stay the summer through in that neighborhood, moving only as the flock required.

Jean Baptiste he knew must come to the hills as surely as the swallow to the eves or the stork to her chimney, but he was perplexed by the thought that in the years that had passed so many changes had come to them both that they might unwittingly meet and pass each other. He wished that he might find other messengers than the wind and the rain-washed rocks and the fast-obliterating pines. And while Gabriel pondered these things with a sore heart, two thousand of the Los Alamos sheep poured down upon his meadow from the upper pass.

Their shuddering bleat, their jangling bells, sounded unseen among the tamarack pines all the half of one day before they found him. But when they came into the open and saw him feeding down the stream-side among the dwarf willows, the shepherds of Los Alamos promised themselves great sport.

Le Berge, walking lazily at the head of his flock, spoke a word to his dogs, and the dogs in their own fashion spoke to the flock, and straightway the sheep began to pour steadily down the meadow and around the flock of Gabriel; for that was a way they of Los Alamos had—compelling small shepherds to keep their sheep parted out at their own cost.

"And what do you here, friend?" said Le Berge, when he had reached Gabriel.

"I feed my flock," answered the old man. "The pasture is free. Also I seek my son."

The under-shepherds came hurrying, expecting to be greatly entertained, and one called to another, "Hi, Mule, here is work for you!"

The man so called came slowly and in silence, a short man, but close-knit and broad in the shoulders, a wrestler by the look of him, and leaning upon his staff until his part of the entertainment should begin.

"Free is it," said Le Berge, still to Gabriel. "Yes, free to those who can hold it. By the turn of your tongue you should be from Bourdonne. Here, Mule, is a countryman of thine. Come teach him the law of the feeding-ground."

"I am an old man," said Gabriel, "and I wish no harm. Help me out with my flock and I will be gone. But you," he said to The Mule, "are you truly of Bourdonne? I am Gabriel Lausanne, and I seek my son, Jean Baptiste, whom I love. We also are of Bourdonne; it may be you can tell where he is to be found."

"Enough said," cried Le Berge. "Up with him, Mule."

IV

AND then the shepherds of Los Alamos looked with mouths agape to see that The Mule stood still, and the knuckles of the hand that grasped his staff were strained and white. The voice of Gabriel quavered on amid the bleating of the sheep:

"If you are surely of Bourdonne you will earn an old man's blessing; and say to him that his mother is dead, and his father has come to find him. Say to my son, 'Jean Baptiste, your father loves you.'" The old man stooped a little, that he might meet The Mule eye to eye.

"Jean Baptiste," he said again, and then his staff shook in his hands, though there was no wind, and his voice shook, too, with a sudden note of hope and doubt and wistful inquiry. "Jean Baptiste," he cried, "your father loves you! Jean Baptiste—"

Jean Baptiste, called The Mule, dropped his staff and wept with his face between his hands, and his whole strong frame shook with emotion, and his father fell on his neck and kissed him.

So Gabriel found his son.

V

AND now it is said that there are no better shepherds in the Sierras than the two Lausannes, the one famed for his skill with the lambs, the other for his knowledge of the feeding-grounds.

They will not be hired apart, and it is believed that it will be so until the end; for it is said at shearings, as a joke that is half believed, that when father Gabriel is too old to walk, The Mule will carry him.

They are a silent pair, and well content to be so; but as often as they come by Manache, when they sit by the twilight fire at the day's end, Gabriel puts out his hand to his son, saying softly, as of old habit, "Jean Baptiste, your father loves you"; and The Mule, patting the hand upon his arm, makes answer, "Ay, father; Jean Baptiste knows."

HIS HERO

By Margaret Minor

February, 1900

IT was an October afternoon, and through Indian summer's tulle-like haze a low-swinging sun sent shafts of scarlet light at the highest peaks of the Blue Ridge. The sweet-gum leaves looked like blood-colored stars as they floated slowly to the ground, and brown chestnuts gleamed satin-like through their gaping burs; while over all there rested a dense stillness, cut now and then by the sharp yelp of a dog as he scurried through the bushes after a rabbit.

Surrounded by this splendid autumn beauty stood Mountain Top Inn, near the crest of the Blue Ridge in Rockfish Gap, its historical value dating from the time when Jefferson, Madison, and Monroe, after a long and spirited discussion in one of its low-ceiled rooms, decided upon the location of the University of Virginia.

On the porch of this old inn there now sat a little boy, idly swinging a pair of sun-tanned legs. Occasionally he tickled an old liver-colored hound that lay dozing in a limp heap; but being rewarded only by toothless snaps at very long intervals, he finally grew tired of this amusement, and stretching himself out on his back, he began to dream with wide-open eyes. At these dream-times, when he let his thoughts loose, they always bore him to the very same field, and here his fancy painted pictures with the vivid colors of a boy's imagination: pictures so strong that they left him flushed and tingling with pride; again, pictures that brought a cool, choking feeling to his throat; and at times pictures that made his childish mouth quiver and droop. Among all of these thought-born scenes, at intervals there would stand out the real ones, scenes that were etched on the clean walls of his memory in everlasting strokes.

He never tired thinking of that first morning—that morning when all the world seemed gilded with sunshine and throbbing with martial music. His grandfather had lifted him up on one of the "big gate" posts to see the soldiers march by. With mingled feelings of admiration and childish envy he had watched them drill for many weeks, but they had never seemed such real, grand soldiers until now, as they came marching by with quick, firm steps, keeping time to the clear staccato notes, marching off to real battle-fields. It was all so beautiful, splendid, and gay—the music, the soldiers, the people, the hurrahing! It stirred his sentient little body through and through with a kind of joy, and he thought it so strange that his mother's eyes were full of tears.

Just a few days later he had listened eagerly to the sharp, crackling sound of guns and the rumbling thunder of cannon, so near that the air seemed to vibrate. He and another little boy had stood and talked in high, quick tones, bragging and predicting breathlessly the result of the battle as they used the term "our men."

Finally they climbed the tallest oak on the lawn, and strained their young eyes to see which was "gettin' whipped."

A little while after this he remembered following his father through the long hospital ward. Over the first bed he saw him stoop and loosen the white cotton bandages of a wounded man. On the next narrow cot there was a slender boy of fifteen, who lay with clenched hands watching the work of the surgeon. Then they passed a woman, who was gently bathing the forehead of a man whose soldier days seemed likely to come to an early end.

Some weeks had gone by, when one day he followed a party of men to Marye's Heights. It was a short time after the battle of Fredericksburg. A light snow had fallen the night before, which the wind whirled and sifted about the dead, in a way that made them appear to be shuddering. Once a sharp gust blew the snow off a body lying on its face, and the boy's eyes filled. He scarcely heeded the talk of the men with whom he had gone. His thoughts were held fast by the awful scene which lay spread before his young eyes.

How often since then had the boy pictured himself a grown man, seated on just such a fine horse and following Lee! It was always Lee; in his dreamland through the heart of the battle he always followed General Robert E. Lee, his hero, whom he had never seen, but whom he had carried halo-crowned in his heart ever since he could remember.

And then the very saddest day in his life had come—the day when the first news of Lee's surrender lay heavy on the hearts of the household. For a while he had followed his mother as she went silently, with closed white lips, from one duty to another. Finally he went out to seek comfort from Uncle Jake, whom he found sitting with his back propped against the side of the corn-crib, drawing little quick puffs of smoke from his pipe.

"Uncle Jake," he said, "Lee's just *had* to s'render."

"Yes, honey, I done heahud 'bout hit." And as he looked into Uncle Jake's little red, watery eyes, he saw no comfort there, and turned away. Then Uncle Jake said very tenderly: "Nuvvuh you min', son; ef you had be'n uh grow'd-up man you'd uh whipped um sho! Unc' Jake gwine tuh tek you possum-huntin' Sa'd'y night."

Seven months had gone by since the war had ended; still, on this October afternoon, as the boy lay stretched out on the porch of the old inn, he dreamed his boyish dreams of romance and heroism.

Suddenly his attention was attracted by the sound of hoofs, and turning his head he saw a man riding slowly down the road. A new arrival at the inn was always most interesting. An eager light came into the boy's eyes as he watched the rider, who was now near enough for him to see how firmly he sat in his saddle. The man seemed a very part of the strongly built horse, which carried him with an ease that indicated long habit.

A wiry little Negro had also seen the approaching horseman, and was now hurrying across the lawn to meet him.

"May I spend the night here, my man?" asked the stranger.

"Yessuh—yessuh!" answered Uncle Jake, quickly, and opening the gate he stepped out and caught the bridle near the bit, as the horseman swung out of the creaking saddle to the ground.

"Uncle Jake, take the horse around to the stable!" called out the boy, who felt that the honors of hospitality rested on him, there being no one else in sight. Then he ran briskly down the walk to meet the stranger, who extended his fine, strong hand with a little smile, and said very kindly:

"How do you do, sir?"

"I'm well," replied the boy.

"And what is your name?"

"Jimmy."

"Jimmy? Well, Jimmy is a nice name," he said. Then he turned, and still held the boy's hand as he watched the little old Negro, who stood with his head under the saddle-skirt, tiptoeing and straining in his effort to unfasten the girth. Finally, when he succeeded, he flung the saddle on the ground, and the horse, feeling relieved of his burden, first shook himself violently, and then expressed his comfort again and again in deep chest-tones.

During all this time Jimmy's eyes had been fastened on the stranger's spurs, and a peculiar feeling of incredulity gradually filled his mind.

Silver, indeed? He could not fool him! No one was rich enough to have real silver spurs! So sternly did he resent what he thought to be an attempt at deception that he drew his small brown hand slowly out of the stranger's gentle clasp.

After slipping off the bridle from the horse's head and dropping it by the saddle, Uncle Jake led him away by his forelock to the stable, and Jimmy walked toward the inn with his guest, who said as they reached the steps:

"Jimmy, we will sit here for a while, and then I will go over to the stable and see about my horse."

As they sat down the old hound came cautiously down the steps, wheezing out a husky greeting.

"She is too old to hurt any one," said Jimmy.

"Is she yours?"

"No, sir. Tip's mine. Listen!" he exclaimed, as the sharp yelp of a dog again broke the stillness. "That's Tip! He goes off and runs rabbits all by himself."

"Perhaps he is after a fox."

"No, sir; Tip won't run a fox."

"Jimmy, can you tell from a dog's cry whether he is running a fox or a rabbit?"

"No, sir."

"Well, if he is trailing a rabbit he does not bark continually, but if he is after a fox he does; so you can always tell if you listen carefully."

"Never heard about that before," replied Jimmy, with a smile.

After this there followed a long pause, during which the stranger looked about inquiringly, then said:

"Jimmy, how long have you been living here?"

"Not very long. We refugeed over in North Carolina the first part of the war. Then we came back to Spottsylvania County while father was in prison. Why, we just came here after the s'render. You remember when Lee just had to s'render?" he asked, looking up into the stranger's face.

The boy's mouth, as usual, quivered as he uttered the word "s'render," but the man did not appear to see this. He seemed to be looking at a far-off mountain peak. After a pause he replied, "Yes, I remember," as he arose and started toward the stable.

"I'll show you the way," said Jimmy.

"Thank you, sir," he answered gravely.

When they entered the stable the big gray horse greeted his master with some soft little nickerings. "Oh, he knows you without even looking!" exclaimed Jimmy, in tones expressing delight and surprise.

"Yes, he knows me pretty well," the man replied, as he looked with anxious sympathy at a saddle-galled place on the horse's back.

Jimmy had climbed up on the side of the stall, and was also looking with much interest. Suddenly he exclaimed: "I know what's good for that! Some stuff down in the bottom of the chalybeate spring."

He pronounced each syllable of the word "chalybeate" very clearly, for it was a newly learned word, and he was proud of his ability to use it.

"Why, yes; the iron in it ought to be healing. How far is the spring?"

"Oh, just a little way; I'll show you," Jimmy replied, jumping to the ground and quickly opening the stable door. "Let me lead him," he added.

"Hadn't you rather ride him, Jimmy?"

"Yes, sir," he replied, in rather shy but pleased tones.

"All right," said the man, as he swung

the little fellow up on the horse. "There! Sit farther back, so you will not hurt that galled place. Now I'll lead him, and you tell me in which direction to go."

"Down the road there, just on the other side of the ice-pond," said Jimmy, pointing in that direction as they moved off.

The boy was happy as he cupped his bare legs close around the body of the horse, and watched the square shoulders of the man who walked slowly ahead. He thought him exceedingly nice and kind, and his feelings in regard to the spurs were not nearly so intense. The desire to ask if they were real silver, though, was strong, but he felt that perhaps it would not be polite, so he said nothing.

After they had gone some distance Jimmy exclaimed, "There's the spring!" Then he slid quickly to the ground, and without other words knelt down and, baring one arm, dipped out of the bottom of the spring a handful of rust-colored flakes.

"This is what you put on his back," he said. "Just lay it right on. It doesn't hurt; it just feels cool."

The directions were quietly obeyed, and the horse made no movement, save a slight quiver of the skin, as if to shake off a fly.

"Uncle Jake says that doctors can't make any finer medicine than this," he said, as he scooped up another handful.

"Well, Jimmy, I am very much obliged to you, and I'm sure that my horse is also," said the stranger, as they started on back to the stable.

In the meantime the saddle left by Uncle Jake near the horse-rack had attracted the attention of a young man as he came through the front gate. After looking at it for a few minutes, idle curiosity prompted him to turn it over with his foot, and as he did so three bright brass letters—"R. E. L."—greeted him. He looked sharply at them at first, then his eyes dilated, and a little prickly thrill ran through him. "I won-

der if it can be!" he said. Suddenly some convincing feeling seemed to fill his mind, and then he almost ran to the house. On reaching the steps, he sprang up them two at a time, and entered the hall, where he met Mrs. Claverly.

"Mrs. Claverly—" he began, and stopped.

"Well?" she asked, smiling at his hesitation. "What is it, Charley?"

"Ah, do you know, Mrs. Claverly, I think that General Lee is here." His voice was husky with excitement.

"General Lee! Where?" But without waiting for a reply, she stepped quickly to the door of the old-fashioned parlor, and exclaimed in soft, suppressed tones to a group of women sitting there:

"They think that General Lee is here!"

"What makes them think so?" asked a thin, gray-haired woman, as she hastily arose.

"Why," replied the young man, his tones now quite positive, "his saddle with 'R. E. L.' on it is out there by the gate."

"There he comes now," said one of the group, eagerly; "at least, I suppose that it is he."

"Let me see," said Mrs. Claverly, going rapidly to the window. "I saw him once at the Greenbrier White, and I am sure that I would know him. Yes, it is he!" she exclaimed, as she looked at the man coming slowly across the lawn, talking earnestly to the barefoot boy at his side. His thoughts were so completely occupied by what he was saying that not until he was quite near the inn did he see the group on the porch, and his face flushed slightly as he realized that they were there to greet him. Lifting his hat, he ascended the steps with bared head. Mrs. Claverly walked quickly forward, and extended her slim white hand.

"General Lee, I believe."

"Yes, madam," he replied gravely, as he bowed low over her hand.

At the sound of Lee's name Jimmy's eyes

grew round, and filled with astonishment. For one brief moment he stood gazing up at the stately old soldier, whom every one was greeting, then he backed slowly away until he reached the door. There he stood another moment, seeing nothing but his hero.

Suddenly he turned and darted down the long hall, up the stairway, and into his mother's room.

"Mother!" he exclaimed in breathless wonderment, "mother! General Lee is downstairs, and he is just splendid, and— er—mother, he's just exactly like anybody else!"

THE LITTLE RED APPLE TREE
By James Whitcomb Riley

October, 1890

THE Little Red Apple Tree!
  Oh, the Little Red Apple Tree!
When I was the little-est bit of a boy,
  And you were a boy with me!
The bluebird's flight from the topmost boughs,
  And the boys up there—so high
That we rocked over the roof of the house,
  And whooped as the winds went by!

Ho! the Little Red Apple Tree!
  With the garden beds below,
And the old grape-arbor so welcomely
  Hiding the rake and hoe—
  Hiding, too, as the sun dripped through
  In spatters of wasted gold,
Frank and Amy away from you
  And me, in the days of old.

Ah! the Little Red Apple Tree!
  In the edge of the garden-spot,
Where the apples fell so lavishly
  Into the neighbor's lot;
So do I think of you,
  Brother of mine, as the tree—
Giving the ripest wealth of your love
  To the world as well as me.

Oh, the Little Red Apple Tree!
  Sweet as its juiciest fruit
Spanged on the palate spicily,
  And rolled o'er the tongue to boot,
Is the memory still and the joy
  Of the Little Red Apple Tree,
When I was the little-est bit of a boy,
  And you were a boy with me!

MRS. PETERKIN'S TEA-PARTY
By Lucretia P. Hale

June, 1877

It was important to have a tea-party, as they had all been invited by everybody—the Bromwiches, the Tremletts, and the Gibbonses. It would be such a good chance to pay off some of their old debts, now that the lady from Philadelphia was back again, and her two daughters, who would be sure to make it all go off well.

But as soon as they began to make out the list, they saw there were too many to have at once, for there were but twelve cups and saucers in the best set.

"There are seven of *us* to begin with," said Mr. Peterkin.

"We need not all drink tea," said Mrs. Peterkin.

"I never do," said Solomon John. The little boys never did.

"And we could have coffee, too," suggested Elizabeth Eliza.

"That would take as many cups," objected Agamemnon.

"We could use the every-day set for the coffee," answered Elizabeth Eliza; "they are the right shape. Besides," she went on, "they would not all come. Mr. and Mrs. Bromwich, for instance; they never go out."

"There are but six cups in the every-day set," said Mrs. Peterkin.

The little boys said there were plenty of saucers; and Mr. Peterkin agreed with Elizabeth Eliza that all would not come. Old Mr. Jeffers never went out.

"There are three of the Tremletts," said Elizabeth Eliza; "they never go out together. One of them, if not two, will be sure to have the headache. Ann Maria Bromwich would come, and the three Gibbons boys, and their sister Juliana; but the other sisters are out West, and there is but one Osborne."

It really did seem safe to ask "everybody." They would be sorry, after it was over, that they had not asked more.

"We have the cow," said Mrs. Peterkin, "so there will be as much cream and milk as we shall need."

"And our own pig," said Agamemnon. "I am glad we had it salted; so we can have plenty of sandwiches."

"I will buy a chest of tea," exclaimed Mr. Peterkin. "I have been thinking of a chest for some time."

Mrs. Peterkin thought a whole chest would not be needed; it was as well to buy the tea and coffee by the pound. But Mr. Peterkin determined on a chest of tea and a bag of coffee.

So they decided to give the invitations to all. It might be a stormy evening, and some would be prevented.

The lady from Philadelphia and her daughters accepted.

And it turned out a fair day, and more came than were expected. Ann Maria Bromwich had a friend staying with her, and brought her over, for the Bromwiches were opposite neighbors. And the Tremletts had a niece, and Mary Osborne an aunt, that they took the liberty to bring.

The little boys were at the door, to show in the guests; and as each set came to the front gate, they ran back to tell their mother that more were coming. Mrs. Peterkin had grown dizzy with counting those who had come, and trying to calculate how many were to come, and wondering why there were always more and never less, and whether the cups would go round.

36

The three Tremletts all came with their niece. They all had had their headaches the day before, and were having that banged feeling you always have after a headache; so they all sat at the same side of the room on the long sofa.

All the Jefferses came, though they had sent uncertain answer. Old Mr. Jeffers had to be helped in with his cane, by Mr. Peterkin.

The Gibbons boys came, and would stand just outside the parlor door. And Julianna appeared afterward, with the two other sisters, unexpectedly home from the West.

"Got home this morning!" they said. "And so glad to be in time to see everybody—a little tired, to be sure, after forty-eight hours in a sleeping-car!"

"Forty-eight!" repeated Mrs. Peterkin; and wondered if there were forty-eight people, and why they were all so glad to come, and whether all could sit down.

Old Mr. and Mrs. Bromwich came. They thought it would not be neighborly to stay away. They insisted on getting into the most uncomfortable seats.

Yet there seemed to be seats enough while the Gibbons boys preferred to stand. But they never could sit around a tea-table. Elizabeth Eliza had thought they all might have room at the table, and Solomon John and the little boys could help in the waiting.

It was a great moment when the lady from Philadelphia arrived with her daughters. Mr. Peterkin was talking to Mr. Bromwich, who was a little deaf. The Gibbons boys retreated a little farther behind the parlor door. Mrs. Peterkin hastened forward to shake hands with the lady from Philadelphia, saying:

"Four Gibbons girls and Mary Osborne's aunt,—that makes nineteen; and now—"

It made no difference what she said; for there was such a murmuring of talk, that any words suited. And the lady from Philadelphia wanted to be introduced to the Bromwiches.

It was delightful for the little boys. They came to Elizabeth Eliza, and asked:

"Can't we go and ask more? Can't we fetch the Larkins?"

"Oh dear, no!" answered Elizabeth Eliza.

Mrs. Peterkin found time to meet Elizabeth Eliza in the side entry to ask if there were going to be cups enough.

"I have set Agamemnon in the front entry to count," said Elizabeth Eliza, putting her hand to her head.

The little boys came to say that the Maberlys were coming.

"The Maberlys!" exclaimed Elizabeth Eliza. "I never asked them."

"It is your father's doing," cried Mrs. Peterkin. "I do believe he asked everybody he saw!" And she hurried back to her guests.

"What if father really has asked everybody?" Elizabeth Eliza said to herself pressing her head again with her hand.

There was the cow and the pig. But if they all took tea or coffee, or both, the cups could *not* go round.

Agamemnon returned in the midst of her agony.

He had not been able to count the guests, they moved about so, they talked so; and it would not look well to appear to count.

"What shall we do?" exclaimed Elizabeth Eliza.

"We are not a family for an emergency," sighed Agamemnon.

"What do you suppose they do in Philadelphia at the Exhibition, when there are more people than cups and saucers?" asked Elizabeth Eliza. "Could not you go and inquire? I know the lady from Philadelphia is talking about the Exhibition, and telling why she must go back to receive friends. And they must have trouble there! Could not you go in and ask, just as if you wanted to know?"

Agamemnon looked into the room, but there were too many talking with the lady from Philadelphia.

"If we could only look into some book," he said, "the encyclopaedia or the dictionary—they are such a help sometimes!"

At this moment he thought of his *Great Triumphs of Great Men,* that he was reading just now. He had not reached the lives of the Stephensons, or any of the men of modern times. He might skip over to them —he knew they were men for emergencies.

He ran up to his room, and met Solomon John coming down with chairs.

"That is a good thought," said Agamemnon. "I will bring down more upstairs chairs."

"No," said Solomon John, "here are all that can come down; the rest of the bedroom chairs match bureaus, and they never will do!"

Agamemnon kept on to his own room, to consult his books. If only he could invent something on the spur of the moment—a set of bedroom furniture, that in an emergency could be turned into parlor chairs! It seemed an idea; and he sat himself down to his table and pencils, when he was interrupted by the little boys, who came to tell him that Elizabeth Eliza wanted him.

The little boys had been busy thinking. They proposed that the tea-table, with all the things on, should be pushed into the front room, where the company were; and those could take cups who could find cups.

But Elizabeth Eliza feared it would not be safe to push so large a table; it might upset and break what china they had.

Agamemnon came down to find her pouring out tea, in the back room. She called to him:

"Agamemnon, you must bring Mary Osborne to help, and perhaps one of the Gibbons boys would carry round some of the cups."

And so she began to pour out and to send round the sandwiches, and the tea, and the coffee. Let things go as far as they would!

The little boys took the sugar and cream.

"As soon as they have done drinking, bring back the cups and saucers to be washed," she said to the Gibbons boys and the little boys.

This was an idea of Mary Osborne's.

But what was their surprise, that the more they poured out, the more cups they seemed to have! Elizabeth Eliza took the coffee, and Mary Osborne the tea. Amanda brought fresh cups from the kitchen.

"I can't understand it," Elizabeth Eliza said to Amanda. "Do they come back to you, round through the piazza? Surely there are more cups than there were!"

Her surprise was greater when some of them proved to be coffee-cups that matched the set! And they never had had coffee-cups.

Solomon John came in at this moment, breathless with triumph.

"Solomon John!" Elizabeth Eliza exclaimed, "I cannot understand the cups!"

"It is my doing," said Solomon John, with an elevated air. "I went to the lady from Philadelphia, in the midst of her talk. 'What do you do in Philadelphia, when you haven't enough cups?' 'Borrow of my neighbors,' she answered, as quick as she could."

"She must have guessed," interrupted Elizabeth Eliza.

"That may be," said Solomon John. "But I whispered to Ann Maria Bromwich—she was standing by—and she took me straight over into their closet, and old Mr. Bromwich bought this set, just where we bought ours. And they had a coffee-set, too—"

"You mean where our father and mother

bought them. We were not born," said Elizabeth Eliza.

"It is all the same," said Solomon John. "They match exactly."

So they did, and more and more came in. Elizabeth Eliza exclaimed:

"And Agamemnon says we are not a family for emergencies!"

"Ann Maria was very good about it," said Solomon John; "and quick, too. And old Mrs. Bromwich has kept all her set of two dozen coffee and tea cups!"

Elizabeth Eliza was ready to faint with delight and relief. She told the Gibbons boys, by mistake, instead of Agamemnon, and the little boys. She almost let fall the cups and saucers she took in her hand.

"No trouble now!"

She thought of the cow, and she thought of the pig, and she poured on.

No trouble, except about the chairs. She looked into the room—all seemed to be sitting down, even her mother. No, her father was standing, talking to Mr. Jeffers. But he was drinking coffee, and the Gibbons boys were handing things around.

The daughters of the lady from Philadelphia were sitting on shawls on the edge of the window that opened upon the piazza. It was a soft, warm evening, and some of the young people were on the piazza. Everybody was talking and laughing, except those who were listening.

Mr. Peterkin broke away, to bring back his cup and another for more coffee.

"It's a great success, Elizabeth Eliza," he whispered. "The coffee is admirable, and plenty of cups. We asked none too many. I should not mind having a tea-party every week."

Elizabeth Eliza sighed with relief as she filled his cup. It was going off well. There were cups enough, but she was not sure she could live over another such hour of anxiety; and what was to be done after tea?

THE SENSITIVE CAT
By Alice Brown
November, 1905

THERE once was a sensitive cat
Who couldn't abide the word "Scat."
"If you want me to go,"
She yowled, "say so, you know,
But don't be so rude as all that!"

POH-HLAIK, THE CAVE-BOY

By Charles F. Lummis

October, 1903

FIVE hundred years ago the cloudless sun of New Mexico beat as blinding white upon the Pu-yé as it does to-day, and played as quaint pranks of hide-and-seek with the shadows in the face of that dazzling cliff; stealing now behind the royal pines in front, now suddenly leaping out to catch the dark truants that went dodging into the caves.

Now the sun and shadows are the same, and play the same old game—on one side with eager fire, on the other with pleased but timid gentleness. The playground has changed with the centuries, but not so much as to seem unfamiliar. It is the same noble cliff, lofty and long and castellate, towering creamy and beautiful amid the outpost pine groves of the Valles wilderness. From a little way off there seems no bit of change in it.

But ah, what a change there has been, after all! For the very silence of silences lies upon the Pu-yé. Only the deep breath of the pines, the sudden scream of the piñonero blue jay, ever break it now. And time was when the Boy Sun and the Shadow Girls had here a thousand mates in their gambols: mates whose voices flew like birds, and with pattering feet amid the tufa blocks, and the gleam of young eyes—three things that sun and shadows have not, nor had even when they were so much younger. Once these jumbled stones were tall houses against the white face of the cliff; and the caves into which the shadows crowd so were homes.

Then the great cliff of the Pu-yé was not lonely. Hundreds of faint smoke-spirals stole up its face. Here and there among the gray houses strode stalwart men with bow-case on shoulder, and women bringing water in earthen jars upon their heads. As for children, they were everywhere: sitting in the tufa sand and sifting it through their fingers; shouting *"hee-tah-oó"* from their hiding amid the great pumice blocks fallen from the cliff; chasing each other over the rocks, into the caves, down the slope, in that very game of tag which was invented before fire was; making mud tortillas by the pools of the drying brook; hunting each other in mimic war among the pines, or turning small bows and arrows to bring down the saucy piñonero, whose sky-blue feathers should deck bare heads of straight black hair.

Póh-hlaik, up by the cliff corner near where the estufa of the Eagle clan showed its dark mouth, was enjoying himself as much as any one—and a little bit after the game of the sun and the shadows. He was a tall, sinewy lad, with strong white teeth coming to light very often, and supple hands that could bend a bow to the arrow head. Just now he was down on all fours, crouching, pouncing, charging, and roaring in blood-curdling wise when he had breath between laughs. *Mo-keit-cha*, indeed! I would like to *see* the mountain-lion with such contented victims! Póh-hlaik's were half a dozen brown little sisters and cousins who laughed and shrieked and ran and came back to be devoured anew by this insatiate monster. Sometimes in a particularly ferocious rush some one got tipped over or had a toe stepped on by *Mo-keit-cha;* and then she would make a lip and start off

40

crying—whereat the ravening beast would pat her on the head with clumsy tenderness, and call back her dimples by a still grotesquer caper.

But before the victims had been devoured many more times apiece, a sweet, clear voice of a woman came ringing:

"Póh-hlaik!"

"Here, little mother! What wilt thou?" And the cougar of a moment ago rose on his hind legs and ran obediently on them to where a woman leaned through the tiny doorway of a cave. The adobe floor was spotlessly clean, and her modest cotton tunic shone like snow. Floor and tunic and feature should have looked strange enough to the unguessed and unguessing world beyond the seas. But in the face was a presence which any one should know, down to a smallest child, and anywhere—the mother look, which is the same in all the world.

"A goodly man will he be!" she murmured absently, with soft eyes resting on her strong young son. "Ay! It is to seek thy father, carrying this squash and dried meat of the deer. For by now he will be hungry, so long as he is in the estufa. And pray him come, if he will, that he may hear the baby, what it says."

Reaching back, she brought forward a little flat cradle with buckskin flaps laced across it; and from under its buckskin hood peered a brown lump of flesh, with big eyes black as tar.

"Ennah, handful-warrior!
Ennah, little great-man!"

she crooned, tossing the bundle gently on level palms. A funny little crack ran across the fatness, and the eyes lighted up as if they really knew something; and from that uncertain cavity came a decided "dă-dă" —which is just as far as a baby of his age gets with all the civilized progress of this year of grace 1903. We start about even; and it is fairly wonderful in knocking about the world to find how little difference there is, even in the first speech. There is no home nor blood where "papa" and "mama" are not understood. English words? Not a bit of it! They are *human* words, everywhere current, everywhere dear—perhaps remnants to us, with a few more of childhood, of before the Tower of Babel. And everywhere is as great joy when the uncertain lips first say "dă-dă" as was now in the house of Kwé-ya.

"Already he is to talk!" cried Póh-hlaik, with a delighted grin; and patting his mother on the shoulder and the baby on the cheek, he went running and leaping over the rocks like a young deer. Directly he was at the Eagle people's estufa, where the men of his father's clan all slept as well as counseled; for in the queer Indian society, which was not society at all, the men lived in their big sacred room, the women and children in their little houses. Póh-hlaik entered the small door, and stood a moment before his eyes grew used to the darkness. Then he saw his father sitting by the wall smoking a rush, and went to him.

"Here is to eat," he said, handing the bundle. "And my mother says if you will come! For already the small-one calls you!"

"He does? It is good—I will go." The tall, stern-faced Indian rose with slow dignity which was belied by a something in his eyes and voice. Like some men I have remotely heard of in more modern times, P'yá-po was not so "weak" as to betray feeling. But he was strong enough to *have* it—and sometimes a very tiny token of it would leak out in spite of him. Now, though nothing would have induced him to show unseemly haste, he was clearly losing no steps; and already the stately strides had carried him several yards as he turned to say to Póh-hlaik:

"Son, at the White-Corn people's estufa if thou see Enque-Enque, tell him I would speak with him before the night."

"So I will say," answered the boy, respectfully, turning to go to his own estufa—for since his mother was of the White-Corn people, so was Póh-hlaik. With Indians almost everywhere descent is reckoned from the mother's side, and not, as with us, from the father's. Furthermore, a man cannot marry into his own clan, so his sons belong to a different estufa.

Sure enough, Enque-Enque was at the Man-house of the White-Corn clan, and he received the message with a grunt. He was a little sharp-faced man, with the look of one gone sour. If P'yá-po with his mighty head and frame had a lion-like air, this other as clearly suggested the fox. Even the acute features contributed less to this than a way he had of cocking his chin down and to one side, and looking at something else, but seeing you. And it is a thing I have had occasion to learn, that when you are with one of these men who sees all you do without using even "half an eye," you will have none too many eyes to watch him if you use all you have.

Enque-Enque did not so much as look at Póh-hlaik; but the boy (who could have given lessons in these things to any one of us, if able to phrase what he knew) understood that the subordinate Shaman had weighed his face to a feather. Not that there was any secret to read there—he had merely delivered a message of which he knew no import back of the words. He did not *like* Enque-Enque; but trust an Indian face to say nothing of that—and as for his tone, it was the respectful one which no Pueblo boy ever failed to use to an elder. And now he suddenly felt *afraid* of his father's fifth assistant—suddenly, without the slightest tangible excuse, for nothing had happened.

"Shall I say to my father anything?" he ventured at last.

"I will go," answered the man, shortly—which Póh-hlaik needed no interpreter to tell him meant also "Now clear out, boy."

"But that is a queer one!" he was thinking to himself, as he went skipping down the slope. As he turned to come away, he had caught glimpse of about an inch of notched reed projecting from the lion-skin case on Enque-Enque's back. "For the feathers are put differently, and it will be longer, too—since it stands above the rest."

It was a very trifling matter to annoy any one; but that arrow seemed to stick in the boy's mind. You can have no possible notion how tiny a thing the Indian will notice, nor how much it can say to him; for he has kept the eyes that nature gave man to start with, and that we civilized folk have largely frittered away.

At the foot of the slope, where some enormous boulders hid him from the village, his trot dropped to a walk; and presently he sat down upon a block of tufa and began looking very intently at his feet. Whatever he saw there did not serve; for in a few minutes he rose, with a still clouded face, and began climbing a zigzag trail to the left. Here the cliff tapers into a long slope; and after a short trudging over the pumice fragments, he came upon the brow of the mesa among the junipers. A little farther yet, and he suddenly stepped from the woods into a large clearing, in whose center stood a great square pueblo, three stories high, built of tufa blocks from the same white cliff. Here were other brown folk, little and big; for this was the "upstairs town" of the cave pueblo, its ultimate refuge and fortress, and the permanent home of some of its people.

"Ka-ki!" sung out a voice; and a boy of Póh-hlaik's own age came scrambling down a ladder from the tall housetops. "I was just to go for thee. Come, let us make a hunt in the cañon, if we may find the Little Old-Mountain-Man*—for now he is very fat."

"It is well!" answered Póh-hlaik, brightening. "And if not him, we'll at least get trout."

Both boys had their bow-cases on their backs, and in five minutes they had descended the slope and were crossing the plateau to the brink of the cañon. This rift in the upland, four hundred feet deep, was shadowy with royal pines and musical with a lovely brook—as it is to this day. Póh-hlaik and Ka-be descended the precipitous side noiselessly, and began creeping along the brook in the thick underbrush. Fat trout flashed in the pools; but the boys paid no attention to them, for from a thicket on the other side of a little natural glade came the "gobble-obble-obble" and then the *skir-r-r!* of the wild turkey.

"No!" whispered Póh-hlaik to his companion's suggestion. "We will wait here —for he will come out to the brook with his family. But if we try to get to the other side, he can run without our seeing him for the bushes."

They lay quietly in a thick clump of alders, grasping each his bow, with an arrow at the string. The gobbler repeated his cry—and suddenly it was echoed from behind! The boys exchanged startled looks, and Ka-be was about to speak, but Póh-hlaik put his finger to his lips, with a curious flicker in his eye.

Just then there was a faint sighing sound overhead; and close in front of the thicket whence the first gobble had come, an arrow, fallen from the sky, stood quivering in the sward. A tiny rustle in the bushes, and a dark, bare arm reached out and plucked the arrow back out of sight.

* The wild turkey

Ka-be wore a dumbfounded look, but Póh-hlaik's face showed even more of terror than of wonder. He thought he had seen that arrow before! Now there were no more turkey-calls, but dead silence reigned in the cañon.

"Now he will not come!" whispered Ka-be. "Let us creep up the brook and around upon him before that other gets him."

"For your heart, hush you!" breathed Póh-hlaik in the ear of his chum. "See you not that there are no turkeys? And that hand—is that a hand of the Grandchildren of the Sun? It is for us to get to the pueblo *now*, and unseen! For not *our* lives only, but many more, are in the shadow. See!" he added nervously—for two or three fresh alder-leaves came slipping down the current, and then there was the faintest tinge in the limpid water, as of sand stirred up far above. "Come! But more noiseless and hidden than the snakes!"

He stretched upon his belly, and began moving down stream, lizard-like, the still puzzled Ka-be following him. When they had traversed a few hundred feet in this tedious fashion, Póh-hlaik turned to the right, up a little ravine dense with bush. It led to the top; and in a few moments the boys peered from the last bush on the brink of the cañon out among the scattered pines. All was still.

"Now, friend, it is to run as for life—and not straight, but dodging between the trees. Come!" Springing from their shelter, Póh-hlaik dashed off. Ka-be was at his heels—for, though his face showed that he was still mystified, he was one of those who follow.

No living thing was in sight; but before the runners had made four bounds there was a vicious *ish-oo!* and an arrow split the lobe of Póh-hlaik's ear and fell five yards ahead of him. Ka-be gave a wild yell, and leaped ahead like a scared fawn; but as for Póh-hlaik, he only clapped his hand to his ear even as he swerved past a big pine so as to throw it in line behind him. There was another whizz, but not so near; and then no further token.

"Not a word now!" said Póh-hlaik sternly, as they came, still at a smart run, to the cave-village. "For none must know save the Men of Power. My father will know what to do."

Ka-be promised—though a little sullenly at loss of the sensation he wished to noise abroad—and went off along the cliff. Póh-hlaik drew his father into an inner cave-room, and there told him everything just as it had befallen, without comments or surmises. Only, at the end, he could not refrain from adding: "As for the arrow which went as a message to the *barbaro*, I think I saw it once before!"

"Ahu? Was it with Enque-Enque? For if there be a traitor, it is he. It is because he is thought to be treating with the Tin-néh that I summoned him. Two say that they have seen him coming secretly from where the hostiles were. He has never been content since the elders laughed at his pretensions to be Chief Shaman. So in his quiver was the arrow? Well hast thou done, son! Keep the heart of a man and the still tongue. As for me, we will see what is to do."

There was but one thing to be done, in the opinion of the Captain of War. Those who had shot at two boys of the pueblo must be of the savage Tin-néh,* who from time immemorial had harassed the town-dwellers. Since they were in the cañon, he would teach them! Old Mah-quah had been dead but a year, and this was his successor's first chance. He would have no barbarians

* The great tribe now kown as Navajos

prowling about the peace-loving cave-town of the Pu-yé!

In less than half an hour a strong band of warriors, headed by the War Captain and the Chief Shaman, were stealing down into the cañon noiselessly as so many shadows. "Come thou," P'yá-po had said to his son; "for to-day may be the chance to prove thyself a man."

But Póh-hlaik replied: "Wilt thou not let me stay here by the mother? For in my heart something tells me."

"As thou wilt!" his father had given short answer. As he strode off he was thinking: "Will my first son be a mouse?"

But it was not that which kept the boy at home. He dared not say it to his father, but to him the plan of the War Captain seemed reckless. "What if it were even so that Enque-Enque wishes? For else why did he shoot at me again, after failing to kill? Was it not that I might report there were *barbaros* in the cañon, so he would get the warriors sent there? But how shall one dare think so, when the Men of Power decide otherwise?"

But, despite the inbred reverence for authority, Póh-hlaik could not convince himself that all was well; he wandered about restlessly. As the sun went down, the men sat in little groups talking of the matter, ill at ease; for after so many months of quiet, the savage foe was back at the old game. Dusk was closing in as Enque-Enque came strolling around the western turn of the cliff, his stone hoe in his hand. He had been at his field, he explained carelessly; and violent were his curses upon the Tin-néh when he heard the news.

Even as he spoke there came a far clamor—yells of rage, mingled with the fierce war-cry.

"They have trapped ours!" shouted Enque-Enque, leaping upon a rock. "Come!

we must run to their help, for the enemy are many."

A hundred men sprang forward at the word of the sub-Shaman, clutching their bows; but Póh-hlaik stood before them, crying shrilly:

"Not so! This same is the traitor who has sold us to the Tin-néh, and now he would strip the town of its men! Go not, if ye will hear the words of a boy!"

It was an unheard-of thing, thus to defy a medicine-man; but even so he stood erect, so stern and gray-faced that grizzled men looked at him in awe and back to the accused.

Enque-Enque's foxy air did not change in the least. "Bewitched is the boy!" he sneered, running his eyes back along the cliff. Then a sudden light broke across his face, and from his throat poured a wild whoop, even as he drove a swift shaft through the neck of the First Lieutenant of War. In answer rose a hideous yell from all about, and the darkening rocks swarmed with darker forms, and the twilight buzzed with wasps that had need to sting but once. A score of the men of the Pu-yé fell before one had time to turn; and among them was Póh-hlaik, an obsidian-tipped arrow through his shoulder and another deep in his thigh.

The conspirator's plans had worked very well. His hated chief and a majority of the warriors were gone out to the ambush he had laid for them; and his failure to send off the rest of the fighting strength of the town was like to be counterbalanced by the complete surprise. The startled Pueblos fought desperately; but the savages were nearly two to one, and pushed them to the very doors of the caves.

As for Póh-hlaik, he had fallen between two great lava-blocks, fainting with pain and loss of blood. For a few moments he lay there; and then, suddenly gritting his teeth, began dragging himself toward his mother's house. She was alone with the little one.

All around him raged the fight. The air hurtled with arrows, and everywhere were savage whoops and dying screams and the sickly smell of blood. Once two grappled foemen wrestled across him, wringing a howl of pain from him with their tread; and again, he had to crawl over a stark form. But he hunched himself painfully along behind sheltering rocks till close to the cave that was his home. He was about to call out, when suddenly, against the darkening sky, he saw a figure backing out of the low doorway, dragging something. Had he been standing he could not have made it out; but from his prostrate position that dark silhouette against the west was unmistakable. It was Enque-Enque! His bow was gone; but between his teeth was something which could only be the cruel obsidian knife, and both his hands were clenched in the long hair of a woman—who seemed to be bracing against the doorway to keep from being dragged out.

Póh-hlaik's heart lost its count for a moment. His father's enemy knew well where to strike! And at thought of the fate that overhung his mother, he turned deathly sick.

The victim's hold was slipping—already her head and shoulders were through the door. Enque-Enque, as he hauled away, was hidden now by a tall tufa block; only his long, sinewy arms and their prey showed against the sky.

"The Trues give me eyes!" breathed Póh-hlaik devoutly, tugging the bowstring to his ear, though the effort seemed to drive a hundred darts through the wounded shoulder. Truly it was an ill mark, in that grim dusk and from the ground! But the twang of the cord was followed by a howl of rage and pain. The head popped within the doorway again; and Enque-Enque sprawled backward, scrambled up, and fled into the gloom—his two hands spitted one to the other by the clever shaft.

And then there was a new uproar—but this time from the east! And arrows rained doubly thick, and the enemy-yell of the Hero Brothers soared above the savage howls of the Tin-néh. P'yá-po and his men were back, and at last the barbarians fled down the slopes, leaving their dead among the rocks. It would be long before they should forget the Pu-yé. P'yá-po's counsel had saved the impetuous War Captain from the full disaster of the ambuscade: and, scattering that small force by a flank movement, they had hurried back to the village—well understanding now the whole manoeuver.

When all was over and the Chief Shaman came to his wife's house, he found a badly wounded lad crouched within the door, his bow clutched tightly and his lips set. "I have kept them safe for thee, father!" he said huskily—and, with the words, lurched fainting to one side. P'yá-po laid him along the floor and stanched the blood, and sat beside him.

"The heart and the hand of a Man!" he said, with a little shake in the sonorous voice. "And when he is well of his wounds he shall take the place of the unworthy one who has gone."

"He is his father's son!" whispered Kwé-ya proudly. And just then the little one, who had slept through the jaws of death, stirred in the buckskin cradle and called, "Dǎ-dǎ!"

THE CLEVER NURSE
BY MARGARET JOHNSON

Said this clever little nurse
"I'm not a gaby.
I can do more things than tend
this infant, maybe!"
And she trotted, sang & read,
As she plied her nimble thread,
And every one was pleased—
except the Baby

THE STORY OF KING ARTHUR AND HIS KNIGHTS

By Howard Pyle

May, 1903

CHAPTER VI

HOW KING ARTHUR HELD A ROYAL WEDDING, AND ESTABLISHED THE ROUND TABLE.

AND now was come the early fall of the year; that pleasant season when meadowland and wold were still green with the summer that had only just passed; when the sky, likewise, was as of summertime—extraordinarily blue and full of large floating clouds; when a bird might sing here and another there a short song in memory of springtime (as the smaller fowl doth when the year draweth to its ending); when all the air was tempered with warmth and yet the leaves were everywhere turning brown and red and gold, so that when the sun shone through them it was as though a cloth of gold, broidered with brown and crimson and green, hung above the head. Now was come the early autumn season of the year, when it is exceedingly pleasant to be afield among the nut-trees with hawk and hound, or to travel abroad in the yellow world, whether it be ahorse or afoot.

Such was the time of year in which had been set the marriage of King Arthur and the Lady Guinevere at Camelot, and at that place was extraordinary pomp and glory of circumstance. All the world was astir and in a great ferment of joy, for all folk were exceedingly glad that King Arthur was to have a queen.

In preparation for that great occasion the town of Camelot was entirely bedight with magnificence, for the stony street along which the Lady Guinevere must come to the royal castle of the king was strewn thick with fresh-cut rushes, smoothly laid. Moreover, it was in many places spread with carpets of excellent pattern such as might be fit to lay upon the floor of some goodly hall. Likewise all the houses along the way were hung with fine hangings of woven texture interwoven with threads of azure and crimson, and everywhere were flags and bannerets afloat in the warm and gentle breeze against the blue sky, so that all the world appeared to be alive with bright colors.

Thus came the wedding-day of the king—bright and clear and exceeding radiant.

King Arthur sat in his hall, surrounded by his court, awaiting news that the Lady Guinevere was coming thitherward. And it was about the middle of the morning when there came a messenger in haste riding upon a milk-white steed. And the raiment of that messenger and the trappings of his horse were all of cloth of gold embroidered with scarlet and white, and the tabard of the messenger was set with many jewels, so that he glistened from afar as he rode, with a singular splendor of appearance.

So this herald-messenger came straight into the castle where the king abided waiting, and he said: "My Lord King, the Lady Guinevere with her father, the King Leodegrance, and their court draweth nigh unto this place."

Upon this the king immediately arose with great joy, and straightway he went forth with his court of knights, riding in great state. And as he went down that marvelously adorned street, all the people shouted aloud as he passed by, wherefore

47

he smiled and bent his head from side to side; for that day he was wondrous happy.

Thus he rode forward unto the town gate, and out therefrom, and so came thence into the country beyond, where the broad and well-beaten highway ran winding down beside the shining river betwixt the willows and the osiers.

And, behold! King Arthur and those with him perceived the court of the princess where it appeared at a distance, wherefore they made great rejoicing and hastened forward with all speed. And as they came nigh, the sun falling upon the apparels of silk and cloth of gold, and upon golden chains and the jewels that hung therefrom, all of that noble company that surrounded the Lady Guinevere's litter flashed and sparkled with a marvelous radiance.

For seventeen of the noblest knights of King Arthur's court, clad in complete armor, and sent by him as an escort unto the lady, rode in great splendor, surrounding the litter wherein the princess lay. And the framework of that litter was of richly gilded wood, and its curtains and its cushions were of crimson silk embroidered with threads of gold. And behind the litter there rode in gay and joyous array, all shining with many colors, the court of the princess—her damsels in waiting, gentlemen, ladies, pages and attendants. And the sun shone with surpassing brightness, and the river lay like a silver shield, darkened where the small winds breathed upon it; and the swallows darted over the water, dipping here and there to touch its smooth surface; and everything was so exceedingly cheerful with the beauty of the young autumn season that the heart of everyone was expanded with entire joy.

So those parties of the king and the Lady Guinevere drew nigh together until they met.

Then straightway King Arthur dis-mounted from his noble horse, and, all clothed with royalty, he went afoot unto the Lady Guinevere's litter, whilst Sir Gawaine and Sir Ewaine held the bridle of his horse. Thereupon one of her pages drew aside the silken curtains of the Lady Guinevere's litter, and King Leodegrance gave her his hand, and she straightway descended therefrom, all aglow, as it were, with her exceeding beauty. So King Leodegrance led her to King Arthur, and King Arthur came to her, and placed one hand beneath her chin and the other upon her head, and inclined his countenance and kissed her upon her smooth cheek. And all those who were there lifted up their voices in great acclaim.

Thus did King Arthur give welcome unto the Lady Guinevere and unto King Leodegrance her father upon the highway beneath the walls of the town of Camelot, at the distance of half a league from that place. And no one who was there ever forgot that meeting, for it was full of extraordinary grace and noble courtliness.

Then King Arthur and his court of knights and nobles brought King Leodegrance and the Lady Guinevere with great ceremony unto Camelot, and thereby into the royal castle, where, befitting their several states, apartments were assigned unto all, so that the entire place was all alive with joyousness and beauty.

And when high noon had come the entire court went with great state and ceremony unto the cathedral, and there, surrounded by wonderful magnificence, those two noble souls were married by the archbishop.

And all the bells did ring right joyfully, and all the people who stood without the cathedral shouted with loud acclaim; and, lo! the king and the queen came forth all shining, he like unto the sun for splendor and she like unto the moon for beauty.

King Arthur meets the Lady Guinevere.

Drawn by Howard Pyle.

In the castle a great noontide feast was spread, and there sat thereat four hundred eighty and six lordly and noble folk—kings, knights, and nobles, with queens and ladies in magnificent array. And near to the king and the queen there sat King Leodegrance, and Merlin, and Sir Ulfius, and Sir Ector the Trustworthy, and Sir Gawaine, and Sir Ewaine, and Sir Kay, and King Ban, and King Pellinore, and many other famous and exalted folk—so that no man had before that time beheld such magnificent courtliness as they beheld at that famous wedding-feast of King Arthur and Queen Guinevere. So have I told it unto you, so that you might behold, however so dimly, how marvelously pleasant were those days in which dwelt King Arthur and his famous court of knights.

And that day was likewise very famous in the history of chivalry: for in the afternoon the famous Round Table was established; and that Round Table was at once the very flower and the chiefest glory of King Arthur's reign.

For about mid of the afternoon the king and queen, preceded by Merlin and followed by all that splendid court of kings, lords, nobles, and knights in full array, made progression to that certain place where Merlin, partly by magic and partly by skill, had caused to be builded a very wonderful pavilion about the Round Table where it stood.

And when the king and the queen and the court had entered in thereat, they were amazed at the beauty of that pavilion, for they perceived, as it were, a great space that appeared to be a marvelous land of fay. For the walls were all richly gilded and were painted with very wonderful figures of saints and of angels, clad in ultramarine and crimson. And all those saints and angels were depicted playing upon various musical instruments that appeared to be made of gold. And overhead the roof of the pavilion was made to represent the sky, being all of cerulean blue sprinkled over with stars. And in the midst of that painted sky was an image as it were of the sun in his glory. And underfoot was a pavement all of marble stone, set in small squares of black and white, and blue and red, and sundry other colors.

And in the midst of the pavilion was the famous Round Table, with seats thereat exactly sufficient for fifty persons. And the table was covered with a table-cloth of fine linen, as white as snow and embroidered at the hem with threads of silver. And at each of the fifty places was a chalice of gold filled with fragrant wine, and at each place was a platter of gold bearing a manchet of fair white bread. And when the king and his court entered into the pavilion, lo! music began of a sudden for to play with a wonderful sweetness, so that the heart was overjoyed for to listen to it.

Then Merlin came and took King Arthur by the hand and led him away from Queen Guinevere. And he said unto the king: "Lo, Lord King! Behold, this is the Round Table."

And King Arthur said: "Merlin, that which I see is wonderful beyond the telling."

Then Merlin discovered unto the king the marvels of the Round Table. For first he pointed to a high seat, very wonderfully wrought in precious woods and gilded so that it was exceedingly beautiful, and he said: "Behold! Lord King, yonder seat is called the Seat Royal, and that seat is for thyself." And as Merlin spake, lo! there suddenly appeared sundry letters of gold above that seat, and the letters of gold read the name

Arthur, King.

—

And Merlin said, "Lord, yonder seat may well be called the center seat of the Round Table, for, in sooth, thou art indeed the very center of all that is most worthy of true knightliness. Wherefore that seat shall still be called the center seat of all the other seats."

Then Merlin pointed to the seat that stood opposite to the Seat Royal, and that seat also was of a very wonderful appearance, being all of crimson and of azure inlaid with many cunning devices, and with figures of silver inset into the wood. And Merlin said unto the king: "My Lord King, that seat is named the Seat Perilous; for no man but one in all this world shall sit therein, and that man is not yet born upon the earth. And if any other man shall dare to sit therein that man shall either suffer death or a sudden and terrible misfortune for his temerity. Wherefore that seat is called the Seat Perilous."

"Merlin," quoth the king, "all that thou tellest me passeth the bound of understanding for marvelousness. Now I do beseech thee in all haste to find forthwith a sufficient number of knights to fill this Round Table, so that my glory shall be entirely complete."

"My lord," said Merlin, "I may not fill the Round Table for thee at this time. For, though thou hast gathered about thee the very noblest court of chivalry in all of Christendom, yet are there but two-and-thirty knights here present who may be considered worthy to sit at the Round Table."

"Then, Merlin," quoth King Arthur, "I do desire of thee that thou shalt straightway choose me those two-and-thirty."

"That will I do, Lord King," said Merlin.

So Merlin cast his eyes around, and lo! he saw where King Pellinore stood at a little distance. Unto him went Merlin and took him by the hand. "Behold, my Lord King," quoth he unto Arthur, "here is the knight in all of the world next to thyself who is at this time most worthy for to sit at this Round Table. For he is both exceedingly gentle of demeanor unto the poor and needy, and at the same time is so terribly strong and skilful that I know not whether thou or he is the more to be feared in an encounter of knight against knight."

Then Merlin led King Pellinore forward, and behold! upon the high seat that stood upon the left hand of the Seat Royal there appeared of a sudden the name

Pellinore.

And the name was emblazoned in letters of gold that shone with extraordinary luster. And when King Pellinore took this seat great and loud acclaim long continued was given him by all those who stood round about.

Now after Merlin had chosen King Arthur and King Pellinore, he chose from out of the court of King Arthur knights two-and-thirty in all, and they were knights of greatest renown in chivalry who did first establish the Round Table of King Arthur.

And among these knights were Sir Gawaine and Sir Ewaine, who were nephews unto the king, and they sat nigh to him upon the right hand; and there was Sir Ulfius (who held his place but a year and eight months unto the time of his death, after the which Sir Geharris, who was esquire unto his brother Sir Gawaine, held that seat); and there was Sir Kay the Seneschal, who was foster-brother unto the king; and there was Sir Baudwain of Britain (who held his place but three years and two months until his death, after the which Sir Agravaine held that seat); and there was Sir Pellias, and Sir Geraint, and many others, so that the world had never before seen such a splendid array of noble knights gathered together.

And as each of these knights was chosen

by Merlin, and as Merlin took that knight by the hand, lo! the name of that knight suddenly appeared in golden letters, very bright and shining, upon the chair that appertained to him.

And when all had been chosen, behold! King Arthur saw that the seat upon the right hand of the Seat Royal had not been filled and that it bore no name upon it. And he said unto Merlin: "Merlin, how is this, that the seat upon my right hand hath not been filled and beareth no name?"

And Merlin said: "My lord, there shall be a name thereon in a very little while, and he who shall sit therein shall be the greatest knight in all the world until that knight cometh who shall occupy the Seat Perilous."

And King Arthur said, "I would that he who shall sit at my right hand were with us now." And Merlin said, "He cometh anon."

Thus was the Round Table established with great pomp and ceremony of estate. For first the Archbishop of Canterbury blessed each and every seat, progressing from place to place surrounded by his court, the choir whereof sang most musically in accord, whilst others swang censers from which there ascended a vapor of frankincense, filling that entire pavilion as with an odor of heavenly blessedness.

And when the archbishop had thus blessed every one of those seats, the chosen knights took each his stall at the Round Table, and his esquire came and stood behind him, holding the banneret with his coat of arms upon the spear-point above the knight's head. And all those who stood about that place, both knights and ladies, lifted up their voices in loud acclaim.

Then all the knights arose, and each knight held up before him the cross of the hilt of his sword, and each knight spake word for word as King Arthur spake. And this was the covenant of their knighthood of the Round Table: that they should be gentle unto the weak; that they should be courageous unto the strong; that they should be terrible unto the wicked and the evil-doers; that they should defend the helpless who should call upon them for aid; that all women should be held unto them sacred; that they should stand unto the defense of one another whensoever such defense should be required; that they should be merciful unto all men; that they should be gentle of deed, true in friendship, and faithful in love.

This was the covenant unto which each knight vowed upon the cross of his sword, and in witness thereof did kiss the hilt thereof, and thereupon all those present once more gave loud acclaim. Then did all the knights of the Round Table seat themselves, and each knight brake bread from the golden paten and quaffed wine from the golden chalice that stood before him, giving thanks unto God for that which he ate and drank.

Thus was King Arthur wedded unto Queen Guinevere; and thus was the Round Table established. Wherefore all these things have I told unto you that ye might know how that glorious order of knighthood was first established.

And King Arthur was exceedingly uplifted with the great joy that possessed him. Wherefore he commanded that all of Camelot should be feasted at his expense.

And he also proclaimed that there should be feasting and jousting in his court for three days.

HOW TO STUDY PICTURES
By Charles H. Caffin
November, 1904

INTRODUCTION

"Having eyes, see ye not?"

THE world is full of beauty which many people hurry past or live in front of and do not see. There is also a world of beauty in pictures, but it escapes the notice of many, because, while they wish to see it, they do not know how.

The first necessity for the proper seeing of a picture is to try to see it through the eyes of the artist who painted it. This is not a usual method. Generally people look only through their own eyes, and like or dislike a picture according as it does or does not suit their particular fancy. These people will tell you: "Oh, I don't know anything about painting, but I know what I like"; which is their way of saying: "If I don't like it right off, I don't care to be bothered to like it at all."

Such an attitude of mind cuts one off from growth and development, for it is as much as to say: "I am very well satisfied with myself and quite indifferent to the experiences and feelings of other men." Yet it is just this feeling and experience of another man which a picture gives us. If you consider a moment you will understand why. The world itself is a vast panorama, and from it the painter selects his subject—not to copy it exactly, since it would be impossible for him to do this, even if he tried. How could he represent, for example, each blade of grass, each leaf upon a tree? So what he does is to represent the subject as he sees it, as it appeals to his sympathy or interest; and if twelve artists painted the same landscape the result would be twelve different pictures, differ-

ing according to the way in which each man had been impressed by the scene; in fact, according to his separate point of view or separate way of seeing it, influenced by his individual experience and feeling.

It is most important to realize the part which is played by these two qualities of experience and feeling. Experience, the fullness or the deficiency of it, must affect the work of every one of us, no matter what our occupation may be. And if the work is of the kind which appeals to the feelings of others, as in the case of the preacher, the writer, the actor, the painter, sculptor, architect, or art-craftsman, the musician or even the dancer, then it must be affected equally by the individual's capacity of feeling and by his power of expressing what he feels.

Therefore, since none of us can include in ourselves the whole range of possible experience and feeling, it is through the experience and the feeling of others that we deepen and refine our own. It is this that we should look to pictures to accomplish, which, as you will acknowledge, is a very different thing from offhand like or dislike. For example, we may not be attracted at first, but we reason with ourselves: "No doubt this picture meant a good deal to the man who painted it; it embodies his experience of the world and his feeling toward the subject. It represents, in fact, a revelation of the man himself, and if it is true that 'the noblest study of mankind is man,' then possibly in the study of this man, as revealed in his work, there may be much that ought to interest me."

I am far from wishing you to suppose

that all pictures will repay you for such intimate study. For instance, we may quickly discover that an artist's experience of life is meager, his feeling commonplace and paltry. There are not a few men of this sort in the occupation of art, just as in every other walk of life, and their pictures, so far as we ourselves are concerned, will be disappointing. But among the pictures which have stood the test of time we shall always find that the fruits of the artist's experience and feeling are of a kind which make a lasting appeal to the needs of the human heart and mind, and that this fact is one of the causes of their being held in perpetual honor.

There is also another cause: If only experience and feeling were necessary to make an artist, some of us would be better artists than many who follow the profession of art. But there is another necessity—the power of expressing the experience and feeling. This, by its derivation from the Greek, is the real meaning of the word "art," the capacity to "fit" a form to an idea. The artist is the "fitter," who gives shape and construction to the visionary fabric of his imagination; and this method of "fitting" is called his "technique."

So the making of a picture involves two processes: a taking in of the *impression*, and a giving of it out by visible *expression;* a seeing of the subject with the eye and the mind, and a communicating of what has been so seen to the eyes and minds of others; and both these processes are influenced by the experience and feeling of the artist and make their appeal to our own. From this it should be clear that the beauty of a picture depends much less upon its subject than upon the artist's conception and treatment of it. A grand subject will not of itself make a grand picture, while a very homely one, by the way in which it is treated, may be made to impress us profoundly.

The degree of beauty in a picture depends, in fact, upon the artist's feeling for beauty and upon his power to express it; and in order that we may discover how, at successive times and in various countries, different men have conceived of life and have expressed their feeling and experience in pictures, I propose that we shall study this out in a series of comparisons.

Our plan, therefore, will be:

"Look here, upon this picture, and on this"; not to decide offhand which you like the better,—for in some cases perhaps you will not like either, since they were painted in times so remote from ours as to be outside our twentieth-century habit of understanding—but in order that we may get at the artist's way of seeing in each case. In this way I hope, too, that we may be able to piece together the story of modern painting; beginning with its re-birth in the thirteenth century, when it emerged from the darkness of the Middle Ages, and following it through its successive stages in different countries down to our own day.

I

GIOVANNI CIMABUE (1240–1302); GIOTTO [GIOTTO DI BONDONE] (1276–1377), FLORENTINE SCHOOL.

FOR the first comparison I invite you to study the two pictures . . . of "The Madonna Enthroned." One was painted by Cimabue, the other by his pupil, Giotto. Both were painted on wooden panels in distemper, that is to say, with colors that have been mixed with some gelatinous medium, such as the white and the yolk of an egg beaten up together, for it was not until the fifteenth century that the use of oil-colors was adopted. The colors used in Giotto's panel are tints of blue and rose and white;

"THE MADONNA ENTHRONED." BY CIMABUE.

in Cimabue's the blues and reds are deep and dusky, the background in each case being golden.

We notice at once a general similarity between these two pictures, not only in choice of subject but in the manner of presentation: the Madonna seated upon a throne; her mantle drawn over her head; her right hand resting on the knee of the infant Saviour, who has two fingers of his right hand raised in the act of blessing; kneeling angels at the foot, and figures in tiers above them; all the heads being surrounded by the nimbus, or circular cloud of light, showing, like a halo, their sacred character.

'" THE MADONNA ENTHRONED." BY GIOTTO.

The reason of this general similarity is that the choice of a subject in painting and the manner of its presentation were fixed by the Christian Church of that time: for long before this thirteenth century the methods of old Greek art had been lost, and the Church had adopted a form of art known as Byzantine. I will try to explain what this means.

Briefly, the cause of the change was this. In old Greece, art and religion were bound together. The gods and goddesses* in

* Zeus, Ares, Athene, and the rest—or, as the Romans called them, Jupiter. Mars, Minerva, etc.

whom they believed were always represented in sculpture and painting as human beings of a higher order; physical perfection was the ideal alike of religion and of art. But the Christianity of those earlier times met the ideal of physical perfection with the spiritual doctrine of mortifying the flesh, and the pagan art of old Greece was condemned by the Church. Yet pictures of some sort were needed as an aid to the teachings of religion, and the Church found what it required in the art of Byzantium.

This old Greek city stood where Constantinople now stands, and was the gateway between the Eastern and Western worlds. Now the ideals of the East and West are very different. While the Greek artist carved or painted human or animal forms, striving to give them a perfection of shape in every part that would express his ideal, the artist of the East reached his ideal through the perfection of beautiful lines, of beautiful patterns of form and colors. Thus the one art is represented at its best by the sculptures of Phidias on the Parthenon, the other by a decorated porcelain vase.

The arrival, therefore, at Byzantium of this Oriental art, so far removed from the pagan study of the human form, so beautifully decorative, was welcomed by the Church, both for the decorating of the sacred buildings and for the illuminating of the sacred manuscripts; and it was as decorators and illuminators that the Byzantine artists did their finest work. But as the old Greek study of the human figure had been abandoned, the ignorance of the artists regarding the real character of the human form increased; their types of figure became less and less like nature and more and more according to an unnatural figure established by the Church. As "mortifying the flesh" was preached, the figures must be thin and gaunt, their gestures angular, the expression of their emaciated faces one of painful ecstasy. And so, in time, all that was required of or permitted to the painters of those days was to go on reproducing certain chosen subjects in a sort of stencil-like way.

Now, therefore, we can understand why those two pictures of "The Madonna Enthroned," by Cimabue and Giotto, are so similar in arrangement. They both followed the rules prescribed by the Church. Yet the Florentines of Cimabue's day found his picture so superior to anything they had seen before—so much more splendid in color, if not much nearer to the true representation of life—that, when it was completed, they carried it in joyous procession from the artist's home, through the streets of Florence, and deposited it with ceremony in the Church of Santa Maria Novella.

Cimabue had chanced upon the boy Giotto as, like David of old, he watched his flock upon the mountain; and he found him drawing the form of one of the goats upon a rock with a sharp piece of slate. The master must have seen some hint of genius in the work, for he straightway asked the boy if he would like to be his pupil, and, having received a glad assent and the father's permission, carried him off to Florence to his *bottega*. This, the artist's studio of that period and for long after, was rather what we should call a workshop, in which the pupils ground and prepared the colors under the master's direction; and it was not until they had thoroughly mastered this branch of the work, a task which in Giotto's time was supposed to occupy about six years, that they were permitted to use the brushes. How often, as he worked in the gloom of the bottega, must the shepherd-boy have peeped wistfully at the master standing in the shady garden, before a great glory of crimson drapery and golden background, and wondered if he himself should ever acquire so marvelous a skill!

He was destined to accomplish greater things, for in the free air of the mountain the boy's eager eyes had learned to love and study nature. It was the love of *form* that had set him to try to picture a goat upon the surface of the rock; it was the *actual appearance* of objects that he sought to render when in due time he learned to use the brush.

If you turn again to a comparison of his Madonna with that of Cimabue, you will see what strides he had already made toward natural truth. Observe how the figure of the Virgin is made real to us, notwithstanding that it is covered, as in Cimabue's, with drapery; and that the Holy Child in Cimabue's picture is not nearly so strong and firm and lifelike as Giotto's, though he is enveloped in a garment. Examine also the other figures in Giotto's picture; you will find the same suggestion of a substantial form that could be touched and grasped. Notice further how his feeling for truth has affected his arrangement of the forms. The throne actually has length, breadth, and thickness; so have all the figures, and they rest firmly upon the ground; the artist has called in the aid of perspective to enforce the reality of his group.

Now how has he accomplished this appearance of reality? By the use of light and shade, and by making his lines express the structure and character of the object. Compare, again, for example, the figure of the infant Saviour in the two pictures. In Cimabue's the drapery is scored with lines which vaguely hint at folds and obscure the shape of the limbs beneath; but in Giotto's certain parts of the figure are made to project by the use of high lights, and others are correspondingly depressed by shade, while the lines of the drapery serve, as you notice, to indicate the shape of the form beneath.

This use of light and shade by Giotto, while it marks a distinct advance from the flat, pattern-like painting of the Byzantine school, is still very crudely managed, and, as if conscious of the fact, the artist has selected the most simple arrangements of drapery. The picture was painted probably during the years of his apprenticeship to Cimabue, and shows much less freedom and practised skill than the works of Giotto's later years. Giotto was the first artist to introduce the faces of living people of his own time into pictures, and the "Paradise" on the walls of the Bargello in Florence contains the famous portrait of Dante, the great Italian poet, in his early manhood. It had remained covered with whitewash for two hundred years, until once more brought to light in 1840.

All Giotto's paintings were executed in fresco, that is to say, were painted on the plaster before it was dry, with water-colors mixed in a glutinous medium, so that as the surface hardened the colors became fixed and blended in it. While the technical knowledge displayed in them may seem to you hardly greater than that of a school-boy of our own day, yet they are so simple and unaffected, so earnest in feeling, that they arouse the interest and enthusiasm of the modern student.

In his own day Giotto's fame as a painter was supreme. He had numerous followers, and these "Giotteschi," as they were styled, continued his methods for nearly a hundred years. But, like all the great men of the Florentine school, he was a master of more than one craft. "Forget that they were painters," writes Mr. Berenson, "they remain great sculptors; forget that they were sculptors, and still they remain architects, poets, and even men of science."

The beautiful Campanile, which stands beside the cathedral in Florence, and represents a perfect union of strength and elegance, was designed by Giotto and partly erected in his lifetime. Moreover, the sculptured reliefs which decorate its lower part were all from his designs, though he lived to execute only two of them.

Thus, architect, sculptor, painter, friend of Dante and of other great men of his day, Giotto was the worthy forerunner of that brilliant band of artists which a century later made Florence forever renowned as the birthplace of that great revival, or "new birth" of art, generally called "The Renaissance."

II

ALESSANDRO BOTTICELLI (1446–1510), FLOR-ENTINE SCHOOL; HANS MEMLING (1430–1494), FLEMISH SCHOOL.

WE have seen that the revival of painting began with a study of the appearances of objects, and an attempt to represent them as real to the senses of sight and touch; that the painters learned from the sculptors, who themselves had learned from the remains of antique sculpture, and that the result was a closer truth to nature, in the representation of the human form.

We have now to consider the effect produced upon painting by the revival of the study of Greek, which revealed to Italy of the fifteenth century a new light. Botticelli represents this new inspiration, and I have coupled with him the Flemish painter, Memling, because these two artists, though they worked apart and under different conditions, had one quality of mind in common. An unaffected simplicity, frank and artless, fresh and tender, like the child-mind or the opening buds of spring flowers, appears in each.

In the year 1396 Manuel Chrysoloras, a Byzantine scholar, was appointed professor of Greek at Florence. From him and from his pupils the knowledge of Greek literature spread rapidly over Italy, accompanied by an extraordinary enthusiasm for Roman and Greek art, and for Greek thought and Greek ideals. Artists of that time soon began to cherish the old Greek devotion to the beauty of the human form; the scholars gave themselves up to admiration of Plato's philosophy. Artists and scholars thronged the court of Duke Lorenzo de' Medici (Lorenzo the Magnificent), patron of arts and letters, and among the brilliant throng none was more highly honored than Sandro Botticelli. His father was in comfortable circumstances, and he had been "instructed in all such things as children are usually taught before they choose a calling." But he refused to give his attention to reading, writing, and accounts, so that his father, despairing of his ever becoming a scholar, apprenticed him to the goldsmith Botticello; whence the name by which the world remembers him. His own family name was Filipepi.

In those days, as we have noted before, men were often masters of more than one craft. One well-known painter was also a goldsmith; another was goldsmith, painter, and sculptor. Botticello's Sandro, a stubborn-featured youth with large, quietly searching eyes and a shock of yellow hair—he has left a portrait of himself in one of his pictures—would also fain have been a painter, and to that end was placed with a well-known painter, who was also a monk, Fra Philippo Lippi. Sandro made rapid progress, and loved his master. But his own pictures show that Sandro was a dreamer and a poet.

You will feel this if you refer to the two pictures and compare his "Virgin Enthroned" with Memling's. The latter's is much more realistic. It is true that it does not, as a whole, represent a real scene, for the Virgin's throne with its embroidered hanging or *dossal*, the canopy of *baldachin* above it, and the richly decorated arch which frames it in are not what you would expect to see set up in a landscape. These are features repeated, with variations, in so many Madonna pictures intended for altar-pieces.

But how very real are the two bits of

into the world to redress. But Memling was satisfied merely to suggest these things; and then devoted himself to rendering with characteristic truth a little scene of realism. The angel on the left is simply an older child playfully attracting the baby's atten-

"THE VIRGIN ENTHRONED." BY BOTTICELLI.

landscape, which are drawn, we may feel sure, from nature: a great man's castle and a water-mill, two widely separated phases of life, suggesting, perhaps, that the Christ came to save rich and poor alike. Then, too, the introduction of the apple may be intended to remind us of the circumstances of the fall of man, which the Saviour came

tion to an apple; the Christ-child is simply a baby, attracted by the colored, shining object, and the pretty scene is watched intently by the other angel. On the Madonna's face, however, is an abstracted expression, as if her thoughts were far away: not in pursuit of any mystical dreams, but following that quiet, happy pathway along which a young mother's thoughts will roam.

So we find in Memling's picture close studies of the way in which the facts pre-

figures, and in the little story which they are enacting. As I have said, the spirit of the picture is realistic.

But turn to Botticelli's. Here the spirit is

"THE VIRGIN ENTHRONED." BY MEMLING.

sent themselves to the eye. This is seen, too, in the landscape, in the carved and embroidered ornament, in the character of the

imaginative or allegorical. He was fond of allegorical subjects. In the present case the subject is religious, but we may doubt if the Bible version of the story was in the artist's mind. He was commissioned to paint a Madonna and Child with attendant angels, and, poet and dreamer that he was, took the familiar theme and made it the basis of a picture from his own imagination. In the figure of the Christ-child there is a grave dignity, a suggestion of authority. The only gesture of infancy is in the left arm and hand, and the mother's face is bowed in timid meekness, and is rather sad in expression.

But beauty of face he does not give to his Madonna; she is meek and timid—oppressed with gentle sadness. In the faces of the angels, the young fair creatures who stand around the throne, what wistful and unsatisfied yearning!

The strain of sadness, indeed, is in all Botticelli's pictures; they have the note of infinite but ineffectual longing. So that, when we understand this, we forget the ugliness of many of his faces, and find in them a spiritual meaning, which we learn to feel is a very touching and beautiful expression of the artist's own mind, of his particular way of looking at the world of his time.

He looked at it as a poet, moved alike by the love of beauty and by the beauty of love; and out of the world's realities he fashioned for himself dreams, and these he pictured. So his pictures, as I have said, are not records of fact, treated with a very pleasing fancifulness and reverence, as in this Madonna of Memling's, but visions, the beauty of which is rather spiritual than material. It is almost as if he tried to paint not only the flower but also its fragrance, and it was the fragrance that to him seemed the more precious quality.

So now, perhaps, we can begin to understand the difference between his technique—that is to say, his manner of setting down in paint what he desired to express—and Memling's. The latter, serene and happy, had all a child's delight in the appearances of things, attracted by them as the infant in his picture is attracted by the apple, and offering them to us with the same winning grace, and certainty that they will please, as the angel in his picture exhibits. So it is the *facts*, clear to the senses of sight and touch, that he presents, with a loving, tender care to make them as plain to us as possible, working out to perfection even the smallest details.

You have examined the beautiful workmanship in the ornamentation of the arch and in the garlands suspended by the charming little baby forms; but have you discovered the tiny figures in the landscape? And with a reading-glass you will see that the castle drawbridge is down, and a lady on horseback is passing over it, following a gentleman who is evidently riding forth to hunt, as a greyhound comes along behind him. From the mill is issuing a man with a sack of flour on his shoulders, which he will set upon the back of the donkey that waits patiently before the door, while a little way along the road stands a dog, all alert and impatient to start. These incidents illustrate Memling's fondness for detail, and his delight in the representation of facts as facts.

By comparison, Botticelli is a painter, not of facts, but of ideas, and his pictures are not so much a representation of certain objects as a pattern of forms. Nor is his coloring rich and lifelike, as Memling's is; it is often rather a tinting than actual color. His figures do not attract us by their suggestion of bulk, but as shapes of form, suggesting rather a flat pattern of decoration. Accordingly, the lines which inclose the figures are chosen with the first intention of being decorative.

You will see this at once if you compare the draperies of the angels in the two pictures. Those of Memling's are commonplace compared wih the fluttering grace of Botticelli's. But there is more in this flutter of draperies than mere beauty of line: it expresses lively and graceful movement. These angels seem to have alighted like birds, their garments still buoyed up with air and agitated by their speed of flight, each being animated with its individual grace of movement. Compared with the spontaneousness and freedom of these figures, those of Memling look heavy, stock-still, and posed for effect.

Now, therefore, we can appreciate the truth of the remark that Botticelli, "though one of the worst anatomists, was one of the greatest draftsmen of the Renaissance." As an example of false anatomy, you may notice the impossible way in which the Madonna's head is attached to the neck, and other instances of faulty or incorrect form may be found in Botticelli's pictures. Yet, in spite of this, he is recognized as one of the greatest draftsmen, because he gave to "line" not only intrinsic beauty, but also significance—that is to say, his rhythmical and harmonious lines produce an effect upon our imagination corresponding to the sentiment of grave and tender poetry that filled the artist himself.

This power of making every line count, both in significance and beauty, distinguishes the great master draftsmen of all time.

MORNING
By Emily Dickinson
May, 1891

Will there really be a morning?
    Is there such a thing as day?
Could I see it from the mountains
    If I were as tall as they?

Has it feet like water-lilies?
    Has it feathers like a bird?
Is it brought from famous countries
    Of which I have never heard?

Oh, some scholar! Oh, some sailor!
    Oh, some wise man from the skies!
Please to tell a little pilgrim
    Where the place called morning lies!

AT SCHOOL A HUNDRED YEARS AGO.

By Agnes Repplier

September, 1896

IT is a pleasant thing to go to school in this year of grace, 1896. It is a moderately pleasant thing even to go to boarding-school, unless one is hopelessly homesick, and I have the less hesitation in saying this, because I know so many boys and girls who will agree with me. But there was a time—a time not so very, very long ago—when the "hardships of school" was not a fancy phrase, as it is now, to be used effectively in the Christmas holidays, but when it had a real significance for the unlucky little students who were learning what hardship meant.

Only sixty years have passed since the boys of Eton ventured to beg that pipes might be laid in some of the school buildings so that they need not fetch water from the pumps in the freezing winter weather, and the petition was promptly rejected, with the scornful comment that "they would be wanting gas and Turkey carpets next!" At Winchester, another big English school, all the lads had to wash in an open yard called "Moab," where half-a-dozen tubs were ranged around the wall, and it was the duty of one of the juniors to go from tub to tub on frosty mornings, and thaw the ice with a candle. Comfort was deemed a bad thing for boys, lest they should grow up dainty and unmanly. "Cold?" said Dr. Keate, a famous head-master of Eton, to a poor little bit of hu-

manity whom he met shivering and shaking in the hall. "Don't talk to me of being cold! You must learn to bear it, sir! You are not at a girls' school!"

But if he had been at a girls' school, I doubt whether the child would have found himself much warmer. Fires, in our great-grandmothers' time, especially in England, where the winters are less biting than with us, were held to be luxuries more fitting for old age than for youth. Mrs. Sherwood, who lived about seventy years ago, and wrote stories which all little boys and girls used to read, tells us that when she was young she was never permitted to come near the fire, though it blazed brightly away in the family sitting-room. Indeed, the discipline under which she was reared at home was so exceedingly severe that school seemed by comparison a place of pastime and relaxation.

Mothers were then especially anxious that their little daughters should carry themselves properly, and grow up straight and tall. To accomplish this good end, Mrs. Sherwood, from the time she was six until she was thirteen, wore a backboard strapped over her shoulders, and, worse still, an iron collar around her neck, forcing her to hold her chin high in the air. This instrument of torture was put on every morning, and seldom taken off until late in the afternoon. Moreover, she learned and recited all her lessons standing in stocks to turn her toes out. She was not allowed to sit down in her mother's presence, and for breakfast, dinner, and supper she enjoyed an unvarying monotony of bread and milk. Nevertheless, she seems to have been a cheerful and contented little girl; and when the dreadful collar was removed she used to manifest her wild delight by running as hard as ever she could for half a mile or more through her father's beautiful grounds. No wonder that, when sent as a boarder to a famous French school called the Abbey School, she thought it the height of luxury to be awakened at daybreak, and permitted to breakfast near the fire on buttered toast and tea. In fact, she always writes of the Abbey as if it were the abode of perpetual and rather hurtful gaiety; though all we can learn from her letters is that the older girls were allowed to visit and receive their friends, that they had a dance at Christmas time, and that they acted occasionally *The Good Mother,* by Madame de Genlis, and other French plays of a very grave and serious character.

It was not in this joyous fashion, however, that school presented itself to another, and far brighter, little girl, Mary Fairfax, who was born over a hundred years ago, and who afterward became Mrs. Somerville and one of the most learned women in England. Mary was fortunate enough to live the first ten years of her life by the seashore, the happiest, wildest, shyest child that ever played all day long on the yellow sands, and made huge collections of shells, and weeds, and pebbles, and other treasures brought her as playthings by the waves. When it rained, and her mother would not permit her to run out, she read over and over again the three books which formed her library—*The Arabian Nights, Robinson Crusoe,* and *Pilgrim's Progress.* Now and then her father, who was an officer in

the English navy, came home from sea; and finding his little daughter as ignorant as a child could be, he made her read aloud to him every morning a chapter of Hume's "History of England." This was all her education until she was ten years old, when, one dreadful day, her parents sent her to a boarding-school, a small and very expensive boarding-school kept by Miss Primrose, who was so stately and so severe that her pupils used to say they never saw her smile. Thanks to the healthy outdoor life she had always led, little Mary was straight and strong as a young Indian, but that did not save her from the ingenious tortures designed for stooping children, and which she describes for us in her memoirs.

"A few days after my arrival I was enclosed in stiff stays with a steel busk in front, while, above my frock, bands drew my shoulders back till the shoulder-blades met. Then a steel rod, with a semicircle which went under the chin, was clasped to the steel busk in my stays. In this constrained state I and most of the younger children had to prepare our lessons."

Think of it, you luxurious little people who prepare *your* lessons lolling on rocking-chairs, nestling in sofa corners, or lying comfortably on warm hearth-rugs before cheerful fires! Think of studying a whole page of Johnson's dictionary every day, spelling, definitions, even the very position of each word in the long columns, and all the while unable to lean backward or forward, or turn your head from side to side—unable even to see what the girl next to you was doing! That was a discipline which must have made home and the dear shining ocean-sands a picture of Paradise, of Paradise Lost, to poor, tired, timid Mary Fairfax. And the worst of it was, she learned so little at Miss Primrose's school that, when she escaped for her first holidays she covered herself with disgrace by writing *bank-knot* for bank-note, and was severely scolded for being so idle, and wasting such golden opportunities. She was taught to sew, however, very neatly, and in after years she grew so passionately fond of study, of real, hard, severe uncompromising study, that it was necessary, when she was fifteen, to take away her candles, so that she might not sit up half the night over her books. Even then she used to arise at daybreak, wrap herself in a blanket—not being allowed a fire,—and work away at Algebra and Latin until breakfast time. She wrote a number of valuable works on scientific subjects, and she lived to be ninety-two years old, proving that neither hard schools nor hard study are certain to shorten our days.

Miss Edgeworth, that beloved Maria Edgeworth, who has given us some of the best stories ever written for children, and whose shabby, well read volumes were the treasures of old-fashioned nurseries, has told us many things about her early life at school. She was only eight years old when she was first sent away from home, a shy and timid little girl, but too docile and intelligent to be unhappy, even amid strange surroundings. She was taught to sew and embroider very prettily, and to write a neat clear hand which was destined to be much admired. There is a prim little letter sent by her to her father, in which she says:

"School now seems agreeable to me. I have begun French and dancing, and intend to make great improvement in everything I learn. I am sure it will give you satisfaction to know that I am a good girl."

Her real troubles began when she was taken away from this simple, homelike place—where her hardest task had been to work a white satin waistcoat for her father—and sent to a fashionable establishment in London. She was then eleven years old, a small, delicate child, with stooping shoulders, and her appearance gave great displeasure to her teachers. The work of improvement was started at once, and in good earnest. Every day she was strapped to the backboard until she ached all over. Every day the iron collar—that favorite instrument of discomfort—was fastened under her chin. Every day she swung the dumb-bells until her hands could hold them no longer. It is hardly surprising that under this strenuous discipline, from which nothing but the rack appears to have been omitted, school no longer seemed agreeable to the little girl. She lost her gaiety, and moped in quiet corners, reading, or pining for her Irish home and the younger children who filled it merrily; for Miss Edgeworth had more step-brothers and step-sisters than ever fell to the lot of authoress before or since, and she loved every one of them dearly all her life.

Have I written enough about the miseries you might have suffered if you had lived in your great-grandmother's day? Would you like to hear of somebody who really had a good time when she was a child, and whose splendid high spirits neither study nor discipline could daunt? Then read for yourselves the delightful papers in which Miss Mitford describes for us her school-life in London just one hundred years ago. Few things more amusing than these "Early Recollections" have ever been told in print. We know everybody in that school as intimately as Mary Mitford knew them in the year 1796. The English teacher who was so wedded to grammar and arithmetic—Mary hated to study; the French teacher whom she both loved and feared, who had a passion for neatness, and used to hang around the children's necks all their possessions found out of place, from dictionaries and sheets of music to skipping-ropes and dilapidated dolls; the school-girls who came from every part of England and France; above all, the school plays—*The Search after Happiness*, which they were permitted to act as a great treat, because Miss Hannah More had written it. If you know nothing about *The Search after Happiness* you have no real idea how dull a play can be. Four discontented young ladies go forth to seek Urania, whose wisdom will teach them to be happy. They meet Florella, a virtuous shepherdess, who leads them to the grove where Urania lives. Here they are kindly received, and describe all their faults at great length to their hostess, who sends them brimful of good advice to their respective homes. Think of a lot of real school-girls acting such a drama, and speaking to each other in this sedate and meritorious fashion:

"With ever new delight we now attend
    The counsels of our fond maternal friend."

Yet these girls did it, and enjoyed it, too, grateful for even this demure amusement, a hundred years ago.

The Ingenious Little Old Man

By John Bennett
September, 1897

A little old man
    of the sea
Went out in a
        boat for a
            sail:
The water came
        in
Almost up to his chin
And he had nothing with

            which to bail.
        But this little old
            man of the
                sea
            Just drew out his
                jack-knife so
                    stout,
            And a hole with
                its blade
            In the bottom
                he made,
So that all of the water ran out.

—JOHN BENNETT—

MORE THAN CONQUERORS

By Ariadne Gilbert

THE SUNNY MASTER
OF "SUNNYSIDE"

May, 1913

"PLEASE, Your Honor, here's a bairn was named after you." Lizzie, the Scotch nurse, pushed into the shop, dragging a short-legged boy by the arm till they were close to the President's side. "Here's a bairn was named after you," she repeated encouragingly. And then President Washington knew what she meant, and laid his hand on the child's tumbled hair in blessing. The boy who received that blessing was Washington Irving. He lived near by, at 128 William Street, below Fulton Street, in New York City. Eight children were crowded into that two-story city house: William, Ann, Peter, Catharine, Ebenezer, John, Sarah, and Washington. Over the brood presided a stern father and a gentle mother who loved and understood.

Doubtless, as the years advanced, that mother knew that her youngest child, Washington, would learn, like all other children, from every source that claimed his interest. Though he was taught hardly more than his alphabet, in the queer little school in Ann Street, he was taught much else by life in the city. He used to "haunt the pier heads in fine weather," to watch the ships "fare forth" with lessening sails; and there at the wharves, from the smell of salt water, the call of sea-birds, and the flapping canvas, he was learning a love of adventure, and was even planning to sail away as his father had done before the war. At home, he trained himself to the hardships of a sailor's life by eating salt pork, fat and greasy—a thing he loathed: and by getting out of bed at night to lie on the hard floor. Monkey-like, he was learning to climb from roof to roof of the city houses for the pure fun of dropping mysterious stones down mysterious chimneys, and clambering back, half giddy, but chuckling at the wonder he had aroused, for he was always a roguish lad. From the queerly dressed Dutch people, with their queerer language, he was learning that there were other lands besides his own. From the high-vaulted roof of Trinity Church, with its darkness, and beauty, and deep-swelling music, he was learning that there were other religions than the strict Scotch Presbyterianism of his father. He even learned, in time, that dancing and the theater had their own charms; and he secretly took lessons in the one, and let himself down from the attic window to go to the other.

"Oh, Washington, if you were only good!" the dear impulsive mother used to say. And yet, in her secret heart, she must have felt that the child was "good" who was always sweet and sunny and loving.

Perhaps it was because she shared his thirst for adventure that she won his confidence. Not allowed by his father to read *Robinson Crusoe* and *Sindbad the Sailor*, Washington used to read them at night in bed, or under his desk at school. He liked those books better than his book of sums; such stories carried him into the wild world of his longing, and partly quenched his thirst for adventure—a taste that lasted a lifetime.

In 1800, when Irving was seventeen, he made his first voyage up the Hudson to Albany. In those days, a journey from New York to Albany was like a journey to Europe to-day. Washington's older sisters, Ann and Catharine, who had married young, were living near Albany, and he was to visit them. Boylike, he packed his trunk at the first mention of the trip; but as the sloop would not sail without a certain amount of freight and a certain number of passengers, he unpacked and repacked many times before her cargo was ready and the wonderful journey began.

To almost any one, that first sail through the Hudson Highlands is a dream of beauty; to Irving it was a wonder and a rapture. The stern mountains, crowned with forests; the eagles, sailing and screaming; the roar of "unseen streams dashing down precipices"; and then the anchoring at night in the darkness and mystery of the overhanging cliffs, and drifting asleep to the plaintive call of the whippoorwill—it was all new to the city boy, who had never left the New York streets before, except to wander in the woods with dog and gun.

That journey was the beginning of his many travels. Though he went into Mr. Hoffman's office the next year to study law, he did not continue long at the work. An incessant cough soon developed into consumptive tendencies, and, in July, 1803, his employer, who loved him like a father, invited him to join a party of seven on a trip to Canada.

The hardships of this journey, however, were a poor medicine. Beyond Albany, they traveled mainly by wagons, over roads so bad and through woods so thick, that they often had to get out and walk. "The whole country was a wilderness," writes Irving. "We floated down the Black River in a scow; we toiled through forests in wagons drawn by oxen; we slept in hunt-

ers' cabins, and were once four and twenty hours without food; but all was romance to me."

Naturally when he returned home, his family found him worse rather than better. Accordingly, feeling that something must be done to save him, the older brothers put their money together—William, who was best able, giving the greatest share—and engaged his passage on a ship sailing for Bordeaux, May 19, 1804. "There's a chap who will go overboard before we get across," commented the captain, eying Irving suspiciously.

On ship his sleeping quarters were in the cabin, with sixteen others "besides the master and mate." "I have often passed the greater part of the night walking the deck," Washington wrote to William; and again, "When I cannot get a dinner to suit my taste, I endeavor to get a taste to suit my dinner." His letters breathe a spirit of gaiety, and are hopefully full of his own physical improvement, for he was never a man to complain.

And yet his trip was not all joy; now we read of his Christmas at sea, in a dull, pouring rain, with the captain snoring in his berth; now of a "villainous crew of pirates" who attacked the ship.

After Irving reached port, life, like the sea, seemed smoother; but now he fell a prey to the tempting distractions of travel. His greatest fault was, no doubt, a lack of steadiness of aim. Like a bee, he flew from flower to flower, wherever honey seemed the sweetest. To be sure, he had gone abroad for his health; but the brothers who had sent him expected him to turn the time and money to some definitely good account. For a short time, the art galleries in Rome fired Washington with an ambition to "turn painter," for he loved wild landscapes and color, while he declared that "cold, raw tints" gave him rheumatism.

This art craze, however, amounted to a mere temporary dabbling. Moreover, though his expense book gives account of two months' tuition in French and of the purchase of a botanical dictionary, we do not picture Irving as studying either French or botany very hard. His social instincts were a real impediment to any study. William, in bitter disappointment, declared that he was scouring through Italy in too short a time, "leaving Florence on the left and Venice on the right," for the sake of "good company." In fact, the younger brother's bump of sociability was very large. In London he met Mrs. Siddons and the Kembles. Fascinated with foreign life and foreign people, he hated the student side of travel, and was frankly tired of churches, palaces, and cathedrals. All his countries were *peopled*. That is why *Bracebridge Hall* and *The Sketch-Book* are so alive.

We are not surprised, then, to find that, on his return to New York, he plunged into society life; nevertheless he resumed the writing of occasional sketches—a practice which he had begun before leaving his native land. As a partner of Paulding and of William Irving, he issued in twenty numbers a series of brilliant and original papers called *Salmagundi*. These were reprinted in London in 1811.

While Irving was abroad, the harsh news of his father's and his sister Nancy's death had come, so that, on his return, we must picture him living alone with his mother in the old house (now torn down) on the corner of William and Ann Streets. There he wrote his *Letters of Jonathan Oldstyle*, *Salmagundi* and *History of New York*.

Right in the midst of this work came the most terrible bereavement of Irving's life. Under the encouragement of his employer, the fatherly Mr. Hoffman, Irving had attempted to continue the study of the law.

Through Mr. Hoffman's friendship, too, and the openness of his hospitable home, the young man had learned to love Mr. Hoffman's young daughter, Matilda. She was hardly more than a beautiful child, but he loved her for all that she was, and for all that she promised to be. Just when they were happiest, however, Matilda caught a terrible cold, and, within two months, she was taken away from him forever. That sorrow lay too deep for any of Irving's family or any of his friends to touch. He never found words to utter his sorrow. He was twenty-six when she died, and she was only seventeen. But through all his long, lonely life, he cherished her dear love; after his death, was found, among his treasures, a lovely miniature, a lock of fair hair, and a slip of paper bearing her name, "Matilda Hoffman." Through all his travels he had her Bible and prayer-book with him, and through all the years, her memory.

It was nearly thirty years after Matilda's death, that one of Mr. Hoffman's granddaughters, who was rummaging in a drawer for music, found a piece of faded embroidery. "Washington," said Mr. Hoffman, "this is a piece of poor Matilda's work." But Irving had grown suddenly grave and silent, and in a few moments had said good night and gone home.

That Irving tried to lift the clouds from his own spirit is proved by the fact that, in the midst of his sorrow, he continued his *Knickerbocker's History*, a book rippling and sparkling with merriment. He himself was Diedrich Knickerbocker, and it was he who "would sit by the old Dutch housewives with a child on his knee or a purring grimalkin on his lap." If some of the Dutch were nettled by his picture of their ways, others saw that he was writing in "pure wantonness of fun," and that none of his laughter left a sting. Years later, however, Irving himself wrote, "It was a con-

founded impudent thing in such a youngster as I was to be meddling in this way
with old family names."

Yet this special gift of finding fun in little things and interest in nothings filled his
days with life. Except for wide traveling,
there were few events to light his lonely
way. The warmth of his family affections
was always one of the sweetest and strongest things in his nature; now he was helping
Ebenezer and his many children; now bol-
stering up Peter with money loans, always
offered with that sweet graciousness that
was a part of his generous delicacy.

He and Peter and Ebenezer formed a
merchants' firm, to which Washington,
though he detested the "drudgery of regular business," lent his time and interest till it
was firmly on its feet. This required him to
live for a few months in Washington, D.C.
His spirit now, as in all his other travels,
was the same. "I left home determined to
be pleased with everything, or, if not
pleased, to be amused."

On his return to New York the following spring, he went into bachelor quarters,
with his friend Brevoort, on Broadway near
Bowling Green. It was a jovial time, free
and peaceful, but broken, with the peace of
the nation, by news of the War of 1812.
Irving, adventuresome and loyal, joined the
governor's staff posted at Sackett's Harbor.
His letters of that time are full of "breast-
works, and pickets of reinforced militia,"
but also of his own good health, "all the
better for hard traveling," and of "love to
Mother and the family."

Soon after the news of the victory of
New Orleans and the tidings of peace, Irving sailed for Europe, little dreaming that
he would stay for seventeen years. He had
expected to return in a short time and settle
down beside his dear old mother for the
rest of her life. These plans and hopes,
however, were suddenly broken by the
news of her death in 1817. That was the
saddest event of his travels; the happiest
was his friendship with Scott.

At Abbotsford, Scott made Irving more
than welcome, and found in him a kindred
spirit. They were both glad, hearty, natural
men who loved outdoors in the same boyish way. Moreover, Scott found in Irving a
man who needed no explanations—a man
who could tramp with him through his
own Tweedside, and understand all its
beauty. We can imagine how welcome the
Scotchman's cordiality was to Irving's fire-
side heart! To be included as part of Scott's
home, not only by the father and mother
and four children, but by the cat, the packs
of barking dogs, and the noble horses—that
was what Irving loved; for, in spite of his
outward cheer, he suffered from the loneliness of the inner self. As he said, he was not
meant to be a bachelor; and when he writes
letters of blessing on the wives and children
of Brevoort and Paulding and others, there
is an undertone of pathos in the music.
"You and Brevoort have given me the slip.
. . . I cannot hear of my old cronies, snugly
nestled down with good wives and fine
children round them, but I feel for the moment desolate and forlorn."

That is all he *says*, and he puts it jest-
ingly then; but the unsaid thoughts lie
deep. "Irving's smile is one of the sweetest I
know," said a friend: "but he can look
very, very sad."

But enough of the hidden sadness of this
partner of the sunlight. Let us go with the
companionable Irving on his travels, and go
in his spirit—as conquerors of loneliness.

A rapid journey ours must be, a journey
of seventeen years in part of an hour; and
yet we must have time for slow steps in the
silent Abbey—the most hallowed spot of all
England—and time to bow our souls in
reverence while the "deep-laboring organ"
rolls its music up to heaven. And we shall

need time to enjoy the English Christmas as Irving enjoyed it. "While I lay musing on my pillow," he writes, "I heard the sound of little feet pattering outside of the door, and a whispering consultation. Presently a choir of small voices chanted forth an old Christmas carol, the burden of which was

'Rejoice, our Saviour he was born
On Christmas Day in the morning.'

"I rose softly, slipped on my clothes, opened the door suddenly, and beheld one of the most beautiful little fairy groups that a painter could imagine. It consisted of a boy and two girls, the eldest not more than six, and lovely as seraphs. They were going the rounds of the house and singing at every chamber door; but my sudden appearance frightened them into mute bashfulness. They remained for a moment playing on their lips with their fingers, and now and then stealing a shy glance from under their eyebrows, until, as if by one impulse, they scampered away, and as they turned an angle of the gallery, I heard them laughing in triumph at their escape."

Friendly and glad, Irving was heartily welcomed into the English home; and when he left that brother-land, with what a kindly feeling did he grace its memory to the world! And what a benediction he sheds in his "Peace be within thy walls, oh England! and plenteousness within thy palaces."

So much for his books of English travel; his books on Spain are no less charming. In fact, Spain must have been even more fascinating to a man of Irving's imagination; to the mind that conceived the mystic dwarfs and "wicked flagon" of Rip Van Winkle and the headless horsemen of Sleepy Hollow. Spain was a land rich in legend as well as steeped in beauty. The roads were infested with robbers. Every Andalusian carried a saber. There was often a lantern hidden beneath his cloak.

Sometimes, as Irving rode through the stern country, "the deep tones of the cathedral bell would echo through the valley." Then "the shepherd paused on the fold of the hill, the muleteer in the midst of the road; each took off his hat and remained motionless for a time, murmuring his evening prayer."

"Who wants water—water colder than snow?" came the carrier's cry as they neared the city. The shaggy little donkey, with water jars hung on each side, was all too willing to wait.

Arrived at the Alhambra, Irving found it at once a fortress and a palace, every stone breathing poetry and romance. "A little old fairy queen lived under the staircase, plying her needle and singing from morning till night." The Andalusians lay on the grass or danced to the guitar, and everywhere were groves of orange and citron and the music of singing birds and tinkling fountains. It was an enchanted palace. In the evening, Irving took his lamp and, in a "mere halo of light," stole dreamily through the "waste halls and mysterious galleries." There were no sounds but echoes. Everything, even the garden, was deserted. Nevertheless the scent of roses and laurel, the shimmer of moonlight, the murmur of hidden streams, had made the garden a fairy-land, only it was a fairy-land where flitting bat and hooting owl were much at home. To Irving, the owl had a vast knowledge of "astronomy and the moon," and he respected the knowledge which he could not share. In short, the Alhambra just suited his fancy; and when, as he said, the summons came to return into the "bustle and business of the dusty world," that summons ended one of the pleasantest dreams of his life—"a life, perhaps you may think, too much made up of dreams."

But poets should not be bound, nor birds caged; nor do we need to take the poet at his own low estimate. Given to hospitality, and, consequently, open to many interruptions, inclined to postpone, and hating the labors of rewriting, Irving was, nevertheless, a hard worker. Those seventeen years were not all dreams. To them we owe *The Legend of Sleepy Hollow*, written "by candle-light in foggy London"; *Bracebridge Hall*, dashed off in Paris in six weeks; and *Rip Van Winkle*, which was not, as some have supposed, drawn from life, but was an imagined picture; when Irving wrote that story, he had never visited the Catskills; he had merely seen them from the river on his boyhood's rest journey. To these years, moreover, we owe a longer, harder work than any of the rest—*The Life of Columbus*. When the poet Longfellow took his early morning walks in Madrid, he often saw Irving writing at his open study-window at six o'clock; he had risen at five to work on the *Life*. "I must make enough money," he would say to himself, "to be sure of my bread and cheese."

As a rule, however, Irving had a great indifference to money-getting. Perhaps this will partly account for his rare generosity, though I think generosity was in his blood. With his customary faithfulness, he gave *The Sketch-Book* to his old publisher, Moses Thomas, even at the risk of loss. Utterly without envy, he pushed Bryant's work before the public, popularized Scott in America, gave plots to Poe, and, most generous of all, resigned, in favor of Prescott, his whole scheme for writing on the Conquest of Mexico, though Irving had hugged the hope of such a work since childhood, and had definitely written on it for over a year. Perhaps, blessed with eyesight himself, he thought he would do his blind friend this service. At all events,

without consulting any one, he burned his own manuscript. It was a great sacrifice, but Prescott never knew.

Imagine how hard it was for such a warm nature as Irving's to be misjudged by his best friends. But he was misjudged. Some went so far as to think that those seventeen years spent abroad were a proof that he did not love his country and home; whereas Irving was all too weary of foreign society. He was, to quote his letters, "tired of being among strangers." If ever there was a home-loving man, it was Irving. During those seventeen long years he felt himself

Strange tenant of a thousand homes
And friendless with ten thousand friends.

He called it what it was, "a poor, wandering life." "I have been tossed about 'hither and thither' and whither I would not; have been at the levee and the drawing-room, been at routs and balls, and dinners and country-seats, been hand and glove with nobility and *mob*-ility, until, like Trim, I have satisfied the sentiment, and am now preparing to make my escape from all this splendid confusion."

But the world did not understand. The newspaper attacks hurt him. At last criticism became too keen for his sensitive nature to bear. Then began for him "sleepless nights and joyless days," with the sharp thought that the "kindness of his own countrymen was withering toward him." Even Brevoort and Paulding, even his brothers, began to chide him with not wanting to return.

When he did stand before them once again, however, with his truth-telling, sunlight face, they questioned his love no more. Irving's return to New York was heralded by a dinner in his honor. Now Irving, as Moore said, had never been "strong as a lion," though he was "delightful as a domestic animal." He himself said it was "physically impossible for him to make a speech." A manuscript under his plate did not help at all. When, at a dinner in England, he had been announced with loud cheers, he had simply responded, "I beg to return you my sincere thanks." And now when, before his fellow-countrymen, the toast was proposed, "To our illustrious guest, thrice welcome to his native land," the shy author who hated speech-making could only stammer and blush. "I trembled for him," said one of his friends, "until I saw him seize the handle of a knife and commence gesticulating with that; then I knew he would get on."

"I am asked how long I mean to remain here," Irving said. "They know but little of my heart and feelings who can ask me that question. I answer, As long as I live." He hesitated, stood still, and looked about him, the old genial smile beaming from his dark gray eyes. Then a rousing cheer told him that he had won again the trust of all, and he sat down satisfied—a tired exile welcomed home.

Except as Irving was twice sent to Europe by our nation, once to England as secretary of legation, and once as minister to Spain, he did stay home all the rest of his life. It is as a home-maker and a home-lover that he was happiest and best known, and no part of life was so sweet to him as the life at Sunnyside. Let us visit him there in his own little house among the trees. Though the house is small, and already filled with his nieces, there is always room for one more. Let us take the train from New York for Irvington, near Tarrytown. Sunnyside, a ten-acre farm, bought by Irving in 1835, is only about ten minutes walk from the station. The grounds look out on the blue Hudson. There is a cove and a cozy beach, and a spring "welling up at the bottom of the bank." A stony brook, shaded by trees, "babbles down the ravine, throwing itself into the little cove." On the rock at the edge of the lawn, Irving often sits, resting in his love of the shining river, and building his "castles at seventy" as he did at seven. The house described by Irving is a "little old-fashioned stone mansion, all made up of gable-ends, and as full of angles and corners as an old cocked hat." It used to be called "Wolfert's Roost" (or Rest), and over the door is an old motto meaning "pleasure in quiet," a motto that was written in its master's heart.

Though you may not find any of the old Indian arrow-heads about the place, nor Brom Bones's pumpkin in the garden, you will find the spirit of Wolfert's Roost unchanged. Crickets skip in the grass; humming-birds whir among the trumpet-vines; the phoebe-bird and wren have built under the eaves. The thick mantle of Melrose ivy, which almost hides the eastern end of Sunnyside, grew from one of Scott's slips.

Within, Sunnyside is plainly furnished; there are not even many books. Everything, however, looks comfortable and made for use. For instance, the writing-table is a mass of disorder. It is one of the sweet elements of our welcome that nothing is changed to receive us. And we can visit Irving's "tree-circled farm." Those two elms on the lawn were planted by the author's own hands; he carried the saplings on his shoulder. The fruits and vegetables, he will tell you, were raised at "very little more than twice the market-price." Now, purring thunderously, Imp will come and rub his silky head against you, and Toby will bark a greeting and dash away to the other pets. There are cows and setting geese, cooing pigeons, and "squadrons of snowy" ducks. Dandy and Billy, the old coach-horses, are as "sleek as seals," and "Gentleman Dick," Irving's saddle-horse, puts his cheek against his master's and lays his head on his shoulder. Though Irving will say nothing about it, perhaps you will notice that the saddle hanging near is an old one, furbished up. The father of so many borrowed children could not afford a new saddle.

"Dick now and then cuts daisies with me on his back; but that's to please himself, not me," laughs Irving, patting the horse's glossy side; and perhaps he may add that Gentleman Dick has thrown him once. It was after a second accident, when Irving was seventy-two, that his nieces forced him to sell this "Gentleman that had proved no gentleman." "Poor Dick!" Irving said. "His character was very much misunderstood by all but myself."

That word "all" covered a big household. Irving's dearest brother, Peter, had died, and so had William and John; but Ebenezer, now growing very deaf, and his sister Catharine made their home at Sunny-side, and there were six adoring nieces who kept Irving "almost as happy" as if he were "a married man."

To see how happy he was, we should have visited him at Christmas, when "The Tappan Zee was covered with sparkling ice and the opposite hills with snow," and when holly reddened the hearth of Sunny-side. Then, indeed, the cottage rang with shouts, while the king of the cottage tip-toed round to be first with his "Merry Christmas," acted a jovial Santa Claus, and filled all the stockings with presents.

His understanding of children was wonderful. Once when he had amused two fretful little things on a long train journey, the mother thanked him with, "Any one can see you're a father of a large family." There are two delightful stories of Irving and the boys who robbed his orchard. One day he was met by a little fellow who came up to him with winning secrecy and said,

"I'll show you the old man's best tree, if you'll shake it for me." Agreed. "By George, sir!" laughed Irving, "if he didn't take me to the very best tree on my own place!"

Another time, when he came unexpectedly on an apple squad, he said, picking out the leader, "Boy, these are very poor apples. I know a much better tree." Then he led them on, skulking in the shadows and dodging the gardener, in true boy style. "Be quiet! Keep near the hedge!" he cautioned.

"We're afraid the old gentleman will catch us."

"He's not there now. There, the best tree's just beyond the hedge!"

The prickly hedge tore the boys' trousers and faces and hands, but the seekers were too near their spoil to be daunted.

"Now, boys, this is the tree I spoke of, and I am the owner of it—Mr. Irving." There was a pause, during which the boys intently studied the grass. "Don't be afraid," Irving went on, "I sha'n't punish you; the prickly hedge has done that. I only wish that when you take my fruit, you would come to me and ask for it." He gave them a genial, forgiving smile, and was gone, the dear old man with the heart of a boy and the immortal spirit of play.

Up to the very end of life, at seventy-six, he could laugh at pain and sleeplessness, and at weariness of mind and body. Let no one under-rate the heroism of those last years—the hard work wrought with aching hands. With the press dogging Irving's heels, the *Life of Goldsmith* was written in sixty days. He spoke of his writings as "literary babblings," or as "water spilt on the ground." Many times during the composition of the *Life of Washington*, his last work, he was at the point of putting it into the fire. His letters and journal show that writing had become a "toil of head, a fagging of the pen." Often he would be scribbling in his study at half-past twelve at night, long after the family were abed and asleep or he would "rise at midnight, light his lamp, and write for an hour or two." If he rested in the evening, with the girls sewing round him, it was because he had "passed the whole morning in his study hard at work," and had "earned his recreation."

Through those last years, though he made a pitiful struggle for sleep, asthma and nervousness combined against him, except when he slept from pure exhaustion. And still he made merry. Turning to one of his nieces, he said: "I am apt to be rather fatigued, my dear, by my night's rest."

Always he kept his sunniness. "Happy is he who can grow smooth as an old shilling as he wears out; he has endured the rubs of life to some purpose," he said.

And he did grow smooth and tuneful and placid. Though his voice was hoarse and his step faltering, his gray eyes held their twinkle, and his heart was young and singing to the end.

One frosty November day, the solemn bells told the farmers and sailors, the boys who loved the apples, and all the waiting neighbors of the glen, that the master of Sunnyside had gone.

Sunnyside was left, as we might expect, to Ebenezer and his daughter, "to be kept forever as an Irving rally place." But Irving left a far greater bequest to all who will but take it. Besides his books, rich in humor and kindliness, and written in "the language of the heart," he left the dear example of one who loved and lost, and smiled, and gave; of one who sought the good and found it, whether in music or pictures, free country, books, or people; and of one who sheds a constant blessing, even now, like the sunshine from the sky.

THE LITTLE ELF
By John Kendrick Bangs

September, 1893

I MET a little Elf-man, once,
    Down where the lilies blow.
I asked him why he was so small
    And why he didn't grow.

He slightly frowned, and with his eye
    He looked me through and through.
"I'm quite as big for me," said he,
    "As you are big for you."

THE FESTIVAL OF TAPERS

By Charles Dudley Warner

March, 1876

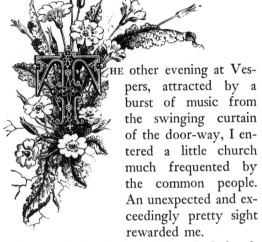

HE other evening at Vespers, attracted by a burst of music from the swinging curtain of the door-way, I entered a little church much frequented by the common people. An unexpected and exceedingly pretty sight rewarded me.

It was All Souls' Day. Here in Italy almost every day is set apart for some festival, or belongs to some saint or another, and I suppose that when leap-year brings round the extra day, there is a saint ready to claim the twenty-ninth of February. Whatever the day was to the elders, the evening was devoted to the children. The first thing I noticed was that the quaint old church was lighted up with innumerable wax tapers—an unusual sight, for the darkness of a Catholic church in the evening is usually relieved only by a candle here and there, and by a blazing pyramid of them on the high altar.

Then I saw that each taper belonged to a little boy or girl, and that groups of children were scattered all about the church. There was a group by every side altar and chapel, all the benches were occupied by knots of them, and there were so many circles of them seated on the pavement that I could with difficulty make my way among them. There were hundreds of children in the church, all dressed in their holiday apparel, and all intent upon the illumination, which seemed to be a private affair to each one of them.

And not much effect had their tapers upon the darkness of the vast vaults above them. The tapers were little spiral coils of wax, which the children unrolled as fast as they burned, and when they were tired of holding them, they rested them on the ground and watched the burning. I stood some time by a group of a dozen seated in a corner of the church. They had massed all the tapers in the center and formed a ring about the spectacle, sitting with their legs straight out before them and their toes turned up. The light shone full in their happy faces, and made the group, enveloped otherwise in darkness, like one of Correggio's pictures of children or angels. Correggio was a famous Italian artist of the sixteenth century, who painted cherubs like children who were just going to heaven, and children like cherubs who had just come out of it. But, then, he had the Italian children for models, and they get the knack of being lovely very young. An Italian child finds it as easy to be pretty as an American child does to be good.

One could not but be struck with the patience these little people exhibited in their occupation, and the enjoyment they got out of it. There was no noise; all conversed in subdued whispers, and behaved in the most gentle manner to each other, especially to the smallest, and there were many of them so small that they could only toddle about by the most judicious exercise of their equilibrium. I do not say this by way of reproof to any other kind of children.

These little groups, as I have said, were scattered all about the church; and they made with their tapers little spots of light, which looked in the distance very much like Correggio's picture which is at Dresden—the Holy Family at night, and the light from the Divine Child blazing in the faces of all the attendants. Some of the children were infants in the nurse's arms, but no one was too small to have a taper, and to run the risk of burning its fingers. There is nothing that a baby likes more than a lighted candle, and the church has understood this longing in human nature, and found means to gratify it by this festival of tapers.

The groups do not all remain long in place, you may imagine; there is a good deal of shifting about, and I see little stragglers wandering over the church, like fairies lighted by fire-flies. Occasionally they form a little procession and march from one altar to another, their lights twinkling as they go.

But all this time there is music pouring out of the organ-loft at the end of the church, and flooding all its spaces with its volume. In front of the organ is a choir of boys, led by a round-faced and jolly monk, who rolls about as he sings, and lets the deep bass noise rumble about a long time in his stomach before he pours it out of his mouth. I can see the faces of all of them quite well, for each singer has a candle to light his music-book.

And next to the monk stands THE BOY—the handsomest boy in the whole world probably at this moment. I can see now his great, liquid, dark eyes, and his exquisite face, and the way he tossed back his long, waving hair when he struck into his part. He resembled the portraits of Raphael, when that artist was a boy; only I think he looked better than Raphael, and without trying, for he seemed to be a spon-taneous sort of boy. And how that boy did sing! He was the soprano of the choir, and he had a voice of heavenly sweetness. When he opened his mouth and tossed back his head, he filled the church with exquisite melody.

He sang like a lark, or like an angel. As we never heard an angel sing, that comparison is not worth much. I have seen pictures of angels singing—there is one by Jan and Hubert Van Eyck in the Gallery at Berlin—and they open their mouths like this boy, but I can't say as much for their singing. The lark, which you very likely never heard either—for larks are as scarce in America as angels—is a bird that springs up from the meadow and begins to sing as he rises in a spiral flight, and the higher he mounts the sweeter he sings, until you think the notes are dropping out of heaven itself, and you hear him when he is gone from sight, and you think you hear him long after all sound has ceased.

And yet this boy sang better than a lark, because he had more notes and a greater compass, and more volume, although he shook out his voice in the same gleesome abundance.

I am sorry that I cannot add that this ravishingly beautiful boy was a good boy. He was probably one of the most mischievous boys that was ever in an organ-loft. All the time that he was singing the Vespers, he was skylarking like an imp. While he was pouring out the most divine melody he would take the opportunity of kicking the shins of the boy next to him, and while he was waiting for his part he would kick out behind at any one who was incautious enough to approach him. There never was such a vicious boy; he kept the whole loft in a ferment. When the monk rumbled his bass in his stomach, the boy cut up monkey-shines that set every other boy into a laugh, or he stirred up a row that set them all at fisticuffs.

And yet this boy was a great favorite. The jolly monk loved him best of all, and bore with his wildest pranks. When he was wanted to sing his part and was skylarking in the rear, the fat monk took him by the ear and brought him forward, and when he gave the boy's ear a twist, the boy opened his lovely mouth and poured forth such a flood of melody as you never heard. And he didn't mind his notes; he seemed to know his notes by heart, and could sing and look off, like a nightingale on a bough. He knew his power, that boy, and he stepped forward to his stand when he pleased, certain that he would be forgiven as soon as he began to sing. And such spirit and life as he threw into the performance, rollicking through the Vespers with a perfect abandon of carriage, as if he could sing himself out of his skin if he liked.

While the little angels down below were pattering about with their wax tapers, keeping the holy fire burning, suddenly the organ stopped, the monk shut his book with a bang, the boys blew out the candles, and I heard them all tumbling down stairs in a gale of noise and laughter. And the Beautiful Boy I saw no more.

THE STAFF

By Emilie Poulsson

June, 1897

I.

The lines upon the treble clef
Are lettered E, G, B, D, F.

"Encourage girls by double fun"
When all their practising is done.

The treble clef has furthermore
The letters, on its spaces four,
For spelling "F A C E, face."

(Put F upon the lowest space.)

II.

Base-clef lines G, B, D, F, A,—
Please put them in your mind to stay:
"Good boys deserve fun always." Now!

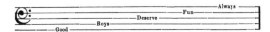

The boys will learn that anyhow.

The bass-clef spaces—lettered thus:
A, C, E, G—won't trouble us;
Upon the first space put the "A"—
"All Candy Eaten Gladly," say.

Con well this lesson o'er and o'er;
The staff will puzzle you no more.

CURIOUS FACTS ABOUT FIGURES
By Mrs. E. T. Corbett

June, 1897

IF the readers of *St. Nicholas* would like something curious in figures, here it is:

Choose *any* number, either in hundreds, thousands, or tens of thousands, and write it down.

Add the figures composing this number together. Subtract their sum from the first number written.

Now add together the figures of this remainder: you will find that they *always* amount either to 9, or to multiple of 9. Let us take a number by way of example:

Suppose you take 8357
These figures, added together, make .   23

8334

Now add these last figures, and you get 18—or twice 9.

This curious fact is the basis of a very pretty puzzle, with which one can mystify those who are not acquainted with it.

It is done thus: Ask any one to write down a number without telling you the figures. Then tell him to add the figures and to subtract, as above. Now ask him to strike out *one* figure from the answer last obtained. Ask him to add the remaining figures, and give you the sum of them.

You will be able at once to name the figure struck out, in this way: Take the sum just given, for example. Suppose the 8 was struck out; then the sum of the other three figures is 10. When you are told that 10 is the sum of the figures remaining, you know that 8 is the figure that will bring the whole amount to the next higher multiple of 9. If some other figures had been written down, and you had been told that the sum of the remaining figures was 20, for in-

stance, you would be certain that the next higher multiple of 9 was 27, and that therefore 7 would be the figure struck out—as follows:

8790

  24 = sum of above figures.

8766 — these amount to 20.

The fact that you do not know the figures chosen, or any of the answers, and that you ask for only the sum of the remaining figures, renders this a very puzzling feat.

One thing more: do not let any one strike out ciphers—always figures.

Here is another curious fact about figures: Write down in a row all the numerals except the number 8, thus:

12345679

Now choose any one of these numerals and multiply it by 9. Suppose we choose 2, which multiplied by 9 will of course give us 18.

Then multilply your row of figures by this 18, thus:

12345679
18

98765432
12345679

222222222

The answer, you see, is all 2's. If you had chosen 3, the answer then would have been all 3's—and so on with each number chosen.

Another curious fact is that if you write down any sum in three different figures, and then reverse those figures and subtract the lesser amount, you will find that the middle figure of the answer is *always* 9. Try it, thus:

Write 763
Now reverse that 367
─────
396

Now reverse again, but this time
add the amounts 693
─────
1089

Your answer will *always* be the same, 1089, except in one instance: if the first two figures you write are alike, as 778, and the last figure next in regular order, as 887,776, 998. In that case you will get 99 for your answer; but by again adding this, and then adding the sum reversed, you come back to your 1089. Example:

                        776
Reversed . . .   677 subtracted.
                 ─────
                   99
   "   . . .   99 added.
                 ─────
                  198
   "   . . .   891 added.
                 ─────
                 1089

TWENTY
QUESTIONS.

September, 1897

THE poet's daughter sat on a toadstool at sunset by the great sea, and ate her bowl of porridge. And while she was dazzling her eyes watching the setting sun, a flying-dragon came crawling up over the rocks. He fanned the little girl with his wing, and when she thanked him politely he begged her not to mention it. So she finished eating her porridge very comfortably, and when he saw that it was gone he cleared his throat and said timidly:

"Do you ever play Twenty Questions?"

"Yes, indeed," said the poet's daughter.

"Do you want to play now?"

"I should like it very much."

Then the dragon was full of joy, for he was fond of the game, and had not played for two hundred years.

"You think of something," said he ea-gerly, "and I'll ask the questions. Are you ready? Yes? Animal, mineral, or vegetable?"

"Neither," said the poet's daughter.

"Is it something you can see?" "Yes."

"Hear?" "Yes."

"Living?" "No."

"Is it something men make?" "Yes."

"Is it useful?" "Ye-e-s."

"Ornamental?" "Yes."

"Has it any color?" "No."

"Something you can see and hear, that men make, is useful and ornamental, and has no color," said the dragon, thought-fully. "Hum! Let me think." He put his head under his wing and thought for three minutes. "Can you play it?"

"No," said the poet's daughter, shaking her head and laughing.

"Then," said the dragon, "not a game or

music? Hum! Is it used for saying things?"

"Yes."

"Made by men—that makes ten," said the dragon, puzzled. "Did you ever make one?"

"Yes."

"Have I?"

"Yes!" she said laughing, "just now!"

"It must be something one can say," the dragon said, after thinking a minute. "Is it something I made by speaking?"

"Yes."

"Is it a sentence?"

"No."

"Is it a question?"

"No."

"Is it made of words?"

"Yes."

"This," said the dragon, "is really not easy! I must be very slow, but, really, I don't know. Have I made more than one?"

"Yes," said the poet's daughter, laughing.

"Is it any sort of a mistake?"

"No."

"Is it any sort of a try—like a guess or question?"

"No."

"One more makes the score. Is it any sort of a story?"

"No."

"Now I have three guesses," said the dragon, wrinkling his eyebrows. "Is it any sort of a remark or observation? Or a joke? Or a—oh, I see! I have it now! It is a—"

And this time he was right!

But it *was* a hard one, for he made three of them before he knew what it was!

THE CLOWN AND THE FEATHER.

RUDYARD KIPLING, MAKER OF MAGIC
By Hildegarde Hawthorne
February, 1915

WHEN I was a child, one of the friends of our family of whom I was particularly fond was Richard Henry Stoddard, the poet, then an old man, with a handsome, patriarchal aspect emphasized by a sweeping white beard.

One day he said to me:

"My dear, it isn't often that you will hear one poet say he would like to have written the verses of another poet. But that is what I say now. I would give a great deal to have written 'The Ballad of East and West,' by a man called Kipling. It's a great, a very great, poem."

That was the first time I had ever heard of Kipling.

That song was written in 1889, and Rudyard Kipling, who was born December 30, 1865, at Bombay, had then been writing some three years; at least, his first published book, *Departmental Ditties,* had been out that long. He had been sub-editor on the *Lahore Civil and Military Gazette* since he was seventeen, and had, of course, written for that publication, but so far he showed little sign of the greatness that lay in him, beyond several remarkable stories in *Plain Tales from the Hills,* and this ballad so highly praised by Stoddard.

Kipling left off being a boy very early indeed. He came back from England, where he had gone to be educated at the United Services College, in Devon, a man, almost an old man, so precocious, so cynical, so cock-sure of himself was he. But really this was no more than college grown-upness, made the more marked by the Indian background of his childhood, which ripens boy or girl quickly. He has grown a great deal younger since those days of his 'teens and first twenties, younger with a real youth, that sees wonder and miracle in so-called common things, as well as in the simplest of human beings. There is not a shred of cynicism left in Kipling now, but instead a tremendous reverence for and interest in the works of God and man, a huge sort of tenderness and a perception of infinite meanings, even in iron and steam and machinery.

His early boyhood, nursed on the strange stories of India told him by the ayahs to whose gentle care he was committed, as are all English children born in that far country, was filled full with mystery and magic. The old, old civilization of the East wrapped him close, and has never let him go. With this went the familiar view of the English soldier on his round of duties, naturally a delightful interest for the boy, strong, sturdy, and patriotic. Between the two influences arose an intense appreciation of England's work and responsibilities, of her larger aspects, her world character. This, too, has remained with him.

Next came the experience of school-life, and this must have been a big experience to the quick, sensitive, and yet somewhat rough nature of the lad. The story of *Stalky and Co.* tells us what this English school-life was, or, at least, what it was to the writer. It is not a pleasant story; the boys are a lot of young savages, the rules and ethics of their contact with each other being such as would shock a clan of aborigines. But there is nothing half-alive or weakly about the story. Hard knocks and swift reprisals, fierce enmities and passionate friendships, woke all there was in the boys. So far as actual learning went, the young Kipling couldn't have acquired any vast amount; his education has been a thing of his own doing, not of other persons'.

Kipling's father, John Lockwood Kipling, who died in 1911, was an artist of considerable charm, for almost twenty years curator of the Central Museum at Lahore, in India. There were two other artists in the family, for one of his mother's sisters was married to Sir Edward Burne-Jones, the great preRaphaelite painter, and another to Sir Edward Poynter, who followed Sir John Millais as President of the Royal Academy of Art. But there seems to have been no writer before Rudyard.

There never was any one more difficult to classify. As soon as people had him labeled as doing one thing, he would begin another. First he wrote sarcastic, cynical tales of the English in India. Then he became the poet of his beloved Tommy Atkins. Then he started in to interpret the native life of India as no one had ever done. Then he revealed himself as a supreme writer for children. Suddenly he sent a thrill through all the British Empire with his "White Man's Burden" and "The Recessional." Next he became intensely modern in his poems and stories of the mechanical achievements of our age, a prophet of yet greater achievements.

He is a man who is at home anywhere in the world. East was east and West was west to him from childhood, both familiar, each clearly defined. Since then he has traveled far and wide, living several years in the United States before at length settling in England. He stirred up all America with his notes on our ways and peculiarities in *From Sea to Sea,* yet, when he lay ill here, the very newsboys were interested in his condition, calling out that "Kipling's better, here y' are, extry, one cent!" The man is so big, so real, so intensely sincere, that he takes the heart of the world much as Mark Twain takes it. Yet both these men could and did slash at faults and weakness and pretense with a terrible fierceness.

One day my father took me into the editorial offices of *The Century* for a chat with Mr. Gilder. One of the first things he said to us was, "Kipling's round here somewhere; don't you want to meet him?" My father had met him before, but I was tremendously excited. I had read everything of his I could get hold of since Mr. Stoddard's remark to me, and I was having all the fun of real hero-worship for the author.

We went into Mr. Gilder's own office and met Kipling there. I looked at him hard. I wanted to be sure of him. He was broad and short and big-headed, with eyes that glowed, a brownish skin, and black hair already graying slightly. I was not disappointed in him. He gave you the feeling that here was force, power, control, and a something genial and warm that I had not looked for. I expected to be afraid of him, and, instead, I felt perfectly at home and at ease with him. He sat down by me and talked and laughed, made fun of several things, though now I cannot remember what they were, and praised the American offices. "Nothing like this sort of thing in England," he said, waving an arm round in a short, quick gesture. "There you have to scramble along narrow dark halls, open doors, fall down stairs, kick some one who has preceded you, and finally reach an ill-lighted, chilly, barren little room with two or three miserable clerks writing at desks."

The contrast between this picture and the beautiful room in which we sat was so great that I have never forgotten that description, nor yet the slight horror with which I heard that he kicked the unfortunate creature who had preceded him. For I believed every word.

It was not until 1894 that Kipling published, in your own beloved *St. Nicholas,* his first *Jungle Stories,* revealing a whole new expanse of his genius, and suddenly turning to you young folk from the older readers who had been his public till then. Nothing like these stories had ever been done. They are magic, fairy, full of a wondrous make-believe. Yet they are amazing in their knowledge of animal facts, of natural history, of the forest life of the tropics. They are absolutely true and absolutely imaginary at the same time. And that is just the kind of story-magic that a child wants and understands.

After that came the second book about the jungle, and then the fascinating *Just So Stories,* meant for young children. But do we ever grow too big to delight in them, I wonder? Some of us don't, I know! That's one of the main things about this Kipling:

he tells you his stories in such a way that you enjoy them at whatever age. After all, a child, or a boy, or a man, looking through a window at a street full of crowded life, where things were happening all the time, odd people and creatures passing, fights going on, songs being sung, soldiers arm in arm, elephants carrying mysterious burdens, all this and much, much more—man, boy, child, wouldn't each of them be tremendously interested, though possibly in different aspects of the show? Of course! And Kipling is such a window. Through him you see into a street that has neither beginning nor end, that leads out on the seven seas and back again, and that is constantly thronged with life. And you don't see only the outside of this life. He shows you what is going on in the minds and hearts of that motley train, even into the feelings of a tiger or an ape. When he tells you about boys, you know he tells the truth, because you are one yourself. And if you are a man or a woman, you know, too, that he is telling the truth. So when he tells you of things you do not know, you don't bother to wonder and doubt; you know those things are true, too.

The two *Jungle Books* were about animals, the *Just So Stories* were fanciful conceptions. When Rudyard Kipling turned to write *Puck of Pook's Hill,* he went to history.

But have you ever known history to be so up and doing as that book? Here is nothing dry and faded. It is all full of color, movement, the very thrill of life. And such good stories! For though the people are in, the story is never left out, as will sometimes happen with writers who are not born to the true romance, as this man surely is.

Kipling is essentially a man of our own generation, and it is the thing that is happening now that most deeply interests him. But he knows that a man is a man whether it be to-day or a thousand years ago, even as he writes in the ballad I spoke of at the beginning of this article—

But there is neither East nor West, Border,
  nor Breed, nor Birth,
When two strong men stand face to face, tho'
  they come from the ends of the earth!

—or the ends of time. That is why he makes history as real as it was, as alive as it was. While he writes about it, it is To-day, not Yesterday. Then in his *Captains Courageous* he shows how he grasped the Yankee character, writing a story as American as the Cape Cod drawl. Is not such a man a master of magic?

Kipling is the kind of man who has all sorts of strong opinions on a great many subjects. It doesn't matter whether or not you agree with all of them. The important point is that he believes them earnestly, and is willing to say so clearly. That is a rare trait, as I think you'll find, and it is a splendid help in getting ideas settled. When one side is honestly and definitely set forth, why, then, the opposing side can be as thoroughly stated, even if only in your own mind. To know what you believe on many subjects, and why you believe it, is worth a good deal. And to realize that there are things you will not be able to understand, because you are so entirely honest in your mind, is another important thing.

In stories like "They" and "The Brushwood Boy," Kipling confesses the things, or some of them, he does not understand, and yet which he feels exist. Reading them, and reading the *Barrack-room Ballads,* and the machine stories and songs, and the Mulvaney stories, with the others I have been talking about, we, too, find it difficult to understand that they can be the work of one man. That he could write such a book as *Kim,* which all of you must read some day (because not to do it would be to miss traveling through a whole world of wonder, a world entirely removed from ours of America or Europe), and also "McAndrew's Hymn," seems impossible. But there it is!

In 1907 Kipling was presented by the Stockholm Academy with the greatest reward in literature, the Nobel Prize.

There's another thing about Kipling, and that is the spirit of manliness, devotion to duty, law and order, clean sanity and serene courage, which you get from all he writes. That doesn't mean that he leaves all bad men and women and deeds out of his books. He could not do that and tell truth. But, like all the really big writers, it is goodness and strength and honor and self-denial that reach out to you from all he writes. And, if any of you are not sure of this, will you get his poem called "If" and read it carefully? Boy or girl, live up to that poem, and you can meet your Master's eye without shame:

When Earth's last picture is painted and the
  tubes are twisted and dried . . .

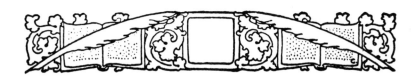

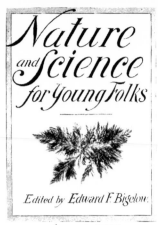

Nature and Science for Young Folks

Edited by Edward F. Bigelow

August, 1900

EGGS ON OR NEAR A ROCK

MOST birds are very skilful in nest-making, strongly weaving together sticks, twigs, and grass or bits of string for the exterior, sometimes cementing the whole together with mud, and often lining the interior with very soft material, But the nighthawk is a surprising exception, for she usually lays her two mottled eggs on the top of a flat rock in the pasture or other open field without any nest. A hollow place on the top of the rock is often selected, and sometimes the two eggs are placed on or near the highest point, where a slight touch would send them rolling off the rock. Less frequently the mother bird places the eggs on the ground near the rock.

The mottled color of the eggs is so much like that of the rock that they are not easily seen. But, strangest of all, the eggs are sometimes laid on a nearly flat roof of a city house!

THE NIGHTHAWK.

THE LIMPET THAT CAN FIND ITS WAY HOME

EVERY reader of *St. Nicholas* has heard of homing pigeons, who, when let loose—it may be hundreds of miles from home—are strong of wing and stout of heart and keen of wit enough to find the way back. But did ever anybody hear of a snail or a slug who was bright as that? We talk about the snail's "carrying his house on his back," and never dream that he cares at all where he sets it down; and, for aught I know, neither does he care. But he has an English cousin, called a limpet, who lives near the sea, and is a true Briton in his love for home. This little fellow has a shell like a long, low tent, and whenever the waves are rough or some big and hungry body comes along, he pulls his shell close down over him and clings so fast to the rock that "sticking like a limpet" has passed into a proverb. If the rock on

THE LIMPET ON A ROCK.

which he lives is soft limestone, the juices of his body gradually dissolve it away and make a little hollow, perhaps quarter of an inch deep, in which he lives. When the tide goes down and his home is dry, he climbs out of his hollow and crawls away in search of the little plants which serve for his dinner. And when he has had enough, and has, we may imagine, taken the little airing which everybody should take after his lunch, he goes back to his hollow with as much certainty as if he were a little boy going home from school.

But now comes the most wonderful part. We might guess, if this were all, that as he crawled away from home he left some sort of track which he could recognize though we could not, and which served to guide him back. But a wise Welshman has been studying the little fellows, and he finds that he can pick them up and put them down six inches, twelve inches, sometimes even as much as two feet, away from their hollows in any direction, and that, though they have no eyes worth the name, they will almost always find their way back. Sometimes, indeed, it may take them as much as two days to do it, and always a few get lost. About five sixths of those he tested came back, when they were put down not more than eighteen inches away, which we must know is a long distance to the little limpet. If they were carried farther from home, they were more likely to be lost.

Now, the English limpet has a good many cousins in America, most of which are found on the shores of the Pacific. But there is one who lives on the New England coast from Cape Cod northward. You may look for him in the little pools left by the outgoing tides, under the wet rockweed, or even on large rocks between tide-marks. The picture shows you what he looks like. He is usually brown and mottled, and everybody to whom I show him exclaims, "How much he looks like a turtle!" I think we may safely give him the name by which he is called in England—the tortoise-shell limpet. The children about Nahant, Massachusetts, call the shells "sugar-bowl covers," and use them to set their dolls' tea-tables.

People have been too busy in America to take time to learn much about our smaller animals; but I have heard from one wise old fisherman that our limpet has the same habit of coming back to his home that the English one has, though on our hard New England rocks he makes no hollow. Perhaps some reader of *St. Nicholas* will like to try, this summer, to see whether the old fisherman is right. When you have found your limpet, you must watch him very quietly, long enough to be quite sure that he is at home instead of being out for a walk and scared into momentary quiet by your coming. Then you can mark both shell and rock, perhaps with enamel paint, and come back every day or two to see whether you always find him there. And if you do, you will have made friends with a little fellow who, in this respect at least, is cleverer, so far as we know, than any other creature that wears a shell.

M. A. WILCOX

THE BURYING-BEETLE,
FULL SIZE.

FROM OUR "YOUNG OBSERVERS"

THE BURYING-BEETLE

103 COTTAGE STREET, BRIDGEPORT, CONN.

DEAR ST. NICHOLAS: One day last summer when I was in Newtown, two ladies were sitting on the veranda, when one of them said: "Look at that toad." The other one said: I don't see any toad, but I see a snake." So they called a man to kill it. After the snake had been killed, mama and I were going home when mama saw the snake raise its head, and she said: "Look out! that snake is alive." But I wasn't afraid; so I stopped to look at it, and I saw that it was not alive, but that three beetles were burying it. The next day one of the children and I went out to see it, and we coiled it up, and the beetles straightened it out. First, they dug a trench under it and piled the sand in a heap; then they dug a hole back of it, and commenced to bury it, tail first. Two of them lay on their backs and pushed with their feet, while the other one pulled it by the tail. After they had buried it they rolled a small stone to the entrance of the hole. Afterward a man pulled it out, and they buried it again.

About two weeks after the mate was killed, but where it was killed the soil was quite hard. They ran around it for about half a day, then they decided to eat it without burying it. The snake had just swallowed a toad. I found out, by asking my uncle, who is a naturalist, that the name of the beetle is the burying- or sexton-beetle. They bury the snake, then they lay their eggs on the snake, and when the young come out they feed on the snake. I found out a good many things from my uncle, who is in the scientific society in Bridgeport. Perhaps you may know him. His name is Mr. C. K. Averill. He once killed a heron, and when he went to the same spot the next day, the beetles had buried it all but the head.

LUCY S. ROBINSON

The young naturalist's mother writes: "I watched the beetles and the snake enough to confirm all that my little daughter has written, but she watched it all—hour after hour in the broiling sun."

This is an excellent example of the right spirit for a lover and student of nature. First, patient, careful observation; second, seeking further information from persons or books; and last, not least, telling others of the interesting discoveries, sharing our pleasures with them.

Entomologists—those who study insects as this little girl has begun to do—give many interesting accounts of the sagacity and remarkable strength of these burying-beetles. They have been known to roll a large dead rat or bird several feet in order to get in a suitable place for burying.

THE ENGLISH SPARROW AS A WORKER

NEW ORLEANS, LA.

DEAR ST. NICHOLAS: I have been very much interested in watching the little English sparrows at work building their nests. Two of them were very busy. They would go off one at a time and bring back a large supply of horsehairs, moss, twigs, and banana-leaves. Another thing they did was to take turns at building the nest. While one was building, the other was resting. I noticed that the male bird did the most work, too. The next morning the nest was finished and looked very cozy. The English sparrows are troublesome, but they are very hard workers.

Your little reader,
EUGENE HUNTER COLEMAN
(Age 8 years)

You are right. The English sparrows surely are faithful workers. So much has been said and written against them that it will be only justice to them to point out their good qualities. The most despised birds and people, young or old, are far from wholly bad. Who can tell us other good things about the English sparrows?

THE ENGLISH SPARROW.

DO SALAMANDERS SING?

SCARSDALE, N. Y.

DEAR ST. NICHOLAS: Do salamanders have voices?

HERBERT E. ANGELL

You will find an extended and interesting discussion of this question in the chapter entitled "Songless Batrachians" of the book *Familiar Life in Field and Forest*, written by F. Schuyler Mathews. The chapter also contains eleven illustrations and many interesting statements of the habits of salamanders. The author claims twenty years' experience with salamanders, and has never heard one sing, and seems to think that those who claim to have heard them sing were mistaken.

Dr. O. P. Hay, a naturalist of considerable experience, has heard from one "a shrill sound somewhat like a whistle or the peeping of a young chicken."

John Burroughs, in his book *Pepacton*, claims not only that the red salamander can make a noise, but that "the mysterious piper may be heard from May to November. It makes more music in the woods in autumn than any bird."

Gibson, in *Sharp Eyes*, has an extended and illustrated chapter entitled "The Autumn Pipers." Dr. Abbott, Professors Cope and Eimer claim to have heard these salamanders' voices.

THE RED SALAMANDER, FOUND IN COLD SPRINGS AND BROOKS.

Here is a good field for observation. What do our young folks say about it? Who has watched salamanders and heard the voice or song?

September.

By Katharine Pyle

September, 1890

We made ourselves a castle
　　Once after school was out;
We raked the leaves together
　　To wall it all about .

We made a winding pathway
　　Down to the school-yard gate,
And there we worked with might and main
　　Until the day grew late;

Until one bright star twinkled
　　Above the maple tree,
And lights shone down the village street
　　As far as we could see .

We planned that every recess
　　We'd come out there to play,
But in the night it blew so hard
　　Our castle blew away .

K. Pyle.

92

·The Goblin of Valestrand·

(An Incident in the Boyhood of Ole Bull.)

By Margaret Johnson

December, 1900

"There's a goblin in the wood,"
Said the folk of Valestrand,
In the far Norwegian land;
So they read the fearsome riddle,
Blessed themselves, and trembling stood.
"There's a troll that in the middle
Of the night, a fairy fiddle
Plays, where white the waters leap
And the chilly moonbeams creep!"

For, belated in the dark,
   Wanderers hastening homeward heard
   All the air about them stirred
  With a music strange and eery,
While they feared to pause and hark.
   Wailings of a spirit weary,
   Moans that made the midnight dreary,
From the gloomy forest stole
Where there dwelt no human soul.

Up and down the startled glen
   Now there pealed a burst of glee,
   Elfin laughter, wild and free,
  On the night wind, rippling, ringing,
Till the echoes laughed again,
   And a sudden tender singing
   Hushed the mocking mirth upspringing,
And with murmurs soft as prayer
Melted on the moonlit air.

"There's a goblin in the wood!"
   And they shunned the forest's edge,
   Trembling at the wind-blown sedge,
  Till at last there came one bolder—
"I would find him if I could!"
   Plunged, with pick upon his shoulder,
   Straight into the forest, colder,
Where the branches, dim and deep,
Hid the moon, and sighed, asleep.

Guided by the music's thread,
   Fast he followed, fast and still,
   Where the laughter sounded shrill,
  Or a moaning, strange and hollow,
Made his hair rise up with dread.
   Stoutly still he tried to follow.
   "I will find this Jack or Moll, oh,
Who, the simple folk to scare,
Juggles thus with empty air!"

On he pressed by rock and tree.
   Nearer, clearer, rang the strain;
   Pattering notes, as quick as rain,
  Gay as feet of nymphs, light-hearted,
Dancing on the daisied lea;
  Till, where swift a streamlet darted,
  Suddenly he paused and started,
Gazing down with blanching cheek
At the thing he came to seek.

Down into a hollow scooped
  In the hillside's rocky frame,
  Whence the elfin music came,
  With the rippled water flowing,
Where the purple harebell drooped,
  And a charmèd wind was blowing,
  Gazed with wide eyes, wider growing,
First in fear, and then, behold,
With a sudden laughter bold!

There, upon a mossy shelf,
  With his bare feet in the dew,
  Where, the parted branches through,
  Poured a flood of moonlight mellow,
Sat—nor goblin, fay, nor elf,
  But—a little blue-eyed fellow,
  Human, mortal, with a yellow
Plaything of a violin
Pressed beneath his boyish chin!

Slipping softly from his bed
  While the world about him slept,
  Forth into the woods he crept,
  By the passion, strong, forbidden,
In his childish bosom led;
  Wandered through the shadow-hidden
  Forest paths, alone, unchidden,
Played, with all his heart in tune,
To the midnight and the moon.

"There's a goblin in the wood!"
  Said the folk of Valestrand;
  "Playing with enchanted hand,
  Playing loudly, playing lowly."
So at last they understood,
  Smiled, and shook their wise heads slowly,
  Knowing it was only Ole,
(Who one day the world should win!)
Ole with his violin.

The Untutored Giraffe

By Oliver Herford

February, 1891

A CHILD at school who fails to pass
    Examination in his class
    Of Natural History will be
    So Shaky in Zoölogy,
That, should he ever chance to go
To foreign parts, he scarce will know
The common *Mus Ridiculus*
From *Felis* or *Caniculus*.
And what of boys and girls is true
Applies to other creatures, too,
As you will cheerfully admit
When once I've illustrated it.

Once on a time a young Giraffe
(Who when at school devoured the chaff,
And trampled underneath his feet
The golden grains of Learning's wheat)
Upon his travels chanced to see
A Python hanging from a tree,
A thing he'd never met before

All neck it seemed and nothing more;
And, stranger still, it was bestrown
With pretty spots much like his own.
"Well, well! I've often heard," he said,
"Of foolish folk who lose their head;
But really it's a funnier joke
To meet a head that's lost its folk."

95

Dear me! Ha! ha! it makes me laugh.
Where *has* he left his other half?
If he could find it he would be
A really fine Giraffe, like me."

The Python, waking with a hiss,
Exclaimed, "What kind of snake is this?
Your spots are really very fine,
Almost as good, in fact, as mine,

But with those legs I fail to see
How you can coil about a tree.
Take away half, and you would make
A very decent sort of snake—
Almost as fine a snake as I;
Indeed, it's not too late to try."

A something in the Python's eye
Told the Giraffe 'twas best to fly,
Omitting all formality.
And afterward, when safe at home,
He wrote a very learned tome,
Called, "What I Saw beyond the Foam."
Said he, "The strangest thing one sees
Is a Giraffe who hangs from trees,
And has—(right here the author begs
To state a *fact*) and has *no legs!*"

The book made a tremendous hit.
The public all devoured it,
Save one, who, minding how he missed
Devouring the author—*hissed*.

THISTLEDOWN
By Lizette Woodworth Reese
August, 1902

WHEN the nights are long and dust is deep,
   The shepherd's at the door;
Hillo, the little white woolly sheep
   That he drives on before!

Never a sound does the shepherd make;
   His flock is as still as he;
Under the boughs their road they take,
   Whatever that road may be.

And one may catch on a shriveling brier,
   And one drop down at the door,
And some may lag, and some may tire,
   But the rest go on before.

The wind is that shepherd so still and sweet,
   And his sheep are the thistledown;
All August long, by alley and street,
   He drives them through the town.

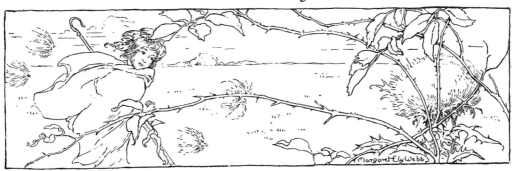

From Our Scrap-Book

July, 1897

HOW THE TURKS CAME BY THEIR CRESCENT

WHEN Philip of Macedon approached by night with his troops to scale the walls of Byzantium, the moon, then new or in crescent, shone out and discovered his design to the besieged, who repulsed him. The crescent was after that adopted as the favorite badge of the city. When the Turks took Byzantium they found the crescent in every public place, and believing it to possess some magical power, adopted it themselves.

A CHAPEL BELL

THE largest bell in the world is the one called "King of Bells," in Moscow, Russia. It was cast in 1733, but fell during a fire, and remained buried in the earth till 1836. It is more than three times as high as a man, being over nineteen feet high, and weighs as much as two hundred and twenty common cart-loads of coal. There is a large piece broken out of one side, so that it cannot be rung as a bell; but it is set upon a stone foundation, and used as a chapel, of which the broken place is the door.

TEN THOUSAND TELEGRAMS AT ONCE

IN 1871, at a celebration held in New York in honor of Professor Morse, the original instrument invented by him was exhibited, connected at that moment by wire with every one of the ten thousand instruments then in use in the country. At a signal a message from the inventor was sent vibrating throughout the United States, and was read at the same time in every city from New York to New Orleans and San Francisco.

THE TRUE "REBECCA"

SIR WALTER SCOTT'S model for the Rebecca of *Ivanhoe* was a young Jewish lady in Philadelphia, named Rebecca Gratz. She was beautiful, and noted for her devotion to the Jewish faith. One of the most intimate friends of her family was Washington Irving. Irving visited Scott, and spoke of Miss Gratz, her beauty and her devotion. Scott was deeply impressed, and planned the story of *Ivanhoe*, naming his heroine Rebecca.

AUSTERLITZ PLANNED BY JOHN MILTON

NAPOLEON declared to Sir Colin Campbell, who had charge of the exile on the isle of Elba, that he was a great admirer of Milton's *Paradise Lost*, and that he had read it to some purpose. He said further that he had borrowed the idea or plan of the battle of Austerlitz from the sixth book of that poem, where Satan brings his artillery to bear upon Michael and his angelic host with such dire effect:

Training his devilish enginery impaled
On every side with shadowing squadrons deep to hide the fraud.

PRETTY NAMES FOR BOOKS

THE following are some of the curious titles of old English books:

1. *A Most Delectable Sweet Perfumed Nosegay for God's Saints to Smell at.*

2. *Biscuit Baked in the Oven of Charity, carefully conserved for the Chickens of the Church, the Sparrows of the Spirit, and the sweet Swallows of Salvation.*

3. *A Sigh of Sorrow for the Sinners of Zion breathed out of a Hole in the Wall of an Earthly Vessel known among men by the name of Samuel Fish* (a Quaker who had been imprisoned).

4. *Eggs of Charity Layed for the Chickens of the Covenant and Boiled with the Water of Divine Love. Take ye out and eat.*

5. *Seven Sobs of a Sorrowful Soul for Sin.*

6. *The Spiritual Mustard-Pot to make the Soul Sneeze with Devotion.*

Most of these were published in the time of Cromwell.

ORIGIN OF "BOZ"

CHARLES DICKENS signed the name "Boz" to his earliest articles. It was a nickname which he had given to his younger brother, whom for fun he called Moses, pronouncing it through his nose, like "Boses," and then shortening it to "Boz."

ICELAND'S MILLENNIAL

IN 1874 Iceland celebrated the one-thousandth anniversary of its colonization. At the same time it became independent of Denmark, though still subject to the king as head of the government. Its new government is thoroughly republican in spirit, all citizens having equal rights and perfect religious liberty. There are in Iceland no officers answering to our policemen, and no prisons.

THE LION

April, 1877

IF any of you ever saw a lion, I am quite sure that he would be in a cage. Now a lion in a cage is a noble-looking beast, but he never seems so grand and king-like—you know some people call the lion the King of Beasts—as he does when he is free. Of course, almost any living creature will look happier and better when it is free than when it is shut up; but there is another reason why the lions we see in cages do not seem so grand as those which are free.

We almost always go to see wild animals in the day-time, and animals of the cat-kind, of which the lion is one, like to take the day for their sleeping time. So, when we see them, they are drowsy and lazy, and would much rather take a good nap than be bothered with visitors. If we could go and look at them at night, it is likely we should find them much more lively.

Lions are natives of Africa and Asia, and there they roam around at night and are not afraid of any living creature. They sometimes stand and roar as if they wished all other animals to know that a lion was about, and that they would do well to behave themselves.

When a lion is hungry, he kills a deer or an antelope, or some such animal, and eats it. But sometimes he comes near to men's houses and fields, and kills an ox or a cow, and carries it away. A lion must be very strong if he can even drag away a great ox.

The male lion is much handsomer and finer looking than the female, or lioness. He has a large head, with a great mane of hair hanging down all around his head and over his shoulders. This gives him a very noble look. The lioness has no mane at all.

Baby lions are funny fellows. They look something like clumsy dogs, and are quite playful. But long before they are full-grown they begin to look grave and sober, as if they knew that it was a very grand thing to be a lion.

Two half-grown lions that I saw not long ago looked just as quiet and sedate as their old father, who was in the next cage. But perhaps they had their play and fun at night, when there was nobody there to see.

Some lions are quite easily tamed, and often learn to like their keepers. I suppose you have seen performing lions in cages. The keeper goes into the cage and makes the lions, and sometimes leopards and other animals, jump about and do just as he tells them.

As the lion seems to have a better disposition than most other savage beasts, he sometimes becomes so tame that his keepers do not appear to be at all afraid of him.

But he is really a wild beast at heart, and it would never do to let the very tamest lion think that he could go where he pleased, and choose his dinner for himself. It would not be long before he would be seen springing upon a cow or a horse—if he did not fancy some little boy or girl.

So, after all, there are animals which have much nobler dispositions than the lion, and among these are elephants and dogs—who not only are often trusted servants of man, but also seem to have some reasoning powers, and are known to do actions that are really good and kind.

JACK-IN-THE-PULPIT

October, 1895

BACK again to school,
   Hear the bells a-ringing!
Feet a-dancing, heads a-whirl,
Shouting boy and smiling girl,
Apron trim and shining curl,
   Here they come a-singing
     Back again to school.
Back again to school,
   Clear September weather,
Wayside goldenrods ablow;
Eyes a-sparkle, cheeks aglow,
Down the grassy ways they go,
   Merry mates together
     Back again to school.

So sings your friend Dorothy Deane in a song lately sent you in Jack's care, my young book-devourers; and your Jack heartily joins in the invisible chorus of good will and fine spirits.

CORKS

WHO knows where corks come from? This question was asked of the children of the red school-house one day, and some funny answers came.

One child said, "From bottles"; another timidly shouted, "The druggist's"; another said, "Off of trees"; and the dear Little Schoolma'am began to feel rather discouraged. Suddenly a freckled little fellow of eight summers held up his hand.

"Well, Eddie," said the Little Schoolma'am, encouragingly.

"I think corks are trees,—I mean there are cork-trees—and all sorts of things are made out of them, such as life-preservers and everything."

"Very good," said the dear Little Schoolma'am. And then she read to the class a little paper about the cork-tree.

To-day every one of those children knows that Spain is a great country for cork-trees. Some of them know more yet on the subject, for they have inquired, and also have looked in the cyclopedia. You may follow the same plan, my chicks, whenever you feel like doing so.

What sort of tree is it, I wonder, big or little? Does it bear flowers? Is the trunk all cork, or is the cork only the bark, or else the center of the trunk? My birds don't seem to know. One traveled fellow says that the cork-tree is "a kind of oak." Now, is that possible, my wise ones?

THAT FLORIDA LEAF

MANY letters have come to this pulpit in answer to the message I gave you in April from Lutie E. D. I should like to show all these notes to you, my friends, but that is not practicable. Rita C., who writes pleasantly from St. Leo, Florida, says that her papa calls the plant the Bryophyllum; Ida May Ingersoll sends word from Florida that where she is living, and in Cuba also, it is called the Chandelier plant; E. J. H., now in Pernambuco, Brazil, says: "I have seen hundreds of these wonderful plants growing here in Brazil. I often pick one and put it away in a drawer, and in two weeks instead of one leaf there are many."

Next comes Cecil Barr, whose letter tells us about the leaf. He says:

> I have read of a sprig of this life-leaf plant about fifteen feet long, cut from a banyan tree on this island of Nassau, which sprouted three months after it was cut, without water or earth, and with no other culture than being first packed in a trunk, and then hung up on a nail!

Last of all comes a delightful letter from a young girl of fourteen. It is so satisfactory and interesting, you shall have it entire:

> MY DEAR "JACK-IN-THE-PULPIT": I think this is the first letter you have had from Uruguay or even from South America, because I have never seen any from here among the letters to you. I am writing in answer to the letter about the "Florida Leaf" in the April number of ST. NICHOLAS, 1895. From the description given I think it must be "The Life Plant," or "Leaf of Life" (Bryophyllum calycinum, natural order Grassulaceæ—Stone Crop and House-Leek family). It is a native of Asia, found in the Malaccas; it is a tall plant and grows to about three feet high with thick, bright green, succulent leaves, notched, leaving rounded segments; the stem of the plant is a pinkish brown color, the flowers are large and pendulous, of a greenish yellow, sometimes turning to purple. It is a greenhouse plant, but grows wild in Jamaica, West Indies, Brazil, and in Entre Rios, Argentine Republic. In Jamaica it is considered a great curiosity by the Creoles on account of its tenacity of the living principle, whence it is called the "Leaf of Life." A single leaf, if broken off and hung by a thread in a room, or put into a box or book, will begin to grow from every notch in little pink buds that soon turn green and form little leaves with long rootlets like threads. It grows if thrown upon the ground even if the leaves are cut in halves. It can only be dried to be put in a herbarium by first killing it with a hot iron or by boiling water. In its native country it grows in the hottest, stoniest places. Here, where I live, it grows very well, although it does not belong to this country and has not yet flowered. The hot climate suits it, and a small sprig that was brought here from Rio Janeiro nearly two years ago has given us about a hundred plants.
>
> A. D.

A St NICHOLAS ANTHOLOGY
WINTER

CONTENTS

THE CREATURE WITH NO CLAWS

By Joel Chandler Harris

October 1889

"W'en you git a leetle bit older dan w'at you is, honey," said Uncle Remus to the little boy, "you'll know lots mo' dan you does now."

The old man had a pile of white oak splits by his side and these he was weaving into a chair-bottom. He was an expert in the art of "bottoming chairs," and he earned many a silver quarter in this way. The little boy seemed to be much interested in the process.

"Hit's des like I tell you," the old man went on; "I done had de speunce un it. I done got so now dat I don't b'lieve w'at I see, much less w'at I year. It got ter be whar I kin put my han' on it en fumble wid it. Folks kin fool deyse'f lots wuss dan yuther folks kin fool um, en ef you don't b'lieve w'at I'm a-tellin' un you, you kin des ax Brer Wolf de nex' time you meet 'im in de big road."

"What about Brother Wolf, Uncle Remus?" the little boy asked, as the old man paused to refill his pipe.

"Well, honey, 'tain't no great long rigamarole; hit's des one er deze yer tales w'at goes in a gallop twel it gits ter de jumpin'-off place.

"One time Brer Wolf wuz gwine 'long de big road feelin' mighty proud en highstrung. He wuz a mighty high-up man in dem days, Brer Wolf wuz, en 'mos all de yuther creeturs wuz feard un 'im. Well, he wuz gwine 'long lickin' his chops en walkin' sorter stiff-kneed, wh'en he happen ter look down 'pon de groun' en dar he seed a track in de san'. Brer Wolf stop, he did, en look at it, en den he 'low:

"'Heyo! w'at kind er creetur dish yer? Brer Dog ain't make dat track, en needer is

Brer Fox. Hit's one er deze yer kind er creeturs w'at ain't got no claws. I'll des 'bout foller 'im up, en ef I ketch 'im he'll sholy be my meat.'

"Dat de way Brer Wolf talk. He followed 'long atter de track, he did, en he look at it close, but he ain't see no print er no claw. Bimeby de track tuck'n tu'n out de road en go up a dreen whar de rain done wash out. De track wuz plain dar in de wet san', but Brer Wolf ain't see no sign er no claws.

"He foller en foller, Brer Wolf did, en de track git fresher en fresher, but still he ain't see no print er no claw. Bimeby he come in sight er de creetur, en Brer Wolf stop, he did, en look at 'im. He stop stock-still en look. De creetur wuz mighty quare-lookin', en he wuz cuttin' up some mighty quare capers. He had big head, sharp nose, en bob tail; en he wuz walkin' roun' en roun' a big dog-wood tree, rubbin' his sides ag'in it. Brer Wolf watch 'im a right smart while, he act so quare, en den he 'low:

"'Shoo! dat creetur done bin in a fight en los' de bes' part er he tail; en w'at make he scratch hisse'f dat away? I lay I'll let 'im know who he foolin' 'long wid.'

"Atter 'while, Brer Wolf went up a leetle nigher de creetur, en holler out:

"'Heyo, dar! w'at you doin' scratchin' yo' scaly hide on my tree, en tryin' fer ter break hit down?'

"De creetur ain't make no answer. He des walk 'roun' en 'roun' de tree scratchin' he sides en back. Brer Wolf holler out:

"'I lay I'll make you year me ef I hatter come dar whar you is!'

"De creetur des walk 'roun' en 'roun' de

105

tree, en ain't make no answer. Den Brer Wolf hail 'im ag'in, en talk like he mighty mad:

"'Ain't you gwine ter min' me, you imperdent scoundul? Ain't you gwine ter mozey outer my woods en let my tree 'lone?'

"Wid dat, Brer Wolf march todes de creetur des like he gwine ter squ'sh 'im in de groun'. De creetur rub hisse'f ag'in de tree en look like he feel mighty good. Brer Wolf keep on gwine todes 'im, en bimeby w'en he git sorter close de creetur tuck 'n sot up on his behime legs des like you see squir'ls do. Den Brer Wolf, he 'low, he did:

"'Ah-yi! you beggin', is you? But 'tain't gwine ter do you no good. I mout er let you off ef you'd a-minded me w'en I fus' holler atter you, but I ain't gwine ter let you off now. I 'm a-gwine ter l'arn you a lesson dat 'll stick by you.'

"Den de creetur sorter wrinkle up he face en mouf, en Brer Wolf 'low:

"'Oh, you nee'n'ter swell up en cry, you 'ceitful vilyun. I'm a-gwine ter gi' you

a frailin' dat I boun' you won't forgit.'

"Brer Wolf make like he gwine ter hit de creetur, en den—"

Here Uncle Remus paused and looked all around the room and up at the rafters. When he began again his voice was very solemn.

"Well, suh, dat creetur des fotch one swipe dis away, en 'n'er swipe dat away, en mos' 'fo' you can wink yo' eye-balls, Brer Wolf hide wuz mighty nigh teetotally tor'd off 'n 'im. Atter dat de creetur sa'ntered off in de woods, en 'gun ter rub hisse'f on 'n'er tree."

"WELL, SUH, DAT CREETUR DES FOTCH ONE SWIPE DIS AWAY, EN 'N'ER SWIPE DAT AWAY."

"What kind of a creature was it, Uncle Remus?" asked the little boy.

"Well, honey," replied the old man in a confidential whisper, "hit want nobody on de top-side er de yeth but ole Brer Wildcat."

"BRER WOLF MAKE LIKE HE GWINE TER HIT DE CREETUR, EN DEN ——"

ON A MOUNTAIN TRAIL

By Harry Perry Robinson

March, 1890

WE had no warning. It was as if they had deliberately lain in ambush for us at the turn in the trail. They seemed suddenly and silently to rise on all sides of the sleigh at once.

It is not often that the gray timber-wolves, or "black wolves," as the mountaineers call them, are seen hunting in packs, though the animal is plentiful enough among the foot-hills of the Rockies. As a general rule they are met with singly or in pairs. At the end of a long and severe winter, however, they sometimes come together in bands of fifteen or twenty; and every old mountaineer has a tale to tell—perhaps of his own narrow escape from one of their fierce packs, perhaps of some friend of his who started one day in winter to travel alone from camp to camp, and whose clean-picked bones were found beside the trail long afterward.

It was in February, and we, Gates and myself, were driving from Livingston, Montana, to Gulch City, fifty miles away, with a load of camp supplies—a barrel of flour and some bacon, coffee, and beans; a blanket or two, and some dynamite (or "giant powder," as the miners call it) for blasting; a few picks and shovels, and other odds and ends. We had started at daybreak. By five o'clock in the evening, with some ten miles more to travel, the worst of the trail was passed. There had been little snow that winter, so that even in the gulches and on the bottoms the exposed ground was barely covered; while, on the steep slopes, snow had almost entirely disappeared, leaving only ragged patches of white under overhanging boughs, and a thin coating of ice in the inequalities of the hard, frost-bound trail, making a treacherous footing for the horses' hoofs.

The first forty miles of the road had lain entirely over hills—zigzagging up one side of a mountain only to zigzag down the other—with the dense growth of pine and tamarack and cedar on both sides, wreathed here and there in mist. But at last we were clear of the foot-hills and reached the level. The tall forest trees gave place to a wilderness of thick underbrush, lying black in the evening air, and the horses swung contentedly from the steep grade into the level trail, where at last they could let their legs move freely in a trot.

Hardly had they settled into their stride, however, when both animals shied violently to the left side of the trail. A moment later they plunged back to the right side so suddenly as almost to throw me off into the brush.

Then, out of the earth and the shadow of the bushes, the grim, dark forms seemed to rise on all sides of us. There was not a sound—not a snap nor a snarl; but in the gathering twilight of the February evening, we saw them moving noiselessly over the thin coat of snow which covered the ground. In the uncertain light, and moving as rapidly as we did, it was impossible to guess how many they were. An animal which was one moment in plain sight, running abreast of the horses, would, the next moment, be lost in the shadow of the bushes, while two more dark, silent forms would edge up to take its place. So, on both sides of us, they kept appearing and disappearing. In the rear, half a dozen jostled one another to push up nearer to the flying sleigh—a black mass that filled the whole width of the trail. Behind those again, others, less clearly visible, crossed and recrossed the roadway from side to side. They might be twenty in all—or thirty—or forty. It was impossible to tell.

For a minute I did not think of danger. The individual wolf is the most skulking and cowardly of animals, and only by some such experience as we had that night does a hunter learn that wolves can be dangerous. But soon the stories of the old mountaineers came crowding into my mind, as the horses, terrified and snorting, plunged wildly along the narrow trail, while the ghost-like forms glided patiently alongside —appearing, disappearing, and reappearing. The silent pertinacity with which, apparently making no effort, they kept pace beside the flying horses was horrible. Even a howl or a yelp or a growl would have been a relief. But not so much as the sound of their footfalls on the snow was to be heard.

At the first sight of the wolves, I had drawn my revolver from the leather case in which it hung suspended from my belt. Gates, handling the reins, was entirely occupied with the horses; but I knew, without need of words, that he saw our pursuers and understood the peril as well as I.

"Have you your gun?" I shouted in his ear.

A negative shake of the head was all the answer. So we must trust to the six cartridges in my revolver.

"How many wolves are there, do you suppose?" again I called.

Again he shook his head, as if to say that he could not guess.

So the minutes passed and we swept on, rising and falling and swaying with the inequalities in the trail. The dark forms, growing more indistinct each minute, were hanging doggedly to the sleigh.

Suddenly I became aware that a wolf was almost at my elbow: its head was on a level with my waist as I sat in the low sleigh. In the darkness I could plainly see the white teeth, and the dim circle of the eyes. I hardly had to lean over at all to place the muzzle of the revolver within a foot of the great round head before I fired. I saw the black form roll over and over in the snow as we went by. Simultaneously, two other shadowy shapes that had been running abreast of the horses, in advance of the animal that was shot, dropped back; and looking over my shoulder I could see them throw themselves upon their wounded fellow. As the sea-gulls, following in the wake of a vessel in mid-ocean, swoop from all directions upon some floating scrap that has been thrown overboard, so from both sides of the trail the dark figures rushed together into one struggling mass behind the sleigh; and for the first time we heard them snapping and snarling at one another, as they tore their comrade to pieces.

The horses appeared to know that in some way a gleam of hope had come. They ceased plunging and seemed to throw all their energies into putting as wide a space as possible between them and the yelping pack behind.

How long would the respite be? Seconds passed until half a minute had gone. Then a minute. Could it be that they had left us—that the horrible race was over?

But even as the hope was forming itself in my mind, I became aware of a dim, gray thing moving beside me. A moment later another appeared, close by the horses' heads, and behind us the trail was again full of the jostling pack.

It was terrible beyond expression, the utter noiselessness with which they resumed their places—apparently tireless; keeping pace with the racing horses without a sign of effort; patient as fate itself. Have you ever been on a fast steamship— say a "P. and O." * boat in Indian waters where the sea is transparent—and, leaning

* Peninsular and Oriental

over the stern, watched a shark following the vessel? If so, you remember how, hour after hour and day after day, the dark, vaguely outlined body, not more distinct than the shadow of a cloud upon the waves, stayed, motionless to all appearance, just so many feet aft in the ship's wake, no matter how fast she moved. To me, and I think to every one who has seen it, that silent, persistent, haunting presence is the very embodiment of ruthlessness and untiring cruelty. There, in the twilight and shadow, was the same silence, the same indistinctness, the same awing impression of motionless speed, the same horror of the inevitable, in that pursuit by the wolves.

But soon their tactics changed. Either they had grown bolder, or the wolf they had eaten among them had put a keener edge upon their appetites. There were now four or five of the ghostlike forms moving abreast of the horses on my side of the sleigh alone. On the other side more were visible. They were now closing in upon us, with determination. Suddenly I saw one make a spring at the throat of the off horse, and, missing his aim, fall back. The horses had been terrified before; from that moment they lost all control of themselves. Neither the driver's voice nor his hands upon the reins had any influence upon them as they tore wildly down the narrow path between the bushes, snorting, throwing their heads from side to side, and breaking now and again into short, shrill neighs of terror. The breath from their nostrils and the steam from their bodies made a white cloud in the wintry night air, almost enveloping them and us, and at times blotting out of sight the wolves beneath.

But the pack was again closing in. In front of all, I could see one running under the very noses of the horses, keeping just beyond the reach of their hoofs, and evidently waiting for the right moment to make a final leap at their throats. Leaning

forward, and steadying my aim as well as I could in the rocking sleigh, I fired full at the whole dark mass in front. Apparently the ball passed harmlessly through them, but in an instant all had vanished—behind and into the bushes—as a swarm of flies vanish at the waving of a handkerchief. Only for a second, however, and one after another they were back again.

A second shot, fired again at random into the mass, was more successful; and once more we saw them drop back and crowd together in the trail behind us while the snapping and snarling grew fainter as the horses plunged on.

Half of the last ten miles had now been traveled, and five miles more would bring us to Gulch City and security. The excitement of that race was unspeakable: the narrow lane of the trail lying white ahead of us and behind us between the dark borders of the brush, seen fitfully through the stream from the maddened horses.

But the respite this time was shorter than before. Once more our relentless foes gathered round us, silently, one by one. The wolves seemed to know as well as we, that time was short and escape lay not far away; for hardly had the pack settled in their places round us before I saw one animal throw himself recklessly at the horses' throats. There was a sudden mad rearing up of both the horses, a wild, despairing neigh, a short yelp from the wolf's throat, and the dark form that had seemed to hang for a moment, leech-like, to the chest of one of our brave beasts was beaten down under the hoofs.

The others did not wait even for the sleigh to pass, but leaped upon the struggling form even as the runners were upon it. In my excitement I did a foolish thing. Leaning over, and thrusting my revolver almost against the skins of the fierce brutes, I fired two shots in quick succession. They had their effect, I know, for I saw one of the dark figures throw itself convulsively out of the mass into the brush, where others sprang upon it, and a death-cry went up in the night air. But we could ill spare the ammunition.

This idea evidently occurred to Gates. Leaning suddenly toward me, but with his eyes fixed on the horses and the road ahead, he called:

"How many shots have you left?"

"Only one."

"Not even one apiece for us?"

And I knew that he was in earnest. I knew also that he was right; that it would be better to die so, than to be torn to pieces by that snarling, hungry crew.

But it was too late now. Five shots out of the six were spent, and twenty minutes yet must pass before we could reach the camp. And even while these few words were being said the pack was close upon us again. Fiercer now, and more determined than ever to make an end of it, they crowded around. One even flung himself at the low side of the sleigh to snap at me, and his teeth caught for a moment in the sleeve of my coat as I struck him on the head with the clenched hand holding the pistol. On both sides, too, they jostled each other, to reach the flying horses, and I knew that in a few seconds more I must sacrifice the last cartridge in my revolver.

As a forlorn hope I snatched the buffalo-robe which lay on Gates' knees, and threw it to them. But they hardly stopped to tear it to pieces. There was more satisfying food in the sleigh. And they closed around the horses again.

For the first time Gates turned to look at me.

"Jack!" he called excitedly, "the giant powder!"

For a moment I did not grasp his meaning. Seeing my indecision he shouted again:

"The giant powder, Jack!"

Then it came to me. Thrusting the pistol into its case, I scrambled over into the rear part of the sleigh, and as I did so the wolves that were following behind fell back a few feet. Hastily fumbling among the various supplies, I found the old sack in which the sticks of dynamite were wrapped, and with them the small package of caps and fuse. Taking three of the sticks, I tied them tightly together with my handkerchief and, quickly fitting the end of an inch of fuse—for, in this case, the shorter the piece the better—into a cap, I thrust the latter into the center of the three sticks. I was still at work, when a sudden swing of the sleigh and a cry from Gates warned me that something was the matter. The horses were plunging violently, and as the near horse reared I saw that a wolf had leaped upon its withers and was clinging, with its teeth apparently in the side of the horse's neck. In their terror, the horses had stopped, and were actually backing us into the brush. Something had to be done, and with some vague hope, I fired the last shot from the revolver into the dark circle which already surrounded the plunging horses. The shot had its effect, for one of the brutes leaped into the air with a yelp and fell backward into the bushes. The horse, too, sprang suddenly forward, and the wolf that was clinging to it fell to the ground and was trampled under the hoofs. In an instant, those of the pack that had not already flung themselves upon the wounded animal in the bushes, rushed upon this one that was lying lifeless or stunned from the horses' feet; and once more, for a few seconds, we had breathing space, and the sleigh sped along through the keen air, our enemies snarling and quarreling behind us.

But the last shot was spent!

Turning my attention again to the giant powder, I fixed the cap and fuse more firmly in their place, and taking off my belt wound that tightly round the whole. Round that again I wrapped one of the old sacks, and tearing off my coat made an extra covering of that, knotting the sleeves tightly on the outside, that the ravenous teeth might be delayed in tearing the bundle apart. Crouching down in the sleigh, I lighted a match, and, as I did so, I saw that the wolves were upon us again, apparently as numerous and as tireless as ever. The match went out; and a second. Crouching lower still, I made a barricade against the wind with anything I could lay my hands on in the sleigh, and at last a dull red spark caught the end of the fuse.

The pack was already crowding round the terrified horses, which, it seemed to me, were almost worn out, and moved more heavily than heretofore. And how slowly the fuse burned! Nursing it carefully with my hands, I blew upon the spark and kept it glowing as it ate its way slowly into the cotton. Why had I not made it shorter? Every moment I expected to feel the sudden jolt which told that the wolves had pulled down one of the horses and that the end had come!

At last the dull red glow had almost reached the end of the cap. A few seconds more and it would explode. Thrusting the bundle hastily into another sack, forgetting even the wolves in my terror lest it should explode in my hands, I threw it with all my force into the midst of the moving forms abreast of the horses.

The beasts flung themselves upon it, and as we swept by, the whole pack was again collected into a struggling, snarling heap beside the trail. We were sweeping round a curve in the road, and before the horses had taken a dozen strides, the brush shut out the path behind us and the wolves.

A moment later and the air and the earth shook around us. I was still standing, clutching the low side of the sleigh, and the concussion threw me upon my face. The report was not the crash of a cannon nor the sharp noise of gunpowder, but a dull, heavy roar like an instantaneous clap of distant thunder. The stillness that followed was intense, but I thought that I heard, from the direction where the wolves had been, one broken, muffled howl.

What had been the effect of it? Both Gates and myself leaned forward and with voice and hand urged the horses on. When would those grim, gray, ruthless forms disappear? The seconds passed; minute followed minute, and the horses, breathing painfully, labored on over the level trail. With every yard traveled, hope grew stronger, until leaning over again I said to Gates:

"I don't believe they're coming, Charlie."

But his only reply was a shake of the reins and another word to the horses.

Then suddenly there came a twinkle of light in the distance. The brush fell away from the trail and the white expanse of the clearing of Gulch City was before us.

For a distance of fifty yards, at a point about a mile and a half north of Gulch City, the old Livingston trail had to be abandoned. It would have been more labor to repair it than to clear a new pathway through the brush. And when I left that part of the country two years afterward, the packers would still turn out of their way for a minute to look at "Giant Hole," and to kick up out of the weeds and brush that had grown around it the skull or part of the skeleton of a wolf.

LOST ON THE PLAINS
By Joaquin Miller

October, 1884

ONLY sixteen or seventeen miles a day. A long, creeping, creaking line of covered white ox-wagons, stretching away to the west across the vast and boundless brown plains. Not a house for thousands of miles, not a tree, not a shrub, not a single thing in sight, except now and then, dotted down here and there, a few great black spots in the boundless sea of brown.

That is the way it was when my parents took me, then only a lad, across the plains, more than thirty years ago. How different now, with the engines tearing, smoking, screeching and screaming across at the rate of five hundred miles or more a day!

There are many houses on the plains now. The pioneers have planted great forests of trees, and there are also vast cornfields, and the song of happy harvesters is heard there. But the great black spots that dotted the boundless sea of brown are gone forever. Those dark spots were herds of countless bison, or buffalo—as they were more generally called.

One sultry morning in July, as the sun rose up and blazed with uncommon ardor, a herd of buffalo was seen grazing quietly close to our train, and some of the younger boys who had guns and pistols, and were "dying to kill a buffalo," begged their parents to let them ride out and take a shot.

As it was only a natural desire, and seemed a simple thing to do, a small party of boys was soon ready. The men were obliged to stay with the train and drive the oxen; for the tents had already been struck, and the long white line had begun to creep slowly away over the level brown sea toward the next water, a little blind stream that stole through the willows fifteen miles away to the west.

There were in our train two sons of a rich and rather important man. And they were now first in the saddle and ready to take the lead. But as they were vain and selfish, and had always had a big opinion of themselves, their father knew they had not learned much about anything else. There was also in the train a sad-faced, silent boy, barefooted and all in rags; for his parents had died with the cholera the day after we crossed the Missouri river, and he was left helpless and alone. He hardly ever spoke to any one. And as for the rich man's boys, they would sooner have thought of speaking to their cook than to him.

As the boys sat on their horses ready to go, and the train of wagons rolled away, the rich man came up to the barefooted boy, and said:

"See here, 'Tatters,' go along with my boys and bring back the game."

"But I have no horse, sir," replied the sad-faced boy.

"Well, take mine," said the anxious father; "I will get in the wagon and ride there till you come back."

"But I have no gun, no pistols nor knife," added the boy.

"Here!" cried the rich man. "Jump on my horse 'Ginger,' and I'll fit you out."

When the barefooted boy had mounted the horse, the man buckled his own belt about the lad and swung his rifle over the saddle-bow.

How the boy's face lit up! His young heart was beating like a drum with delight as the party bounded away after the buffalo.

The wagons creaked and crawled away to the west over the great grassy plains; the herd of buffalo sniffed the young hunters, and lifting their shaggy heads, shook them angrily, and then turned away like a dark retreating tide of the sea, with the boys bounding after them in hot pursuit.

It was a long and exciting chase. "Tatters" soon passed the other boys, and pressing hard on the herd, after nearly an hour of wild and splendid riding, threw himself from the saddle and, taking aim, fired.

The brothers came up soon, and dismounting as fast as their less practiced limbs would let them, also fired at the retreating herd.

When the dust and smoke cleared away, a fine fat buffalo lay rolling in the grass before them. Following the example of "Tatters," they loaded their guns where they stood, as all cautious hunters do, and then went up to the game.

The barefooted boy at once laid his finger on a bullet hole near the region of the heart and looked up at the others.

"I aimed about there!" shouted one. "And so did I!" cried the other eagerly.

Without saying a word, but with a very significant look, the barefooted boy took out his knife, and, unobserved, pricked two holes with the point of it close by the bullet hole. Then he put his finger there and again looked up at the boys. They came down on their knees, wild with delight, in an instant.

They had really helped kill a buffalo! In fact, they had killed it! "For are not two bullets better than one!" they cried.

" 'Tatters,' cut me off the tail," said one.

"And cut me off the mane; I want it to make a coat-collar for my father," shouted the other.

Without a word, the boy did as he was bid, and then securely fastened the trophies on behind their saddles.

"Now let's overtake the train, and tell father all about killing our first buffalo," cried the elder of the two brothers.

"And won't he be delighted!" said the other, as he clambered up to the saddle, and turned his face in every direction, looking for the wagons.

"But where are they?" he cried.

At first the brothers laughed a little. Then they grew very sober.

"That is the way they went," said one, pointing off. "Ye-ye-yes, I think that's the way they went. But I wonder why we can't see the wagons?"

"We have galloped a long way; and then they have all the time been going in the other direction. If you go that way, you will be lost. When we started, I noticed that the train was moving toward sunset, and that the sun was over our left shoulder as we looked after the train. We must go in this direction, or we shall be lost," mildly and firmly said the barefooted boy, as he drew his belt tighter and prepared for work.

The other boys only looked disdainfully at the speaker as he sat his horse and, shading his eyes with his lifted hand, looked away in the direction he wished to go. Then they talked a moment between themselves, and taking out their pocket compasses, pretended to look at them very knowingly.

Now, many people think a compass will lead them out of almost any place where they are lost. This is a mistake.

A compass is only of use when you can not see the sun. And even then you must have coolness and patience and good sense to get on with it at all. It can at best only guide you from one object to another, and thus keep you in a straight line, and so prevent you from going around and around and around.

But when the plain is one vast level sea, without a single object rising up out of it as a guide, what is a boy to do? It takes a cool head, boy's or man's, to use a compass on the plains.

"Come on! that is right," cried the elder

of the two hunters, and they darted away, with "Tatters" far in the rear. They rode hard and hot for a full hour, getting more frightened, and going faster at every jump. The sun was high in the heavens. Their horses were all in a foam.

"I see something at last," shouted the elder, as he stood up in his stirrups, and then settling back in his seat, he laid on whip and spur, and rode fast and furious straight for a dark object that lay there in the long brown grasses of the broad unbroken plains. Soon they came up to it. It was the dead buffalo! They knew now that they were lost on the plains. They had been riding in the fatal circle that means death if you do not break it and escape.

Very meek and very penitent felt the two boys as "Tatters" came riding up slowly after them. They were tired and thirsty. They seemed to themselves to have shrunken to about half their usual size.

Meekly they lifted their eyes to the despised boy, and pleaded silently and pitifully for help. Tears were in their eyes. Their chins and lips quivered, but they could not say one word.

"We must ride with the sun on the left shoulder, as I said, and with our faces all the time to the west. If we do not do that, we shall die. Now, come with me," said "Tatters" firmly, as he turned his horse and took the lead. And now meekly and patiently the others followed.

But the horses were broken in strength and spirit. The sun in mid-heaven poured its full force of heat upon the heads of the thirsty hunters, and they could hardly keep their seats in the hot saddles. The horses began to stumble and stagger as they walked.

And yet there was no sight or sound of anything at all, before, behind, or left or right. Nothing but the weary, dreary, eternal and unbroken sea of brown.

Away to the west, the bright blue sky shut down sharp and tight upon the brown and blazing plain. The tops of the long untrodden grass gleamed and shimmered with the heat. Yet not a sign of water could be anywhere discerned. Silence, vastness, voiceless as when the world came newly from the hand of God.

No one spoke. Steadily and quietly the young leader of the party led on. Now and then he would lift his eyes under his hat to the blazing sun over his left shoulder, and that was all.

There comes a time to us all, I believe, sooner or later, on the plains, in the valley, or on the mountain, in the palace or cottage, when we too can only lift our eyes, silent and helpless, to something shining in heaven.

At last the silent little party heard a faint sound beyond them, a feeble, screeching cry that seemed to come out from the brown grass beneath them as they struggled on.

Then suddenly they came through and out of the tall brown grass into an open plain that looked like a plowed field. Only, all about the outer edge of the field were little hills or forts as high as a man's knee. On every one of these little forts stood a soldier-sentinel, high on his hind legs and barking with all his might.

The lost hunters had found a dog-town, the first they had ever seen.

Some owls flew lazily over the strange little city, close to the ground; and as they rode through the town, a rattlesnake now and then glided into the hole on the top of one of the ten thousand little forts. The prairie dogs, also, as the boys rode close upon them, would twinkle their heels in the air and disappear, head first, only to jump up, like a jack-in-a-box, in another fort, almost instantly.

The party rode through the town and looked beyond. Nothing! Behind? Nothing! To the right? Nothing! To the left?

"HE RODE SLOWLY AND QUIETLY AROUND THE PRAIRIE-DOG CITY."

Nothing; nothing but the great blue sky shut tight down against the boundless level sea of brown!

"Water," gasped one of the boys; "I am dying for water."

"Tatters" looked him in the face and saw that what he said was true. He reflected a moment, and then said, "Wait here for me." Then, leaving the others, he rode slowly and quietly around the prairie-dog city with his eyes closely scanning the ground. As he again neared the two boys waiting patiently for him, he uttered a cry of delight, and beckoned them to come.

"Look there! Do you see that little road there winding along through the thick grass? It is a dim and small road, not wider than your hand, but it means everything to us."

"Oh, I am dying of thirst!" exclaimed one of the brothers. "What does it mean?"

"It means water. Do you think a great city like that can get on without water? This is their road to water. Come! Let us follow this trail till we find it."

Saying this, "Tatters" led off at a lively pace, for the horses, cheered by the barking dogs, and somewhat rested, were in better spirits now. And then it is safe to say that they, too, saw and understood the meaning of the dim and dusty little road that wound along under their feet.

"Hurrah! hurrah! hurrah!" Gallant "Tatters" turned in his saddle and shook his cap to cheer the poor boys behind, as he saw a long line of fresh green willows starting up out of the brown grass and moving in the wind before him.

And didn't the horses dip their noses deep in the water! And didn't the boys slide down from their saddles in a hurry and throw themselves beside it! That same morning, two of these young gentlemen would not have taken water out of the same cup with "Tatters." Now they were drinking with the horses. And happy to do it, too. So happy! Water was never, never so sweet to them before.

The boys all bathed their faces, and the horses began to nibble the grass, as the riders sat on the bank and looked anxiously at the setting sun. Were they lost forever? Each one asked himself that question. Water was good; but they could not live on water.

"Stop here," said "Tatters," "and hold the horses till I come back."

He went down to the edge of the water and sat there watching the clear, swift little stream long and anxiously.

At last he sprang up, rolled his ragged pants above his knees, and dashed into the water. Clutching a little white object in his hands, he looked at it a second, and then with a beaming face hurried back to the boys:

"There! see that! a chip! They are camped up this stream somewhere, and they can't be very far away from here!"

Eagerly the boys mounted their horses, and pressed close on after "Tatters."

"And how do you know they are close by?" queried one.

"The chip was wet only on one side. It had not been ten minutes in the water." As "Tatters" said this, the boys exchanged glances. They were glad, so glad, to be nearing their father once more.

But it somehow began to dawn upon them very clearly that they did not know quite everything, even if their father was rich.

Soon, guns were heard firing for the lost party. And turning a corner in the willowy little river, they saw the tents pitched, the wagons in corral, and the oxen feeding peacefully beyond.

THE CASTLE OF BIM

By Frank R. Stockton

October, 1881

Loris was a little girl, about eleven years old, who lived with her father in a very small house among the mountains of a distant land. He was sometimes a wood-cutter, and sometimes a miner, or a plowman, or a stone-breaker. Being an industrious man, he would work at anything he could do, when a chance offered; but, as there was not much work to do in that part of the country, poor Jorn often found it very hard to make a living for himself and Loris.

One day, when he had gone out early to look for work, Loris was in her little sleeping-room, under the roof, braiding her hair. Although she was so poor, Loris always tried to make herself look as neat as she could, for that pleased her father. She was just tying the ribbon on the end of the long braid, when she heard a knock at the door below.

"In one second," she said to herself, "I will go. I must tie this ribbon tightly, for it would never do to lose it."

And so she tied it, and ran down-stairs to the door. There was no one there.

"Oh, it is too bad!" cried Loris; "perhaps it was some one with work for Father. He told me always to be very careful about answering a knock at the door, for there was no knowing when some one might come with a good job; and now somebody has come and gone!" cried Loris, looking about in every direction for the person who had knocked. "Oh, there he is! How could he have got away so far in such a short time? I must run after him."

So away she ran, as fast as she could, after a man she saw walking away from the cottage in the direction of a forest.

"Oh dear!" she said, as she ran, "how fast he walks! and he is such a short man, too!

He is going right to the hut of Laub, that wicked Laub, who is always trying to get away work from Father; and he came first to our house, but thought there was nobody at home!"

Loris ran and ran, but the short man did walk very fast. However, she gradually gained on him, and just as he reached Laub's door, she seized him by the coat.

"Stop, sir, please!" she said, scarcely able to speak, she was so out of breath.

The man turned and looked at her. He was a very short man indeed, for he scarcely reached to Loris's waist.

"What do you want?" he said, looking up at her.

"Oh, sir," she gasped, "you came to our house first, and I ran to the door almost as quick as I could, and, if it's any work, Father wants work, ever so bad."

"Yes," said the short man, "but Laub wants work, too. He is very poor."

"Yes, sir," said Loris, "but—but you came for Father first."

"True," said the short man, "but nobody answered my knock, and now I am here. Laub has four young children, and sometimes they have nothing to eat. It is never so bad with you, is it?"

"No, sir," said Loris.

"Your father has work sometimes. Is it not so?" asked the short man.

"Yes, sir," answered Loris.

"Laub is often without work for weeks, and he has four children. Shall I go back with you, or knock here?"

"Knock," said Loris, softly.

The short man knocked at the door, and instantly there was heard a great scuffling and hubbub within. Directly all was quiet, and then a voice said, "Come in!"

"He did not wait so long for *me*," thought Loris.

The short man opened the door and went in, Loris following him. In a bed, in a corner of the room, were four children, their heads just appearing above a torn sheet, which was pulled up to their chins.

"Hello! what's the matter?" said the short man, advancing to the bed.

"Please, sir," said the oldest child, a girl of about the age of Loris, with tangled hair and sharp black eyes, "we're all sick, and very poor, and our father has no work. If you can give us a little money to buy bread—"

"All sick, eh?" said the short man. "Any particular disease?"

"We don't know about diseases, sir," said the girl; "we've never been to school."

"No doubt of that," said the man. "I have no money to give you, but you can tell your father that if he will come to the mouth of the Ragged Mine to-morrow morning, he can have a job of work which will pay him well."

So saying, the short man went out.

Loris followed him, but he simply waved his hand to her, and, in a few minutes, he was lost in the forest. She looked sadly after him for a minute, and then walked slowly toward her home.

The moment their visitors had gone, the Laub children sprang out of bed as lively as crickets.

"Ha! ha!" cried the oldest girl; "Loris came after him to get it, and he wouldn't give it to her, and Father's got it. Served her right, the horrid thing!"

And all the other children shouted, "Horrid thing!" while one of the boys ran out and threw a stone after Loris. And then they shut the door, and sat down to finish eating a meat-pie which had been given them.

"Well," said Jorn, that evening, when Loris told him what had happened, "I'm sorry, for I found but little work to-day; but it can't be helped. You did all you could."

"No, Father," said Loris, "I might have gone to the door quicker."

"That may be," said Jorn, "and I hope you will never keep any one waiting again."

Two or three days after this, as Loris was stooping over the fire in the back room of the cottage, preparing her dinner, she heard a knock.

Springing to her feet, she dropped the pan she held in her hand, and made a dash at the front door, pulling it open with a tremendous fling. No one should go away this time, she thought.

"Hello! Ho! ho!" cried a person outside, giving a skip backward. "Do you open doors by lightning, here?"

"No, sir," said Loris, "but I didn't want to keep you waiting."

"I should think not," said the other. "Why, I had hardly begun to knock."

This visitor was a middle-sized man, very slight, and, at first sight, of a youthful appearance. But his hair was either powdered or gray, and it was difficult to know whether he was old or young. His face was long and smooth, and he nearly always looked as if he were just going to burst out laughing. He was dressed in a silken suit of light green, pink, pale yellow, and sky-blue, but all the colors were very much faded. On his head was stuck a tall, orange-colored feather.

"Is your father in?" said this strange personage.

"No, sir," said Loris; "he will be here this evening, and I can give him any message you may leave for him."

"I haven't any message," said the queer-looking man. "I want to see him."

"You can see him about sunset," said Loris, "if you will come then."

"I don't want to come again. I think I'll wait," said the man.

Loris said, "Very well," but she wondered what he would do all the afternoon. She brought out a stool for him to sit upon, for it was not very pleasant in the house, but he did not sit down. He walked all around the house, looking at the chicken-house, where there were no chickens; the cow-house, where there was no cow; and the pig-sty, where there were no pigs. Then he skipped up to the top of a little hillock, near by, and surveyed the landscape. Loris kept her eye upon him, to see that he did not go away without leaving a message, and went on with her cooking.

When her dinner was ready, she thought it only right to ask him to have some. She did not want to do it, but she could not see how she could help it. She had been taught good manners. So she went to the door and called him, and he instantly came skipping to her.

"I thought you might like to have some dinner, sir," she said. "I haven't much but—"

"Two people don't want much," he said. "Where shall we have it? In the house, or will you spread the cloth out here on the grass?"

"There is not much use in spreading a cloth, sir," she said, pointing to what she had prepared for dinner. "I have only one potato, and some salt."

"That's not a dinner," said the other, cheerfully. "A dinner is soup, meat, some vegetables (besides potatoes, and there ought to be two of them, at least), some bread, cheese, pudding, and fruit."

"But I haven't all that, sir," said Loris, with her eyes wide open at this astonishing description of a dinner.

"'SIT DOWN!' SAID HE. 'DON'T LET THINGS GET COLD!'"

"Well then, if you haven't got them, the next best thing is to go and get them."

Loris smiled faintly. "I couldn't do that, sir," she said. "I have no money."

"Well then, if you can't go, the next best thing is for me to go. The village is not far away. Just wait dinner a little while for me." And so saying, he skipped away at a great pace.

Loris did not wait for him, but ate her potato and salt. "I'm glad he is able to buy his own dinner," she said, "but I'm afraid he won't come back. I wish he had left a message."

But she need not have feared. In a half-hour the queer man came back, bearing a great basket, covered with a cloth. The latter he spread on the ground, and then he set out all the things he had said were necessary to make up a dinner. He prepared a place at one end of the cloth for Loris, and one at the other end for himself.

"Sit down," said he, seating himself on the grass; "don't let things get cold."

"I've had my dinner," said Loris; "this is yours."

"Whenever you're ready to begin," said the man, lying back on the grass and looking placidly up to the sky, "I'll begin, but not until then."

Loris saw he was in earnest, and, as she was a sensible girl, she sat down at her end of the cloth.

"That's right!" gayly cried the queer man, sitting up again; "I was afraid you'd be obstinate, and then I should have starved."

When the meal was over, Loris said:

"I never had such a good dinner in my life!"

The man looked at her and laughed.

"This is a funny world, isn't it?" said he.

"Awfully funny!" replied Loris, laughing.

"You don't know what I am, do you?" said the man, as Loris put the dishes, with what was left of the meal, into the basket.

"No, sir; I do not," answered Loris.

"I am a Ninkum," said the other. "Did you ever meet with one before?"

"No, sir, never," said Loris.

"I am very glad to hear that," he said; "it's so pleasant to be fresh and novel."

And then he went walking around the house again, looking at everything he had seen before. Then he laid himself down on the grass, near the house, with one leg thrown over the other, and his hands clasped under his head. For a long time he lay in this way, looking up at the sky and the clouds. Then he turned his head and said to Loris, who was sewing by the door-step:

"Did you ever think how queer it would be if everything in the world were reversed?—if the ground were soft and blue, like the sky? and if the sky were covered with dirt, and chips, and grass? and if fowls and animals walked about on it, like flies sticking to a ceiling?"

"I never thought of such a thing in my life," said Loris.

"I often do," said the Ninkum. "It expands the mind."

For the whole afternoon, the Ninkum lay on his back and expanded his mind; and then, about sunset, Loris saw her father returning. She ran to meet him, and told him of the Ninkum who was waiting to see him. Jorn hurried to the house, for he felt sure that his visitor must have an important job of work for him, as he had waited so long.

"I am glad you have come," said the Ninkum. "I wanted to see you, for two things; the first was that we might have supper. I'm dreadfully hungry, and there's enough in that basket for us all. The second thing can wait. It's business."

So Loris and the Ninkum spread out the remains of the dinner, and the three made a hearty supper. Jorn was highly pleased. He had expected to come home to a meal very different from this.

"Now, then," said the Ninkum, "we'll talk about the business."

"You have some work for me, I suppose," said Jorn.

"No," said the Ninkum, "none that I know of. What I want is for you to go into partnership with me."

"Partnership!" cried Jorn. "I don't understand you. What kind of work could we do together?"

"None at all," said the Ninkum, "for I never work. Your part of the partnership will be to chop wood, and dig, and plow, and do just what you do now. I will live here with you, and will provide the food, and the clothes, and the fuel, and the pocket-money for the three of us."

"But you couldn't live here!" cried Loris. "Our house is so poor, and there is no room for you."

"There need be no trouble about that," said the Ninkum. "I can build a room right here, on this side of the house. I never work," he said to Jorn, "but I hate idleness; so what I want is to go into partnership with a person who will work—an industrious person like you—then my conscience will be at ease. Please agree as quickly as you can, for it's beginning to grow dark, and I hate to walk in the dark."

Jorn did not hesitate. He agreed instantly to go into partnership with the Ninkum, and the latter, after bidding them good-night, skipped gayly away.

The next day, he returned with carpenters, and laborers, and lumber, and timber, and furniture, and bedding, and a large and handsome room was built for him on one side of the house; and he came to live with Jorn and Loris. For several days he had workmen putting a fence around the yard, and building a new cow-house, a new chicken-house, and a new pig-sty. He bought a cow, pigs, and chickens; had flowers planted in front of the house, and made everything look very neat and pretty.

"Now," said he one day to Loris and Jorn, as they were eating supper together, "I'll tell you something. I was told to keep it a secret, but I hate secrets. I think they all ought to be told as soon as possible. Ever so much trouble has been made by secrets. The one I have is this: That dwarf who came here, and then went and hired old Laub to work in his mine—"

"Was that a dwarf?" asked Loris, much excited.

"Yes, indeed," said the Ninkum, "a regular one. Didn't you notice how short he was? Well, he told me all about his coming here. The dwarfs in the Ragged Mine found a deep hole, with lots of gold at the bottom of it, but it steamed and smoked, and was too hot for dwarfs. So the king dwarf sent out the one you saw, and told him to hire the first miner he could find, to work in the deep hole, but not to tell him how hot it was until he had made his contract. So the dwarf had to come first for you, Jorn, for you lived nearest the mine, but he hoped he would not find you, for he knew you were a good man. That was the reason he just gave one knock, and hurried on to Laub's house. And then he told me how Loris ran after him, and how good she was to agree to let him give the work to Laub, when she thought he needed it more than her father. 'Now,' says he to me, 'I want to do something for that family, and I don't know anything better that could happen to a man like Jorn, than to go into partnership with a Ninkum.'"

At these words, Jorn looked over the

well-spread supper-table, and he thought the dwarf was certainly right.

"So that's the way I came to live here," said the Ninkum, "and I like it first-rate."

"I wish I could go and see the dwarfs working in their mine," said Loris.

"I'll take you," exclaimed the Ninkum. "It's not a long walk from here. We can go to-morrow."

Jorn gave his consent, and the next morning Loris and the Ninkum set out for the Ragged Mine. The entrance was a great jagged hole in the side of a mountain, and the inside of the mine had also a very rough and torn appearance. It belonged to a colony of dwarfs, and ordinary mortals seldom visited it, but the Ninkum had no difficulty in obtaining admission. Making their way slowly along the rough and somber tunnel, Loris and he saw numbers of dwarfs, working with pick and shovel, in search of precious minerals. Soon they met the dwarf who had come to Jorn's house, and he seemed glad to see Loris again. He led her about to various parts of the mine, and showed her the heaps of gold and silver and precious stones, which had been dug out of the rocks around them.

The Ninkum had seen these things before, and so he thought he would go and look for the hot hole, where Laub was working. That would be a novelty.

He soon found the hole, and just as he reached it, Laub appeared at its opening, slowly climbing up a ladder. He looked very warm and tired, and throwing some gold ore upon the ground, from a basket which he carried on his back, he sat down and wiped the perspiration from his forehead.

"That is warm work, Laub," said the Ninkum, pleasantly.

"Warm!" said Laub, gruffly. "It's hot. Hot as fire. Why, the gold down at the bottom of that hole burns your fingers when you pick it up. If I hadn't made a contract with these rascally dwarfs to work here for forty-one days, I wouldn't stay another minute; but you can't break a contract you make with dwarfs."

"It's a pretty hard thing to have to work here, that is true," said the Ninkum, "but you owe your ill-fortune to yourself. It's all because you're known to be so ill-natured and wicked. When the dwarf was sent to hire a man to come and work in this hole, he had to go to Jorn's house first, because that was the nearest place, but he just gave one knock there, and hurried away, hoping Jorn wouldn't hear, for it would be a pity to have a good man like Jorn to work in such a place as this. Then he went after you, for he knew you deserved to be punished by this kind of work."

As the Ninkum said this, Laub's face grew black with rage.

"So that's the truth!" he cried. "When I get out of this place, I'll crush every bone in the body of that sneaking Jorn!" and having said this, he turned, as Loris came near, and rushed down into the hot hole.

"Perhaps I ought not to have told him all that," said the Ninkum, as he walked away, "but I hate secrets. They always make mischief."

Presently Loris said: "Do let us go home, now. I have seen nearly everything, and it is so dark and gloomy." Taking leave of the kind dwarf, the two made their way out of the mine.

"I do not like such gloomy places any better than you do," said the Ninkum. "Disagreeable things are always happening in them. I like to have things bright and lively. I'll tell you what would be splendid! To make a visit to the Castle of Bim."

"What is that, and where is it?" asked Loris.

"It's the most delightful place in the whole world," said the Ninkum. "While you're there, you do nothing and see nothing but what is positively charming, and everybody is just as happy and gay as can be. It's all life, and laughter, and perfect delight. I know you would be overjoyed if you were there."

"I should like very much to go," said Loris, "if Father would let me." "I'll go and ask him this minute," said the Ninkum. "I know where he is working. You can run home, and I will go to him, and then come and tell you what he says."

So Loris ran home, and the Ninkum went to the place where Jorn was cutting wood.

"Jorn," said the Ninkum, "suppose that everything in this world were reversed, that you chopped wood standing on your head, and that you split your ax instead of the log you struck. Would not that be peculiar?"

"Such things could not be," said Jorn. "What is the good of talking about them?"

"I think a great deal about such matters," said the Ninkum. "They expand my mind. And now, Jorn, reversibly speaking, will you let Loris go with me to the Castle of Bim?"

"Where is that?" asked Jorn.

"It is not far from here. I think we could go in half a day. I would get a horse in the village."

"And how long would you stay?"

"Well, I don't know. A week or two, perhaps. Come, now, Jorn, reversibly speaking, may she go?"

"No, indeed," said Jorn, "on no account shall she go. I could not spare her."

"All right," said the Ninkum, "I will not keep you from your work any longer. Good-morning." And as soon as he was out of Jorn's sight, the Ninkum began to run home as fast as he could.

"Get ready, Loris," he cried, when he reached the house. "Your father says, rever-

sibly speaking, that on every account you must go. He can well spare you."

"But must we go now?" said Loris; "can not we wait until he comes home, and go to-morrow?"

"No, indeed," said the Ninkum; "there will be obstacles to our starting to-morrow; so let us hasten to the village and hire a horse. Your father will get along nicely here by himself, and he will be greatly pleased with your improvement when you return from the Castle of Bim."

So Loris, who was delighted with the idea of the journey, hastened to get ready, and, having put the house-key under the front door-stone, she and the Ninkum went to the village, where they got a horse and started for the Castle of Bim.

The Ninkum rode in front, Loris sat on a pillion behind, and the horse trotted along gayly. The Ninkum was in high good spirits, and passed the time in telling Loris of all the delightful things she would see in the Castle of Bim.

Late in the afternoon, they came in sight of a vast castle, which rose up at the side of the road like a little mountain.

"Hurrah!" cried the Ninkum, as he spurred the horse, "I knew we were nearly there!"

Loris was very glad that they had reached the castle, for she was getting tired of riding, and when the Ninkum drew up in front of the great portal, she imagined that she was going to see wonderful things, for the door, to begin with, was she felt sure the biggest door in the whole world.

"You need not get off," said the porter, who stood by the door, to the Ninkum, who was preparing to dismount; "you can ride right in."

Accordingly, the Ninkum and Loris rode right into the castle through the front door. Inside, they found themselves in a high and wide hall-way, paved with stone, which led back to what appeared to be an inner court. Riding to the end of this hall, they stopped in the door-way there and looked out. In the center of the court, which was very large, there stood, side by side, and about twenty feet apart, some great upright posts, like the trunks of tall pine-trees. Across two of these, near their tops, rested a thick and heavy horizontal pole, and on this pole a giant was practicing gymnastics. Hanging by his hands, he would draw himself up until his chin touched the pole; and he kept on doing this until the Ninkum said in a whisper:

"Twelve times! I did not think he could do it!"

The giant now drew up his legs and threw them over the bar, above his head; then, by a vigorous effort, he turned himself entirely over the bar, and hung beneath it by his hands. After stopping a minute or two to breathe, he drew up his legs again, and, putting them under the bar between his hands, as boys do when they "skin the cat," he turned partly over, and hung in this position. His face was now toward the door-way, and for the first time he noticed his visitors on their horse.

"Hello!" said he to the Ninkum; "could you do that?"

"Not on that pole," answered the Ninkum, smiling.

"I should think not," said the giant, dropping to his feet and puffing a little. "Ten years ago, when I did not weigh so much, I could draw myself up twenty-seven times. Come in with me and have some supper; it is about ready now. Is that your little daughter?"

"No," said the Ninkum: "I am her guardian for the present."

"Ride right upstairs," said the giant; "my wife is up there, and she will take care of the little girl."

"I am afraid," said the Ninkum, "that my horse can not jump up those great steps."

"Of course not," said the giant. "Let me help you up, and then I will go down and bring your horse."

"Oh, that won't be necessary," said the Ninkum, and Loris laughed at the idea.

"You may want to look at the house," said the giant, "and then you'll need him."

So the giant took the Ninkum and Loris upstairs, and then came down and brought up the horse. The upper story was as vast and spacious as the lower part of the castle, and by a window the giant's wife sat, darning a stocking. As they approached her, the Ninkum whispered to Loris:

"If there were such holes in my stockings, I should fall through."

The giantess was very glad to see Loris, and she took her up in her hand and kissed her, very much as a little girl would kiss a canary-bird. Then the giant children were sent for—two big boys and a baby-girl, who thought Loris was so lovely that she would have squeezed her to death if her mother had allowed her to take the little visitor in her hands.

During supper, Loris and the Ninkum sat in chairs with long legs, like stilts, which the giant had had made for his men and women visitors. They had to be very careful, lest they should tip over and break their necks.

After supper, they sat in the great upper hall, and the giant got out his guitar and sang them a song.

"I hope there are not many more verses," whispered the Ninkum to Loris; "my bones are almost shaken apart."

"How did you like that?" asked the giant, when he had finished.

"It was very nice," said the Ninkum. "It reminded me of something I once heard before. I think it was a wagon-load of copper pots, rolling down a mountain, but I am not sure."

The giant thanked him, and, soon after, they all went to bed. Loris slept in the room with the giantess, on a high shelf, where the children could not reach her.

Just before they went to their rooms, the Ninkum said to Loris:

"Do you know that I don't believe this is the Castle of Bim?"

"It didn't seem to be like the place you told me about," said Loris, "but what are we to do?"

"Nothing, but go to bed," said the Ninkum. "They are very glad to see us, and to-morrow we will bid them good-bye, and push on to the Castle of Bim."

With this, the Ninkum jumped on his horse and rode to his room.

The next day, after they had gone over the castle and seen all its sights, the Ninkum told the giant that he and Loris must pursue their journey to the Castle of Bim.

"What is that?" said the giant, and when the Ninkum proceeded to describe it to him, he became very much interested.

"Ho! ho! good wife!" he cried. "Suppose we go with these friends to the Castle of Bim! It must be a very pleasant place, and the exercise will do me good. I'm dreadfully tired of gymnastics. What do you say? We can take the children."

The giantess thought it would be a capital idea, and so they all put on their hats and caps, and started off, leaving the castle in charge of the giant's servants, who were people of common size.

They journeyed all that day, Loris and Ninkum riding ahead, followed by the giant, then by the giantess, carrying the baby, and, lastly, the two giant boys, with a basket of provisions between them.

That night they slept on the ground, under some trees, and the Ninkum admitted that the Castle of Bim was a good deal farther off than he had supposed it to be.

Toward afternoon of the next day, they found themselves on some high land, and coming to the edge of a bluff, they saw, in the plain below, a beautiful city. The giant was struck with admiration.

"I have seen many a city," said he, "but I never saw one so sensibly and handsomely laid out as that. The people who built that place knew just what they wanted."

"Do you see that great building in the center of the city?" cried the Ninkum. "Well, that is the Castle of Bim! Let us hurry down."

So away they all started, at their best speed, for the city.

They had scarcely reached one of the outer gates, when they were met by a citizen on horseback, followed by two or three others on foot. The horseman greeted them kindly, and said that he had been sent to meet them.

"We shall be very glad," he said to the Ninkum, "to have you and the little girl come into our city to-night, but if those giants were to enter, the people, especially the children, would throng the streets to see them, and many would unavoidably be trampled to death. There is a great show-tent out here, where the giants can comfortably pass the night, and to-morrow we will have the streets cleared, and the people kept within doors. Then these great visitors will be made welcome to walk in and view the city."

The giants agreed to this, and they were conducted to the tent, where they were made very comfortable, while the Ninkum and Loris were taken into the city and lodged in the house of the citizen who had come to meet them.

The next day, the giants entered the city, and the windows and doors in the streets which they passed through were crowded with spectators.

The giant liked the city better and better as he walked through it. Everything was so admirably planned, and in such perfect order. The others enjoyed themselves very much, too, and Loris was old enough to un-

THE NINKUM AND LORIS RIDE THROUGH THE CITY, FOLLOWED BY THE GIANT AND HIS FAMILY.

derstand the beauty and convenience of many of the things she saw around her.

Toward the end of the day, the Ninkum came to her.

"Do you know," said he, "that the Castle of Bim is not here? That large building is used by the governors of the city; and what a queer place it is! Everything that they do turns out just right. I saw a man set a rat-trap, and what do you think? He caught the rat! I couldn't help laughing. It is very funny."

"But what are you going to do?" asked Loris.

"We will stay here to-night," said the Ninkum, "as the citizens are very kind, and treat us well; to-morrow we will go on to the Castle of Bim."

The next day, therefore, our party again set out on their journey. The Ninkum had told the citizen, who had entertained him, where they were going, and his accounts of the wonderful castle induced this worthy man to go with him.

"In our city," said he, "we try to be governed, in everything, by the ordinary rules of common sense. In this way we get along very comfortably and pleasantly, and everything seems to go well with us. But we are always willing to examine into the merits of things which are new to us, and so I should like to go to this curious castle, and come back and report what I have seen to my fellow-citizens."

His company was gladly accepted, and all set out in high good humor, the citizen riding by the side of Loris and the Ninkum. But when they had gone several miles, the giantess declared that she believed she would go back home. The baby was getting very heavy, and the boys were tired. The giant could tell her about the Castle of Bim on his return. So the weary giantess turned back with her children, her husband kissing her good-bye, and assuring her that he would not let her go back by herself if he did not feel certain that no one would molest her on the way.

The rest of the party now went on at a good pace, the giant striding along as fast as the horses could trot. The Ninkum did not seem to know the way as well as he had said he did. He continually desired to turn to the right, and when the others inquired if he was sure that he ought to do this, he said he had often been told that the best thing a person could do when a little in doubt was to turn to the right.

The citizen did not like this method of reasoning, and he was going to say something about it, when a man was perceived, sitting in doleful plight by the side of the road. The Ninkum, who was very kind-hearted, rode up to him to inquire what had happened to him, but the moment the man raised his head, and before he had time to say a word, Loris slipped off the horse and threw her arms around his neck.

"Oh, Father! Father!" she cried, "how came you here?"

It was, indeed, Jorn,—ragged, wounded, and exhausted. In a moment, every one set to work to relieve him. Loris ran for water, and bathed his face and hands; the citizen gave him some wine from a flask; the giant produced some great pieces of bread and meat, and the Ninkum asked him questions.

Jorn soon felt refreshed and strengthened, and then he told his story.

He had been greatly troubled, he said, when he found that Loris had gone away against his express orders.

"Why, Father!" cried Loris, at this point, "you said I could go!"

"Never," said Jorn. "Of course not. I said you could not go."

"Reversibly speaking," said the Ninkum, smiling, "he consented. That was the way I put the question to him. If I hadn't put it that way, I should have told a lie."

Everybody looked severely at the Ninkum and Loris was very angry; but her father patted her on the head, and went on with his story. He would have followed the Ninkum and his daughter, but he did not know what road they had taken, and, as they were on a horse, he could not, in any case, expect to catch up with them; so he waited, hoping they would soon return. But before long he was very glad that Loris was away. The wicked Laub, who, in some manner, had found out that he had been made to work in the dwarfs' mine instead of Jorn—who had been considered too good for such disagreeable labor—had become so enraged that he broke his contract with the dwarfs, and, instead of continuing his work in the mine, had collected a few of his depraved companions, and had made an attack upon Jorn's house. The doors had been forced, poor Jorn had been dragged forth, beaten, and forced to fly, while Laub and his companions took possession of the house and everything in it.

"But how could you wander so far, dear Father?" asked Loris.

"It's not far," said Jorn. "Our home is not many miles away."

"Then you have been going in a circle," said the citizen to the Ninkum, "and you are now very near the point you started from."

"That seems to be the case," said the Ninkum, smiling.

"But we won't talk about that now," said the citizen. "We must see what we can do for this poor man, who has been treated so unjustly. He must have his house again."

"I would have asked the dwarfs to help me," said Jorn, "but I believe they would have killed Laub and the others if they had resisted, and I didn't want any bloodshed."

"No," said the citizen, "I think we can manage it better than that. Our large friend here will be able to get these people out of your house without killing them."

panions, prepared to resist every attempt to enter.

But his efforts were useless.

The giant knelt down before the house, and, having easily removed the door, he thrust in his arm, and, sweeping it around the room, quickly caught three of the invaders. He then put his other arm through the window of the Ninkum's room, and soon pulled out Laub, taking no notice of his kicks and blows.

The giant then tied the four rascals in a bunch, by the feet, and laid them on the grass.

"Now," said the citizen to the Ninkum, "as there seems to be nothing more to be

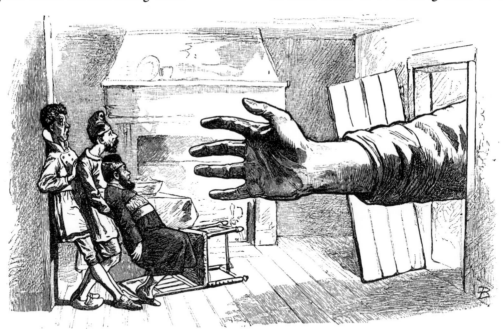

"THE GIANT THRUST HIS ARM THROUGH THE DOOR-WAY."

"Oh, yes," said the giant, quietly, "I'll soon attend to that."

Jorn being now quite ready to travel, the party proceeded, and soon reached his house. When Laub perceived the approach of Jorn and his friends, he barricaded all the doors and windows, and, with his com-

done for this good man and his daughter, suppose you tell me the way to the Castle of Bim. I think I can find it if I have good directions, and I do not wish to waste any more time."

"I do not know the exact road," answered the Ninkum.

"What!" cried the other, "have you never been there?"

"No," said the Ninkum.

"Well, then, did not the person who told you about it tell you the way?"

"No one ever told me about it," replied the Ninkum, looking very serious. "But I have thought a great deal on the subject, and I feel sure that there must be such a place; and I think the way to find it is to go and look for it."

"Well," said the citizen, smiling, "you are a true Ninkum. I suppose we have all thought of some place where everything shall be just as we want it to be; but I don't believe any of us will find that place. I am going home."

"And I, too," said the giant, "and on my way I will stop at the Ragged Mine, and leave these fellows to the care of the dwarfs. They are little fellows, but, I'm sure, will see that these rascals molest honest men no more."

"And I think I will go, too," said the Ninkum. "I liked this place very much, but I am getting tired of it now."

"That will be a good thing for you to do," said the citizen, who had heard the story of how the Ninkum had been sent to Jorn and Loris as a reward. "You have lived for a time with these good people, and have been of some service to them; but I think they must now feel that partnership with a Ninkum is a very dangerous thing, and should not be kept up too long."

"No doubt that's true," said the Ninkum. "Good-bye, my friends; I will give you my room, and everything that is in it."

"You have been very kind to us," said Loris, as she shook hands with the Ninkum.

"Yes," said Jorn, "and you got me work that will last a long time."

"Yes, I did what I could," cried the Ninkum, mounting his horse, and gayly waving his hat around his head, "and, reversibly speaking, I took you to the Castle of Bim."

THE EAGLE AND THE SERPENT
(From the Spanish)
By William Cullen Bryant

July, 1874

A SERPENT saw an eagle gain,
 On soaring wing, a mountain height,
And envied him, and crawled with pain
 To where he saw the bird alight.
So fickle fortune oftentimes
 Befriends the cunning and the base,
And oft the groveling reptile climbs
 Up to the eagle's lofty place.

THE VOYAGE OF THE *NORTHERN LIGHT*

By J. T. Trowbridge

December, 1896

I HAD just completed my sophomore term [said the Harvard man], when I narrowly escaped having my college course cut short in the middle by the strange thing that happened to me that summer.

I passed my vacation chiefly on Cape Breton and Prince Edward Island; and in the month of August found myself at Charlottetown, undecided as to the route by which I should return to the United States. There, one afternoon, as I was sauntering about the harbor, I fell in with the captain of a coasting schooner, the *Northern Light,* who was getting his craft ready for sea.

He was bluff and blunt, but good-natured, and easily drawn into conversation. He told me he was bound for Boston; and when I remarked that he couldn't have much freight aboard, the schooner's sides rising high out of the water, he answered, with a significant quirk of the mouth which provoked my curiosity: "She'll wet 'em 'fore ever she gets out of the Strait, if freight is all that's wanted."

He went on to say that he was waiting for a wind to run over to a small port on the south shore, where he was to take in building-stone from the Nova Scotia quarries.

He showed me his cabin, which, for the cabin of a coaster, was neat and comfortable; and interested me so much in the life he led, and in his own simple, genial character, that I said impulsively:

"If it was by daylight, and you would take a passenger, I might be tempted to try a voyage with you, as far as the south shore."

"I can give you a bunk, and we've got a decent sort of a cook," he replied. "You'll be welcome, if you won't mind roughing it."

I said it would be just what I should like.

"Then you'd better come aboard this evening," he went on. "We can't beat out into the Strait with this light southerly breeze; but if I know the signs, it will shift about and freshen 'fore morning, and the sunrise will see our sheets taut and sails bellying."

There was a touch of poetry in the man's nature, in piquant contrast with his weather-roughened visage and chubby form.

In the evening I went on board with my valise—a little to his surprise, I thought, for he had evidently expected my heart would fail me at the last moment; and after watching the moonlight on the water, for a while, took possession of the berth allotted me in the small cabin. I slept soundly, and did not waken until noises on deck and the harsh creak-creak of the hoisting-tackle warned me that we were getting under sail.

I hurried on my clothing, and putting my head out over the gangway saw that the schooner was spreading her white wings, like some huge croaking crane preparing to take flight. We had already swung off into the stream, heading down the harbor; the wind had freshened, and got into the northwest; the canvas filled, the masts swayed, the lightly-ballasted hull yielded and careened, and we were off, with the dim shores flitting away from us, and the waves gurgling under our wales. The east brightened behind over the hills, and we had hardly passed the point and entered the

130

open Strait when the clouds on the horizon broke into fiery flakes, and the first beams of the sunrise gilded our spars.

I had a keen appetite for the cook's good breakfast of fried bacon and potatoes, and enjoyed the passage with as fine a zest as I had felt for anything so far in my vacation. It took us about five hours to run over to the landing on the north coast of Nova Scotia, where our cargo, from a neighboring sandstone quarry, was to be taken aboard. We drifted into a little cove, and the mate stood ready to fling a line to the pier, when my attention was called to a boy who came forward to catch it.

He had a singularly solemn countenance for a boy of his age (he could hardly have been more than seventeen), bare feet and legs, and a brown neck, exposed by his coarse woolen shirt wide open at the throat. He had on an old straw hat with a ripped crown, showing the top of his uncombed head through the gap.

"Wide awake, Jake!" called out the captain.

"Jake's wide awake," the boy answered back, extending his open hands to catch the line.

"Good for you, Jake!" cried the captain, as the hawser was hauled in from the schooner.

"I know what's good," said Jake, simply.

"You know better than some folks that think they know a great deal more. Here—ketch that!" cried the captain. Then, as the boy stooped to pick up a Canadian copper flung to him on the wharf, he added:

"Jake never'll dam the St. Lawrence, but he's good as gold all through."

My voyage over had been so delightful that I was much inclined to accept an invitation from the captain to take the trip to Boston with him; although he warned me

that the *Northern Light* wouldn't sail so dashingly with heavy freight as she did with light ballast. Anyhow, I would spend the time on shore, while the schooner was lading, visit the quarries, and explore the country a little. There were a few houses in sight, grouped about the cove.

As I stepped to the wharf with my valise, I asked Jake to show me a good boarding-place.

"Want a place to stop?" he said in his solemn, earnest way. "Ma'll let you in. I'll tell her. Come on"; and he took my valise.

He went on before. I followed amid piles of quarry-stone, and along a path that led over a high bank to a dingy little house on the terrace of the hills. It commanded a fine view of the coast and the sea, but nothing else could be said in its favor. I shrank back, feeling that I had made an awkward mistake in accepting Jake's guidance; but he threw the door open, calling out: "Ma, here's a man come to stop with us! I said you'd let him in."

The surprised face of a stooping little gray-haired woman peered out.

"Why, Jakey," she said, "how could you!" She gave me a kindly but distressed smile. "I'd like to be hospitable, but I hain't a speck of room, nor a spare bed."

"He can sleep with me," said Jake, generously; "or I'll sleep on the floor."

I relieved her embarrassment by saying, "Jake is altogether too kind. If he will show the way to some house you can recommend, I shall be as much obliged to him as if I turned him out of his bed."

"Oh, yes," she exclaimed quickly; "Mr. Kendall's. Jakey will go with you." Her voice softened as she added, with a tearful sort of smile, "Jakey is good-hearted as you ever see, but he don't always use good judgment. Go along with the gentleman, Jakey dear."

Jake appeared disappointed that they were not to have me as a guest; he backed up the offer of his bed with a proposal to "ketch a lunker" for my dinner, by which a big fish was meant; then, as even that failed to tempt me, he faced about abruptly, and, with a curt "Come on!" he set off to guide me to the nearest farmhouse.

I saw a good deal of him while I stayed in the nighborhood. I took him with me in my excursions, and enjoyed his quaint and often shrewd sayings, and his simple kind-heartedness. The Kendalls, with whom I lodged, gave him credit for the gift of second-sight, inherited from his Scotch ancestry; and told a curious story of his having seen a certain coaster go down in the Strait three days before it actually did go down, and in the way he described. I concluded, however, that he made more misses than hits in his predictions, as forecasters of the future commonly do; and that the gift had been attributed to him on account of an abrupt and sententious way of saying things.

Having decided to make the voyage to Boston with Captain Cameron, I wrote to assure my friends at home that they would have no cause for anxiety if they missed my letters for a few days, or failed to see me as soon as they expected. Then one afternoon I sat on the wharf, watching the last of the building-blocks as they were lowered by the derrick through the schooner's main hatch into the hold.

"We'll be off by sundown, if the wind stays to the west'ard," said the captain; "just a jolly breeze for running out of the Strait!"

That was joyful news to me, but not so to Jake, who came and sat by my side.

"I shall hate to have you go," he exclaimed earnestly. And when I asked him why: "Cause you've been good to me.

Some folks poke fun at me; but you never do that. I don't like to have fun poked at me, more 'n anybody does, though I know I ain't bright," he said, with a pathos that was touching, it was so simple and unconscious.

I was trying to frame some comforting reply to this affecting speech, when he said, "I'm going to make you a present," and handed out to me an old pocket-knife with a much-worn blade and a cracked horn handle.

I couldn't help smiling as I asked how he could think of parting with such a treasure.

"You've made me presents," he replied; "you give me this hat, and the shoes I've got on; and you lost your knife when we was out in the boat fishing."

This was true; and he had heard me lament that I couldn't buy another good knife at the country store where I had purchased his hat and shoes.

"But, you dear fellow," I exclaimed, "I can't take your knife!"

He was evidently hurt, seeming to think I had slighted his humble offering. After a moment's silence he said, still holding the knife in open palm—and I remember just how it looked, with one end of the whitish horn handle broken away at a rivet, showing the polished iron rim, and how I had to wink the glimmering moisture from my eyes in order to see it at all:

"Time'll come, and 't won't be long first,"—he spoke slowly and earnestly— "when you'll be glad to give a thousand dollars for a jack-knife no better 'n that. Then you'll think of what I tell ye."

"I haven't got a thousand dollars in the world," I said, laughing; "so give it to me." And I took it to please him.

But I knew how much he prized the poor old battered thing, and felt guilty of a heartless robbery when I thought of carrying it off in my pocket, So, as he was accompanying me to the schooner an hour later, I left him to walk on with my valise, while I stopped at his mother's door to bid her good-by.

"And here is the knife which your son gave me," I said. "It was very, very kind in him; but of course I can't keep it."

She said she was "afraid Jakey would feel awful bad" if I didn't, and she took it with reluctance.

"Hide it away from him awhile," I said; "then some day put it where he will find it, and perhaps he will have forgotten all about giving it away."

"I'll do just as you wish," she replied, tears rising in her eyes as I shook her hand with sincere cordiality. "I know 't wa'n't no sort of a present for him to make a person like you; but, as I said to you once before, and as you've had a chance to find out for yourself, my poor boy don't always use good judgment." I tried to say something reassuring, but faltered, and she went on: "You've been dreadful good to him, and I know how he'll miss you!"

I hurried away, and bade Jake good-by on board the schooner.

"Wish I was going with you," he said. "I would in a minute, if 't wa'n't for ma."

"She needs you," I answered. "You're a great comfort to her, Jake; and I hope you never will leave her. Now go ashore, my good Jake, and good-by!"

Without a word he walked to the wharf and dropped down on a block of stone, where he remained seated, sadly watching us as we made sail and got under way—as pathetic a picture of Patience on a monument as you can well imagine. His disconsolate, motionless figure grew indistinct across the tossing waves, until a jutting headland hid him from view.

We went out with a good breeze, but the schooner was laden and her progress was prosaic enough compared with the fine dash she had made in coming over from the island. But I was altogether at my ease on board. The captain was good company; I had in my valise two or three interesting books which, so far on my trip, I had not taken time to read; and I did not easily tire of watching the waves, the gulls, the clouds, and the shores, which were sometimes quite near.

We passed through the Gulf of Canso partly by daylight, and were becalmed in Chedabucto Bay until a strong east wind sprang up, against which we had a rather dull time beating out into the Atlantic. The captain took good fortune and bad with equal cheerfulness, and when I expressed a wish that the wind would change back again to the westward, he said:

"Be patient, young man! We can't have everything our own way. Let the wind hold, and after we pass Cape Canso it will give us a straight run to Massachusetts Bay."

Night came on—our second night—and we were still knocking about inside the cape. The schooner heaved on the long swells that came rolling in from the Atlantic; but the evening, though cool, was fine; and I was glad to keep the deck with the captain.

He told tales of his seafaring life, one of which I had good reason to remember, from the bearing it had upon my own subsequent strange adventure. It was of a brother of his, who sailed with him as his mate a few years before, and was lost overboard and drowned under his very eyes, when he might have been saved if there had been any convenient object at hand to fling after him so as to keep him afloat till a boat could be lowered.

"Since then," he said, "I have always kept a life-buoy ready for the man at the wheel to cast overboard, in case of such an accident. We have never had to use it yet, and I hope we never shall; but there it is, and there it will always be found as long as I walk the deck."

I had noticed it, a circular life-preserver, with a sort of line attached, such as one often sees on passenger steamers, but rarely on board of a common sailing-vessel. Buoy and line were held together by a smaller cord which a quick pull at a bow-knot would untie, and the whole was hung securely on a cleat under the stern-rail.

I was sitting on the box over the steering-gear, and the captain was himself at the wheel; our own green and red lights were in the rigging, when we noticed, off our port bow, the lights of a steamer coming in sight around the cape. She was evidently entering the bay, and as we were directly in her path I expressed some anxiety as to her course.

"We have the right of way," said the captain; "she sees our lights, and she'll pass astern of us. That's what she's doing," he added, after a minute's careful observation.

He called the mate to the wheel, while he himself stood watching the stranger. There was something mysterious and awe-inspiring in the gradual approach of her lights, like two great eyes, one green and one red, in the immense darkness; and in the slow, far-off, monotonous clank of her machinery, growing upon the silence of the night and of the sea.

The ship's bell rang, and a steam-signal responded, booming across the water. Soon I could make out a dim object looming on the horizon; at the same time there was a gradual veering of the steamer's lights.

"She's changing her course!" cried the captain. "What does that mean?" It was the first time I had heard him speak in a tone indicating any excitement.

"She means to cross our bows," said the mate.

"She can't do that!" the captain ex-

claimed. "She'll be aboard of us, sure as fate!"

Moments of terrible uncertainty ensued. The ship's bell clanged. The sailors in the forecastle came tumbling up on deck. We were all on our feet, every man getting ready to obey whatever orders were called out to him in the emergency: a never-to-be-forgotten scene of hurry and apprehension, lighted by the lanterns in the shrouds over our heads.

On came the great black hull, towering above us—for we were comparatively low in the water—and rushing down upon our port bow. Our captain roared out at her, and there was all at once a wild movement of human figures visible along her rail. She veered again, and the schooner at the same time fell off from her course, both vessels endeavoring to bear away from each other; but it was too late. There was a tremendous crash, and I thought for a moment the steamer was actually walking over us. I could see her prow rise out of the water, as if she had struck a ledge. She recoiled, settled back, and immediately drifted away from us, disappearing in the darkness.

The schooner made a horrible lurch under the shock, then rolled back in the other direction, lifting barrels of water on her bow, and spilling it across the deck. I hurried forward with the captain to see what damage had been done. The steamer had cut us down to the top layer of blocks of stone that composed our freight, and the sea was spouting in through the gap.

There was but one chance of saving her—to check the incoming torrent by means of objects thrust down over the crushed side, while she was headed for the shore, in the hope of running her aground before she sank. Planks, hatch-covers, potato-bags, the cabin door—wrenched off in mad haste—hammer and spikes, a rope to support a sailor, up to his waist in the water, over her side—every available object was used, and every effort made, but all to no purpose; the flood rushed in beneath and around and through the obstructions; then a great wave swept by, undoing all that had been done. Meanwhile the schooner was steadily settling in that direction, and the farther she went over the faster the sea poured in.

"No use!" cried the captain. "We must try to launch the boat."

There was but one, and it had not been hanging from the stern davits at any time during the voyage; it had been carried lying bottom up on deck, against the bulwarks that were cut down by the collision. The streamer's stem had struck it and shoved it from its position, giving it a bad wrench, but without crushing it; and there was hope that it would still prove seaworthy. But no sooner was it lowered by ropes over the side than it began to fill with water.

A sort of panic followed, but the captain did not once lose his head.

"Don't pile into her!" he shouted to the sailors scrambling overboard. "Keep her afloat! Hold on to her rail till she's bailed out and the leak stanched! Get her off, so she won't be sucked down!"

I knew what that meant. Until then I had hardly realized that the danger was so imminent. I had such confidence in the captain that I stood eagerly watching him, and waiting to obey his orders or follow his example.

He and I were alone on the deck by this time. We looked down upon a tumultuous scene, half in shadow and half lighted by the ship's lanterns, one man in the boat with a bucket bailing with all his might; another trying to stuff burlaps into the opened seams; two or three up to their shoulders in the water, clinging to the gunwales, and endeavoring, by swimming and

by pushing with an oar, to get her away from the schooner. But few words were uttered, and those in quick, half-stifled tones, like the voices of men in a death-struggle.

"You are doing well, boys!" the captain called out cheerily. "And you!"—he caught me roughly by the arm, and turned my face toward the stern—"the life-buoy for you! And be quick!"

I had thought of that, but still had hopes that the boat would be emptied and saved and brought back alongside before the schooner went down.

"And you, captain?" I said; "take the life-buoy yourself!"

"Start!" he exclaimed. "Don't you see we are sinking?"

I lost no more precious moments, but ran for the life-buoy, released it from its fastenings, put my feet through it, and slipped it up under my arms. I gave one glance at the captain as his stumpy form disappeared over the schooner's side, then threw the loosened coils of the buoy-line overboard, and jumped after it.

In my excitement I didn't much mind the shock of the immersion, although the water was very cold and I was unaccustomed to sea-bathing. I could swim a little, but I knew well that without some support I couldn't have kept my head above the waves many minutes.

What did I think about? I can hardly tell. In that frightful crisis I suppose my past life should have flashed before my mind, and I ought to have thought of my friends at home; for I was well aware that, even with my life-preserver on, I might perish before I could be rescued.

But, incredible as it may seem, some of my thoughts were facetious, and it is chiefly those that I remember. Whether I could read the name on the stern or not (it seems to me now that I could), I looked up to where it was, and said to myself, "The

Northern Light will soon be quenched!" Then, "Where was Moses when the light went out?" It was the jocularity of terrible excitement, something like Hamlet's after the interview with his father's ghost.

It could hardly have lasted half a minute. Things were rushing to a climax faster than I can tell them. I had drifted a few yards away from the stern, and was paddling to increase the distance, when I discovered that the line attached to the life-buoy did not come free when I pulled at it. On the contrary, I was pulling myself back to the schooner. In short, the line had caught on something when I flung it over; it was spliced to the buoy, and I was in the buoy. As I continued pulling in one direction, the schooner began pulling in the other—she was making her final, wallowing, gurgling plunge to the bottom drawing me down with her!

It was impossible to untie or break the line, though I might have cut it, even while I felt myself hauled rapidly after the wreck. I struggled frantically, and I believe I shrieked out, just as my head was going under:

"A THOUSAND DOLLARS FOR A JACK-KNIFE!"

How far down I was drawn I haven't the slightest notion. It seemed to me a long way; and what was probably but a few seconds of agony appeared many minutes. I remember a ringing in my head, and vivid flashes of light; then all at once there was nothing for me to struggle against, and I rose rapidly to the surface. I had succeeded in freeing myself from the buoy.

Something was floating near. I grasped it. It was a ship's fender. Then a boat bore down upon me, pulled by plashing oars; if I hadn't shrieked out, it might have passed over me. It was a boat from the steamer that had run us down. I was quickly pulled in over the gunwale; and afterward the captain and all our crew were picked up from the foundering boat and other floating objects.

The steamer was also injured by the collision, but not disabled; and we received the kindest treatment on board. The captain had strangely mistaken our distance when he attempted to cross our bows; we were much nearer than he supposed. She was a tramp steamer, but her owners were responsible; and as we were not in any way at fault, they had heavy damages to pay. I was told that if I put in a personal claim, it would be settled; but I never did.

And as for Jake's prediction, which was so singularly fulfilled? I have related the circumstances as I remember them, and am willing to leave the question of prophecy or coincidence to anybody's unbiased judgment. Some very strange things happen in this world of ours—things it is useless to argue much about; and this I regard as one of them.

Oh!—well, yes; I reached home in time to get ready for the fall term, and completed my college course.

BUFFALO HUNTING

By Theodore Roosevelt.

December, 1889

HEN Independence was declared in 1776, and the United States of America appeared among the powers of the earth, the continent beyond the Alleghenies was one unbroken wilderness; and the buffaloes, the first animals to vanish when the wilderness is settled, roved up to the crests of the mountains which mark the western boundaries of Pennsylvania, Virginia, and the Carolinas. They were plentiful in what are now the States of Ohio, Kentucky, and Tennessee. But by the beginning of the present century they had been driven beyond the Mississippi; and for the next eighty years they formed one of the most distinctive and characteristic features of existence on the great plains. Their numbers were countless—incredible. In vast herds of hundreds of thousands of individuals, they roamed from the Saskatchewan to the Rio Grande and westward to the Rocky Mountains. They furnished all the means of livelihood to the tribes of Horse Indians, and to the curious population of French Metis, or Half-breeds, on the Red River, as well as those dauntless and archtypical wanderers, the white hunters and trappers. Their numbers slowly diminished; but the decrease was very gradual until after the Civil War. They were not destroyed by the settlers, but by the railways and by the skin hunters.

After the ending of the Civil War, the work of constructing transcontinental railway lines was pushed forward with the utmost vigor. These supplied cheap and indispensable, but hitherto wholly lacking, means of transportation to the hunters; and at the same time the demand for buffalo robes and hides became very great, while the enormous numbers of the beasts, and the comparative ease with which they were slaughtered, attracted throngs of adventurers. The result was such a slaughter of big game as the world had never before seen; never before were so many large animals of one species destroyed in so short a time. Several million buffaloes were slain. In fifteen years from the time the destruction fairly began, the great herds were exterminated. In all probability there are not now, all told, a thousand head of wild buffaloes on the American continent; and no herd of a hundred individuals has been in existence since 1884.

The first great break followed the building of the Union Pacific Railway. All the buffaloes of the middle region were then destroyed, and the others were then split into two vast sets of herds, the northern and the southern. The latter were destroyed first, about 1878; the former not until 1883. My own experience with buffaloes was obtained in the latter year, among small bands and scattered individuals, near my ranch on the Little Missouri; I have related it elsewhere. But two of my relatives were more fortunate, and took part in the chase of these lordly beasts when the herds still darkened the prairie as far as the eye could see.

During the first two months of 1877, my brother Elliott, then a lad not seventeen years old, made a buffalo-hunt toward the edge of the Staked Plains in northern Texas. He was thus in at the death of the southern herds, for all, save a few scattering bands, were destroyed within two years of this time.

My brother was with my cousin, John Roosevelt, and they went out on the range with six other adventurers—a German-American, a Scotchman who had been in the Confederate cavalry and afterward in Maximilian's Mexican body-guard, and four Irishmen. It was a party of just such young men as frequently drift to the frontier. All were short of cash, and all were hardy, vigorous fellows eager for excitement and adventure. My brother was much the youngest of the party, and the least experienced; but he was well-grown, strong and healthy, and very fond of boxing, wrestling, running, riding, and shooting; moreover, he had served an apprenticeship in hunting deer and turkeys. Their mess-kit, ammunition, bedding, and provisions were carried in two prairie wagons, each drawn by four horses. In addition to the teams they had six saddle-animals—all of them shaggy, unkempt mustangs. Three or four dogs, setters and half-bred greyhounds, trotted along behind the wagons. Each man took his turn for two days as teamster and cook; and there were always two with the wagons, or camp, as the case might be, while the other six were off hunting, usually in couples. The expedition was undertaken partly for sport and partly with the hope of profit; for, after purchasing the horses and wagons, none of the party had any money left, and they were forced to rely upon selling skins and hides and, when near the forts, meat.

They started on January 2d, and shaped their course for the head-waters of the Salt Fork of the Brazos, the center of abundance for the great buffalo herds. During the first few days they were in the outskirts of the settled country, and shot only small game—quail and prairie fowl; then they began to kill turkey, deer, and antelope. These they "swapped" for flour and feed, at the ranches or squalid, straggling frontier towns. On several occasions the hunters were lost, spending the night out in the open, or sleeping at a ranch if one was found. Both towns and ranches were filled with rough customers; all of my brother's companions were muscular, hot-headed fellows; and as a consequence they were involved in several savage "free fights," in which, fortunately, nobody was seriously hurt. My brother kept a very brief diary, the entries being fairly startling from their conciseness. A number of times, the mention of their arrival, either at a halting-place, a little village, or a rival buffalo-camp is followed by the laconic remark, "big fight," or "big row"; but once they evidently concluded discretion to be the better part of valor, the entry for January 20th being, "On the road—passed through Belknap—too lively, so kept on to the Brazos—very late." The buffalo-camps in particular were very jealous of one another, each party regarding itself as having exclusive right to the range it was the first to find; and on several occasions this feeling came near involving my brother and his companions in serious trouble.

While slowly driving the heavy wagons to the hunting-grounds they suffered the usual hardships of plains travel. The weather, as in most Texas winters, alternated between the extremes of heat and cold. There had been little rain; in consequence water was scarce. Twice they were forced to cross wild, barren wastes, where the pools had dried up, and they suffered terribly from thirst. On the first occasion the horses were in good condition, and they traveled steadily, with only occasional short halts, for over thirty-six hours, by which time they were across the waterless country. The journal reads: "January 29th.—Big hunt—no water and we left Quinn's blockhouse this morning at 3 A.M. —on the go all night—hot. January 28th.— No water—hot—at seven we struck water and by eight Stinking Creek—grand 'hurrah.'" On the second occasion, the horses were weak and traveled slowly, so the party went forty-eight hours without drinking. "February 19th.—Pulled on twenty-one miles—trail bad—freezing night, no water, and wolves after our fresh meat. 20th.—Made nineteen miles over prairie; again only mud, no water, freezing hard—frightful thirst. 21st.—Thirty miles to Clear Fork, fresh water." These entries were hurriedly jotted down at the time, by a boy who deemed it unmanly to make any especial note of hardship or suffering; but every plainsman will understand the real agony implied in working hard for two nights, one day, and portions of two others, without water, even in cool weather. During the last few miles the staggering horses were only just able to drag the lightly loaded wagon—for they had but one with them at the time—while the men plodded

along in sullen silence, their mouths so parched that they could hardly utter a word. My own hunting and ranching were done in the North where there is more water; so I have never had a similar experience. Once I took a team in thirty-six hours across a country where there was no water; but by good luck it rained heavily in the night, so that the horses had plenty of wet grass, and I caught the rain in my slicker, and so had enough water for myself. Personally, I have but once been as long as twenty-six hours without water.

The party pitched their permanent camp in a cañon of the Brazos known as Cañon Blanco. The last few days of their journey they traveled beside the river through a veritable hunter's paradise. The drought had forced all the animals to come to the larger watercourses, and the country was literally swarming with game. Every day, and all day long, the wagons traveled through the herds of antelopes that grazed on every side, while, whenever they approached the cañon brink, bands of deer started from the timber that fringed the river's course; often, even the deer wandered out on the prairie with the antelopes. Nor was the game shy; for the hunters, both red and white, followed only the buffaloes until the huge, shaggy herds were destroyed, and the smaller beasts were in consequence but little molested.

Once my brother shot five antelopes from a single stand, when the party were short of fresh venison; he was out of sight and to leeward, and the antelopes seemed confused rather than alarmed at the rifle-reports and the fall of their companions. As was to be expected where game was so plenty, wolves and coyotes also abounded. At night they surrounded the camp, wailing and howling in a kind of shrieking chorus throughout the hours of darkness; one night they came up so close that the frightened horses had to be hobbled and guarded. On another occasion a large wolf actually crept into camp, where he was seized by the dogs, and the yelling, writhing knot of combatants rolled over one of the sleepers; finally, the long-toothed prowler managed to shake himself loose, and vanished in the gloom. One evening they were almost as much startled by a visit of a different kind. They were just finishing supper when an Indian stalked suddenly and silently out of the surrounding darkness, squatted down in the circle of firelight, remarked gravely, "Me Tonk," and began helping himself from the stew. He belonged to the friendly tribe of Tonkaways, so his hosts speedily recovered their equanimity; as for him, he had never lost his, and he sat eating by the fire until there was literally nothing left to eat. The panic caused by his appearance was natural; for at that time the Comanches were a scourge to the buffalo-hunters, ambushing them and raiding their camps; and several bloody fights had taken place.

Their camp had been pitched near a deep pool or water-hole. On both sides the bluffs rose like walls, and where they had crumbled and lost their sheerness, the vast buffalo herds, passing and repassing for countless generations, had worn furrowed trails so deep that the backs of the beasts were but little above the surrounding soil. In the bottom, and in places along the crests of the cliffs that hemmed in the cañon-like valley, there were groves of tangled trees, tenanted by great flocks of wild turkeys. Once my brother made two really remarkable shots at a pair of these great birds. It was at dusk, and they were flying directly overhead from one cliff to the other. He had in his hand a thirty-eight-caliber Ballard rifle, and, as the gobblers winged their way heavily by, he brought them both down with two successive bullets. This was of course mainly a piece of mere luck; but it meant good shooting, too. The Ballard was a very accurate, handy little weapon; it belonged to me, and was the first rifle I ever owned or used. With it I had once killed a deer, the only specimen of large game I had then shot; and I presented the rifle to my brother when he went to Texas. In our happy ignorance we deemed it quite good enough for buffalo or anything else; but out on the plains my brother soon found himself forced to procure a heavier and more deadly weapon.

When camp was pitched the horses were turned loose to graze and refresh themselves after their trying journey, during which they had lost flesh woefully. They were watched and tended by the two men who were always left in camp, and save on rare occasions, were only used to haul in the buffalo-hides. The camp-guards for the time being acted as cooks; and, though coffee and flour both ran short and finally gave out, fresh meat of every kind was abundant. The camp was never without buffalo-beef, deer and antelope venison, wild turkeys, prairie-chickens, quails, ducks, and rabbits. The birds were simply "potted," as occasion required; when the quarry was deer or antelope, the hunters took the dogs with them to run down the wounded animals. But almost the entire attention of the hunters was given to the buffalo. After an evening spent in lounging round the camp-fire, and a sound night's sleep, wrapped in robes and blankets, they would get up before daybreak, snatch a hurried breakfast, and start off in couples through the chilly dawn. The great beasts were very plentiful; in the first day's hunt, twenty were slain; but the herds were restless and ever on the move. Sometimes they would be seen right by the camp, and again it would need an all-day's tramp to find them. There was no difficulty in spying them—the chief trouble with forest game;

for on the prairie a buffalo makes no effort to hide, and its black, shaggy bulk looms up as far as the eye can see. Sometimes they were found in small parties of three or four individuals, sometimes in bands of about two hundred, and again in great herds of many thousand; and solitary old bulls, expelled from the herds, were common. If on broken land, among hills and ravines, there was not much difficulty in approaching from the leeward; for, though the sense of smell in the buffalo is very acute, they do not see well at a distance through their overhanging frontlets of coarse and matted hair. If, as was generally the case, they were out on the open, rolling prairie, the stalking was far more difficult. Every hollow, every earth hummock and sagebush had to be used as cover. The hunter wriggled through the grass flat on his face, pushing himself along for perhaps a quarter of a mile by his toes and fingers, heedless of the spiny cactus. When near enough to the huge, unconscious quarry the hunter began firing, still keeping himself carefully concealed. If the smoke was blown away by the wind, and if the buffaloes caught no glimpse of the assailant, they would often stand motionless and stupid until many of their number had been slain; the hunter being careful not to fire too high, aiming just behind the shoulder, about a third of the way up the body, that his bullet might go through the lungs. Sometimes, even after they saw the man, they would act as if confused and panic-struck, huddling up together and staring at the smoke puffs—but generally they were off at a lumbering gallop as soon as they had an idea of the point of danger. When once started, they ran for many miles before halting, and their pursuit on foot was extremely laborious.

One morning my cousin and brother had been left in camp as guards. They were sitting, idly warming themselves in the first sunbeams, when their attention was sharply drawn to four buffaloes who were coming to the pool to drink. The beasts came down a game trail, a deep rut in the bluff, fronting where they were sitting, and they did not dare stir for fear of being discovered. The buffaloes walked into the pool, and, after drinking their fill, stood for some time with the water running out of their mouths, idly lashing their sides with their short tails, enjoying the bright warmth of the early sunshine; then, with much splashing and the gurgling of soft mud, they left the pool and clambered up the bluff with unwieldy agility. As soon as they turned, my brother and cousin ran for their rifles; but before they got back the buffaloes had crossed the bluff crest. Climbing after them, the two hunters found, when they reached the summit, that their game, instead of halting, had struck straight off across the prairie at a slow lope, doubtless intending to rejoin the herd they had left. After a moment's consultation, the men went in pursuit, excitement overcoming their knowledge that they ought not, by rights, to leave the camp. They struck a steady trot, following the animals by sight until they passed over a knoll, and then trailing them. Where the grass was long, as it was for the first four or five miles, this was a work of no difficulty, and they did not break their gait, only glancing now and then at the trail. As the sun rose and the day became warm, their breathing grew quicker; and the sweat rolled off their faces as they ran across the rough prairie sward, up and down the long inclines, now and then shifting their heavy rifles from one shoulder to the other. But they were in good training, and they did not have to halt. At last they reached stretches of bare ground, sun-baked and grassless, where the trail grew dim; and here they had to go very slowly, carefully examining the faint dents and marks made in the soil by the heavy hoofs, and unraveling the trail from the mass of old foot-marks. It was tedious work, but it enabled them to completely recover their breath by the time that they again struck the grass land; and but a few hundred yards from its edge, in a slight hollow, they saw the four buffaloes just entering a herd of fifty or sixty that were scattered out grazing. The herd paid no attention to the newcomers, and these immediately began to feed greedily. After a whispered consultation, the two hunters crept back, and made a long circle that brought them well to leeward of the herd, in line with a slight rise in the ground. They then crawled up to this rise and, peering through the tufts of tall, rank grass, saw the unconscious beasts a hundred and twenty-five or fifty yards away. They fired together, each mortally wounding his animal, and then, rushing in as the herd halted in confusion, and following them as they ran, impeded by numbers, hurry, and panic, they eventually got three more.

On another occasion, the same two hunters nearly met with a frightful death, being overtaken by a vast herd of stampeded buffaloes. All animals that go in herds are subject to these instantaneous attacks of uncontrollable terror, under the influence of which they become perfectly mad, and rush headlong in dense masses on any form of death. Horses, and more especially cattle, often suffer from stampedes; it is a danger against which the cowboys are compelled to be perpetually on guard. A band of stampeded horses, sweeping in mad terror up a valley, will dash against a rock or tree with such violence as to leave several dead animals at its base, while the survivors race on without halting; they will overturn and destroy tents and wagons, and a man on foot caught in the rush has but a small

chance for his life. A buffalo stampede is much worse—or rather was much worse, in the old days—because of the great weight and immense numbers of the beasts, who, in a fury of heedless terror, plunged over cliffs and into rivers, and bore down whatever was in their path. On the occasion in question, my brother and cousin were on their way homeward. They were just mounting one of the long, low swells into which the prairie was broken when they heard a low, muttering, rumbling noise, like far-off thunder. It grew steadily louder, and, not knowing what it meant, they hurried forward to the top of the rise. As they reached it, they stopped short in terror and amazement, for before them the whole prairie was black with madly rushing buffaloes.

Afterward they learned that another couple of hunters, four or five miles off, had fired into and stampeded a large herd. This herd, in its rush, gathered others, all thundering along together in uncontrollable and increasing panic.

The surprised hunters were far away from any broken ground or other place of refuge; while the vast herd of huge, plunging, maddened beasts was charging straight down on them not a quarter of a mile distant. Down they came!—thousands upon thousands, their front extending a mile in breadth, while the earth shook beneath their thunderous gallop, and as they came closer, their shaggy frontlets loomed dimly through the columns of dust thrown up from the dry soil. The two hunters knew that their only hope for life was to split the herd, which, though it had so broad a front, was not very deep. If they failed they would inevitably be trampled to death.

Waiting until the beasts were in close range, they opened a rapid fire from their heavy breech-loading rifles, yelling at the top of their voices. For a moment the result seemed doubtful. The line thundered steadily down on them; then it swayed violently, as two or three of the brutes immediately in their front fell beneath the bullets, while the neighbors made violent efforts to press off sideways. Then a narrow wedge-shaped rift appeared in the line, and widened as it came up closer, and the

on toward the horizon, save five individuals who had been killed or disabled by the shots.

On another occasion, when my brother was out with one of his Irish friends, they fired at a small herd containing an old bull; the bull charged the smoke, and the whole herd followed him. Probably they were simply stampeded, and had no hostile in-

A THRILLING EXPERIENCE OF LIFE ON THE PLAINS. "SPLITTING" A HERD OF STAMPEDED BUFFALOES.

buffaloes, shrinking from their foes in front, strove desperately to edge away from the dangerous neighborhood; the shouts and shots were redoubled; the hunters were almost choked by the cloud of dust through which they could see the stream of dark huge bodies passing within rifle-length on either side; and in a moment the peril was over, and the two men were left alone on the plain, unharmed, though with their nerves terribly shaken. The herd careered

tention; at any rate, after the death of their leader, they rushed by without doing any damage.

But buffaloes sometimes charged with the utmost determination, and were then dangerous antagonists. My cousin, a very hardy and resolute hunter, had a narrow escape from a wounded cow which he followed up a steep bluff or sand cliff. Just as he reached the summit, he was charged, and was only saved by the sudden appearance of his dog, which distracted the cow's attention. He thus escaped with only a tumble and a few bruises.

My brother also came in for a charge, while killing the biggest bull that was slain by any of the party. He was out alone, and saw a small herd of cows and calves at some distance, with a huge bull among them, towering above them like a giant. There was no break in the ground, nor any tree nor bush near them, but by making a half-circle, my brother managed to creep up against the wind behind a slight roll in the prairie surface, until he was within seventy-five yards of the grazing and unconscious beasts. There were some cows and calves between him and the bull, and he had to wait some moments before they shifted position as the herd grazed onward and gave him a fair shot; in the interval they had moved so far forward that he was in plain view. His first bullet struck just behind the shoulder; the herd started and looked around, but the bull merely lifted his head and took a step forward, his tail curled up over his back. The next bullet likewise struck fair, nearly in the same place, telling with a loud "pack!" against the thick hide, and making the dust fly up from the matted hair. Instantly the great bull wheeled and charged in headlong anger, while the herd fled in the opposite direction. On the bare prairie, with no spot of refuge, it was useless to try to escape, and the hunter, with reloaded rifle, waited until the bull was not far off, then drew-up his weapon and fired. Either he was nervous, or the bull at the moment bounded over some obstacle, for the ball went a little wild; nevertheless, by good luck, it broke a

"THE GREAT BEAST CAME CRASHING TO THE EARTH."

"THEY WERE IN GOOD TRAINING, AND THEY DID NOT HAVE TO HALT."

fore leg, and the great beast came crashing to the earth, and was slain before it could struggle to its feet.

Two days after this event, a war party of Comanches swept down along the river. They "jumped" a neighboring camp, killing one man and wounding two more, and at the same time ran off all but three of the horses belonging to our eight adventurers. With the remaining three horses and one wagon they set out homeward. The march was hard and tedious; they lost their way and were in jeopardy from quicksands and cloudbursts; they suffered from thirst and cold, their shoes gave out and their feet were lamed by cactus spines. At last they reached Fort Sniffin in safety, and great was their ravenous rejoicing when they procured some bread—for during the final fortnight of the hunt they had been without flour or vegetables of any kind, or even coffee, and had subsisted on fresh meat "straight." Nevertheless, it was a very healthy, as well as a very pleasant and exciting experience; and I doubt if any of those who took part in it will ever forget their great buffalo-hunt on the Brazos.

THE SKEE-HUNTERS
By Charles Frederick Holder

March, 1900

A SNOW-STORM, heavy even for the high altitudes of Colorado and Montana, had just come to an end. The wind had literally blown itself out, and the mountains, peaks, and cañons of the great inland plateau were covered with snow, heaped and piled in marvelous drifts that changed the entire appearance of the country, raising great mounds of white in unexpected places, and covering the land for thousands of square miles with a mantle of dazzling white—the winter quilt of nature, protecting the resting trees, shrubs, and other vegetation from the deadly blizzard that swept so relentlessly over the land.

The wind had gone down, and there had followed a cold so intense that the upper surface of the snow had frozen into an icy sheet, glistening in the sunlight like silver, throwing back a thousand hues and rays.

One deep cañon in particular presented a singular appearance. It was a perfect cradle of snow, many hundred feet deep, with sloping sides, and trees like huge pompons rising on the summits of them, the interior being perfectly smooth. On the morning after the storm several furred and muffled figures could be seen stealing along beneath the trees. Each had those peculiar snowshoes, called "skees," fastened to his feet, and each held a long pole firmly in his hand. The skees were pieces of wood seven feet in length and half an inch thick, turned up tightly at the end, and were really little sleds on which the men walked and slid along.

The latter were not ordinary hunters, but men famous in their county for their skill in skee-racing, and trained in the dangerous art of sliding down a mountain-side at a speed inconceivable to any one who has not witnessed it in the northern counties of California, where skee-racing is a favorite pastime, and men become very skilful. These men were engaged in a more serious work. They were the hunters who supply wild animals to the zoölogical gardens, or the circus, or to any one who desires living wild animals. Every man was a tried woodsman; every one had killed the great game of the Rocky Mountain country—grizzlies, mountain-sheep, black bear, mountain-lion, and many more; and to-day they were in search of the elk, specimens of which were desired to stock a great game-preserve in the East.

It would have been an easy matter to go and shoot an elk, as the men could have crept upon them from some concealment; but it was necessary to take them alive and uninjured, and this explained the stealthy movements of the men as they crept along the upper edge of the great cañon that dropped away beneath them. They walked from tree to tree, keeping on the side away from the edge, but occasionally they would creep to it and glance carefully over into the cañon, looking up and down.

Suddenly one of the party stopped and uttered a low whistle. Looking in the direction indiciated, the others saw a herd of elk standing deep in the snow in a secluded corner. The hunters at once left the edge of the cañon, and, now out of sight, hurried on until they reached a point directly opposite the herd. Here they held a hasty consultation, and then, at the orders of the leader, they crept out and found themselves directly above the herd.

Grasping their poles more firmly, they

146

swung themselves lightly over the edge, and then began one of the most exciting and remarkable races possible to imagine: five men rushing down the mountain-side with the speed of the wind—now sliding along the smooth surface, now rising on a slight incline and bounding into the air. They seemed more like shadows gliding down the white sides of the cañon than like mere men.

The herd had seen the hunters at once, and, terror-stricken, dashed away, breaking through the crust, plunging through the deep snow, and becoming, in a moment, at the mercy of the flying men, who, with loud shouts, dashed down among them, even going some distance up the other side in their wild race. But they turned to slide again among the terrified elk, that now headed down the cañon, urged on by the hunters, who easily approached them. The men, by cries and shouts, added to the animals' alarm.

The object of the men was to drive them out upon the level plain below, and so, selecting the animals they wished to capture, they threw their lariats over the branching horns and literally "drove" before them the elk steeds they had chosen.

The cañon was presently left behind, and at its entrance the men selected the two elk they wished to keep, and a photographer took their pictures as they are here shown—plunged deep in the snow, no doubt trembling with fear at the strange instrument aimed at them, defenseless and helpless, though the open country was before them.

When the elk could no longer be driven, they were caught, bound, placed upon sleds brought for the purpose, and hauled to the ranch. Here they were released in a game corral, and were fed until spring, and until the snow had melted so the railway could be reached. They were then hauled to the nearest station and shipped to the game preserve for which they were captured.

In this way, by plunging down with great velocity among the animals, scattering them here and there, and forcing them to break through the snow-crust, nearly all elk are taken. Even bears and wolves are sometimes captured in the same manner, though the latter are more often followed by wolf-hounds that have been carefully trained for the purpose.

HER SOLILOQUY
By Frederick B. Opper

March, 1895

I love my little brother:
  He's a cunning, rosy elf;
But I wish—somehow or other—
  That he could rock himself!

BETWEEN SEA AND SKY
By Hjalmar Hjorth Boyesen

February, 1887

I

CELAND is the most beautiful land the sun doth shine upon," said Sigurd Sigurdson to his two sons.

"How can you know that, Father," asked Thoralf, the elder of the two boys, "when you have never been anywhere else?"

"I know it in my heart," said Sigurd devoutly.

"It is, after all, a matter of taste," observed the son. "I think, if I were hard pressed, I might be induced to put up with some other country."

"You ought to blush with shame," his father rejoined warmly. "You do not deserve the name of an Icelander, when you fail to see how you have been blessed in having been born in so beautiful a country."

"I wish it were less beautiful and had more things to eat in it," muttered Thoralf. "Salted codfish, I have no doubt, is good for the soul, but it rests very heavily on the stomach, especially when you eat it three times a day."

"You ought to thank God that you have codfish, and are not a naked savage on some South Sea isle, who feeds like an animal on the herbs of the earth."

"But I like codfish much better than smoked puffin," remarked Jens, the younger brother, who was carving a pipe-bowl. "Smoked puffin always makes me sea-sick. It tastes like cod liver oil."

Sigurd smiled, and, patting the younger boy on the head, entered the cottage.

"You shouldn't talk so to Father, Thoralf," said Jens, with superior dignity; for his father's caress made him proud and happy. "Father works so hard, and he does not like to see any one discontented."

"That is just it," replied the elder brother; "he works so hard, and yet barely manages to keep the wolf from the door. That is what makes me impatient with the country. If he worked so hard in any other country he would live in abundance, and in America he would become a rich man."

This conversation took place one day, late in the autumn, outside of a fisherman's cottage on the northwestern coast of Iceland. The wind was blowing a gale down from the very ice-engirdled pole, and it required a very genial temper to keep one from getting blue. The ocean, which was but a few hundred feet distant, roared like an angry beast, and shook its white mane of spray, flinging it up against the black clouds. With every fresh gust of wind, a shower of salt water would fly hissing through the air and whirl about the chimney-top, which was white on the windward side from dried deposits of brine. On the turf-thatched roof big pieces of driftwood, weighted down with stones, were laid lengthwise and crosswise, and along the walls fishing-nets hung in festoons from wooden pegs. Even the low door was draped, as with decorative intent, with the folds of a great drag-net, the clumsy cork-floats of which often dashed into the faces of those who attempted to enter. Under a driftwood shed which projected from the northern wall was seen a pile of peat, cut into square blocks, and a quantity of the same useful material might be observed down at the beach, in a boat which the boys had been unloading when the storm blew up. Trees no longer grow in the island, except the crippled and twisted dwarf-birch, which creeps along the ground like a snake, and, if it ever dares lift its head, rarely grows more than four or six feet high. In the olden time, which is described in the so-called sagas of the twelfth and thirteenth centuries, Iceland had very considerable forests of birch and probably also of pine. But they were cut down; and the climate has gradually been growing colder, until now even the hardiest tree, if it be induced to strike root in a sheltered place, never reaches maturity. The Icelanders therefore burn peat, and use for building their houses driftwood, which is carried to them by the Gulf Stream from Cuba and the other well-wooded isles along the Mexican Gulf.

"If it keeps blowing like this," said Thoralf, fixing his weather eye on the black horizon, "we shan't be able to go a-fishing; and Mother says the larder is very nearly empty."

"I wish it would blow down an Englishman or something on us," remarked the younger brother; "Englishmen always have such lots of money, and they are willing to pay for everything they look at."

"While you are a-wishing, why don't you wish for an American? Americans have mountains and mountains of money, and they don't mind a bit what they do with it. That's the reason I should like to be an American."

"Yes, let us wish for an American or two to make us comfortable for the winter. But I am afraid it is too late in the season to expect foreigners."

The two boys chatted together in this strain, each working at some piece of wood-carving which he expected to sell to some foreign traveler. Thoralf was sixteen years old, tall of growth, but round-shouldered, from being obliged to work when he was too young. He was rather a handsome lad, though his features were square and weather-beaten, and he looked prematurely old. Jens, the younger boy, was fourteen years old, and was his mother's darling. For even up under the North Pole mothers love their children tenderly, and sometimes they love one a little more than another; that is, of course, the merest wee bit of a fraction of a trifle more. Icelandic mothers are so constituted that when one child is a little weaker and sicklier than the rest, and thus seems to be more in need of petting, they are apt to love their little weakling above all their other children, and to lavish the tenderest care upon that one. It was because little Jens had so narrow a chest, and looked so small and slender by the side of his robust brother, that his mother always singled him out for favors and caresses.

II

ALL night long the storm danced wildly about the cottage, rattling the windows, shaking the walls, and making fierce assaults upon the door, as if it meant to burst in. Sometimes it bellowed hoarsely down the chimney, and whirled the ashes on the hearth, like a gray snowdrift, through the room. The fire had been put out, of course; but the dancing ashes kept up a fitful patter, like that of a pelting rainstorm against the walls; they even penetrated into the sleeping alcoves and powdered the heads of their occupants. For in Iceland it is only well-to-do people who can afford to have separate sleeping-rooms; ordinary folk sleep in little closed alcoves, along the walls of the sitting-room; masters and servants, parents and children, guests and wayfarers, all retiring at night into square little holes in the walls, where they undress behind sliding trapdoors which may be opened again, when the lights have been put out, and the supply of air threatens to become exhausted. It was in a little closet of this sort that Thoralf and Jens were lying, listening to the roar of the storm. Thoralf dozed off occasionally, and tried gently to extricate himself from his frightened brother's embrace; but Jens lay with wide-open eyes, staring into the dark, and now and then sliding the trapdoor aside and peeping out, until a blinding shower of ashes would again compel him to slip his head under the sheepskin coverlet. When at last he summoned courage to peep out, he could not help shuddering. It was terribly cheerless and desolate. And all the time, his father's words kept ringing ironically in his ears: "Iceland is the most beautiful land the sun doth shine upon." For the first time in his life he began to question whether his father might not possibly be mistaken, or, perhaps, blinded by his love for his country. But the boy immediately repented of this doubt, and, as if to convince himself in spite of everything, kept repeating the patriotic motto to himself until he fell asleep.

It was yet pitch dark in the room, when he was awakened by his father, who stood stooping over him.

"Sleep on, child," said Sigurd; "it was your brother I wanted to wake up, not you."

"What is the matter, Father? What has happened?" cried Jens, rising up in bed, and rubbing the ashes from the corners of his eyes.

"We are snowed up," said the father quietly. "It is already nine o'clock, I should judge, or thereabouts, but not a ray of light comes through the windows. I want Thoralf to help me open the door."

Thoralf was by this time awake, and finished his primitive toilet with much dispatch. The darkness, the damp cold, and the unopened window-shutters impressed him ominously. He felt as if some calamity had happened or were about to happen. Sigurd lighted a piece of driftwood and

stuck it into a crevice in the wall. The storm seemed to have ceased; a strange, tomb-like silence prevailed without and within. On the low hearth lay a small snowdrift which sparkled with a starlike glitter in the light.

"Bring the snow-shovels, Thoralf," said Sigurd. "Be quick; lose no time."

"They are in the shed outside," answered Thoralf.

"That is very unlucky," said the father; "now we shall have to use our fists."

The door opened outward, and it was only with the greatest difficulty that father and son succeeded in pushing it ajar. The storm had driven the snow with such force against it that their efforts seemed scarcely to make any impression upon the dense white wall which rose up before them.

"This is of no earthly use, Father," said the boy; "it is a day's job at the very least. Let me rather try the chimney."

"But you might stick in the snow and perish," objected the father anxiously.

"Weeds don't perish so easily," said Thoralf.

"Stand up on the hearth, Father, and I will climb up on your shoulders," urged the boy.

Sigurd half reluctantly complied with his son's request, who crawled up his father's back, and soon planted his feet on the paternal shoulders. He pulled his knitted woolen cap over his eyes and ears so as to protect them from the drizzling soot which descended in intermittent showers. Then, groping with his toes for a little projection of the wall, he gained a securer foothold, and, pushing boldly on, soon thrust his sooty head through the snow-crust. A chorus as of a thousand howling wolves burst upon his bewildered sense; the storm raged, shrieked, roared, and nearly swept him off his feet. Its biting breath smote his face like a sharp whip-lash.

"Give me my sheepskin coat," he cried

down into the cottage; "the wind chills me to the bone."

The sheepskin coat was handed to him on the end of a pole, and seated upon the edge of the chimney, he pulled it on and buttoned it securely. Then he rolled up the edges of his cap in front and cautiously exposed his eyes and the tip of his nose. It was not a pleasant experiment, but one dictated by necessity. As far as he could see, the world was white with snow, which the storm whirled madly around, and swept now earthward, now heavenward. Great funnel-shaped columns of snow danced up the hillsides and vanished against the black horizon. The prospect before the boy was by no means inviting, but he had been accustomed to battle with dangers since his earliest childhood, and he was not easily dismayed. With much deliberation, he climbed over the edge of the chimney, and rolled down the slope of the roof in the direction of the shed. He might have rolled a great deal farther, if he had not taken the precaution to roll against the wind. When he had made sure that he was in the right locality, he checked himself by spreading his legs and arms; then, judging by the outline of the snow where the door of the shed was, he crept along the edge of the roof on the leeward side. He looked more like a small polar bear than a boy, covered, as he was, with snow from head to foot. He was prepared for a laborious descent, and raising himself up he jumped with all his might, hoping that his weight would carry him a couple of feet down. To his utmost astonishment he accomplished considerably more. The snow yielded under his feet as if it had been eider-down, and he tumbled headlong into a white cave right at the entrance to the shed. The storm, while it had packed the snow on the windward side, had naturally scattered it very loosely on the leeward, which left a considerable space unfilled under the projecting eaves.

Thoralf picked himself up and entered the shed without difficulty. He made up a large bundle of peat, which he put into a basket which could be carried, by means of straps, upon the back. With a snow-shovel he then proceeded to dig a tunnel to the nearest window. This was not a very hard task, as the distance was not great. The window was opened and the basket of peat, a couple of shovels, and two pairs of skees* (to be used in case of emergency) were handed in. Thoralf himself, who was hungry as a wolf, made haste to avail himself of the same entrance. And it occurred to him as a happy afterthought that he might have saved himself much trouble if he had selected the window instead of the chimney, when he sallied forth on his expedition. He had erroneously taken it for granted that the snow would be packed as hard everywhere as it was at the front door. The mother, who had been spending this exciting half-hour in keeping little Jens warm, now lighted a fire and made coffee; and Thoralf needed no coaxing to do justice to his breakfast, even though it had, like everything else in Iceland, a flavor of salted fish.

III

FIVE days had passed, and still the storm raged with unabated fury. The access to the ocean was cut off, and, with that, access to food. Already the last handful of flour had been made into bread, and of the dried cod which hung in rows under the ceiling only one small and skinny specimen remained. The father and the mother sat with mournful faces at the hearth, the former reading in his hymn-book, the latter stroking the hair of her youngest boy. Thoralf, who was carving at his everlasting pipe-bowl (a corpulent and short-leg-

* Skees are a kind of snowshoe, four to six feet long, bent upward in front, with a band to attach it to the foot in the middle.

ged Turk with an enormous mustache),
looked up suddenly from his work and
glanced questioningly at his father.

"Father," he said abruptly, "how would
you like to starve to death?"

"God will preserve us from that, my
son," answered the father devoutly.

"Not unless we try to preserve ourselves," retorted the boy earnestly. "We
can't tell how long this storm is going to
last, and it is better for us to start out in
search of food now, while we are yet
strong, than to wait until later, when, as
likely as not, we shall be weakened by
hunger."

"But what would you have me do, Thoralf?" asked the father sadly. "To venture
out on the ocean in this weather would be
certain death."

"True; but we can reach the Pope's Nose
on our skees, and there we might snare or
shoot some auks and gulls. Though I am
not partial to that kind of diet myself, it is
always preferable to starvation."

"Wait, my son, wait," said Sigurd earnestly. "We have food enough for to-day,
and by tomorrow the storm will have
ceased, and we may go fishing without en-
dangering our lives."

' As you wish, Father," the son replied, a
trifle hurt at his father's unresponsive manner; "but if you will take a look out of the
chimney, you will find that it looks black
enough to storm for another week."

The father, instead of accepting this
suggestion, went quietly to his book-case,
took out a copy of Livy, in Latin, and sat
down to read. Occasionally he looked up a
word in the lexicon (which he had borrowed from the public library at
Reykjavik), but read nevertheless with apparent fluency and pleasure. Though he
was a fisherman, he was also a scholar, and
during the long winter evenings he had
taught himself Latin and even a smattering

of Greek.* In Iceland the people have to
spend their evenings at home; and especially since their millennial celebration in
1876, when American scholars † presented
the people with a large library, books are
their unfailing resource. In the case of Sigurd Sigurdson, however, books had become
a kind of dissipation, and he had to be
weaned gradually of his predilection for
Homer and Livy. His oldest son especially
looked upon Latin and Greek as a vicious
indulgence, which no man with a family
could afford to foster. Many a day when
Sigurd ought to have been out in his boat
casting his nets, he staid at home reading.
And this, in Thoralf's opinion, was the
chief reason why they would always remain poor and run the risk of starvation,
whenever a stretch of bad weather prevented them from going to sea.

The next morning—the sixth since the
breaking of the storm—Thoralf climbed up
to his post of observation on the chimney
top, and saw, to his dismay, that his prediction was correct. It had ceased snowing,
but the wind was blowing as fiercely as
ever, and the cold was intense.

"Will you follow me, Father, or will you
not?" he asked, when he had accomplished
his descent into the room. "Our last fish is
now eaten, and our last loaf of bread will
soon follow suit."

"I will go with you, my son," answered
Sigurd, putting down his Livy reluctantly.
He had just been reading for the hundredth
time about the expulsion of the Tarquins
from Rome, and his blood was aglow with
sympathy and enthusiasm.

* Lord Dufferin tells, in his *Letters from High
Latitudes,* how the Icelandic pilots conversed with
him in Latin, and other travelers have many similar tales to relate.
† Prof. Willard Fiske, of Cornell University, was
instrumental in collecting in the United States a
library of several thousand volumes, which he presented to the Icelanders on the one thousandth
birthday of their nation.

"Here is your coat, Sigurd," said his wife, holding up the great sheepskin garment, and assisting him in putting it on.

"And here are your skees and your mittens and your cap," cried Thoralf, eager to seize the moment when his father was in the mood for action.

Muffled up like Eskimos to their very eyes, armed with bows and arrows and long poles with nooses of horse-hair at the ends, they sallied forth on their skees. The wind blew straight into their faces, forcing their breaths down their throats and compelling them to tack in zigzag lines like ships in a gale. The promontory called "The Pope's Nose" was about a mile distant; but in spite of their knowledge of the land, they went twice astray, and had to lie down in the snow, every now and then, so as to draw breath and warm the exposed portions of their faces. At the end of nearly two hours, they found themselves at their destination, but to their unutterable astonishment, the ocean seemed to have vanished, and as far as their eyes could reach, a vast field of packed ice loomed up against the sky in fantastic bastions, turrets, and spires. The storm had driven down this enormous arctic wilderness from the frozen precincts of the pole; and now they were blockaded on all sides, and cut off from all intercourse with humanity.

"We are lost, Thoralf," muttered his father, after having gazed for some time in speechless despair at the towering icebergs; "we might just as well have remained at home."

"The wind, which has blown the ice down upon us, can blow it away again too," replied the son with forced cheerfulness.

"I see no living thing here," said Sigurd, spying anxiously seaward.

"Nor do I," rejoined Thoralf; "but if we hunt, we shall. I have brought a rope, and I am going to pay a little visit to those auks

and gulls that must be hiding in the sheltered nooks of the rocks."

"Are you mad, boy?" cried the father in alarm. "I will never permit it!"

"There is no help for it, Father," said the boy resolutely. "Here, you take hold of one end of the rope; the other I will secure about my waist. Now, get a good strong hold, and brace your feet against the rock there."

Sigurd, after some remonstrance, yielded, as was his wont, to his son's resolution and courage. Stepping off his skees, which he stuck endwise into the snow, and burrowing his feet down until they reached the solid rock, he tied the rope around his waist and twisted it about his hands and at last, with quaking heart, gave the signal for the perilous enterprise. The promontory, which rose abruptly to a height of two or three hundred feet from the sea, presented a jagged wall full of nooks and crevices glazed with frozen snow on the windward side, but black and partly bare to leeward.

"Now, let go!" shouted Thoralf; "and stop when I give a slight pull at the rope."

"All right," replied his father.

And slowly, slowly, hovering in mid-air, now yielding to an irresistible impulse of dread, now brave, cautious, and confident, Thoralf descended the cliff, which no human foot had ever trod before. He held in his hand the pole with the horse-hair noose, and over his shoulder hung a foxskin hunting-bag. With alert, wide-open eyes he spied about him, exploring every cranny of the rock, and thrusting his pole into the holes where he suspected the birds might have taken refuge. Sometimes a gust of wind would have flung him violently against the jagged wall if he had not, by means of his pole, warded off the collision. At last he caught sight of a bare ledge, where he might gain a secure foothold; for the rope cut him terribly about the waist, and made him anxious to relieve the strain, if only for a moment. He gave the signal to his father, and by the aid of his pole swung himself over to the projecting ledge. It was uncomfortably narrow, and, what was worse, the remnants of a dozen auk's nests had made the place extremely slippery. Nevertheless, he seated himself, allowing his feet to dangle, and gazed out upon the vast ocean, which looked in its icy grandeur like a forest of shining towers and minarets. It struck him for the first time in his life that perhaps his father was right in his belief that Iceland was the fairest land the sun doth shine upon; but he could not help reflecting that it was a very unprofitable kind of beauty. The storm whistled and howled overhead, but under the lee of the sheltering rock it blew only in fitful gusts with intermissions of comparative calm. He knew that in fair weather this was the haunt of innumerable seabirds, and he concluded that even now they could not be far away. He pulled up his legs, and crept carefully on hands and feet along the slippery ledge, peering intently into every nook and crevice. His eyes, which had been half-blinded by the glare of the snow, gradually recovered their power of vision. There! What was that? Something seemed to move on the ledge below. Yes, there sat a long row of auks, some erect as soldiers, as if determined to face it out; others huddled together in clusters, and comically woebegone. Quite a number lay dead at the base of the rock, whether from starvation or as the victims of fierce fights for the possession of the sheltered ledges could scarcely be determined. Thoralf, delighted at the sight of anything eatable (even though it was poor eating), gently lowered the end of his pole, slipped the noose about the neck of a large, military-looking fellow, and, with a quick pull, swung him out over

the ice-field. The auk gave a few ineffectual flaps with his useless wings,* and expired. His picking off apparently occasioned no comment whatever in his family, for his comrades never uttered a sound nor stirred an inch, except to take possession of the place he had vacated. Number two met his fate with the same listless resignation; and numbers three, four, and five were likewise removed in the same noiseless manner, without impressing their neighbors with the fact that their turn might come next. The birds were half-benumbed with hunger, and their usually alert senses were drowsy and stupefied. Nevertheless, number six, when it felt the noose about its neck, raised a hubbub that suddenly aroused the whole colony, and, with a chorus of wild screams, the birds flung themselves down the cliffs or, in their bewilderment, dashed headlong down upon the ice, where they lay half stunned or helplessly sprawling. So through all the caves and hiding-places of the promontory the commotion spread, and the noise of screams and confused chatter mingled with the storm and filled the vault of the sky. In an instant, a great flock of gulls was on the wing, and circled with resentful shrieks about the head of the daring intruder who had disturbed their wintry peace. The wind whirled them about, but they still held their own, and almost brushed with their wings against his face, while he struck out at them with his pole. He had no intention of catching them; but, by chance, a huge burgomaster gull † got its foot into the noose. It made an ineffectual attempt to disentangle itself, then, with piercing screams, flapped its great wings, beating the air

---

* The auk can not fly well, but uses its wings for swimming and diving.

† The burgomaster gull is the largest of all gulls. It is thirty inches long, exclusive of its tail, and its wings have a span of five feet.

desperately. Thoralf, having packed three birds into his hunting-bag, tied the three others together by the legs, and flung them across his shoulders. Then, gradually trusting his weight to the rope, he slid off the rock, and was about to give his father the signal to hoist him up. But, greatly to his astonishment, his living captive, by the power of its mighty wings, pulling at the end of the pole, swung him considerably farther into space than he had calculated. He would have liked to let go both the gull and the pole, but he perceived instantly that if he did, he would, by the mere force of his weight, be flung back against the rocky wall. He did not dare take that risk, as the blow might be hard enough to stun him. A strange, tingling sensation shot through his nerves, and the blood throbbed with a surging sound in his ears. There he hung suspended in mid-air, over a terrible precipice—and a hundred feet below was the jagged ice-field with its sharp, fiercely-shining steeples! With a powerful effort of will, he collected his senses, clenched his teeth and strove to think clearly. The gull whirled wildly eastward and westward, and he swayed with its every motion like a living pendulum between sea and sky. He began to grow dizzy, but again his powerful will came to his rescue, and he gazed resolutely up against the brow of the precipice and down upon the projecting ledges below, in order to accustom his eye and his mind to the sight. By a strong effort he succeeded in giving a pull at the rope, and expected to feel himself raised upward by his father's strong arms. But to his amazement, there came no response to his signal. He repeated it once, twice, thrice; there was a slight tugging at the rope, but no upward movement. Then the brave lad's heart stood still, and his courage well-nigh failed him.

"Father!" he cried, with a hoarse voice of despair; "why don't you pull me up?"

His cry was lost in the roar of the wind, and there came no answer. Taking hold once more of the rope with one hand, he considered the possibility of climbing; but the miserable gull, seeming every moment to redouble its efforts at escape, deprived him of the use of his hands unless he chose to dash out his brains by collision with the rock. Something like a husky, choked scream seemed to float down from above, and staring again upward, he saw his father's head projecting over the brink of the precipice.

"The rope will break," screamed Sigurd. "I have tied it to the rock."

Thoralf instantly took in the situation. By the swinging motion, occasioned both by the wind and his fight with the gull, the rope had become frayed against the sharp edge of the cliff, and his chances of life, he coolly concluded, were now not worth a sixpence. Curiously enough, his agitation suddenly left him, and a great calm came over him. He seemed to stand face to face with eternity; and as nothing else that he could do was of any avail, he could at least steel his heart to meet death like a man and an Icelander.

"I am trying to get hold of the rope below the place where it is frayed," he heard his father shout during a momentary lull in the storm.

"Don't try," answered the boy; "you can't do it, alone. Rather, let me down on the lower ledge, and let me sit there until you can go and get some one to help you."

His father, accustomed to take his son's advice, reluctantly lowered him ten or twenty feet until he was on a level with the shelving ledge below, which was broader than the one upon which he had first gained foothold. But—oh, the misery of it! —the ledge did not project far enough! He could not reach it with his feet! The rope, of which only a few strands remained, might break at any moment and—he dared not think what would be the result! He had scarcely had time to consider, when a brilliant device shot through his brain. With a sudden thrust he flung away the pole, and the impetus of his weight sent him inward with such force that he landed securely upon the broad shelf of rock.

The gull, surprised by the sudden weight of the pole, made a somersault, strove to rise again, and tumbled, with the pole still depending from its leg, down upon the ice-field.

It was well that Thoralf was warmly clad, or he could never have endured the terrible hours while he sat through the long afternoon, hearing the moaning and shrieking of the wind and seeing the darkness close about him. The storm was chilling him with its fierce breath. One of the birds he tied about his throat as a sort of scarf, using the feet and neck for making the knot, and the dense, downy feathers sent a glow of comfort through him, in spite of his consciousness that every hour might be his last. If he could only keep awake through the night, the chances were that he would survive to greet the morning. He hit upon an ingenious plan for accomplishing this purpose. He opened the bill of the auk which warmed his neck, cut off the lower mandible, and placed the upper one (which was as sharp as a knife) so that it would inevitably cut his chin in case he should nod. He leaned against the rock and thought of his mother and the warm, comfortable chimney-corner at home. The wind probably resented this thought, for it suddenly sent a biting gust right into Thoralf's face, and he buried his nose in the downy breast

of the auks until the pain had subsided. The darkness had now settled upon sea and land; only here and there white steeples loomed out of the gloom. Thoralf, simply to occupy his thought, began to count them. But all of a sudden one of the steeples seemed to move, then another—and another.

The boy feared that the long strain of excitement was depriving him of his reason. The wind, too, after a few wild arctic howls, acquired a warmer breath and a gentler sound. It could not be possible that he was dreaming. For in that case he would soon be dead. Perhaps he was dead already, and was drifting through this strange icy vista to a better world. All these imaginings flitted through his mind, and were again dismissed as improbable. He scratched his face with the foot of an auk in order to convince himself that he was really awake. Yes, there could be no doubt of it; he was wide awake. Accordingly he once more fixed his eyes upon the ghostly steeples and towers, and—it sent cold shudders down his back—they were still moving. Then there came a fusilade as of heavy artillery, followed by a salvo of lighter musketry; then came a fierce grinding, and cracking, and creaking sound, as if the whole ocean were of glass and were breaking to pieces. "What," thought Thoralf, "if the ice is breaking to pieces!" In an instant, the explanation of the whole spectral panorama was clear as the day. The wind had veered round to the southeast, and the whole enormous ice-floe was being driven out to sea. For several hours—he could not tell how many—he sat watching this superb spectacle by the pale light of the aurora borealis, which toward midnight began to flicker across the sky and illuminated the northern horizon. He found the sight so interesting that for a while he forgot to be sleepy. But toward morning, when the aurora began to fade and the clouds to cover the east, a terrible weariness was irresistibly stealing over him. He could see glimpses of the black water beneath him: the shining spires of ice were vanishing in the dusk, drifting rapidly away upon the arctic currents with death and disaster to ships and crews that might happen to cross their paths.

It was terrible at what a snail's pace the hours crept along! It seemed to Thoralf as if a week had passed since his father left him. He pinched himself in order to keep awake, but it was of no use; his eyelids would slowly droop and his head would incline—horrors! what was that? Oh, he had forgotten; it was the sharp mandible of the auk that cut his chin. He put his hand up to it, and felt something warm and clammy on his fingers. He was bleeding. It took Thoralf several minutes to stay the blood—the wound was deeper than he had bargained for; but it occupied him and kept him awake, which was of vital importance.

At last, after a long and desperate struggle with drowsiness, he saw the dawn break faintly in the east. It was a mere feeble promise of light, a remote suggestion that there was such a thing as day. But to the boy, worn out by the terrible strain of death and danger staring him in the face, it was a glorious assurance that rescue was at hand. The tears came into his eyes—not tears of weakness, but tears of gratitude that the terrible trial had been endured. Gradually the light spread like a pale, grayish veil over the eastern sky, and the ocean caught faint reflections of the presence of the unseen sun. The wind was mild, and thousands of birds that had been imprisoned by the ice in the crevices of the rocks whirled triumphantly into the air and plunged with wild screams into the tide below. It was hard to imagine where they all had been, for the air seemed alive with them, the cliffs teemed with them; and they

fought, and shrieked, and chattered, like a howling mob in times of famine. It was owing to this unearthly tumult that Thoralf did not hear the voice which called to him from the top of the cliff. His senses were half-dazed by the noise and by the sudden relief from the excitement of the night. Then there came two voices floating down to him—then quite a chorus. He tried to look up, but the beetling brow of the rock prevented him from seeing anything but a stout rope, which was dangling in mid-air and slowly approaching him. With all the power of his lungs he responded to the call; and there came a wild cheer from above—a cheer full of triumph and joy. He recognized the voices of Hunding's sons, who lived on the other side of the promontory; and he knew that even without their father they were strong enough to pull up a man three times his weight. The difficulty now was only to get hold of the rope, which hung too far out for his hands to reach it.

"Shake the rope hard," he called up; and immediately the rope was shaken into serpentine undulations; and after a few vain efforts, he succeeded in catching hold of the knot. To secure the rope about his waist and to give the signal for the ascent was but a moment's work. They hauled vigorously, those sons of Hunding—for he rose, up, along the black walls—up—up—up —with no uncertain motion. At last, when he was at the very brink of the precipice, he saw his father's pale and anxious face leaning out over the abyss. But there was another face too! Whose could it be? It was a woman's face. It was his mother's. Somebody swung him out into space; a strange, delicious dizziness came over him; his eyes were blinded with tears; he did not know where he was. He only knew that he was inexpressibly happy. There came a tremendous cheer from somewhere—for Icelanders know how to cheer—but it penetrated but faintly through his bewildered senses. Something cold touched his forehead; it seemed to be snow; then warm drops fell, which were tears. He opened his eyes; he was in his mother's arms. Little Jens was crying over him and kissing him. His father and Hunding's sons were standing with folded arms, gazing joyously at him.

The little toy dog so covered with dust
But sturdy and staunch he stands,
And the little toy soldier is red with rust
And his musket molds in his hands
Time was when the little toy dog was new,
And the soldier was passing fair;
That was the time when our Little Boy Blue
Kissed them and put them there.

"Now don't you go 'til I come," he said
"And don't you make any noise"—
So, toddling off to his trundle bed,
He dreamt of the pretty toys.
And, as he was dreaming, an angel song
Awakened our Little Boy Blue—
Oh, the years are many, the years are long,
But the little toy friends are true!

Aye, faithful to Little Boy Blue, they stand,
Each in the same old place —
Awaiting the touch of a little hand,
The smile of a little face.
And they wonder — as waiting the long years thro'
In the dust of that little chair —
What has become of our Little Boy Blue,
Since he kissed them and put them there.

FROM THE ORIGINAL ENGROSSED COPY MADE BY EUGENE FIELD.
ORIGINAL OWNED BY MRS. A. C. BALLANTYNE, CHICAGO.

Eugene Field

BABY SYLVESTER
By Bret Harte

July, 1874

It was at a little mining camp in the California Sierras that he first dawned upon me in all his grotesque sweetness.

I had arrived early in the morning, but not in time to intercept the friend who was the object of my visit. He had gone "prospecting"—so they told me on the river—and would not probably return until late in the afternoon. They could not say what direction he had taken; they could not suggest that I would be likely to find him if I followed. But it was the general opinion that I had better wait.

I looked around me. I was standing upon the bank of the river; and, apparently, the only other human beings in the world were my interlocutors, who were even then just disappearing from my horizon down the steep bank toward the river's dry bed. I approached the edge of the bank.

Where could I wait?

O, anywhere; down with them on the river-bar, where they were working, if I liked! Or I could make myself at home in any of those cabins that I found lying round loose. Or, perhaps it would be cooler and pleasanter for me in my friend's cabin on the hill. Did I see those three large sugarpines? And, a little to the right, a canvas roof and chimney over the bushes? Well, that was my friend's—that was Dick Sylvester's cabin. I could stake my horse in that little hollow, and just hang round there

till he came. I would find some books in the shanty; I could amuse myself with them. Or I could play with the baby.

Do what?

But they had already gone. I leaned over the bank and called after their vanishing figures:

"What did you say I could do?"

The answer floated slowly up on the hot, sluggish air:

"Pla-a-y with the ba-by."

The lazy echoes took it up and tossed it languidly from hill to hill, until Bald Mountain opposite made some incoherent remark about the baby, and then all was still.

I must have been mistaken. My friend was not a man of family; there was not a woman within forty miles of the river camp; he never was so passionately devoted to children as to import a luxury so expensive. I must have been mistaken.

I turned my horse's head toward the hill. As we slowly climbed the narrow trail, the little settlement might have been some exhumed Pompeian suburb, so deserted and silent were its habitations. The open doors plainly disclosed each rudely-furnished interior—the rough pine table, with the scant equipage of the morning meal still standing; the wooden bunk, with its tumbled and disheveled blankets. A golden lizard—the very genius of desolate stillness—had stopped breathless upon the threshold of one cabin; a squirrel peeped impudently into the window of another; a woodpecker, with the general flavor of undertaking which distinguishes that bird, withheld his sepulchral hammer from the coffin-lid of the roof on which he was professionally engaged, as we passed. For a moment, I half-regretted that I had not accepted the invitation to the river-bed; but, the next moment, a breeze swept up the long, dark cañon, and the waiting files of the pines beyond bent toward me in salutation. I think my horse understood as well as myself that it was the cabins that made the solitude human, and therefore unbearable, for he quickened his pace, and with a gentle trot brought me to the edge of the wood and the three pines that stood like videttes before the Sylvester outpost.

Unsaddling my horse in the little hollow, I unslung the long *riata* from the saddle-bow, and tethering him to a young sapling, turned toward the cabin. But I had gone only a few steps when I heard a quick trot behind me, and poor Pomposo, with every fibre tingling with fear, was at my heels. I looked hurriedly around. The breeze had died away, and only an occasional breath from the deep-chested woods, more like a long sigh than any articulate sound, or the dry singing of a cicada in the heated cañon, were to be heard. I examined the ground carefully for rattlesnakes, but in vain. Yet here was Pomposo shivering from his arched neck to his sensitive haunches, his very flanks pulsating with terror. I soothed him as well as I could, and then walked to the edge of the wood and peered into its dark recesses. The bright flash of a bird's wing, or the quick dart of a squirrel, was all I saw. I confess it was with something of superstitious expectation that I again turned toward the cabin. A fairy child, attended by Titania and her train, lying in an expensive cradle, would not have surprised me; a Sleeping Beauty, whose awakening would have repeopled these solitudes with life and energy, I am afraid I began to confidently look for, and would have kissed without hesitation.

But I found none of these. Here was the evidence of my friend's taste and refinement in the hearth swept scrupulously clean, in the picturesque arrangement of the fur skins that covered the floor and furniture, and the striped *serápe** lying on the wooden couch. Here were the walls fancifully papered with illustrations from the *London News;* here was the wood-cut portrait of Mr. Emerson over the chimney, quaintly framed with blue jays' wings; here were his few favorite books on the swinging shelf; and here, lying upon the couch, the latest copy of *Punch.* Dear Dick! The floursack was sometimes empty, but the gentle satirist seldom missed his weekly visit.

I threw myself on the couch and tried to read. But I soon exhausted my interest in my friend's library, and lay there staring through the open door on the green hillside beyond. The breeze again sprang up, and a delicious coolness, mixed with the rare incense of the woods, stole through the cabin. The slumbrous droning of bumble-bees outside the canvas roof, the faint cawing of rooks on the opposite mountain, and the fatigue of my morning ride, began to droop my eyelids. I pulled the *serápe* over me, as a precaution against the freshening mountain breeze, and in a few moments was asleep.

I do not remember how long I slept. I must have been conscious, however, during my slumber, of my inability to keep myself covered by the *serápe*, for I awoke once or twice, clutching it with a despairing hand as it was disappearing over the foot of the couch. Then I became suddenly aroused to the fact that my efforts to retain it were resisted by some equally persistent force, and, letting it go, I was horrified at seeing it swiftly drawn under the couch. At this point I sat up completely awake; for

* A fine Mexican blanket, used as an outer garment for riding.

immediately after, what seemed to be an exaggerated muff began to emerge from under the couch. Presently it appeared fully, dragging the *serápe* after it. There was no mistaking it now—it was a baby bear. A mere suckling, it was true—a helpless roll of fat and fur—but, unmistakably, a grizzly cub.

I cannot recall anything more irresistibly ludicrous than its aspect as it slowly raised its small wondering eyes to mine. It was so much taller on its haunches than its shoulders—its fore-legs were so disproportionately small—that in walking, its hind-feet invariably took precedence. It was perpetually pitching forward over its pointed, inoffensive nose, and recovering itself always, after these involuntary somersaults, with the gravest astonishment. To add to its preposterous appearance, one of its hind-feet was adorned by a shoe of Sylvester's, into which it had accidentally and inextricably stepped. As this somewhat impeded its first impulse to fly, it turned to me; and then, possibly recognizing in the stranger the same species as its master, it paused. Presently, it slowly raised itself on its hind-legs, and vaguely and deprecatingly waved a baby paw, fringed with little hooks of steel. I took the paw and shook it gravely. From that moment we were friends. The little affair of the *serápe* was forgotten.

Nevertheless, I was wise enough to cement our friendship by an act of delicate courtesy. Following the direction of his eyes, I had no difficulty in finding, on a shelf near the ridge-pole, the sugarbox and the square lumps of white sugar that even the poorest miner is never without. While he was eating them I had time to examine him more closely. His body was a silky, dark, but exquisitely modulated grey, deepening to black in his paws and muzzle. His fur was excessively long, thick, and soft as eider down; the cushions of flesh beneath,

perfectly infantine in their texture and contour. He was so very young that the palms of his half-human feet were still tender as a baby's. Except for the bright blue, steely hooks, half-sheathed in his little toes, there was not a single harsh outline or detail in his plump figure. He was as free from angles as one of Leda's offspring. Your caressing hand sank away in his fur with dreamy languor. To look at him long was an intoxication of the senses; to pat him was a wild delirium; to embrace him, an utter demoralization of the intellectual faculties.

When he had finished the sugar, he rolled out of the door with a half-diffident, half-inviting look in his eye, as if he expected me to follow. I did so, but the sniffing and snorting of the keen-scented Pomposo in the hollow, not only revealed the cause of his former terror, but decided me to take another direction. After a moment's hesitation, he concluded to go with me, although I am satisfied, from a certain impish look in his eye, that he fully understood and rather enjoyed the fright of Pomposo. As he rolled along at my side, with a gait not unlike a drunken sailor, I discovered that his long hair concealed a leather collar around his neck, which bore for its legend the single word, "Baby!" I recalled the mysterious suggestion of the two miners. This, then, was the "baby" with whom I was to "play."

How we "played"; how Baby allowed me to roll him down hill, crawling and puffing up again each time, with perfect good humor; how he climbed a young sapling after my Panama hat, which I had "shied" into one of the topmost branches; how after getting it he refused to descend until it suited his pleasure; how when he did come down he persisted in walking about on three legs, carrying my hat, a crushed and shapeless mass, clasped to his breast with the remaining one; how I missed him at last, and finally discovered him seated on a table in one of the tenant-less cabins, with a bottle of syrup between his paws, vainly endeavoring to extract its contents—these and other details of that eventful day I shall not weary the reader with now. Enough that when Dick Sylvester returned, I was pretty well fagged out, and the baby was rolled up, an immense bolster at the foot of the couch, asleep. Sylvester's first words after our greeting were:

"Isn't he delicious?"

"Perfectly. Where did you get him?"

"Lying under his dead mother, five miles from here," said Dick, lighting his pipe. "Knocked her over at fifty yards; perfectly clean shot—never moved afterwards! Baby crawled out, scared but unhurt. She must have been carrying him in her mouth, and dropped him when she faced me, for he wasn't more than three days old, and not steady on his pins. He takes the only milk that comes to the settlement—brought up by Adams Express at seven o'clock every morning. They say he looks like me. Do you think so?" asked Dick, with perfect gravity, stroking his hay-colored moustachios, and evidently assuming his best expression.

I took leave of the baby early the next morning in Sylvester's cabin, and out of respect to Pomposo's feelings, rode by without any postscript of expression. But the night before I had made Sylvester solemnly swear, that in the event of any separation between himself and Baby, it should revert to me. "At the same time," he had added, "it's only fair to say that I don't think of dying just yet, old fellow, and I don't know of anything else that would part the cub and me."

Two months after this conversation, as I was turning over the morning's mail at my office in San Francisco, I noticed a letter bearing Sylvester's familiar hand. But it was post-marked "Stockton," and I opened it with some anxiety at once. Its contents were as follows:

O FRANK!—Don't you remember what we agreed upon anent the baby? Well, consider me as dead for the next six months, or gone where cubs can't follow me—East. I know you love the baby; but do you think, dear boy—now, really, do you think you *could* be a father to it? Consider this well. You are young, thoughtless, well-meaning enough; but dare you take upon yourself the functions of guide, genius or guardian to one so young and guileless? Could you be the mentor to this Telemachus? Think of the temptations of a metropolis. Look at the question well, and let me know speedily, for I've got him as far as this place, and he's kicking up an awful row in the hotel-yard, and rattling his chain like a maniac. Let me know by telegraph at once.

P.S.—Of course he's grown a little, and doesn't take things always as quietly as he did. He dropped rather heavily on two of Watson's "purps" last week, and snatched old Watson himself, bald-headed, for interfering. You remember Watson: for an intelligent man, he knows very little of California fauna. How are you fixed for bears on Montgomery Street—I mean in regard to corrals and things?

P.P.S.—He's got some new tricks. The boys have been teaching him to put up his hands with them. He slings an ugly left.—S.

I am afraid that my desire to possess myself of Baby overcame all other considerations, and I telegraphed an affirmative at once to Sylvester. When I reached my lodgings late that afternoon, my landlady was awaiting me with a telegram. It was two lines from Sylvester:

ALL RIGHT. BABY GOES DOWN ON NIGHT-BOAT. BE A FATHER TO HIM.—S.

It was due, then, at one o'clock that night. For a moment I was staggered at my own precipitation. I had as yet made no preparations—had said nothing to my land-lady about her new guest. I expected to arrange everything in time; and now, through Sylvester's indecent haste, that time had been shortened twelve hours.

Something, however, must be done at once. I turned to Mrs. Brown. I had great reliance in her maternal instincts; I had that still greater reliance, common to our sex, in the general tender-heartedness of pretty women. But I confess I was alarmed. Yet, with a feeble smile, I tried to introduce the subject with classical ease and lightness. I even said, "If Shakespeare's Athenian clown, Mrs. Brown, believed that a lion among ladies was a dreadful thing, what must—" But here I broke down, for Mrs. Brown, with the awful intuition of her sex, I saw at once was more occupied with my manner than my speech. So I tried a busi-ness *brusquerie*, and, placing the telegram in her hand, said hurriedly, "We must do something about this at once. It's perfectly absurd, but he will be here at one to-night. Beg thousand pardons, but business pre-vented my speaking before—" and paused, out of breath and courage.

Mrs. Brown read the telegram gravely, lifted her pretty eyebrows, turned the paper over and looked on the other side, and then, in a remote and chilling voice, asked me if she understood me to say that the mother was coming also.

"O dear no," I exclaimed, with con-siderable relief; "the mother is dead, you know. Sylvester—that is my friend, who

sent this—shot her when the Baby was only three days old—" But the expression of Mrs. Brown's face at this moment was so alarming, that I saw that nothing but the fullest explanation would save me. Hastily, and I fear not very coherently, I told her all.

She relaxed sweetly. She said I had frightened her with my talk about lions. In-deed, I think my picture of poor Baby—albeit a trifle highly-colored—touched her motherly heart. She was even a little vexed at what she called Sylvester's "hard-heartedness." Still, I was not without some apprehension. It was two months since I had seen him, and Sylvester's vague allusion to his "slinging an ugly left" pained me. I looked at sympathetic little Mrs. Brown, and the thought of Watson's pups covered me with guilty confusion.

Mrs. Brown had agreed to sit up with me until he arrived. One o'clock came, but no Baby. Two o'clock—three o'clock passed. It was almost four when there was a wild clatter of horses' hoofs outside, and with a jerk a wagon stopped at the door. In an in-stant I had opened it and confronted a stranger. Almost at the same moment, the horses attempted to run away with the wagon.

The stranger's appearance was, to say the least, disconcerting. His clothes were badly torn and frayed; his linen sack hung from his shoulders like a herald's apron; one of his hands was bandaged; his face scratched, and there was no hat on his disheveled head. To add to the general effect, he had evidently sought relief from his woes in drink, and he swayed from side to side as he clung to the door-handle; and, in a very thick voice, stated that he had "suthin" for me outside. When he had finished, the horses made another plunge.

Mrs. Brown thought they must be fright-ened at something.

"Frightened!" laughed the stranger, with bitter irony. "Oh no! Hossish ain't frightened! On'y ran away four timesh comin' here. Oh no! Nobody's frightened. Everythin's all ri'. Ain't it, Bill?" he said, addressing the driver. "On'y been overboard twish; knocked down a hatchway once. Thash nothin'! On'y two men unner doctor's han's at Stockton. Thash nothin'! Six hunner dollarsh cover all dammish."

I was too much disheartened to reply, but moved toward the wagon. The stranger eyed me with an astonishment that almost sobered him.

"Do you reckon to tackle that animile yourself?" he asked, as he surveyed me from head to foot.

I did not speak, but, with an appearance of boldness I was far from feeling, walked to the wagon and called "Baby!"

"All ri'. Cash loose them straps, Bill, and stan' clear."

The straps were cut loose, and Baby—the remorseless, the terrible—quietly tumbled to the ground, and rolling to my side, rubbed his foolish head against me.

I think the astonishment of the two men was beyond any vocal expression. Without a word the drunken stranger got into the wagon and drove away.

And Baby? He had grown, it is true, some larger; but he was thin, and bore the marks of evident ill-usage. His beautiful coat was matted and unkempt, and his claws—those bright steel hooks—had been ruthlessly pared to the quick. His eyes were furtive and restless, and the old expression of stupid good humor had changed to one of intelligent distrust. His intercourse with mankind had evidently quickened his intellect without broadening his moral nature.

I had great difficulty in keeping Mrs. Brown from smothering him in blankets and ruining his digestion with the delicacies of her larder; but I at last got him completely rolled up in the corner of my room and asleep. I lay awake some time later with plans for his future. I finally determined to take him to Oakland, where I had built a little cottage and always spent my Sundays, the very next day. And in the midst of a rosy picture of domestic felicity, I fell asleep.

When I awoke it was broad day. My eyes at once sought the corner where Baby had been lying. But he was gone. I sprang from the bed, looked under it, searched the closet, but in vain. The door was still locked; but there were the marks of his claws upon the sill of the window, that I had forgotten to close. He had evidently escaped that way—but where? The window opened upon a balcony, to which the only other entrance was through the hall. He must be still in the house.

My hand was already upon the bell-rope, but I stayed it in time. If he had not made himself known, why should I disturb the house? I dressed myself hurriedly, and slipped into the hall. The first object that met my eyes was a boot lying upon the stairs. It bore the marks of Baby's teeth; and as I looked along the hall, I saw too plainly that the usual array of freshly-blackened boots and shoes before the lodgers' doors was not there. As I ascended the stairs I found another, but with the blacking carefully licked off. On the third floor were two or three more boots, slightly mouthed; but at this point Baby's taste for blacking had evidently palled. A little further on was a ladder, leading to an open scuttle. I mounted the ladder, and reached the flat roof, that formed a continuous level over the row of houses to the corner of the street. Behind the chimney on the very last roof something was lurking. It was the fugitive Baby. He was covered with dust and dirt and fragments of glass. But he was sitting on his hind-legs, and was eating an enormous slab of pea-nut candy, with a look of mingled guilt and infinite satisfaction. He even, I fancied, slightly stroked his stomach with his disengaged fore-paw, as I approached. He knew that I was looking for him, and the expression of his eye said plainly, "The past, at least, is secure."

I hurried him, with the evidences of his guilt, back to the scuttle, and descended on tip-toe to the floor beneath. Providence favored us; I met no one on the stairs, and his own cushioned tread was inaudible. I think he was conscious of the dangers of detection, for he even forebore to breathe, or much less chew the last mouthful he had taken; and he skulked at my side, with the syrup dropping from his motionless jaws. I think he would have silently choked to death just then, for my sake: and it was not until I had reached my room again, and threw myself panting on the sofa, that I saw how near strangulation he had been. He gulped once or twice, apologetically, and then walked to the corner of his own accord, and rolled himself up like an immense sugar-plum, sweating remorse and treacle at every pore.

I locked him in when I went to breakfast, when I found Mrs. Brown's lodgers in a state of intense excitement over certain mysterious events of the night before, and the dreadful revelations of the morning. It appeared that burglars had entered the block from the scuttles; that being suddenly alarmed, they had quitted our house without committing any depredation, dropping even the boots they had collected in the halls; but that a desperate attempt had been made to force the till in the confectioner's shop on the corner, and that the glass show-cases had been ruthlessly smashed. A courageous servant in No. 4 had seen a masked burglar, on his hands and knees, attempting to enter their scuttle; but

on her shouting, "Away wid yees," he instantly fled.

I sat through this recital with cheeks that burned uncomfortably; nor was I the less embarrassed on raising my eyes to meet Mrs. Brown's fixed curiously and mischievously on mine. As soon as I could make my escape from the table, I did so; and running rapidly up stairs, sought refuge from any possible inquiry in my own room. Baby was still asleep in the corner. It would not be safe to remove him until the lodgers had gone down town; and I was revolving in my mind the expediency of keeping him until night veiled his obtrusive eccentricity from the public eye, when there came a cautious tap at my door. I opened it. Mrs. Brown slipped in quietly, closed the door softly, stood with her back against it and her hand on the knob, and beckoned me mysteriously towards her. Then she asked, in a low voice:

"Is hair-dye poisonous?"

I was too confounded to speak.

"O do! you know what I mean," she said, impatiently. "This stuff." She produced suddenly from behind her a bottle with a Greek label—so long as to run two or three times spirally around it from top to bottom. "He says it isn't a dye; it's a vegetable preparation, for invigorating—"

"Who says?" I asked, despairingly.

"Why, Mr. Parker, of course," said Mrs. Brown, severely, with the air of having repeated the name a great many times—"the old gentleman in the room above. The simple question I want to ask," she continued, with the calm manner of one who has just convicted another of gross ambiguity of language, "is only this: If some of this stuff were put in a saucer and left carelessly on the table, and a child or a baby or a cat, or any young animal, should come in at the window and drink it up—a whole saucer full—because it had a sweet taste, would it be likely to hurt them?"

I cast an anxious glance at Baby, sleeping peacefully in the corner, and a very grateful one at Mrs. Brown, and said I didn't think it would.

"Because," said Mrs. Brown, loftily, as she opened the door, "I thought if it was poisonous, remedies might be used in time. Because," she added suddenly, abandoning her lofty manner and wildly rushing to the corner, with a frantic embrace of the unconscious Baby, "because if any nasty stuff should turn its boofull hair a horrid green or a naughty pink, it would break its own muzzer's heart, it would!"

But before I could assure Mrs. Brown of the inefficiency of hair-dye as an internal application, she had darted from the room.

That night, with the secrecy of defaulters, Baby and I decamped from Mrs. Brown's. Distrusting the too emotional nature of that noble animal, the horse, I had recourse to a hand-cart, drawn by a stout Irishman, to convey my charge to the ferry. Even then, Baby refused to go unless I walked by the cart, and at times rode in it.

"I wish," said Mrs. Brown, as she stood by the door wrapped in an immense shawl, and saw us depart, "I wish it looked less solemn—less like a pauper's funeral."

I must admit, that as I walked by the cart that night, I felt very much as if I were accompanying the remains of some humble friend to his last resting-place; and that, when I was obliged to ride in it, I never could entirely convince myself that I was not helplessly overcome by liquor, or the victim of an accident, *en route* to the hospital. But, at last, we reached the ferry. On the boat I think no one discovered Baby except a drunken man, who approached me to ask for a light for his cigar, but who suddenly dropped it and fled in dismay to the gentlemen's cabin, where his incoherent ravings were luckily taken for the earlier indications of *delirium tremens*.

It was nearly midnight when I reached my little cottage on the outskirts of Oakland; and it was with a feeling of relief and security that I entered, locked the door, and turned him loose in the hall, satisfied that henceforward his depredations would be limited to my own property. He was very quiet that night, and after he had tried to mount the hat-rack, under the mistaken impression that it was intended for his own gymnastic exercise, and knocked all the hats off, he went peaceably to sleep on the rug.

In a week, with the exercise afforded him by the run of a large, carefully-boarded enclosure, he recovered his health, strength, spirits, and much of his former beauty. His presence was unknown to my neighbors, although it was noticeable that horses invariably "shied" in passing to the windward of my house, and that the baker and milkman had great difficulty in the delivery of their wares in the morning, and indulged in unseemly and unnecessary profanity in so doing.

At the end of the week, I determined to invite a few friends to see the Baby, and to that purpose wrote a number of formal invitations. After descanting, at some length, on the great expense and danger attending his capture and training, I offered a programme of the performances of the "Infant Phenomenon of Sierran Solitudes," drawn up into the highest professional profusion of alliteration and capital letters. A few extracts will give the reader some idea of his educational progress:

1. He will, rolled up in a Round Ball, roll down the Wood Shed, Rapidly, illustrating His manner of Escaping from His Enemy in His Native Wilds.

2. He will Ascend the Well Pole, and remove from the Very Top a Hat, and as much of the Crown and Brim thereof as May be Permitted.
3. He will perform in a pantomine, descriptive of the Conduct of the Big Bear, The Middle-Sized Bear, and The Little Bear of the Popular Nursery Legend.
4. He will shake his chain Rapidly, showing his Manner of striking Dismay and Terror in the Breasts of Wanderers in Ursine Wildernesses.

The morning of the exhibition came, but an hour before the performance the wretched Baby was missing. The Chinese cook could not indicate his whereabouts. I searched the premises thoroughly, and then, in despair, took my hat and hurried out into the narrow lane that led toward the open fields and the woods beyond. But I found no trace nor track of Baby Sylvester. I returned, after an hour's fruitless search, to find my guests already assembled on the rear verandah. I briefly recounted my disappointment, my probable loss, and begged their assistance.

"Why," said a Spanish friend, who prided himself on his accurate knowledge of English, to Barker, who seemed to be trying vainly to rise from his reclining position on the verandah, "Why do you disengage yourself from the verandah of our friend? and why, in the name of Heaven, do you attach to yourself so much of this thing, and make to yourself such unnecessary contortion? Ah," he continued, suddenly withdrawing one of his own feet from the verandah with an evident effort, "I am myself attached! Surely it is something here!"

It evidently was. My guests were all rising with difficulty—the floor of the verandah was covered with some glutinous substance. It was—syrup!

I saw it all in a flash. I ran to the barn; the keg of "golden syrup," purchased only the day before, lay empty upon the floor. There were sticky tracks all over the enclosure, but still no Baby.

"There's something moving the ground over there by that pile of dirt," said Barker.

He was right; the earth was shaking in one corner of the enclosure like an earthquake. I approached cautiously. I saw, what I had not before noticed, that the ground was thrown up; and there, in the middle of an immense grave-like cavity, crouched Baby Sylvester, still digging, and slowly, but surely, sinking from sight in a mass of dust and clay.

What were his intentions? Whether he was stung by remorse, and wished to hide himself from my reproachful eyes, or whether he was simply trying to dry his syrup-besmeared coat, I never shall know, for that day, alas! was his last with me.

He was pumped upon for two hours, at the end of which time he still yielded a thin treacle. He was then taken and carefully enwrapped in blankets and locked up in the store-room. The next morning he was gone! The lower portion of the window sash and pane were gone too. His successful experiments on the fragile texture of glass at the confectioner's, on the first day of his entrance to civilization, had not been lost upon him. His first essay at combining cause and effect ended in his escape.

Where he went, where he hid, who captured him if he did not succeed in reaching the foot-hills beyond Oakland, even the offer of a large reward, backed by the efforts of an intelligent police, could not discover. I never saw him again from that day until—

Did I see him? I was in a horse-car on Sixth Avenue, a few days ago, when the horses suddenly became unmanageable and left the track for the sidewalk, amid the oaths and execrations of the driver. Immediately in front of the car a crowd had gathered around two performing bears and a showman. One of the animals—thin, emaciated, and the mere wreck of his native strength—attracted my attention. I endeavored to attract his. He turned a pair of bleared, sightless eyes in my direction, but there was no sign of recognition. I leaned from the car-window and called, softly, "Baby!" But he did not heed. I closed the window. The car was just moving on, when he suddenly turned, and, either by accident or design, thrust a callous paw through the glass.

"It's worth a dollar-and-half to put in a new pane," said the conductor, "if folks will play with bears!—"

GREEDY
By Sydney Dayre

February, 1890

A GREEDY fellow? I should say!
They passed the apples round this way
And then he snatched—he couldn't wait—
The biggest one upon the plate.

Such greediness I do despise!
I had been keeping both my eyes
Upon that apple, for, you see,
The plate was coming, next, to me.

'T was big and mellow, just the kind
A greedy chap would like to find.
He laughed as if he thought it fun—
I meant to take that very one.

THE BOYS OF MY BOYHOOD

By William Cullen Bryant

December, 1876

THE conductor of ST. NICHOLAS has asked me for a talk with the boys who read this magazine. If she had not at the same time suggested a subject, I am pretty sure that I should not have complied with the request; but when she mentioned "The Boys of My Boyhood," there was something in the words which carried my mind back to the early years of my life, and made me think that I might be able to hold the attention of the readers of the ST. NICHOLAS for a little while in discoursing of those who began life with me.

The boys of the generation to which I belonged—that is to say, who were born in the last years of the last century or the earliest of this—were brought up under a system of discipline which put a far greater distance between parents and their children than now exists. The parents seemed to think this necessary in order to secure obedience. They were believers in the old maxim that familiarity breeds contempt. My own parents lived in the house with my grandfather and grandmother on the mother's side. My grandfather was a disciplinarian of the stricter sort, and I can hardly find words to express the awe in which I stood of him—an awe so great as almost to prevent anything like affection on my part, although he was in the main kind, and, certainly, never thought of being severe beyond what was necessary to maintain a proper degree of order in the family.

The other boys in that part of the country, my school-mates and play-fellows, were educated on the same system. Yet there were at that time some indications that this very severe discipline was beginning to relax. With my father and mother I was on much easier terms than with my grandfather. If a favor was to be asked of my grandfather, it was asked with fear and trembling; the request was postponed to the last moment, and then made with hesitation and blushes and a confused utterance.

One of the means of keeping the boys of that generation in order was a little bundle of birchen rods, bound together by a small cord, and generally suspended on a nail against the wall in the kitchen. This was esteemed as much a part of the necessary furniture as the crane that hung in the kitchen fireplace, or the shovel and tongs. It sometimes happened that the boy suffered a fate similar to that of the eagle in the fable, wounded by an arrow fledged with a feather from his own wing; in other words, the boy was made to gather the twigs intended for his own castigation.

It has never been clear to me why the birch was chosen above all other trees of the wood to yield its twigs for this purpose. The beech of our forests produces sprays as slender, as flexible, and as tough; and farmers, wherever the beech is common, cut its long and pliant branches for driving oxen. Yet the use of birchen rods for the correction of children is of very great antiquity. In his *Discourse on Forest Trees*, written three hundred years ago, Evelyn speaks of birchen twigs as an implement of the school-master; and Loudon, in his *Arboretum*, goes yet further back. He says: "The birch has been used as the instrument of correction in schools from the earliest ages." The English poets of the last century make frequent mention of this use of birchen twigs; but in Loudon's time, whose book was published thirty years since, he remarks that the use of these rods, both in schools and private families, was fast passing away—a change on which the boys, both of England and the United States may well be congratulated—for the birchen rod was, in my time, even more freely used in the school than in the household.

The chastisement which was thought so wholesome in the case of boys, was at that time administered, for petty crimes, to grown-up persons. About a mile from where I lived stood a public whipping-post, and I remember seeing a young fellow, of about eighteen years of age, upon whose back, by direction of a justice of the peace, forty lashes had just been laid, as the punishment for a theft which he had committed. His eyes were red, like those of one who had been crying, and I well remember the feeling of curiosity, mingled with pity and fear, with which I gazed on him. That, I think, was the last example of corporal punishment inflicted by law in that neighborhood. The whipping-post stood in its place for several years afterward, the memorial of a practice which had passed away.

The awe in which the boys of that time held their parents extended to all elderly persons, toward whom our behavior was more than merely respectful, for we all observed a hushed and subdued demeanor in their presence. Toward the ministers of the gospel this behavior was particularly marked. At that time, every township in Massachusetts, the State in which I lived, had its minister, who was settled there for life, and when he once came among his people was understood to have entered into a connection with them scarcely less lasting than the marriage tie. The community in which he lived regarded him with great veneration, and the visits which from time to time he made to the district schools

seemed to the boys important occasions, for which special preparation was made. When he came to visit the school which I attended, we all had on our Sunday clothes, and we were ready for him with a few answers to the questions in the *Westminster Catechism*. He heard us recite our lessons, examined us in the catechism, and then began a little address, which I remember was the same on every occasion. He told us how much greater were the advantages of education which we enjoyed than those which had fallen to the lot of our parents, and exhorted us to make the best possible use of them, both for our own sakes and that of our parents, who were ready to make any sacrifice for us, even so far as to take the bread out of their own mouths to give us. I remember being disgusted with this illustration of parental kindness which I was obliged to listen to twice at least in every year.

The good man had, perhaps, less reason than he supposed to magnify the advantages of education enjoyed in the common schools at that time. Reading, spelling, writing and arithmetic, with a little grammar and a little geography, were all that was taught, and these by persons much less qualified, for the most part, than those who now give instruction. Those, however, who wished to proceed further took lessons from graduates of the colleges, who were then much more numerous in proportion to the population than they now are.

The profound respect shown to the clergy in those days had this good effect—that wherever there was a concourse of people, their presence prevented the occurrence of anything disorderly or unseemly. The minister, therefore, made it one of his duties to be present on those occasions which brought people together in any considerable numbers. His appearance had somewhat the effect which that of a policeman now has at a public assembly in one of our large towns. At that time there was, in each township, at least one company of militia, which was required to hold several meetings in the course of the year, and at these, I remember, the minister was always present. The military parade, with the drums and fifes and other musical instruments, was a powerful attraction for the boys, who came from all parts of the neighborhood to the place at which the militia mustered. But on these occasions there was one respect in which the minister's presence proved but a slight restraint upon excess. There were then no temperance societies, no temperance lectures held forth, no temperance tracts were ever distributed, nor temperance pledges given. It was, to be sure, esteemed a shame to get drunk; but as long as they stopped short of this, people, almost without exception, drank grog and punch freely without much fear of a reproach from any quarter. Drunkenness, however, in that demure population, was not obstreperous, and the man who was overtaken by it was generally glad to slink out of sight.

I remember an instance of this kind. There had been a muster of a militia company on the church green for the election of one of its officers, and the person elected had treated the members of the company and all who were present to sweetened rum and water, carried to the green in pailfuls, with a tin cup to each pail for the convenience of drinking. The afternoon was far spent, and I was going home with other boys, when we overtook a young man who had taken too much of the election toddy, and in endeavoring to go quietly home, had got but a little way from the green, when he fell in a miry place, and was surrounded by three or four persons, who assisted in getting him on his legs again. The poor fellow seemed in great distress, and his new nankeen pantaloons, daubed with the mire of the road, and his dangling limbs, gave him a most wretched appearance. It was, I think, the first time that I had ever seen a drunken man. As I approached to pass him by, some of the older boys said to me, "Do not go too near him, for if you smell a drunken man it will make you drunk." Of course I kept at a good distance, but not out of hearing, for I remember hearing him lament his condition in these words: "Oh dear, I shall die!" "Oh dear, I wish I hadn't drinked any!" "Oh dear, what will my poor Betsy say?" What his poor Betsy said I never heard, but I saw him led off in the direction of his home, and I continued on my way with the other boys, impressed with a salutary horror of drunkenness and a fear of drunken men.

One of the entertainments of the boys of my time was what were called the "raisings," meaning the erection of the timber frames of houses or barns, to which the boards were to be afterward nailed. Here the minister made a point of being present, and hither the able-bodied men of the neighborhood, the young men especially, were summoned, and took part in the work with great alacrity. It was a spectacle for us next to that of a performer on the tight-rope, to see the young men walk steadily on the narrow footing of the beams at a great height from the ground, or as they stood to catch in their hands the wooden pins and the braces flung to them from below. They vied with each other in the dexterity and daring with which they went through with the work, and when the skeleton of the building was put together, some one among them generally capped the climax of fearless activity by standing on the ridge-pole with his head downward and his heels in the air. At that time, even the presence of the minister was no restraint upon the flow of milk punch and grog, which in some cases was taken to excess. The practice of calling the neighbors to these "raisings" is now discontinued in the rural neighborhoods; the carpenters provide their own workmen for the business of adjusting the timbers of the new building to each other, and there is no consumption of grog.

Another of the entertainments of rustic life in the region of which I am speaking was the making of maple sugar. This was a favorite frolic of the boys. The apparatus for the sugar camp was of a much ruder kind than is now used. The sap was brought in buckets from the wounded trees and poured into a great caldron which hung over a hot fire from a stout horizontal pole supported at each end by an upright stake planted in the ground. Since that time they have built in every maple grove a sugarhouse—a little building in which the process of making sugar is carried on with several ingenious contrivances unknown at that time, when everything was done in the open air.

From my father's door, in the latter part of March and the early part of April, we could see perhaps a dozen columns of smoke rising over the woods in different places where the work was going on. After the sap had been collected and boiled for three or four days, the time came when the thickening liquid was made to pass into the form of sugar. This was when the sirup had become of such a consistency that it would "feather"—that is to say, when a beechen twig, formed at the small end into a little loop, dipped into the hot sirup and blown upon by the breath, sent into the air a light, feathery film. The huge caldron was then lifted from the fire, and its contents were either dipped out and poured into molds, or stirred briskly till the sirup cooled and took the form of ordinary brown sugar in loose grains. This process was exceedingly inter-esting to the boys who came to watch its different stages and to try from time to time the sirup as it thickened.

In autumn, the task of stripping the husks from the ears of Indian corn was made the occasion of social meetings, in which the boys took a special part. A farmer would appoint what was called "a husking," to which he invited all his neighbors. The ears of maize in the husk, sometimes along with part of the stalk, were heaped on the barn floor. In the evening, lanterns were brought, and, seated on piles of dry husks, the men and boys stripped the ears of their covering, and breaking them from the stem with a sudden jerk, threw them into baskets placed for the purpose. It was often a merry time; the gossip of the neighborhood was talked over, stories were told, jests went round, and at the proper hour the assembly adjourned to the dwelling-house and were treated to pumpkin pie and cider, which in that season had not been so long from the press as to have parted with its sweetness.

Quite as cheerful were the "apple-parings," which on autumn evenings brought together the young people of both sexes in little circles. The fruit of the orchards was pared and quartered and the core extracted, and a supply of apples in this state provided for making what was called "applesauce," a kind of preserve of which every family laid in a large quantity every year.

The cider-making season in autumn was, at the time of which I am speaking, somewhat correspondent to the vintage in the wine countries of Europe. Large tracts of land in New England were overshadowed by rows of apple-trees, and in the month of May a journey through that region was a journey through a wilderness of bloom. In the month of October the whole population was busy gathering apples under the trees, from which they fell in heavy showers as the branches were shaken by the strong arms of the farmers. The creak of the cider-mill, turned by a horse moving in a circle, was heard in every neighborhood as one of the most common of rural sounds. The freshly pressed juice of the apples was most agreeable to boyish tastes, and the whole process of gathering the fruit and making the cider came in among the more laborious rural occupations in a way which diversified them pleasantly, and which made it seem a pastime. The time that was given to making cider, and the number of barrels made and stored in the cellars of the farm-houses, would now seem incredible. A hundred barrels to a single farm was no uncommon proportion, and the quantity swallowed by the men of that day led to the habits of intemperance which at length alarmed the more thoughtful part of the community, and gave occasion to the formation of temperance societies and the introduction of better habits.

From time to time, the winter evenings, and occasionally a winter afternoon, brought the young people of the parish together in attendance upon a singing-school. Some person who possessed more than common power of voice and skill in modulating it, was employed to teach psalmody, and the boys were naturally attracted to his school as a recreation. It often happened that the teacher was an enthusiast in his vocation, and thundered forth the airs set down in the music-books with a fervor that was contagious. A few of those who attempted to learn psalmody were told that they had no aptitude for the art, and were set aside, but that did not prevent their attendance as hearers of the others. In those days a set of tunes were in fashion mostly of New England origin, which have since been laid aside in obedience to a more fastidious taste. They were

in quick time, sharply accented, the words clearly articulated, and often running into fugues in which the bass, the tenor, and the treble chased each other from the middle to the end of the stanza. I recollect that some impatience was manifested when slower and graver airs of church music were introduced by the choir, and I wondered why the words should not be sung in the same time that they were pronounced in reading.

The streams which bickered through the narrow glens of the region in which I lived were much better stocked with trout in those days than now, for the country had been newly opened to settlement. The boys all were anglers. I confess to having felt a strong interest in that "sport," as I no longer call it. I have long since been weaned from the propensity of which I speak; but I have no doubt that the instinct which inclines so many to it, and some of them our grave divines, is a remnant of the original wild nature of man. Another "sport," to which the young men of the neighborhood sometimes admitted the elder boys, was the autumnal squirrel-hunt. The young men formed themselves into two parties equal in number, and fixed a day for the shooting. The party which on that day brought down the greatest number of squirrels was declared the victor, and the contest ended with some sort of festivity in the evening.

I have not mentioned other sports and games of the boys of that day—that is to say, of seventy or eighty years since—such as wrestling, running, leaping, base-ball, and the like, for in these there was nothing to distinguish them from the same pastimes at the present day. There were no public lectures at that time on subjects of general interest; the profession of public lecturer was then unknown, and eminent men were not solicited, as they now are, to appear before audiences in distant parts of the country, and gratify the curiosity of strangers by letting them hear the sound of their voices. But the men of those days were far more given to attendance of public worship than those who now occupy their place, and of course they took their boys with them. They were not satisfied with the morning and afternoon services, but each neighborhood held a third service of its own in the evening. Here some lay brother made a prayer, hymns were sung by those who were trained at the singing-schools, a sermon was read from the works of some orthodox divine, and now and then a word of exhortation was addressed to the little assembly by some one who was more fluent in speech than the rest.

Every parish had its tything-men, two in number generally, whose business it was to maintain order in the church during divine service, and who sat with a stern countenance through the sermon, keeping a vigilant eye on the boys in the distant pews and in the galleries. Sometimes, when he detected two of them communicating with each other, he went to one of them, took him by the button, and leading him away, seated him beside himself. His power extended to other delinquencies. He was directed by law to see that the Sabbath was not profaned by people wandering in the fields and angling in the brooks. At that time a law, no longer in force, directed that any person who absented himself unnecessarily from public worship for a certain length of time, should pay a fine into the treasury of the country. I remember several persons of whom it was said that they had

been compelled to pay this fine, but I do not remember any of them who went to church afterward.

For the boys of the present day an immense number of books have been provided, some of them excellent, some mere trash or worse, but scarce any are now read which are not of recent date. The question is often asked, What books had they to read seventy or eighty years since? They had books, and some of great merit. There was *Sanford and Merton*, and *Little Jack*; there was *Robinson Crusoe*, with its variations *The Swiss Family Robinson* and *The New Robinson Crusoe;* there was Mrs. Trimmer's *Knowledge of Nature* and Berquin's lively narratives and sketches translated from the French; there was *Philip Quarll*, and Watts's *Poems for Children*, and Bunyan's *Pilgrim's Progress* and Mrs. Barbauld's writings, and the *Miscellaneous Poems* of Cowper. Later, we had Mrs. Edgworth's *Parent's Assistant* and *Evenings at Home*. All these, if not numerous, were at least often read, and the frequent reading of a few good books is thought to be at least as improving—as useful in storing the mind and teaching one to think—as the more cursory reading of many. Of elementary books there was no lack, nor, as I have already intimated, any scarcity of private instructors, principally clergymen, educated at the colleges.

I have here set down such particulars as now occur to me of the employments, the amusements, and the studies amidst which the boys of my time grew up and were trained for the duties of manhood.

THE STORY OF THE SPHINX
By Emma J. Arnold

February, 1900

ONCE upon a time, Prince Tehuti-mes, the son of the King of Egypt, went on a hunting expedition in the desert which stretches behind the Pyramids. On your map of Africa you will find Egypt in the right-hand upper corner, and near the city of Cairo you will see three little triangular figures marked "Pyramids of Gizeh." It was in the desert country to the left of these pyramids that Prince Tehuti-mes went hunting. From early dawn till midday he spent the hours shooting brazen bolts at a target, and hunting lions in the Valley of the Gazelles. A servant was with him, and they rode on a two-wheeled chariot with a span of horses "swifter than the wind."

Now, it must have been very hot work hunting lions in a desert, where there are no trees and the ground is all sand. In Egypt it seldom rains. No clouds shade the sun, whose burning rays beat down hour after hour and make the sands very hot.

Well, by noon-time Tehuti-mes was hot and exceedingly tired by his exertions, so he said to his servant:

"Drive me back as far as the Sphinx. There is a nice long shadow under his chin, and it will be a fine, cool place to take a nap."

You may believe people in a desert are generally glad if they can find a shadow, be it ever so small a one. Now, I suppose you are wondering what kind of an object it was whose chin cast a shadow large enough to cover Prince Tehuti-mes; so I will tell you about the great figure known as the Sphinx.

Long, long ago—five or six thousands of years ago—the little country of Egypt, whose whole territory, desert and all, is only about twice the size of the State of Illinois, was yet the greatest kingdom on the earth. That certainly was more than five thousand years before Christopher Columbus sailed across the Atlantic Ocean and discovered America. Egypt had a large population even then. Thousands, perhaps millions, of people swarmed along the banks of the river Nile, and rowed their little boats in and out of the network of canals which led the waters of the "sacred river" between the cultivated fields. The religion of these people was what we call polytheism—that is, the worship of many gods. The Egyptians, like all pagan nations, made images of their gods, and built temples where they might be worshiped. It was the business of the priests to carry on this worship, and a very profitable business they made of it, too.

When the Egyptians saw how beautiful and bright the sun was, and how at his rising each morning the ugly black darkness disappeared, they thought that he, too, must be a god, and so they worshiped him among the rest. Some among the Egyptians thought that the sun god died every night when he set in the west, and came to life again the next morning; others believed that he spent the night-hours fighting against evil spirits and horrible monsters who tried to kill him. But he always conquered them, and the next morning there he was in the east again, and rose anew, as bright and beautiful as ever, to give light and warmth to the earth.

Now, the Egyptians had many names for their sun-god, among these, one for the rising sun, one for the midday sun, and one for the sun when he set in the west. The rising-sun god was called *Hor-em-akhu,* which means in English, "Horus-on-the-horizon." The very biggest idol they ever made was to represent this sun-god. It is what we call the "Great Sphinx of Gizeh." No one knows who made this Sphinx, or when it was made; but, in all likelihood, it was already there in the desert more than six thousand years ago, when the first King of Egypt whom we know anything about ruled over the country.

No temple was ever built over Hor-em-akhu. He is too immense. He is one hundred and ninety feet long and sixty-five feet high. His head would reach above the top of a six-story house. His face is thirteen and a half feet wide, and between his lips, if he could open them, you might drive a good-sized carriage, and have room to spare on each side. A portion of his body is an immense rock which lay partly out of the sand. The Egyptian workmen put upon it bricks and plaster enough to give it the shape of a lion; and on the neck of this lion they placed a man's head, surmounted with a royal crown. A great stone beard hung from the Sphinx's chin, and I suspect that in the shadow cast by this beard Prince Tehuti-mes took his noonday nap.

The Egyptian people thought they could not have any better place to bury their dead than near the image of their beautiful sun-god. So, year after year, the kings and the princes and the nobles made their graves in the desert land. And it is thus in the midst of a great cemetery that you would find the Sphinx, if you should go now to look at him.

Not far from this cemetery was once a great city called Memphis. Sixty centuries ago it was the capital city of Egypt. It had thousands of houses, and magnificent temples and obelisks, besides a famous citadel, in which were kept a great many soldiers to guard the city. But to-day, if you should visit the place where this famous city once stood, you would see nothing but mounds of earth with palm-trees growing upon them, and here and there, scattered over the ground, blocks of stone, which are all there is left of those magnificent buildings built and adorned by the kings of Egypt.

Now, the burial-ground in which the Sphinx is was the cemetery of Memphis, and it stretched for forty miles along the river Nile. In it there were over sixty pyramids, which are the big tombs built by the kings. The nobles and the princes also built very large tombs, the walls of which are covered with colored pictures, very beautiful to look at.

But you have not yet learned whether Prince Tehuti-mes took his nap. He went to sleep, and he dreamed; and it seemed to him that the god in whose shadow he lay opened his great stone lips and spoke to him; and this is what the god said:

"Behold me! Look upon me, my son Tehuti-mes! I am thy father, Hor-em-akhu. Thou shalt be a mighty king, and rule over all the land. The whole world shall be thine in its length and in its breadth, as far as the light of the eye of the Lord of the Universe shines. Plenty and riches shall be thine. Long years shall be granted thee as thy term of life. My heart clings to thee.

"But the sand of the desert has covered me up. Promise me that thou wilt clear it away. Then shall I know that thou art my son, my helper."

Tehuti-mes awoke, and his dream had been so very real that as he looked up in adoration at the mighty stone face above him he half expected to see the big lips open anew to answer the devout prayers by which he promised obedience to the god's command. He laid up the words in his heart, and vowed that when he became king he would do all that his god had commanded. Some years after this his father died, and the prince ascended the throne of Egypt and was King Tehuti-mes IV. I will tell you now how it happened that we have found out whether he did what he made up his mind to do the day when he slept in the shadow of the Sphinx.

You have learned that the desert is mostly sand. Egypt does not have snow and hail and rain, as we do; hence its sand keeps exceedingly dry and powdery. Often there are terrific gales of wind, and then the sand is whirled along through the air in such quantities that it is worse for people to be out in than a rain-storm or snow-storm. Each gust of wind carries along just as much sand as it can support, and when anything obstructs the path of the wind, then and there the sand is dropped, and falls again to the ground.

Now, on the day when Prince Tehuti-mes had his dream, these sand-storms had been blowing around the Sphinx for more than two thousand years, so you can imagine what a pile of sand had accumulated against him. In fact, he was all covered up, except his head.

And he was covered up in the year 1818, eighty-one years ago, when an Englishman named Caviglia undertook the task of digging him out. He had heard many interesting stories about the great Sphinx. In a book written by the celebrated Roman, Pliny, it was stated that a king was buried under it. Caviglia desired to find the tomb of this king, so he engaged a large number of laborers—men to dig and women and children to carry off the sand in baskets on their heads. They dug over a space of more than a hundred feet, carrying away the sand for days, and finally, what do you think they found? Right under the chin of the monstrous idol, at the end of a long passage between its paws, they found a little temple. The back wall of this temple was one huge block of red granite, covered

all over with pictures and writing. Perhaps you think the writing was in English or German or French, or even in Greek or Latin. In not one of these. It was in a strange language that nobody could read. In fact, it did not look at all like a language. It looked for all the world just like a lot of pictures.

You must know that, ages before the dawn of history, there was no such thing as an alphabet. Letters had not been invented, and when people wished to send a written message anywhere, they did it by making pictures of what they wished to tell. This is the way the ancient Egyptians commenced to write. By and by, one at a time, they learned to make each picture stand for the sound of a letter or syllable, and so they spelled out their words. You may imagine that it was a very long, tedious process to write in this way. This is the kind of writing which Mr. Caviglia found on the stone in the little house between the paws of the Sphinx. It is called the ancient Egyptian hieroglyphic writing. A Frenchman named Champollion first found out how to read it, and he had to study over it a long time before he could do so.

In 1896 an American, Colonel Raum of San Francisco, made another attempt to uncover the Sphinx and find the buried king. With the help of a hundred Arabs, men and boys, he dug out the rubbish from a hole about forty feet deep, which had been cut down into solid rock of the lion's body ages ago. The bottom of this hole was blocked up with stones. The Egyptian government would not allow him to remove them, so he was obliged to stop just at the very spot where is probably the entrance to an ancient tomb. He cleaned out the little temple, and found in it a piece of the stone beard, which had broken off and been buried for centuries. And more interesting still it was to find a part of the royal crown.

This stone crown was gigantic. It was ten feet across and about fifteen or twenty feet high, and fitted into a hole in the head by a stem seven feet long.

When the writing upon the stone which Mr. Caviglia found was finally deciphered, it was learned from it that King Tehuti-mes IV had built this little temple in the first year of his reign, more than three thousand years ago! Upon the stone he had had engraved in big hieroglyphics the whole story of his hunting expedition, his dream, and the command of the god. And of course he must have cleared away the sand, else he could not have set up the stone. But the sand soon drifted back again, and ever since, though it has been several times dug out, the Sphinx is always being covered up by the drifting sands, and perhaps some day it will be overwhelmed and disappear altogether.

This is the story of the great sun-god Hor-em-akhu, which we call the Sphinx; and if, some day, you go to Egypt, you can see it for yourself—that is, if it is not buried by that time.

TWO VALENTINES
By Tudor Jenks

February, 1900

You never saw anything so fine
As the Princess Clementine's valentine!
It glittered with gold; it shimmered with lace;
Pink Cupids poised with dainty grace,
Plump of limb and sly of face;
Poems and posies, garlands gay,
Were mixed in a decorative way.
'T was all complete in a silver box
With tiniest of keys and locks,
And left by a page as sly as a fox,
Who had never even a word to say,
But handed it in on a silver tray,
Took to his heels, and ran away.
I'm sure the page was not to blame
That the princess knew from whom it came—
A very rich prince of a noble name.
The princess yawned while she agreed
'T was a very rich valentine indeed.

Then the gift was stowed away
In a steel strong-box—and it's there to-day.

On his way home, the page did stray
From the beaten path to a woodland way
Which brought him, just at close of day,
To a neat little cottage where he knew
A sweet little maid, who sweeter grew
Each day she was his sweetheart true.
On tippiest tiptoe, soft and still,
The dapper page crept near, until
He left a rose on the window-sill;
Attached to the rose with this billet-doux:

> The rose is red, the violet blue,
> Sugar is sweet, and so are you;
> If you love me as I love you,
> No knife can cut our love in two.

'T was trite—but the best that he could do.

> When the maiden finds the rose,
> Rosy pink her sweet face glows.

The strong-box gift to strong-box went;
The rose from heart to heart was sent.
They say a brook, whate'er its course,
Can rise no higher than its source.

THE PORCUPINE

By John Burroughs

May, 1896

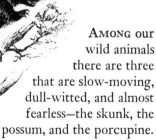

THE PORCUPINE

AMONG our wild animals there are three that are slow-moving, dull-witted, and almost fearless—the skunk, the possum, and the porcupine. The two latter seem to be increasing in most parts of the country. The possum is becoming quite common in the valley of the Hudson, and the porcupine is frequently met with in parts of the country where it was rarely or never seen forty years ago.

When the boys in late fall now go cooning where I used to go cooning in my youth, the dogs frequently run on a porcupine or drive him up a tree, and thus the sport is interrupted. Sometimes the dog comes to them with his mouth stuck full of quills, and is then compelled to submit to the painful operation of having them withdrawn.

A sportsman relates that he once came upon a dead porcupine and a dead bald eagle lying upon the ground within a few yards of each other. The eagle had partly torn the porcupine to pieces, but in attacking it with its beak it had driven numerous spines of the animal into its throat, and from their effect had apparently died as soon as its victim.

The quill of a porcupine is like a bad habit: if it once gets hold it constantly works deeper and deeper, though the quill has no power of motion in itself; it is the live, active flesh that draws it in by means of the barbed point. One day my boy and I encountered a porcupine on the top of one of the Catskills, and we had a little circus with him; we wanted to wake him up and make him show a little excitement if possible. Without violence or injury to him we succeeded to the extent of making his eyes fairly stand out from his head, but quicken his motion he would not—probably could not.

What astonished and alarmed him seemed to be that his quills had no effect upon his enemies; they laughed at his weapons. He stuck his head under a rock and left his back and tail exposed. This is the porcupine's favorite position of defense. "Now come if you dare," he seems to say. Touch his tail, and like a trap it springs up and strikes your hand full of little quills. The tail is the active weapon of defense; with this the animal strikes. It is the outpost that delivers its fire before the citadel is reached. It is doubtless this fact that has given rise to the popular notion that the porcupine can shoot its quills, which of course it cannot do.

With a rotten stick we sprang the animal's tail again and again, till its supply of quills began to run low, and the creature grew uneasy. "What does this mean?" he seemed to say, his excitement rising. His shield upon his back, too, we trifled with, and when we finally drew him forth with a forked stick, his eyes were ready to burst from his head. Then we laughed in his face and went our way. Before we had reached our camp I was suddenly seized with a strange, acute pain in one of my feet. It seemed as if a large nerve were being roughly sawed in two. I could not take another step. Sitting down and removing my shoe and stocking, I searched for the cause of the paralyzing pain. The foot was free from mark or injury, but what was this little thorn or fang of thistle doing on the ankle? I pulled it out and found it to be one of the lesser quills of the porcupine. By some means, during our "circus," the quill had dropped inside my stocking, the thing had "took," and the porcupine had his revenge for all the indignities we had put upon him. I was well punished. The nerve which the quill struck had unpleasant memories of it for many months afterward.

When you come suddenly upon the porcupine in his native haunts he draws his head back and down, puts up his shield, trails his broad tail, and waddles slowly away. His shield is the sheaf of larger quills upon his back, which he opens and spreads out in a circular form so that the whole body is quite hidden beneath it.

I once passed a summer night alone upon the highest peak of the Catskills, Slide Mountain. I soon found there were numerous porcupines that desired to keep me company. The news of my arrival in the afternoon soon spread among them. They probably had scented me. After resting awhile I set out to look up the spring, and met a porcupine on his way toward my camp. He turned out in the grass, and then, as I paused, came back into the path and passed directly over my feet. He evidently felt that he had as good a right to the road as I had; he had traveled it many times before me. When I charged upon him with a stick in my hand he slowly climbed a small balsam fir. I soon found the place of the spring, and, having dredged it and cleaned it, I sat down upon a rock and waited for the water to slowly seep in. Presently I heard something in the near bushes, and in a moment a large porcupine came into view. I thought that he, too, was looking for water, but no, he was evidently on his way to my camp. He, too, had heard the latest rumor on the mountain top. It was highly amusing to watch his movements. He came teetering along in the most aimless, idiotic way. Now he drifted off a little to the right, then a little to the left; his blunt nose seemed vaguely to be feeling the air; he fumbled over the ground, tossed about by loose boulders and little hillocks; his eyes wandered stupidly about; I was in plain view within four or five yards of him, but he heeded me not. Then he turned back a few paces, but some slight obstacle in his way caused him to change his mind. One thought of a sleepwalker; uncertainty was stamped upon every gesture and movement; yet he was really drifting towards camp. After a while he struck the well-defined trail, and his gray, shapeless body slowly disappeared up the hill. In five or six minutes I overtook him shuffling along within sight of the big rock upon which rested my blanket and lunch. As I came up to him he depressed his tail, put up his shield, and slowly pushed off into the wild grass. While I was at lunch I heard a sound, and there he was, looking up at me from the path a few feet away. "An uninvited guest," I said; "but come on." He hesitated, and then turned aside into the bracken; he would wait till I had finished and gone to sleep, or had moved off.

How much less wit have such animals—animals like the porcupine, possum, skunk, turtle—that nature has armed against all foes, than the animals that have no such ready-made defenses, and are preyed upon by a multitude of enemies. The price paid for being shielded against all danger, for never feeling fear or anxiety, is stupidity. If the porcupine were as vulnerable to its enemies as, say, the woodchuck, it would probably soon come to be as alert and swift of foot as that marmot.

For an hour or more, that afternoon on the mountain top, my attention was attracted by a peculiar continuous sound that seemed to come from far away to the east. I queried with myself, "Is it the sound of some workman in a distant valley hidden by the mountains, or is its source nearer by me on the mountain side?" I could not determine. It was not a hammering or a grating or the filing of a saw, though it suggested such sounds. It had a vague, distant, ventriloquial character. In the solitude of the mountain top there was something welcome and pleasing. Finally I set out to try to solve the mystery. I had not gone fifty yards from camp when I knew I was near the sound. Presently I saw a porcupine on a log, and as I approached the sound ceased, and the animal moved away. A curious kind of chant he made, or note of wonder and surprise at my presence on the mountain—or was he calling together the clan for a midnight raid upon my camp?

I made my bed that night of ferns and balsam boughs under an overhanging rock, where the storm that swept across the mountain just after dark could not reach me. I lay down, rolled in my blankets, with a long staff by my side, in anticipation of visits from the porcupines. In the middle of the night I was awakened, and, looking out of my den, saw a porcupine outlined against the starlit sky. I made a thrust at him with my staff when, with a grunt or grumble, he disappeared. A little later I was awakened again by the same animal, or another, and repelled him as before. At intervals during the rest of the night they visited me in this way; my sleep was by short stages from one porcupine to another. These animals are great gnawers. They seem to be specially fond of gnawing any tool or object that has been touched or used by human hands. They would probably have gnawed my shoes or lunch basket or staff had I lain still. A settler at the foot of the mountain told me they used to prove very annoying to him by getting into his cellar or wood-shed at night, and indulging their ruling passion by chewing upon his tool-handles or pails or harness. "Kick one of them outdoors," he said, "and in half an hour he is back again."

In winter they usually live in trees, gnawing the bark and feeding upon the inner layer. I have seen large hemlocks quite denuded and killed in this way.

KEPT AFTER SCHOOL

By Agnes Lewis Mitchill

March, 1894

"I AM sorry," said their teacher,
"To keep you, Tom and Joe;
I do not like to punish you,
Because it grieves me so."
But hopeful Tommy whispered
To naughty little Joe,
"If she's so *very* sorry,
Maybe she'll let us go!"

A SNOW BATTLE
By Daniel C. Beard

January, 1881

It was a year when the Indian-summer had been prolonged into the winter. Christmas had come and gone and a new year begun, but no snow had fallen on the river bank or neighboring hills.

Such was the condition of things one January morning, in a Kentucky town, upon the banks of the Ohio River, where I and some sixty other boys were gathered in a little frame school-house.

We had about made up our minds that old Jack Frost was a humbug, and winter a myth; but when the bell tapped for recess, the first boy out gave a shout which passed from mouth to mouth, until it became a universal cheer as we reached the play-ground, for, floating airily down from a dull, gray sky came myriads of white snow-flakes!

Winter had come! Jack Frost was no longer a humbug! Before the bell again recalled us to our study, the ground was whitened with snow, and the school divided into two opposing armies. That night was a busy one. All hands set to work manufacturing ammunition-sleds and shields for the coming battle. It was my fortune to be chosen as one of the garrison of the fort. There was not a boy late next morning—in fact, when the teachers arrived to open the school, they found all the scholars upon the play-grounds, rolling huge snow-balls. All night the snow had continued to fall, and it was now quite deep. When we went out at noon, a beautifully modeled fort of snowy whiteness stood ready for us, and from a mound in the center floated the battle-flag.

Our company took their places inside the fortifications. We could see the enemy gathered around their captain at their camp, some two hundred yards distant, their ammunition-sleds loaded with snow-balls. The lieutenant bore their battle-flag.

Our teachers showed their interest by standing shivering with wet feet in the deep snow to watch the battle. At a blast from a tin horn, on rushed the foe! They separated, and came in two divisions, approaching us from the left and right.

"Now, boys!" cried our captain. "Don't throw a ball until they are within range."

Then, calling the pluckiest amongst us, a flaxen-haired country-boy, to his side, he whispered a word or two and pointed to the flag in the enemy's camp. The boy, who had been nicknamed "Daddy," on account of his old-looking face, slipped quietly over the rear wall of the fort, dodged behind a snow-drift, and then behind a fence, and was lost to sight. Forward marched the enemy, their battle-flag borne in advance of the party to the right. Their captain was at the head of the division to the left.

Having engaged our attention on the two flanks, where we stood ready to receive them, as they neared us, by a quick and well executed maneuver, rushing obliquely toward each other, the two divisions unexpectedly joined, and advanced, shield to shield, with the ammunition-sleds in the rear. It was in vain we pelted them with snow-balls; on they came, encouraged by a cheer from the teachers and some spectators who by this time had gathered near the school-house.

Three times had our noble captain been tumbled from his perch upon the mound in the center of the fort, when another burst of applause from the spectators announced some new development, and, as we looked, we could see "Daddy" with the colors of the enemy's camp in his arms, his tow hair flying in the wind, as he ran for dear life.

In an instant, the line of the enemy was all in confusion; some ran to head off "Daddy," while others in their excitement stood and shouted. It was our turn now, and we pelted their broken ranks with snow until they looked like animated snow-men. Another shout, and we looked around to find our captain down and the hands of one of the besieging party almost upon our flag. It was the work of a second to pitch the intruder upon his back outside the fort. Then came the tug of war. A rush was made to capture our standard, several of our boys were pulled out of the fort and taken prisoners, and the capture of the fort seemed inevitable. Again and again a number of the enemy, among whom was their color-bearer, gained the top of our breast-works, and again and again were they tumbled off, amid a shower of snow-balls that forced them to retire to gain breath and clear their eyes from the snow. Once, their lieutenant, with the red-bordered battle-flag, had actually succeeded in reaching the mound upon which stood our colors, when a combined attack that nearly resulted in his being made prisoner, drove him from the fort to gather strength for another rush. "Daddy" was now a prisoner, and the re-captured flag again floated over the ene-my's camp, when the school-bell called us, fresh and glowing with exercise and health-ful excitement, to our lessons. The battle was left undecided, and our fort was soon captured by a force stronger than any our companions were able to bring against it, for a warm south wind sprang up from the lowlands down the river, our fortification quickly yielded to its insidious attack, and the snow-campaign was over.

A NEW YEAR'S MEETING
By Tudor Jenks
January, 1896

"Do you know how to get to grandpa's?—
  I went on New Year's day—
You climb the hill where the pine-trees grow,
  And grandpa comes half-way.

"He waits in the road for mama and me,
  And plays he's a robber bold.
Then, when I can't help laughing,
  How grandpa pretends to scold!

"He threatens me with his cane, and says:
  'A kiss or your life, my dear!'
And then with a regular bear-hug
  I wish him a Happy New Year!"

HOW THE ELEPHANTS TURNED BACK

December, 1879

A LONG time ago, two hundred and seventeen years before Christ, there was a king of Egypt, Ptolemy the Fourth, who was returning, proud and victorious, from a war with his enemies. On his way home, he passed through Jerusalem; and there, feeling that such a mighty conqueror had a right to go where he pleased, he endeavored to enter the most sacred precinct of the Jewish Temple—the "Holy of Holies." No one among his own people could prevail upon him to give up his rash plan; but in answer to a prayer by the High-Priest of the Temple, who stood undismayed before him, this great king fell senseless to the ground.

He did not try again to penetrate into this sacred place, but he became very much enraged against the Jewish people; and, when he returned to Alexandria, he ordered all the Jews in that city to give up their religion and to practice the heathenish rites of Egypt. Only a few Jews consented to do this; nearly all of them boldly refused. Then the angry king commanded that all the Jews in the country around about, as well as those in the city, should be arrested and confined in the Hippodrome, or great circus, just outside of the town.

When, after a good many failures and difficulties, this had at last been done, Ptolemy prepared to carry out his great and novel plan of vengeance. This was to have these poor people trampled to death by elephants. Such a performance in the circus would make a grand show for the heathen king and his heathen people.

But it was not to be expected that ele-phants, who are good-natured creatures, would be willing to trample upon human beings unless they were in some way excited or enraged. Therefore, a great many elephants were drugged and intoxicated; and, when they had thus been made wild and reckless, they were let loose in the great arena of the Hippodrome, where the trembling Jews were gathered together in groups, awaiting their fate.

In rushed and stumbled the great monsters, and the Egyptian king and vast crowds of the Egyptian people sat in their seats to see what would happen to the Jews.

But, suddenly, up rose Eleazer, an aged priest of the Jews; and, lifting his hands toward heaven, he prayed for deliverance.

Then, all at once, the elephants stopped. They snorted and threw their trunks into the air, they ran backward and sidewise in wild confusion, and then they turned, and with savage cries and tossing trunks, they plunged over the low parapet around the arena, and ran trampling madly among the people who had come to see the show!

The scene was a terrible one, and the punishment of the Egyptians was very great. The king sat high above all, and out of danger; but he was struck with fear, and determined no longer to endeavor to punish a people who were so miraculously defended. When at last the elephants were driven back and this awful performance at the circus had come to an end, the king let the Jews go free. And this day of their wonderful deliverance was made an annual festival among them.

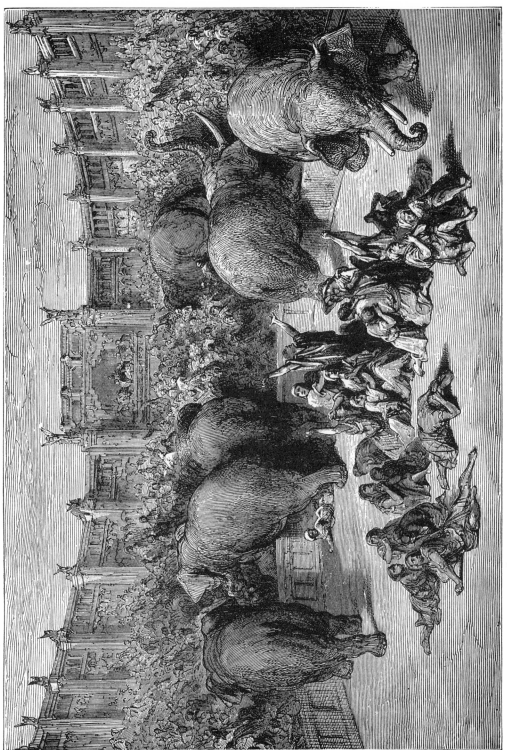

"THE ELEPHANTS TURNED, AND, WITH TOSSING TRUNKS, PLUNGED OVER THE LOW PARAPET."

ABRAM MORRISON

By John Greenleaf Whittier

December, 1879

'MIDST the men and things which will
Haunt an old man's memory still,
Drollest, quaintest of them all,
With a boy's laugh I recall
    Good old Abram Morrison.

When the Grist and Rolling Mill
Ground and rumbled by Po Hill,
And the old red school-house stood
Midway in the Powow's flood,
    Here dwelt Abram Morrison.

From the Beach to far beyond
Bear-Hill, Lion's Mouth and Pond,
Marvelous to our tough old stock,
Chips o' the Anglo-Saxon block,
    Seemed the Celtic Morrison.

Mudknock, Balmawhistle, all
Only knew the Yankee drawl,
Never brogue was heard till when,
Foremost of his countrymen,
    Hither came Friend Morrison;

Irish of the Irishes,
Pope nor priest nor church were his;
Sober with his Quaker folks,
Merry with his quiet jokes
    On week days was Morrison.

Half a genius, quick to plan
As to blunder; Irishman
Rich in schemes, and, in the end,
Spoiling what he could not mend,
    Such was Abram Morrison.

Back and forth to daily meals,
Rode his cherished pig on wheels,
And to all who came to see:
"Aisier for the pig an' me,
    Sure it is," said Morrison.

Careless-hearted, boy o'ergrown!
Jack of all trades, good at none,
Shaping out with saw and lathe
Ox-yoke, pudding-slice, or snath,
    Whistled Abram Morrison.

Well we loved the tales he told
Of a country strange and old,
Where the fairies danced till dawn;
And the goblin Leprecaun
    Looked, we thought, like Morrison.

First was he to sing the praise
Of the Powow's winding ways;
And our straggling village took
City grandeur to the look
    Of its prophet Morrison.

All his words have perished. Shame
On the saddle-bags of Fame,
That they bring not to our time
One poor couplet of the rhyme
    Made by Abram Morrison!

When, on clam and fair First Days,
Rattled down our one-horse chaise
Through the blossomed apple-boughs
To the Quaker meeting-house,
    There was Abram Morrison.

Underneath his hat's broad brim
Peered the queer old face of him;
And with Irish jauntiness
Swung the coat-tails of the dress
    Worn by Abram Morrison.

Still, in memory, on his feet,
Leaning o'er the old, high seat,
Mingling with a solemn drone,
Celtic accents all his own,
    Rises Abram Morrison.

"Don't," he's pleading—"don't ye go,
Dear young friends, to sight and show;
Don't run after elephants,
Learned pigs and presidents
        And the likes!" said Morrison.

On his well-worn theme intent,
Simple, child-like innocent,
Heaven forgive the half-checked smile
Of our careless boyhood, while
        Listening to Friend Morrison!

Once a soldier, blame him not
That the Quaker he forgot,
When, to think of battles won,
And the red-coats on the run,
        Laughed aloud Friend Morrison.

Dead and gone! But while its track
Powow keeps to Merrimack,
While Po Hill is still on guard,
Looking land and ocean ward,
        They shall tell of Morrison!

After half a century's lapse,
We are wiser now, perhaps,
But we miss our streets amid
Something which the past has hid,
        Lost with Abram Morrison.

Gone forever with the queer
Characters of that old year!
Now the many are as one;
Broken is the mold that run
        Men like Abram Morrison.

CHICKADEES
By Edith M. Thomas

December, 1899

BLACKCAP, madcap!
Never tired of play,
What's the news to-day?
"Faint-heart, faint-heart!
Winter's coming up this way;
And the winter comes to stay!"

Blackcap, madcap!
In the snow and sleet,
What have you to eat?
"Faint-heart, faint-heart!
Seeds and berries are a treat,
When the frost has made them sweet!"

Blackcap, madcap!
Whither will you go,
Now the storm-winds blow?
"Faint-heart, faint-heart!
In the pine-boughs, thick and low,
There is shelter from the snow!"

Blackcap, madcap!
Other birds have flown
To a sunnier zone!
"Faint-heart, faint-heart!
When they're gone, we blackcaps own
Our white playground all alone!"

THE OUTDOOR WORLD

February, 1900

QUEER HOMES IN ICY PALACES

UNDER the ice of the pond or brook, in queer little homes or cases, are the interesting creatures known as the caddis-worms or caddis-larvae. They can be obtained by breaking the ice and plunging in a long-handled dipper or net.

A common glass dish (not a jar) makes an excellent aquarium in which to place them and study their habits. Cover the bottom with sand, add tiny gravel stones, a twig, a few leaves (willow preferred), and a piece of water-starwort, or some other plant that grows in water, and your little guests will have all that they require to make and repair their overcoats, and you will find, by watching the various species, that their manners and customs differ from each other almost as widely as the shapes and materials of their cases. Whether there is any connection between the strength of

A CADDIS-HOME OF BITS OF BARK AND LITTLE STICKS.

MOLANNA'S HOME IN CASE OF SAND.

the case and the habits of its maker, is an interesting problem for all of us to study.

For example, there is the well-protected caddis known as the *Molanna* larva, that moves with curious, intermittent jerks; and

as its flat case of sand allows neither head nor legs to be seen from above, the effect is as if a patch of sand were traveling about by itself.

The larvae of two other kinds are very pretty swimmers. One makes a slender, pointed case, of bits of water-starwort arranged in a spiral; the other makes a short tube of sand and bark; and both protrude their fore legs and swim about merrily.

The larger larva, called the *Neuronia*, has a striped yellow face, and an overcoat made of large pieces of leaves fastened by their edges into a cylinder. I call it the "Iroquois," because it is forever on the war-path, traveling restlessly about the aquarium, pausing only to kill and eat other insects, so that, unless the aquarium is to be depopulated, it is necessary to keep this small savage in a dish by himself, where he can be fed on rare beef. While his manner

THE "LOG-CABIN" HOMES OF LITTLE STICKS WITH ROUND CAP

HOME OF THE "IROQUOIS" IN BITS OF LEAVES FASTENED TOGETHER.

seems to us very savage, that manner is, doubtless, from his point of view only greater industry in seeking food.

A species of about the same size, which I name "Huronian," after a more peaceable

A MUSKRAT'S SNOW-COVERED HOME, OF STICKS AND LEAVES, IN A SWAMP.

tribe of Indians, clothes itself in a sort of log-cabin of crosswise twigs, has a gray face with a mild expression, and is gentle in its temper and tranquil in its movements. C. H. C.

A MUSKRAT.

THE WINTER HOMES OF THE MUSKRAT

ALTHOUGH most boys have seen muskrats and know that they burrow in the banks of streams and ponds, perhaps they do not all know that there are some muskrats who build more pretentious winter homes for themselves. These furry aristocrats select as a site for their house a shallow spot in some swamp or quiet stream, and on a moonlight night in the fall of the year they may be seen at work on their new dwelling. Some gather sticks, and others dried grass and bunches of fallen leaves. With this building material in their mouths, they swim out to the spot they have chosen, and begin to build a mound, leaving a hollow space in the middle. When the house is finished, it looks very much like a pile of leaves such as the gardeners rake up on the lawns in the autumn; but in reality it is very firm, for besides the strength given by the sticks which are laid between the layers of leaves, the whole mass is soon frozen stiff, and often remains so all winter.

But within the thick walls in a snug little chamber, where the muskrats sleep in the daytime, sometimes on a flat stone or log over which the house has been built, and sometimes on a sort of shelf made on purpose. The doorways are under the water, and the owners have to dive if they wish to go in or out. When the river or swamp is frozen over, the rats sometimes have to swim for a long distance under the ice, and the bubbles of air which they breathe out as they shoot along may often be seen from above.

They generally go out at night, and landing at some opening near the shore, canter off to a corn-field, to glean the ears left here and there by the farmers. Sometimes they will visit an old barn and carry off apples, turnips, or almost any other vegetables which may be stored there. They are also very fond of fresh-water mussels, and gnawed mussel-shells will generally be found along streams inhabited by muskrats.

THE SNOW CRYSTALS

How beautiful is the snow, as the flakes fall, winging their way night and day to the fields, trees, and houses! We like to watch them as they come so silently and gracefully, and we like to see the white covering over the earth. In the parks and in the country the trees are very attractive in their rich ornaments, of which Lowell says:

> The poorest twig on the elm-tree
> Was ridged inch-deep with pearl.

Then what a variety of sports comes with the snow! There's snow-balling fort-building, sliding, and sleighing with the musical bells. But these are not all the beauty and enjoyment to be obtained from the snow. The snowflakes are made up of beautiful crystals. In each storm, and in different parts of the same storm, there are presented new patterns of the little flakes.

Without any aid to our eyes we can see much beauty in the flakes as they fall on our clothes, and by examining them with a pocket-lens, on a piece of black cloth or card, we can see still more, and can easily

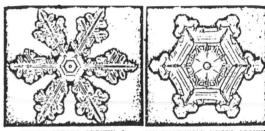

ROUGH SPEARS AROUND A JEWELED CENTERPIECE.   SIX THREEFOLD KNOTS AROUND A PRETTY "MAT."

A MAGNIFIED SNOWFLAKE WITH FEATHERY AND VERY ORNAMENTAL ARMS.

make a sketch of the forms. For several years, Mr. W. A. Bentley of Nashville, Vermont, has been photographing them through a microscope, and he sends us a few beautiful pictures of these magnified forms from his large collection. He finds that in some storms the crystals are large and feathery, in others solid like little balls, and often they are little rough, glistening, icy needles.

Not all are beautiful, nor all in the flowery form. Because the very best are rare, there will be all the greater joy in hunting for them.

Press a broom-splint lightly upon the edge of the crystal, and it will stick to it so it can be put on a card or glass for examination or drawing. The most beautiful specimens are to be found in from five to fourteen storms each winter.

AT HOME

EVERY girl and boy may have one of the largest astronomical observatories in the world. Possibly many will say, "That can't be, for I have read of the Yerkes Observatory at Williams Bay, Wisconsin, and the Lick, at Mount Hamilton, California, and the other large observatories, and I cannot hope to have one as large as those."

You mean that those have large telescopes and large buildings. Let us look at the *Century Dictionary*, and see what an observatory is. Here is the part of the definition that applies to your observatory: "A *place* or building . . . for making observations. An astronomical observatory is so planned as to secure . . . an unobstructed view, together with such arrangements as will otherwise facilitate observations."

So your observatory, one of the largest in the world, is the *place* near your home where you can get the best view of the starry sky, from the point directly overhead, called the zenith, to the great circle where earth and sky seem to meet, called the horizon. Other places may have large buildings and instruments, but no more of the sky than from zenith to horizon can be seen. Find your best observatory—that is, where you can get the most "unobstructed view"—and make "such arrangements" of easy-chairs, dark lanterns, star-maps, and opera- and field-glasses as you may be able to obtain. Even with no aid from glasses, you may see stars billions of miles away, and the beautiful groups called constellations, that have been named and written and talked about for centuries. Try this on the next starry, moonless night.

By Anna Marion Smith

March, 1907

OLD KING COLE

"Old King Cole was a merry old soul.
And a merry old soul was he:
He called for his pipe, and he called for his bowl,
And he called for his fiddlers three.
Every fiddler had a fine fiddle,
And a very fine fiddle had he:
(Twee - tweedle - dee, tweedle - dee, went the
fiddlers three) —
Oh, there's none so rare as can compare
With King Cole and his fiddlers three!"

I

GOOD Queen Kate was his royal mate,
  And a right royal mate was she:
She would frequently state that carous-
  ing till late
Was something that never should be.
But every fiddler had such a fine fiddle, —
  Oh, such a fine fiddle had he, —
That old King Cole, in his inmost soul,
  Was as restive as he could be.

II

WHEN thus spoke she to his majesty,
  He planted his crown on tight.
"We will wait," whispered he to
  the fiddlers three,
"Till the Queen has retired for the night."
Every fiddler then tuned up his fiddle,
  And tuned it as true as could be:
While old King Cole got his pipe and bowl
  And replenished them secretly.

III

SO gay they grew as
    the night hours flew,
  He forgot how the time sped away;
Till swift overhead he heard the Queen's tread
As she sprang out of bed, when he hurriedly said
  They might finish the tune the next day.
Every fiddler he had a fine fiddle,
  And a very fine fiddle had he:
Oh, 't was not fair such a concert rare
  Should be ended so suddenly!

PUSSY SITS BESIDE THE FIRE

Pussy sits beside the fire
How can she be fair?
Then comes in the little dog,
"Pussy, are you there?
So so, dear Mistress Pussy,
Pray tell me how you do?"
"Indeed, I thank you little dog,
I'm very well just now."

"Fy, pussy, what a lazy cat,
On such a pleasant day
To sit and drowse beside the fire
And sleep the hours away!
A self-respecting dog would think
Himself a sorry cur,
If he did nothing all day long
But fold his arms and purr!"

"Now, sir, you need n't criticize
Because I sit and blink,
For while my eyes are shut, like this,
I think, and think, and think.
And when I purr, please understand
I work with all my might,
A-humming over songs I sing
When I go out at night.

"Excuse me. Now I 'll close my
eyes,
And think a little more.
On busy days like this, I show
My visitors the door.
'T is only little dogs who judge
That one must idle be,
Unless one 's chasing round and
round
Or barking up a tree."

THE NORTH WIND DOTH BLOW

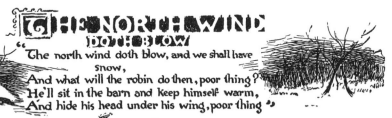

"The north wind doth blow, and we shall have
snow,
And what will the robin do then, poor thing?
He'll sit in the barn and keep himself warm,
And hide his head under his wing, poor thing"

But never a word of plaint will be
heard
From robin, no matter how tired
and cold;

For well will he know that the
winter will go,
And the blossoms and greenness
of spring unfold.

And when the warm sun says
winter is done,
He 'll gladden us all with his
cheery song;
And never will fret if the season
is wet,
Or wail that the winter was hard and long.

A SONG OF POPCORN

BY NANCY BYRD TURNER.

Sing a song of popcorn
When the snow-storms rage;
Fifty little brown men
Put into a cage.
Shake them till they laugh
and leap,
Crowding to the top;
Watch them burst their
little coats—
Pop! Pop! Pop!

Sing a song of popcorn
In the firelight:
Fifty little fairies
Robed in fleecy white.
Through the shining wires see
How they skip & prance
To the music of the
flames:
Dance, dance,
dance.

Sing a song of popcorn—
Done the frolicing;
Fifty little fairies
Strung upon a
string.

Cool & happy, hand in hand,
Sugar-spangled, fair:
Isn't that a necklace fit
For any child to
wear?

Albertine
Randall
Wheelan

CHRISTMAS EVERY DAY
By W. D. Howells

January, 1886

The little girl came into her papa's study, as she always did Saturday morning before breakfast, and asked for a story. He tried to beg off that morning, for he was very busy, but she would not let him. So he began:

"Well, once there was a little pig—"

She put her hand over his mouth and stopped him at the word. She said she had heard little pig stories till she was perfectly sick of them.

"Well, what kind of story *shall* I tell, then?"

"About Christmas. It's getting to be the season. It's past Thanksgiving already."

"It seems to me," argued her papa, "that I've told as often about Christmas as I have about little pigs."

"No difference! Christmas is more interesting."

"Well!" Her papa roused himself from his writing by a great effort. "Well, then, I'll tell you about the little girl that wanted it Christmas every day in the year. How would you like that?"

"First-rate!" said the little girl; and she nestled into comfortable shape in his lap, ready for listening.

"Very well, then, this little pig— Oh, what are you pounding me for?"

"Because you said little pig instead of little girl."

"I should like to know what's the difference between a little pig and a little girl that wanted it Christmas every day!"

"Papa," said the little girl, warningly, "if you don't go on, I'll *give* it to you!" And at this her papa darted off like lightning, and began to tell the story as fast as he could.

Well, once there was a little girl who liked Christmas so much that she wanted it to be Christmas every day in the year; and as soon as Thanksgiving was over she began to send postal cards to the old Christmas Fairy to ask if she mightn't have it. But the old Fairy never answered any of the postals; and, after a while, the little girl found out that the Fairy was pretty particular, and wouldn't notice anything but letters, not even correspondence cards in envelopes; but real letters on sheets of paper, and sealed outside with a monogram—or your initial, any way. So, then, she began to send her letters; and in about three weeks —or just the day before Christmas, it was— she got a letter from the Fairy, saying she might have it Christmas every day for a year, and then they would see about having it longer.

The little girl was a good deal excited already preparing for the old-fashioned, once-a-year Christmas that was coming the next day, and perhaps the Fairy's promise didn't make such an impression on her as it would have made at some other time. She just resolved to keep it to herself, and surprise everybody with it as it kept coming true; and then it slipped out of her mind altogether.

She had a splendid Christmas. She went to bed early, so as to let Santa Claus have a chance at the stockings, and in the morning she was up the first of anybody and went and felt them, and found hers all lumpy with packages of candy, and oranges and grapes, and pocket-books and rubber balls and all kinds of small presents, and her big brother's with nothing but the tongs in them, and her young lady sister's with a new silk umbrella, and her papa's and mamma's with potatoes and pieces of coal wrapped up in tissue paper, just as they always had every Christmas. Then she waited around till the rest of the family were up, and she was the first to burst into the library, when the doors were opened, and look at the large presents laid out on the library-table—books, and portfolios, and boxes of stationery, and breast-pins, and dolls, and little stoves, and dozens of handkerchiefs, and ink-stands, and skates, and snow-shovels, and photograph-frames, and little easels, and boxes of water-colors, and Turkish paste, and nougat, and candied cherries, and dolls' houses, and waterproofs—and the big Christmas-tree, lighted and standing in a waste-basket in the middle.

She had a splendid Christmas all day. She ate so much candy that she did not want any breakfast; and the whole forenoon the presents kept pouring in that the express-man had not had time to deliver the night before; and she went 'round giving the presents she had got for other people, and came home and ate turkey and cranberry for dinner, and plum-pudding and nuts and raisins and oranges and more candy, and then went out and coasted and came in with a stomach-ache, crying; and her papa said he would see if his house was turned into that sort of fool's paradise another year; and they had a light supper, and pretty early everybody went to bed cross.

Here the little girl pounded her papa in the back again.

"Well, what now? Did I say pigs?"

"You made them *act* like pigs."

"Well, didn't they?"

"No matter; you oughtn't to put it into a story."

"Very well, then, I'll take it all out."

Her father went on:

The little girl slept very heavily, and she slept very late, but she was wakened at last by the other children dancing 'round her bed with their stockings full of presents in their hands.

"What is it?" said the little girl, and she rubbed her eyes and tried to rise up in bed.

"Christmas! Christmas! Christmas!" they all shouted, and waved their stockings.

"Nonsense! It was Christmas yesterday."

Her brothers and sisters just laughed. "We don't know about that. It's Christmas to-day, any way. You come into the library and see."

Then all at once it flashed on the little girl that the Fairy was keeping her promise, and her year of Christmases was beginning. She was dreadfully sleepy, but she sprang up like a lark—a lark that had overeaten itself and gone to bed cross—and darted into the library. There it was again! Books, and portfolios, and boxes of stationery, and breast-pins—

"You needn't go over it all, Papa; I guess I can remember just what was there," said the little girl.

Well, and there was the Christmas-tree blazing away, and the family picking out their presents, but looking pretty sleepy, and her father perfectly puzzled, and her mother ready to cry. "I'm sure I don't see how I'm to dispose of all these things," said her mother, and her father said it seemed to him they had had something just like it the day before, but he supposed he must have dreamed it. This struck the little girl as the best kind of a joke; and so she ate so much candy she didn't want any breakfast, and went 'round carrying presents, and had turkey and cranberry for dinner, and then went out and coasted, and came in with a—

"Papa!"

"Well, what now?"

"What did you promise, you forgetful thing?"

"Oh! oh, yes!"

Well, the next day, it was just the same thing over again, but everybody getting crosser; and at the end of a week's time so many people had lost their tempers that you could pick up lost tempers anywhere; they perfectly strewed the ground. Even when people tried to recover their tempers they usually got somebody else's, and it made the most dreadful mix.

The little girl began to get frightened, keeping the secret all to herself; she wanted to tell her mother, but she didn't dare to; and she was ashamed to ask the Fairy to take back her gift, it seemed ungrateful and ill-bred, and she thought she would try to stand it, but she hardly knew how she could, for a whole year. So it went on and on, and it was Christmas on St. Valentine's Day, and Washington's Birthday just the same as any day, and it didn't skip even the First of April, though everything was counterfeit that day, and that was some *little* relief.

After a while, coal and potatoes began to be awfully scarce, so many had been wrapped up in tissue paper to fool papas and mammas with. Turkeys got to be about a thousand dollars apiece—

"Papa!"

"Well, what?"

"You're beginning to fib."

"Well, *two* thousand, then."

And they got to passing off almost anything for turkeys—half-grown humming-birds, and even rocs out of the "Arabian Nights"—the real turkeys were so scarce. And cranberries—well, they asked a diamond apiece for cranberries. All the woods and orchards were cut down for Christmas-trees, and where the woods and orchards used to be, it looked just like a stubble-field, with the stumps. After a while they had to make Christmas-trees out of rags, and stuff them with bran, like old-fashioned dolls; but there were plenty of rags, because people got so poor, buying presents for one another, that they couldn't get any new clothes, and they just wore their old ones to tatters. They got so poor that everybody had to go to the poor-house, except the confectioners, and the fancy store-keepers, and the picture-booksellers, and the ex-pressmen; and *they* all got so rich and proud that they would hardly wait upon a person when he came to buy; it was perfectly shameful!

Well, after it had gone on about three or four months, the little girl, whenever she came into the room in the morning and saw those great ugly lumpy stockings dangling at the fire-place, and the disgusting presents around everywhere, used to just sit down and burst out crying. In six months she was perfectly exhausted; she couldn't even cry any more; she just lay on the lounge and rolled her eyes and panted. About the beginning of October she took to sitting down on dolls, wherever she found them—French dolls, or any kind—she hated the sight of them so; and by Thanksgiving she was crazy, and just slammed her presents across the room.

By that time people didn't carry presents around nicely any more. They flung them over the fence or through the window, or anything; and, instead of running their tongues out and taking great pains to write "For dear Papa," or "Mamma," or "Brother," or "Sister," or "Susie," or "Sammie," or "Billie," or "Bobby," or "Jimmie," or "Jennie," or whoever it was, and troubling to get the spelling right, and then signing their names, and "'Xmas, 188—," they used to write in the gift-books, "Take it, you horrid old thing!" and then go and bang it against the front door. Nearly everybody had built barns to hold their presents, but pretty soon the barns overflowed, and then they used to let them lie out in the rain, or anywhere. Sometimes the police used to come and tell them to shovel their presents off the sidewalk, or they would arrest them.

"I thought you said everybody had gone to the poor-house," interrupted the little girl.

"They did go, at first," said her papa; "but after a while the poor-houses got so full that they had to send the people back to their own houses. They tried to cry, when they got back, but they couldn't make the least sound."

"Why couldn't they?"

"Because they had lost their voices, saying 'Merry Christmas' so much. Did I tell you how it was on the Fourth of July?"

"No; how was it?" And the little girl nestled closer, in expectation of something uncommon.

Well, the night before, the boys staid up to celebrate, as they always do, and fell asleep before twelve o'clock, as usual, expecting to be wakened by the bells and cannon. But it was nearly eight o'clock before the first boy in the United States woke up, and then he found out what the trouble was. As soon as he could get his clothes on, he ran out of the house and smashed a big cannon-torpedo down on the pavement; but it didn't make any more noise than a damp wad of paper, and, after he tried about twenty or thirty more, he began to pick them up and look at them. Every single torpedo was a big raisin! Then he just streaked it upstairs, and examined his fire-crackers and toy-pistol and two-dollar collection of fireworks, and found that they were nothing but sugar and

candy painted up to look like fireworks! Before ten o'clock, every boy in the United States found out that his Fourth of July things had turned into Christmas things; and then they just sat down and cried— they were so mad. There are about twenty million boys in the United States, and so you can imagine what a noise they made. Some men got together before night, with a little powder that hadn't turned into purple sugar yet, and they said they would fire off *one* cannon, any way. But the cannon burst into a thousand pieces, for it was nothing but rock-candy, and some of the men nearly got killed. The Fourth of July orations all turned into Christmas carols, and when anybody tried to read the Declaration, instead of saying, "When in the course of human events it becomes necessary," he was sure to sing, "God rest you, merry gentlemen." It was perfectly awful.

The little girl drew a deep sigh of satisfaction.

"And how was it at Thanskgiving?" she asked.

Her papa hesitated. "Well, I'm almost afraid to tell you. I'm afraid you'll think it's wicked."

"Well, tell, anyway," said the little girl.

Well, before it came Thanksgiving, it had leaked out who had caused all these Christmases. The little girl had suffered so much that she had talked about it in her sleep; and after that, hardly anybody would play with her. People just perfectly despised her, because if it had not been for her greediness, it wouldn't have happened; and now, when it came Thanksgiving, and she wanted them to go to church, and have squash-pie and turkey, and show their gratitude, they said that all the turkeys had been eaten up for her old Christmas dinners, and if she would stop the Christmases, they would see about the gratitude. Wasn't it dreadful? And the very next day the little girl began to send letters to the Christmas Fairy, and then telegrams, to stop it. But it didn't do any good; and then she got to calling at the Fairy's house, but the girl that came to the door always said "Not at home," or "Engaged," or "At dinner," or something like that; and so it went on till it came to the old once-a-year Christmas Eve. The little girl fell asleep, and when she woke up in the morning—

"She found it was all nothing but a dream," suggested the little girl.

"No, indeed!" said her papa. "It was all every bit true!"

"Well, what *did* she find out then?"

"Why, that it wasn't Christmas at last, and wasn't ever going to be, any more. Now it's time for breakfast."

The little girl held her papa fast around the neck.

"You sha'n't go if you're going to leave it so!"

"How do you want it left?"

"Christmas once a year."

"All right," said her papa; and he went on again.

Well, there was the greatest rejoicing all over the country, and it extended clear up into Canada. The people met together everywhere, and kissed and cried for joy. The city carts went around and gathered up all the candy and raisins and nuts, and dumped them into the river; and it made the fish perfectly sick; and the whole United States, as far out as Alaska, was one blaze of bonfires, where the children were burning up their gift-books and presents of all kinds. They had the greatest *time!*

The little girl went to thank the old Fairy because she had stopped its being Christmas, and she said she hoped she would keep her promise, and see that Christmas never, never came again. Then the Fairy frowned, and asked her if she was sure she knew what she meant; and the little girl asked her, why not? and the old Fairy said that now she was behaving just as greedily as ever, and she'd better look out. This made the little girl think it all over carefully again, and she said she would be willing to have it Christmas about once in a thousand years; and then she said a hundred, and then she said ten, and at last she got down to one. Then the Fairy said that was the good old way that had pleased people ever since Christmas began, and she was agreed. Then the little girl said, "What're your shoes made of?" And the Fairy said, "Leather." And the little girl said, "Bargain's done forever," and skipped off, and hippity-hopped the whole way home, she was so glad.

"How will that do?" asked the papa.

"First-rate!" said the little girl; but she hated to have the story stop, and was rather sober. However, her mamma put her head in at the door, and asked her papa:

"Are you never coming to breakfast? What have you been telling that child?"

"Oh, just a moral tale."

The little girl caught him around the neck again.

"We know! Don't you tell *what*, Papa! Don't you tell *what!*"

THE SECRET DOOR
(A Christmas Story)
By Susan Coolidge

December, 1876

KNOWLE, in Kent, is an ancient manor-house. It stands knee-deep in rich garden and pasture lands, with hay-fields and apple-orchards stretching beyond, and solemn oak woods which whisper and shake their wise heads when the wind blows, as though possessed of secrets which must not be spoken. It is a real place, and the room which you see in the picture is a real room. That makes the picture much more interesting; don't you think so?

Very much as it looks to-day, it looked two hundred and thirty years ago, when Charles the First was king of England. That was the Charles who had his head cut off, you may remember. Blue Christmas smokes curled from the twisted chimneys in 1645, just as they will this year if the world lasts a month longer. The same dinner fragrance filled the air, for good cheer smells pretty much alike in all ages and the world over. A few changes there may be—thicker trees, beds of gay flowers which were not known in that day; and where once the moat—a ditch-like stream of green water covered with weeds and scum—ran round the walls, is now a trimly cut border of verdant turf. But these changes are improvements, and in all important respects the house keeps its old look, undisturbed by modern times and ways.

In the same nursery where modern boys and girls eat, sleep and learn their A, B, C to-day, two children lived. You see them in the picture—little Ralph Tresham and his sister Henrietta. Quaint, old-fashioned creatures they would look to us now; but, in spite of their formal dresses and speech, they were bright and merry and happy as any children you can find among your acquaintances. Ralph's name was pronounced "Rafe," and he always called his sister "Hexie."

Christmas did not come to Knowle in its usual bright shape in 1645. Gloom and sadness and anxiety overshadowed the house; and though the little ones did not understand what the cause of the anxiety was, they felt something wrong, and went about quietly whispering to each other in corners, instead of whooping and laughing, as had been their wont. They had eaten their Christmas beef, and toasted the king in a thimbleful of wine, as usual, but their mother cried when they did so; and Joyce, the old butler, had carried off the pudding with a face like a funeral. So, after dinner, they crept away to the nursery, and there, by the window, began a long whispering talk. Hexie had something very exciting to tell.

"Nurse thought I was asleep," she said, "but I wasn't quite; and when they began to talk I woke up. That wasn't wrong, was it, Rafe? I couldn't sleep when I couldn't, could I?"

"I suppose not; but you needn't have listened," said Rafe, whose notions about honor were very strict.

"I did pull the pillow over my ear, but the words would get in," went on Henrietta, piteously. "And it was so interesting. Did you know that there were such creatures as Bogies, Rafe? Dorothy thinks we have got one in our house, and that its hole is in the great gallery, because once when she was there dusting the armor, she heard a queer noise in the wall, and what else

200

could it be? It eats a great deal, does the Bogie. That's the reason nurse is sure we have got one. It ate all the cold sheep's-head yesterday, and the day before half the big pasty. No victual is safe in the larder, the Bogie has such a big appetite, nurse says."

"I remember about the sheep's-head," said Rafe, meditatively. "Almost all of it was left, and I looked to see it come in cold; but when I asked, Joyce said there was none. Cold sheep's-head is very good. Do you remember how much Humphrey used to like it?"

"I don't remember exactly, it is so long ago," replied Hexie. "How long is it, brother?—since Humphrey went away, I mean. Won't he ever come back?"

"I asked Winifred once, but she only said God knew, that nothing had been heard of him since the battle when the king was taken. He might be dead, or he might be escaped into foreign parts—and then she cried, oh, so hard, Hexie! Poor Humphrey! I hope he isn't dead. But, about the Bogie, how curious it must be to meet one! Oh, I say, let us go to the gallery now, and see if we hear any strange noises there. Will you?"

"Oh, Rafe! I'm afraid. I don't quite like—"

"But you can't be afraid if I'm there," said Rafe valiantly; "besides, I'll put on Humphrey's old sword which he left behind. Then if the Bogie comes—we shall see!"

Rafe spoke like a conquering hero, Hexie thought; so, though she trembled, she made no further objection, but stood by while he lifted down the sword, helped to fasten its belt over his shoulder, and followed along the passage which led to the gallery. The heavy sword clattered and rattled as it dragged on the floor, and the sound was echoed in a ghostly way, which renewed Hexie's fears.

"Rafe! Rafe! let us go back!" she cried.

"Go back yourself if you are afraid," replied Ralph, stoutly; and as going back alone through the dim passage seemed just then worse than staying where she was, Hexie stayed with her valiant brother.

Very softly they unlatched the gallery door, and stole in. It was a long, lofty apartment, paneled with cedar-wood, to which time had given a beautiful light-brown color. The ceiling, of the same wood, was carved, here and there, with shields, coats of arms, and other devices. There was little furniture: one tall cabinet, a few high-backed Dutch chairs, and some portraits hanging on the walls. The sun, not yet quite set, poured a stream of red light across the polished floor, leaving the far corners and the empty spaces formidably dusk. The children had seldom been in the gallery at this hour, and it looked to them almost like a strange place, not at all as it did at noonday when they came to jump up and down the slippery floor, and play hide-and-seek in the corners which now seemed so dark and dismal.

Even Rafe felt the difference, and shivered in spite of his bold heart and the big sword by his side. Timidly they went forward, hushing their footsteps and peering furtively into the shadows. Suddenly Hexie stopped with a little scream.

Close to them stood a huge suit of armor, larger and taller than a man. The empty eye-holes of the helmet glared out quite like real eyes, and the whole figure was terrible enough to frighten any little girl. But it was not at the armor that Hexie screamed; the iron man was an old friend of the children's. Many a game of hide-and-seek had they played around, and behind, and even inside him; for Humphrey had contrived a cunning way by which the figure could be taken to pieces and put together again; and more than once Rafe had been popped inside, and had lain shaking with laughter while Hexie vainly searched for him through all the gallery. This had not happened lately, for Rafe was hardly strong enough to manage by himself the screws and hinges which opened the armor; but he knew the iron man too well to scream at him, and so did Hexie. The object which excited her terror was something different, and so strange and surprising that it is no wonder she screamed.

Close by the armor, half hidden by a curtain of heavy tapestry, was an open door, where never door had been known to be. It stood ajar, and dimly visible inside was a narrow staircase winding upward.

"The hole of the Bogie!" gasped Hexie, clutching at Rafe's arm. He started, and felt for the sword. It rattled fearfully, and the sound completed Hexie's terror. She burst away, flew like a scared lapwing down the gallery, along the passages, and never stopped till she reached the nursery and her own bed, where, with two pillows and the quilt drawn over her head, she lay sobbing bitterly at the thought of Ralph left behind, to be eaten perhaps by the Bogie! Poor little Hexie!

Ralph, meanwhile, stood his ground. His heart beat very fast, but he would not run away—that was for girls. It must be owned, however, that when a moment later the sound of muffled voices became audible down the stairs, he trembled extremely, and was guilty of the unmanlike act of hiding behind the curtain. He was only ten years old, which must plead his excuse with bigger boys who are confident that they could never, under any circumstances, hide themselves or be afraid.

The voices drew nearer, steps sounded, and two figures came out of the narrow door-way. Could there be two Bogies? No wonder they ate so much. But in another minute all thought of Bogies vanished from Ralph's mind, for in one of the figures he recognized his own sister Winifred.

Her companion was a man. There was something familiar in his form. It moved forward, and Ralph jumped so that the big sword rattled again. Bogie number two was his brother Humphrey, mourned as dead ever since the summer before, when so many brave gentlemen gave up their lives for King Charles at the battle of Naseby.

"What noise was that?" whispered Winifred, fearfully.

"Some sound from below," replied Humphrey, after listening a moment. "Must you go, Winnie?"

"I must, dear Humphrey. I dare not absent myself longer lest I be missed and suspected. Oh, if to-morrow were but over, and you safe on the French lugger and over the sea! I cannot breathe while this hiding and danger go on."

"I suppose I ought to be glad also," said Humphrey, ruefully; "but to me that French lugger means exile, and loneliness, and poverty, for the rest of my life, perhaps. Better have laid down my life with the rest at Naseby, in striking one last blow for the king."

"Don't, don't speak so!" protested Winifred, tearfully. "You are alive, thank God; and once these wars are over we may rejoin you, and have a happy home somewhere, if not in the land of our fathers. Now, dear Humphrey, have you all you need for the night?"

"Christmas cheer," said Humphrey, in a would-be cheerful voice. "Beef and ale— what better fare could be? You are a gallant provider, my Winnie, and there is need, for since I have lain in that hole with nothing else to do, my appetite has raged like a wolf. That sheep's-head was wondrous savory. I say though, Winnie, what do the servants think of the famine I create in the larder?"

"Oh, the stupid creatures fancy that a Bogie has taken up his residence here. A very hungry Bogie, Joyce calls the creature!"

The brother and sister laughed; then they kissed each other.

"Good-night, dearest Winifred."

"Good-night, brother"; and Humphrey vanished up the stairs. Winifred lingered a moment; then, as if remembering something, opened the door again and ran after him. Ralph marked that she laid her hand on a particular boss in the carved wainscot, and pressed it in hard, whereon the door sprang open. He stole out, laid his hand on the same boss, and felt the spring give way under his touch. Some undefined idea of stealing in later, to make Humphrey a visit, was in his head; but he heard Winifred returning, and hurried out of the gallery. Putting back the sword in its place, he entered the nursery. No Hexie was visible, but a sobbing sound drew his attention to a tumbled heap on the bed.

"Is that you, Hexie? Why, what are you crying about?" pulling away the pillow which she held tight.

"Oh, Rafe! Then the Bogie didn't eat you, after all!" And Hexie buried her tear-stained face in his shoulder.

"Bogie! Nonsense! There are no such things as Bogies!"

"What was it, then, that lived up that dreadful stairs?"

"I can't tell you; only it was nothing at all dreadful. And, Hexie, don't say a word about that door to any one, will you? It might make great trouble if you did."

"I did tell Deborah, when she fetched the candle and asked why I cried, that I saw a strange door in the gallery," faltered Hexie, truthful, though penitent.

"Oh! Hexie, how could you? I don't like Deborah, and her father is a crop-eared knave. Humphrey said so one day. How could you talk to her about the door, Hexie?"

"I—don't know. I was frightened, and she asked me," sobbed Hexie. "Will it do any harm, Rafe?"

"It may," said Rafe, gloomily. "But don't cry, Hexie. You meant no harm, at all events."

"Oh, don't speak so gravely and so like Joyce," said Hexie, much troubled. She cried herself to sleep that night. Deborah, who undressed her, asked many questions about the gallery and the door.

"It was very dark, and perhaps she mistook"—that was all Hexie could be made to say. Ralph was disturbed and wakeful, and slept later than usual next morning. He jumped up in a hurry and made what haste he could with dressing and breakfast, but it seemed as though they never took so much time before; and all the while he ate he was conscious of a stir and bustle in the house, which excited his curiosity very much. Knocking—the sound of feet—something unusual was going on.

As soon as possible he slipped away from nurse and ran to the gallery. The door was half open. He looked in, and stood still with terror. Men, in brown uniforms and steel caps, were there sounding the walls and tapping the floor-boards with staves. The gallery seemed full of them, though when Rafe counted there were but five.

"This man of iron was, in all likelihood, a Malignant also," he heard one of them say, striking the armor with his fist.

"He is somewhat old for that. Methinks that is armor of the time of that man of blood, Harry the Eighth. Move it aside, Jotham, that we may search the farther panel."

So the heavy figure was thrust into a corner, and the men went on tapping with their wands. Rafe groaned within himself when he heard them declare that the wall sounded hollow, and saw them searching for a spring. Twenty times it seemed as though they must have lighted on the right place. Twenty times they just missed it.

"We were ill advised to come without tools," declared the man who seemed leader of the party. "Come thou to my shop, Peter Kettle, and thou, Bartimeus and Zerrubabel, and we will fetch such things as are needful. Jotham, stay thou here, to see that no man escapeth from the concealment behind the wall."

So four of the men went away, leaving Jotham striding up and down as on guard. Presently came a shout from beneath the window:

"Jotham! our leader hath dropped his pouch in which are the keys of the smithy. Hasten and bring it to the outer door."

"Aye, aye!" answered Jotham, and, pouch in hand, he ran down the stairs. Now was Rafe's opportunity. Like a flash he was across the gallery, his hand on the boss. The door flew open, and he fell into the arms of Humphrey, who, sword in hand and teeth set, stood on the lower step of the staircase, prepared to sell his liberty as dearly as possible.

"Rafe! little Rafe!" he exclaimed.

"Hush! The man will come back," panted Rafe. "Come away—hide—oh, where?" Then with a sudden inspiration he dragged his brother toward the iron man. "Get inside," he cried. "They will never think of searching there! Oh, Humphrey—make haste! Get inside!"

There was no time to be lost. With the speed of desperation, Humphrey unscrewed, lifted, stepped inside the armor. Rafe slipped the fastenings together, whispered "shut your eyes," and flew back to his hiding-place. Just in time, for Jotham's step was on the stair, and next moment he entered the gallery, and resumed his march up and down, little dreaming that the man sought for was peeping through the helmet holes at him, not three feet away.

Presently the other soldiers came back with hammers and wrenches, and in a short time the beautiful wainscot, split into pieces, lay on the floor. Suddenly there was a shout. The secret door had flown open, and the staircase stood revealed. Four of the men, with pikes and pistols, prepared to ascend, while the fifth guarded the opening below.

At that moment Winifred entered the gallery from the farther end. She turned deadly pale when she saw the open door and the men.

"Oh! Heaven have mercy!" she cried, and dropped half fainting into a chair.

Rafe darted across the floor and seized her hand.

"Hush," he whispered. "Don't say a word, sister. *He* is safe."

"He? Who?" cried the amazed Winifred.

But now voices sounded from above. The men were coming down. Winifred rallied her courage, rose, and went forward. She was very white still, but she spoke in a steady voice. Her two brothers, Humphrey in his hiding-place and little Rafe by her side, both admired her greatly.

"What is the meaning of this, Jotham Green?" she demanded. "By what warrant do you enter and spoil our house?"

"By the warrant which all true men have to search for traitors," said Jotham.

"You will find none such here," responded Winifred firmly.

"We find the lurking-place in which one such has doubtless lain," said Zerrubabel. "Where holes exist, look out for vermin."

"You are less than civil, neighbor. An old house like this has many strange nooks and corners of which the inhabitants may have neither use nor knowledge. If your search is done, I will beg you to make good the damage you have caused as best you may, and with as little noise as possible, that my mother be not alarmed. Jotham Green, you are a good workman, I know. I recollect how deftly you once repaired that cabinet for us."

All the men knew Winifred, and her calm and decided manner made its impression. Jotham slowly picked up the fragments of the paneling and began to fit them together. The rest consulted, and at last rather sheepishly, and with a muttered half apology about "wrong information," went away, taking with them the injured woodwork, which Jotham undertook to repair. Rafe's first words after they disappeared were:

"Winifred, you must dismiss Deborah. It is she that has betrayed us."

"How do you know that, Rafe?"

Then it all came out. Winifred listened to the tale with streaming tears.

"Oh, Rafe, my darling, how brave you were! You played the man for us to-day, and have saved—I trust you have saved—our Humphrey. The men will not return to-day, and to-night the lugger sails."

And Humphrey was saved. Before morning, well disguised, he had made his way across country to a little fishing-port, embarked, and reached France without farther accident.

So that strange Christmas adventure ended happily. It was all long, long ago. Humphrey and Winifred and Rafe lived their lives out, and lay down to rest a century and a half since under the daisy-sprinkled English sod. Little Hexie died an aged woman, before any of us was born. But still the beautiful old manor-house stands amid its gardens and pasture lands, with the silvery look of time on its gray walls. Still the armed figure keeps guard beside the secret staircase, the tapestry hangs in the old heavy folds, evening reddens the cedar walls and the polished floor, and everything occupies the same place and wears the same look that it did when little Rafe played the man in that gallery, and saved his brother Humphrey more than two hundred years ago.

THE TARDY SANTA CLAUS
By Kate D. Wiggin
January, 1896

I AM a little Santa Claus
   Who somehow got belated;
My reindeer didn't come in time,
   And so of course I waited.
I found your chimneys plastered tight,
   Your stockings put away,

I heard you talking of the gifts
   You had on Christmas Day;
So will you please to take me in
   And keep me till November?
I'd rather start Thanksgiving Day
   Than miss you *next* December!

February, 1875

NICHOLAS! ST. NICHOLAS!

The "Ice-Boat Song," from "Hans Brinker."

GEORGE J. HUSS

1. Friend of sail - ors
2. While through wintry
3. Sun - ny spar - kles
4. Pret - ty gifts and

With Spirit.

1 and of children! Dou-ble claim have we
2 air we're rushing, As our voic-es blend,
3 bright before us Chase a - way the cold!
4 lov-ing les - son, Fes - ti - val and glee,

As in youth-ful joy we're sailing O'er a fro - zen sea!
Are you near us? do you hear us, Nich-o - las, our friend?
Hearts where sunny thoughts are welcome, Never can grow old.
Bid us thank thee as we're sailing O'er the froz - en sea.

1 Nich - o-las! Saint Nich-o-las!
2 Nich - o-las! Saint Nich-o-las!
3 Nich - o-las! Saint Nich-o-las!
4 Nich - o-las! Saint Nich-o-las!

Let us sing to thee.
Love can nev-er end.
Nev - er can grow old.
So we sing to thee!

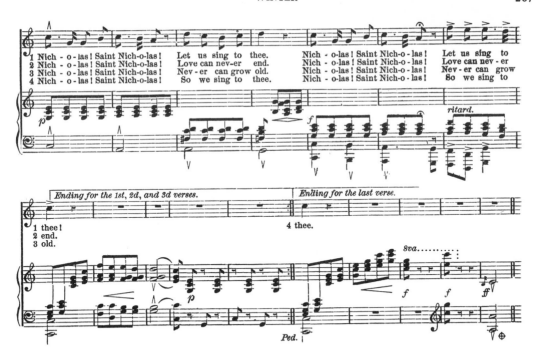

1 Nich - o - las! Saint Nich-o-las! Let us sing to thee. Nich - o-las! Saint Nich-o - las! Let us sing to
2 Nich - o - las! Saint Nich-o-las! Love can nev-er end. Nich - o-las! Saint Nich-o - las! Love can nev - er
3 Nich - o - las! Saint Nich-o-las! Nev - er can grow old. Nich - o-las! Saint Nich-o - las! Nev - er can grow
4 Nich - o - las! Saint Nich-o-las! So we sing to thee. Nich - o-las! Saint Nich-o - las! So we sing to

Ending for the 1st, 2d, and 3d verses.   Ending for the last verse.

1 thee!   4 thee.
2 end.
3 old.

THE ANTIPODES
By E. P.

February, 1875

HERE all the world is winter-time,
  And gusty breezes blow
On violets that sleep beneath
  A counterpane of snow.

The sparrows huddle in the rain
  Or hardly try to sing,
But go to bed at five instead
  To dream about the spring.

And yet, in the antipodes—
  A word I learned last week,
With several other pleasant terms
  (They tell me that it's Greek)—

In Sydney and Van Diemen's Land,
  December days are bright,
And while we mourn a winter day
  They sing a summer night.

'Tis winter here, 'tis summer there;
  Likewise in every town
They justify the weather chart
  By walking upside down.

Now, I should like, when summer's gone
  And winter brings the rain,
To turn the world the wrong way round
  And find the spring again!

POMPEY'S CHRISTMAS.

By Carolyn Wells

December, 1899

IF aught of history
 you 've been
 told,
 Of course you
 know
That long ago
There lived a war-
 rior brave
 and bold,
 And Pompey was
 his name—
"Pompey the Great" he was enrolled
Upon the lists of fame.

So skilfully his darts he hurled
He conquered nearly all the world.
 But this occurred,
 As you have heard,
When Pompey was a man.
And as I 'm sure that you 'd enjoy
A tale of Pompey when a boy,
 I 'll tell you all I can.

Young Pompey had a pleasant home
In the old, well-known town of Rome;
The house was wondrous to behold,

Adorned with ivory and gold;
The "atrium" and the "peristyle"
 (They 're rooms, you know,
 Of long ago)
Were decked with marble, glass, and tile,
 Rich woven goods
 And precious woods,
And statues in the aisle.

When Pompey with his parents dined,
Upon low couches they reclined,
 And thus in state
 Rare viands ate
Of every sort and kind.
For clothing Pompey round him draped
A Roman garment queerly shaped—
 A "toga" of white wool,
 Exceeding long and full;
And on his feet the funny chap
Wore sandals buckled with a strap.

 Now, Pompey had his joys
 As well as modern boys.
His native town of Rome could boast
Of seven hills down which to coast;

"AND THUS IN STATE RARE VIANDS ATE."

Or, if he cared to see a show,
To Circus Maximus he 'd go;
    Then, he could read a scroll
    Or a papyrus roll;
      Or, if he 'd wish,
      In Tiber fish;
And there were many Roman games—
I have forgotten their queer names.

But shall I tell you of the way
Young Pompey spent one Christmas Day
    In merriment and cheer?
    And would you like to hear
      How this young lad
      His presents had?
    The tale is rather queer.

Imagine Pompey's boyish head
Pillowed upon his ivory bed,
    So sound asleep
    In slumber deep,
    He could not hear the tread
Of Santa Claus, who stealthily
Came, laden with a Christmas tree
    That I declare,
    Had you been there,
    You would have laughed to see.

"SEVEN HILLS DOWN WHICH TO COAST."

Of course in Italy's warm clime
They cannot find at Christmas-time
    A fir or spruce
    For Christmas use;
    So Santa Claus, you see,
    Had brought a tall palm-tree;

For worse than stockings full of holes
It is to fill a pair of soles.
But he accomplished it some way,
And then, as it was almost day,
  He slung his pack
  Across his back
And drove off in his sleigh.

And oh, when Christmas morning broke,
  And Pompey from his dreams awoke,
  Just try to picture his delight!
  But *no!* why—*wait!* this is n't right!
    How *could* I make
    Such a mistake?
  The story is all wrong! Oh, dear!
  I 'll have to stop the tale right here.
  You *can't* imagine Pompey's joy,
  Because when Pompey was a boy

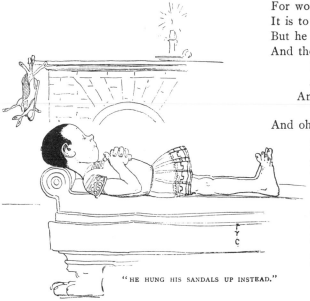

"HE HUNG HIS SANDALS UP INSTEAD."

And when with gifts and toys arrayed,
Quite a fair Christmas tree it made,
Although 't was very high. Indeed,
A tall step-ladder one would need
  To reach the toys and things,
  Even when hung by strings.

As you have often heard before,
No stockings Roman people wore;
And so, ere Pompey went to bed,
He hung his sandals up instead.
  And Santa Claus
  Was at a loss;

Of Christmas presents he had none;
For Christmases had not begun
  When Pompey was a boy!

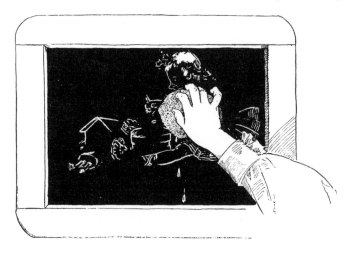

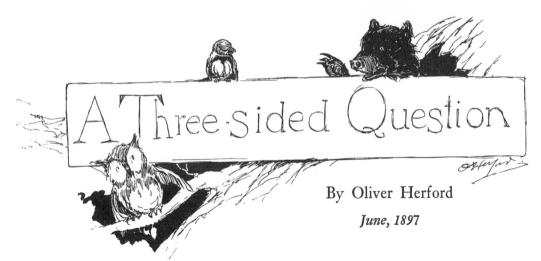

A Three-sided Question

By Oliver Herford

June, 1897

A WOODLAND COMEDY
SCENE: *A hollow tree in the woods.*
TIME: *December, evening.*
PERSONS: *Mr. Owl, Mr. Sparrow, Mr. Bear.*

MR. OWL *(stretching his wings):*
EIGHO! It's dark! How fast the daylight goes! I must have overslept. It's time I rose
And went about my breakfast to prepare.
I should keep better hours; I declare
Before I got to bed 'twas broad daylight!
That must be why I'm getting up to-night
With such a sleepy feeling in my head.
Heigho! Heigho! *(Yawns.)*

Enter MR. SPARROW.

MR. SPARROW: Why don't you go to bed,
If you're so very sleepy!—it's high time!
The sun has set an hour ago, and I'm
Going home myself as fast as I can trot.
Night is the time for sleep.

MR. OWL: The time for *what?*
The time for *sleep,* you say?
MR. SPARROW: That's what I said.
MR. OWL:
Well, my dear bird, your reason must have fled!
MR. SPARROW *(icily):*
I do not catch your meaning quite, I fear.
MR. OWL:
I mean you're talking nonsense. Is that clear?
MR. SPARROW *(angrily):*
Say that again—again, sir, if you dare!
Say it again!
MR. OWL: As often as you care.
You're talking nonsense—stuff and nonsense
    —there!
MR. SPARROW *(hopping one twig higher up):*
You are a coward, sir, and *impolite!*
        (Hopping on a still higher twig)
And if you weren't beneath me I would fight.
MR. OWL:
I *am* beneath you, true enough, my friend,
By just two branches. Will you not descend?

211

Or shall I—

MR. SPARROW (*hastily*):

　　　　No, don't rise.　Tell me instead
What was the nonsense that you thought I
　　said.

MR. OWL:

It may be wrong, but if I heard aright,
You said the proper time for sleep was night.

MR. SPARROW:

That's what I said, and I repeat it too!

MR. OWL:

Then you repeat a thing that is not true.
Day is the time for sleep, not *night*.

MR. SPARROW:　　　　　　　Absurd!
Who's talking nonsense now?

MR. OWL:　　　　　　Impudent bird!

How dare you answer back, you upstart
　　fowl!

MR. SPARROW:

How dare you call me upstart—you—you
　　Owl!

MR. OWL:

This is too much! I'll stand no more, I vow!
Defend yourself!

MR. BEAR (*looking out of hollow tree*):
Come, neighbors, stop that row!
What you're about I'm sure I cannot think.

I only know I haven't had one wink
Of sleep. Indeed, I've borne it long enough.
'Twould put the mildest temper in a huff;
　　And I am but a bear. Why don't you go
　　To bed like other folks, I'd like to know?
Summer is long enough to keep awake—
Winter's the time when honest people take
Their three months' sleep.

　　　　MR. SPARROW: That settles me! I
　　　　fly!

Dear Mr. Owl and Mr. Bear, good-
　　by!　　　　　　　　　[*Exit.*

MR. OWL:

I must go too, to find another wood
Every one's mad in this queer neigh-
　　　　borhood!

It is not safe such company to keep.
Good evening, Mr. Bear.　　[*Exit.*
MR. BEAR: *Now* I shall sleep.

　　　　CURTAIN.

The Queen's Jewels

A Nonsense Rhyme

for

Chess Players

by

Charles Love Benjamin

June, 1897

IN Chess-board Land there dwelt a ,
  And he was quite forlorn
Because his mate the , had been
  Obliged her jewels to
(As Isabel of Castile did
  Long, long ere you were born).

And so, unchecked, the  she grieved
  Within the  walls;
She gave up theater-going,
  She never went to balls;
"And say I 'm not at home," said she,
  Unless the  calls."

The  called upon the ,
  He brought with him a  —
I don't remember clearly —

Now, was he black, or white?
But, anyway, he said that he
  Could get the jewels bright.

"But can we trust him," said the ;
  "With gems so rich and rare?
These  , alas, lead checkered lives.
  One must proceed with care."
This , wretched punster, said
  This  was "on the square."

"Go then, and quickly!" said the ;
  So forth the brave  set:
But how his tour was ended
  I really quite forget.
Perhaps he found the gems at last —
  Perhaps he 's riding yet.

From Our Scrap-Book

-C.T.HILL-

July, 1897

WHY GONDOLAS ARE BLACK

In former times the nobles of Venice spent such immense sums in decorating their gondolas that the government passed a law that all should be alike, and all have since been painted black. Some gondolas have been on the lakes of Central Park, and many were used in Chicago at the time of the World's Fair, in 1893.

WHY "BEACON" STREET?

BEACON STREET, in Boston, derives its name from a beacon which stood on the summit of the hill so that, in case of an invasion, the country could be roused by setting fire to a barrel of tar kept there. The beacon was blown down by the violence of the wind in 1789. Beacon Hill was the highest of the three hills which gave Boston its original name, Trimountain.

FOUNDING OF HARVARD UNIVERSITY

THE General Court of Massachusetts voted in 1636 to give £400 to found a college at Newtown, afterward called Cambridge. It is said that "This was the first legislative assembly in which the people, through their representatives, gave their own money to found a place of education."

A WILLOW FROM NAPOLEON'S GRAVE

OVER the grave of Cotton Mather in Copp's burying-ground (near Bunker Hill, Boston) is a weeping-willow tree which was grown from a cutting of the willow-tree that shaded the grave of Napoleon at St. Helena.

MICHELANGELO AS ARCHITECT

THE great artist Michelangelo was as famous an architect or designer as he was a painter. He designed the church of St. Peter at Rome, which is built in the form of a Latin cross. He also designed another church in Rome, and, besides these, planned a number of famous structures.

THE PEACOCK AT HOME

THE real home of the peacock or peafowl is in India. There they were and are hunted, and their flesh is used for food. As these birds live in the same region as the tiger, peacock-hunting is a very dangerous sport. The long train of the peacock is not its tail, as many suppose, but is composed of feathers which grow out just above the tail, and are called the tail-coverts. Peacocks have been known for many hundred years. They are mentioned in the Bible:

Job mentions them, and they are mentioned too in I Kings, 10. Hundreds of years ago in Rome many thousand peacocks were killed for the great feasts which the emperors made. The brains of the peacock were considered a great treat, and many had to be killed for a single feast.

"THE MISSISSIPPI OF STREETS"

BROADWAY is five miles long, with nearly half its line as straight as an arrow flies, so that the eye may look upward from the quaint little Bowling Green near the Battery to the graceful spire of Grace Church—almost up to Union Square. From this point it turns from its straight course, and nearly two miles beyond reaches Central Park, from which, under the name of the Boulevard, it is prolonged nine miles farther. It was with reason that Lady Mary Wortley Montagu called this the "lengthy Mississippi of streets."

ST. CLEMENTE, ROME

THERE is a church in Rome, called St. Clemente, which is a very curious building. Here we find four buildings, one on top of the other. The uppermost one is the present church, built in 1108. There is another below this which was the church of the early Christians, and first mentioned in 392. Below this one are the remains of an old Roman building of the time of the emperors; and still below this are great walls belonging to a building of the time of the Roman republic.

A KNOCK ON THE DOOR, IN ANCIENT TIMES

WINCKELMANN, quoting the comedies of Plautus and Terence, says that Grecian doors opened outward, so that a person leaving the house knocked first within, lest he should open the door in the face of a passer-by. Hinges were not then in use, and at Rome, Pompeii, and Herculaneum doors have at top and bottom pivots which turn in sockets.

VARIOUS ITEMS

THE Revolutionary War, from its first outbreak at Lexington, April 19, 1775, to the final disbanding of the army, April 19, 1783, lasted *just eight years* to a day.

THE Second Epistle of St. John is a letter to a lady.

LEONARDO DA VINCI, the great painter, who painted the famous picture of the Last Supper, is said to have invented the wheelbarrow.

SAMUEL ADAMS first originated the idea of declaring the American colonies independent of Great Britain.

THE tusks of the elephant never stop growing till the animal dies.

THE goldfish is a native of China, and was seen in England first in 1691.

ANCIENT soldiers were taught to fight equally well with either hand.

IN France St. Nicholas's day is the fête-day for boys, and St. Catherine's day is the fête-day for girls.

CARTHAGE was destroyed 146 B.C. It was twenty-four miles in circumference, and is said to have been burning seventeen days.

IN winding up the clock of Trinity Church, New York, it is said that the crank or handle has to be turned round eight hundred and fifty times.

WHAT THE PARROT
TAUGHT THE LITTLE GIRL

October, 1887

PECKY was just a poor poll parrot, with nothing of his own but his pretty gray feathers and sharp beak, that could bite little fingers when they came too near his cage; and yet this same Pecky taught Katie Scott a very useful lesson. When he was first brought home, Katie was just the happiest little girl! "Mamma!" she cried. "Mamma, please, he must be placed where he can see Libbie and Mary play croquet!"

Libbie and Mary lived next door, and, when the weather was fine, the three friends—Katie, Libbie and Mary—used to have fine games on the lawn between the two houses.

There were four friends when Pecky came, for he was put close by the window, where he could see the fun. Before long, he learned many new words. He would cry, "Croquet her away! Take care, Katie! I have won! Ha! ha! ha!" And he could laugh louder than any of them. They thought there never was such a wonderful pet.

Katie told her mamma it was "just the *cunningest*, nicest little polly in the world." So it was; and Katie was one of the nicest little girls in the world when she could have what she wanted, but sometimes little people want what is not good for them. One day, at dinner, mama said:

"You can't have any more melon, Katie dear; it will make you ill!"

I hope none of the little girls and boys who read this would do as Katie Scott did—I am really sorry to have to tell it—she threw herself on the floor, and kicked and screamed so loudly, that Libbie and Mary, who were playing outside, heard her.

"What is that noise?" asked Mary.

"Oh!" said Libbie, "it is just Katie Scott—*Cry-baby!*"

Libbie did not know that she was heard, but such was the case. Mr. Pecky had two little sharp ears open, and turning one up and then the other, he walked up and down chuckling to himself, as much as to say: "I guess I know what *that* means!" And then he cried softly, imitating Katie's voice: "Boo—hoo! Boo, hoo, hoo!"

He did not forget it for a whole week, and I am glad to say that, for a while, his little mistress was a perfectly good girl.

But there came a day—a damp, cold day—and mamma said there could be no croquet. Katie forgot that she was trying to be good, and, lying down near Pecky's perch, screamed like a very naughty child.

Pecky thought so, I know. He watched her some time, then jumped down to the floor of his cage, crying: "Bo-o-o-o! Boo, hoo! Bo-o-o-o!" Katie very quickly stopped crying, peeped up at him, and ran out of the room very much ashamed. Mamma and Aunt Jane laughed, and Pecky thought: "I must have done something very funny. I'll just do it again! Oh, yes, I'll do it again!"

And he did it all that day, whenever any one came into the room.

When mamma was putting Katie to bed that evening, a little voice whispered: "Mamma, *won't* you make Pecky stop doing *that?*"

What do you think mamma said? She whispered to Katie: "When Polly does not see any little girl doing so, I am sure he will forget it."

"Then I'll never do so any more!" said Katie. And she kept her word.

JACK-IN-THE-PULPIT

December, 1894

As you all know right well, my friends, your Jack is not a summer Jack-in-the-pulpit; neither does he belong to winter, autumn, or spring. He is an outdoor-loving, all-the-year Jack, at your service, thriving in the sunlight of young lives, and blooming best in the warmth and merriment of young hearts. Therefore is he specially alive in December, the last month of the twelve, and the cheeriest, for it sets the Christmas bells a-ringing and brings in the glow of Christmas-tide.

And this reminds me of a little song sent to this pulpit by Emilie Poulsson, in the desire that you learn it by heart, and in time for the coming day:

WHILE stars of Christmas shine,
  Lighting the skies,
Let only loving looks
  Beam from your eyes.

While bells of Christmas ring
  Joyous and clear,
Speak only happy words,
  All mirth and cheer.

Give only loving gifts,
  And in love take;
Gladden the poor and sad
  For love's dear sake.

SWIFT TRAVELERS

DEAR JACK-IN-THE-PULPIT: Not very long ago you told your ST. NICHOLAS hearers of hawks being able to fly at the rate of 150 miles an hour. Here are some interesting facts concerning the traveling powers of certain other birds.

The paisano, road-runner, or chaparral cock runs faster than a fleet horse.

The ostrich sometimes runs at the rate of 30 miles an hour.

The carrier-pigeon will fly at least 30 miles an hour, and some have been known to travel at the rate of 60 or even 90 miles an hour.

Wild pigeons often fly hundreds of miles a day to feed, returning to their roosts at night. Audubon says they travel a mile a minute.

The condor of the Andes flies to the height of six miles.

The bald eagle rises in circular sweeps until it disappears from view, and then glides to the earth with such velocity that the eye can scarcely follow it.

The humming-bird, although the smallest bird known, possesses great power and rapidity of flight, and travels many miles in one day.

Yours truly,   B. L. B.—

Here is a message from the Red School-house:

DEAR JACK-IN-THE-PULPIT: A young girl only thirteen years of age has sent me these very clever nonsense rhymes—her own unaided work, she says—and so, dear Jack, without ado I'll hand them to your "chicks" and you.

Very truly yours
Little Schoolma'am

THE *BUGABOO*

Now heed my tale, so strange and true:
The good ship called the *Bugaboo*
Sailed forth one day from Timbuctoo.
Of men it had a goodly crew,
A captain and a boatswain too.
Of passengers there were but few:
A Chinaman who wore a queue,
A Frenchman, African, and Jew.
The animals would frighten you:
A llama, and a kangaroo,
An elephant, and caribou,
A cow, dog, owl, pig, cat, and gnu,
Six hens, a rooster and a ewe,
And more—enough to form a Zoo.

It took them many days to hew
The slender masts of oak and yew.
At last when naught was left to do,
And all had said their last adieu,
The boiler puffed, the whistle blew,
And they were off with small ado.

Far out upon the ocean blue,
Where naught but water greets the view,
A fearful storm began to brew.
The birds up to the rigging flew,
The chickens clucked, the rooster crew,
The frightened cow began to moo,
The dog to bark, the cat to mew.
In vain they hollered "scat!" and "shoo!"
And many missiles at them threw;
The noises only louder grew.
But greater trouble did ensue—
Their coming they began to rue:
A whirlpool in the vessel drew,
The crew declared it nothing new,
A way to reach the land they knew,
So all set off in a canoe.
When food grew scarce, the cock they slew
And made his flesh into a stew.
They sighted land, took hope anew;
But all were gone but one or two
When land was reached. Alas, 'tis true,
The natives boiled and ate them, too.
And now my simple tale is through.

Flora W. Smith

A St. NICHOLAS ANTHOLOGY
SPRING

CONTENTS

BREWSTER'S DEBUT

By Ralph Henry Barbour

September, 1903

I

THE gong clanged, the last man sprang aboard, and the car trundled away to the accompaniment of a final lusty cheer from the crowd which still lingered in front of the hotel. Then a corner was turned, and the last long-drawn *"Er-r-rskine!"* was cut short by intercepting walls. The throngs were streaming out to the field where, on the smooth green diamond, the rival nines of Robinson and Erskine were to meet in the deciding game of the season. For a while the car with its dozen or so passengers followed the crowds, but presently it swung eastward toward the railroad, and then made its way through a portion of Collegetown which, to one passenger at least, looked far from attractive.

Ned Brewster shared one of the last seats with a big leather bat-bag, and gave himself over to his thoughts. The mere fact of his presence there in the special trolley car as a substitute on the Erskine varsity nine was alone wonderful enough to keep his thoughts busy for a week. Even yet he had not altogether recovered from his surprise.

Ned had played the season through at center field on the freshman nine, and had made a name for himself as a batsman. On Thursday the freshman team had played its last game, had met with defeat, and had disbanded. Ned, trotting off the field, his heart bitter with disappointment at the outcome of the final contest, had heard his name called, and had turned to confront "Big Jim" Milford, the varsity captain.

"I wish you would report at the varsity table to-night, Brewster," Milford had said. Then he had turned abruptly away, per-haps to avoid smiling outright at the expression of bewilderment on the freshman's countenance. Ned never was certain whether he had made any verbal response; but he remembered the way in which his heart had leaped into his throat and stuck there, as well as the narrow escape he had had from dashing his brains out against the locker-house, owing to the fact that he had covered most of the way thither at top speed. That had been on Thursday; to-day, which was Saturday, he was a substitute on the varsity, with a possibility—just that and no more—of playing for a minute or two against Robinson and so winning his E in his freshman year, a feat accomplished but seldom!

Ned had been the only member of the freshman nine taken on the varsity that spring. At first this had bothered him; there were two or three others—notably Barrett, the freshman captain—who were, in his estimation, more deserving of the good fortune than he. But, strange to say, it had been just those two or three who had shown themselves honestly glad at his luck, while the poorest player on the nine had loudly hinted at favoritism. Since Thursday night Ned had, of course, made the acquaintance of all the varsity men, and they had treated him as one of themselves. But they were all, with the single exception of Stilson, seniors and juniors, and Ned knew that a freshman is still a freshman, even if he does happen to be a varsity substitute. Hence he avoided all appearance of trying to force himself upon the others, and so it was that on his journey to the grounds he had only a bat-bag for companion.

The closely settled part of town was left

221

behind now, and the car was speeding over a smooth, elm-lined avenue. Windows held the brown banners of Robinson, but not often did a dash of purple meet the gaze of the Erskine players. At the farther end of the car McLimmont and Housel and Lester were gathered about "Baldy" Simson, the trainer, and their laughter rose above the talk and whistling of the rest. Nearer at hand, across the aisle, sat "Lady" Levett, the big first-baseman. Ned wondered why he was called "Lady." There was nothing ladylike apparent about him. He was fully six feet one, broad of shoulder, mighty of chest, deep of voice, and dark of complexion—a jovial, bellowing giant whom everybody liked. Beside Levett sat Page, the head coach, and Hovey, the manager. Then there were Greene and Captain Milford beyond, and across from them Hill and Kesner, both substitutes. In the seat in front of Ned two big chaps were talking together. They were Billings and Stilson, the latter a sophomore.

"I'll tell you what I'll do," Billings was saying. "If we lose I'll buy you a dinner at the Elm Tree Monday night; if we win you do the same for me."

"Oh, I don't bet!"

"Get out! That's fair, isn't it, Brownie?"

A little round-faced chap across the aisle nodded laughingly. His name was Browne and he played short-stop. He wrote his name with an *e*, and so his friends gave him the full benefit of it.

"Yes, that's fair," said Browne. "We're bound to lose."

"Oh, what are you afraid of?" said Stilson.

"No; that's straight! We haven't much show; we can't hit Dithman."

"*You* can't, maybe," jeered Stilson.

"I'll bet you can't either, my chipper young friend!"

"I'll bet I get a hit off him!"

"Oh, *one!*"

"Well, two, then. Come, now!"

"No; I won't bet," answered Browne, grinning. "If there's a prize ahead, there's no telling what you'll do; is there, Pete?"

"No; he might even make a run," responded Billings. "But it's going to take more than two hits to win this game," he went on, dropping his voice, "for I'll just tell you they're going to pound Hugh all over the field."

"Well, what if they do get a dozen runs or so?" said Stilson. "Haven't we got a mighty batter, imported especially for the occasion, to win out for us?"

"Whom do you mean?" asked Billings.

"I mean the redoubtable Mr. Brewster, of course—the freshman Joan of Arc who is to lead us to vict—"

"Not so loud," whispered Browne, glancing at Ned's crimsoning cheeks.

Stilson swung around and shot a look at the substitute, then turned back grinning.

"Cleared off nicely, hasn't it?" he observed with elaborate nonchalance.

Ned said to himself, "He's got it in for me because he knows that if I play it will be in his place."

The car slowed down with much clanging of gong, and pushed its way through the crowd before the entrance to the field. Then, with a final jerk, it came to a stop. "All out, fellows!" cried Hovey; and Ned followed the others through the throng, noisy with the shouts of ticket and score-card venders, to the gate and dressing-room.

II

NED sat on the bench. With him were Hovey, the manager, who was keeping score, Hill and Kesner, substitutes like himself, and, at the farther end, Simson, the trainer, and Page, the head coach. Page had pulled his straw hat far over his eyes, but from under the brim he was watching sharply every incident of the diamond, the while he talked with expressionless countenance to "Baldy." Back of them the grand stand was purple with flags and ribbons, but at a little distance on either side the purple gave place to the brown of Robinson. Back of third base, at the west end of the stand, the Robinson College band held forth brazenly at intervals, making up in vigor what it lacked in tunefulness. In front of the spectators the diamond spread deeply green, save where the base-lines left the dusty red-brown earth exposed, and marked with lines and angles of lime, which gleamed snow-white in the afternoon sunlight. Beyond the diamond the field stretched, as smooth and even as a great velvet carpet, to a distant fence and a line of trees above whose tops a turret or tower here and there indicated the whereabouts of town and college.

Ned had sat there on the bench during six innings, the sun burning his neck and the dust from the batsman's box floating into his face. In those six innings he had seen Erskine struggle pluckily against defeat—a defeat which now, with the score 12 to 6 in Robinson's favor, hovered, dark and ominous, above her. Yet he had not lost hope; perhaps his optimism was largely due to the fact that he found it difficult to believe that Fate could be so cruel as to make the occasion of his first appearance with the varsity team one of sorrow. He was only seventeen, and his idea of Fate was a kind-hearted, motherly old soul with a watchful interest in his welfare. Yet he was forced to acknowledge that Fate, or somebody, was treating him rather shabbily. The first half of the seventh was as good as over, and still he kicked his heels idly beneath the bench. Page didn't seem to be even aware of his presence. To be sure,

there were Hill and Kesner in the same box, but that didn't bring much comfort. Besides, any one with half an eye could see that Stilson should have been taken off long ago; he hadn't made a single hit and already had three errors marked against him. Ned wondered how his name would look in the column instead of Stilson's, and edged along the bench until he could look over Hovey's shoulder. The manager glanced up, smiled in a perfunctory way, and credited the Robinson runner with a stolen base. Ned read the batting list again:

BILLINGS, r. f.
GREENE, l. f.
MILFORD, 2b., Capt.
LESTER, p.
BROWNE, ss.
HOUSEL, c.
McLIMMONT, 3b.
LEVETT, 1b.
STILSON, c. f.

There was a sudden burst of applause from the seats behind, and a red-faced senior with a wilted collar balanced himself upon the railing and begged for "one more good one, fellows!" The first of the seventh was at an end, and the Erskine players, perspiring and streaked with dust, trotted in. "Lady" Levett sank down on the bench beside Ned with a sigh, and fell to examining the little finger of his left hand, which looked very red and which refused to work in unison with its companions.

"Hurt?" asked Ned.

"Blame thing's bust, I guess," said "Lady," disgustedly. "Oh, Baldy, got some tape there?"

The trainer, wearing the anxious air of a hen with one chicken, bustled up with his black bag, and Ned watched the bandaging of the damaged finger until the sudden calling of his name by the head coach sent his heart into this throat and brought him leaping to his feet with visions of hopes fulfilled. But his heart subsided again in the instant, for what Page said was merely:

"Brewster, you go over there and catch for Greene, will you?" And then, turning again to the bench, "Kesner, you play left field next half."

Ned picked up a catcher's mitt, and for the rest of the half caught the balls that the substitute pitcher sent him as he warmed up to take Lester's place. Greene didn't keep him so busy, however, that he couldn't watch the game. Milford had hit safely to right field and had reached second on a slow bunt by Lester. The wavers of the purple flags implored little Browne to "smash it out!" But the short-stop never found the ball, and Housel took his place and lifted the sphere just over second-baseman's head into the out field. The bases were full. The red-faced senior was working his arms heroically and begging in husky tones for more noise. And when, a minute later, McLimmont took up his bat and faced the Robinson pitcher, the supporters of the purple went mad up there on the sun-smitten stand and drowned the discordant efforts of the Robinson band.

McLimmont rubbed his hands in the dust, rubbed the dust off on his trousers, and swung his bat. Dithman, who had puzzled Erskine batters all day and had pitched a magnificent game for six innings, shook himself together. McLimmont waited. No, thank you, he didn't care for that outshoot; nor for that drop; nor for— What? A strike, did he say? Well, perhaps it did go somewhere near the plate, though to see it coming you'd have thought it was going to be a passed ball! One and two, wasn't it? Thanks; there was no hurry then, so he'd just let that in-curve alone, wait until something worth while came along, and—*Eh!* what was that? Strike two! Well, well,

well, of all the umpires this fellow must be a beginner! Never mind that, though. But he'd have to look sharp now or else—

Crack!

Off sped the ball, and off sped McLimmont. The former went over first-baseman's head; the latter swung around the bag like an automobile taking a corner, and raced for second, reaching it on his stomach a second before the ball. There was rejoicing where the purple flags fluttered, for Captain Milford and Lester had scored.

But Erskine's good fortune ended there. McLimmont was thrown out while trying to steal third, and Levett popped a short fly into the hands of the pitcher. Greene trotted off to the box, and Ned walked dejectedly back to the bench. Page stared at him in surprise. Then, "Didn't I tell you to play center field?" he ejaculated.

Ned's heart turned a somersault and landed in his throat. He stared dumbly back at the head coach and shook his head. As he did so he became aware of Stilson's presence on the bench.

"What? Well, get a move on!" said Page.

Get a move on! Ned went out to center as though he had knocked a three-bagger and wanted to get home on it. Little Browne grinned at him as he sped by.

"Good work, Brewster!" he called softly.

Over at left, Kesner, happy over his own good fortune, waved congratulations. In the Erskine section the desultory hand-clapping which had accompanied Ned's departure for center field died away, and the eighth inning began with the score 12 to 8.

III

FROM center field the grand stands are very far away. Ned was glad of it. He felt particularly happy and wanted to have a good comfortable grin all to himself. He had won his E. Nothing else mattered very much now. So grin he did to his heart's content, and even jumped up and down on his toes a few times; he would have liked to sing or whistle, but that was out of the question. And then suddenly he began to wonder whether he had not, after all, secured the coveted symbol under false pretense; would he be able to do any better than Stilson had done? Robinson's clever pitcher had fooled man after man; was it likely that he would succeed where the best batsmen of the varsity nine had virtually failed? Or, worse, supposing he showed up no better here in the out-field than had Stilson! The sun was low in the west and the atmosphere was filled with a golden haze; it seemed to him that it might be very easy to misjudge a ball in that queer glow. Of a sudden his heart began to hammer at his ribs sickeningly. He was afraid—afraid that he would fail, when the trial came, there with the whole college looking on! Little shivers ran up his back, and he clenched his hands till they hurt. He wished, oh, how he wished it were over! Then there came the sharp sound of bat against ball, and in an instant he was racing in toward second, his thoughts intent upon the brown speck that sailed high in air, his fears all forgotten.

Back sped second-baseman, and on went Ned. "My ball!" he shouted. Milford hesitated an instant, then gave up the attempt. "All yours, Brewster!" he shouted back. "Steady!" Ned finished his run and glanced up, stepped a little to the left, put up his hands, and felt the ball thud against his glove. Then he fielded it to second and trotted back; and as he went he heard the applause, loud and hearty, from the stands. After that there was no more fear. Robinson failed to get a man past first, and presently he was trotting in to the bench side by side with Kesner.

"Brewster at bat!" called Hovey, and, with a sudden throb at his heart, Ned selected a stick and went to the plate. He stood there swinging his bat easily, confidently as one who is not to be fooled by the ordinary wiles of the pitcher, a well-built, curly-haired youngster with blue eyes, and cheeks in which the red showed through the liberal coating of tan.

"The best batter the freshmen had," fellows whispered one to another.

"Looks as though he knew how, too, eh? Just you watch him, now!"

And the red-faced senior once more demanded three long Erskines, three times three, and three long Erskines for Brewster! And Ned heard them—he couldn't very well have helped it!—and felt very grateful and proud. And five minutes later he was back on the bench, frowning miserably at his knuckles, having been struck out without the least difficulty by the long-legged Dithman. The pride was all gone. "But," he repeated silently, "wait until next time! Just wait until next time!"

Billings found the Robinson pitcher for a two-bagger, stole third, and came home on a hit by Greene. Erskine's spirits rose another notch. Three more runs to tie the score in this inning, and then—why, it would be strange indeed if the purple couldn't win out! Captain Milford went to bat in a veritable tempest of cheers. He looked determined; but so did his adversary, the redoubtable Dithman.

"We've got to tie it this inning," said Levett, anxiously. "We'll never do it next, when the tail-enders come up."

"There's one tail-ender who's going to hit that chap in the box next time," answered Ned.

"Lady" looked amused.

"You'll be in luck if it comes around to you," he said. "We all will. Oh, thunder! Another strike!"

A moment later they were on their feet,

and the ball was arching into left field; and "Big Jim" was plowing his way around first. But the eighth inning ended right there, for the ball plumped into left-fielder's hands. "Lady" groaned, picked up his big mitt, and ambled to first, and the ninth inning began with the score 12 to 9.

Greene was determined that Robinson should not increase her tally, even to the extent of making it a baker's dozen. And he pitched wonderful ball, striking out the first two batsmen, allowing the next to make first on a hit past short-stop, and then bringing the half to an end by sending three glorious balls over the corner of the plate one after another, amid the frantic cheers of the Erskine contingent and the dismay of the puzzled batsman. Then the rival nines changed places for the last time, and Robinson set grimly and determinedly about the task of keeping Erskine's players from crossing the plate again.

And Milford, leaning above Hovey's shoulder, viewed the list of batting candidates and ruefully concluded that she would not have much trouble doing it.

The stands were emptying and the spectators were ranging themselves along the base-lines. The Robinson band had broken out afresh, and the Robinson cheerers were confident. The sun was low in the west, and the shadows of the stands stretched far across the diamond. Kesner, who had taken Lester's place in the batting list, stepped to the plate and faced Dithman, and the final struggle was on.

Dithman looked as calmly confident as at any time during the game, and yet, after pitching eight innings of excellent ball, it scarcely seemed likely that he could still command perfect form. Kesner proved a foeman worthy of his steel; the most seductive drops and shoots failed to entice him, and with three balls against him Dithman was forced to put the ball over the plate.

The second time he did it, Kesner found it and went to rest on a clean hit into the out-field past third, and the purple banners flaunted exultantly. Milford's face took on an expression of hopefulness as he dashed to first and whispered his instructions in Kesner's ear. Then he retired to the coaches' box and put every effort into getting the runner down to second. But Fate came to his assistance and saved him some breath. Dithman lost command of the dirty brown sphere for one little moment, and it went wild, striking Greene on the thigh. And when he limped to first Kesner went on to second, and there were two on bases, and Erskine was mad with joy. Milford and Billings were coaching from opposite corners, Milford's bellowing being plainly heard a quarter of a mile away; he had a good, hearty voice, and for the first time that day it bothered the Robinson pitcher. For Housel, waiting for a chance to make a bunt, was kept busy getting out of the way of the balls, and after four of them was given his base.

Erskine's delight was now of the sort best expressed by turning somersaults. As somersaults were out of the question owing to the density of the throng, her supporters were forced to content themselves with jumping up and down and shouting the last breaths from their bodies. Bases full and none out! Three runs would tie the score! Four runs would win! And they'd get them, of course; there was no doubt about that—at least, not until McLimmont had struck out and had turned back to the bench with miserable face. Then it was Robinson's turn to cheer. Erskine looked doubtful for a moment, then began her husky shouting again; after all, there was only one out. But Dithman, rather pale of face, had himself in hand once more. To the knowing ones, Levett, who followed McLimmont, was already as good as out;

the way in which he stood, the manner in which he "went down" for the balls, proved him nervous and over-anxious. With two strikes and three balls called on him, he swung at a wretched out-shoot. A low groan ran along the bench. Levett himself didn't groan; he placed his bat carefully on the ground, kicked it ten yards away, and said "Confound the luck!" very forcibly.

"You're up, Brewster," called Hovey.

"Two gone! Last man, fellows!" shouted the Robinson catcher, as Ned tapped the plate.

"Last man!" echoed the second-baseman. "He's easy!"

"Make him pitch 'em, Brewster!" called Milford. The rest was drowned in the sudden surge of cheers from the Robinson side. Ned faced the pitcher with an uncomfortable empty feeling inside of him. He meant to hit that ball, but he greatly feared he wouldn't; he scarcely dared think what a hit meant. For a moment he wished himself well out of it—wished that he were back on the bench and that another had his place and his chance to win or lose the game. Then the first delivery sped toward him, and much of his nervousness vanished.

"Ball!" droned the umpire.

Milford and Levett were coaching again; it was hard to say whose voice was the loudest. Down at first Housel was dancing back and forth on his toes, and back of him Milford, kneeling on the turf, was roaring: "Two gone, Jack, remember. Run on anything! Look out for a passed ball! Now you're off! Hi, hi, hi! *Look out!* He won't throw! Take a lead—go on! Watch his arm; go down with his arm! Now you're off! *Now, now, now!*"

But if this was meant to rattle the pitcher it failed of its effect. Dithman swung his arm out, danced forward on his left foot, and shot the ball away.

"Strike!" said the umpire.

Ned wondered why he had let that ball go by; he had been sure that it was going to cut the plate, and yet he had stood by undecided until it was too late. Well! He gripped his bat a little tighter, shifted his feet a few inches, and waited again. Dithman's expression of calm unconcern aroused his ire; just let him get one whack at that ball and he would show that long-legged pitcher something to surprise him! A palpable in-shoot followed, and Ned staggered out of its way. Then came what was so undoubtedly a ball that Ned merely smiled at it. Unfortunately at the last instant it dropped down below his shoulder, and he waited anxiously for the verdict.

"Strike two!" called the umpire.

Two and two! Ned's heart sank. He shot a glance toward first. Milford was staring over at him imploringly. Ned gave a gasp and set his jaws together firmly. The pitcher had the ball again, and was signaling to the catcher. Then out shot his arm, the little one-legged hop followed, and the ball sped toward the boy at the plate. And his heart gave a leap, for the delivery was a straight ball, swift, to be sure, but straight and true for the plate. Ned took one step forward, and ball and bat met with a sound like a pistol-shot, and a pair of purple-stockinged legs were flashing toward first.

Up, up against the gray-blue sky went the sphere, and then it seemed to hang for a moment there, neither rising nor falling. And all the time the bases were emptying themselves. Kesner was in ere the ball was well away, Greene was close behind him, and now Housel, slower because of his size, was swinging by third; and from second sped a smaller, lithe figure with down-bent head and legs fairly flying. Coaches were shouting wild, useless words, and none but themselves heard them; for four thousand voices were shrieking frenziedly, and four thousand pairs of eyes were either watching the flight of the far-off ball, or were fixed anxiously upon the figure of left-fielder, who, away up near the fence and the row of trees, was running desperately back.

Ned reached second, and, for the first time since he had started around, looked for the ball. And, as he did so, afar off across the turf a figure stooped and picked something from the ground and threw it to center-fielder. And center-fielder threw it to third-baseman. And meanwhile Ned trotted over the plate into the arms of "Big Jim" Milford, and Hovey made four big black tallies in the score-book. Three minutes later and it was all over, Billings flying out to center field, and the final score stood 13 to 12. Erskine owned the field, and Ned, swaying and slipping dizzily about on the shoulders of three temporary lunatics, looked down upon a surging sea of shouting, distorted faces, and tried his hardest to appear unconcerned—and was secretly very, very happy. He had his E; best of all, he had honestly earned it.

SPRING CLEANING
By Thomas Tapper

O MARCH wind, blow with all your might!
Set disordered things aright.
Rustle every dry leaf down;
Chase the cold all out of town;
Sweep the streets quite free of dust;
Blow it off with many a gust.
Make the earth all clean again,
And ready for the April rain.

THE FLOWER-FED BUFFALOES
By Vachel Lindsay

The flower-fed buffaloes of the spring
In the days of long ago,
Ranged where the locomotives sing
And the prairie flowers lie low:—
The tossing, blooming, perfumed grass
Is swept away by the wheat,
Wheels and wheels and wheels spin by
In the spring that still is sweet.

But the flower-fed buffaloes of the spring
Left us, long ago.
They gore no more, they bellow no more,
They trundle around the hills no more:—
With the Blackfeet, lying low.
With the Pawnees, lying low,
Lying low.

EDITHA'S BURGLAR

By Frances Hodgson Burnett

February, 1880

I WILL begin by saying that Editha was always rather a queer little girl, and not much like other children. She was not a strong, healthy little girl, and had never been able to run about and play; and, as she had no sisters or brothers, or companions of her own size, she was rather old-fashioned, as her aunts used to call it. She had always been very fond of books, and had learned to read when she was such a tiny child, that I should almost be afraid to say how tiny she was when she read her first volume through. Her papa wrote books himself, and was also the editor of a newspaper; and, as he had a large library, Editha perhaps read more than was quite good for her. She lived in London; and, as her mamma was very young and pretty, and went out a great deal, and her papa was so busy, and her governess only came in the morning, she was left to herself a good many hours in the day, and when she was left to herself, she spent the greater part of her time in the library reading her papa's big books, and even his newspapers.

She was very fond of the newspapers, because she found so many curious things in them—stories, for instance, of strange events which happened every day in the great city of London, and yet never seemed to happen anywhere near where she lived. Through the newspapers, she found that there were actually men who lived by breaking into people's houses and stealing all the nice things they could carry away, and she read that such men were called burglars. When she first began to read about burglars, she was very much troubled. In the first place, she felt rather timid about going to bed at night, and, in the second place, she felt rather sorry for the burglars.

"I suppose no one ever taught them any better," she thought.

In fact, she thought so much about the matter, that she could not help asking her papa some questions one morning when he was at breakfast. He was reading his paper and eating his chops both at once when she spoke to him.

"Papa," she said, in a solemn little voice, and looking at him in a very solemn manner, "papa dear, what do you think of burglars—as a class?" (She said "as a class," because she had heard one of her papa's friends say it, and as he was a gentleman she admired very much, she liked to talk as he did.) Her papa gave a little jump in his chair, as if she had startled him, and then he pushed his hair off his forehead and stared at her.

"Burglars! As a class!" he said, and then he stared at her a minute again in rather a puzzled way. "Bless my soul!" he said. "As a class, Nixie!" (That was his queer pet name for her.) "Nixie, where is your mother?"

"She is in bed, papa dear, and we mustn't disturb her," said Editha. "The party last night tired her out. I peeped into her room softly as I came down. She looks so pretty when she is asleep. What *do* you think of burglars, papa?"

"I think they're a bad lot, Nixie," said her papa, "a bad lot."

"Are there no good burglars, papa?"

"Well, Nixie," answered papa, "I should say not. As a rule you know—" and here he began to smile, as people often smiled at Editha when she asked questions. "As a rule, burglars are not distinguished for moral perspicuity and blameless character."

But Editha did not understand what moral perspicuity meant, and besides she was thinking again.

"Miss Lane was talking to me the other day, about some poor children who had never been taught anything; they had never had any French or music lessons, and scarcely knew how to read, and she said they had never had any advantages. Perhaps that is the way with the burglars, papa—perhaps they have never had any advantages—perhaps if they had had advantages they mightn't have been burglars."

"Lessons in French and music are very elevating to the mind, my dear Nixie," papa began in his laughing way, which was always a trial to Editha, but suddenly he stopped, and looked at her rather sadly.

"How old are you, Nixie?" he asked.

"I am seven," answered Editha, "seven years, going on eight."

Papa sighed.

"Come here, little one," he said, holding out his strong white hand to her.

She left her chair and went to him, and he put his arms around her, and kissed her, and stroked her long brown hair.

"Don't puzzle your little brain too much," he said, "never mind about the burglars, Nixie."

"Well," said Editha, "I can't help thinking about them a little, and it seems to me that there must be, perhaps, one good burglar among all the bad ones. You see, they must have to be up all night, and out in the

rain sometimes, and they can't help not having had advantages."

It was strange that the first thing she heard, when she went up to her mamma's room, was something about burglars.

She was very very fond of her mamma, and very proud of her. She even tried to take care of her in her small way; she never disturbed her when she was asleep, and she always helped her to dress, bringing her things to her, buttoning her little shoes and gloves, putting the perfume on her handkerchiefs, and holding her wraps until she wanted them.

This morning, when she went into the dressing-room, she found the chamber-maid there before her, and her dear little mamma looking very pale.

"Ah, mem! if you please, mem!" the chamber-maid was saying, "what a blessing it was they didn't come here!"

"Who, Janet?" Editha asked.

"The burglars, Miss, that broke into Number Eighteen last night, and carried off all the silver, and the missus's jewelry."

"If burglars ever do break in here," said mamma, "I hope none of us will hear them, though it would almost break my heart to have my things taken. If I should waken in the night, and find a burglar in my room, I think it would kill me, and I know I should scream, and then there is no knowing what they might do. If ever you think there is a burglar in the house, Nixie, whatever you do, don't scream or make any noise. It would be better to have one's things stolen, than to be killed by burglars for screaming."

She was not a very wise little mamma, and often said rather thoughtless things; but she was very gentle and loving, and Editha was so fond of her that she put her arms round her waist and said to her:

"Mamma, dearest, I will never let any

burglars hurt you or frighten you if I can help it. I do believe I could persuade them not to. I should think even a burglar would listen to reason."

That made her mamma laugh, so that she forgot all about the burglars and began to get her color again, and it was not long before she was quite gay, and was singing a song she had heard at the opera, while Editha was helping her to dress.

But that very night Editha met a burglar.

Just before dinner, her papa came up from the city in a great hurry. He dashed up to the front door in a cab, and, jumping out, ran upstairs to mamma, who was sitting in the drawing-room, while Editha read aloud to her.

"Kitty, my dear," he said, "I am obliged to go to Glasgow by the 'five' train. I must throw a few things into a portmanteau and go at once."

"Oh, Francis!" said mamma. "And just after that burglary at the Norris's! I don't like to be left alone."

"The servants are here," said papa, "and Nixie will take care of you; won't you, Nixie? Nixie is interested in burglars."

"I am sure Nixie could do more than the servants," said mamma. "All three of them sleep in one room at the top of the house when you are away, and even if they awakened they would only scream."

"Nixie wouldn't scream," said papa laughing; "Nixie would do something heroic. I will leave you in her hands."

He was only joking, but Editha did not think of what he said as a joke; she felt that her mamma was really left in her care and that it was a very serious matter.

She thought about it so seriously that she hardly talked at all at dinner, and was so quiet afterward that her mamma said, "Dear me, Nixie, what *are* you thinking of? You look as solemn as a little owl."

"I am thinking of you, mamma," the child answered.

And then her mamma laughed and kissed her, and said: "Well, I must say I don't see why you should look so grave about me. I didn't think I was such a solemn subject."

At last bed-time came, and the little girl went to her mother's room, because she was to sleep there.

"I am glad I have you with me, Nixie," said mamma, with a rather nervous little laugh. "I am sure I shouldn't like to sleep in this big room alone."

But, after she was in bed, she soon fell asleep, and lay looking so happy and sweet and comfortable that Editha thought it was lovely to see her.

Editha did not go to sleep for a long time. She thought of her papa trying to sleep on the train, rushing through the dark night on its way to Scotland; she thought of a new book she had just begun to read; she thought of a child she had once heard singing in the street; and when her eyes closed at length, her mind had just gone back to the burglars at Number Eighteen. She slept until midnight, and then something wakened her. At first she did not know what it was, but in a few minutes she found that it was a queer little sound coming from down-stairs—a sound like a stealthy filing of iron.

She understood in a moment then, because she had heard the chamber-maid say that the burglars broke into Number Eighteen by filing through the bars of the shutters.

"It is a burglar," she thought, "and he will awaken mamma."

If she had been older, and had known more of the habits of burglars, she might have been more frightened than she was. She did not think of herself at all, however, but of her mother.

She began to reason the matter over as quickly as possible, and she made up her mind that the burglar must not be allowed to make a noise.

"I'll go down and ask him to please be as quiet as he can," she said to herself, "and I'll tell him why."

Certainly, this was a queer thing to think of doing, but I told you when I began my story that she was a queer little girl.

She slipped out of bed so quietly that she scarcely stirred the clothes, and then slipped just as quietly out of the room and down the stairs.

The filing had ceased, but she heard a sound of stealthy feet in the kitchen; and, though it must be confessed her heart beat rather faster than usual, she made her way to the kitchen and opened the door.

Imagine the astonishment of that burglar when, on hearing the door open, he turned round and found himself looking at a slender little girl, in a white frilled night-gown, and with bare feet—a little girl whose large brown eyes rested on him in a by no means unfriendly way.

"I'll be polite to him," Editha had said, as she was coming down-stairs. "I am sure he'll be more obliging if I am very polite. Miss Lane says politeness always wins its way."

So the first words she spoke were as polite as she could make them.

"Don't be frightened," she said, in a soft voice. "I don't want to hurt you; I came to ask a favor of you."

The burglar was so amazed that he actually forgot he was a burglar, and staggered back against the wall. I think he thought at first that Editha was a little ghost. "You see I couldn't hurt you if I wanted to," she went on, wishing to encourage him. "I'm too little. I'm only seven—and a little over—and I'm not going to scream, because that would waken mamma, and that's just what I don't want to do."

That did encourage the burglar, but still he was so astonished that he did not know what to do.

"Well, I'm blowed," he said in a whisper, "if this aint a rummy go!" which was extremely vulgar language; but, unfortunately, he was one of those burglars who, as Miss Lane said, "had not had any advantages," which is indeed the case with the majority of burglars of my acquaintance.

Then he began to laugh—in a whisper also, if one can be said to laugh in a whisper. He put his hand over his mouth, and made no noise, but he laughed so hard that he doubled up and rocked himself to and fro.

"The rummiest go!" he said, in his uneducated way. "An' she haint agoin' to 'urt me. Oh, my heye!"

He was evidently very badly educated, indeed, for he not only used singular words, but sounded his h's all in the wrong places. Editha noticed this, even in the midst of her surprise at his laughter. She could not understand what he was laughing at. Then it occurred to her that she might have made a mistake.

"If you please," she said, with great delicacy, "are you really a burglar?"

He stopped laughing just long enough to answer her.

"Lor' no, miss," he said, "by no manner o' means. I'm a dear friend o' yer Par's, come to make a evenin' call, an' not a wishin' to trouble the servants, I stepped in through the winder."

"Ah!" said Editha, looking very gravely at him; "I see you are joking with me, as papa does sometimes. But what I wanted to say to you was this: Papa has gone to Scotland, and all our servants are women, and mamma would be so frightened if you were to waken her, that I am sure it would make her ill. And if you are going to burgle, would you please burgle as quietly as you can, so that you won't disturb her?"

"Well, I'll be blowed!"

"Why don't you say, 'I'll be blown?'" asked Editha. "I'm sure it isn't correct to say you'll be blowed."

She thought he was going off into one of his unaccountable fits of laughter again, but he did not; he seemed to check himself with an effort.

"There haint no time to waste," she heard him mutter.

"No, I suppose there isn't," she answered. "Mamma might wake and miss me. What are you going to burgle first?"

"You'd better go upstairs to yer mar," he said, rather sulkily.

Editha thought deeply for a few seconds.

"You oughtn't to burgle anything," she said. "Of course you know that, but if you have really made up your mind to do it, I would like to show you the things you'd better take."

"What, fer instance?" said the burglar, with interest.

"You mustn't take any of mamma's things," said Edith, "because they are all in her room, and you would waken her, and besides, she said it would break her heart; and don't take any of the things papa is fond of. I'll tell you what," turning rather pale, "you can take my things."

"What kind o' things?" asked the burglar.

"My locket, and the little watch papa gave me, and the necklace and bracelets my grandmamma left me—they are worth a great deal of money, and they are very pretty, and I was to wear them when I grew to be a young lady, but—you can take them. And—then—" very slowly, and

with a deep sigh, "there are—my books. I'm very fond of them, but—"

"I don't want no books," said the burglar.

"Don't you?" exclaimed she. "Ah, thank you."

"Well," said the burglar, as if to himself, and staring hard at her brightening face, "I never see no sich a start afore."

"Shall I go upstairs and get the other things?" said Editha.

"No," he said. "You stay where you are—or stay, come along o' me inter the pantry, an' sit down while I'm occypied."

He led the way into the pantry, and pushed her down on a step, and then began to open the drawers where the silver was kept.

"It's curious that you should know just where to look for things and that your key should fit, isn't it?" said Editha.

"Yes," he answered, "it's werry sing'lar, indeed. There's a good deal in bein' eddicated."

"Are you educated?" asked Editha, with a look of surprise.

"Did yer think I wasn't?" said the burglar.

"Well," said Editha, not wishing to offend him, "you see, you pronounce your words so very strangely."

"It's all a matter o' taste," interrupted the burglar. "Oxford an' Cambridge 'as different vocabillaries."

"Did you go to Oxford?" asked Editha, politely.

"No," said he, "nor yet to Cambridge."

Then he laughed again, and seemed to be quite enjoying himself as he made some forks and spoons up into a bundle. "I 'ope there haint no plated stuff 'ere," he said. "Plate's wulgar, an' I 'ope yer parents haint wulgar, cos that'd be settin' yer a werry bad example an' sp'ilin' yer morals."

"I am sure papa and mamma are not vulgar," said Editha.

The burglar opened another drawer, and chuckled again, and this suggested to Editha's mind another question.

"Is your business a good one?" she suddenly inquired of him.

" 'Taint as good as it ought to be, by no manner o' means," said the burglar. "Every one haint as hobligin' as you, my little dear."

"Oh!" said Editha. "You know you obliged me by not making a noise."

"Well," said the burglar, "as a rule, we don't make a practice o' makin' no more noise than we can help. It haint considered 'ealthy in the perfession."

"Would you mind leaving us a few forks and spoons to eat with, if you please? I beg pardon for interrupting you, but I'm afraid we shall not have any to use at breakfast."

"Haint yer got no steel uns?" inquired the burglar.

"Mamma wouldn't like to use steel ones, I'm sure," Editha answered. "I'll tell you what you can do: please leave out enough for mamma, and I can use steel. I don't care about myself, much."

The man seemed to think for a moment, and then he was really so accommodating as to do as she asked, and even went to the length of leaving out her own little fork and knife and spoon.

"Oh! you are very kind," said Editha, when she saw him do this.

"That's a reward o' merit, cos yer didn't squeal," said the burglar.

He was so busy for the next few minutes that he did not speak, though now and then he broke into a low laugh, as if he were thinking of something very funny, indeed. During the silence, Editha sat holding her little feet in her night-gown, and watching him very curiously. A great many new thoughts came into her active brain, and at last she could not help asking some more questions.

"Would you really rather be a burglar than anything else?" she inquired, respectfully.

"Well," said the man, "p'r'aps I'd prefer to be Lord Mayor, or a member o' the 'Ouse o' Lords, or heven the Prince o' Wales, honly for there bein' hobstacles in the way of it."

"Oh!" said Editha; "you couldn't be the Prince of Wales, you know. I meant wouldn't you rather be in some other profession? My papa is an editor," she added. "How would you like to be an editor?"

"Well," said the burglar, "hif yer par ud change with me, or hif he chanced to know hany heditor with a roarin' trade as ud be so hobligin' as to 'and it hover, hit's wot I've allers 'ad a leanin' to."

"I am sure papa would not like to be a burglar," said Editha, thoughtfully; "but perhaps he might speak to his friends about you, if you would give me your name and address, and if I were to tell him how obliging you were, and if I told him you really didn't like being a burglar."

The burglar put his hand to his pocket and gave a start of great surprise.

"To think o' me a forgettin' my card-case," he said, "an' a leavin' it on the pianner when I come hout. I'm sich a bloomin' forgetful cove. I might hev knowed I'd hev wanted it."

"It is a pity," said Editha; "but if you told me your name and your number, I think I could remember it."

"I'm afeared yer couldn't," said the burglar regretfully, "but I'll try yer. Lord Halgernon Hedward Halbert de Pentonville, Yde Park. Can you think o' that?"

"Are you a lord?" exclaimed Editha. "Dear me, how strange!"

"It is sing'lar," said the burglar, shaking

his head. "I've hoften thought so myself. But not wishin' to detain a lady no longer than can be 'elped, s'pose we take a turn in the lib'ery among yer respected par's things."

"Don't make a noise," said Editha, as she led the way.

But when they reached the library her loving little heart failed her. All the things her father valued most were there, and he would be sure to be so sorry if one thing was missing when he returned. She stood on the threshold a moment and looked about her.

"Oh," she whispered, "please do me another favor, wont you? Please let me slip quietly upstairs and bring down my own things instead. They will be so easy to carry away, and they are very valuable, and—and I will make you a present of them if you will not touch anything that belongs to papa. He is so fond of his things and, besides that, he is so good."

The burglar gave a rather strange and disturbed look at her.

"Go an' get yer gimcracks," he said in a somewhat grumbling voice.

Her treasures were in her own room, and her bare feet made no sound as she crept slowly up the staircase and then down again. But when she handed the little box to the burglar her eyes were wet.

"Papa gave me the watch, and mamma gave me the locket," she whispered, tremulously; "and the pearls were grandmamma's, and grandmamma is in heaven."

It would not be easy to know what the burglar thought; he looked queerer than ever. Perhaps he was not quite so bad as some burglars and felt rather ashamed of taking her treasures from a little girl who loved other people so much better than she loved herself. But he did not touch any of papa's belongings, and, indeed, did not remain much longer. He grumbled a little when he looked into the drawing-room, saying something to himself about "folks never 'avin' no consideration for a cove, an' leavin' nothin' portable 'andy, a expectin' of him to carry off seventy-five pound bronze clocks an' marble stattoos;" but though Editha was sorry to see that he appeared annoyed, she did not understand him.

After that, he returned to the pantry and helped himself to some cold game pie, and seemed to enjoy it, and then poured out a tumbler of wine, which Editha thought a great deal to drink at once.

"Yer 'e'lth, my dear," he said, "an' 'appy returns, an' many on 'em. May yer grow up a hornyment to yer sect, an' a comfort to yer respected mar an' par."

And he threw his head very far back, and drank the very last drop in the glass, which was vulgar, to say the least of it.

Then he took up his bundles of silver and the other articles he had appropriated, and seeing that he was going away, Editha rose from the pantry step.

"Are you going out through the window?" she asked.

"Yes, my dear," he answered with a chuckle, "it's a little 'abit I've got into. I prefers 'em to doors."

"Well, good-bye," she said, holding out her hand politely. "And thank you, my lord."

She felt it only respectful to say that, even if he had fallen into bad habits and become a burglar.

He shook hands with her in a quite friendly manner, and even made a bow.

"Yer welcome, my dear," he said. "An' I must hadd that if I ever see a queerer or better behaved little kid, may I be blowed—or, as yer told me it would be more correcter to say, I'll be blown."

Editha did not know he was joking; she thought he was improving, and that if he had had advantages he might have been a very nice man.

It was astonishing how neatly he slipped through the window; he was gone in a second, and Editha found herself standing alone in the dark, as he had taken his lantern with him.

She groped her way out and up the stairs, and then, for the first time, she began to feel cold and rather weak and strange; it was more like being frightened than any feeling she had had while the burglar was in the house.

"Perhaps, if he had been a very bad burglar, he might have killed me," she said to herself, trembling a little. "I am very glad he did not kill me, for—for it would have hurt mamma so, and papa too, when he came back, and they told him."

Her mamma wakened in the morning with a bright smile.

"Nobody hurt us, Nixie," she said. "We are all right, aren't we?"

"Yes, mamma dear," said Editha.

She did not want to startle her just then, so she said nothing more, and she even said nothing all through the excitement that followed the discovery of the robbery, and indeed, said nothing until her papa came home, and then he wondered so at her pale face, and petted her so tenderly, and thought it so strange that nothing but her treasures had been taken from upstairs, that she could keep her secret no longer.

"Papa," she cried out all at once in a trembling voice, "I gave them to him myself."

"You, Nixie! You!" exclaimed her papa, looking alarmed. "Kitty, the fright has made the poor little thing ill."

"No, papa," said Editha, her hands shaking, and the tears rushing into her eyes, she did not know why. "I heard him, and—I knew mamma would be so frightened—and

it came into my mind to ask him—not to waken her—and I crept down-stairs—and asked him—and he was not at all unkind though he laughed. And I stayed with him, and—and told him I would give him all my things if he would not touch yours nor mamma's. He—he wasn't such a bad burglar, papa—and he told me he would rather be something more respectable."

And she hid her face on her papa's shoulder.

"Kitty!" papa cried out. "Oh, Kitty!"

Then her mamma flew to her and knelt down by her, kissing her, and crying aloud:

"Oh, Nixie! if he had hurt you—if he had hurt you."

"He knew I was not going to scream, mamma," said Editha. "And he knew I was too little to hurt him. I told him so."

She scarcely understood why mamma cried so much more at this, and why even papa's eyes were wet as he held her close up to his breast.

"It is my fault, Francis," wept the poor little mamma. "I have left her too much to herself, and I have not been a wise mother. Oh, to think of her risking her dear little life just to save me from being frightened, and to think of her giving up the things she loves for our sakes. I will be a better mother to her, after this, and take care of her more."

But I am happy to say that the watch and locket and pearls were not altogether lost, and came back to their gentle owner in time. About six months after, the burglar was caught, as burglars are apt to be, and, after being tried and sentenced to transportation to the penal settlements (which means that he was to be sent away to be a prisoner in a far country), a police officer came one day to see Editha's papa, and he actually came from that burglar, who was in jail and wanted to see Editha for a special reason. Editha's papa took her to see him, and the moment she entered his cell she knew him.

"How do you do, my lord?" she said, in a gentle tone.

"Not as lively as common, miss," he answered, "in consekence o' the confinement not bein' good fer my 'e'lth."

"None of your chaff," said the police officer. "Say what you have to say."

And then, strange to say, the burglar brought forth from under his mattress a box, which he handed to the little girl.

"One o' my wisitors brought 'em in to me this mornin'," he said. "I thought yer might as well hev 'em. I kep' 'em partly 'cos it was more convenienter, an' partly 'cos I took a fancy to yer. I've seed a many curi's things, sir," he said to Editha's papa, "but never nothin' as bloomin' queer as that little kid a-comin' in an' tellin' me she wont 'urt me, nor yet wont scream, and please wont I burgle quietly so as to not disturb her mar. It brought my 'art in my mouth when first I see her, an' then, lor', how I larft. I almost made up my mind to give her things back to her afore I left, but I didn't quite do that—it was agin human natur'."

But they were in the box now, and Editha was so glad to see them that she could scarcely speak for a few seconds. Then she thanked the burglar politely.

"I am much obliged to you," she said, "and I'm really very sorry you are to be sent so far away. I am sure papa would have tried to help you if he could, though he says he is afraid you would not do for an editor."

The burglar closed one eye and made a very singular grimace at the police officer, who turned away suddenly and did not look round until Editha had bidden her acquaintance good-bye.

And even this was not quite all. A few weeks later, a box was left for Editha by a very shabby queer-looking man, who quickly disappeared as soon as he had given it to the servant at the door; and in this box was a very large old-fashioned silver watch, almost as big as a turnip, and inside the lid were scratched these words:

To the little Kid,
From 'er fr'end and wel wisher,
Lord halgernon hedward halbert
de pentonwill, ide park.

AN ONTEORA VISITOR

By Candace Wheeler

September, 1895

It was long past midnight, and yet I was leaning on the rough tree-rail of the high piazza, enjoying my garden. It is not often at that hour that one has opportunity to enjoy a flower-garden, and I certainly should not have had except for a little rankling needle of anxiety, that made its point felt in every inch of consciousness whenever I tried to sleep. The anxiety was about the boys, who had gone off on a bear-hunt, and the point that kept turning itself, so that I felt the prick every minute in a new place, was whether they had killed the bear or the bear had killed them.

We had all been sitting together quietly in the big family room, watching the little flashes and living tongues of flame which flickered out from the spent logs of our summer-evening fire, and thinking it was time to light the candles and go to bed, when the loose rattling of a country one-horse wagon had broken the quiet of our road-track, and coming to a stop in front of the door with a suddenness that had the effect of a bang, had been followed by a tremulous hammering of the knocker.

Generally we say, "Come in," when any one knocks, for that is received Onteora custom; but in this case Harry opened the door. When the upper square of it swung back, it seemed to open from a framed half-length portrait of a good-looking country boy, with a blue moonlit sky for a background, the face well lit up by our interior lamp- and fire-light.

The portrait looked relieved when it recognized Harry, and there was at once a low communication between them, of which we heard only an occasional word— "bear," "upper pasture," "half an hour";

and now there were three boys' heads together, for Dunham had joined the others.

Our boys are great hunters. Harry has killed his grizzly bear and mountain sheep in the Rocky Mountains during his college vacations, and Dunham can shoot almost as well as he. Consequently the armament of these boys, as well as their prowess, is a matter discussed in all the barns of all the farms along the side of the mountains. One corner of the family room is called "the armory"; for it is occupied entirely by guns and rifles, boxes of shells, and the things which hunters seem never to have enough of; and our hunters cannot understand why bottles of oil and oily black rags, and steel rods with brushes on the ends are not legitimate garnishings of the dinner-table during the hours when meals are not served.

Of course the colloquy at the door ended by a rush to the armory corner, and a selection of certain things which were handed out to the portrait, while a three-at-a-time mounting of the stairs and back again effected a change into big boots and leather jackets with pockets into which shells and things were quickly stuffed.

The rattly wagon was turned around by this time. There was a little consultation about dogs, which ended in the two big staghounds, "Cooper" and "Hewitt," and horrid little "Snap," Harry's Rocky Mountain mongrel, being let out of the outside kitchen, and all prancing off together in the brilliant moonlight—the lean old farm-horse, the two country boys, who belonged on a wild farm a mile or so away, our two boys, and the trio of dogs.

The reason we all detested Snap was that one day, soon after Harry brought him to Onteora, he and Dunham had decided to drive over to Catskill Mountain House and interview Mr. Beech about the prospects of the season for game; and as Snap insisted upon being of the party, Harry had taken him up-stairs to his bedroom, and shut him in while he and Dunham drove away.

While the bedrooms were being "done up" we heard the most explosive and tremendous barking, then a slam of a door, and Mary came half tumbling down the stairs, looking frightened and confused, and showing us a bleeding wrist with marks of teeth upon it. She had opened Harry's door, and the dog had tried to keep her out; and when she paid no attention to him, he had flown at her and bitten her on the wrist.

Of all possible elements of dismay to introduce into a houseful of women a mad dog is one of the worst, and we felt sure that Snap was mad. Everything was against him: his uncertain origin, his wild life in the far-off Rockies, his habits of subsistence upon the flesh of wild animals—we were sure that his sudden transference from that kind of life to civilization had driven him mad. And what could we do for Mary, with the only doctor in the two-mile-away village, and the boys off with the horses? What we did was to hunt up a razor, and try to bring her courage to the point of cross-slashing the tooth-prints, and to wash the wounds well with salt and water, and start her off on a long tramp to the village to be cauterized. And when a day of much anxiety was over, broken by occasional visits to Harry's door, every creak of the floor being greeted by loud barkings from within, Harry and Dunham returned, full of enjoyment from their excursion. "Harry! Harry!" I exclaimed as soon as his

foot was on the piazza, "Snap has gone mad and bitten Mary!"

"Why, Gran, where is he? How do you know?"

"He is up in your room. He flew at her when she went in to make the bed, and he goes into perfect frenzies if one goes near the door."

A sudden red look of guilt appeared on Harry's face, and the anxiety and astonishment seemed to melt away.

"Why, Gran, he isn't *mad!* He thought he was *keeping camp!*"

"Keeping camp," said I slowly, while a perfect comprehension of the truth flashed into my mind. "What do you mean?"

"Why, you know when we went on long hunts away from camp we used to put Snap in charge, and neither man nor beast could come near it. We never had a pound of provision stolen while Snap was in charge." And under cover of this defense he disappeared up the stairs, bringing the wriggly, leaping, barking dog down with him.

But I would have none of him. "He bit Mary," I reiterated in answer to all Harry's excuses; and although I was inexpressibly relieved by the explanation, the incongruity of a camp-keeper of this character, and our well-bred and peaceful cabin in the Catskills, was always present in my mind.

About this time Mark Twain came to visit us, and he had a habit of making midday lunch his principal meal, so when six-o'clock dinner came he would walk up and down the room, crossing it diagonally, and telling the most amusing stories while we ate our dinner. He always put on low-heeled slippers for this promenade, and something about the singularity of the proceeding as a whole inspired Snap with distrust. He followed Mr. Clemens up and down, up and down, the room, occasionally sniffing at the low-heeled slippers; and when a louder burst of laughter than usual greeted some of the delightful stories, Snap would growl and try to worry the peripatetic foot-gear, until Mr. Clemens became conscious of him, and slowly turned a wondering consideration upon him.

This was Snap, who had gone off, wriggling and prancing, with the stately great staghounds, without the slightest consciousness of his own vulgar plane of character in the dog world. Whenever I characterize Snap as a vulgar dog, Harry always says:

"Gran, you are very narrow and aristocratic in your notions. There *must* be grades of dogs and men in the world, or the different kinds of work would never be done." All the same, I cannot understand the good-natured tolerance of boys and men for dogs and people who are not up to the mark.

Now, all this was far enough away from my thoughts while I sat that late August night, leaning on the rough piazza rail, and looking out at my garden.

It was beautiful in the moonlight, but I noticed that you could not see the blue flowers. The great patch of larkspur which was so brilliantly, almost burningly, blue in the day-time was just a part of the night, and could not be distinguished; and the yellow and orange nasturtiums did not show themselves nearly so bravely as by daylight. They quite melted into the shadow of the stone wall along which they grew, leaves and flowers and all. You might have thought all the flowers were leaves, and all the leaves were flowers; but the blossoms sent up a spicy odor into the moonlit air, which encircled the garden like an invisible wreath. You knew they were there by their breath, even if you could not distinguish them.

But the scarlet flowers you could see

very well. There were three or four great double poppies, which seemed to burn faintly in the moonlight. It looked as if the garden had been stuck here and there with a smoldering torch; and all along the middle path, where the sweet-peas were growing thickly, there was a swarm of blossoms, white and pink, which was even more beautiful by night than by day. The little dots of color were just softened by the moonlight, and melted together, and you could almost see the odor. I fancied it rising in a thread-like spiral from each flower until at a certain height it began to spread into a little pink and pearly mist, and fuse itself with the odor of the others, and become an invisible cloud of fragrance which spread itself and blew hither and thither in the soft night air. Some part of it was constantly touching my face, little edges of it which floated now near me and now away. I had a fancy, since I could feel it melt along my lips, to stretch out my hands and waft it toward me, until I was enveloped in a cloud of heavenly sweetness. And why not? We know now that sound has shape, and shape means body, even if it is impalpable, and we perceive that odors must have cloud-like bodies, even although they are too ethereal for sight. I thought of it as the breath of the flowers, and felt a sense of living the night in company with all these breathing efforts of nature's beauty.

Oh, my dear garden! It is like living with cherubs and angels and birds of paradise to live neighbor to you, and breathe your breath, and enter into your beauty by day and by night. All the great solemn night bent over us, over the garden, and over me. I felt myself brooded by it, as if it cared for and were conscious of me.

Right at my hand, where I could put it out and touch their bluish bloom, rose up the tops of two slender young spruce-trees, and over near the great boulder-piled wall stood a fifteen-year-old apple-tree, with all the charm of youth upon it, although it was filled and clustered with ripe, red, sweet apples.

The youth of trees always has a peculiar charm for me—the charm of girlhood and boyhood. Some trees are like young athletes—you can almost fancy them throwing themselves into attitudes, and playing strong and graceful games together, like a field of college boys. And how feminine is my young, sweet apple-tree!—a smart young Hebe, bringing globes of solid wine, and offering them with out-stretched fingers to all comers.

How heavenly gracious I feel it to be of all this beauty to live and flourish under my very house-eaves, to cluster next the family, to be a part of it! I am sure it makes us good; for who could be churlish, or ungrateful, or selfish, with a garden full of wonder-growing miracles in color and form and fragrance leaning against the family life.

Now, as I leaned over and enjoyed my garden, my beds of softly breathing pansies and gay young phlox, my two strong young spruces, with their slender steeples of blue bloom, my apple-tree, red in the moonlight with its overgrowing richness of fruit, I was suddenly conscious of something which intruded, something which seemed not quite harmonious with the blue and gold night, and the near beauty of the garden, and the far beauty of the hills.

Yes, there was something strong, and gross, and animal; a black and clumsy shape moving on softly padded feet, but with rustling and clumsy body, along the stone wall of the garden. It was chumping and mouthing my ripe, sweet apples, where they had fallen on the wet grass from the out-reaching branches. I felt my hair rise in a sort of antagonism at the musky grossness of the creature, even before I recognized it, and knew it for a bear.

My thoughts flew to the boys who were dragging through the rough, dew-wet woods miles away, looking for this very beast or its mate, and I felt a sort of indignation mingling with my surprise and dislike. Suddenly the shape rose on its hind feet, and surveyed the garden; then, with a motion that seemed altogether too light for its great bulk, dropped over on the garden side, among my flowers, among my apples, and, worse than all, near to a bench spread with bowls of fresh, clear crab-apple jelly, left out to harden in the air.

I had made it, and I knew that it was the perfection of jelly, clear as spring water, pink as blossoms, and flavored with sprigs of lemon verbena. It was perfection when it was made, and my leaving it for twenty-four hours in the garden was a sentiment, a sort of charm, a baptism of sun and dew; and now it was in close view and neighborhood of this gross, moving compactness of animalism! All the poetry of my beautiful success at his mercy! But the very neighborhood of the creature was enough to destroy it, I thought angrily, and it might as well complete the destruction; and in a moment I saw the great hairy muzzle mouthing and slobbering over the bowls, rolling them around, and breaking them against one another, and all with a bestial enjoyment which was inexpressibly exasperating, and which made me almost frantic. Looking about for the form of words suited to the occasion, I laid hands first upon my heavy glass inkstand, of the kind warranted not to upset, and launched it at the creature. It must have grazed his ear, for, without stopping his slobberings, he wiped the ear with his paw, and paid no further attention. Then I explored my wood-box, and found a quantity of hard chunks of wood, which had been chopped for my little bedroom stove. All these I carried out, and aimed one after another at this natural enemy, and sent them flying at him through the air.

They were to him like so many mosquitos. The bear never looked up until he had finished my ethereal food, and then he lifted his head, and regarded me stupidly and yet cunningly, exactly as a pig will look at you from his pen. He evidently took in the sense of the position perfectly, recognized my feelings, in short, and weighed the circumstances. It was not worth while to attempt to retaliate. The posts of the upper piazza were slender and high; he knew that this accounted for my attack, and with a grunt of derision and contempt he dropped himself over the wall and seemed to melt at once into the woods, and was gone.

It was curious how all the harmony and beauty of the night seemed to have gone too—broken up and destroyed by his presence, by the aggressive animal power and influence. It was as if the better part of it—the spirit of it all—had flown off on unseen wings, and left a soulless beauty in its place; and while I sat discontentedly feeling this, there came up the road and along the air the unmistakable rattle of the one horse farm-wagon, and there were the boys again.

I unbolted the front door, and brought out a plate of sandwiches to them and their driver companions, and gave the limp, tired dogs each one, and waited until they were shut up, and the boys were in the house stripping off their jackets, before I said:

"Well, did you see the bear?"

"No; we followed it over the crest of North Mountain, but it was no good trying to get down the front, and the dogs got dead discouraged. They had two or three tussles with it, but it got away before we could get anywhere near, and finally we gave it up and came home."

"What a pity you went," said I, "for if you had been at home you might have shot one in my flower-garden."

This statement was received in silence, but with rather a puzzled look at each other, which seemed to say: "Well, we'll have to stand the chaffing anyway."

And I let it rest there, for I knew those boys were capable of rousing out the dogs again, and following the bear over ledges and precipices into the East Kill Valley; but I had it all out at breakfast the next morning, and took them into the garden, and showed them the ruins of my jelly bowls and the prints of great padded feet on the flower-beds.

"Jee-whillikens!" said Harry.

A BOY OF GALATIA

By Samuel Scoville, Jr.

April, 1900

It was court-day in far-away Galatia, northernmost of all the Grecian provinces. Before the great gate of Ancyra, the capital, a long line of accused and accusers passed the ivory chair of the archon, or ruler, who judged every cause that touched not the life of a freeman. Now a thief was scourged, now a pledge redeemed, and case after case was heard and passed upon in a few brief words. Finally a pathetic little group, that seemed oddly out of place in the line of petty criminals, came before the judgment-seat. A tall woman, with the noble oval face that marked the highest type of Grecian beauty, leaned on the arm of a youth, while a little fair-haired boy clung to her skirt. In the background stood a lame slave with eyes fixed on the ground, while the edge of a ghastly scar running underneath his tunic gave a reason for the withered limb. The archon regarded the four for a moment in silence, and then addressed them in a voice cold and impassive as his face. "Ladas and Nestor, children of him that was Milo, captain of the soldiers, and Egeria, wife of the same, hither have you been summoned at the instance of your creditors. Debts to the amount of the half of one talent are recorded against you. Your home is but a hovel, your land untilled and barren, and your one slave a worthless cripple. Therefore the city allows one year for the cancelation of these lawful debts. At the end of that time, the same remaining unpaid, this family shall be sold as slaves in the public mart for the benefit of its creditors. Thus saith the law of Galatia."

"'Tis a hard law," cried the boy, facing the archon unflinchingly, while the mother sobbed aloud, "that enslaves the family of one who died in battle for his city, and whose friends are in exile!"

"Speak not evil of the law, boy!" responded the archon, sternly. "No fault of the law is it that thy father became surety for those who belonged to the accursed Athenian faction and were rightly driven into exile, or that the family of a man are liable for his surety debts."

And the archon, who had come into office when the Athenian party was driven into exile, and hated Athens and all things Athenian with the race-hatred that belonged to his Macedonian blood, called the next case.

It was a sad home-going for the little family. In the west the afterglow of the sunset had begun to pale long before the rude dwelling, now their only shelter, was reached. That night, after the little boy had fallen asleep, Ladas and his mother sat long in the wavering firelight before the hearth, that sacred heart of a Grecian home. Back in the shadow sat their slave, Phraanes the Dumb; for never since the time that his wound had healed, leaving him with a shrunken limb, had he been heard to speak. Captured in some foray of the city against a tribe of the desert, he had been assigned to Milo, the leader of the hoplites, in the division of the spoil.

Between his master and this strange, silent man, who could outrun and, with his own weapons, outfight any one of the hoplites, there had sprung up a friendship deeper than any suspected. Ever in battle was the slave permitted to fight at his captain's side among the freemen of Galatia. Then came that terrible day when, in a skirmish against the horde of northern barbarians that had swarmed down upon Galatia, the company of Milo had been cut off from the main army by an overwhelming force. They found his body afterward in the midst of a ring of slain, covered with wounds, lying prostrate across Phraanes, who was still breathing. The latter was brought home, and, under Egeria's tender nursing, had at last recovered. Always taciturn, he now became dumb, and, with bowed head and eyes always fixed on the ground, wrought ever at such labor as his crippled state would allow. He had been the mainstay of the family during dark days of debt and shame. For the leader of the hoplites had been a surety to several of his friends who belonged to the Athenian party in the city, and whom the Macedonian faction, upon coming into power, had driven into exile. Then, by the stern Galatian code, Milo, and his family after him, became liable for all the debts that the fugitives had been forced to leave unpaid.

For a long time Egeria gazed at the fire with hot dry eyes.

"Ah, the cruelty and shame of it all!" she broke forth at last, "that the sons of my blood, and I myself whose ancestors were of the gods, should be sold as slaves! Ah, I cannot bear it!" And the stricken woman burst into a passion of weeping, withal vainly trying to keep back her sobs lest the little Nestor should be awakened.

Ladas strove to console her, his heart nearly broken the while, for never before had he seen his mother so give way, not even when the dead body of Milo was borne home.

"A year is long," he said, striving to speak hopefully, "and I have a plan, mother mine. Before the time has gone come the great Olympic Games. By toiling mightily, perchance I can gain enough to pay Timon the trainer to teach me the lore of racing. For I am fleet of foot, and the family of him who could win the race need, as thou knowest, never fear debt nor want throughout all Greece, even to the farthest province."

Suddenly from out of the darkness came a voice unheard throughout long years —the voice of the slave. It was to the mother almost as if the dead Milo had spoken. Into the circle of the firelight strode Phraanes, no longer the Dumb. The eyes, downcast so weary long, burned level under the black brows. The bent form stood again erect, and, in spite of the shriveled limb, it was no longer a broken-spirited cripple, but Phraanes the Swift, Phraanes the Warrior, who spoke.

"Art sure of the words thou saidst, O Ladas, son of my lord?" slowly questioned the slave, in a voice hoarse and faltering from long disuse.

Ladas was too startled by the transformation to do more than nod assent.

"Then hear me, O race of Milo," continued Phraanes, and his voice rang now clear and compelling as a trumpet-note. "Between Milo, the commander of troops, and me, a slave, was such love as only strong men feel who have stood back to back amid the deadly din of blows, and won through many a hard-fought day together. At the last came that battle when, hemmed in by the enemy, the Greeks fought until none were on their feet, save only Milo the captain and Phraanes the slave. Then did it chance that one ran within the sword-sweep, and down my thigh ripped a curved blade, for always fought I uncovered, as my fathers before me. The accursed one was dead before he could withdraw the knife, but my strength flowed with the blood, and even in the midst of a stroke I fell forward on my face.

Nothing more I knew until they lifted the body of my lord from mine, protecting me even in death."

There was a pause, broken only by a sob from Egeria, as the remembrance of that bitter day came back to her.

"Then came the time that I found myself no longer a man worthy to fight among men,"—and the voice dropped low—"but only a 'worthless cripple,' as thou heardst the archon say this day, and in the despair of my heart I became dumb, nor could I face my kind. Long ago would I have dared to die, but that, even in my worthlessness, some use might I be to the race of my lord."

"A helper indeed hast thou been, our Phraanes," said Egeria, softly, and her eyes became very tender as she remembered how the cripple, hopeless, bent, and dumb, had labored always, night and day, for them all.

Phraanes bent low before his mistress, touching his forehead to her outstretched hand. Then he turned to the boy, and there was the ring of absolute conviction to his words.

"O my Ladas, thou speakest of Timon the trainer. I say to thee that to his mind omens avail more than practice, and sacrifices than speed. I, too, have viewed the Olympic Games and the racers therein, and have marveled that such running should win. Slower are the Grecians in the start than the wild dog of the wilderness, who must follow his prey from sun to sun ere, wearied, it be o'ertaken. In the race they wave their arms and waste breath crying on the gods to grant them speed. To you Greeks running has been but a pastime; among my nation speed means life or death, for, as thou knowest, we desert-dwellers of the north have no horsemen, and the fate of battles must turn on the swiftness of our

warriors' feet. Among a nation of runners my father, Aisnax, was swiftest. In the great races of the desert, wherein contended all the peoples that live a life of wanderings in tents, never did he see the back of a runner at the finish. And his fame went forth throughout all the vastness of Scythia, even to the dwellers in the north, the Hyperboreans.

"To me, Phraanes, his son, he told all the wile and wisdom of the track, and the traditions of our tribe, until it came to pass that in the races I was ever at his shoulder. And, O my master, all this within the year can I teach to thee, and thou shalt win the race, an thou wilt take old Phraanes as a trainer."

He finished, and laid his massive arm, knotted and gnarled with the hard muscle like to the ribbed branch of some gray old oak, caressingly across the shoulders of Ladas.

"Thou shalt train me, my Phraanes," cried the boy, fired by the slave's words, which came to him almost like a revelation. "If I win, my statue stands before the temple in the ring of the Olympic winners from Galatia; I, and all that bear my name, live as the city's guests, honored in the public hall, and our debts the city takes upon itself; while thou, thou who fought by my dead father's side, shalt dwell with us, a friend and freeman!"

Months after this speaking of Phraanes came the day, long proclaimed by a herald throughout the length and breadth of the province, when every athlete of Galatia met in the games of the city. The winners of each event would be sent with their trainers to Olympia, there to contend in the great quadrennial games for the glory of the province. Even before the dawn, every man, woman, and child of all Galatia, save and sick and slaves, were gathered around the level field just outside the city walls, where the games of the province were held. The aulos, shortest yet most important of the races, came first. Each runner, as he took his place, was greeted with shouts of applause from his friends, save one alone, who, attended only by a limping slave, came to the line almost unnoticed. Only when, at the second word of the starter, the long rank of runners stiffened into position, did he attract any attention. All the others bent forward, one foot on the starting-line, one arm outstretched, the other back—the regulation starting position of a Grecian runner. The last youth alone crouched, and, with both hands on the line and muscles all tense, awaited the final signal.

At the first sound of the word he was off, and yards ahead of the rest before they fairly came into their stride. The fleetest runners of the province heretofore, they strained every muscle to overtake the flying body that flashed along ahead of them, gleaming in the sunlight. But in vain, in vain, do they cry on Hermes of the winged feet, god of runners, or on the swift Apollo. Like the smooth movement of a coursing hound is the long, even stride of Ladas, while the white arms swinging alternately and the lithe and even poise of the body show the effects of Phraanes's training. As the boy crossed the line marking the finish easily a winner, the spectators thronged about him, and inquiries as to his name and blood were on every tongue. The Elders, the members of the Council, and all the notables of the city pressed up to congratulate one whose speed surpassed any ever seen on a Galatian course.

"He shall join my squad at once," said Timon the trainer, authoritatively pushing his way through the crowd, "be he who he may. I doubt not that by a due observance of the auguries I can increase his speed, albeit I like not that barbarian start of his."

"Nay, but I have a trainer," the boy answered quickly, and he laid his bare arm, moist with the sweat of the race, upon the swarthy shoulder of Phraanes, who stood behind him bearing his mantle.

"What, that slave, a limping—" But the trainer ceased speaking suddenly, as with a swift movement Phraanes stepped forward and fixed his fierce eyes upon those of Timon with a look so strangely menacing that the latter shrank back involuntarily.

"Let the lad have whom he will," observed one who wore the insignia of the Council. "Such running hath never before been seen in this city, whoever has taught him."

Long months passed—months to Ladas of the sternest training and the most rigorous practice. At last came the eve of the one hundred and thirty-first Olympiad, and the little city of Olympia, usually so quiet, that stood near the sacred groves and famed course, in a lonely corner of Hellas, was alive with the vast crowd of visitors, who were thronging its streets during the "truce of God" that heralds had proclaimed throughout the Grecian world, the sacred month of the Olympic Games. Such a motley assemblage was never seen at any other time, nor could it have been gathered there save for the month's safe-conduct extended to all who came.

Richly garmented Athenians jostled against stern-faced, simply clad men of Sparta, while those slept side by side in the crowded inns who, mayhap, a few short weeks before, had met on a battle-field where quarter was not asked or given. Men of every rank and age were there—soldiers, philosophers, and poets, young and old. Only the women stayed lonely at home, by edict of the rulers.

Nor was the throng merely a Grecian one. Everywhere were seen barbarians from the unknown outer world, whose grim faces and garbs were strange to all save those veterans who had seen service in distant provinces. Here a black-robed Egyptian priest, carrying himself with the dignity that the learning of the Pyramids gave, moves slowly through the excited throngs. A little farther on, the vast thews and dark muscles of an Ethiopian from the far-away South-land attract general attention, but the menace of the sable warrior's long javelin and curved belt-dagger discourage curiosity. A slant-eyed, yellow-faced Scythian, from a region as yet beyond even the conquering march of the Macedonian troops, is not so fortunate. The furs that have kept out the cold of arctic winters afford no protection against the storm of ridicule that his odd appearance excites among the laughter-loving Greeks, and the squat figure seems to become even more dwarfed as he strives to hide himself in the throng.

Beside a fountain in the market-place stands a Phrygian flute-player. The shrill notes drown the plash of the water, and reap a rich harvest of coins from the appreciative bystanders. Suddenly the crowd parts. Down the main street sweeps a swaying, dancing band of worshipers on their way to the pillared temple of Dionysus, and the wild, sweet cadence of their chorus sounds high above the many-voiced clamor.

Far across the plain of Elis, in the dark olive-groves where stood the temple of Zeus, slept those who were to compete for the wild-olive wreaths, the winning of which bore with them world-wide fame and fortune. Among the athletes was Ladas, with Phraanes, his silent trainer, who had been there for the last ten months under the supervision of the Hellenodikae, or rulers of the games. On the morrow he was to run, not only for fame—for if he won the aulos his name would be given to the Olympiad, and forever would those four years of Grecian history be known as the Olympiad of Ladas—but to save himself and those dear to him from shame; for that week expired the year allowed him by Galatian law to cancel his debts. Swiftest of all the Galatian racers had Ladas proved himself, but to-morrow he was to meet the chosen runners of Athens, of Sparta, and of all the provinces, and, in spite of the comforting words of Phraanes, it was but a sleepless night for Ladas.

Morning came at last, and as the red dawn-light crept into the eastern-sky, the two attired themselves and hastened to the temple of mighty Zeus. Behind the great altar of Pentelic marble, stained with the life-blood of a quivering victim, was the vast gold-and-ivory statue of the ruler of the gods, the life-work of inspired Phidias. The grand figure, seated in its ivory chair, towered forty feet from the ground, and, extending the eagle-crowned scepter that swayed Olympus, demanded the reverence of mortals. No man could meet the majestic gaze of that deathless face with a lie on his lips. Before the crouched lions that supported the golden footstool of the god were grouped the competitors from all Greece and her provinces, while facing them, beneath the winged spike that stood in the god's left hand, were the ten silent judges of the games, whose stern eyes watched and weighed each athlete that stepped forward, as his name was called, to prove by witnesses the integrity of his character and to take the oath of the Olympic Games.

One by one the awed athletes came forward, until at last, "Ladas, son of Milo, of the city of Ancyra of the province of Galatia, stand forth!" shouted the herald of the games, and his mighty voice echoed among the temple pillars.

"Who answers for this youth?" again, as Ladas stood before the altar.

"I, Chryses, of the Inner Council of the city of Ancyra, answer for him," responded a calm voice from the group of witnesses, and a man of majestic bearing stepped forth. "Before great Zeus, this youth is without blemish or stain."

"Take the oath, O Ladas!" rang the great voice again.

The boy laid his right hand in the flowing life-blood of the sacrifice, gazed straight up at the mighty face that towered above him, and unfalteringly repeated the oath of the games:

"Hear, O Zeus! I who stand before thee now am of pure Hellenic blood, a free son of free parents, neither branded with dishonor nor guilty of any sacrilege. I have duly undergone for ten months the training to fit me to contend before thee, and will so contend, striving earnestly by all lawful means, and without bribery, to obtain victory."

Later, in the northwest corner of the great Altis, filled with the statues of former victors, Ladas and Phraanes waited in the dim dawn-light for the trumpet-note which would summon the former to the stadium.

"Thou art drawn in the third heat," said Phraanes, laying his arm across the boy's shoulders, all a-tremble under the terrible strain of suspense. "Run thou that with the ordinary upright start such as all will use. There are none against thee save new men from distant provinces; but in the last heat Phaedo of Athens will push thee hard, for this is but thy first year, and sixteen wreaths has he won at games—Olympic, Pythian, Nemean, and Isthmian. Thou must needs remember every wile that I have taught thee, to touch the marble at the finish in front of him. See to it that—"

But here a trumpet-note cut short all further conversation. The two then separated, Phraanes hastening to the place on the hill Kronion reserved for the men of Galatia, while Ladas joined the little group of competitors that passed through the vaulted passage leading to the stadium.

On each side were long rows of brazen Zanes, whose grim, cold faces had seen generation after generation of runners hasten down the echoing steps toward the stadium to strive for the honor of provinces and cities. As Ladas stepped forth into the brightening sunlight it was into a tempest of sound. The vast crowd that darkened the sides of the hill Kronion, feverish from a night of waiting, rose to its feet, and a human roar surged across the stadium like the voice of some vast unearthly thing. Through the serried ranks passed the Hellenodikae with their wands of office, whose slightest motion was law even to the most frenzied of the spectators.

Half stunned by the tumult, Ladas stretched himself on the narrow space of turf next the track, where the runners awaited their heats, pressed his burning face deep into the cool grass, and drew in long breaths of its dewy fragrance. Although the air was warm, he shivered and wrapped himself more closely in the great *chlamys*, or fleece-lined cloak that was the conventional garb of waiting athletes.

Then the wands of the Hellenodikae were lifted, and in an instant there was a silence, broken only by the high, monotonous tone of the herald as he announced the names and cities of the competitors in the first heat. As they bent forward in a line that reached across the stadium, the muscles of Ladas stiffened involuntarily with theirs. Then came the short, sharp trumpet-note, and they were off.

As Ladas watched the line that flashed forward he saw much to hearten him. Some of the racers cried out shrilly to their gods as they ran, and the awkward play of their arms and legs was far different from the clean, machine-like motion that old

Phraanes had taught the boy. Unconsciously Ladas sat up, and the loud beating of his heart no longer seemed to fill his ears. "I could give any of those five cubits and overtake them on the start," he thought joyously.

But the next heat dispelled rudely his dreams of an easy victory. Phaedo, the Athenian, ran in that heat, and Ladas saw instantly that there was a competitor whose speed far outstripped all that he had seen. His left arm to the shoulder was red with the blood of a wild deer, sacrificed that morning to Hermes, the winged one; for Phaedo believed much in sacrifice. At the trumpet-note he was off a stride before the others, and his every motion showed the training and experience that years of competition at the four great sacred games had given him. Half-way down the stadium he led by nearly double his own length.

Then, with a quick glance over his shoulder at the laboring runners behind him, by degrees his pace slackened; for Phaedo was no novice, to make any unnecessary effort in what was only a preliminary heat. As he half turned to look back Ladas saw the red emblem of the sea-god, an image of a fish, burned deeply in just above the heart, showing with strange vividness against the snowy skin, and he remembered that Phaedo was of the Poseidonic Brotherhood, one of the oldest and most powerful of those mystic orders whose origin went back to the days when the gods still dwelt among men. To this none were eligible save certain of the priesthood—who prepared themselves for the dread honor only by years of endurance—and the winners of the Isthmian Games, whose bravery had been proved by dread initiatory rites. Free were these Brethren of the Sea to voyage on any vessel of Greece, the provinces, or the isles, while even the Phoenicians, those sea-rovers who feared no man, granted all

honor to the wearer of the symbol of great Dagon, the fish-god; for the Brethren were forever exempt from all perils of wreck or storm, and Poseidon extended like protection to the ship and the crew with whom they were associated.

This honor, which only age and a life of endeavor could bring to other men, Phaedo, still in his youth, had won almost in a day, and Ladas remembered certain ringing lines of the blind Homer that his mother had read to him: "Throughout life a man hath naught more glorious than what he wins with his hands or his feet." And if he but won to-day, what glory greater than all would be his—the glory of restoring those of his race and blood to the proud place they had once held in the city, the glory of saving his mother, his brother, and himself from unspeakable shame! And the boy's teeth clenched together grimly, and very suddenly all the tremor, all the fear, was gone; the dogged fighting blood that had come down to him through a long line of warrior ancestors was stirred. 'Twas a fight with all Greece, and the odds against him, but win he would; and the boy felt the strange calm that comes to him who has once nerved himself to fight undauntedly, desperately, despairingly it may be, but still to fight through to the end, whatever that end may be.

The great voice of the herald sounded along the hillside, and the first name was "Ladas of the province of Galatia." A shout to the patron god of the province went up from the northeastern end of the hill: "Galatia! Galatia! Ares for Galatia!" And Ladas thrilled all over as he heard the voice of his city, and realized how dear to him was his birthplace, and how to-day its honor lay in his hands. He listened intently as, one by one, the other contestants were called and ranged themselves by his side. All were unknown novices. Every runner who during recent years had achieved aught of reputation, either in the national or provincial races, had become known to Ladas, by name at least, during these last few months of training. With a feeling of intense relief, he faced up the stadium as the starter gave the first word, and assumed the position for the Grecian start, in accordance with Phraanes's directions. Bending lithely forward, he darted off at the last signal a little ahead of the other runners, despite the unfamiliar method of starting. Before he had taken half a score of strides, by that indefinable instinct that comes to a runner, he knew, without glancing back, that he was easily drawing away from the others.

Imperceptibly he slackened his pace when once assured that his opponents were running at the limit of their speed, and foot by foot they crept up. The awkward fling, too, of their limbs he imitated somewhat, disguised the smooth, rhythmic beat of his feet by clumsy movements, ran as if greatly exhausted, and finally staggered in, a winner by a few inches. It was of the craft of Phraanes that none should know of his pupil's real speed until the last heat; for the old racer well knew that, especially in a short race, a surprise might turn the scale.

"'Tis but a young runner that wins," quoth the grizzled Athenian trainer to Phaedo, who stood watching the heat critically. "Not till another Olympiad will he be skilled enough to hasten thee. To-day it is the Wolf from Sparta and that accursed 'Girl' from Corinth whom thou must fear."

Like words spoke all the trainers to their charges ere Ladas joined the group of waiting athletes, that was waning with every heat. He alone of all the runners was attended by no trainer, for none save freeborn men of Hellenic parents were allowed to enter the sacred inclosure of the stadium.

Lonely he wrapped the fleecy cloak around his bare shoulders and paced back and forth, while the others looked at him askance, and the trainers sneered audibly at the young runner who competed unattended; but on Ladas's left wrist was the gleaming golden circlet that the elder of the judges had clasped on for him as winner of an Olympiad heat—an honor in itself that was worth years of striving—and in his ears still rang the great shout of triumph that had gone up from the men of Galatia at the words of the herald: "Ladas of the province of Galatia wins the third course!"

The next heat went to Lycaon the Spartan, the "Wolf"—so named from that grim winter's night when, alone and on foot, he had run down a gray wolf of the forest, and killed him with no other weapons than his hands and teeth.

The last heat was taken by Arcesilaus, the runner from Corinth, surnamed the "Girl," from the fairness of his face and the effeminacy of his manners; yet underneath that soft exterior was concealed a fire and a fury of courage that had made him one of the most noted of all the Grecian racers in long or short races.

Now came a brief interval of rest, while the trainers with supple hands and limpid oil rubbed out the last vestige of fatigue from limbs on whose speed that day depended the honor of a city. As the mighty-voiced herald called forth the names and cities of the heat-winners, they ranged themselves at the start in the order of their names.

First was a Thessalian, a heavy-featured, sturdily built mountaineer; next to him stood a Cretan, sly-faced and treacherous-eyed: slow runners both, who chanced to be the swiftest in their heats. Then came Ladas, with Phaedo of Athens next. Side by side with Phaedo was the Wolf of Sparta, while, last of all, on the farthest right was the Girl of Corinth, twirling a freshly plucked rose in his white be-ringed fingers.

As the runners ranged themselves in line, far down the sandy course, back of the sunken marble slab that marked the goal, rose the elder of the judges to call down the blessing of great Zeus, the ruler of the gods, upon the coming Olympiad; for each Olympiad bore the name of the winner of the race. The Olympiad of Phaedo was drawing to its close, and this race determined whose name the next four years of Greece should bear.

"Look well, O Hellas!" cried the elder from his carved marble seat, holding aloft the sacred cup of the games, brimming with the crimson wine. "Is there aught of evil known against these who run to-day before the deathless, all-knowing gods?" An instant of silence, and "The blessing of great Zeus be on the coming Olympiad, and him who names it!" cried the elder, and the crimson drops fell as an oblation upon the goal-slab. Scarcely had they stained the snowy marble when there sounded the trumpet-note that warned the runners to take their positions. Instantly the line bent forward, and all save the runner of Galatia leaned over with arm outstretched, left foot on the mark, ready to stride forth at the last trumpet-call. Ladas alone crouched at the feet of the others, both hands white to the knuckles with the pressing on the starting-line, and every muscle in his lithe body tense to shoot him forward at the first sound of the trumpet.

A murmur of astonishment went up from the audience as, for the first time, the barbarian start of the desert was seen on an Olympic stadium. From the corner of his eye Phaedo saw, with a vague feeling of uneasiness, the figure crouching below him, while at the farther end the Girl of Corinth lost somewhat of his unconcerned bearing; there was a troubled frown on the Wolf's stern face, and the whole line was pervaded with the anxiety that something unexpected causes. Insensibly the strained attention for the first sound of the starting note relaxed.

It came, the clear call to every man to run that day for all that life held dear.

At the first throb of sound on the air, Ladas, with a panther-like spring, is off and into his stride an instant before his startled opponents. A third of the way down the course he is leading by over his own length. Back of him on the left he can hear the muttered ejaculations of the Thessalian and the runner from Crete, as they cry to the gods for fleetness, but cry in vain, for with every stride the others draw away from them. Nearest to Ladas is Phaedo, surprised at such swiftness from one whom he had considered an untrained novice, but running craftily as ever, waiting for the finish, where he counts upon the tremendous burst of speed that has snatched for him so many races out of the very jaws of defeat. On the far right, the Corinthian, his assumed girlishness cast aside, is running like a demon neck and neck with the Wolf of Sparta, the two but half a stride behind Phaedo.

But it is to Phaedo that the knowing ones look to win the race, for the leader from Galatia is but an unknown runner. On the right the madness of the race has fallen upon the farther two, and, though lessening the space that separates them from the leaders, they are running at the very limit of their speed in this first third of the race. But Phaedo seems to be husbanding his strength for a last desperate effort. There is no sound from the watching multitude, and in the tense silence the beat of the runners' feet upon the yellow sand, the gasping intake of their quick breathing, and their murmured cries to patron gods all are heard with strange distinctness. As the warm blood rushes through the veins of the Galatian boy, it carries away all the fear, all the oppression, that has weighed upon him. As in a dream, outside of himself, he seems to be watching, watching the race and his own speed dispassionately, impersonally.

Never before has every faculty acted with such absolute coolness and accuracy. Every word of the counsel that Phraanes has again and again given him for this his life-race comes to him now. With slanting, backward glance he sees the runners on the left dropping back, those on the right doing their uttermost; only Phaedo he sees not—Phaedo, crafty as swift.

Little by little he slackens his speed to spare himself for what is to be the final struggle with Phaedo; and now the mad rush of the two on the right brings them up beside Ladas. The boy lengthens his stride, and for a moment the dark, swarthy visage of the Wolf, with the veins all swollen and black from struggling, the face of the Girl, wild-eyed, with a tiny crimson stream staining the dainty chin where the clenched teeth have pierced the lower lip, and the calm, uneager countenance of Ladas are in line.

But soon the straining efforts of the two on the right begin to tell, and slowly they draw away from the boy until there is a clear space between. Ladas holds the same pace, watching only that the little gap shall not widen. Still Phaedo makes no sign, though near enough for Ladas to hear his rapid breathing close at his shoulder; nor, though the boy lags all that he dares, will Phaedo draw up side by side; and Ladas knows that to-day the race is between Athens and Galatia, for already his practised eyes see the tiny fatal falter in the stride of the leaders. That desperate struggling from the very start is beginning to tell, and the

life and dash at the finish which wins a race has gone.

And now the white goal-stone of the young boys, who run a shorter course at the games than the men, is reached. The last third of the race is at hand.

Scarcely have they swung by it when, with a mad rush, Phaedo shoots past Ladas, running as Ladas never saw man run before, eyes fixed on the goal, flaming under his heavy brows like altar-coals, his blood-stained arm gleaming back and forth with every quick, plunging stride.

A voice shrilled and broken, with a passion of pleading in its tone, sounds above the hoarse monotone of the Spartan, who shouts to the patron god of Lacedaemon. "Hear, O Poseidon, hear!" it calls. "The race grant thou to me, to me who shed my blood for thee on the Shore of Dread!"

Unlawful words are they, words telling what many a priest in the vast audience trembled to hear. Only the desperation of the finish could have wrung them from Phaedo, for, though he has flashed past the laboring leaders, right at his heel comes the rapid footfall of the Galatian boy. Clearer and clearer it sounds, run as he will. Every faculty and fiber in Ladas's mind and body is concentrated on keeping unbroken the long, swift stride that Phraanes has taught him, which eats up the ground like fire. With elbows held well in, and swinging arms that lengthen every stride, he wastes no breath shouting invocations.

A single slip or falter will be fatal now, with the goal distant but a few short lengths, and as his limbs weaken under the terrible strain, the strength of his will sustains his flagging muscles, and still the flying feet spurn the loose sand with never a break in their motion. Deep down within himself Ladas feels yet remaining an iota of reserve power. The temptation is almost irresistible to make his effort now, now to end the suspense and decide the race; but to his mind come the words of crafty old Phraanes: "With a stout heart and cool head the race can be won in the very last stride," and the supreme moment is delayed. Just ahead a flying figure dances before his dimming sight, and he wonders how feels Phaedo, and whether aught of his strength also has been saved. And now a mad shout from the crowded seats of the Athenians roars forth across the stadium as they see Phaedo in the lead at the very finish. "Athene! Athene!" they shout. "Pallas Athene gives us the race!" The cheers of the little group of Galatians are swallowed up in the great cry, but Ladas needs no applause to nerve him on. Now, at the very last, the wan, beautiful face of his mother is before him, and he remembers the two, lonely at home, waiting, waiting for the outcome of this day, for their glory or for their shame. Already the goal is scarce three strides away, and Phaedo laughs with triumph, when suddenly the face of Ladas shoots up even with his. For an instant, that seems hours of struggling, the two waver side by side, and then with a last desperate effort the boy of Galatia draws ahead and touches the goal-slab, even while the foot of the Athenian hangs above it.

With the mighty shout of an assembled world begins the Olympiad of Ladas.

A VICTOR IN THE OLYMPIC GAMES ENTERING THE TEMPLE OF ZEUS.

THE STORY OF A PROVERB

By Sidney Lanier

May, 1877

ONCE upon a time,—if my memory serves me correctly, it was in the year 6⅞—His Intensely-Serene-and-Altogether-Perfectly-Astounding Highness the King of Nimporte was reclining in his royal palace. The casual observer (though it must be said that casual observers were as rigidly excluded from the palace of Nimporte as if they had been tramps) might easily have noticed that his majesty was displeased.

The fact is, if his majesty had been a little boy, he would have been whipped and sent to bed for the sulks; but even during this early period of which I am writing, the strangeness of things had reached such a pitch, that in the very moment at which this story opens the King of Nimporte arose from his couch, seized by the shoulders his grand vizier (who was not at all in the sulks, but was endeavoring, as best he could, to smile from the crown of his head to the soles of his feet), and kicked him down-stairs.

As the grand vizier reached the lowest step in the course of his tumble, a courier covered with dust was in the act of putting his foot upon the same. But the force of the grand vizier's fall was such as to knock both the courier's legs from under him; and as, in the meantime, the grand vizier had wildly clasped his arms around the courier's body, to arrest his own descent, the result was such a miscellaneous rolling of the two men, that for a moment no one was able to distinguish which legs belonged to the grand vizier and which to the courier.

"Has she arrived?" asked the grand vizier, as soon as his breath came.

"Yes," said the courier, already hastening up the stairs.

At this magic word, the grand vizier again threw his arms around the courier, kissed him, released him, whirled himself about like a teetotum, leaped into the air and cracked his heels thrice before again touching the earth, and said:

"Allah be praised! Perhaps now we shall have some peace in the palace."

In truth, the King of Nimporte had been waiting two hours for his bride, whom he had never seen; for, according to custom, one of his great lords had been sent to the court of the bride's father, where he had married her by proxy for his royal master, and whence he was now conducting her to the palace. For two hours the King of Nimporte had been waiting for a courier to arrive and announce to him that the cavalcade was on its last day's march over the plain, and was fast approaching the city.

As soon as the courier had delivered his message, the king kicked him down-stairs (for not arriving sooner, his majesty incidentally remarked), and ordered the grand vizier to cause that a strip of velvet carpet should be laid from the front door of the grand palace, extending a half-mile down the street in the direction of the road by which the cavalcade was approaching; adding that it was his royal intention to walk this distance, for the purpose of giving his bride a more honorable reception than any bride of any king of Nimporte had ever before received.

The grand vizier lost no time in carrying out his instructions, and in a short time the king appeared stepping along the carpet in the stateliest manner, followed by a vast and glittering retinue of courtiers, and encompassed by multitudes of citizens who had crowded to see the pageant.

As the king, bareheaded and barefooted (for at this time everybody went barefoot in Nimporte), approached the end of the carpet, he caught sight of his bride, who was but a few yards distant on her milk-white palfrey.

Her appearance was so ravishingly beautiful, that the king seemed at first dazed, like a man who has looked at the sun; but, quickly recovering his wits, he threw himself forward, in the ardor of his admiration, with the intention of running to his bride and dropping on one knee at her stirrup, while he would gaze into her face with adoring humility. And as the king rushed forward with this impulse, the populace cheered with the wildest enthusiasm at finding him thus capable of the feelings of an ordinary man.

But in an instant a scene of the wildest commotion ensued. At the very first step which the king took beyond the end of the carpet, his face grew suddenly white, and, with a loud cry of pain, he fell fainting to the earth. He was immediately surrounded by the anxious courtiers; and the court physician, after feeling his pulse for several minutes, and inquiring very carefully of the grand vizier whether his majesty had on that day eaten any green fruit, was in the act of announcing that it was a violent attack of a very Greek disease indeed, when the bride (who had dismounted and run to her royal lord with wifely devotion) called the attention of the excited courtiers to his majesty's left great toe. It was immediately discovered that, in his first precipitate step from off the carpet to the bare ground, his majesty had set his foot upon a very rugged pebble, the effect of which upon tender feet accustomed to nothing but velvet, had caused him to swoon with pain.

As soon as the King of Nimporte opened his eyes in his own palace, where he had been quickly conveyed and ministered to by the bride, he called his trembling grand vizier and inquired to whom belonged the houses at that portion of the street where his unfortunate accident had occurred. Upon learning the names of these unhappy property-owners, he instantly ordered that they and their entire kindred should be beheaded, and the adjacent houses burned for the length of a quarter of a mile.

The king further instructed the grand vizier that he should instantly convene the cabinet of councilors and devise with them some means of covering the whole earth with leather, in order that all possibility of such accidents to the kings of Nimporte might be completely prevented—adding that if the cabinet should fail, not only in devising the plan, but in actually carrying it out within the next three days, then the whole body of councilors should be executed on the very spot where the king's foot was bruised.

Then the king kissed his bride, and was very happy.

But the grand vizier, having communicated these instructions to his colleagues of the cabinet—namely, the postmaster-general, the praetor, the sachem, and the three Scribes-and-Pharisees—proceeded to his own home, and consulted his wife, whose advice he was accustomed to follow with the utmost faithfulness. After thinking steadily for two days and nights, on the morning of the third day the grand vizier's wife advised him to pluck out his beard, to tear up his garments, and to make his will; declaring that she could not, upon the most mature deliberation, conceive of any course more appropriate to the circumstances.

The grand vizier was in the act of separating his last pair of bag-trousers into very minute strips indeed, when a knocking at the door arrested his hand, and in a moment afterward the footman ushered in a young man of very sickly complexion, attired in the seediest possible manner. The grand vizier immediately recognized him as a person well known about Nimporte for a sort of loafer, given to mooning about the clover-fields, and to meditating upon things in general, but not commonly regarded as ever likely to set a river on fire.

"O grand vizier!" said this young person (the inhabitants of Nimporte usually pronounced this word much like the French *personne*, which means nobody), "I have come to say that if you will procure the attendance of the king and court to-morrow morning at eleven o'clock in front of the palace, I will cover the whole earth with leather for his majesty in five minutes."

Then the grand vizier arose in the quietest possible manner, and kicked the young person down the back-stairs; and when he had reached the bottom stair, the grand vizier tenderly lifted him in his arms and carried him back to the upper landing, and then kicked him down the front-stairs—in fact, quite out of the front gate.

Having accomplished these matters satisfactorily, the grand vizier returned with a much lighter heart, and completed a draft of his last will and testament for his lawyer, who was to call at eleven.

Punctually at the appointed time—being exactly three days from the hour when the grand vizier received his instructions—the King of Nimporte and all his court, together with a great mass of citizens, assembled at the scene of the accident to witness the decapitation of the entire cabinet. The headsman had previously arranged his apparatus; and presently the six unfortunate wise men were seen standing with hands tied behind, and with heads bent forward meekly over the six blocks in a row.

The executioner advanced and lifted a long and glittering sword. He was in the act of bringing it down with terrific force upon the neck of the grand vizier, when a stir was observed in the crowd, which quickly increased to a commotion so great that the king raised his hand and bade the executioner wait until he could ascertain the cause of the disturbance.

In a moment more, the young person appeared in the open space which had been reserved for the court, and with a mingled air of proud self-confidence and of shrinking reserve, made his obeisance before the king.

"O king of the whole earth!" he said, "if within the next five minutes I shall have covered the whole earth with leather for your majesty, will your gracious highness remit the sentence which has been pronounced upon the wise men of the cabinet?"

It was impossible for the king to refuse.

"Will your majesty then be kind enough to advance your right foot?"

The young person kneeled, and drawing a bundle from his bosom, for a moment manipulated the king's right foot in a manner which the courtiers could not very well understand.

"Will your majesty now advance your majesty's left foot?" said the young person again; and again he manipulated.

"Will your majesty now walk forth upon the stones?" said the young person; and his majesty walked forth upon the stones.

"Will your majesty now answer: If your majesty should walk over the entire globe, would not your majesty's feet find leather between them and the earth the whole way?"

"It is true," said his majesty.

"Will your majesty further answer: Is not the whole earth, so far as your majesty is concerned, now covered with leather?"

"It is true," said his majesty.

"O king of the whole earth, what is it?" cried the whole court in one breath.

"In fact, my lords and gentlemen," said the king, "I have on, what has never been known in the whole, great kingdom of Nimporte until this moment, a pair of—of—"

And here the king looked inquiringly at the young person.

"Let us call them—shoes," said the young person.

Then the king, walking to and fro over the pebbles with the greatest comfort and security, looked inquiringly at him. "Who are you?" asked his majesty.

"I belong," said the young person, "to the tribe of the poets—who make the earth tolerable for the feet of man."

Then the king turned to his cabinet, and pacing along in front of the six blocks, pointed to his feet, and inquired:

"What do you think of this invention?"

"I do not like it; I cannot understand it: I think the part of wisdom is always to reject the unintelligible; I therefore advise your majesty to refuse it," said the grand vizier, who was really so piqued, that he would much rather have been beheaded than live to see the triumph of the young person whom he had kicked down both pairs of stairs.

It is worthy of note, however, that when the grand vizier found himself in his own apartments, alive and safe, he gave a great leap into the air and whirled himself with joy, as on a former occasion.

The postmaster-general also signified his disapproval. "I do not like it," said he; "they are not rights and lefts; I therefore advise your majesty to refuse the invention."

The praetor was like minded. "It will not do," he said; "It is clearly obnoxious to the overwhelming objection that there is abso-lutely nothing objectionable about it; in my judgment, this should be sufficient to authorize your majesty's prompt refusal of the expedient and the decapitation of the inventor."

"Moreover," added the sachem, "if your majesty once wears them, then every man, woman and child, will desire to have his, her and its whole earth covered with leather; which will create such a demand for hides, that there will shortly be not a bullock or a cow in your majesty's dominions: if your majesty will but contemplate the state of this kingdom without beef and butter!—there seems no more room for argument!"

"But these objections," cried the three Scribes-and-Pharisees, "although powerful enough in themselves, O king of the whole earth, have not yet touched the most heinous fault of this inventor, and that is, that there is no reserved force about this invention; the young person has actually done the very best he could in the most candid manner; this is clearly in violation of the rules of art—witness the artistic restraint of our own behavior in this matter!"

Then the King of Nimporte said: "O wise men of my former cabinet, your wisdom seems folly; I will rather betake me to the counsels of the poet, and he shall be my sole adviser for the future; as for you, live—but live in shame for the littleness of your souls!" And he dismissed them from his presence in disgrace.

It was then that the King of Nimporte uttered that proverb which has since become so famous among the Persians; for, turning away to his palace, with his bride on one arm and the young person on the other, he said:

"To him who wears a shoe, it is as if the whole earth were covered with leather."

ON A GLACIER IN GREENLAND

By Albert White Vorse

April, 1894

FOR a boy of twelve Kywingwa knew many things. He could pick out the likeliest situations for fox-traps; he knew how to stalk an arctic hare, and to shoot her with his bow and arrow; he could point to the spot in the water where a seal which had dived would probably rise. With the whip he was, for a *mickanniny* (child), really expert; for not only had he ceased now to slash himself in the back of the neck, when he whirled the long, unwieldy lash, but also he was beginning to direct his strokes with accuracy. And in one exercise he was preëminent above all the other boys in Greenland. That exercise was throwing the harpoon. Even the older Eskimos were accustomed to gather when with his comrades he practised harpooning, and to praise the accuracy of his aim, and the power of his delivery.

In other than physical things also was Kywingwa versed. He had unconsciously acquired a knowledge of human nature beyond his years. Eskimo emotions are comparatively simple, and the lad had learned to guess pretty accurately the motives for the actions of his friends. But he was utterly bewildered by the strange conduct of a party of seemingly crazy people with white faces, who had come from across the sea, and had built a wonderful house on the shores of the bay upon which Kywingwa lived. The house was as big as many Eskimo *igloos* (huts) together, and it was constructed not of sealskins, nor even of stones, but of wood. Kywingwa had never before seen a piece of wood larger than a harpoon-shaft. The Eskimos treasured with the greatest care even small splinters of the precious substance. Ky-wingwa himself had rather a large piece, with moreover a sharp spike of iron in its end, which made it more valuable. This instrument, used to prevent a seal from escaping after you had once fastened to him with your harpoon, had been handed down to Kywingwa from his great-grandfather. It was called a *pusheemut*. Kywingwa had been very proud of owning a pusheemut. But when he saw the great quantities of wood possessed by the white people his pride departed from him. They had not only enough long, broad pieces to build the great igloo, but also a vast number of smaller sticks left over. Curiously enough, they did not seem to value them very highly; they would give one to you almost always if you would help them with the queer things that they were constantly doing.

Some of them wandered along the beach and picked up shells, and they liked to have you bring them all the unusual shells that you could find. Others gathered different kinds of flowers, and were much pleased if you discovered for them a variety that they had not come across. One of them had a net not unlike the net the Eskimos were accustomed to use in catching little auks, only of much finer mesh, and made of a soft material that was not sealskin string. With it the white man pursued, not birds, but insects: butterflies, and bumblebees, and spiders, and all the other kinds of small creatures that abound in Greenland during the warm summer. He was a very enthusiastic white man, and the Eskimos named him after his favorite prey, Arhiveh, the spider.

Whenever Kywingwa was not asleep he was sure to be either at the white man's igloo, or else away upon some excursion with the butterfly-hunter, whom he liked best of all. In return, the white man showed a warm affection for Kywingwa. He taught him to catch butterflies, and made for him a little net. And when they went forth together he once or twice even let the boy bear the glacier implement which Kywingwa thought the most beautiful of all created things.

It was a wonderful implement: a long, springy, wooden shaft with a head made of some substance as hard as iron, but so shiny that you could see your face in it, just as in a pool of water. One side of the head was a blade with which you could chop ice; the other side was a long, sharp spike.

"What a fine thing for seal-hunting!" exclaimed all the Eskimos when they saw it. Kywingwa more than the others admired it. He was wont to stand before it as it hung in the great wooden igloo and gaze at it, and touch the keen edge of the blade softly with his fingers. Once or twice Arhiveh saw him thus caressing it, and laughed.

"Good?" he inquired in his broken Eskimo.

"Infinitely good!" Kywingwa cried.

He admired it humbly, however, and without hope of possessing it. It was not for Eskimos to aspire to things so perfect: they were for white people only.

But the most noteworthy event in Kywingwa's life occurred and changed entirely his point of view. Entering the wooden igloo upon a certain waking-time he saw Arhiveh bending over a tiny brown butterfly which he held in his palm. The white man appeared to be disturbed in mind.

"*Agai* (come), Kywingwa!" he said.

Obediently approaching, the lad perceived that the insect lacked one wing.

"*Takoo* (observe), Kywingwa," said Arhiveh, "you capture butterfly, good but-

terfly. Not like this—" he stood erect, with one arm behind him, and moved the other arm vigorously up and down. "Like this—" both arms going hard. Kywingwa laughed with glee and nodded to show that he comprehended.

"*Peook* (very well)!" continued Arhiveh, "you catch butterfly, I give you—"

He paused, and the boy was seized with a strange impulse he could not control.

"*That!*" he cried, and pointed to the glacier implement.

The butterfly-hunter seemed a good deal surprised, and Kywingwa was breathless.

At last Arhiveh laughed.

"*Peook!*" he said, "you catch good butterfly. I give you—yes, I give you *that*."

What Kywingwa did next he does not remember. Arhiveh has told him that he stood as if dazed for a moment, and then rushed out. The first memory that comes to him is of seeking for his net among the harpoons, and pieces of ivory, and sealskin water-buckets in his father's tent, and of repeating over and over:

"A tiny brown butterfly with *two* wings!"

He at last found his net, and after a moment's thought he took his pusheemut. The white people usually carried their glacier implements on important excursions. Kywingwa was going upon an excursion that he deemed very important, and the pusheemut was the best substitute for a glacier implement that he had. Recently, Arhiveh had sharpened the spike and the pusheemut was much more efficient than of old. A piece of seal-flipper also he picked up, and started forth, repeating to himself: "A tiny brown butterfly."

The valley where butterflies lived was a long distance up toward the head of the bay. Kywingwa had been there several times with Arhiveh, but always in a woman's boat with four men to propel it. To walk there would take a long time and would probably tire him, but he was too much excited to dwell upon that thought, and he set out briskly.

But after a long time he did grow very weary. The walking was exceedingly bad; there was no path but the beach between the sea and the vast cliffs, and it was covered with sharp stones which hurt his feet, for he had forgotten to stuff grass between the soles of his boots and his dogskin stockings.

The sun completed more than half its circular course in the sky, dipped till its edge touched the mountains across the bay to the north, and then began to rise once more. Kywingwa had never been so long away from home alone before, but whenever discouragement threatened, he thought of the glacier implement and plodded on. And at last, just as the sun reached his highest point, the lad rounded a promontory and came into the valley of butterflies. He found a small stream, and threw himself down beside it to rest, eat his seal-meat, and survey his territory.

Between little smooth hills small brooks ran; and along these brooks grew vividly green grass and bright flowers. It was among the flowers that the butterflies lived.

The seal-flipper was good; he ate it all, drank of the pure cold water that had flowed from the melting snow on the plateau, and started forth. Up and down the little streams he wandered, following one back as far as the cliffs, then crossing to the next one and tracing it down to its mouth. He saw plenty of bumblebees, plenty of flies, even plenty of brown butterflies, dancing in the hot sunlight, but none like that Arhiveh had shown him.

"What shall I do?" he asked himself.

He decided to try the next valley.

The next valley was filled by a great white glacier. Evidently there were no butterflies there. But across the front of the glacier Kywingwa discerned a third valley that looked promising. Grown Eskimos rarely crossed glaciers, and he was but a *mickanniny*. But he was still borne onward by the thought of the glacier implement. Out toward the center of the glacier, huge masses were splitting off with tremendous crashes and plunging into the sea. The torrent at the side roared; the noise was almost deafening.

Not to be daunted by noise, Kywingwa passed up the gorge along the side of the glacier, and found a place where he could cross the torrent, on some stones, to a part of the glacier which sloped away and was accessible. Presently he came to rougher ice; from the surface of the glacier rose in all directions sharp peaks. Yawning cracks appeared and then chasms so wide that he had to make long detours around them, or to cross by dangerous snow-bridges.

Upon one of these bridges a misfortune happened to Kywingwa. The snow appeared hard and perfectly solid; nevertheless an impulse led the lad to test it. With the handle of his butterfly-net he prodded, and the handle passed through the snow. Kywingwa lost his balance and fell. Down crashed the snow-bridge into the crevasse. Kywingwa's head and right arm hung over the abyss. It was some minutes before he recovered from the shock, and then he found that his butterfly-net had fallen into the chasm. He had lost his net, but he remembered that he had caught many butterflies in his hand before the net had been his. He determined to proceed to the other side of the glacier, trusting that fortune would send him the butterfly.

In his path lay a stream altogether too broad to be jumped, and, though rather shallow, too swift to be waded. It had worn a deep bed in the hard ice—a bed as blue as the sky, and so smooth, so exquisitely smooth, that the water hardly rippled as it rushed along. Not the length of a harpoon-line away from the spot where Kywingwa stood it plunged into a deep crevasse, whence rose a heavy rumbling.

Patiently Kywingwa followed up the stream till he came to an ice-bridge. He crossed it, meeting with no further obstructions, and presently stood upon the edge of the glacier, and looked up and down the gorge at its side.

Far down by the bay, toward the end of the great white mass, the cliffs receded, the land was low, the sun shone; it seemed just the place for butterflies. Kywingwa found a sloping spot where he could descend into the gorge, and turned toward the fertile spot.

As he emerged from the shadow of the cliffs, he came out into full sunlight, and found himself surrounded by rivulets, by flowers, and by insects. And before he could well note these things, lo! from under his feet rose and settled again the very object of his search—the little brown butterfly!

Kywingwa stole toward it, came within his own length of it, leaped with open hands upon it. In vain! The little creature darted from his grasp. Kywingwa, always keeping it in view, scrambled to his feet and gave chase. Down nearly to the beach it led him; then it doubled, dodged him, and made off up the hills toward the cliffs. Kywingwa tried to follow, but to no purpose; it alighted far away, and out of sight. Bitterly disappointed, the boy shuffled through the grass, hoping to scare up the insect once more; but his efforts were futile. And presently he was aware that the sun had gone behind the hills, and that not only his butterfly, but also all the other insects, had disappeared.

Kywingwa was far from home—nearly two sleeps. He was footsore. Moreover, he was without food. These things troubled him but little; he had been hungry, lame, and astray many times before. But he was utterly cast down because the butterfly had escaped. His journey was useless; he had lost his net; he had failed to win the glacier implement.

"I am good for nothing, good for nothing!" he cried, and threw himself in despair upon the ground. In a moment he was sound asleep.

Awakening, he perceived that the sun was shining brightly once more, and that the insects were playing briskly. He must have slept a very long while. He was ravenously hungry.

"I will try if I can hit a little auk with a stone," he said, and trudged back to certain rocks near the glacier, whence came the chatter of the small birds.

But just as he arrived at the foot of the ice, he heard a shrill sound. He knew at once what produced it; it came from one of those curious little wooden instruments which the white people carried, and which shrieked when you blew into them. Looking up, he beheld Arhiveh, with butterfly-net in one hand, and glacier implement in the other, standing firmly, in his boots shod with sharp spikes, upon the very edge of the ice-wall. Kywingwa felt a pang of disappointment at sight of the glacier implement; but he forgot it in his surprise because Arhiveh was alone. White men did not usually venture upon glaciers by themselves; something extraordinary must have occurred.

The little Eskimo hastened to the ice-bridge, crossed the torrent, and in a moment was by Arhiveh's side. The white man's voice was gruff, as he accosted the boy.

"Not dead, Kywingwa?" he inquired. "Mother say you lost. Say you food all gone. She go like this—" he rubbed his eyes with his hand, in imitation of a weeping woman. "White men all go look. I come woman's boat. Woman's boat there," he added, pointing to the opposite corner of the glacier. "Come on!"

"I tried to catch the butterfly," explained Kywingwa, as they started. "I wanted to win the glacier implement. But my net dropped into a crevasse. I saw a butterfly, but I could not capture him."

"You very much no good! You lost, Mother afraid," was the ungracious reply. Kywingwa felt that he was in disgrace. He took thankfully some seal-meat that Arhiveh had brought him, and ate it silently, being very miserable.

Presently Arhiveh reached the stream, and turned to the left to find the ice-bridge.

A tiny brown something fluttered before Kywingwa's gaze. He paused in amazement and rubbed his eyes.

"Arhiveh, Arhiveh!" cried Kywingwa; *"takoo iblee! takoo!* (see there—see!) butterfly!"

The white man seized the net and dashed after the tiny creature. Kywingwa watched him eagerly. The butterfly fluttered aimlessly about for a moment, and then crossed the stream. Arhiveh sprang recklessly after it, missed his footing, and fell into the water.

Kywingwa burst out into laughter, and waited gleefully to greet his companion, scrambling, soaked with ice-cold water, from the stream. But no head appeared above the bank, and Kywingwa ran to see what was the matter.

The white man had not risen. He was lying in the water, with his head downstream. He was struggling violently. He was floating rapidly down; the cataract was close at hand.

All at once the meaning of the situation burst upon Kywingwa's mind. Arhiveh could not rise—the bottom of the stream was too slippery. He was trying to use the spikes in his shoes, but to no purpose, for his feet were upstream. Faster and faster he swept helplessly along.

In an instant Kywingwa saw what he must do. He sprang upon a mound of ice that almost overhung the water. Balanced as a harpoon in his hand was his sharp pusheemut.

Down came the helpless Arhiveh, now floating rapidly; in another instant he would be opposite the Eskimo's position. Then, with all his force, Kywingwa hurled his pusheemut. Its point entered the hard ice-bed of the current and the weapon stood upright. The white man was borne against it; instinctively he clutched it. It held for an instant, then the ice about it chipped and it gave way. But that instant was enough. Arhiveh had swung around, his feet were downstream, his course was checked. Before the powerful little brook could take hold of him again, he had driven his shoe-spikes into the ice, and using the pusheemut as a rest, had risen to his feet. He stood as if dazed, while Kywingwa brought the glacier implement, and lying flat, reached it down to him. Then he cut notches for himself and ascended out of the bed of the brook. The pusheemut floated away.

Kywingwa was ready to laugh with him over his escape. But white people always acted so oddly! Arhiveh stood, when he was once more safe on the surface of the glacier, and simply looked about him. He gazed across the white expanse of ice to the cliffs, tinted with red lichen and green grass. He looked out over the bay to the blue sea. He looked at the sun, which, as all Eskimos know, is a bad thing to do: it ruins the eyes. Finally, he walked to the crevasse, and peered down into the dark depths into which he would have been swept by the rushing water, but for Kywingwa's quick wit and sure aim.

Kywingwa looked cautiously down, too, and wondered where his pusheemut was. Presently, the white man turned toward him.

"Pusheemut?" asked Kywingwa, shyly. "Did you see my pusheemut? It is lost, isn't it?"

"Pusheemut!" exclaimed Arhiveh vehemently. "See, Kywingwa, I not talk Eskimo. But you very good! You go white man's *igloo*—I give you plenty pusheemuts. *Peook iblee ami-i-i-ishwa!* (You are a splendid fellow!) *Takoo*, I give you this."

And as he received from Arhiveh's outstretched hand the shining glacier implement, Kywingwa was unspeakably happy.

DISCONTENT
By Sarah O. Jewett

February, 1876

Down in a field, one day in June,
    The flowers all bloomed together,
Save one, who tried to hide herself,
    And drooped, that pleasant weather.

A robin who had soared too high,
    And felt a little lazy,
Was resting near a buttercup
    Who wished she were a daisy.

For daisies grow so trig and tall;
    She always had a passion
For wearing frills about her neck
    In just the daisies' fashion.

And buttercups must always be
    The same old tiresome color,
While daisies dress in gold and white,
    Although their gold is duller.

"Dear robin," said this sad young flower,
    "Perhaps you'd not mind trying
To find a nice white frill for me,
    Some day, when you are flying?"

"You silly thing!" the robin said;
    "I think you must be crazy!
I'd rather be my honest self
    Than any made-up daisy.

"You're nicer in your own bright gown,
    The little children love you;
Be the best buttercup you can,
    And think no flower above you.

"Though swallows leave me out of sight,
    We'd better keep our places;
Perhaps the world would all go wrong
    With one too many daisies.

"Look bravely up into the sky,
    And be content with knowing
That God wished for a buttercup,
    Just here where you are growing."

LOST IN THE FOG
(A Tale of Adventure)

By Irving Bacheller
(Author of *Eben Holden*)

February, 1901

IT's odd how some people take to geese. As a boy I never could understand, for the life of me, how one could ever have any love of a goose in him. When I came out in the glory of my first trousers a whole flock of geese came after me, tweaking the sacred garment with their bills, and hissing me to shame of my new dignity, and screaming in derision as they pulled me down. After that and for long I treasured a most unrighteous hatred of the whole goose family. They were to me a low, waddling tribe with the evil spirit of envy in them. The worst thing about Mother Tipton was her geese, I used to think. She lived in a shanty all by herself—a lonely man-hater—and the bit of land that climbed to the ridges on either side of it was known as Mother Tipton's Hollow. Every day skirmishers, sentinels, and reserves of geese covered the green slopes of the Hollow, and a white squadron of them was always sailing the black waters of the pond in its center. I came betimes, of a summer day, and peered over the circling ridge in a tremble of fear, whereupon a stir of white wings and a yell of defiance greeted me. Mother Tipton herself was a kindly creature who rescued me whenever I was captured by that noisy rabble of boy-haters. She was an Englishwoman, the daughter of a rich man, I believe, in the city of Bristol, and turned out of her home for some reason—we never knew why. I know she had in her shanty wonderful trinkets of gold and silver, the relics of a better day, and more than once I had the inestimable pleasure of holding them in my hands. The Hollow was half a mile from the shore of the broad Sound, and Mother Tipton took her geese and feathers to market in a rowboat. There was a big town across the bay, and she went always from the end of Shirley Point when the weather was fine, rowing as strong an oar as any man of all the many that made their living on those waters.

One morning—I was then a boy of eight years—I got permission to go with her in the boat. I remember she had a cargo of ten young geese, that were stowed away, their legs tied together, in the bow of the boat.

It was a mile and a half across the bay, and the water lay like a mill-pond, with scarcely a ripple showing. A thin mist hovered about the farther shore as we pulled away, but we could see the dock clearly and the building that lay beyond it.

"Land o' Goshen!" Mother Tipton cried, after rowing a few minutes, "it's foggin'"; then she sat a long time, as it seemed to me, looking over the water at a misty wall that lay not far ahead of us. Of a sudden she began to pull vigorously on the right oar.

"It's the ebb-tide," said she, "and we must get back as quick as we can or we'll be in trouble."

Evidently she saw it coming, for she began to pull with redoubled energy. I could just see the dim outline of rocks on Shirley Point as we turned about.

"The tide has taken us half over," she muttered. "It runs like a mill-race."

Now I could see mist rising on the water under the side, as if it had turned hot sud-

264

denly. The fog thickened fast, and presently the boat had seemed to lengthen, and we to go far apart, so that I could see but dimly the face of Mother Tipton. Then I could hear her groan and breathe heavily as she put all her strength to the oars. She was lifting the bow from the water every stroke now, but suddenly I heard the snap of an oar, and the boat turned in the tide; then a splash of water hit my face.

Mother Tipton rose in the boat and shouted a long halloo. We listened for some answer, but, hearing none, she called "Help!" a dozen times, at the top of her voice. Between her cries we could hear nothing but the tide rippling under the boat.

I felt a fine thrill then, having little sense at best, and none of our danger. I remember growing very manly and chivalrous when I saw Mother Tipton crying in her seat, and did my best to comfort her.

She was up to shouting for help again presently, but not a sound came back to us. We drifted of course, with the tide, and could see nothing. She kept calling all the time, and when my tongue was dry for the need of water, and the thought of cake and cookies kept crowding on me, I lost a bit of my bravery. It was time to be getting home—there was no longer any doubt of that.

"Mother Tipton," I said, "where do you suppose we are?"

"The Lord only knows, child," was her answer. "I'm afraid we're out in the deep water half over to Long Island. But the tide has turned, and it may take us back before night comes. We'll just sit still and keep calling."

I was lying on my back in the stern, resting my head on the seat behind me, and was feeling very miserable indeed, when I heard a great disturbance among the geese.

"Willie, come here," said Mother Tipton.

Two of the geese were lying in her lap, and she was unwinding a long fish-line.

"Tie it tightly," said she, "just above the big joint of the leg. Wait—let's cut it first into even lengths. That's right—now cut it."

She measured for me, and I cut the line, as she held it, into ten pieces, with probably as many feet in each. Then we tied them securely to the geese, above the big joint of the legs, and fastened the loose ends together, winding them with a bit of string. We tied another fish-line to this ten-stranded cable, cut the geese apart, and let them all go at once. They flew for a little distance, and, being not all of a mind, came down in a rather bad tangle. I had hold of the line, and if I had not paid it out quickly we would surely have lost them. They ducked their heads in the water, and shook their wings, and screamed as if delighted with their liberty. Meanwhile they had begun to pull like a team of horses, and I could feel the stretch of the line. It had parted in a minute—and a thick, strong line it was at that—and I had gone overboard and was clutching for the loose end. There was a thunder of wings when they saw me coming upon them, and when I got my hand on the cord they began to pull me through the water at a great rate. I was a good swimmer, but was glad to lie over on my back and rest a little after the violence of my exertion. Then, suddenly, I heard the voice of Mother Tipton calling me, and it seemed far away. I looked in the direction it came from, and then I got a scare I hope never to have again. I could see nothing of the boat. The geese were swimming with the tide, and over all, the fog lay on the sea as thick as darkness. I was breathing hard, and lay for a long time floating on my back, my fingers clutching the tight strings.

When I turned over and got a little of

the water out of my eyes, I could hear faintly in the distance the voice of Mother Tipton calling the geese just as I had heard her many a time over there in the Hollow. I could see them turn and listen, and then the whole flock veered about, cackling together as if they knew the meaning of it. The ten of them were now swimming comfortably. Every moment I could hear more distinctly the voice of Mother Tipton, and after a little I could hear the water on the boat. Suddenly its end broke through the wall of fog, and I saw my companion looming above me in the thick air, her head showing first. She answered with a cheery "Thank Heaven!" as I called to her, and the whole flock rose out of the water and tried to fly.

The geese came up to the boat-side, and she touched their beaks fondly with her hand as she came to help me in. The water had chilled me through, and I was glad enough to set my feet on the boat-bottom, and to take off my coat and wrap my shoulders in the warm shawl that Mother Tipton offered. You may be sure I kept a good hold of the strings, and before I sat down we made them fast to some ten feet of the small anchor-rope and tied it at the bow. Then those that had got their feet over the traces were carefully attended to. They lay quietly under the gunwale as Mother Tipton fussed with them, sometimes lifting one above another. She shooed them off in a moment, and they made away, turning their heads knowingly as she began to paddle.

"I believe those creatures will have sense enough to go ashore. They know more than we do about a good many things," said she. "That old gray gander of mine goes a mile away sometimes, but he'll get home, if it *is* foggy, every night of his life."

It was growing dark, and in five minutes we couldn't see our team. I was kneeling in the bow, my hand on the rope, peering to get a view of the geese, when I heard a loud quacking and a big ripple in the water just ahead. I was about to speak, when I saw a drift of dark objects on either side of the boat. I made out what they were, and caught one of them by the neck just as Mother Tipton shouted, "Ducks!" Then there was a roar of wings that made me jump back, and that set the geese in a panic. I hung on to my captive, and brought him in flapping and drenching my sleeve with spray.

"Bring him here," said Mother Tipton, as I crept to the middle seat, the poor creature fighting me desperately all the way.

"We shall need him for our supper, my dear child," said she, as she took him. "I think we're coming to shore somewhere, and I know you're hungry.

It was not long before we heard our boat-bottom grinding on the sand, but it was very dark. Mother Tipton went to the bow of the boat, and I was near the middle seat.

"Thank Heaven, we're somewhere!" I heard her say; and then she stood up, and I heard her paddle strike in the sand, and felt the boat lift forward and go up on the dry beach. I was out pulling in a moment, and I tell you the firm earth had never so good a feeling. I felt my way up the beach, and Mother Tipton came after me. It was so dark and foggy we could see nothing. After a little I felt the grass under me, and my companion lit a match and touched it to a bit of paper she had taken off of a bundle in the boat.

"Make haste, now," she said, "and pick up all the bits of small wood you see around."

The dry drift lay all around us, and in half a minute a good bit of it was crackling on that flaming wad of paper. Then we brought sticks as thick as a man's leg, and fed the flames until they leaped higher than our heads and lit the misty reaches of the shore a good distance.

"Lawsy me!" said she, presently, "I think we're on Charles Island." Then she took a brand out of the fire, and walked away in the thick grass, waving it above her head. She was calling me in a moment.

"Bring the fish-line and the tin pail!" she shouted.

I went to the boat for them, and was shortly groping through the tall grass in the direction of that flickering torch. She was not nearly so far away as I thought, the fog had such a trick of deepening the perspective in every scene. I found her by an old ruin of a house, peering into a deep well, the cover of which had mostly rotted away. We were not long tying that line to the pail and dropping it down the well-hole. The line raced through my fingers, and the pail bounded as it struck, and rang like a bell on the splashing water. When I had hauled it up, we sat looking at the slopping cylinder of cold, clear water, the golden flare of the torch shining in it, each insisting that the other must drink first, until I was quite out of patience.

She took the pail at last, and buried her mouth at the rim, and nearly smothered herself with the water. I thanked her with a good heart when I got my hands on it, for I had a mighty fever of thirst in me. When my dry tongue was soaking in the sweet, pure water, I could feel my heart lighten, and soon it was floating off its rock of despair.

"Now let's take a pailful with us, and get supper," said Mother Tipton. "We're on Charles Island, five miles from home, but it isn't more than half a mile from Milford. We'd better stop here for the night, and maybe it'll be clear before morning."

I took the torch, and she dragged behind her a bit of the fallen roof that had once covered the old house. By the light of the fire we began to dig clams with the oar and paddle. In ten minutes we had enough for a fine bake, and laid them out on a rock, and raked the hot coals over them. Mother Tipton had killed and dressed the duck, and while I tended the clams she was cutting turf and shaking the clay off it into a hollow she scooped out of the sand. She wet the clay then with salt water, and, when it was thick and sticky, rolled the duck in it until the bare skin was coated. Then she poked it into the ashes under the hot fire, and came to help me uncover the clams. We ate them with sharpened sticks, and, while some butter would have helped a bit, they went with a fine relish. The duck came out of the fire looking like a boulder of gray granite. Mother Tipton broke the hard clay with a stone, and the duck came out clean and smoking hot, leaving its skin in the shell. A more tender and delicious bit of fowl I have never eaten, the salt clay having given it the right savor.

After supper we untied the flock and set it free, and dragged the boat above tidewater. Then we drove two stakes in front of a rock near the fire, and set our strip of roofing over all. Under it we threw a good layer of hot sand from near the fire, and built high ridges on either side of our shelter. There were sacks of down for pillows, and my overcoat and the big woolen shawl as covering. Though it is so long ago—I was, as I said, only eight years old—I remember still when Mother Tipton told me to creep in and draw up the wraps around me. The warm sand gave me a grateful sense of comfort. I lay for a time and looked at the dying firelight, but before very long I fell asleep.

As I awoke, next day, I could hear the bellow of a great fog-siren, away in the distance, that sent its echoes crashing through the dungeon of mist. Next I noticed the sound of the noisy water on the rocks near by. It was growing light, and somebody was poking the fire. When I lifted my head I felt a warm breeze and saw that the fog had gone. A man with a wooden leg and a patch of gray whiskers on his chin was standing by the fire. I crept out and greeted him, rubbing my eyes with drowsiness.

"Ketched in the fog, I suppose," said he, kicking the fire.

"Yes, sir," I answered; "we were caught by the tide and lost, yesterday."

"Hum!" he muttered, as he glanced under the lean-to roof of our shanty and took a good look at Mother Tipton. "Rather a tidy bit of a woman—stout as an ox an' a good-looker."

"I'd thank you not to disturb her," I said with indignation.

"Not for the world," he answered, returning and shying another bit of wood at the fire. "I like t' see 'em sleep—it's good for 'em. Got anything for breakfus'?"

"I'm going to dig some clams," I answered.

"You jes' wait," he said, winking at me, "an' I'll go off to the tug an' bring ye some coffee an' fish an' bread an' butter. Got loads of it aboard there. No trouble at all."

He made off for his boat, that lay on the beach near by, and rowed around the point. I walked down the shore a few rods, and from a high rock saw the tug lying at anchor a little way off the shore. He came back in a short time, bringing a basket of provisions. Mother Tipton was up, and by that time I had a good fire going.

"Madam," he said, laying down the basket, "may I be so bold as to offer you su'-thin' for your breakfus'? Here's a snack o' coffee an' fish an' a tidy bit o' bread an' butter."

She thanked him politely, and while we were getting breakfast, he told us that he was a menhaden-fisherman "—as owned his own tug." Then we told him our story. Afterward he insisted on taking us home. We were glad to accept his kindness, and the sun was shining brightly when we put off for the tug, with all our geese in the boat; I made Mother Tipton promise me that not one of them would ever be sold. The captain brought a big armchair and made her very comfortable in the bow of the boat. We were home in an hour, and I was as glad to get there as all were to see me. The adventure resulted in great good, for it gave me some respect for geese, and gave Mother Tipton a greater regard for men. It was not long after that she added to her museum in the Hollow a man with a wooden leg; and you may be sure I went to the wedding.

THE FESTIVAL OF EGGS.

By C. F. HOLDER.

May, 1897

KAITAE was just sixteen years old. It was his birthday, and he rose bright and early, and was abroad before any of his companions; for, exhausted with the games and contests of the previous day, they were sleeping heavily in the curious caves or stone houses that even to this day mark the location of Orongo.

Kaitae was a prince, the lineal descendant of King Kaitae of Waihu, the strange volcanic island in the South Pacific better known as Easter Island.

The young prince, stepping lightly over two sleeping comrades, stole out of the cave and with a joyful heart bounded away. For some distance he ran quickly, then, coming to a large platform of stone, he stopped at last near a group of curious objects.

The sun was just rising over the sea, seeming to Kaitae to illumine the scene with a mysterious radiance. He stood upon the side of an ancient volcano, the steep slope of which fell precipitously a thousand feet to the sea; and before him were many faces of gigantic size, staring, gaunt, lifeless stone, their enormous eyes turned to the north. The great heads alone appeared, as if the bodies were embedded in the hardened lava that had poured over and formed the base of the outer slope of the famous volcano Rana Roraka. The youth gazed long and wonderingly at them, as in his mind they were associated with the gods, and he reverently touched one, being able just to reach its huge lips.

Kaitae was a bright boy, with long, dark hair and brilliant, piercing eyes, and he presented a strange contrast to the wonderful old face that looked so steadfastly to the north. What was it looking at? What did it see? he asked himself; and climbing up to the brink of Rana Roraka, he gazed steadily to the north, then, turning, peered down into the vast crater of the volcano. The great abyss was nearly circular, a mile across, and its sides were deeply jagged. On the sides, half-way down, were other faces, lying in strange confusion, as if they had been hurriedly left, or thrown down by some convulsion of nature.

Kaitae had heard from his father that in ancient times Tro Kaiho, a son of King Mohuta Ariiki, had made the first of these images. Here they had been for ages, for all

269

he knew, marking the spot where the remains of his ancestors lay.

Kaitae, however, was not abroad so early in the morning to study these strange monuments of his ancestors. It was a famous holiday time—the Festival of the Sea-birds' Eggs—and the entire male population of Waihu was gathered at Orongo to celebrate it. The festival was an ancient custom, and the stone houses of Orongo had been built long in the past by these people to shelter them during this season.

The festival consisted of a race for the first gull's egg deposited upon the islands of Mutu Rankan and Mutu Nui, mere volcanic rocks which peered above the surface a few hundred yards from the rocky shore of the island of Orongo. The object was to reach the island first, secure an egg, and bring it back in safety. The one who accomplished this was greeted by the entire community as a hero; and, more important yet, the return with the unbroken egg was supposed to bring with it the approval of the great spirit Meke Meke; and the fortunate one was the recipient of many gifts from his fellows throughout the ensuing year.

There was keen rivalry among the young men and boys; and Kaitae had determined this year to be the first to discover gulls on the islands. Running down the slope of the volcano, past the great stone images weighing many tons, he made his way quickly to an observation tower, about thirty feet in height, resting upon a platform of rock over the tombs of his people. Here, in the season, the men watched for turtles and signaled to their fellows. From the top of this lookout Kaitae gazed over the blue water. There were the little islands below him, and—yes, about them hovered numbers of white objects, the long-looked-for gulls, which evidently had arrived during the night. With a joyous shout, Kaitae sprang

down, and was soon bounding over the rocks to convey the news to the natives. At once they all came swarming out of their stone burrows like ants, and before long began to move in the direction of the coast. When all had gathered at the cliff, the king addressed them, repeating the time-honored rules for the race.

At his word they were to start for the island, and the one who returned to him first with an unbroken egg would have the especial favor of the great spirit Meke Meke.

The band of excited men and boys stood in various expectant postures, some with one foot in advance, others with arms eagerly stretched to the front, ready for the word from the king.

Kaitae stood near his father, his eyes flashing, and determination expressed in every motion. He had decided upon a dangerous course. The cliff where the start was made was a precipitous, jagged wall rising far above the sea, and breasting it with a bold front. From it numerous paths led down to the water; and Kaitae knew that many a fierce struggle would take place to reach the water's edge. He had determined to take the cliff jump, a perilous feat that had not been attempted since the king, his grandfather, a famous athlete, had performed it when a boy.

Finally, when all in line were in readiness, the king gave the signal, and on rushed the crowd of islanders with loud cries and shouts. Out from among them shot the form of a boy, straight as an arrow, his long, black hair flying in the wind. Not to the lower beach, not to the narrow trails made by his ancestors, but directly to the brink of the precipice. The train of dusky figures paused breathless, and the king rushed forward to see Kaitae dive out into space and gracefully disappear into the depths below. Up he soon came, a black spot on the waters, and before the astonished natives could recover from their excitement he was far on his way to the island.

Down the narrow trails worn in the lava swept the crowd, pushing one another over in their rush to the shore, diving, leaping, and hurling themselves into the sea in eager endeavor to reach the island. But Kaitae was far in advance; and before the crowd of egg-seekers were half-way over he had gained the rocky point of Mutu Nui, and amid the threatening cries of the birds had clambered up. Dozens of speckled eggs were strewn about. Seizing one, Kaitae placed it in his mouth as the safest place, and, springing again into the water, was homeward bound.

No one seemed discouraged because Kaitae was ahead. A hundred accidents might yet befall him. The current was strong against the return; the egg might break—it generally did; he might slip on the rocks in the quick ascent; he might be injured, even killed—such things had been known. So the contestants swam on, and soon scores of dark forms could be seen crawling out from the water over the moss-covered rocks, slipping, sliding, falling; then darting this way and that in search of an egg. Having found one, each plunged quickly into the sea. Altogether it was a scene strange and exciting, even to the king who had witnessed every race for many years. Some of the men broke their eggs and were obliged to return, while others could not find any, and were pecked at and buffeted by the enraged birds that filled the air with their cries, and swooped down to avenge this intrusion.

Kaitae reached the shore of Orongo well ahead of all except one man who had won the race more than once in former years—a daring climber, a rapid and powerful swimmer. But Kaitae drew himself up on the rocks carefully, that the egg might not be broken, then sped away up the face of the cliff. For days he had studied the steep ascent, and a score of times had scaled its rough face, but never before with a large egg in his mouth. When half-way up he was breathing hard. His mouth became dry and parched, and the egg seemed to be choking him. But still he held on, climbing higher and higher, spurred on by the shouts of his companions, who were now landing in large numbers.

One more effort, and he reached the top, and running forward, he held out the egg, unbroken, to the king. He was just in time, for his nearest rival, breathless Tahana, came rushing up the narrow trail, followed, a few moments later, by a score of disappointed contestants.

As victor, Kaitae was the center of interest for the remainder of the day. Many gifts and favors fell to him, and he sat in the seat of honor next to the king at the dance and the merrymakings on that and succeeding nights.

Kaitae was much more intelligent than many of his comrades, and while he joined in their games and pastimes he as much enjoyed listening to his elders when they related stories of the wonders of Waihu in the olden time. He learned that in those days the island was inhabited by many tribes of men, all under his ancestor the king; and that the curious platforms and monuments that have since made Easter Island famous over the entire world were long before erected by his ancestors, just as in our parks we set up statues to commemorate our own distinguished men; and that the platforms were tombs as much revered by the natives of the island as Westminster Abbey is revered by patriotic Englishmen.

During the boyhood of Kaitae several strange ships bearing white men visited the island, and traded with the islanders. But some difficulties occurred, and numbers of his people were killed; and once a horde of native enemies came in canoes, drove them to their hidden caves, destroyed their homes, and killed hundreds of the people. When Kaitae and his friends came out from their hiding-places they found the statues in many cases thrown down or broken in pieces, and the tombs destroyed. The heads of the images weighed tons, and many could not be replaced; and there they lie, to this day, prone upon the side of the great volcano.

A descendant of King Kaitae, also bearing his name, is, or was a few years ago, still living at Easter Island—an old man, over eighty years of age, who delighted in talking to foreigners of the wonders of his native Waihu in ancient days.

A few years ago an American man-of-war visited Waihu, and made a careful examination of the island. Among the many interesting relics brought to the United States was one of the ancient faces or heads by one of which Kaitae stood on the morning of his sixteenth birthday when he won the race; and readers of *St. Nicholas* who visit Washington may see this great stone image, for it is exhibited in the National Museum.

"KAITAE REVERENTLY TOUCHED ONE OF THE GREAT STONE FACES, BEING ABLE JUST TO REACH ITS HUGE LIPS."

LETTERS TO YOUNG FRIENDS

By Robert Louis Stevenson
With Introduction and Notes by
Lloyd Osbourne

December, 1895

INTRODUCTION

I suppose there are few boys and girls who have not heard of Robert Louis Stevenson, the great author. It was Mr. Stevenson's good fortune that his book should not only be widely read and admired, but that, as they read first one and then another, people began to like the man who wrote them, until he became not a mere name on the title-page, but the invisible member of many households and the personal friend of those who had never seen him; so that at last, when death stopped his pen forever, the light grew dim in many a pleasant home and the world seemed emptier to thousands who speak the English tongue.

It is due to this wide-spread feeling that the Editor of *St. Nicholas* has obtained for the magazine, in the belief that they will interest its young readers, a number of Mr. Stevenson's letters to his ward, Austin Strong, and to several little girls in England. These letters were not written for publication, and were not expected to have more of a circulation than perhaps among Master Austin's chums, or the mamas and favorite aunts of the little English lasses; but now they have been unearthed from desk and locker, to be read again in a bigger play-room than their author dreamed of. And as you read them you will wonder about this "Vailima" plantation, and the brown men and black; and how it was that Mr. Stevenson came to live in so outlandish a country, so far from civilization that nobody goes there except good missionaries, and other white men (not always so good) who barter cotton-print and knives and kerosene oil for dried coconut kernels. And you will wonder too, doubtless, as to this Master Austin—whether he had a gun or a pony, and whether he had lessons every day, and did sums, as little boys must everywhere, even in those far-off isles of the Pacific Ocean.

Mr. Stevenson knew as little as you do about Samoa and the remote South Seas when, several years ago, he came to San Francisco and set sail in a beautiful schooner yacht, hoping the Trade Wind would blow him to some pleasant isle where he might get well and strong again. The "Shining Ship" (for that was what the natives called her) poked her sharp nose into many a sweet bay and dark-blue lagoon, and passed from island to island through calm and storm, and picked her way through surf-swept reefs where the sharks played like minnows beneath her keel, but she came no nearer the haven for which she was in search. At last she reached an island called Oahu, which was so pleasant to look at, and so agreeable to live in, that Mr. Stevenson thought his voyage was over. The King of Oahu was a very agreeable man, too, and wished Mr. Stevenson never to go away, but to stay with him all his life and be his friend. So Mr. Stevenson stayed many months in Oahu, and would have been very happy and contented had it not been for the Trade Wind, who was always telling him about the fine islands further on, until he was persuaded to say good-by to the king and set sail again. The

Trade Wind took him a long road and through many queer and dangerous places before he brought him within sight of Upolu in Samoa, and told him to pack up and go ashore; which Mr. Stevenson was very glad to do, for he quite agreed with the Trade Wind that Upolu was the finest island in the whole ocean. Here he bought a large tract of land, which he called "Vailima," and built a big house, and planted bananas and breadfruit trees and coconuts and mangos and other trees with strange names, in order to feed the brown people who gathered about him and made him the head of their tribe. They called him "Tusitala," or the "Writer of Tales," for his own name was too hard for them to say. In a short time Mr. Storyteller grew well and strong, just as he hoped he would, and remained grateful all his days to the Trade Wind for bringing him to Upolu; and he always made a point of speaking kindly about it in his books.

The first three letters are to some little girls in a Convalescent Home in England, where a friend of Mr. Stevenson's had a share of the management of the institution. This lady used to hear so frequently of the "boys" in Vailima, that she wrote and asked Mr. Stevenson for news of them, as it would so much interest her little girls. In the tropics, for some reason or other that it is impossible to understand, servants and work-people are always called "boys," though the years of Methuselah may have whitened their heads, and great-grandchildren prattle about their knees. Mr. Stevenson was amused to think that his "boys," who ranged from eighteen years of age to three score and ten, should be mistaken for little youngsters; but he was touched to hear of the sick children his friend tried so hard to entertain, and gladly wrote a few letters to them. He would have written more but for the fact that his friend left the home, being transferred elsewhere.

In Samoa the name "black boy" is used to distinguish the negroes of the New Hebridean, Solomon, and New Guinea archipelagos from the Samoan natives, whose color is scarcely darker than that of a Spaniard or a South Italian. "Bush" is another South Sea word, and is applied to the high, dense forest that covers all but a few square miles of Samoa.

LETTER I

Vailima Plantation

Dear Friend:

Please salute your pupils in my name, and tell them that a long, lean, elderly man who lives right through on the underside of the world, so that down in your cellar you are nearer him than the people in the street, desires his compliments.

This man lives in an island which is not very long and is extremely narrow. The sea beats round it very hard, so that it is difficult to get to shore. There is only one harbour where ships come, and even that is very wild and dangerous; four ships of war were broken there a little while ago, and one of them is still lying on its side on a rock clean above water, where the sea threw it as you might throw your fiddle-bow upon the table. All round the harbour the town is strung out: it is nothing but wooden houses, only there are some churches built of stone. They are not very large, but the people have never seen such fine buildings. Almost all the houses are of one story. Away at one end of the village lives the king of the whole country. His palace has a thatched roof which rests upon posts; there are no walls, but when it blows and rains, they have Venetian blinds which they let down between the posts, making all very snug. There is no furniture, and the king and the queen and the courtiers sit and eat on the floor, which is of gravel: the lamp stands there too, and every now and then it is upset.

These good folk wear nothing but a kilt about their waists, unless to go to church or for a dance on the New Year, or some great occasion. The children play marbles all along the street; and though they are generally very jolly, yet they get awfully cross over their marbles, and cry and fight just as boys and girls do at home. Another amusement in country places is to shoot fish with a little bow and arrow. All round the beach there is bright shallow water, where the fishes can be seen darting or lying in shoals. The child trots round the shore, and whenever he sees a fish, lets fly an arrow, and misses, and then wades in after his arrow. It is great fun (I have tried it) for the child, and I never heard of it doing any harm to the fishes: so what could be more jolly?

The road to this lean man's house is uphill all the way and through forests; the trees are not so much unlike those at home, only here and there some very queer ones are mixed with them—coconut palms, and great trees that are covered with bloom like red hawthorn but not near so bright; and from them all thick creepers hang down like ropes, and ugly-looking weeds that they call orchids grow in the forks of the branches; and on the ground many prickly things are dotted, which they call pineapples. I suppose everyone has eaten pineapple drops.

On the way up to the lean man's house, you pass a little village, all of houses like the king's house, so that as you ride by you can see everybody sitting at dinner, or, if it is night, lying in their beds by lamplight; because all the people are terribly afraid of ghosts and would not lie in the dark for anything. After the village, there is only one more house, and that is the lean man's. For the people are not very many and live all by the sea, and the whole inside of the island is desert woods and mountains. When the lean man goes into the forest, he is very much ashamed to own it, but he is always in a terrible fright. The wood is so great, and empty, and hot, and it is always filled with curious noises: birds cry like children, and bark like dogs; and he can hear people laughing and felling trees; and the other day (when he was far in the woods) he heard a sound like the biggest mill-wheel possible, going with a kind of dot-and-carry-one movement like a dance. That was the noise of an earthquake away down below him in the bowels of the earth; and that is the same thing as to say away up toward you in your cellar in Kilburn. All these noises make him feel lonely and scared, and he doesn't quite know what he is scared of. Once when he was just about to cross a river, a blow struck him on the top of his head, and knocked him head-foremost down the bank and splash into the water. It was a nut, I fancy, that had fallen from a tree, by which accident people are sometimes killed. But at the time he thought it was a Black Boy.

"Aha," say you, "and what is a Black Boy?" Well, there are here a lot of poor people who are brought to Samoa from distant islands to labor for the Germans. They are not at all like the king and his people, who are brown and very pretty; for these are black . . . and as ugly as sin, poor souls, and in their own land they live all the time at war, and cook and eat men's flesh. The Germans make them work; and every now and then some run away into the Bush, as the forest is called, and build little sheds of leaves, and eat nuts and roots and fruits, and dwell there by themselves. Sometimes they are bad, and wild, and people whisper to each other that some of them have gone back to their horrid old habits, and catch men and women in order to eat them. But it is very likely not true; and the most of them are poor, half-starved, pitiful creatures, like frightened dogs. Their life is all very well when the sun shines, as it does eight or nine months in the year. But it is very different the rest of the time. The wind rages then most violently. The great trees thrash about like whips; the air is filled with leaves and branches flying like birds; and the sound of the trees falling shakes the earth. It rains, too, as it never rains at home. You can hear a shower while it is yet half a mile away, hissing like a shower-bath in the forest; and when it comes to you, the water blinds your eyes, and the cold drenching takes your breath away as though some one had struck you. In that kind of weather it must be dreadful indeed to live in the woods, one man alone by himself. And you must know that if the lean man feels afraid to be in the forest, the people of the island and the Black Boys are much more afraid than he; for they believe the woods to be quite filled with spirits; some like pigs, and some like flying things; but others (and these are thought the most dangerous) in the shape of beautiful young women and young men, beautifully dressed in the island manner, with fine kilts and fine necklaces, and crosses of scarlet seeds and flowers. Woe betide him or her who gets to speak with one of these! They will be charmed out of their wits, and come home again quite silly, and go mad and die. So that the poor runaway Black Boy must be always trembling, and looking about for the coming of the demons.

Sometimes the women-demons go down out of the woods into the villages, and here is a tale the lean man heard last year: One of the islanders was sitting in his house, and he had cooked fish. There came along the road two beautiful young women, dressed as I told you, who came into his house, and asked for some of his fish. It is the fashion in the islands always to give what is asked, and never to ask folks' names. So the man gave them fish, and talked to them in the island jesting way. Presently he asked one of the women for her red necklace; which is good manners and their way: he had given the fish, and he had a right to ask for something back. "I will give it you by and by," said the woman, and she and her companion went away; but he thought they were gone very suddenly, and the truth is they had vanished. The night was nearly come, when the man heard the voice of the woman crying that he should come to her, and she would give the necklace. He looked out, and behold! she was standing calling him from the top of the sea, on which she stood as you might stand on the table. At that, fear came on the man; he fell on his knees and prayed, and the woman disappeared.

It was said afterward that this was once a woman, indeed, but she should have died a thousand years ago, and has lived all that while as an evil spirit in the woods beside the spring of a river. Sau-mai-afe* is her name, in case you want to write to her.

Ever your friend (for whom I thank the stars), TUSITALA (Tale-writer)

[Austin Strong, who is mentioned in the following letter, was a ward of Mr. Stevenson's. His fate was a sad one; for though his "fort" was stout, the palisade high, and his trusty air-gun and wooden sword lay ever within his reach, he was inopportunely captured and sent to Monterey in California, to school.—L. O.]

LETTER II

VAILIMA PLANTATION, 14 Aug., 1892
. . . The lean man is exceedingly ashamed

* "Come-a-thousand."

of himself, and offers his apologies to the little girls in the cellar just above. If they will be so good as to knock three times upon the floor, he will hear it on the other side of his floor, and will understand that he is forgiven.

I left you and the children still on the road to the lean man's house, where a great part of the forest has now been cleared away. It comes back again pretty quick, though not quite so high; but everywhere, except where the weeders have been kept busy, young trees have sprouted up, and the cattle and the horses cannot be seen as they feed. In this clearing there are two or three houses scattered about, and between the two biggest I think the little girls in the cellar would first notice a sort of thing like a gridiron on legs, made of logs of wood. Sometimes it has a flag flying on it, made of rags of old clothes. It is a fort (as I am told) built by the person here who would be much the most interesting to the girls in the cellar. This is a young gentleman of eleven years of age, answering to the name of Austin. It was after reading a book about the Red Indians that he thought it more prudent to create this place of strength. As the Red Indians are in North America, and this fort seems to me a very useless kind of building, I anxiously hope that the two may never be brought together. When Austin is not engaged in building forts, nor on his lessons, which are just as annoying to him as other children's lessons are to them, he walks sometimes in the Bush, and if anybody is with him, talks all the time. When he is alone I don't think he says anything, and I dare say he feels very lonely and frightened, just as the Samoan does, at the queer noises and the endless lines of the trees.

He finds the strangest kinds of seeds, some of them bright-colored like lollipops, or really like precious stones; some of them in odd cases like tobacco-pouches. He finds and collects all kinds of little shells with which the whole ground is scattered, and that, though they are the shells of land creatures like our snails, are of nearly as many shapes and colours as the shells on our sea-beaches. In the streams that come running down out of our mountains, all as clear and bright as mirror-glass, he sees eels and little bright fish that sometimes jump together out of the surface of the brook in a spray of silver, and fresh-water prawns which lie close under the stones, looking up at him through the water with eyes the colour of a jewel. He sees all kinds of beautiful birds, some of them blue and white, and some of them colored like our pigeons at home; and these last, the little girls in the cellar may like to know, live almost entirely on wild nutmegs as they fall ripe off the trees. Another little bird he may sometimes see, as the lean man saw him only this morning: a little fellow not so big as a man's hand, exquisitely neat, of a pretty bronzy black like ladies' shoes, who sticks up behind him (much as a peacock does) his little tail, shaped and fluted like a scallop-shell.

Here there are a lot of curious and interesting things that Austin sees all round him every day; and when I was a child at home in the old country I used to play and pretend to myself that I saw things of the same kind—that the rooms were full of orange and nutmeg trees, and the cold town gardens outside the windows were alive with parrots and with lions. What do the little girls in the cellar think that Austin does? He makes believe just the other way: he pretends that the strange great trees with their broad leaves and slab-sided roots are European oaks; and the places on the road up (where you and I and the little girls in the cellar have already gone) he calls old-fashioned, far-away European names, just as if you were to call the cellar-stair and the corner of the next street—if you could only manage to pronounce their names—Upolu and Savaii. And so it is with all of us, with Austin, and the lean man, and the little girls in the cellar: wherever we are, it is but a stage on the way to somewhere else, and whatever we do, however well we do it, it is only a preparation to do something else that shall be different.

But you must not suppose that Austin does nothing but build forts, and walk along the woods, and swim in the rivers. On the contrary, he is sometimes a very busy and useful fellow; and I think the little girls in the cellar would have admired him very nearly as much as he admired himself, if they had seen him setting off on horseback with his hand on his hip, and his pocket full of letters and orders, at the head of quite a procession of huge white cart-horses with pack-saddles, and big, brown native men with nothing on but gaudy kilts. Mighty well he managed all his commissions; and those who saw him ordering and eating his single-handed luncheon in the queer little Chinese restaurant on the beach, declare he looked as if the place, and the town, and the whole archipelago belonged to him.

But I am not going to let you suppose that this great gentleman at the head of all his horses and his men, like the King of France in the old rhyme, would be thought much of a dandy on the streets of London. On the contrary, if he could be seen with his dirty white cap and his faded purple shirt, and his little brown breeks that do not reach his knees, and the bare shanks below, and the bare feet stuck in the stirrup-leathers—for he is not quite long enough to reach the irons—I am afraid the little girls and boys in your part of the town might be very much inclined to give him a penny in charity. So you see that a very big man in one place might seem very small

potatoes in another, just as the king's palace here (of which I told you in my last) would be thought rather a poor place of residence by a Surrey gipsy. And if you come to that, even the lean man himself, who is no end of an important person, if he were picked up from the chair where he is now sitting, and slung down, feet-foremost, in the neighborhood of Charing Cross, would probably have to escape into the nearest shop, or take the risk of being mobbed. And the ladies of his family, who are very pretty ladies, and think themselves uncommon well-dressed for Samoa, would (if the same thing were to be done to them) be extremely glad to get into a cab. . . .

TUSITALA

[The German Company, from which we got our black boy Arick, owns and cultivates many thousands of acres in Samoa, and keeps at least a thousand black people to work on its plantations. Two schooners are always busy in bringing fresh batches to Samoa, and in taking home to their own islands the men who have worked out their three years' term of labor. This traffic in human beings is called the "labor trade," and is the life's blood, not only of the great German Company, but of all the planters in Fiji, Queensland, New Caledonia, German New Guinea, the Solomon Islands, and the New Hebrides. The difference between the labor trade, as it is now carried on under government supervision, and the slave trade is a great one, but not great enough to please sensitive people. In Samoa the missionaries are not allowed by the Company to teach these poor savages religion, or to do anything to civilize them and raise them from their monkey-like ignorance. But in other respects the Company is not a bad master, and treats its people pretty well. The system, however, is one that cannot be defended and must sooner or later be suppressed.—L. O.]

LETTER III

VAILIMA, 4th Sept., 1892

DEAR CHILDREN IN THE CELLAR: I told you before something of the Black Boys who come here to work on the plantations, and some of whom run away and live a wild life in the forests of the island. Now I want to tell you of one who lived in the house of the lean man. Like the rest of them here, he is a little fellow, and when he goes about in old battered cheap European clothes, looks very small and shabby. When first he came he was as lean as a tobacco-pipe, and his smile (like that of almost all the others) was the sort that half makes you wish to smile yourself, and half wish to cry. However, the boys in the kitchen took him in hand and fed him up. They would set him down alone to table, and wait upon him till he had his fill, which was a good long time to wait. The first thing we noticed was that his little stomach began to stick out like a pigeon's breast; and then the food got a little wider spread, and he started little calves to his legs; and last of all, he began to get quite saucy and impudent. He is really what you ought to call a young man, though I suppose nobody in the whole wide world has any idea of his age; and as far as his behaviour goes, you can only think of him as a big little child with a good deal of sense.

When Austin built his fort against the Indians, Arick (for that is the Black Boy's name) liked nothing so much as to help him. And this is very funny, when you think that of all the dangerous savages in this island Arick is one of the most dangerous. The other day, besides, he made Austin a musical instrument of the sort they use in his own country—a harp with only one string. He took a stick about three feet long and perhaps four inches round. The under side he hollowed out in a deep trench to serve as sounding-box; the two ends of the upper side he made to curve upward like the ends of a canoe, and between these he stretched the single string. He plays upon it with a match or a little piece of stick, and sings to it songs of his own country, of which no person here can understand a single word, and which are, very likely, all about fighting with his enemies in battle, and killing them, and, I am sorry to say, cooking them in a ground-oven, and eating them for supper when the fight is over.

For Arick is really what you call a savage, though a savage is a very different sort of a person, and very much nicer than he is made to appear in little books. He is the kind of person that everybody smiles to, or makes faces at, or gives a smack as he goes by; the sort of person that all the girls on the plantation give the best seat to and help first, and love to decorate with flowers and ribbons, and yet all the while are laughing at him; the sort of person who likes best to play with Austin, and whom Austin, perhaps (when he is allowed), likes best to play with. He is all grins and giggles and little steps out of dances, and little droll ways to attract people's attention and set them laughing. And yet, when you come to look at him closely, you will find that his body is all covered with *scars!* This happened when he was a child. There was war, as is the way in these wild islands, between his village and the next, much as if there were war in London between one street and another; and all the children ran about playing in the middle of the trouble, and, I dare say, took no more notice of the war than you children in London do of a general election. But sometimes, at general elections, English children may get run over by processions in the street; and it chanced that as little Arick was running about in the Bush, and very busy about his playing, he ran into the midst of the warriors on the other side. These speared him with a poisoned spear; and his own people, when they had found him, in order to cure him of the poison scored him with knives that were probably made of fish-bone.

This is a very savage piece of child-life; and Arick, for all his good nature, is still a very savage person. I have told you how the Black Boys sometimes run away from the plantations, and live alone in the forest, building little sheds to protect them from the rain and sometimes planting little gardens for food; but for the most part living the best they can upon the nuts of the trees and the yams that they dig with their hands out of the earth. I do not think there can be anywhere in the world people more wretched than these runaways. They cannot return, for they would only return to be punished; they can never hope to see again their own people—indeed, I do not know what they can hope, but just to find enough yams every day to keep them from starvation. And in the wet season of the year, which is our summer and your winter, when the rain falls day after day far harder and louder than the loudest thunder-plump that ever fell in England, and the room is so dark that the lean man is sometimes glad to light his lamp to write by, I can think of nothing so dreary as the state of these poor runaways in the houseless bush. You are to remember, besides, that the people of the island hate and fear them because they are cannibals; sit and tell tales of them about their lamps at night in their own comfortable houses, and are sometimes afraid to lie down to sleep if they think there is a lurking Black Boy in the neighborhood. Well, now, Arick is of their own race and language, only he is a little more lucky because he has not run away; and

how do you think that he proposed to help them? He asked if he might not have a gun. "What do you want with a gun, Arick?" was asked. He answered quite simply, and with his nice, good-natured smile, that if he had a gun he would go up into the High Bush and shoot Black Boys as men shoot pigeons. He said nothing about eating them, nor do I think he really meant to; I think all he wanted was to clear the plantation of vermin, as gamekeepers at home kill weasels or rats.

The other day he was sent on an errand to the German Company where many of the Black Boys live. It was very late when he came home. He had a white bandage round his head, his eyes shone, and he could scarcely speak for excitement. It seems some of the Black Boys who were his enemies at home had attacked him, one with a knife. By his own account, he had fought very well; but the odds were heavy. The man with the knife had cut him both in the head and back; he had been struck down; and if some Black Boys of his own side had not come to the rescue, he must certainly have been killed. I am sure no Christmas box could make any of you children so happy as this fight made Arick. A great part of the next day he neglected his work to play upon the one-stringed harp and sing songs about his great victory. To-day, when he is gone upon his holiday, he has announced that he is going back to the German Firm to have another battle and another triumph. I do not think he will go, all the same, or I should be uneasy; for I do not want to have my Arick killed; and there is no doubt that if he begin this fight again, he will be likely to go on with it very far. For I have seen him once when he saw, or thought he saw, an enemy.

It was one of those dreadful days of rain, the sound of it like a great waterfall, or like a tempest of wind blowing in the forest; and there came to our door two runaway

Black Boys seeking refuge. In such weather as that my enemy's dog (as Shakspere says) should have had a right to shelter. But when Arick saw the two poor rogues coming with their empty stomachs and drenched clothes, one of them with a stolen cutlass in his hand, through the world of falling water, he had no thought of any pity in his heart. Crouching behind one of the pillars of the veranda, to which he clung with his two hands, his mouth drew back into a strange sort of smile, his eyes grew bigger and bigger, and his whole face was just like the one word MURDER in big capitals.

But I have told you a great deal too much about poor Arick's savage nature, and now I must tell you of a great amusement he had the other day. There came an English ship-of-war into the harbor, and the officers good-naturedly gave an entertainment of songs and dances and a magic lantern, to which Arick and Austin were allowed to go. At the door of the hall there were crowds of Black Boys waiting and trying to peep in, as children at home lie about and peep under the tent of a circus; and you may be sure Arick was a very proud person when he passed them all by, and entered the hall with his ticket.

I wish I knew what he thought of the whole performance; but a friend of the lean man, who sat just in front of Arick tells me what seemed to startle him most. The first thing was when two of the officers came out with blackened faces, like minstrels, and began to dance. Arick was sure that they were really black and his own people, and he was wonderfully surprised to see them dance in this new European style.

But the great affair was the magic lantern. The hall was made quite dark, which was very little to Arick's taste. He sat there behind my friend, nothing to be seen of him but eyes and teeth, and his heart was beating finely in his little scarred breast. And presently there came out on the white sheet that great bright eye of light that I am sure all you children must have often seen. It was quite new to Arick; he had no idea what would happen next, and in his fear and excitement he laid hold with his little slim black fingers like a bird's claw on the neck of the friend in front of him. All through the rest of the show, as one picture followed another on the white sheet, he sat there grasping and clutching, and goodness knows whether he were more pleased or frightened.

Doubtless it was a very fine thing to see all those bright pictures coming out and dying away again, one after another; but doubtless it was rather alarming also, for how was it done? At last when there appeared upon the screen the head of a black woman (as it might be his own mother or sister), and this black woman of a sudden began to roll her eyes, the fear or the excitement, whichever it was, wrung out of him a loud, shuddering sob. I think we all ought to admire his courage when, after an evening spent in looking at such wonderful miracles, he and Austin set out alone through the forest to the lean man's house. It was late at night and pitch dark when some of the party overtook the little white boy and the big black boy, marching among the trees with their lantern. I have told you this wood has an ill name, and all the people of the island believe it to be full of evil spirits; it is a pretty dreadful place to walk in by the moving light of a lantern, with nothing about you but a curious whirl of shadows, and the black night above and beyond. But Arick kept his courage up, and I dare say Austin's, too, with a perpetual chatter, so that the people coming after heard his voice long before they saw the shining of the lantern. TUSITALA

NATURE AND SCIENCE FOR YOUNG FOLKS

EDITED BY
EDWARD F. BIGELOW

THE OUTDOOR WORLD

March, 1900

MISCHIEVOUS AND PRETTY RACCOON

A FEW years ago, in the top of a large hollow tree in a moist bit of woods in northern Pennsylvania, there lived a family of four young raccoons. Their mother, with a feeling common to all mothers, thought these four, fluffy, frolicsome youngsters to be the finest babies in the world. All went well with the little fellows while they remained in the hollow tree, under the care of their wise old mother. As they grew older, however, they felt a desire to see the big world outside, and, accordingly, fell into the habit of taking long rambles by night.

It was while returning home, early one morning, from one of these rambles, that the prettiest one of the lot came face to face with a bright-eyed boy of about fourteen. For a moment both were too frightened to move; but the boy soon recovered, and made a prisoner of the poor little raccoon. For a time the little captive bore his imprisonment very sullenly; but good food and kind treatment soon changed his wild, shy nature into a spirit of love and confidence. When he had attained full size, his appearance was between that of a fox and bear, on a smaller scale, of course.

For the benefit of our girls and boys interested in nature, our friend Mr. E. A. Sterling sends a photograph of this pretty and intelligent little animal climbing up the big limb of a tree.

THE RACCOON ON A BRANCH OF A TREE.

In the wild state the raccoon always conducts himself like a perfect little gentleman. His favorite feeding-grounds are along the shady banks of streams, or in some swampy bit of woods, where can be found those large delicious frogs he loves so well. He has however, no scruples against going out into the fields and orchards in search of nuts, fruits, and green corn; and, moreover, when Dame Fortune puts nice fat poultry in his way, Mr. Raccoon is too much of a gentleman to refuse them, which often gets him into trouble with the farmer. He also eats mice, rats, insects, eggs—in fact is almost omnivorous. He is active day and night.

A curious and interesting habit of raccoons is that of washing all their food in water. It matters not whether they have an ear of corn, a nice clean berry, or a big fat bug, they will always seek a little pool of water and carefully dip the object in it several times before conveying it to their mouth.

In the left end of our heading, "Nature and Science," he is represented as looking out from his winter home, a hollow tree, while a woodpecker is a visitor to the home, getting the insect's eggs and larvae from the bark.

GATHERING COCOONS

MARCH is a good time to go out to gather cocoons from the bushes and also from the trees growing by the roadside.

The worm of the cecropia-moth spins rather a large brownish-gray cocoon, not very far above the ground, on several different kinds of twigs. You can find them often on vines winding over the stone walls, on stout rough stalks growing low under the trees, and sometimes on currant-bushes in the gardens.

They are usually three inches long, bag-shaped at the lower end, pointed at the upper. The moth that hatches from them late in the spring is handsome enough to repay all the trouble of searching for it. When hatched, its wings expand about five inches, are trimmed with spots of black inside a rim of blue, with red and white stripes upon the edges, and the main coloring is a dusky gray. Its body has a row of red spots extending along each side, and it is known as one of our handsomest New England moths.

The polyphemus-moth has a cocoon

POLYPHEMUS COCOON WITH LEAVES ON IT

CECROPIA COCOON.

rounded at both ends, about an inch and a half long, usually made with a leaf or two fastened closely to the sides, and difficult to find on that account, as the real cocoons look exactly like dead leaves swinging in the wind. You have really to take hold of them to find the difference. This moth varies in color from a cinnamon brown to a yellowish gray, and is distinguished by a handsome "eye"-spot on each lower wing.

If you want the cocoons to hatch well, do not keep them in a warm place or they will get too dry and not come out in good shape. Put them where it is cool until late in the spring, then bring them into a warmer place, and by the last of May or first of June you will find wings, some day, where before there was only a homely case.

SARAH F. BEL

THE FIRST WILD FLOWER

YES, this is a spring month; the winter is nearly past, and one wild flower, at least, is here. Even if there is snow upon the ground the greater part of March, and the wind blows fierce and cold, there will be some sunny days when we shall take a walk in the fields and woods. The trees are bare. The buds, with possibly the exception of the pussy-willows, have not yet started.

We will be guided by the hum of the honey-bees that are buzzing around the wood-pile, getting the sweet sap from the recently sawed and split pieces of maple and birch. Down in the pasture we shall find them where there may be a little sap from the injured bark at the base of the maple-tree, or from the stump of the tree cut down this past winter.

We pass through the dense clump of bushes and follow the brook down the ravine. Here the hum of the bee is as loud as at the wood-pile, for the bees know that the first spring flower, the skunk-cabbage, is here, and they are visiting the queer flowers for the pollen, which they will pile on their flat legs and take home to the baby honey-bees in the hive.

THE SKUNK-CABBAGE, "THE ADVANCE-GUARD OF OUR FLORAL ARMY."

The skunk-cabbage pushes itself up through the leaves even before the snow is gone. John Burroughs says, "If you look closely upon the ground, you will find that sturdy advance-guard of our floral army thrusting his spear-point up through the ooze, and spring will again quicken your pulse."

It is evident that the shell-like or hooded covering called a spathe protects the flower from the harsh winds. The leaves are pushing up and will unfold in cabbage-like form. All is inviting and refreshing—except the rank perfume. But we'll forgive them that, for they bring us the good news that spring is coming—yes, is even already here!

THE HOOT-OWL IN THE SWAMP

"Whoo-whoo! whoo, whoo-whoo, oo-whoo-ah!"

What's that? Listen, and hear it again. You and I are on this country road, just a little after the sun has set, and it is growing dark. That strange sound comes from the depths of that big swamp. We will not be frightened, for it is only the hooting-owl, called also the "barred owl," from the rows of feathers like bars on its breast.

The owl is the first wild bird to lay its eggs, the great horned owl beginning the latter part of February, the barred owl about the middle of March in the New England and Middle States, selecting, as pictured, an old hawk's nest, sometimes a crow's nest, and frequently laying the two to four white eggs in a hollow tree. Our

THE BARRED OWL AND ITS FIRST EGG, LAID IN AN OLD HAWK'S NEST ABOUT THE MIDDLE OF MARCH.

barred owl is rightly called *the* hoot-owl, for, while other owls hoot or screech, this is the noisiest of the whole family. It feeds mostly on mice, upon which it drops, seizing them in its claws, very silently, because its very soft feathers prevent the wings making any noise. The owl has been called "a cat in feathers."

Mr. John H. Sage tells the following story:

I had a funny experience with a barred owl once, in Maine. It was in the daytime, and the bird was perched among some thick trees, apparently asleep. I "squeaked" (that is, imitated a bird that was hurt) several times from the bushes where I was concealed. His owlship was soon awake, and turned his head from side to side, endeavoring to find out where the noise came from. He jumped up from the limb on which he stood, perhaps three inches, turned around in the air, and landed on the same limb, but facing in the opposite direction. This operation was repeated several times, facing alternate directions. Disgusted in its endeavor to locate the wounded bird, it finally closed its eyes and went to sleep again. The owl seemed fairly crazy in puzzled eagerness to ascertain the source of the sound when I first commenced to "squeak," but did not offer to leave the limb.

MERRY MONTH OF MARCH

Ah, March! we know thou art
Kind-hearted, spite of ugly looks and threats,
And, out of sight, art nursing April's violets.

WHETHER "March comes in like a lamb and goes out like a lion," she is always merry in anticipations. When the young folks are to have a party there are always jolly times before-hand, talking it over and making plans. So our young nature-lovers are making plans this month. Who will see the first of each kind of spring birds? What a pleasure it will be to watch for the opening of the buds! And then, oh, what a treasure will be the first bouquet of spring

INDOORS

wild flowers! We may have joined with the older people, two months ago, in making good resolutions and plans; but there are new ones to be renewed this month. The first spring month! Think of it and of what it means to us who are interested in nature. And who isn't? If any there be, we are sorry for them—especially this month. Our joy is wide-spreading.

SLEPT ALL WINTER

THE young grizzly-bear, "Wahb," became very sleepy in the autumn, sometimes sleeping all day. Mr. Thompson tells us that the little bear had a very comfortable nest under a root, and one day, as it began to blow and snow, he crawled into this and curled up to sleep. The storm increased, and the snow fell deeper and deeper. It piled up over Wahb's den, shutting out the cold of winter, and Wahb slept, and slept, and slept all winter without waking. When spring came and aroused him, he knew that he had been asleep a long time.

ONE OF NATURE'S LITTLE JOKES

In the life of our commonest plants and animals there is much well worth careful attention. Some plants do not live what we might call an ordinary life, distinct to themselves, for they are like actors, mimicking some other plants or animals or surroundings, either for protection or to secure food. Such special traits we shall observe from time to time.

In nature are some things not only interesting but laughable—ludicrous in the extreme, as if nature were playing a joke for no purpose except "the fun of the thing."

Among the most noticeable of these (perhaps we will call it the clown of a fancied nature show) is the chrysalis of the Harvester butterfly, its very odd markings looking decidedly like a monkey's face. The eggs of this butterfly are laid on the leaves of alder-bushes, among the aphids, or plant-lice, which the larvae eat. Thus living on animal food, they are carnivorous, as it is called.

The larvae of a few other butterflies (especially those belonging to the same family) have been known to turn cannibal and eat their brothers and sisters in times of famine, but this Harvester larva is the only one truly carnivorous among our own butterflies.

From Our Scrap-Book

October, 1897

SCHOOL A PLACE OF LEISURE

OUR word "school" is derived from a Greek word meaning "leisure." The education of men was obtained not so much from books in ancient Greece as from lectures on philosophy, the public assembly, the theater, the games, and the law-courts, where most of their unoccupied time was spent.

THE GRAVE OF "PETER THE HEADSTRONG"

THE church known as "St. Mark's in the Bowery," New York, contains an ancient colonial shrine inclosing the tomb of Petrus Stuyvesant, the last of the Dutch governors of New York.

AN ACRE

AN acre was originally as much as a yoke of oxen could plow in a day, but in the thirteenth century it was made by law of its present size. The word "acre" is from the Latin *ager*, a cultivated field.

THE PILGRIM'S SCALLOP

THE scallop abounds on the coast of Palestine, and in old times pilgrims returning from the Holy Land used to wear one on their hats to show that they had been there.

A CURIOUS SUPERSTITION

AMONG the superstitions of the Seneca Indians was one most beautiful one: When a young maiden died they imprisoned a young bird until it first began to try its powers of song; and then, loading it with caresses and messages, they loosed its bonds over her grave, in the belief that it would not fold its wing nor close its eye until it had flown to the spirit-land and delivered its precious burden of affection to the loved and lost one.

VENEZUELA

WHEN Columbus discovered South America, near the mouth of the Orinoco, the Spaniards found an Indian village built over the water on piles. As it reminded them of Venice, they called it Venezuela, or "little Venice."

HOW A MEDICINE WAS NAMED

QUININE is made from Peruvian bark—the outer part of a medicinal plant, called *Cinchona*. It was so named from the wife of Count Cinchon of Peru, in the seventeenth century, who, by its use was cured of intermittent fever.

THE SHIP OF THE DESERT

THE scent of the camel for water is said to be very keen. He can smell it a great way off; and oftentimes the travelers who are suffering for water will let the camel take his own way, and he will take them often to a place where water may be found.

E PLURIBUS UNUM

WE are indebted to John Adams for our national motto, *E pluribus unum*. While he was minister to England, Sir John Prestwick suggested it to Mr. Adams as a good motto to indicate the union of the colonies. It was submitted to Congress, and adopted by Act of Congress, June, 1782. The eagle in its beak bears a ribbon on which is the motto. In the early days of its use the eagle bore also in its talons a bundle of thirteen arrows; but when in 1841 a new seal was made to take the place of the old one, which had become worn, only six arrows were placed in the talons. Whether this change was ordered by law or not is not known. The old Latin motto was in use in England as far back as 1730 on the *Gentleman's Magazine*.

THE SKYLARK'S SONG

IN winter the skylark of England does not sing; but in the early days of spring the great flocks of these birds break up, and then go in pairs to look for places to build their nests and rear their young ones. And then the charming song of the skylark is heard in all its sweetness. While the mother bird is brooding over her eggs to warm them, her mate often rises into the air, and then with quivering wings mounts vertically upward so far that he looks like a mere speck in the sky, and all the time pouring forth his rich and beautiful song, but at last ceases his song before descending again to the nest. One of the most beautiful poems in the English language is Shelley's "Ode to the Skylark."

HOW FISHES BREATHE

WATER has mixed with it a good deal of air, or fishes could not live in it. They breathe in oxygen and breathe out carbonic acid gas, and the carbonic acid gas is used up, and oxygen given out by the sea plants, the same as is done by plants on land. If there were no plants in the sea the carbonic acid gas would increase so as to kill all the fishes and other animals living in it.

A LONG WALK

IF any one were to undertake to walk, one way only, through all the streets of London, he would be obliged to go a distance of 2,600 miles, or as far as it is across the American continent from New York to San Francisco. This will give an idea of the distance one would have to go to see thoroughly even the greater part of the city of London—the largest city in the world.

ITEMS

IT is estimated that Australia contains nearly seven thousand species of plants not found elsewhere.

HARD or anthracite coal was not discovered till 1790. This bed of Pennsylvania hard coal is the richest in the world.

THE Bible was written by degrees during a period of 1,600 years. It was anciently called "The Books," but for the past 700 years the "Bible."

THE great Thirty Years' War began at Prague and ended at Prague.

A NOCTURNE

By Julia B. Chapman

April, 1900

THE day was done, and in the west
The glowing sun sank to his 𝄩 ;
Gleamed in the heavens the first faint stars,
The cows were at the pasture ▱ .
The wild fowl, rising from the pines,
Flew in two long, converging ≡ .
Straight where the sky and sea connect
Their leader took his course ∿
(While yet the sunset glories burn),
Nor ever swerved, nor made a ∿.
Out on the lake rocked a small boat,
And in it two who took no ♩
Of time, until the darkening sky
Warned them to land, their boat to ⏜ ;
And, to remove of risk all trace,
They fastened to a stake a { .

Soon from the boat they took some carp,
Which they had caught with fish-hooks ♯ ,
And, with a joyful smile ironic,

Drew out a bottle labeled " 𝄞♯♩ ."

Their rods and guns, and this and that,
They laid upon a rock quite ♭.
Their camp-fire lit, they did not fail,

Ere cooking, first each fish to ♫♫♩♪♪♪♪ .

They supped, and smoked, and laughed at straws,
And rattled on without a ⌢ .
Each tried the other's tale to beat,
As wondrous stories they'd ▦ .
Wearied, at length, with mirth and jest,
They laid them down and went to ━ .

JUNE ATHLETICS

June, 1897

BREAKING A RECORD AT THE STANDING HIGH JUMP.

MEADOW TALK

By Caroline Leslie

July, 1878

A BUMBLE-BEE, yellow as gold,
    Sat perched on a red-clover top,
When a grasshopper, wiry and old,
    Came along with a skip and a hop.
"Good-morrow!" cried he, "Mr. Bumble-Bee!
    You seem to have come to a stop."

    "We people that work,"
      Said the bee with a jerk,
"Find a benefit sometimes in stopping;
    Only insects like you,
    Who have nothing to do,
Can keep up a perpetual hopping."

The grasshopper paused on his way,
    And thoughtfully hunched up his knees;
"Why trouble this sunshiny day,"
    Quoth he, "with reflections like these?
I follow the trade for which I was made;
    We all can't be wise bumble-bees.

    "There's a time to be sad,
      And a time to be glad;
A time both for working and stopping;
    For men to make money,
    For you to make honey,
And for me to do nothing but hopping."

MAY QUEENS

May, 1904

Each little girl is neat and sweet, and all are quaintly dressed.
How *can* we choose one May-Queen and leave out all the rest?
Which is the neatest, which is the sweetest, and which do you like the best?

A MAY-DAY SHOWER
By M. A. Thomson

May, 1896

BIRDS are singing,
Bells are ringing,
Children bringing
  Garlands fair;
Maids are scorning
Clouds of warning;
Gay adorning
  Girls will wear.

Rain is falling,
Hearts appalling;
Some one's calling,
  "Homeward skip!"
Isabella's,
Ruth's and Ella's,
Maud's and Stella's
Wet umbrellas—
  How they drip!

"Hat and feather,
Altogether
Spoiled by weather,"
  Ruth bemoans;
Dress and frilling,
Sash and quilling,
All so killing,
Maud, unwilling,
  "Ruined!" owns.

Hey day! Hey day!
Choose not May-Day
For a play-day
  Out of doors:
Or, prepare ye;
New gear spare ye;
Old clothes wear ye;
Never care ye
  When it pours.

The Song of the Skipping Rope

By Anna B. Patten

May, 1896

WINTER-TIME has fled away,
Spring has had her gentle sway,
Summer surely must be near
When the skipping-ropes appear;
    With a skip, skip,
    And a trip, trip,
As thus we rise and fall;
    In yard and street
    The little feet
Are coming to the call!

Oh, so many tricks to do
That our mothers also knew!
"In the Front Door," "Baking Bread,"
"Chase the Fox," and" Needle Thread."
    With a skip, skip,
    And a trip, trip,
For so the leader saith—
    With a hop, jump,
    And a thump, thump,
Until you're out of breath.

Hear the counting, sure and slow;
To a hundred they must go.
Not a hand or arm should swerve,
While the rope describes its curve;
    With a skip, skip,
    And a trip, trip,
Until the task is done;
    With cheeks so red,
    And ruffled head,
Bravo, my little one!

Boys may leap and vault so high,
But none was ever known to try
To master this soft, little spring
That is so intricate a thing!
    With a skip, skip,
    And a trip, trip.
Oh, may I always hear
    That pit-pat-pit
    That seems to fit
This blossom-time of year!

The Elf & the Dormouse

By Oliver Herford

February, 1892

UNDER a toadstool
  Crept a wee Elf,
Out of the rain
  To shelter himself.

Under the toadstool,
  Sound asleep,
Sat a big Dormouse
  All in a heap.

Trembled the wee Elf,
  Frightened, and yet
Fearing to fly away
  Lest he get wet.

To the next shelter—
  Maybe a mile!
Sudden the wee Elf
  Smiled a wee smile,

Tugged till the toadstool
  Toppled in two.
Holding it over him
  Gaily he flew.

Soon he was safe home
  Dry as could be.
Soon woke the Dormouse—
  "Good gracious me!

Where is my toadstool?"
  Loud he lamented.
—And that's how umbrellas
  First were invented.

THE ELF AND THE SPIDER
By M. M. D.

August, 1881

PERCHED on a stool of the fairy style,
An elf-boy worked with a mischievous smile.
"That careless spider!" said he, "to leave
His web unfinished! But I can sew:
I'll spin, or sew, or darn, or weave—
Whatever they call it—so none will know
That his spidership didn't complete it himself,
Or I'm a very mistaken young elf!"

Well, the wee sprite sewed, or wove, or spun,
Plying his brier and gossamer thread;
And, quick as a ripple, the web, all done,
Was softly swaying against his head
As he laughed and nodded in joyful pride.
   Ho! ho! it's done!
   Ha! ha! what fun!
And then he felt himself slowly slide—
Slide and tumble—stool and all—
In the prettiest sort of a fairy fall!
Up he jumped, as light as air;
But oh, what a sight,

What a sorry plight—
The web was caught in his sunny hair!
When, *presto!* on sudden invisible track,
That horrible spider came lumbering back:
"WHO'S BEEN AT MY WEB? WHAT HO! COME ON!"
And he knotted for fight,
The horrid fright!
Poor, frightened fay!
But the elf was gone—
Nothing was seen but a tattered sheen,
Trailing and shining upon the green.

But all that night, with dainty care,
An elf sat tugging away at his hair.
And 'tis whispered in Elf-land to this day
That any spider under the sun
May go and leave his web undone,
With its filmy thread-end swinging free
Or tied to the top of a distant tree,
With never a fear that elfin-men
Will meddle with spider-work again.

THE SKYLARK'S SONG

By John Bennett

September, 1987

ARRANGED FOR THE PIANO
BY CARL KIEFEN

WORDS FROM "MASTER SKYLARK";
AIR BY JOHN BENNETT

1. Hey! lad-die, hark, to the merry, mer-ry lark, How high he sing-eth clear. Oh, a morn in Spring is the sweetest thing That cometh in all the year: Oh, a morn in Spring is the sweet-est thing That com-eth in all the year!

2. God save us all, my jol-ly gen-tle-men! We'll mer-ry be to-day; For the cuc-koo sings till the greenwood rings, And it is the month of May: For the cuc-koo sings till the greenwood rings, And it is the month of May!

REFRAIN. *Vivace*

Ring! Ting! It is the mer-ry

Ped.

Spring - time. How full of heart a bod - y feels! Sing hey trol - ly

Repeat Refrain after 2d Stanza.

lol - ly! O to live is to be jol - ly, When Spring-time cometh with the Summer at her heels!

"OVER THE ROOFS OF THE HOUSES
I HEAR THE BARKING OF LEO"

By R. W. Gilder

December, 1890

I

OVER the roofs of the houses I hear the barking of Leo—
Leo the shaggy, the lustrous, the giant, the gentle Newfoundland.
Dark are his eyes as the night, and black is his hair as the midnight;
Large and slow is his tread till he sees his master returning,
Then how he leaps in the air, with motion ponderous, frightening!
Now as I pass to my work, I hear o'er the roar of the city—
Far over the roofs of the houses, I hear the barking of Leo;
For me he is moaning and crying, for me in measure sonorous
He raises his marvelous voice, for he is waiting and calling.

II

None can assuage his grief though but for a day is the parting,
Though morn after morn 'tis the same, though home every night comes his
    master,
Still will he grieve when we sever, and wild will be his rejoicing
When at night his master returns and lays but a hand on his forehead.
No lack will there be in the world, of faith, of love, and devotion,
No lack for me and for mine, while Leo alone is living—
While over the roofs of the houses I hear the barking of Leo.

THE DROLL LITTLE FOLK OF SLEEPY DELL

By John Vance Cheney

June, 1899

THEY sleep the livelong day,
And in the starlight play,
The tiny people hid so well,
The wee, wee folk of Sleepy Dell.
I have never found in any book
The words to tell you how they look;
But every hue of the wood they wear,
And softest colors won from the air—
Pale greens and browns and yellows and
grays,
Mixed secretly by the nights and days.
Some time you may meet them on their
round,
Marching about the mossy mound,
Or sitting in rows by the singing brook;
Then you will know just how they look.
If only I could paint a summer day,
Or tell what sunbeams to the daisies say,
Or what is the dream of the cloud asleep,
Curled up so snug where the blue is soft
and deep,

Then I would try to make you see
How the quaint little people look to me.
Their homes are so frail, when the winds
come out
And run on the roofs, they rock about,
And swing this way and that, like weeds at
play,
Shy, all alone beside the summer way.
It's a very, very hard thing to tell
Of the wee, wee folk of Sleepy Dell!
'T would make the witches wink and think
To name the dainties they eat and drink.
I know some three or four—
That many and no more:
The breath of leaves and flowers,
The sighs of midnight hours,
The dreams that now and then
Float from the sleep of men—
I really thought I knew one more,
But they told me only three, not four.
The midget mischiefs hid so well,
The wee, wee folk of Sleepy Dell!

"MISS MUFFET"

March, 1877

LITTLE TRADJA of Norway,
She sat in the door-way,
  Eating her reindeer broth;

There came a big badger,
And little Miss Tradja
  Soon carried her meal further north.

THE GIN-GER-BREAD BOY

As told by Nova Nestrick

May, 1875

Now you shall hear a sto-ry that some-bod-y's great, great-grand-moth-er told a lit-tle girl ev-er so ma-ny years a-go:

There was once a lit-tle old man and a lit-tle old wom-an, who lived in a lit-tle old house in the edge of a wood. They would have been a ver-y happy old coup-le but for one thing,—they had no lit-tle child, and they wished for one ver-y much. One day, when the lit-tle old wom-an was bak-ing gin-ger-bread, she cut a cake in the shape of a lit-tle boy, and put it in-to the ov-en.

Pres-ent-ly, she went to the ov-en to see if it was baked. As soon as the ov-en door was o-pened, the lit-tle gin-ger-bread boy jumped out, and be-gan to run a-way as fast as he could go.

The lit-tle old wom-an called her hus-band, and they both ran aft-er him. But they could not catch him. And soon the gin-ger-bread boy came to a barn full of thresh-ers. He called out to them as he went by, say-ing:

"I've run a-way from a lit-tle old wom-an,
A lit-tle old man,
And I can run a-way from you, I can!"

Then the barn full of thresh-ers set out to run aft-er him. But, though they ran fast, they could not catch him. And he ran on till he came to a field full of mow-ers. He called out to them:

"I've run a-way from a lit-tle old wom-an,
A lit-tle old man,
A barn full of thresh-ers,
And I can run away from you, I can!"

Then the mow-ers be-gan to run aft-er him, but they couldn't catch him. And he ran on till he came to a cow. He called out to her:

"I've run a-way from a lit-tle old wom-an,
    A lit-tle old man,
    A barn full of thresh-ers,
    A field full of mowers,
And I can run a-way from you, I can!"

But, though the cow start-ed at once, she couldn't catch him. And soon he came to a pig. He called out to the pig:

"I've run a-way from a lit-tle old wom-an,
    A lit-tle old man,
    A barn full of thresh-ers,
    A field full of now-ers
    A cow,
And I can run a-way from you, I can!"

But the pig ran, and couldn't catch him. And he ran till he came a-cross a fox, and to him he called out:

"I've run a-way from a lit-tle old wom-an,
    A lit-tle old man,
    A barn full of thresh-ers,
    A field full of mow-ers,
    A cow and a pig,
And I can run a-way from you, I can!"

Then the fox set out to run. Now fox-es can run ver-y fast, and so the fox soon caught the gin-ger-bread boy and be-gan to eat him up.

Pres-ent-ly the gin-ger-bread boy said: "O dear! I'm quar-ter gone!" And then: "Oh, I'm half gone!" And soon: "I'm three-quarters gone!" And at last: "I'm all gone!" And never spoke a-gain.

JACK-IN-THE-PULPIT

March, 1895

'Tis March, and the winds are high;
The clouds are scurrying by,
    And, peeping through,
    One sees the blue,
As they go hurrying by.
    For blow, blow,
    Winter must go,
With the clouds that are hurrying by.

'Tis March, and the winds are high;
But soon comes a summer sky;
    The first bluebird
    Has brought the word—
He sings of a summer sky.
    Then blow, blow,
    Winter must go,
And clouds must scatter and fly.

So says William Zachary Gladwin, in his verses sent to this pulpit; and your Jack warmly seconds the motion.

VOLTAIRE'S RIDDLE

WHAT is the longest and the shortest thing in the world; the swiftest and the slowest; the most divisible and the most extended; the least valued and the most regretted; without which nothing can be done; which devours everything, however small, and yet gives life and spirit to all things, however great?

TO HELP YOUR MEMORY

ALICE MAY DOUGLAS sends this message to you, my hearers:

"A great man has told us that, when reading, he always stopped at the bottom of every page and thought over what he had just read.

"If you do this, it may not make a great man or woman of you; but it surely will improve your memory, and at the same time help you to form a very valuable habit."

HERE is a simple story, in straightforward rhyme, that says precisely what it means to say. It was written for this congregation by ANNIE E. TYNAN; and Deacon Green says if he were a school-boy he would be tempted to learn it for a recitation piece.

THE UNCLE FROM OVER THE SEA

WILKINSON LUNN was sixty years old;
His coffers were full to their covers with gold,
His rent-roll was long as a baron could boast,
For he owned half a town on the New Jersey coast.
That he'd earned it himself made his opulence sweet,
But he still needed something to make life complete;
And, pondering the question, this answer he drew:
To double a pleasure, divide it by two!
"I'll look up my nephew," said Wilkinson Lunn,
"And if he is worthy I'll make him my son."

In Manchester, England, a small, narrow street
Runs into a square where four broader ones meet.
It was far down this street, where stores looked ill-kept,
Where stoops were untidy and sidewalks unswept,
That Wilkinson Lunn at last found a store
With the name of his nephew hung over the door.
A soiled scrap of paper was pinned to the jamb;
It read: "I'll be back in an hour. H. Lamb."
"An hour"—the uncle looked thoughtfully down.
"An hour?"—he lifted his head with a frown.
"An hour!"—he stamped as he read it again—
"My gem of a nephew, an hour from *when?*"

He peered through the finger-marked panes of the door;
Saw a chair, an old pipe, and a scrap-littered floor.
He rattled the door-knob: it needed a screw;
He looked in the window: disorder there, too;
He stepped to the sidewalk, took one long survey.
Then shook his gray head and went sadly away.

The nephew came back to his pipe and his chair,
But never once dreamed of the guest who'd been there.
He berated his luck—'tis the lazy man's way—
That his profits were small and his rent was to pay;
And he never once thought that his shortness of pelf
Was due, not to fortune, but just to himself.

If ever it happens that *you* keep a store,
Don't pin "I'll be back" to the jamb of the door,
But stay there, and keep both your wares and yourself
As clean and attractive as new polished delf.
You will find that your trade soon will grow like the trees
If your shop is well kept and you try hard to please;
And then, if he happens to come, there you'll be
To welcome your uncle from over the sea.

IN DAKOTA

MISS VIRGINIA SHARPE-PATTISON has written to this Pulpit a letter describing "A Strange Use of Trees," "Mr. Jack-rabbit in Winter," and a few other matters:

How would your boys and girls [she asks] like to have their mother's pantry of good things high up in a tree instead of on the ground floor, as it is in their well-regulated homes? It would be rather an odd place for a larder, it is true; but the soldiers in camp on Cannon Ball River a few winters ago found it exceedingly convenient to step out of their mess-tents and cut from a bough a few prairie-chickens or rabbits which were there suspended, ready for the cook's basting-spoon.

Once in a while, however, an ill-mannered cat would get there before them, and lessen the number of good things by stealing a nice pullet, and sneaking off without even a purr or thanks.

Great white rabbits with fur soft as silk are brought into camp for sale by the Indians who are skilled in securing this game.

In winter Mr. Jack-rabbit looks like a snowball, so perfectly white does his coat become during the cold season. This appears to be a wise provision for his protection, as to an ordinary eye he is easily confounded with the general whiteness of the landscape in that climate of hoarfrosts and blizzards. But the wily redskinned hunter is not so easily deceived, and these winter rabbits are a constant means of revenue to him when there is a camp of pale-faces near by which he can supply with wild meats.

It must be owned that these coppercolored meat-venders are not the artless children of the forest pictured in the pages of Longfellow's *Hiawatha*—they know how to bargain and dicker almost as well as if they had a drop or two of Yankee blood in their veins. Before buying of them it is well to know something of Indian arithmetic; and old Black Bull, whose Indian name is "Tatankasapa," will graciously teach you that wahzhee means 1; nopo, 2; yaminee, 3; topah, 4; zaptah, 5; shakopee, 6; shakoin, 7; shakalocha, 8; nuptchoakah, 9; wickchuminee, 10. After obtaining this information, customers must look out for themselves.

A St. NICHOLAS ANTHOLOGY
SUMMER

CONTENTS

MIDSUMMER PIRATES.

By Richard H. Davis

August, 1889

HE BOYS living at the Atlantic House, and the boys boarding at Chadwick's, held mutual sentiments of something not unlike enmity—feelings of hostility from which even the older boarders were not altogether free. Nor was this unnatural under the circumstances.

When Judge Henry S. Carter and his friend Dr. Prescott first discovered Manasquan, such an institution as the Atlantic House seemed an impossibility, and land improvement companies, Queen Anne cottages, and hacks to and from the railroad station, were out of all calculation. At that time "Captain" Chadwick's farmhouse, though not rich in all the modern improvements of a seaside hotel, rejoiced in a table covered three times a day with the good things from the farm. The river, back of the house, was full of fish, and the pinewoods along its banks were intended by Nature expressly for the hanging of hammocks.

The chief amusements were picnics to the head of the river (or as near the head as the boats could get through the lily-pads), crabbing along the shore, and races on the river itself, which, if it was broad, was so absurdly shallow that an upset meant nothing more serious than a wetting and a temporary loss of reputation as a sailor.

But all this had been spoiled by the advance of civilization and the erection of the Atlantic House.

The railroad surveyors, with their high-top boots and transits, were the first signs of the approaching evils. After them came the Ozone Land Company, which bought up all the sand hills bordering on the ocean, and proceeded to stake out a flourishing "city by the sea" and to erect sign-posts in the marshes to show where they would lay out streets, named after the directors of the Ozone Land Company and the Presidents of the United States.

It was not unnatural, therefore, that the Carters, and the Prescotts, and all the Judge's clients, and the Doctor's patients, who had been coming to Manasquan for many years, and loved it for its simplicity and quiet, should feel aggrieved at these great changes. And though the young Carters and Prescotts endeavored to impede the march of civilization by pulling up the surveyor's stakes and tearing down the Land Company's sign-posts, the inevitable improvements marched steadily on.

I hope all this will show why it was that the boys who lived at the Atlantic House—and dressed as if they were still in the city, and had "hops" every evening—were not pleasing to the boys who boarded at Chadwick's, who never changed their flannel suits for anything more formal than their bathing-suits, and spent the summer nights on the river.

This spirit of hostility and its past history were explained to the new arrival at Chadwick's by young Teddy Carter, as the two sat under the willow tree watching a game of tennis. The new arrival had just expressed his surprise at the earnest desire manifest on the part of the entire Chadwick establishment to defeat the Atlantic House people in the great race which was to occur on the day following.

"Well, you see, sir," said Teddy, "considerable depends on this race. As it is now, we stand about even. The Atlantic House beat us playing base-ball—though they had to get the waiters to help them—and we

beat them at tennis. Our house is great on tennis. Then we had a boat-race, and our boat won. They claimed it wasn't a fair race, because their best boat was stuck on the sand-bar, and so we agreed to sail it over again. The second time the wind gave out, and all the boats had to be poled home. The Atlantic House boat was poled in first, and her crew claimed the race. Wasn't it silly of them? Why, Charley Prescott told them, if they'd only said it was to be a *poling* match, he'd have entered a mud-scow and left his sail-boat at the dock!"

"And so you are going to race again to-morrow?" asked the new arrival.

"Well, it isn't exactly a race," explained Teddy. "It's a game we boys have invented. We call it 'Pirates and Smugglers.' It's something like tag, only we play it on the water, in boats. We divide boats and boys up into two sides; half of them are pirates or smugglers, and half of them are revenue officers or man-o'-war's-men. The 'Pirate's Lair' is at the island, and our dock is 'Cuba.' That's where the smugglers run in for cargoes of cigars and brandy. Mr. Moore gives us his empty cigar boxes, and Miss Sherrill (the lady who's down here for her health) lets us have all the empty Apollinaris bottles. We fill the bottles with water colored with crushed blackberries, and that answers for brandy.

"The revenue officers are stationed at Annapolis (that's the Atlantic House dock), and when they see a pirate start from the island, or from our dock, they sail after him. If they can touch him with the bow of their boat, or if one of their men can board him, that counts one for the revenue officers; and they take down his sail and the pirate captain gives up his tiller as a sign of surrender.

"Then they tow him back to Annapolis, where they keep him a prisoner until he is exchanged. But if the pirate can dodge the

Custom House boat, and get to the place he started for, without being caught, that counts one for him."

"Very interesting, indeed," said the new arrival; "but suppose the pirate won't be captured or give up his tiller, what then?"

"Oh, well, in that case," said Teddy, reflectively, "they'd cut his sheet-rope, or splash water on him, or hit him with an oar, or something. But he generally gives right up. Now, to-morrow the Atlantic House boys are to be the revenue officers and we are to be the pirates. They have been watching us as we played the game, all summer, and they think they understand it well enough to capture our boats without any trouble at all."

"And what do you think?" asked the new arrival.

"Well, I can't say, certainly. They have faster boats than ours, but they don't know how to sail them. If we had their boats, or if they knew as much about the river as we do, it would be easy enough to name the winners. But, as it is, it's about even."

Every one who owned a boat was on the river, the following afternoon, and those who didn't own a boat, hired, or borrowed one—with or without the owner's permission.

The shore from Chadwick's to the Atlantic House dock was crowded with people. All Manasquan seemed to be ranged in line along the river's bank. Crab-men and clam-diggers mixed indiscriminately with the summer boarders; and the beach-wagons and stages from Chadwick's grazed the wheels of the dog-carts and drags from the Atlantic's livery-stables.

It does not take much to overthrow the pleasant routine of summer-resort life, and the state of temporary excitement existing at the two houses on the eve of the race was not limited to the youthful contestants.

The proprietor of the Atlantic House had already announced an elaborate supper in honor of the anticipated victory, and every father and mother whose son was to take part in the day's race felt the importance of the occasion even more keenly than the son himself.

"Of course," said Judge Carter, "it's only a game, and for my part, so long as no one is drowned, I don't really care who wins; *but,* if our boys" ("our boys" meaning all three crews) "allow those young whipper-snappers from the Atlantic House to win the pennant, they deserve to have their boats taken from them and exchanged for hoops and marbles!"

Which goes to show how serious a matter was the success of the Chadwick crews.

At three o'clock the amateur pirates started from the dock to take up their positions at the island. Each of the three small cat-boats held two boys: one at the helm and one in charge of the center-board and sheet-rope. Each pirate wore a jersey striped with differing colors, and the head of each bore the sanguinary red, knitted cap in which all genuine pirates are wont to appear. From the peaks of the three boats floated black flags, bearing the emblematic skull and bones, of Captain Kidd's followers.

As they left the dock the Chadwick's people cheered with delight at their appearance and shouted encouragement, while the remaining youngsters fired salutes with a small cannon, which added to the uproar as well as increased the excitement of the moment by its likelihood to explode.

At the Atlantic House dock, also, the excitement was at fever heat.

Clad in white flannel suits and white duck yachting-caps with gilt buttons, the revenue officers strolled up and down the pier with an air of cool and determined purpose such as Decatur may have worn as he paced the deck of his man-of-war and scanned the horizon for Algerine pirates. The stars-and-stripes floated bravely from the peaks of the three cat-boats, soon to leap in pursuit of the pirate craft which were conspicuously making for the starting-point at the island.

At half-past three the judges' steam-launch, the *Gracie*, made for the middle of the river, carrying two representatives from both houses and a dozen undergraduates from different colleges, who had chartered the boat for the purpose of following the race and seeing at close quarters all that was to be seen.

They enlivened the occasion by courteously and impartially giving the especial yell of each college of which there was a representative present, whether they knew him or not, or whether he happened to be an undergraduate, a professor, or an alumnus. Lest some one might inadvertently be overlooked, they continued to yell throughout the course of the afternoon, giving, in time, the shibboleth of every known institution of learning.

"Which do I think is going to win?" said the veteran boat-builder of Manasquan to the inquiring group around his boat-house. "Well, I wouldn't like to say. You see, I built every one of those boats that sails to-day, and every time I make a boat I make it better than the last one. Now, the Chadwick boats I built near five years ago,

"'WHICH DO I THINK IS GOING TO WIN?' SAID THE VETERAN BOAT-BUILDER TO THE INQUIRING GROUP AROUND HIS BOAT-HOUSE."

and the Atlantic House boats I built last summer, and I've learned a good deal in five years."

"So you think our side will win?" eagerly interrupted an Atlantic House boarder.

"Well, I didn't say so, did I?" inquired the veteran, with crushing slowness of speech. "I didn't say so. For though these boats the Chadwick's boys have is five years old, they're good boats still; and those boys know every trick and turn of 'em—and they know every current and sand-bar just as though it was marked with a piece of chalk. So, if the Atlantic folks win, it'll be because they've got the best boats; and if the Chadwick boys win, they'll win because they're the better sailors."

In the fashion of all first-class aquatic contests, it was fully half an hour after the time appointed for the race to begin before the first pirate boat left the island.

The *Ripple*, with Judge Carter's two sons in command, was the leader; and when her sail filled and showed above the shore, a cheer from the Chadwick's dock was carried to the ears of the pirate crew who sat perched on the rail as she started on her first long tack.

In a moment, two of the Atlantic House heroes tumbled into the *Osprey*, a dozen over-hasty hands had cast off her painter, had shoved her head into the stream, and the great race was begun.

The wind was down the river, or toward the island, so that while the *Osprey* was sailing before the wind, the *Ripple* had her sail close-hauled and was tacking.

"They're after us!" said Charley Carter, excitedly. "It's the *Osprey*, but I can't make out who's handling her. From the way they are pointing, I think they expect to reach us on this tack as we go about."

The crew of the *Osprey* evidently thought so too, for her bow was pointed at a spot on the shore, near which the *Ripple* must turn if she continued much longer on the same tack.

"Do you see that?" gasped Charley, who was acting as lookout. "They're letting her drift in the wind so as not to get there before us. I tell you what it is, Gus, they know what they're doing, and I think we'd better go about now."

"Do you?" inquired the younger brother, who had a lofty contempt for the other's judgment as a sailor. "Well, I don't. My plan is simply this: I am going to run as near the shore as I can, then go about sharp, and let them drift by us by a boat's length. A boat's length is as good as a mile, and then, when we are both heading the same way, I would like to see them touch us!"

"What's the use of taking such risks?" demanded the elder brother. "I tell you we can't afford to let them get so near as that."

"At the same time," replied the man at the helm, "that is what we are going to do. I am commanding this boat, please to remember, and if I take the risks I am willing to take the blame."

"You'll be doing well if you get off with nothing but blame," growled the elder brother. "If you let those kids catch us, I'll throw you overboard!"

"I'll put you in irons for threatening a superior officer if you don't keep quiet," answered the younger Carter, with a grin, and the mutiny ended.

It certainly would have been great sport to have run almost into the arms of the revenue officers, and then to have turned and led them a race to the goal, but the humor of young Carter's plan was not so apparent to the anxious throng of sympathizers on Chadwick's dock.

"What's the matter with the boys! Why don't they go about?" asked Captain Chadwick, excitedly. "One would think they were trying to be caught."

As he spoke, the sail of the *Ripple* fluttered in the wind, her head went about sharply, and, as her crew scrambled up on the windward rail, she bent and bowed gracefully on the homeward tack.

But, before the boat was fully under way, the *Osprey* came down upon her with a rush. The Carters hauled in the sail until their sheet lay almost flat with the surface of the river, the water came pouring over the leeward rail, and the boys threw their bodies far over the other side, in an effort to right her. The next instant there was a crash, the despised boat of the Atlantic House struck her fairly in the side and one of the Atlantic House crew had boarded the *Ripple* with a painter in one hand and his hat in the other.

Whether it was the shock of the collision, or disgust at having been captured, no one could tell; but when the *Osprey's* bow struck the *Ripple,* the younger Carter calmly let himself go over backward and remained in the mud with the water up to his chin and without making any effort to help himself, until the judges' boat picked him up and carried him, an ignominious prisoner-of-war, to the Atlantic House dock.

The disgust over the catastrophe to the pirate crew was manifested on the part of the Chadwick sympathizers by gloomy silence or loudly expressed indignation. On the whole, it was perhaps just as well that the two Carters, as prisoners-of-war, were forced to remain at the Atlantic House dock, for their reception at home would not have been a gracious one.

Their captors, on the other hand, were received with all the honor due triumphant heroes, and were trotted off the pier on the shoulders of their cheering admirers; while the girls in the carriages waved their parasols and handkerchiefs and the colored waiters on the banks danced up and down and shouted like so many human calliopes.

The victories of John Paul Jones and the rescue of Lieutenant Greely became aquatic events of little importance in comparison. Everybody was so encouraged at this first success, that Atlantic House stock rose fifty points in as many seconds, and the next crew to sally forth from that favored party felt that the second and decisive victory was already theirs.

Again the black flag appeared around the bank of the island, and on the instant a second picked crew of the Atlantic House was in pursuit. But the boys who commanded the pirate craft had no intention of taking nor giving any chances. They put their boat about, long before the revenue officers expected them to do so, forcing their adversaries to go so directly before the wind that their boat rocked violently. It was not long before the boats drew nearer and nearer together, again, as if they must certainly meet at a point not more than a hundred yards from the Atlantic House pier, where the excitement had passed the noisy point and had reached that of titillating silence.

"Go about sharp!" snapped out the captain of the pirate boat, pushing his tiller from him and throwing his weight upon it. His first officer pulled the sail close over the deck, the wind caught it fairly, and, almost before the spectators were aware of it, the pirate boat had gone about and was speeding away on another tack. The revenue officers were not prepared for this. They naturally thought the pirates would run as close to the shore as they possibly could before they tacked, and were aiming for the point at which they calculated their opponents would go about, just as did the officers in the first race.

Seeing this, and not wishing to sail too

close to them, the pirates had gone about much farther from the shore than was needful. In order to follow them the revenue officers were now forced to come about and tack, which, going before the wind as they were, they found less easy. The sudden change in their opponents' tactics puzzled them, and one of the two boys bungled. On future occasions each confidentially informed his friends that it was the other who was responsible; but, however that may have been, the boat missed stays, her sail flapped weakly in the breeze, and, while the crew were vigorously trying to set her in the wind by lashing the water with her rudder, the pirate boat was off and away, one hundred yards to the good, and the remainder of the race was a procession of two boats with the pirates easily in the lead.

And now came the final struggle. Now came the momentous "rubber," which was to plunge Chadwick's into gloom, or keep them still the champions of the river. The appetites of both were whetted for victory by the single triumph each had already won, and their representatives felt that, for them, success or a watery grave were the alternatives.

The Atlantic House boat, the *Wave*, and the boat upon which the Chadwicks' hopes were set, the *Rover*, were evenly matched, their crews were composed of equally good sailors, and each was determined to tow the other ignominiously into port.

The two Prescotts watched the *Wave* critically and admiringly, as she came toward them with her crew perched on her side and the water showing white under her bow.

"They're coming entirely too fast to suit *me*," said the elder Prescott. "I want more room and I have a plan to get it. Stand ready to go about." The younger brother stood ready to go about, keeping the *Rover*

on her first tack until she was clear of the island's high banks and had the full sweep of the wind; then, to the surprise of her pursuers and the bewilderment of the spectators, she went smartly about, and, turning her bow directly away from the goal, started before the wind back past the island and toward the wide stretch of river on the upper side.

"What's your man doing that for?" excitedly asked one of the Atlantic House people, of the prisoners-of-war.

"I don't know, certainly," one of the Carters answered, "but I suppose he thinks his boat can go faster before the wind than the *Wave* can, and is counting on getting a long lead on her before he turns to come back. There is much more room up there, and the opportunities for dodging are about twice as good."

"Why didn't *we* think of that, Gus?" whispered the other Carter.

"We were too anxious to show what smart sailors we were, to think of anything!" answered his brother, ruefully.

Beyond the island the *Rover* gained rapidly; but, as soon as she turned and began beating homeward, the *Wave* showed that tacking was her strong point and began, in turn, to make up all the advantage the *Rover* had gained.

The *Rover's* pirate-king cast a troubled eye at the distant goal and at the slowly but steadily advancing *Wave*.

His younger brother noticed the look.

"If one could only *do* something," he exclaimed, impatiently. "That's the worst of sailing races. In a rowing race you can pull till you break your back, if you want to; but here you must just sit still and watch the other fellow creep up, inch by inch, without being able to do anything to help yourself. If I could only get out and push, or pole! It's this trying to keep still that drives me crazy."

"I think we'd better go about, now," said the commander quietly, "and instead of going about again when we are off the bar, I intend to try to cross it."

"What!" gasped the younger Prescott, "go across the bar at low water? You can't do it. You'll stick sure. Don't try it. Don't think of it!"

"It is rather a forlorn hope, I know," said his brother; "but you can see, yourself, they're bound to overhaul us if we keep on—we don't draw as much water as they do, and if they try to follow us we'll leave them high and dry on the bar."

The island stood in the center of the river, separated from the shore on one side by the channel, through which both boats had already passed, and on the other by a narrow stretch of water which barely covered the bar the *Rover* purposed to cross.

When she pointed for it, the *Wave* promptly gave up chasing her, and made for the channel with the intention of heading her off in the event of her crossing the bar.

"She's turned back!" exclaimed the captain of the *Rover*. "Now, if we only can clear it, we'll have a beautiful start on her. Sit perfectly still, and, if you hear her center-board scrape, pull it up, and balance so as to keep her keel level."

Slowly the *Rover* drifted toward the bar; once her center-board touched, and as the boat moved further into the shallow water the waves rose higher in proportion at the stern.

But her keel did not touch, and as soon as the dark water showed again, her crew gave an exultant shout and pointed her bow toward the Chadwick dock, whence a welcoming cheer came faintly over the mile of water.

"I'll bet they didn't cheer much when we were crossing the bar!" said the younger

brother, with a grim chuckle. "I'll bet they thought we were mighty foolish."

"We couldn't have done anything else," returned the superior officer. "It was risky, though. If we'd moved an inch she would have grounded sure."

"I was scared so stiff that I couldn't have moved if I'd tried to," testified the younger sailor with cheerful frankness.

Meanwhile, the wind had freshened, and whitecaps began to show over the roughened surface of the river, while sharp, ugly flaws struck the sails of the two contesting boats from all directions, making them bow before the sudden gusts of wind until the water poured over the sides.

But the sharpness of the wind made the racing only more exciting, and such a series of maneuvers as followed, and such a naval battle, was never before seen on the Manasquan River.

The boys handled their boats like veterans, and the boats answered every movement of the rudders and shortening of the sails as a thoroughbred horse obeys its bridle. They ducked and dodged, turned and followed in pursuit, now going free before the wind, now racing, close-hauled, into the teeth of it. Several times a capture seemed inevitable, but a quick turn of the tiller would send the pirates out of danger. And, as many times, the pirate crew almost succeeded in crossing the line, but before they could reach it the revenue cutter would sweep down upon them and frighten them away again.

"We can't keep this up much longer," said the elder Prescott. "There's more water in the boat now than is safe; and every time we go about we ship three or four bucketfuls more."

As he spoke, a heavy flaw keeled the boat over again, and, before her crew could right her, the water came pouring over the side with the steadiness of a small waterfall. "That settles it for us," exclaimed Prescott, grimly; "we *must* pass the line on this tack, or we sink."

"They're as badly off as we are," returned his brother. "See how she's wobbling—but she's gaining on us, just the same," he added.

"Keep her to it, then," said the man at the helm. "Hold on to that sheet, no matter how much water she ships."

"If I don't let it out a little, she'll sink!"

"Let her sink, then," growled the chief officer. "I'd rather upset than be caught."

The people on the shore and on the judges' boat appreciated the situation fully as well as the racers. They had seen, for some time, how slowly the boats responded to their rudders and how deeply they were sunk in the water.

All the maneuvering for the past ten minutes had been off the Chadwick dock, and the Atlantic House people, in order to get a better view of the finish, were racing along the bank on foot and in carriages, cheering their champions as they came.

The *Rover* was pointed to cross an imaginary line between the judges' steamlaunch and Chadwick's dock. Behind her, not three boat-lengths in the rear, so close that her wash impeded their headway, came the revenue officers, their white caps off, their hair flying in the wind, and every muscle strained.

Both crews were hanging far over the sides of the boats, while each wave washed the water into the already half-filled cockpits.

"Look out!" shouted the younger Prescott, "here comes another flaw!"

"Don't let that sail out!" shouted back his brother, and as the full force of the flaw struck her, the boat's rail buried itself in the water and her sail swept along the surface of the river.

For an instant it looked as if the boat was swamped, but as the force of the flaw passed over her, she slowly righted again, and with her sail dripping and heavy, and rolling like a log, she plunged forward on her way to the goal.

When the flaw struck the *Wave*, her crew let their sheet go free, saving themselves the inundation of water which had almost swamped the *Rover*, but losing the headway, which the *Rover* had kept.

Before the *Wave* regained it, the pirate craft had increased her lead, though it was only for a moment.

"We can't make it," shouted the younger Prescott, turning his face toward his brother so that the wind might not drown his voice. "They're after us again, and we're settling fast."

"So are they," shouted his brother. "We can't be far from the line now, and as soon as we cross that, it doesn't matter what happens to us!"

As he spoke another heavy gust of wind came sweeping toward them, turning the surface of the river dark blue as it passed over, and flattening out the waves.

"Look at that!" groaned the pirate-king, adding, with professional disregard for the Queen's English, "We're done for now, that's certain!" But before the flaw reached them, and almost before the prophetic words were uttered, the cannon on the judges' boat banged forth merrily, and the crowds on the Chadwick dock answered its signal with an unearthly yell of triumph.

"We're across, we're across!" shouted the younger Prescott, jumping up to his knees in the water in the bottom of the boat and letting the wet sheet-rope run freely through his stiff and blistered fingers.

But the movement was an unfortunate one.

The flaw struck the boat with her heavy sail dragging in the water, and with young Prescott's weight removed from the rail. She reeled under the gust as a tree bows in a storm, bent gracefully before it, and then turned over slowly on her side.

The next instant the *Wave* swept by her, and as the two Prescotts scrambled up on the gunwale of their boat the defeated crew saluted them with cheers, in response to which the victors bowed as gracefully as their uncertain position would permit.

The new arrival, who had come to Manasquan in the hope of finding something to shoot, stood among the people on the bank and discharged his gun until the barrels were so hot that he had to lay the gun down to cool. And every other man and boy who owned a gun or pistol of any sort, fired it off and yelled at the same time, as if the contents of the gun or pistol had entered his own body. Unfortunately, every boat possessed a tin horn with which the helmsman was wont to warn of his approach the keeper of the draw-bridge. One evil-minded captain blew a blast of triumph, and in a minute's time the air was rent with tootings little less vicious than those of the steam whistle of a locomotive.

The last had been so hard-fought a race, and both crews had acquitted themselves so well, that their respective followers joined in cheering them indiscriminately.

The *Wave* just succeeded in reaching the dock before she settled and sank. A dozen of Chadwick's boarders seized the crew by their coat-collars and arms as they leaped from the sinking boat to the pier and assisted them to their feet, forgetful in the excitement of the moment that the sailors were already as wet as sponges on their native rocks.

"I suppose I should have stuck to my ship as Prescott did," said the captain of the *Wave* with a smile, pointing to where the judges' boat was towing in the *Rover* with her crew still clinging to her side; "but I'd already thrown you my rope, you know, and there really isn't anything heroic in sticking to a sinking ship when she goes down in two feet of water."

As soon as the Prescotts reached the pier they pushed their way to their late rivals and shook them heartily by their hands. Then the Atlantic House people carried their crew around on their shoulders, and the two Chadwick's crews were honored in the same embarrassing manner. The proprietor of the Atlantic House invited the entire Chadwick establishment over to a dance and a late supper.

"I prepared it for the victors," he said, "and though these victors don't happen to be the ones I prepared it for, the victors must eat it."

The sun had gone down for over half an hour before the boats and carriages had left the Chadwick dock, and the Chadwick people had an opportunity to rush home to dress. They put on their very best clothes, "just to show the Atlantic people that they *had* something else besides flannels," and danced in the big hall of the Atlantic House until late in the evening.

When the supper was served, the victors were toasted and cheered and presented with a very handsome set of colors, and then Judge Carter made a stirring speech.

He went over the history of the rival houses in a way that pleased everybody, and made all the people at the table feel ashamed of themselves for ever having been rivals at all.

He pointed out in courtly phrases how excellent and varied were the modern features of the Atlantic House, and yet how healthful and satisfying was the old-fashioned simplicity of Chadwick's. He expressed the hope that the two houses would learn to appreciate each other's virtues, and hoped that in the future they would see more of each other.

To which sentiment everybody assented most noisily and enthusiastically, and the proprietor of the Atlantic House said that, in his opinion, Judge Carter's speech was one of the finest he had ever listened to, and he considered that part of it which touched on the excellent attractions of the Atlantic House as simply sublime, and that, with his Honor's permission, he intended to use it in his advertisements and circulars, with Judge Carter's name attached.

SERGEANT McTIGUE'S TWINS

By Lt. Charles Dudley Rhodes

November, 1900

To ONE who had once seen them together, there could be no question that they were twin brother and sister, so marvelous was the resemblance in height, form, feature, and even in voice. When quite small, and still in kilts, they had often been mistaken, the one for the other; and it had been a common occurrence to hear, "Please, sir, I'm not Billy, I'm Betty"; or, "I'm not a girl, sir. I'm Billy McTigue, not Betty!"—this with a touch of youthful indignation.

But the resemblance ended with their external characteristics, for their respective natures differed in a very marked degree. Betty was bold and aggressive, a leader in all that she undertook; Billy, timid, retiring, and painfully sensitive to ridicule.

Thus it was that when Tommy Bowen, the quartermaster-sergeant's little son, fell through the ice on the skating-pond, Betty alone had the presence of mind to push a board forward on the brittle ice, crawl out on it, and pull the struggling lad from the water, none the worse for the ducking. Billy had stood by, horror-stricken, and when the rescue was finally accomplished, was as white as the snow which covered the prairie.

Then there was the occasion when Bessie Scott, the adjutant's five-year-old, had run a nail in her tiny foot, Betty, without waiting for older counsels, had carefully hurried the little tot up to the post hospital, where the old surgeon had taken steps to prevent dangerous consequences. Billy meanwhile had run off to inform the adjutant, and between fright and loss of breath, had barely made himself understood.

All this had happened in the years when the twins were very small; but time had not changed the two natures in the least. Betty was a decidedly feminine little woman, and Billy a very sturdy little man, but every one said that Betty should have been a boy, and Billy a girl. One cannot account for some of Dame Nature's doings; perhaps the good old lady enjoys a little variety with the best of us. Be this as it may, despite the difference in the dispositions of the twins, their affection for each other was something it was wonderful and beautiful to behold.

None of the big boys had again dared to brave Betty's wrath, after the lecture she gave Jim Kerrigan, the ordnance-sergeant's boy, when he called Billy a "girl," and threw sand down his neck, on the way from school. And as Betty's womanly self-reliance developed more and more, while Billy's timidity and reticence daily increased, she acted the part of a mother to him—their own mother being too busy to look properly after them; and Betty's maternal solicitude for Billy's welfare was as amusing as it was touching.

And so they had grown up, before the eyes of the regiment, during the long sojourn in Arizona and New Mexico; and that soldier was a "Johnny-come-lately" who did not know all about Billy and Betty McTigue.

And now indeed had come an eventful time in the lives of the twins. Billy, having arrived at an age when his father thought he should be doing something in the world, had been enlisted as a trumpeter to Captain Cratty, in Troop M of "Ours," and a new life opened before him.

Betty, to be sure, did not at first favor a change which would take Billy away from

316

her care, but she was a practical little woman, and soon the reasons for the step commended themselves to her mind. Moreover, she was a soldier herself, heart and soul, and I believe she must often have envied Billy's opportunity to enlist, while she, being a girl, was debarred.

Billy had permission to visit his home at any time when not on duty, and in his neat and soldierly appearance could be recognized his twin-sister's handiwork. Never had Billy a button off his trim-fitting blouse; and such a thing as a spot on the army-blue trousers was something unheard of. Some of the "recruities" had once attempted to tease the boy about his shining trumpet, insinuating that Betty had even polished this for him; but Flathers and some of the older men had given the jokers such a talking to as precluded any further nonsense of that character.

Time went on apace, and a year had swiftly passed since Billy's enlistment. With a natural ear for music, he had learned his trumpet-calls well, and he blew them with sensitive appreciation of their beauty. The way he blew "taps" over the grave of poor Ned Kennedy is still remembered and talked about with feeling in the regiment.

But the boy shrank from the roughness of a soldier's life, and did not seem to take kindly to the atmosphere of the barrack-room. His natural timidity made him appear more and more reserved and undemonstrative; and among the men he was more than ever characterized, in private, as a "regular sissy."

"I believe if that boy'd see an Injun, he'd never stop a-runnin'," old Sergeant Jewett had said; and the time came when the veteran fully expected to see his prediction verified.

Spring was beginning, and with it came rumors of general restlessness at the Apache camp down on the Red Fork; and when, one night, a telegram came from the department commander, directing one troop of cavalry to be sent to Pinal to cut off some renegades who had bolted from the Agency, no one was very much surprised.

As luck would have it, the colonel selected M Troop to go, probably because it was the one longest from detached service of this character. Then, indeed, were there hurryings to and fro in the darkness between the barracks and stables, the drawing of field-rations, the packing of saddles and the loading of pack-mules, the saying of good-bys, and in a remarkably short time the troop was ready for service in the field.

But where was Billy? As Captain Cratty rode down the long line of men, "standing to horse" in front of the stables, he noticed that his trumpeter was not in his usual place behind him.

But while the troopers, left foot in stirrup, were waiting the final command to mount, up rode the familiar figure at a gallop, reining in his horse behind the captain so sharply as almost to throw the animal back on its haunches. Then, with trumpet unslung, he was just in time to give the final note which caused the long line to swing into saddle as one man. And as they successively wheeled by twos to the right, the captain and his diminutive trumpeter took their places at the head of the column, and the little command wound its way over the brown sand-hills toward the southwest, the straggling pack-mules following as fast as the experienced packers could urge them.

For an hour the column pushed on through the darkness, and then came a short halt to tighten girths and to give the horses a hearty drink from the creek—the last water in any abundance for some time to come; then ahead again for three hours with another halt. They should then, the captain thought, be near Bear Spring, where he intended to have a hasty breakfast prepared, where the smoke of the cook's fire could not be seen and would not give warning to the renegades miles away to the southwest.

Telling his trumpeter to follow, the troop commander spurred ahead to reconnoiter. Half a mile on the trail they turned abruptly to the left, a fainter trail leading straight up to the foot of a rocky butte, where, by the light of the moon just peeping over the foot-hills, could be seen the small spring which was to contribute to the troop's coffee.

The captain dismounted, and his trumpeter hastened to do likewise and hold his commander's horse. The latter, a high-strung, mettlesome Kentuckian, champed at his bit, not at all pleased with the change of proprietorship. Small wonder is it, then, that as the trumpeter turned his back on the animal, and peered anxiously down the long slope in the direction of the column, the thoroughbred should suddenly seize the yielding campaign-hat in his strong white teeth, and with a proud toss of his head, fling it high in the air.

One sudden shriek, which, strangely enough, sounded suspiciously feminine, and the trumpeter made haste to find the lost head-covering. But an authoritative "Trumpeter!" from the captain brought the soldier to attention in an instant, and then—Captain Cratty saw that it was not Billy at all. But there before him in the moonlight stood Betty, her eyes cast down, and her long golden hair, which had been knotted up under the campaign-hat, flowing over the shoulders of her blue blouse—as natty a young trumpeter as ever wore the uniform.

"Why, Betty!—what on earth are you doing here?" exclaimed the captain.

A sob was the only answer, and the bluff old trooper thought to himself that here, indeed, was a pretty state of things. But he had daughters of his own, and the soft place in his big heart softened still more as he took the bridles from the trembling girl with a kindness which was not without its effect.

"O, Captain!" Betty stammered, "I thought you would never know me and—and I thought it would save Billy from disgrace, and—and, oh, I am *so* disappointed!" And covering her face with her gauntleted hands, she sobbed and sobbed.

"Come, come, Betty, there's no harm done, I am sure; and no one shall know of it. So stop your crying, child, and tell me all about it."

"Well, sir," began Betty, gradually drying her eyes and plucking up courage, "when the order came for the troop to go out, I bustled about and got Billy's field-clothes ready for him—he always leaves them at the house; and—and when Billy didn't come to get ready, I was just frantic for fear he'd miss going. And at last, when I'd wondered and wondered where he could be, I stole up to his old room, and there, stretched out on the bed—oh, Captain, you won't ever tell any one!—was Billy, so white and scared-looking that he was all of a tremble. And I stole away again, and he never knew I had seen him. But how sorry I felt for him! He really isn't a coward, Captain; he just can't help it. Indeed, he's always been that way. And I thought if I could get away with the troop I could take Billy's place. I can blow the trumpet nearly as well as he can, and—surely, Captain, you wouldn't send me back now!"

The brave young face looked very determined as she looked beseechingly into the tall trooper's face.

"Why, Betty, you certainly cannot remain with us. You ought to know that. We may be gone for months, and may have to fight these renegades very, very soon. You can do Billy infinitely more good by going back, and sending him on to join us at once. If he doesn't come he will be court-martialed, whether you go in his place or not."

This argument had an immediate effect on Betty, who dried her eyes, and picking up the broad-brimmed campaign-hat, carefully tucked away her long locks again beneath its capacious crown.

"I'll go back, sir," she said bravely. "I never thought of it in just that way."

"Spoken like a soldier," exclaimed the captain. "Now, take this side trail off to the right, and you will avoid meeting the troop. Push along hard and fast, so that you may reach the post and see Billy by daylight. Quick, now! the troop will be here in a few moments." And the officer waved her toward her horse. "Above all things, make that brother of yours reach us before we arrive at Pinal!"

Then with "Good night, sir"—"Good night, Betty, and good luck to you," Betty's horse, holding its nose high in air as it heard the approaching troop, went galloping back with her toward the far-away army post.

A tin cup of coffee all around—hot, though a trifle weak—bacon and hard bread in plenty, and the troop was again ready for the march, and, if necessary, for a fight.

An hour later, as the column crossed a little valley, and began the ascent of the steep trail on the opposite side, the troop-commander glanced over his shoulder, and looked back. What was his amazement to see a mounted horseman speeding at a gallop across the sandy expanse, a glittering trumpet shining in the moonlight as it swung from the cord about the rider's body.

The captain was perplexed. Betty returning contrary to orders? No; she was too good a soldier to disobey; perhaps, indeed, she had met with some accident. Nevertheless, the troop did not stop, but, arrived at the top of the rugged slope, pushed on across the barren mesa. Ten, fifteen, twenty minutes passed, and then, galloping up past the troop to his place at the head, halting only after saluting his captain, came the trumpeter. It was the same horse surely, but on him was none other than the long-looked-for Billy. The captain and he rode to the front; and the officer saw so much shame, contrition, and suffering on the boy's face, that he had not the heart to reproach him.

"I haven't a word to say, sir," began Billy, impulsively. "I deserve a court-martial if any one ever did; but do, Captain, give me one more chance. I *was* afraid to start—it's born in me, I guess. And I *did* hide from the men, like the coward that I was. And then, when I at last discovered that Betty had taken my extra field-uniform, I began to suspect; and, afterward, when I found both horse and trumpet gone, it all dawned upon me, and made me almost too ashamed to live. So without letting a soul know, I jumped on an extra horse, and followed the troop as hard as I could ride. Over the butte there I met Betty riding back, and she gave me the horse and trumpet."

"Let this be a lesson, Billy," said Captain Cratty, solemnly; for he felt that the boy needed no other punishment than the shame which his own weakness had caused.

"I really don't think, sir," Billy continued, after a moment's pause, "that I am a coward at heart—only I couldn't help feeling the most awful dread when I heard of our order to cut off those Apaches." A smothered sob shook the boy's frame—he was very young.

"There, there, boy, cheer up! The future is before you, and no one shall ever know of your neglect of duty. Drop back to your place now; and if we do meet those Apaches, think of the brave sister who all but went in your place."

Belly fell back to his place among the men, who fully believed that he had been with the command throughout the night; and as the dawning light made objects more and more distinct, their thoughts were fixed on the probability of cutting off the renegades, or were busy with the question whether it would be necessary to pursue them into the fastnesses of the Sierra Madre.

And so they rode, a thin, black line on that landscape of red cliffs and brown plains; riding where the dust would not rise to betray their approach—behind hills, through cañons and ravines, and around precipitous bluffs, silently, and still more silently as the day began to dawn.

And near the head rode a boy, with a dancing trumpet slung from the shoulder, and at his hip an army revolver as large as his forearm. His drab campaign-hat was pulled well over his eyes, for he was heart-heavy; but there was determination in the way he sat the saddle, and a world of resolution in his firm pressed lips.

The little army post was bathed in summer sunshine. The grasshoppers buzzed across the parade with a lazy uncertainty of purpose, characteristic of the day, the hot glare from the adobe buildings wearied the eye, and the post-flag hung limp as a rag from the tall staff in front of the guard-house.

"Number One" felt sleepy, decidedly sleepy, as he tramped back and forth on the guard-house porch, and the carbine on his shoulder leaned in a comfortable way toward the horizontal. The old sergeant in charge of the guard, seated on the bench in the shade of the wall, was the first one to see a mounted courier as he cautiously picked his way down the narrow trail leading from the San Michel; and as he afterward sped across the plain toward the post like one possessed. The sergeant sprang to his feet, and at the sound "Number One" wakened to a perceptible interest in things around him.

"Trumpeter Kerrigan," the veteran thundered to an individual within the building, "run across to headquarters, and report to the adjutant that a courier from Captain Cratty is coming down the San Michel trail. Off with ye now, as fast your legs can carry ye!"

The trumpeter hurried away, and the guard poured forth from the guard-room to get a look at the distant horseman. Except when hidden now and then by the lay of the land, the horseman could be plainly seen galloping across the long stretch of level toward the south.

And on her fleet little pony, Betty was at that very time racing toward the approaching courier. For had she not all day been watching that far-away niche in the hills where the trail led over the divide, with the pony saddled and waiting in the little shed behind the house? And was it not Betty herself who learned from Sergeant Jewett all the details of the fight, a good half-hour before even the colonel and his adjutant?

We struck the Apaches [so the despatch briefly ran] at Gallisteo Cañon—a larger party than was reported from Department Headquarters. Three Indians are killed, and one mortally wounded. Three escaped, and are being pursued by Lieutenant Murlin with troop, toward the Nutria. Our casualties consist of Sergeant Sullivan, wounded in shoulder; and myself, bullet through thigh, received while imprudently reconnoitering ahead of troop. Both of us doing well. Trumpeter McTigue behaved with great gallantry—without a doubt saving my life under fire. Request ambulance to be sent at once.

CRATTY.

And Betty, too jubilant to remain long in one place, moved about hither and thither, with joy in her heart, and Billy's beloved name ever upon her lips.

It all came out later in the oral report of Captain Cratty, who, with Sergeant Sullivan, was carried into the post a day or two later, in the Red Cross ambulance. The troop had cut the trail of the renegades at Pinal, and, turning abruptly to the left, had pushed hard after them into the hilly country, the trail becoming fresher and fresher with each succeeding mile that they urged their jaded horses. When the command reached Gallisteo Cañon the pace was made slower on account of numerous obstacles, and Captain Cratty, telling his trumpeter to follow, had trotted ahead of the main party, hoping from the cañon's mouth to secure, through his field-glasses, a view of the Indians on the plain beyond.

Suddenly a volley of bullets from the rocks on each side had come rattling down upon them without warning. The captain and his horse, both pierced by the same bullet, had rolled over together, the animal in his agony plunging and kicking. Without an instant's hesitation, Billy had pulled his commander away from the struggling horse, and, in the twinkling of an eye, had helped him on his own frightened but uninjured steed. The officer, too weak to do aught but grasp the pommel of the saddle, shouted to the boy to save himself. But Billy, seizing the reins, had led the horse up the cañon at a run, the bullets flying about them like hail, until a projecting rock interposed. One bullet had clipped the edge of the saddle, and another had ruined forever Billy's handsome brass trumpet; but the captain was saved, even if he had received a flesh wound in the thigh.

The Indians did not wait to try conclusions with the rapidly approaching troops (they had hoped to throw the party into confusion by killing its commander), but jumped on their ponies, and made off. The latter, however, ill-fed and worn out by the long flight from the Agency, could not outstrip the trooper's comparatively fresh horses. So that on the rocky hill-tops some of the Indians were overtaken—the troopers jumping from their horses, and, carbine in hand, continuing the chase on foot. In this way, as has already been mentioned, four of the renegades had been killed or wounded, and three had escaped over the Mexican line into the Sierra Madre.

Six months later (for the mills of the government grind slowly) a medal of honor reached the little Arizona army post from far-away Washington; and in front of the entire command, one evening at dress-parade, it was pinned by the colonel on the breast of Trumpeter McTigue. And the order announcing it stated that it was presented to

> Trumpeter William McTigue, Troop M, 11th Cavalry, who at the risk of his life rescued his wounded captain from under fire of hostile Apaches, at Gallisteo Cañon, Arizona, May 20, 18–.

And Captain Cratty, leaning on his cane by the gate at Quarters No. 10, knew what no one else knew, except Billy and Betty; for he knew that Billy might never have become thus distinguished, had it not been for the brave little heroine who stood at his side witnessing the ceremony with a heart overflowing with joy and pride. But the old cavalryman wished with all his heart that Betty, too, might have shared in the honor she so well deserved. And he knew if the matter had been placed in his hands, in short order there would have been *twin* medals of honor for the McTigue twins.

THE DOZEN FROM LAKERIM.

By Rupert Hughes
(Author of *The Lakerim Athletic Club*)

May, 1899

You may not find the town of Lakerim on the map in your geography. And yet it was very well known to the people who lived in it. And the Lakerim Athletic Club also was very well known to them. And the Lakerim Athletic Club, or at least the twelve founders of the club, were as blue as the June sky, because it seemed to them that Father Time—old Grandaddy Longlegs that he is—was "playing a mean trick" upon them.

For hadn't they given all their brain and muscle to building up an athletic club that should be a credit to the town and a terror to outsiders? And hadn't they given up every free hour for two years to working like Trojans? Though, for that matter, who ever heard of any work the Trojans ever did that amounted to anything—except the spending of ten years in getting themselves badly defeated by a big wooden hobby-horse?

But while all of the Dozen were deep in the dumps, and had their brows tied up like a neglected fish-line, the loudest complaint was made, of course, by the one who had done the least work in building up the club—a lazy-bones who had been born tired, and had spent most of his young life

in industriously earning for himself the name of "Sleepy."

"It's a shame," growled he, "for you fellows to go and leave the club in the lurch this way, after all the trouble we have had organizing it."

"Yes," assented another, who was called "B. J." because he had jumped from a high bridge once too often, and who read more wild Western romances than was good for his peace of mind or his conversation; "it looks as if you fellows were renegades to the cause."

None of the Twelve knew exactly what a renegade was, and so, although it sounded unpleasant, the men to whom the term was applied did not lose their tempers, and the debate went on in a peaceful manner.

The trouble with this: Some of you who are up on the important works of history may have heard how these twelve youth of the High School at Lakerim organized themselves into an athletic club that won many victories, and how they begged, borrowed, and earned enough money to build themselves a club-house after a year of hard work and harder play.

Well, now, after they had gone to all this trouble and expense, and had enjoyed the fruits of their labors barely a year, lo and behold, one third of the Dozen were planning to desert the club, leave the town, and take their good muscles to another town, where there was an academy! The worst of it was that this academy was the very one that had worked hardest to keep the Lakerim Athletic Club from being admitted into the league known as the Tri-State Interscholastic.

And now that the Lakerim Club had forced its way into the League, and had won the pennant the very first year, it seemed hard that some of the most valuable of the Lakerimmers should even consider joining forces with their rival. The president of the club himself was one of the deserters; and the rest of the Dozen grew very bitter, and the arguments often reached a point where it needed only one word more to bring on a scrimmage—a scrimmage that would make a lively football game seem tame by comparison.

And now the president, or "Tug," as he was always called, had been "baited" long enough. He rose to his feet and proceeded to deliver an oration with all the fervor of a Fourth-of-July orator.

"I want you fellows to understand once for all," he cried, "that no one loves the Lakerim Athletic Club more than I do, or is more patriotic toward it. But now that I have graduated from the High School, I can't consider that I know everything that is to be known. There are one or two things to learn yet, and I intend to go to a preparatory school, and then through college; and the best thing you fellows can do is to make your plans to do the same thing. Well, now, seeing that my mind is made up to go to college, and seeing that I've got to go to some preparatory school, and seeing there is no preparatory school in Lakerim, and seeing that I must therefore go to some other town, and seeing that at Kingston

there is a fine preparatory school, and seeing that the Athletic Association of the Kingston Academy has been kind enough specially to invite three of us fellows to go there and has promised to give us an especially good show on the athletic team, why, seeing all this, I don't see that there is any kick coming to you fellows if we three fellows take advantage of our opportunities like sensible people; and the best advice I can give you is to make up your minds, and make up your father's and mothers' minds, to come along to Kingston Academy with us. Then there won't be any talk about our being traitors to the Dozen, for we'll just pick the Dozen up bodily and carry it over to Kingston! The new members we've elected can take care of the club and the club-house."

Tug sat down amid a silence that was more complimentary than the wildest applause; for he had done what few orators do: he had set his audience to thinking. Only one of the Twelve had a remark to make for some time, and that was a small-framed, big-spectacled gnome called "History." He leaned over and said to his elbow-companion, "Bobbles":

"Tug is a regular Demoserenes!"

"Who's Demoserenes?" whispered Bobbles.

"Why, don't you remember Demoserenes?" said History, proudly.

The fate of the Dozen was a still more serious matter, because the Dozen had existed before the club or the club-house, and their hearts ached at the mere thought of breaking up the old and dear associations that had grown up around their partnership in many an hour of victory and defeat.

But where there are many souls there are many minds, and it seemed impossible to keep the Twelve together for another year. It was settled that Tug and Jumbo and Punk should accept the invitation of the

Kingston Athletic Association, and their parents were glad to pay their expenses, knowing the high standing of Kingston among preparatory schools.

History was also sure to go, for his learning had won him a free scholarship in a competitive examination. "B.J.," "Quiz," and "Bobbles" were to be sent to other academies—to Charleston, to Troy, and to Greenville; but they made life miserable for their fathers and mothers by their pleadings, until they, too, were permitted to join their fellows at Kingston.

Sleepy was the only one who did not want to go, and he insisted that he had learned all that was necessary for his purpose in life; that he simply could not endure the thought of laboring over books any longer. But just as the Dozen had resigned themselves to losing the companionship of Sleepy (he was a good man to crack jokes about, if for no other purpose), Sleepy's parents announced to him that his decision was not final, and that, whether or not he wanted to go, go he should. And then there were eight.

The handsome and fashionable young "Dozener," known to his friends as Edward Parker, and to fame as "Pretty," was won over with much difficulty. He had completely made up his mind to attend the Troy Latin School—not because he loved Latin, but because Troy was the seat of much social gaiety. He was, however, at length cajoled into consenting to pitch his tent at Kingston. And then there were nine.

The Phillips twins, "Reddy" and "Heady," were the next source of trouble, for they had recently indulged in an unusually violent squabble, even for them, and each had vowed that he would never speak to the other again, and would sooner die than go to the same boarding school. The father of this fiery couple knew that the boys really loved each other dearly at the bottom of their hearts, and decided to teach them how much they truly cared for each other; so he yielded to their prayer that they be allowed to go to different academies. The boys, in high glee, tossed up a penny to decide which should go with the Dozen to Kingston, and which should go to the Brownsville School for Boys. Reddy won Kingston, and rejoiced greatly. But though Heady was very "blue," as he expressed it, over his enforced separation from "the fellows," yet nothing could persuade him to "tag along after his brother," as he phrased it. And so there were ten.

The deepest grief of the Dozen was the plight of the beloved giant, "Sawed-Off." There seemed to be no possible way of getting him to Kingston, much as they thought of his big muscles, and more as they thought of his big heart. His sworn pal, the tiny Jumbo, was well-nigh distracted at the thought of severing their two knitted souls; but Sawed-Off's father was dead, and his mother was too poor to pay for his schooling, so they mournfully gave him up for lost.

Heady was the first to leave town. He slipped away on an early morning train without telling any one, for he felt very much ashamed of his stubbornness; and he and his brother shook hands with each other very nervously.

A few days later the five sixths of the Dozen that were booked for Kingston stood on the crowded platform of the Lakerim railroad station, bidding good-by to all the parents they had, and all the friends.

Just as the engine began to ring its warning bell, and the conductor to wave the people aboard, there was a loud clatter of hoofs, and the rickety old Lakerim carryall came dashing up, drawn by the lively horses Sawed-Off had once saved from destroying themselves and the Dozen in one fell swoop down a steep hill. The carryall lurched up to the station, came to a sudden stop, and out bounced—who but Sawed-Off himself, loaded down with bundles, and yelling at the top of his voice:

"Stop the train and wait for me! I'm going to Kingston, too!"

There was just time to dump his trunk in the baggage-car, and bundle him and his bundles on to the platform, before the train steamed away; and the eleven Lakerimmers were so busy waving farewell to the crowd at the station that it was some minutes before they could find time to ask Sawed-Off how he came to be among them. When he explained that he had made arrangements to work his way through the Academy, they took no thought for the hard struggle before him, they were so glad to have him along. Jumbo and he sat with their arms around each other all the way to Kingston, their hearts too full for anything but an occasional "Hooray!"

The journey to Kingston brought no adventures with it—except that History, of course, had lost his spectacles and his ticket, and had to borrow money of Pretty to keep from being put off the train, and that when they reached Kingston they came near forgetting Sleepy entirely, for he had curled up in a seat, and was in his usual state of harmless slumber.

It might be useful to insert here a little sketch of Kingston Academy. The town itself was a drowsy old village that claimed a thousand inhabitants, but could never have mustered that number without counting in all the sleepy horses, mules, cows, and pet dogs that roamed the streets as freely as the other inhabitants. The chief industry of the people of Kingston seemed to be that of selling school-books, mince-pies, and other necessaries of life to the boys at the Academy. The grown young men of the town spent their lives in trying to get away to some other cities. The younger youth of the town spent their lives trying to interfere with the pleasures of the Kingston academicians. So there were many of the old-time "town-and-gown" squabbles; and it was well for the comfort of the Kingston Academy boys that they rarely went around town except in groups of two or three; and it was very bad for the comfort of any of the town fellows if they happened to be caught within the Academy grounds.

The result of being situated in a half-dead village, which was neither loved nor loving, did not make life at the Academy tame, but quite the opposite; for the boys were forced to find their whole entertainment in the Academy life, and in one another, and the campus was therefore a little republic in itself—a Utopia. Like every other republic, it had its cliques and its struggles, its victories and its defeats, its friendships and its enmities, and everything else that makes life lively and lifelike.

The campus was beautiful enough and large enough to accommodate its citizens handsomely. Its trees were many and tall, venerable old monarchs with foliage-like tents for shade and comfort to any little groups that cared to lounge upon the mossy divans beneath.

The school-grounds were spacious enough to furnish not only football and baseball fields and tennis-courts, but meadows where wild flowers grew in the spring, and a little lake where the ice grew in the winter. Miles away—just enough to make a good "Sabbath-day's journey"—was a wonderful region called the "Ledges," where glaciers had once resided, and left huge boulders, scratched and scarred. As Jumbo put it, it seemed, from the chasms and caves and curious distortions of stone and soil, that "nature must once have had a fit there."

But this is more than enough description,

and you must imagine for yourselves how the Lakerim eleven, often as they thought of home, and homesick as they were in spite of themselves now and then, rejoiced in being thrown on their own resources, and made somewhat independent citizens in a little country of their own. Unwilling to make selections among themselves, more unwilling to select room-mates from the other students (the "foreigners," as the Lakerimmers called them), the eleven drew lots for each other, and the lots decided that they should room together thus: Tug and Punk were on the ground floor of the building known as South College, in room No. 2; in the room just over them were Quiz and Pretty; and on the same floor, at the back of the building, were Bobbles and Reddy. Reddy insisted upon this room because it had a third bedroom off its study-room; while, of course, he never expected to see Heady there, and didn't much care, of course, whether he came or not, "still, a fellow never can tell, you know." On the same floor were B. J. and Jumbo. Jumbo did not stoop to flatter B. J. by pretending that he would not have preferred Sawed-Off for his room-mate; but Sawed-Off was working his way through, and the principal of the Academy had offered to help him out not only with a free scholarship, but with a free room, as well, in Middle College, an old building which had the gymnasium on the first floor, the chapel on the second, and in the loft a single store-room fixed up as a bedroom.

The lots the fellows drew seemed to be in a joking mood when they selected History and Sleepy for room-mates—the hardest student and the laziest, not only of the Dozen, but of the whole Academy. Sleepy had been too lazy to pay much heed when the diplomatic History had suggested their choosing room No. 13 for theirs, and he assented languidly. History had said that it was the brightest and sunniest room in the building, and if there was one thing that Sleepy loved almost better than baseball, it was a good snooze in the sun after any one of the three meals. His disappointment was keen, however, when he learned that the room chosen by the wily History was on the top floor, with three long flights to climb. After that you could never convince him that thirteen was not an unlucky number.

The Lakerimmers had thus managed quietly to ensconce themselves, all except Sawed-Off, in one building; and it was just as well, perhaps, that they did so establish themselves in a stronghold of their own, for they clung together so steadfastly that there was soon a deal of jealousy among the other students toward them, and all the factions combined together to try to keep the Lakerimmers from any of the good things of academy life.

There was a deal of skylarking the first few weeks after the school opened. Almost every day some of the Lakerimmers would come back from his classes to find his room "stacked"—a word that exactly expresses its meaning. There is something particularly discouraging in going to your room late in the evening, your mind made up to a comfortable hour of reading on a divan covered with cushions made by your home folks, only to find the divan placed in the middle of the bed, with a bureau and a bookcase stuck on top of it, a few chairs and a pet bulldog tied in the middle of the mix-up, and a mirror and a well-filled bowl of water so fixed on the top of the heap that it is well-nigh impossible to move any one of the articles without cracking the looking-glass or dousing yourself with the water. The Lakerimmers tried retaliation for a time; but the pleasure of stacking another man's room was not half so great as the misery of unstacking one's own room, and they finally decided to keep two or three of the men always on guard in the building.

There was a deal of hazing, too, the first few weeks; and as the Lakerimmers were all new men in the Academy, they were considered particularly good candidates for various degrees of torment. Hazing was strictly against the rules of the Academy, but the teachers could not be everywhere at once, and had something to do besides prowl around the dark corners of the campus at all hours of the night. Some of the men furiously resisted the efforts to haze them; but when they once learned that their efforts were vain, and had perforce to submit, none of them were mean enough to peach on their tormentors after the damage was done. The Lakerimmers, however, decided to resist force with force, and stuck by one another so closely, and barricaded their doors so firmly at night, when they must necessarily separate, that time went on without any of them being subjected to any other indignities than the guying of the other Kingstonians.

Sawed-Off had so much and such hard work to do after school-hours that the whole Academy respected him too much to attempt to haze him, though he roomed alone in the old Middle College. Besides, his size was such that nobody cared to be the first one to lay hand on him.

There was just one blot on the happiness of the Dozen at Kingston. Tug and Punk and Jumbo had started the whole migration from Lakerim because they had been invited by the Kingston Athletic Association to join forces with the Academy. The magnificent game of football these three men had played in the last two years had been the cause of this invitation, and they had come with glowing dreams of new worlds to conquer. What was their pain and disgust to find that the captain of the Kingston team, elected before they came, had decided that he had good cause for jealousy of Tug, and had concluded that, since Tug

would probably win all his old laurels away from him if he once admitted him to the eleven, the only way to retain those laurels was to keep Tug off the team. When the Lakerim three, therefore, appeared on the field as candidates for the eleven, they were assigned to the second or scrub team. (The first team was generally called the "varsity," though of course it represented only an academy.)

The Lakerim three, though disappointed at first, determined to show their respect for discipline, and to earn their way; so they submitted meekly, and played the best game they could on the scrub. When the varsity captain, Clayton by name, criticized their playing in a way that was brutal—not because it was frank, but because it was unjust—they stood this injustice as quietly as they could, and went back into the game determined not to repeat the slip that had brought upon them such a deluge of blame.

It soon became evident, however, from the way Clayton neglected the mistakes of the pets of his own eleven, and his constant and petty fault-finding with the three Lakerimmers, that he was determined to keep them from the varsity team, even if he had to keep second-rate players on the team, and even if he imperiled the Academy's chances against rival elevens.

When this unpleasant truth had finally soaked into their minds, the Lakerimmers grew very solemn; and one evening, when the whole scrub eleven happened to be in room No. 2, and when the hosts, Tug and Punk, were particularly sore from the outrageous language used against them in the practice of the afternoon, Punk who was rather easily discouraged, spoke up:

"I guess the only thing for us to do, fellows, is to pack up our duds and go back home. There's no chance for us here."

Tug, who was feeling rather "muggy," only growled:

"Not if I know it! I had rather be a yellow dog than a quitter. I've got a better idea," he said, "and one that will do us more credit. I'll tell you what I'm going to do: I am going to take this matter into my own hands, and drill that scrub team myself, and see if we can't teach the varsity a thing or two. I believe that, with a little practice and a little good sense, we can shove 'em off the earth."

This struck the fellows as the proper and the Lakerim method of doing things, and they responded with a cheer. Tug persuaded Reddy, B. J., Pretty, and Bobbles, who had not been trying for the team, to come out on the field. He even coaxed the busy Sawed-Off into postponing some of his work for a few days to help them out. He thus had almost the old Lakerim eleven at his command; and that very night, in that very room, they concocted and practised a few secret tricks and a few surprises for Clayton, who was neither very fertile in invention nor very quick to understand the schemes of others.

Clayton was too sure of his own position and power to pay any heed to the storm that was brewing for him, and was only too glad to see on the scrub team a few more representatives of the Lakerim men for him to abuse.

Tug did not put into play the whole strength of his eleven, but practised cautiously, and instructed his team in the few ruses Clayton seemed to be fond of. Tug was looking forward to the occasion when a complete game was to be played, before the townspeople, between the varsity and the scrub; and Clayton was looking forward to this same day, and promising himself a great triumph when the Academy and the town should see what a rattling eleven he had made up.

The day came. The whole Academy and most of the town turned out and filled the grand stand and the space along the side lines. It was to be the first full game of the season on the Academy grounds, and every one was eager to renew acquaintance with the excitements of the fall before. It is too warm weather now to describe a football game at any length, and you have doubtless seen and read about more games than enough, and you will be glad to skip the details of this contest. It will be unnecessary to do more than suggest how Clayton was simply dumfounded when he saw his first long kick-off caught by the veteran fullback Punk, and carried forward with express speed under the protection of Tug's men, who were not satisfied with merely running in front of Clayton's tacklers, but bunted into them and bowled them over with a spine-jolting vigor, and covered Punk from attack on the rear, and carried him across the center line and well on into Clayton's territory before Clayton, realizing that several of his pets were mere "straw men," had dashed violently and madly into and through Punk's interference, and downed him on the 15-yard line; how the spectators looked on in silent amazement at this unexpected beginning; how promptly Tug's men were lined up, a broad swath opened with one quick gash in Clayton's line, and the ball shoved through and within five yards of the goal-post, almost before Clayton knew it was in play; how Clayton called his men to one side, and rebuked them, and told them just what to do, and found, to his disgust, that when they had done it, it was just the wrong thing to do; how they could not hold the line against the fury of the scrub team; how the ball was jammed across the line right under the goal-posts, and Clayton's head well whacked against one of these same posts as he was swept off his feet; how Tug's men on the line were taught to avoid foolish attempts to worry their opponents, and taught to reserve their strength for the supreme moment when the call came to split the line; how Sawed-Off, though lighter than Clayton's huge 200-pound center, had more than mere bulk to commend him, and tipped the huge baby over at just the right moment; how Tug now and then followed a series of plain football manoeuvers with some unexpected trick that carried the ball far down the field around one end, when Clayton was scrambling after it in the wrong place; how Tug had perfected his interference until the man carrying the ball seemed almost as safe as if Clayton's men were Spaniards, and he were in the turret of the U.S.S. *Oregon;* how little time Tug's men lost in getting away after the ball had been passed to them; how little they depended on "grand stand" plays by the individual, and how much on team-work; how Tug's men went through Clayton's interference as neatly as a fox through a hedge; how they resisted Clayton's mass plays as firmly as harveyized steel; how Clayton fumed and fretted and "slugged" and fouled, and threatened his men, and called them off to hold conferences that only served to give Tug's men a chance to get their wind after some violent play; how Tug was everywhere at once, and played for more than the pleasure of winning this one game—played as if he were a pair of twins, and only smiled back when Clayton glared at him; how Punk headed off and garnered in the longest punts the varsity fullback could make, and how he kicked the goal after all but one of the many touch-downs the scrub team made; how little Jumbo, as quarter-back, passed the ball with never a fumble and never a bad throw; how, when it came back to his hands, he skimmed almost as closely and as silently and as swiftly over the ground as the shadow of a flying bird, and made long run after long run that won the cheers of the crowd; how

B. J., Sawed-Off, and Pretty, as right-end, center and left-end, responded at just the right moment, and how Pretty dodged and ran with the alertness he had learned in many a championship tennis tournament; and how Reddy, as left half-back, flew across the field like a firebrand, or hurled himself into the line with a fury that seemed to have no regard for the bones or flesh of himself or the Claytonians; how—but did any one ever read such a string of "hows"? I vow this sentence is getting to be longer and more complicated than the game it is pretending not to describe; so here's an end on't, with the plain statement that the game resulted in a victory of 34 to 4 for the scrub team, and that the headlines of the Kingston weekly paper read thus:

SCRUB ELEVEN BEATS THE VARSITY

Kingston Football Team Meets with a Crushing Defeat at the Hands of the Second Eleven.

SCORE, 34 to 4

VARSITY OUTPLAYED AT EVERY POINT

Popular Opinion Forces Captain Clayton to Resign in Favor of "Tug" Robinson.

KINGSTON TEAM TO BE COMPLETELY REORGANIZED

Mr. Robinson Declares that Favoritism will have no Part in the Make-up of the New Team, and Magnanimously Offers Ex-Captain Clayton a Position on the New Eleven.

There is no need telling here the wild emotions in the hearts of Clayton and his faction at the end of the game, and no need of even hinting the wilder delight of the Lakerimmers at the vindication of their cause. The whole eleven of them strolled home in one grand embrace, and used their jaws more for talking than for eating when they reached the long-delayed meal at the boarding-house, and after supper met again at the fence, and sang Lakerim songs of rejoicing, and told and retold to one another the different features of the game, which they all knew without the telling. So much praise was heaped upon Tug by the rest of the Academy, and he was so fêted by the Lakerimmers, that he finally slipped away and went to his room. And little History also bade them good night, on his usual excuse of having to study.

It was very dark before the Lakerimmers had talked themselves tired. Then they voted to go around and congratulate Tug once more upon his victory, and give him three cheers for the sake of auld lang syne. When they went to his room, they were amazed to see the door swinging open and shut in the breeze; they noted that the lock was torn off. They hurried in, and found one of the windows broken, and books and chairs scattered around in confusion; the mantel and cloth and the photographs on it were all awry. It was evident that a fierce struggle had taken place in the room. The nine Lakerimmers stood aghast, staring at one another in stupefaction. Reddy was the first to find tongue, and he cried out:

"I know what's up, fellows: the hazers have got him!"

Now there was an excitement indeed. Punk suggested that perhaps he might be in History's room, and Bobbles scaled the three flights three steps at a time, only to return with a wild look, and declare that History's room was empty, his lock broken, and his student-lamp smoking. Plainly the hazing committee had lost no time in seizing its first opportunity. Plainly the Lakerimmers must lose no time in hurrying to the rescue.

"Up and after 'em, men!" cried B. J.; and, trying to remember what was the proper thing for an old Indian scout to do under the circumstances he started off on a dead run, and the others followed him into the night.

THE CRUISE OF THE *DAZZLER*

By Jack London

July, 1902

This story suggests most forcefully the effect that Jack London's reading of "The Cruise of the Pirate-Ship *Moonraker*," by F. Marshall White, had upon his career. Jack read it in a bound volume of *St. Nicholas* for November, 1884. After he read it, Jack stopped being a bay pirate and offered his services to the state fish-patrol. Ten years later his own story, "The Cruise of the *Dazzler*," appeared in *St. Nicholas*.

CHAPTER I

'FRISCO KID, AND THE NEW BOY

'FRISCO KID was discontented—discontented and disgusted; though this would have seemed impossible to the boys who fished from the dock above and envied him mightily. He frowned, got up from where he had been sunning himself on the top of the *Dazzler*'s cabin, and kicked off his heavy rubber boots. Then he stretched himself on the narrow side-deck and dangled his feet in the cool salt water.

"Now, that's freedom," thought the boys who watched him. Besides, those long sea-boots, reaching the hips and buckled to the leather strap about the waist, held a strange and wonderful fascination for them. They did not know that 'Frisco Kid did not possess such things as shoes; that the boots were an old pair of Pete Le Maire's and were three sizes too large for him; nor could they guess how uncomfortable they were to wear on a hot summer day.

The cause of 'Frisco Kid's discontent was those very boys who sat on the string-piece and admired him; but his disgust was the result of quite another event. Further, the *Dazzler* was short one in its crew, and he had to do more work than was justly his share. He did not mind the cooking, nor the washing down of the decks and the pumping; but when it came to the paint-scrubbing and dish-washing, he rebelled. He felt that he had earned the right to be exempt from such scullion work. That was all the green boys were fit for; while he could make or take in sail, lift anchor, steer, and make landings.

"Stan' from un'er!" Pete Le Maire, captain of the *Dazzler* and lord and master of 'Frisco Kid, threw a bundle into the cockpit and came aboard by the starboard rigging.

"Come! Queeck!" he shouted to the boy who owned the bundle, and who now hesitated on the dock. It was a good fifteen feet to the deck of the sloop, and he could not reach the steel stay by which he must descend.

"Now! One, two, three!" the Frenchman counted good-naturedly, after the manner of all captains when their crews are short-handed.

The boy swung his body into space and gripped the rigging. A moment later he struck the deck, his hands tingling warmly from the friction.

"Kid, dis is ze new sailor. I make your

acquaintance." Pete smirked and bowed, and stood aside. "Mistaire Sho Bronson," he added as an afterthought.

The two boys regarded each other silently for a moment. They were evidently about the same age, though the stranger looked the heartier and the stronger of the two. 'Frisco Kid put out his hand, and they shook.

"So you're thinking of tackling the water, eh?" he asked.

Joe Bronson nodded, and glanced curiously about him before answering. "Yes; I think the Bay life will suit me for a while, and then, when I've got used to it, I'm going to sea in the forecastle."

"In the what? In the *what*, did you say?"

"In the forecastle—the place where the sailors live," he explained, flushing and feeling doubtful of his pronunciation.

"Oh, the fo'c'sle. Know anything about going to sea?"

"Yes—no; that is, except what I've read."

'Frisco Kid whistled, turned on his heel in a lordly manner, and went into the cabin.

"Going to sea!" he remarked to himself as he built the fire and set about cooking supper; "in the 'forecastle,' too—and thinks he'll like it!"

In the meanwhile Pete Le Maire was showing the new-comer about the sloop as though he were a guest. Such affability and charm did he display that 'Frisco Kid, popping his head up through the scuttle to call them to supper, nearly choked in his effort to suppress a grin.

Joe Bronson enjoyed that supper. The food was rough but good, and the smack of the salt air and the sea-fittings around him gave zest to his appetite. The cabin was clean and snug, and, though not large, the accommodations surprised him. Every bit of space was utilized. The table swung to the centerboard-case on hinges, so that when not in use it actually occupied almost no room at all. On either side, and partly under the deck, were two bunks. The blankets were rolled back, and they sat on the well-scrubbed bunk boards while they ate. A swinging sea-lamp of brightly polished brass gave them light, which in the daytime could be obtained through the four dead-eyes, or small round panes of heavy glass which were fitted into the walls of the cabin. On one side of the door were the stove and wood-box, on the other the cupboard. The front end of the cabin was ornamented with a couple of rifles and a shot-gun, while exposed by the rolled-back blankets of Pete's bunk was a cartridge-lined belt carrying a brace of revolvers.

It all seemed like a dream to Joe. Countless times he had imagined scenes somewhat similar to this; but here he was, right in the midst of it, and already it seemed as though he had known his two companions for years. Pete was smiling genially at him across the board. His was really a villainous countenance, but to Joe it seemed only "weather-beaten." 'Frisco Kid was describing to him, between mouthfuls, the last sou'easter the *Dazzler* had weathered, and Joe experienced an increasing awe for this boy who had lived so long upon the water and knew so much about it.

The captain, however, drank a glass of wine, and topped it off with a second and a third, and then, a vicious flush lighting his swarthy face, stretched out on top of his blankets, where he soon was snoring loudly.

"Better turn in and get a couple of hours' sleep," 'Frisco Kid said kindly, pointing Joe's bunk out to him. "We'll most likely be up the rest of the night."

Joe obeyed, but he could not fall asleep so readily as the others. He lay with his eyes wide open, watching the hands of the alarm-clock that hung in the cabin, and thinking how quickly event had followed event in the last twelve hours. Only that very morning he had been a school-boy, and now he was a sailor, shipped on the *Dazzler*, and bound he knew not whither. His fifteen years increased to twenty at the thought of it, and he felt every inch a man—a sailor-man at that. He wished Charley and Fred could see him now. Well, they would hear of it quick enough. He could see them talking it over, and the other boys crowding around. "Who?" "What!—Joe Bronson?" "Yes, he's run away to sea. Used to chum with us, you know."

Joe pictured the scene proudly. Then he softened at the thought of his mother worrying, but hardened again at the recollection of his father. Not that his father was not good and kind; but he did not understand boys, Joe thought. That was where the trouble lay. Only that morning he had said that the world wasn't a play-ground, and that the boys who thought it was were liable to make sore mistakes and be glad to get home again. Well, *he* knew that there was plenty of hard work and rough experience in the world; but *he* also thought boys had some rights and should be allowed to do a lot of things without being questioned. He'd show him he could take care of himself; and, anyway, he could write home after he got settled down to his new life.

A skiff grazed the side of the *Dazzler* softly and interrupted his reveries. He wondered why he had not heard the sound of the rowlocks. Then two men jumped over the cockpit-rail and came into the cabin.

"Bli' me, if 'ere they ain't snoozin'," said the first of the new-comers, deftly rolling 'Frisco Kid out of his blankets with one hand and reaching for the wine-bottle with the other.

Pete put his head up on the other side of the centerboard, his eyes heavy with sleep, and made them welcome.

"'Oo's this?" asked "the Cockney," as 'Frisco Kid called him, smacking his lips over the wine and rolling Joe out upon the floor. "Passenger?"

"No, no," Pete made haste to answer. "Ze new sailor-man. Vaire good boy."

"Good boy or not, he's got to keep his tongue a-tween his teeth," growled the second new-comer, who had not yet spoken, glaring fiercely at Joe.

"I say," queried the other man, "'ow does 'e whack up on the loot? I 'ope as me an' Bill 'av a square deal."

"Ze *Dazzler* she take one share—what you call—one third; den we split ze rest in five shares. Five men, five shares. Vaire good."

It was all Greek to Joe, except he knew that he was in some way the cause of the quarrel. In the end Pete had his way, and the new-comers gave in after much grumbling. After they had drunk their coffee all hands went on deck.

"Just stay in the cockpit an' keep out of their way," 'Frisco Kid whispered to Joe. "I'll teach you the ropes an' everything when we ain't in a hurry."

Joe's heart went out to him in sudden gratitude, for the strange feeling came to him that, of those on board, to 'Frisco Kid, and to 'Frisco Kid only, could he look for help in time of need. Already a dislike for Pete was growing up within him. Why, he could not say—he just simply felt it. A creaking of blocks for'ard, and the huge mainsail loomed above him in the night. Bill cast off the bowline. The Cockney followed with the stern. 'Frisco Kid gave her the jib as Pete jammed up the tiller, and the *Dazzler* caught the breeze, heeling over for mid-channel. Joe heard some talking in low tones of not putting up the sidelights, and of keeping a sharp lookout, but all he could comprehend was that some law of navigation was being violated.

The water-front lights of Oakland began to slip past. Soon the stretches of docks and shadowy ships began to be broken by dim sweeps of marsh-land, and Joe knew that they were heading out for San Francisco Bay. The wind was blowing from the north in mild squalls, and the *Dazzler* cut noiselessly through the landlocked water.

"Where are we going?" Joe asked the Cockney, in an endeavor to be friendly and at the same time satisfy his curiosity.

"Oh, my pardner 'ere, Bill—we're goin' to take a cargo from 'is factory," that worthy airily replied.

Joe thought he was rather a funny-looking individual to own a factory; but conscious that stranger things yet might be found in this new world he was entering, he said nothing. He had already exposed himself to 'Frisco Kid in the matter of his pronunciation of "fo'c'sle," and he had no desire further to show his ignorance.

A little after that he was sent in to blow out the cabin lamp. The *Dazzler* tacked about and began to work in toward the north shore. Everybody kept silent, save for occasional whispered questions and answers which passed between Bill and the captain. Finally the sloop was run into the wind and the jib and mainsail lowered cautiously.

"Short hawse, you know," Pete whispered to 'Frisco Kid, who went for'ard and dropped the anchor, paying out the slightest quantity of slack.

The *Dazzler*'s skiff was brought alongside, as was also the small boat the two strangers had come aboard in.

"See that that cub don't make a fuss," Bill commanded in an undertone, as he joined his partner in his own boat.

"Can you row?" 'Frisco Kid asked as they got into the other boat. Joe nodded his head. "Then take these oars, and don't make a racket."

'Frisco Kid took the second pair, while Pete steered. Joe noticed that the oars were muffled with sennit, and that even the row-lock sockets were protected by leather. It was impossible to make a noise except by a mis-stroke, and Joe had learned to row on Lake Merrit well enough to avoid that. They followed in the wake of the first boat, and glancing aside, he saw they were running along the length of a pier which jutted out from the land. A couple of ships, with riding-lanterns burning brightly, were moored to it, but they kept just beyond the edge of the light. He stopped rowing at the whispered command of 'Frisco Kid. Then the boats grounded like ghosts on a tiny beach, and they clambered out.

Joe followed the men, who picked their way carefully up a twenty-foot bank. At the top he found himself on a narrow railway track which ran between huge piles of rusty scrap-iron. These piles, separated by tracks, extended in every direction, he could not tell how far, though in the distance he could see the vague outlines of some great factory-like building. The men began to carry loads of the iron down to the beach, and Pete, gripping him by the arm and again warning him to not make any noise, told him to do likewise. At the beach they turned their loads over to 'Frisco Kid, who loaded them, first in one skiff and then in the other. As the boats settled under the weight, he kept pushing them farther and farther out, in order that they should keep clear of the bottom.

Joe worked away steadily, though he could not help marveling at the queerness of the whole business. Why should there be such a mystery about it, and why such care taken to maintain silence? He had just begun to ask himself these questions, and a horrible suspicion was forming itself in his mind, when he heard the hoot of an owl from the direction of the beach. Wondering at an owl being in so unlikely a place, he stooped to gather a fresh load of iron. But suddenly a man sprang out of the gloom, flashing a dark lantern full upon him. Blinded by the light, he staggered back. Then a revolver in the man's hand went off. All Joe realized was that he was being shot at, while his legs manifested an overwhelming desire to get away. Even if he had so wished, he could not very well have stayed to explain to the excited man with the smoking revolver. So he took to his heels for the beach, colliding with another man with a dark lantern who came running around the end of one of the piles of iron. This second man quickly regained his feet, and peppered away at Joe as he flew down the bank.

He dashed out into the water for the boat. Pete at the bow oars and 'Frisco Kid at the stroke had the skiff's nose pointed seaward and were calmly awaiting his arrival. They had their oars all ready for the start, but they held them quietly at rest, notwithstanding that both men on the bank had begun to fire at them. The other skiff lay closer inshore, partially aground. Bill was trying to shove it off, and was calling on the Cockney to lend a hand; but that gentleman had lost his head completely, and came floundering through the water hard after Joe. No sooner had Joe climbed in over the stern than he followed him. This extra weight on the stern of the heavily loaded craft nearly swamped them; as it was, a dangerous quantity of water was shipped. In the meantime the men on the bank had reloaded their pistols and opened fire again, this time with better aim. The alarm had spread. Voices and cries could be heard from the ships on the pier, along which men were running. In the distance a police whistle was being frantically blown.

"Get out!" 'Frisco Kid shouted. "You ain't a-going to sink us if I know it. Go and help your pardner!"

But the Cockney's teeth were chattering with fright, and he was too unnerved to move or speak.

"T'row ze crazy man out!" Pete ordered from the bow. At this moment a bullet shattered an oar in his hand, and he coolly proceeded to ship a spare one.

"Give us a hand, Joe," 'Frisco Kid commanded.

Joe understood, and together they seized the terror-stricken creature and flung him over-board. Two or three bullets splashed about him as he came to the surface just in time to be picked up by Bill, who had at last succeeded in getting clear.

"Now," Pete called, and a few strokes into the darkness quickly took them out of the zone of fire.

So much water had been shipped that the light skiff was in danger of sinking at any moment. While the other two rowed, and by the Frenchman's orders, Joe began to throw out the iron. This saved them for the time being; but just as they swept alongside the *Dazzler* the skiff lurched, shoved a side under, and turned turtle, sending the remainder of the iron to the bottom. Joe and 'Frisco Kid came up side by side, and together they clambered aboard with the skiff's painter in tow. Pete had already arrived, and now helped them out.

By the time they had canted the water out of the swamped boat, Bill and his partner appeared on the scene. All hands worked rapidly, and almost before Joe could realize, the mainsail and jib had been hoisted, the anchor broken out, and the *Dazzler* was leaping down the channel. Off a bleak piece of marshland, Bill and the Cockney said good-by and cast loose in their skiff. Pete, in the cabin, bewailed their bad luck in various languages, and sought consolation in the wine-bottle.

The wind freshened as they got clear of the land, and soon the *Dazzler* was heeling it with her lee deck buried and the water churning by half-way up the cockpit-rail. Side-lights had been hung out. 'Frisco Kid was steering, and by his side sat Joe, pondering over the events of the night.

He could no longer blind himself to the facts. His mind was in a whirl of apprehension. If he had done wrong, he reasoned, he had done it through ignorance; and he did not feel shame for the past so much as he did fear of the future. His companions were thieves and robbers—the Bay pirates, of whose unlawful deeds he had heard vague tales. And here he was, right in the midst of them, already possessing information which could send them to State's prison. This very fact, he knew, would force them to keep a sharp watch upon him and so lessen his chances of escape. But escape he would, at the very first opportunity.

At this point his thoughts were interrupted by a sharp squall, which hurled the *Dazzler* over till the sea rushed inboard. 'Frisco Kid luffed quickly, at the same time slacking off the mainsheet. Then, single-handed—for Pete remained below, and Joe sat still looking idly on—he proceeded to reef down.

CHAPTER II

JOE TRIES TAKING FRENCH LEAVE

THE squall which had so nearly capsized the *Dazzler* was of short duration, but it marked the rising of the wind, and soon puff after puff was shrieking down upon them out of the north. The mainsail was spilling the wind, and slapping and thrashing about till it seemed it would tear itself to pieces. The sloop was rolling wildly in the quick sea which had come up. Everything was in confusion; but even Joe's untrained eye showed him that it was an orderly confusion. He could see that 'Frisco Kid knew just what to do, and just how to do it. As he watched him he learned a lesson, the lack of which has made failures of the lives of many men—*knowledge of one's own capacities*. 'Frisco Kid knew what he was able to do, and because of this he had confidence in himself. He was cool and self-possessed, working hurriedly but not carelessly. There was no bungling. Every reef-point was drawn down to stay. Other accidents might occur, but the next squall, or the next forty squalls, would not carry one of these reef-knots away.

He called Joe for'ard to help stretch the mainsail by means of swinging on the peak and throat halyards. To lay out on the long-bowsprit and put a single reef in the jib was a slight task compared with what had been already accomplished; so a few moments later they were again in the cockpit. Under the other lad's directions, Joe flattened down the jib-sheet, and, going into the cabin, let down a foot or so of centerboard. The excitement of the struggle had chased all unpleasant thoughts from his mind. Patterning after the other boy, he had retained his coolness. He had executed his orders without fumbling, and at the same time without undue slowness. Together they had exerted their puny strength in the face of violent nature, and together they had outwitted her.

He came back to where his companion stood at the tiller steering, and he felt proud of him and of himself. And when he read the unspoken praise in 'Frisco Kid's eyes he blushed like a girl at her first compliment. But the next instant the thought flashed across him that this boy was a thief, a common thief, and he instinctively recoiled. His whole life had been sheltered from the harsher things of the world, his reading, which had been of the best, had laid a premium upon honesty and uprightness, and he had learned to look with abhorrence upon the criminal classes. So he drew a little away from 'Frisco Kid and remained silent. But 'Frisco Kid, devoting all his energies to the handling of the sloop, had no time in which to remark this sudden change of feeling on the part of his companion.

Yet there was one thing Joe found in himself that surprised him. While the thought of 'Frisco Kid being a thief was repulsive to him, 'Frisco Kid himself was not. Instead of feeling an honest desire to shun him, he felt drawn toward him. He could not help liking him, though he knew not why. Had he been a little older he would have understood that it was the lad's good qualities which appealed to him—his coolness and self-reliance, his manliness and bravery, and a certain kindliness and sympathy in his nature. As it was, he thought it his own natural badness which prevented him from disliking 'Frisco Kid, and while he felt shame at his own weakness, he could not smother the sort of regard which he felt growing up for this common thief, this Bay pirate.

"Take in two or three feet on the skiff's painter," commanded 'Frisco Kid, who had an eye for everything.

The skiff was towing with too long a painter, and was behaving very badly. Every once in a while it would hold back till the tow-rope tautened, then come leaping ahead and sheering and dropping slack till it threatened to shove its nose under the huge whitecaps which roared hungrily on every hand. Joe climbed over the cockpit-rail upon the slippery afterdeck, and made his way to the bitt to which the skiff was fastened.

"Be careful," 'Frisco Kid warned, as a heavy puff struck the *Dazzler* and careened her dangerously over on her side. "Keep one turn round the bitt, and heave in on it when the painter slacks."

It was ticklish work for a greenhorn. Joe threw off all the turns save the last, which he held with one hand, while with the other he attempted to bring in on the painter. But at that instant it tightened with a tremendous jerk, the boat sheering sharply into the crest of a heavy sea. The rope slipped from his hands and began to fly out over the stern. He clutched it frantically, and was dragged after it over the sloping deck.

"Let her go! Let her go!" 'Frisco Kid roared.

Joe let go just as he was on the verge of going overboard, and the skiff dropped rapidly astern. He glanced in a shamefaced way at his companion, expecting to be sharply reprimanded for his awkwardness. But 'Frisco Kid smiled good-naturedly.

"That's all right," he said. "No bones broke, and nobody overboard. Better to lose a boat than a man any day. That's what I say. Besides, I shouldn't have sent you out there. And there's no harm done. We can pick it up all right. Go in and drop some more centerboard—a couple of feet—and then come out and do what I tell you. But don't be in a hurry. Take it easy and sure."

Joe dropped the centerboard, and returned, to be stationed at the jib-sheet.

"Hard a-lee!" 'Frisco Kid cried, throwing the tiller down and following it with his body. "Cast off! That's right! Now lend a hand on the main-sheet!"

Together, hand over hand, they came in on the reefed mainsail. Joe began to warm up with the work. The *Dazzler* turned on her heel like a race-horse and swept into the wind, her canvas snarling and her sheet slatting like hail.

"Draw down the jib-sheet!"

Joe obeyed, and the head-sail, filling, forced her off on the other tack. This manoeuver had turned Pete's bunk from the lee to the weather side, and rolled him out on the cabin floor, where he lay in drunken stupor.

'Frisco Kid, with his back against the tiller, and holding the sloop off that it might cover their previous course, looked at him with an expression of disgust, and muttered: "The dog! We could well go to the bottom, for all he'd care or do!"

Twice they tacked, trying to go over the same ground, and then Joe discovered the skiff bobbing to windward in the starlit darkness.

"Plenty of time," 'Frisco Kid cautioned, shooting the *Dazzler* into the wind toward it and gradually losing headway.

"Now!"

Joe leaned over the side, grasped the trailing painter, and made it fast to the bitt. Then they tacked ship again and started on their way. Joe still felt sore over the trouble he had caused, but 'Frisco Kid quickly put him at ease.

"Oh, that's nothing," he said. "Everybody does that when they're beginning. Now, some men forget all about the trouble they had in learning, and get mad when a greeny makes a mistake. I never do. Why, I remember—"

And here he told Joe of many of the mishaps which fell on him when, as a little lad, he first went on the water, and some of the severe punishments for the same which were measured out to him. He had passed the running end of a lanyard over the tiller-neck, and, as they talked, they sat side by side and close against each other, in the shelter of the cockpit.

"What place is that?" Joe asked as they flew by a lighthouse perched on a rock headland.

"Goat Island. They've got a naval training-station for boys over on the other side, and a torpedo magazine. There's jolly good fishing, too—rock-cod. We'll pass to the lee of it and make across and anchor in the shelter of Angel Island. There's a quarantine station there. Then, when Pete gets sober, we'll know where he wants to go. You can turn in now and get some sleep. I can manage all right."

Joe shook his head. There had been too much excitement for him to feel in the least like sleeping. He could not bear to think of it, with the *Dazzler* leaping and surging along, and shattering the seas into clouds of spray on her weather bow. His clothes had half dried already, and he preferred to stay on deck and enjoy it. The lights of Oakland had dwindled till they made only a hazy flare against the sky; but to the south the San Francisco lights, topping hills and sinking into valleys, stretched miles upon miles. Starting from the great ferry building and passing on to Telegraph Hill, Joe was soon able to locate the principal places of the city. Somewhere over in that maze of light and shadow was the home of his father, and perhaps even now they were thinking and worrying about him; and over there his sister Bessie was sleeping cozily, to wake up in the morning and wonder why her brother Joe did not come down to breakfast. Joe shivered. It was almost morning. Then, slowly, his head drooped over on 'Frisco Kid's shoulder, and soon he was fast asleep.

"Come! Wake up! We're going into anchor."

Joe roused with a start, bewildered at the unusual scene; for sleep had banished his troubles for the time being, and he knew not where he was. Then he remembered.

The wind had dropped with the night. Beyond, the heavy after-sea was still rolling, but the *Dazzler* was creeping up in the shelter of a rocky island. The sky was clear, and the air had the snap and vigor of early morning about it. The rippling water was laughing in the rays of the sun, just shouldering above the eastern sky-line. To the south lay Alcatraz Island, and from its gun-crowned heights a flourish of trumpets saluted the day. In the west the Golden Gate yawned between the Pacific Ocean and San Francisco Bay. A full-rigged ship, with her lightest canvas, even to the sky-sails, set, was coming slowly in on the flood-tide.

It was a pretty sight. Joe rubbed the sleep from his eyes and remained gazing till 'Frisco Kid told him to go for'ard and make ready for dropping the anchor.

"Overhaul about fifty fathoms of chain," he ordered, "and then stand by." He eased the sloop gently into the wind, at the same time casting off the jib-sheet. "Let go the jib-halyards and come in on the down-haul!"

Joe had seen the manoeuver performed the previous night, and so was able to carry it out with fair success.

"Now! Over with the mud-hook! Watch out for turns! Lively, now!"

The chain flew out with startling rapidity, and brought the *Dazzler* to rest. 'Frisco Kid went for'ard to help, and together they lowered the mainsail, furled it in shipshape manner, made all fast with the gaskets, and put the crutches under the main-boom.

"Here's a bucket." 'Frisco Kid passed him the article in question. "Wash down the decks, and don't be afraid of the water, nor of the dirt, neither. Here's a broom. Give it what for, and have everything shining. When you get that done, bail out the skiff; she opened her seams a little last night. I'm going below to cook breakfast."

The water was soon slushing merrily over the deck, while the smoke pouring from the cabin stove carried a promise of good things to come. Time and again Joe lifted his head from his task to take in the scene. It was one to appeal to any healthy boy, and he was no exception. The romance of it stirred him strangely, and his happiness would have been complete could he have escaped remembering who and what his companions were. But the thought of this, and of Pete in his bleary, drunken sleep below, marred the beauty of the day. He had been unused to such things, and was shocked at the harsh reality of life. But instead of hurting him, as it might a lad of weaker nature, it had the opposite effect. It strengthened his desire to be clean and strong, and to not be ashamed of himself in his own eyes. He glanced about him and sighed. Why could not men be honest and true? It seemed too bad that he must go away and leave all this; but the events of the night were strong upon him, and he knew that in order to be true to himself he must escape.

At this juncture he was called to breakfast. He discovered that 'Frisco Kid was as good a cook as he was sailor, and made haste to do justice to the fare. There were mush and condensed milk, beefsteak and fried potatoes, and all topped off with good French bread, butter, and coffee. Pete did not join them, though 'Frisco Kid attempted a couple of times to rouse him. He mumbled and grunted, half opened his bleared eyes, then went to snoring again.

"Can't tell when he's going to get those spells," 'Frisco Kid explained, when Joe, having finished washing the dishes, came on deck. "Sometimes he won't get that way for a month, and others he won't be decent for a week at a stretch. Sometimes he's good-natured, and sometimes he's dangerous. So the best thing to do is to let him alone and keep out of his way. And don't cross him, for if you do there's liable to be trouble."

"Come on; let's take a swim," he added, abruptly changing the subject to one more agreeable. "Can you swim?"

Joe nodded. "What's that place?" he asked as he poised before diving, pointing toward a sheltered beach on the island, where there were several buildings and a large number of tents.

"Quarantine station. Lots of smallpox coming in now on the China steamers, and they make them go there till the doctors say they're safe to land. I tell you, they're strict about it, too. Why—"

Splash! Had 'Frisco Kid finished his sentence just then, instead of diving overboard, much trouble might have been saved to Joe. But he did not finish it, and Joe dived after him.

"I'll tell you what," 'Frisco Kid suggested half an hour later, while they clung to the bobstay preparatory to climbing out. "Let's catch a mess of fish for dinner, and then turn in and make up for the sleep we lost last night. What'd you say?"

They made a race to clamber aboard, but Joe was shoved over the side again. When he finally did arrive, the other lad had brought to light a pair of heavily leaded, large-hooked lines, and a mackerel-keg of salt sardines.

"Bait," he said. "Just shove a whole one on. They're not a bit partic'lar. Swallow the bait, hook and all, and go—that's their caper. The fellow that don't catch first fish has to clean 'em."

Both sinkers started on their long descent together, and seventy feet of line whizzed out before they came to rest. But at the instant his sinker touched the bottom Joe felt the struggling jerks of a hooked fish. As he began to haul in he glanced at 'Frisco Kid, and saw that he, too, had evidently captured a finny prize. The race between them was exciting. Hand over hand the wet lines flashed inboard; but 'Frisco Kid was more expert, and his fish tumbled into the cockpit first. Joe's followed an instant later—a three-pound rock-cod. He was wild with joy. It was magnificent, the largest fish he had ever landed or ever seen landed. Over went the lines again, and up they came with two mates of the ones already captured. It was sport royal. Joe would have certainly continued till he had fished the Bay empty had not 'Frisco Kid persuaded him to stop.

"We've got enough for three meals now," he said, "so there's no use in having them spoil. Besides, the more you catch, the more you clean, and you'd better start in right away. I'm going to bed."

Joe did not mind. In fact, he was glad he had not caught the first fish, for it helped out a little plan which had come to him while in swimming. He threw the last cleaned fish into a bucket of water, and glanced about him. The quarantine station was a bare half-mile away, and he could make out a soldier pacing up and down at sentry duty on the beach. Going into the cabin, he listened to the heavy breathing of the sleepers. He had to pass so close to 'Frisco Kid to get his bundle of clothes that he decided not to take them. Returning outside, he carefully pulled the skiff alongside, got aboard with a pair of oars, and cast off.

At first he rowed very gently in the direction of the station, fearing the chance of noise if he made undue haste. But gradually he increased the strength of his strokes till he had settled down to the regular stride. When he had covered half the distance he glanced about. Escape was sure now, for he knew, even if he were discovered, that it would be impossible for the *Dazzler* to get under way and head him off before he made the land and the protection of that man who wore the uniform of Uncle Sam.

The report of a gun came to him from

the shore, but his back was in that direction and he did not bother to turn around. A second report followed, and a bullet cut the water within a couple of feet of his oar-blade. This time he did turn around. The soldier on the beach was leveling his rifle at him for a third shot.

CHAPTER III

JOE LOSES LIBERTY, AND FINDS A FRIEND

JOE was in a predicament, and a very tantalizing one at that. A few minutes of hard rowing would bring him to the beach and to safety; but on that beach, for some unaccountable reason, stood a United States soldier who persisted in firing at him.

When Joe saw the gun aimed at him for the third time, he backed water hastily. As a result the skiff came to a standstill, and the soldier, lowering his rifle, regarded him intently.

"I want to come ashore! Important!" Joe shouted out to him.

The man in uniform shook his head.

"But it's important, I tell you! Won't you let me come ashore?"

He took a hurried look in the direction of the *Dazzler*. The shots had evidently awakened Pete; for the mainsail had been hoisted, and as he looked he saw the anchor broken out and the jib flung to the breeze.

"Can't land here!" the soldier shouted back. "Smallpox!"

"But I must!" he cried, choking down a half-sob and preparing to row.

"Then I'll shoot," was the cheering response, and the rifle came to shoulder again.

Joe thought rapidly. The island was large. Perhaps there were no soldiers farther on, and if he only once got ashore he did not care how quickly they captured him. He might catch the smallpox, but even that was better than going back to the Bay pirates. He whirled the skiff half about to

the right, and threw all his strength against the oars. The cove was quite wide, and the nearest point which he must go around a good distance away. Had he been more of a sailor he would have gone in the other direction for the opposite point, and thus had the wind on his pursuers. As it was, the *Dazzler* had a beam wind in which to overtake him.

It was nip and tuck for a while. The breeze was light and not very steady, so sometimes he gained and sometimes they. Once it freshened till the sloop was within a hundred yards of him, and then it dropped suddenly flat, the *Dazzler*'s big mainsail flapping idly from side to side.

"Ah! you steal ze skiff, eh?" Pete howled at him, running into the cabin for his rifle. "I fix you! You come back queeck, or I kill you!" But he knew the soldier was watching them from the shore, and did not dare to fire, even over the lad's head.

Joe did not think of this, for he, who had never been shot at in all his previous life, had been under fire twice in the last twenty-four hours. Once more or less couldn't amount to much. So he pulled steadily away, while Pete raved like a wild man, threatening him with all manner of punishments once he laid hands upon him again. To complicate matters, 'Frisco Kid waxed mutinous.

"Just you shoot him and I'll see you hung for it, see if I don't," he threatened. "You'd better let him go. He's a good boy and all right, and not raised for the life you and I are leading."

"You too, eh!" the Frenchman shrieked, beside himself with rage. "Den I fix you, you rat!"

He made a rush for the boy, but 'Frisco Kid led him a lively chase from cockpit to bowsprit and back again. A sharp capful of wind arriving just then, Pete abandoned the one chase for the other. Springing to the tiller and slacking away on the main-sheet—for the wind favored—he headed the sloop down upon Joe. The latter made one tremendous spurt, then gave up in despair and hauled in his oars. Pete let go the main-sheet, lost steerage-way as he rounded up alongside the motionless skiff, and dragged Joe out.

"Keep mum," 'Frisco Kid whispered to him while the irate Frenchman was busy fastening the painter. "Don't talk back. Let him say all he wants to, and keep quiet. It'll be better for you."

But Joe's Anglo-Saxon blood was up and he did not heed.

"Look here, Mr. Pete, or whatever your name is," he commenced, "I give you to understand that I want to quit, and that I'm going to quit. So you'd better put me ashore at once. If you don't, I'll put you in prison, or my name's not Joe Bronson."

'Frisco Kid waited the outcome fearfully. Pete was aghast. He was being defied aboard his own vessel, and by a boy. Never had such a thing been heard of. He knew he was committing an unlawful act in detaining him, while at the same time he was afraid to let him go with the information he had gathered concerning the sloop and its occupation. The boy had spoken the unpleasant truth when he said he could send him to prison. The only thing for him to do was to bully him.

"You will eh?" His shrill voice rose wrathfully. "Den you come too. You row ze boat last-a night—answer me dat! You steal ze iron—answer me dat! You run away—answer me dat! And den you say you put me in jail? Bah!"

"But I didn't know," Joe protested.

"Ha, ha! Dat is funny. You tell dat to ze judge; mebbe him laugh, eh?"

"I say I didn't," Joe reiterated manfully. "I didn't know I'd shipped along a lot of pirates and thieves."

'Frisco Kid winced at this epithet, and

had Joe been looking at him he would have seen the red flush of shame mount to his face.

"And now that I do know," he continued, "I wish to be put ashore. I don't know anything about the law, but I do know right and wrong, and I'm willing to take my chance with any judge for whatever wrong I have done—with all the judges in the United States, for that matter. And that's more than you can say, Mr. Pete."

"You say dat, eh? Vaire good. But you are one big t'ief—"

"I'm not! Don't you dare call me that again!" Joe's face was pale, and he was trembling—but not with fear.

"T'ief!" the Frenchman taunted back.

"You lie!"

Joe had not been a boy among boys for nothing. He knew the penalty which attached itself to the words he had just spoken, and he expected to receive it. So he was not over-much surprised when he picked himself up from the floor of the cockpit an instant later, his head still ringing from a stiff blow between the eyes.

"Say dat one time more," Pete bullied, his fist raised and prepared to strike.

Tears of anger stood in Joe's eyes, but he was calm and in dead earnest. "When you say I am a thief, Pete, you lie. You can kill me, but still I will say you lie."

"No, you don't!" 'Frisco Kid had darted in like a wildcat, preventing a second blow and shoving the Frenchman back across the cockpit.

"You leave the boy alone," he continued, suddenly unshipping and arming himself with the heavy iron tiller, and standing between them. "This thing's gone just about as far as it's going to go. You big fool, can't you see the stuff the boy's made out of? He speaks true. He's right, and he knows it, and you could kill him and he wouldn't give in. There's my hand on it, Joe." He turned and extended his hand to Joe, who returned the grip. "You've got spunk, and you're not afraid to show it."

Pete's mouth twisted itself in a sickly smile, but the evil gleam in his eyes gave it the lie. He shrugged his shoulders and said: "Ah! So? He does not dee-sire dat I him call pet names. Ha, ha! It is only ze sailor-man play. Let us—what you call—forgive and forget, eh? Vaire good; forgive and forget."

He reached out his hand, but Joe refused to take it. 'Frisco Kid nodded approval, while Pete, still shrugging his shoulders and smiling, passed into the cabin.

"Slack off ze main-sheet," he called out, "and run down for Hunter's Point. For one time I will cook ze dinner, and den you will say dat it is ze vaire good dinner. Ah! Pete is ze great cook!"

"That's the way he always does—gets real good and cooks when he wants to make up," 'Frisco Kid hazarded, slipping the tiller into the rudder-head and obeying the order. "But even then you can't trust him."

Joe nodded his head, but did not speak. He was in no mood for conversation. He was still trembling from the excitement of the last few moments, while deep down he questioned himself on how he had behaved, and found naught to be ashamed of.

The afternoon sea-breeze had sprung up and was now rioting in from the Pacific. Angel Island was fast dropping astern, and the waterfront of San Francisco showing up, as the *Dazzler* plowed along before it. Soon they were in the midst of the shipping, passing in and out among the vessels which had come from the uttermost ends of the earth. Later they crossed the fairway, where the ferry steamers, crowded with passengers, passed backward and forward between San Francisco and Oakland. One came so close that the passengers crowded to the side to see the gallant little sloop and the two boys in the cockpit. Joe gazed almost enviously at the row of down-turned faces. They all were going to their homes, while he—he was going he knew not whither, at the will of Pete Le Maire. He was half tempted to cry out for help; but the foolishness of such an act struck him, and he held his tongue. Turning his head, his eyes wandered along the smoky heights of the city, and he fell to musing on the strange ways of men and ships on the sea.

'Frisco Kid watched him from the corner of his eye, following his thoughts as accurately as though he spoke them aloud.

"Got a home over there somewhere?" he queried suddenly, waving his hand in the direction of the city.

Joe started, so correctly had his thought been anticipated. "Yes," he said simply.

"Tell us about it."

Joe rapidly described his home, though forced to go into greater detail because of the curious questions of his companion. 'Frisco Kid was interested in everything, especially in Mrs. Bronson and Bessie. Of the latter he could not seem to tire, and poured forth question after question concerning her. So peculiar and artless were some of them that Joe could hardly forbear to smile.

"Now tell me about your home," he said, when he at last had finished.

'Frisco Kid seemed suddenly to harden, and his face took on a stern look which the other had never seen there before. He swung his foot idly to and fro, and lifted a dull eye to the main-peak blocks, with which, by the way, there was nothing the matter.

"Go ahead," the other encouraged.

"I haven't no home."

The four words left his mouth as though they had been forcibly ejected, and his lips came together after them almost with a snap.

Joe saw he had touched a tender spot, and strove to ease the way out of it again. "Then the home you did have." He did not dream that there were lads in the world who never had known homes, or that he had only succeeded in probing deeper.

"Never had none."

"Oh!" His interest was aroused, and he now threw solicitude to the winds. "Any sisters?"

"Nope."

"Mother?"

"I was so young when she died that I don't remember her."

"Father?"

"I never saw much of him. He went to sea—anyhow, he disappeared."

"Oh!" Joe did not know what to say, and an oppressive silence, broken only by the churn of the *Dazzler*'s forefoot, fell upon them.

Just then Pete came out to relieve at the tiller, while they went in to eat. Both lads hailed his advent with feelings of relief, and the awkwardness vanished over the dinner, which was all their skipper had claimed it to be. Afterward 'Frisco Kid relieved Pete, and while he was eating, Joe washed up the dishes and put the cabin shipshape. Then they all gathered in the stern, where the captain strove to increase the general cordiality by entertaining them with descriptions of life among the pearl-divers of the South Seas.

In this fashion the afternoon wore away. They had long since left San Francisco behind, rounded Hunter's Point, and were now skirting the San Mateo shore. Joe caught a glimpse, once, of a party of cyclists rounding a cliff on the San Bruno Road, and remembered the time when he had gone over the same ground on his own wheel. That was only a month or two before, but it seemed an age to him now, so much had there been to come between.

By the time supper had been eaten and the things cleared away, they were well down the Bay, off the marshes behind which Redwood City clustered. The wind had gone down with the sun, and the *Dazzler* was making but little headway, when they sighted a sloop bearing down upon them on the dying wind. 'Frisco Kid instantly named it as the *Reindeer*, to which Pete, after a deep scrutiny, agreed. He seemed greatly pleased at the meeting.

"Epont Nelson runs her," 'Frisco Kid informed Joe. "They've got something big down here, and they're always after Pete to tackle it with them. He knows more about it, whatever it is."

Joe nodded and looked at the approaching craft curiously. Though somewhat larger, it was built on about the same lines as the *Dazzler*—which meant, above everything else, that it was built for speed. The mainsail was so large that it was more like that of a racing-yacht, and it carried the points for no less than three reefs in case of rough weather. Aloft and on deck everything was in place; nothing was untidy or useless. From running-gear to standing-rigging, everything bore evidence of thorough order and smart seamanship.

The *Reindeer* came up slowly in the gathering twilight, and went to anchor not a biscuit-toss away. Pete followed suit with the *Dazzler*, and then went in the skiff to pay them a visit. The two lads stretched themselves out on top of the cabin and awaited his return.

"Do you like the life?" Joe broke silence. The other turned on his elbow. "Well—I do, and then again I don't. The fresh air and salt water, and all that, and the freedom—that's all right; but I don't like the—the—" He paused a moment, as though his tongue had failed in its duty, and then blurted out, "the stealing."

"Then why don't you quit it?" Joe liked the lad more than he dared confess, and he felt a sudden missionary zeal come upon him.

"I will, just as soon as I can turn my hand to something else."

"But why not now?"

Now is the accepted time, was ringing in Joe's ears, and if the other wished to leave, it seemed a pity that he did not, and at once.

"Where can I go? What can I do? There's nobody in all the world to lend me a hand, just as there never has been. I tried it once, and learned my lesson too well to do it again in a hurry."

"Well, when I get out of this I'm going home. Guess my father was right, after all. And I don't see—maybe—what's the matter with you going with me?" He said this last impulsively, without thinking, and 'Frisco Kid knew it.

"You don't know what you're talking about," he answered. "Fancy me going off with you! What'd your father say? And—and the rest? How would he think of me? And what'd he do?"

Joe felt sick at heart. He realized that in the spirit of the moment he had given an invitation which, on sober thought, he knew would be impossible to carry out. He tried to imagine his father receiving in his own house a stranger like 'Frisco Kid. No, that was not to be thought of. Then, forgetting his own plight, he fell to racking his brains for some other method by which 'Frisco Kid could get away from his present surroundings.

"He might turn me over to the police," the other went on, "and send me to a refuge. I'd die first, before I'd let that happen

to me. And besides, Joe, I'm not of your kind, and you know it. Why, I'd be like a fish out of water, what with all the things I don't know. Nope; I guess I'll have to wait a little before I strike out. But there's only one thing for you to do, and that's to go straight home. First chance I get, I'll land you, and then deal with Pete—"

"No, you don't," Joe interrupted hotly. "When I leave I'm not going to leave you in trouble on my account. So don't you try anything like that. I'll get away, never fear; and if I can figure it out, I want you to come along too—come along, anyway, and figure it out afterwards. What d' you say?"

'Frisco Kid shook his head, and, gazing up at the starlit heavens, wandered off into daydreams of the life he would like to lead, but from which he seemed inexorably shut out. The seriousness of life was striking deeper than ever into Joe's heart, and he lay silent, thinking hard. A mumble of heavy voices came to them from the *Reindeer;* from the land the solemn notes of a church bell floated across the water; while the summer night wrapped them slowly in its warm darkness.

CHAPTER IV

'FRISCO KID TELLS HIS STORY

AFTER the conversation died away, the two lads lay upon the cabin for perhaps an hour.

Then, without saying a word, 'Frisco Kid went below and struck a light. Joe could hear him fumbling about, and a little later heard his own name called softly. On going into the cabin, he saw 'Frisco Kid sitting on the edge of the bunk, a sailor's ditty-box on his knees, and in his hand a carefully folded page from a magazine.

"Does she look like this?" he asked,

smoothing it out and turning it that the other might see.

It was a half-page illustration of two girls and a boy, grouped in an old-fashioned, roomy attic, and evidently holding a council of some sort. The girl who was talking faced the onlooker, while the backs of the two others were turned.

"Who?" Joe queried, glancing in perplexity from the picture to 'Frisco Kid's face.

"Like—like your sister—Bessie." The name seemed reluctant to come from his lips, and he expressed it with a certain shy reverence, as though it were something unspeakably sacred.

Joe was nonplussed for the moment. He could see no bearing between the two in point, and, anyway, girls were rather silly creatures to waste one's time over. "He's actually blushing," he thought, regarding the soft glow on the other's cheeks. He felt an irresistible desire to laugh, but tried to smother it down.

"No, no; don't!" 'Frisco Kid cried, snatching the paper away and putting it back in the ditty-box with shaking fingers. Then he added more slowly: "I thought I—I kind of thought you would understand, and—and—"

His lips trembled and his eyes glistened with unwonted moisture as he turned hastily away.

The next instant Joe was by his side on the bunk, his arm around him. Prompted by some instinctive monitor, he had done it before he thought. A week before he could not have imagined himself in such an absurd situation—his arm around a boy! but now it seemed the most natural thing in the world. He did not comprehend, but he knew that, whatever it was, it was something that seemed of deep importance to his companion.

"Go ahead and tell us," he urged. "I'll understand."

"No, you won't; you can't."

"Yes—sure. Go ahead."

'Frisco Kid choked and shook his head. "I don't think I could, anyway. It's more the things I feel, and I don't know how to put them in words." Joe's arm wrapped about him reassuringly, and he went on: "Well, it's this way. You see, I don't know much about the land, and people, and homes, and I never had no brothers, or sisters, or playmates. All the time I didn't know it, but I was lonely—sort of missed them down in here somewheres." He placed a hand over his breast to locate the seat of loss. "Did you ever feel downright hungry? Well, that's just the way I used to feel, only a different kind of hunger, and me not knowing what it was. But one day, oh, a long time back, I got a-hold of a magazine, and saw a picture—that picture, with the two girls and the boy talking together. I thought it must be fine to be like them, and I got to thinking about the things they said and did, till it came to me all of a sudden like, and I knew that it was just loneliness was the matter with me.

"But, more than anything else, I got to wondering about the girl who looks out of the picture right at you. I was thinking about her all the time, and by and by she became real to me. You see, it was making believe, and I knew it all the time; and then again I didn't. Whenever I'd think of the men, and the work, and the hard life, I'd know it was make-believe; but when I'd think of her, it wasn't. I don't know; I can't explain it."

Joe remembered all his own adventures which he had imagined on land and sea, and nodded. He at least understood that much.

"Of course it was all foolishness, but to have a girl like that for a friend seemed more like heaven to me than anything else I knew of. As I said, it was a long while back, and I was only a little kid. That's when Nelson gave me my name, and I've never been anything but 'Frisco Kid ever since. But the girl in the picture: I was always getting that picture out to look at her, and before long, if I wasn't square, why, I felt ashamed to look at her. Afterwards, when I was older, I came to look at it in another way. I thought, 'Suppose, Kid, some day you were to meet a girl like that, what would she think of you? Could she like you? Could she be even the least bit of a friend to you?' And then I'd make up my mind to be better, to try and do something with myself so that she or any of her kind of people would not be ashamed to know me.

"That's why I learned to read. That's why I ran away. Nicky Perrata, a Greek boy, taught me my letters, and it wasn't till after I learned to read that I found out there was anything really wrong in Bay-pirating. I'd been used to it ever since I could remember, and several people I knew made their living that way. But when I did find out, I ran away, thinking to quit it for good. I'll tell you about it sometime, and how I'm back at it again.

"Of course she seemed a real girl when I was a youngster, and even now she sometimes seems that way, I've thought so much about her. But while I'm talking to you it all clears up and she comes to me in this light: she stands just for—well, for a better, cleaner life than this, and one I'd like to live; and if I could live it, why, I'd come to know that kind of girls, and their kind of people—your kind, that's what I mean. So I was wondering about your sister and you, and that's why—I don't know; I guess I was just wondering. But I suppose you know lots of girls like that, don't you?"

Joe nodded his head in token that he did.

"Then tell me about them; something—anything," he added, as he noted the fleeting expression of doubt in the other's eyes.

"Oh, that's easy," Joe began valiantly. To a certain extent he did understand the lad's hunger, and it seemed a simple enough task to satisfy him. "To begin with, they're like—hem!—why, they're like—girls, just girls." He broke off with a miserable sense of failure.

'Frisco Kid waited patiently, his face a study in expectancy.

Joe struggled vainly to marshal his ideas. To his mind, in quick succession came the girls with whom he had gone to school, the sisters of the boys he knew, and those who were his sister's friends—slim girls and plump girls, tall girls and short girls, blue-eyed and brown-eyed, curly-haired, black-haired, golden-haired; in short, a regular procession of girls of all sorts and descriptions. But, to save himself, he could say nothing about them. Anyway, he'd never been a "sissy," and why should he be expected to know anything about them? "All girls are alike," he concluded desperately. "They're just the same as the ones you know, Kid. Sure they are."

"But I don't know any."

Joe whistled. "And never did?"

"Yes, once—Carlotta Gispardi. But she couldn't speak English; and she died. I don't care; though I never knew any, I seem to know as much about them as you do."

"And I guess I know more about adventures all over the world than you do," Joe retorted.

Both boys laughed. But a moment later Joe fell into deep thought. It had come upon him quite swiftly that he had not been duly grateful for the good things of life he did possess. Already home, father, and mother had assumed a greater significance to him; but he now found himself placing a higher personal value upon his sister, his chums and friends. He never had appreciated them properly, he thought, but henceforth—well, there would be a different tale to tell.

The voice of Pete hailing them put a finish to the conversation, for they both ran on deck.

"Get up ze mainsail, and break out ze hook!" he shouted. "And den tail on to ze *Reindeer!* No side-lights!"

"Come! Cast off those gaskets! Lively!" 'Frisco Kid ordered. "Now lay onto the peak-halyards—there, that rope; cast it off the pin. And don't hoist ahead of me. There! Make fast! We'll stretch it afterwards. Run aft and come in on the mainsheet! Shove the helm up!"

Under the sudden driving power of the mainsail, the *Dazzler* strained and tugged at her anchor like an impatient horse, till the muddy iron left the bottom with a rush, and she was free.

"Let go the sheet! Come for'ard again, and lend a hand on the chain! Stand by to give her the jib!" 'Frisco Kid, the boy who mooned over a picture of a girl in a magazine, had vanished, and 'Frisco Kid the sailor, strong and dominant, was on deck. He ran aft and tacked about as the jib rattled aloft in the hands of Joe, who quickly joined him. Just then the *Reindeer*, like a monstrous bat, passed to leeward of them in the gloom.

"Ah! dose boys! Dey take all-a night!" they heard Pete exclaim; and then the gruff voice of Nelson, who said: "Never you mind, Frenchy. I learned the Kid his sailor-izing, and I ain't never been ashamed of him yet."

The *Reindeer* was the faster boat, but by spilling the wind from her sails they managed so that the boys could keep them in sight. The breeze came steadily in from the west, with a promise of early increase. The stars were being blotted out by driving masses of clouds, which indicated a greater velocity in the upper strata. 'Frisco Kid surveyed the sky. "Going to have it good and stiff before morning," he prophesied, and Joe guessed so, too.

A couple of hours later both boats stood in for the land, and dropped anchor not more than a cable's-length from the shore. A little wharf ran out, the bare end of which was perceptible to them, though they could discern a small yacht lying to a buoy a short distance away.

As on the previous night, everything was in readiness for hasty departure. The anchors could be tripped and the sails flung out on a moment's notice. Both skiffs came over noiselessly from the *Reindeer*. Nelson had given one of his two men to Pete, so that each skiff was doubly manned. They were not a very prepossessing bunch of men—at least, Joe thought so, for their faces bore a savage seriousness which almost made him shiver. The captain of the *Dazzler* buckled on his pistol-belt and placed a rifle and a small double-block tackle in the boat. Nelson was also armed, while his men wore at their hips the customary sailor's sheath-knife. They were very slow and careful to avoid noise in getting into the boats, Pete pausing long enough to warn the boys to remain quietly aboard and not try any tricks.

"Now'd be your chance, Joe, if they hadn't taken the skiffs," 'Frisco Kid whispered, when the boats had vanished into the loom of the land.

"What's the matter with the *Dazzler?*" was the unexpected answer. "We could up sail and away before you could say Jack Robinson."

They crawled for'ard and began to hoist the mainsail. The anchor they could slip, if necessary, and save the time of pulling it up. But at the first rattle of the halyards on the sheaves a warning "Hist!" came to them through the darkness, followed by a loudly whispered "Drop that!"

Glancing in the direction from which these sounds proceeded, they made out a white face peering at them from over the rail of the other sloop.

"Aw, it's only the *Reindeer*'s boy," 'Frisco Kid said. "Come on."

Again they were interrupted at the first rattling of the blocks.

"I say, you fellers, you'd better let go them halyards pretty quick, I'm a-tellin' you, or I'll give you what for!"

This threat being dramatically capped by the click of a cocking pistol, 'Frisco Kid obeyed and went grumblingly back to the cockpit. "Oh, there's plenty more chances to come," he whispered consolingly to Joe. "Pete was cute, wasn't he? Kind of thought you'd be trying to make a break, and fixed it so you couldn't."

Nothing came from the shore to indicate how the pirates were faring. Not a dog barked, not a light flared; yet the air seemed quivering with an alarm about to burst forth. The night had taken on a strained feeling of intensity, as though it held in store all kinds of terrible things. The boys felt this keenly as they huddled against each other in the cockpit and waited.

"You were going to tell me about your running away," Joe ventured finally, "and why you came back again."

'Frisco Kid took up the tale at once, speaking in a muffled undertone close to the other's ear.

"You see, when I made up my mind to quit the life, there wasn't a soul to lend me a hand; but I knew that the only thing for me to do was to get ashore and find some kind of work, so I could study. Then I figured there'd be more chance in the country than in the city; so I gave Nelson the slip—I was on the *Reindeer* then—one night on the Alameda oysterbeds, and headed back from the Bay. But they were all Portuguese farmers thereabouts, and none of them had work for me. Besides, it was in the wrong time of the year—winter. That shows how much I knew about the land.

"I'd saved up a couple of dollars, and I kept traveling back, deeper and deeper into the country, looking for work and buying bread and cheese, and such things, from the storekeepers. I tell you it was cold, nights, sleeping out without blankets, and I was always glad when morning came. But worse than that was the way everybody looked on me. They were all suspicious, and not a bit afraid to show it, and sometimes they'd sick their dogs on me and tell me to get along. Seemed as though there wasn't no place for me on the land. Then my money gave out, and just about the time I was good and hungry I got captured."

"Captured! What for?"

"Nothing. Living, I suppose. I crawled into a haystack to sleep one night, because it was warmer, and along comes a village constable and arrests me for being a tramp. At first they thought I was a runaway, and telegraphed my description all over. I told them I didn't have no people, but they wouldn't believe me for a long while. And then, when nobody claimed me, the judge sent me to a boys' 'refuge' in San Francisco."

He stopped and peered intently in the direction of the shore. The darkness and the silence in which the men had been swallowed up were profound. Nothing was stirring save the rising wind.

"I thought I'd die in that 'refuge.' Just like being in jail. You were locked up and guarded like any prisoner. Even then, if I could have liked the other boys it wouldn't have been so bad. But they were mostly street-boys of the worst sort, without one spark of manhood or one idea of square dealing and fair play. There was only one thing I did like, and that was the books. Oh, I did lots of reading, I tell you. But that couldn't make up for the rest. I wanted the freedom, and the sunlight, and the salt water. And what had I done to be kept in prison and herded with such a gang? Instead of doing wrong, I had tried to do good, to make myself better, and that's what I got for it. I wasn't old enough, you see.

"Sometimes I'd see the sunshine dancing on the water and showing white on the sails, and the *Reindeer* cutting through it just as you please, and I'd get that sick I wouldn't know hardly what I did. And then the boys would come against me with some of their meannesses, and I'd start in to lick the whole kit of them. Then the men in charge'd lock me up and punish me. After I couldn't stand it no longer, I watched my chance, and cut and run for it. Seemed as though there wasn't no place on the land for me, so I picked up with Pete and went back on the Bay. That's about all there is to it, though I'm going to try it again when I get a little older—old enough to get a square deal for myself."

"You're going to go back on the land with me," Joe said authoritatively, laying a hand on his shoulder; "that's what you're going to do. As for—"

Bang! a revolver-shot rang out from the shore. Bang! bang! More guns were speaking sharply and hurriedly. A man's voice rose wildly on the air and died away. Somebody began to cry for help. Both boys were to their feet on the instant, hoisting the mainsail and getting everything ready to run. The *Reindeer* boy was doing likewise. A man, roused from his sleep on the yacht, thrust an excited head through the skylight, but withdrew it hastily at sight of the two stranger sloops. The intensity of waiting was broken, the time for action come.

CHAPTER I

PERILOUS HOURS

HEAVING in on the anchor-chain till it was up and down, 'Frisco Kid and Joe ceased from their exertions. Everything was in readiness to give the *Dazzler* the jib and go. They strained their eyes in the direction of the shore. The clamor had died away, but here and there lights were beginning to flash. The creaking of a block and tackle came to their ears, and they heard Nelson's voice singing out, "Lower away!" and "Cast off!"

"Pete forgot to oil it," 'Frisco Kid commented, referring to the tackle.

"Takin' their time about it, ain't they?" the boy on the *Reindeer* called over to them, sitting down on the cabin and mopping his face after the exertion of hoisting the mainsail single-handed.

"Guess they're all right," 'Frisco Kid rejoined.

"Say, you," the man on the yacht cried through the skylight, not venturing to show his head. "You'd better go away."

"And you'd better stay below and keep quiet," was the response.

"We'll take care of ourselves. See you do the same," replied the boy on the *Reindeer*.

"If I was only out of this, I'd show you," the man threatened.

"Lucky for you you're not," was the response.

"Here they come!"

The two skiffs shot out of the darkness and came alongside. Some kind of an altercation was going on, as Pete's shrill voice attested.

"No, no!" he cried. "Put it on ze *Dazzler*. Ze *Reindeer* she sail too fast-a, and run away, oh, so queeck, and never more I see it. Put it on ze *Dazzler*. Eh? W'at you say?"

"All right," Nelson agreed. "We'll

whack up afterwards. But hurry up. Out with you, lads, and heave her up. My arm's broke."

The men tumbled out, ropes were cast inboard, and all hands, with the exception of Joe, tailed on. The shouting of men, the sound of oars, and the rattling and slapping of blocks and sails, told that the men on shore were getting under way for the pursuit.

"Now!" Nelson commanded. "All together! Don't let her come back or you'll smash the skiff. There she takes it! A long pull and a strong pull! Once again! And yet again! Get a turn there, somebody, and take a spell."

Though the task was but half accomplished, they were exhausted by the strenuous effort, and hailed the rest eagerly. Joe glanced over the side to discover what the heavy object might be, and saw the vague outlines of a very small office safe.

"Now, all together! Take her on the run, and don't let her stop! Yo, ho! heave, ho! Once again! And another! Over with her!"

Straining and gasping, with tense muscles and heaving chests, they brought the cumbersome weight over the side, rolled it on top of the rail, and lowered it into the cockpit on the run. The cabin doors were thrown apart, and it was moved along, end for end, till it lay on the cabin floor, snug against the end of the centerboard-case. Nelson had followed it aboard to superintend. His left arm hung helpless at his side, and from the finger-tips blood dripped with monotonous regularity. He did not seem to mind it, however; nor even the mutterings of the human storm he had raised ashore, and which, to judge by the sounds, was even now threatening to break upon them.

"Lay your course for the Golden Gate," he said to Pete, as he turned to go. "I'll try to stand by you; but if you get lost in the dark, I'll meet you outside, off the Farralones, in the morning." He sprang into the skiff after the men, and, with a wave of his uninjured arm, cried heartily: "And then it's Mexico, my jolly rovers—Mexico and summer weather!"

Just as the *Dazzler*, freed from her anchor, paid off under the jib and filled away, a dark sail loomed under her stern, barely missing the skiff in tow. The cockpit of the stranger was crowded with men, who raised their voices angrily at sight of the pirates. Joe had half a mind to run for'ard and cut the halyards so that they might be captured. As he had told Pete the day before, he had done nothing to be ashamed of, and was not afraid to go before a court of justice. But the thought of 'Frisco Kid restrained him. He wished to take him ashore with him, but in so doing he did not wish to take him to jail. So he began to experience a keen interest in the escape of the *Dazzler*, after all.

The pursuing sloop rounded up hurriedly to come about after them, and in the darkness fouled the yacht which lay at anchor. The man aboard of her, thinking that at last his time had come, let out one wild yell, and ran on deck, screaming for help. In the confusion of the collision Pete and the boys slipped away into the night.

The *Reindeer* had already disappeared, and by the time Joe and 'Frisco Kid had the running-gear coiled down and everything in shape, they were standing out in open water. The wind was freshening constantly, and the *Dazzler* heeling a lively clip through the comparatively smooth water. Before an hour had passed, the lights of Hunter's Point were well on her starboard beam. 'Frisco Kid went below to make coffee, but Joe remained on deck, watching the lights of South San Francisco grow, and speculating on his destination. Mexico! They were going to sea in such a frail craft! Impossible! At least, it seemed so to him, for his conceptions of ocean travel were limited to steamers and full-rigged ships, and he did not know how the tiny fishing-boats ventured the open sea. He was beginning to feel half sorry that he had not cut the halyards, and longed to ask Pete a thousand questions; but just as the first was on his lips, that worthy ordered him to go below and get some coffee, and then to turn in. He was followed shortly afterward by 'Frisco Kid, Pete remaining at his lonely task of beating down the Bay and out to sea. Twice Pete heard the waves buffeted back from some flying forefoot, and once he saw a sail to leeward on the opposite tack, which luffed sharply and came about at sight of him. But the darkness favored, and he heard no more of it—perhaps because he worked into the wind closer by a point, and held on his way with a rebellious shaking after-leech.

Shortly after dawn the boys were called and came sleepily on deck. The day had broken cold and gray, while the wind had attained half a gale. Joe noted with astonishment the white tents of the quarantine station on Angel Island. San Francisco lay a smoky blur on the southern horizon, while the night, still lingering on the western edge of the world, slowly withdrew before their eyes. Pete was just finishing a long reach into the Raccoon Strait, and, at the same time, studiously regarding a plunging sloop-yacht half a mile astern.

"Dey t'ink to catch ze *Dazzler*, eh? Bah!" And he brought the craft in question about, laying a course straight for the Golden Gate.

The pursuing yacht followed suit. Joe watched her a few moments. She held an apparently parallel course to them, and forged ahead much faster.

"Why, at this rate they'll have us in no time!" he cried.

Pete laughed. "You t'ink so? Bah! Dey outfoot; we outpoint. Dey are scared of ze wind; we wipe ze eye of ze wind. Ah! you wait—you see."

"They're traveling ahead faster," 'Frisco Kid explained, "but we're sailing closer to the wind. In the end we'll beat them, even if they have the nerve to cross the bar, which I don't think they have. Look! See!"

Ahead could be seen the great ocean surges, flinging themselves skyward and bursting into roaring caps of smother. In the midst of it, now rolling her dripping bottom clear, now sousing her deck-load of lumber far above the guards, a coasting steam-schooner was lumbering heavily into port. It was magnificent, this battle between man and the elements. Whatever timidity he had entertained fled away, and Joe's nostrils began to dilate and his eyes to flash at the nearness of the impending struggle.

Pete called for his oilskins and sou'wester, and Joe also was equipped with a spare suit. Then he and 'Frisco Kid were sent below to lash and cleat the safe in place. In the midst of this task Joe glanced at the firm-name gilt-lettered on the face of it, and read, "Bronson & Tate." Why, that was his father and his father's partner. That was their safe! their money! 'Frisco Kid, nailing the last retaining-cleat on the floor of the cabin, looked up and followed his fascinated gaze.

"That's rough, isn't it?" he whispered. "Your father?"

Joe nodded. He could see it all now. They had run in to San Andreas, where his father worked the big quarries, and most probably the safe contained the wages of the thousand men or so whom his firm employed. "Don't say anything," he cautioned.

'Frisco Kid agreed knowingly. "Pete can't read, anyway," he added, "and the chances are that Nelson won't know what your name is. But, just the same, it's pretty rough. They'll break it open and divide up as soon as they can, so I don't see what you're going to do about it."

"Wait and see." Joe had made up his mind that he would do his best to stand by his father's property. At the worst, it could only be lost; and that would surely be the case were he not along; while, being along, he at least held a fighting chance to save or to be in position to recover it. Responsibilities were showering upon him thick and fast. Three days before he had had but himself to consider. Then, in some subtle way, he had felt a certain accountability for 'Frisco Kid's future welfare; and after that, and still more subtly, he had become aware of duties which he owed to his position, to his sister, to his chums, and to friends. And now, by a most unexpected chain of circumstances, came the pressing need of service for his father's sake. It was a call upon his deepest strength, and he responded bravely. While the future might be doubtful, he had no doubt of himself; and this very state of mind, this self-confidence, by a generous alchemy, gave him added strength. Nor did he fail to be vaguely aware of it, and to grasp dimly at the truth that confidence breeds confidence—strength, strength.

"Now she takes it!" Pete cried.

Both lads ran into the cockpit. They were on the edge of the breaking bar. A huge forty-footer reared a foam-crested head far above them, stealing their wind for the moment and threatening to crush the tiny craft like an eggshell. Joe held his breath. It was the supreme moment. Pete luffed straight into it, and the *Dazzler* mounted the steep slope with a rush, poised a moment on the giddy summit, and fell into the yawning valley beyond. Keeping off in the intervals to fill the mainsail, and luffing into the combers, they worked their way across the dangerous stretch. Once they caught the tail-end of the whitecap and were well-nigh smothered in the froth; but otherwise the sloop bobbed and ducked with the happy facility of a cork.

To Joe it seemed as though he had been lifted out of himself, out of the world. Ah, this was life! This was action! Surely it could not be the old, commonplace world he had lived in so long! The sailors, grouped on the streaming deck-load of the steamer, waved their sou'westers, nor, on the bridge, was the captain above expressing his admiration for the plucky craft.

"Ah! You see! You see!" Pete pointed astern.

The sloop-yacht had been afraid to venture it, and was skirting back and forth on the inner edge of the bar. The chase was off. A pilot-boat, running for shelter from the coming storm, flew by them like a frightened bird, passing the steamer as though the latter were standing still.

Half an hour later the *Dazzler* passed beyond the last smoking sea and was sliding up and down on the long Pacific swell. The wind had increased its velocity and necessitated a reefing down of jib and mainsail. Then she laid off again, full and free on the starboard tack, for the Farralones, thirty miles away. By the time breakfast was cooked and eaten they picked up the *Reindeer*, hove to and working offshore to the south and west. The wheel was lashed down, and there was not a soul on deck.

Pete complained bitterly against such a recklessness. "Dat is ze one fault of Nelson. He no care. He is afraid of not'ing. Some day he will die, oh, so vaire queeck! I know, I know."

Three times they circled about the *Reindeer*, running under her weather quarter and shouting in chorus, before they brought anybody on deck. Sail was then made at once, and together the two cockleshells plunged away into the vastness of the Pacific. This was necessary, as 'Frisco Kid informed Joe, in order to have an offing before the whole fury of the storm broke upon them. Otherwise they would be driven on the lee shore of the California coast. "Grub and water," he said, could be obtained by running in to the land when fine weather came. He also congratulated Joe upon the fact that he was not seasick—which circumstance likewise brought praise from Pete, and put him in better humor with his mutinous sailor.

"I'll tell you what we'll do," 'Frisco Kid whispered, while cooking dinner. "Tonight we'll drag Pete down—"

"Drag Pete down?"

"Yes, and tie him up good and snug—as soon as it gets dark. Then put out the lights and make a run for it. Get to port anyway, anywhere, just so long as we shake loose from Nelson. You'll save your father's money, and I'll go away somewhere, over on the other side of the world, and begin all over again."

"Then we'll have to call it off, that's all."

"Call what off?"

"Tying Pete up and running for it."

"No, sir; that's decided upon."

"Now, listen here: I'll not have a thing to do with it—I'll go on to Mexico first—if you don't make me one promise."

"And what's the promise?"

"Just this: you place yourself in my hands from the moment we get ashore, and trust to me. You don't know anything about the land, anyway—you said so. And I'll fix it with my father—I know I can—so that you can get to study, and get an education, and be something else than a Bay pirate or a sailor. That's what you'd like, isn't it?"

Though he said nothing, 'Frisco Kid showed how well he liked it by the expression of his face.

"And it'll be no more than your due, either," Joe continued. "You've stood by me, and you'll have recovered my father's money. He'll owe it to you."

"But I don't do things that way. Think I do a man a favor just to be paid for it?"

"Now you keep quiet. How much do you think it'd cost my father to recover that safe? Give me your promise, that's all, and when I've got things arranged, if you don't like them you can back out. Come on; that's fair."

They shook hands on the bargain, and proceeded to map out their line of action for the night.

But the storm yelling down out of the northwest had something entirely different in store for the *Dazzler* and her crew. By the time dinner was over they were forced to put double reefs in mainsail and jib, and still the gale had not reached its height. The sea, also, had been kicked up till it was a continuous succession of water mountains, frightful and withal grand to look upon from the low deck of the sloop. It was only when the sloops were tossed up on the crests of the waves at the same time that they caught sight of each other. Occasional fragments of seas swashed into the cockpit or dashed aft clear over the cabin, and before long Joe was stationed at the small pump to keep the well dry.

At three o'clock, watching his chance, Pete motioned to the *Reindeer* that he was going to heave to and get out a sea-anchor. This latter was of the nature of a large shallow canvas bag, with the mouth held open by triangularly lashed spars. To this the towing-ropes were attached, on the kite principle, so that the greatest resisting surface was presented to the water. The sloop, drifting so much faster, would thus be held bow on to both wind and sea—the safest possible position in a storm. Nelson waved his hand in response that he understood and to go ahead.

Pete went for'ard to launch the sea-anchor himself, leaving it to 'Frisco Kid to put the helm down at the proper moment and run into the wind.

The Frenchman poised on the slippery foredeck, waiting an opportunity. But at this moment the *Dazzler* lifted into an unusually large sea, and, as she cleared the summit, caught a heavy snort of the gale at the very instant she was righting herself to an even keel.

Thus there was not the slightest yield to this sudden pressure coming on her sails and mast-gear.

Snap! Crash! The steel weather-rigging was carried away at the lanyards, and mast, jib, mainsail, blocks, stays, sea-anchor, Pete—everything—went over the side. Almost by a miracle, the captain clutched at the bobstay and managed to get one hand up and over the bowsprit. The boys ran for'ard to drag him into safety, and Nelson, observing the disaster, put up his helm and instantly ran the *Reindeer* down to the rescue of the imperiled crew.

CHAPTER VI

THE END OF THE CRUISE

PETE was uninjured from the fall overboard with the *Dazzler*'s mast, but the sea-anchor which had gone with him had not escaped so easily. The gaff of the mainsail had been driven through it, and it refused to work. The wreckage, thumping alongside, held the sloop in a quartering slant to the seas—not so dangerous a position as it might be, nor as safe, either.

"Good-by, old-a *Dazzler*. Never no more you wipe ze eye of ze wind. Never no more you kick your heels at ze crack gentleman yachts."

So the captain lamented, standing in the cockpit and surveying the ruin with wet eyes. Even Joe, who bore him great dislike, felt sorry for him at this moment. As the horse is to the Arab, so the ship is to the sailor, and Pete suffered his loss keenly. A heavier blast of the wind caught the jagged crest of a wave and hurled it upon the helpless craft.

"Can't we save her?" Joe spluttered.

'Frisco Kid shook his head.

"Or the safe?"

"Impossible," he answered. "Couldn't lay another boat alongside for a United States mint. As it is, it'll keep us guessing to save ourselves."

Another sea swept over them, and the skiff, which had long since been swamped, dashed itself to pieces against the stern. Then the *Reindeer* towered above them on a mountain of water. Joe caught himself half shrinking back, for it seemed she would fall down squarely on top of them; but the next instant she dropped into the gaping trough, and they were looking down upon her far below. It was a striking picture—one Joe was destined never to forget. The *Reindeer* was wallowing in the snow-white smother, her rails flush with the sea, the water scudding across her deck in foaming cataracts. The air was filled with flying spray, which made the scene appear hazy and unreal. One of the men was clinging to the perilous after-deck and striving to cast off the water-logged skiff. The boy, leaning far over the cockpit-rail and holding on for dear life, was passing him a knife. The second man stood at the wheel, putting it up with flying hands, and forcing the sloop to pay off. By him, his injured arm in a sling, was Nelson, his sou'wester gone and his fair hair plastered in wet, wind-blown ringlets about his face. His whole attitude breathed indomitability, courage, strength. Joe looked upon him in sudden awe, and, realizing the enormous possibilities in the man, felt sorrow for the way in which they had been wasted. A pirate—a robber! In that flashing moment he caught a glimpse of truth, grasped at the mystery of success and failure. Of such stuff as Nelson were heroes made; but they possessed wherein he lacked—the power of choice, the careful poise of mind, the sober control of soul.

These were the thoughts which came to Joe in the flight of a second. Then the *Reindeer* swept skyward and hurtled across their bow to leeward on the breast of a mighty billow.

"Ze wild man! ze wild man!" Pete shrieked, watching her in amazement. "He t'inks he can jibe! He will die! We will all die! He must come about! Oh, ze fool! ze fool!"

But time was precious, and Nelson ventured the chance. At the right moment he jibed the mainsail over and hauled back on the wind.

"Here she comes! Make ready to jump for it!" 'Frisco Kid cried to Joe.

The *Reindeer* dashed by their stern, heeling over till the cabin windows were buried, and so close that it appeared she must run them down. But a freak of the waters lurched the two crafts apart. Nelson, seeing that the manoeuver had miscarried, instantly instituted another. Throwing the helm hard up, the *Reindeer* whirled on her heel, thus swinging her overhanging mainboom closer to the *Dazzler*. Pete was the nearest, and the opportunity could last no longer than a second. Like a cat he sprang, catching the foot-rope with both hands. Then the *Reindeer* forged ahead, dipping him into the sea at every plunge. But he clung on, working inboard every time he emerged, till he dropped into the cockpit, as Nelson squared off to run down to leeward and repeat the manoeuver.

"Your turn next," 'Frisco Kid said.

"No; yours," Joe replied.

"But I know more about the water," 'Frisco Kid insisted.

"I can swim as well as you," said the other.

It would have been hard to forecast the outcome of this dispute; but, as it was, the swift rush of events made any settlement useless. The *Reindeer* had jibed over and was plowing back at breakneck speed, careening at such an angle that it seemed she must surely capsize. It was a gallant sight.

The storm burst in fury, the shouting wind, flattening the ragged crests till they boiled. The *Reindeer* dipped from view behind an immense wave. The wave rolled on, but where the sloop had been the boys noted with startled eyes only the angry waters. Doubting, they looked a second time. There was no *Reindeer*. They were alone on the ocean.

"God have mercy on their souls!"

Joe was too horrified at the suddenness of the catastrophe to utter a sound.

"Sailed her clean under, and, with the ballast she carried, went straight to bottom," 'Frisco Kid gasped when he could speak. "Pete always said Nelson would drown himself that way some day! And now they're all gone. It's dreadful—dreadful. But now we've got to look out for ourselves, I tell you! The back of the storm broke in that puff, but the sea'll kick up worse yet as the wind eases down. Lend a hand, and hang on with the other. We've got to get her head-on."

Together, knives in hand, they crawled for'ard, where the pounding wreckage hampered the boat sorely. 'Frisco Kid took the lead in the ticklish work, but Joe obeyed orders like a veteran. Every minute or so the bow was swept by the sea, and they were pounded and buffeted about like a pair of shuttlecocks. First the main portion of the wreckage was securely fastened to the for'ard bits; then, breathless and gasping, more often under the water than out, it was cut and hack at the tangle of halyards, sheets, stays, and tackles. The cockpit was taking water rapidly, and it was a race between swamping and completing the task. At last, however, everything stood clear save the lee rigging. 'Frisco Kid slashed the lanyards. The storm did the rest. The *Dazzler* drifted swiftly to leeward of the wreckage, till the strain on the line fast to the for'ard bitts jerked her bow into place, and she ducked dead into the eye of the wind and sea.

Pausing but for a cheer at the success of their undertaking, the two lads raced aft, where the cockpit was half full and the dunnage of the cabin all afloat. With a couple of buckets procured from the stern lockers, they proceeded to fling the water overboard. It was heartbreaking work, for many a barrelful was flung back upon them again; but they persevered, and when night fell, the *Dazzler*, bobbing merrily at her sea-anchor, could boast that her pumps sucked once more. As 'Frisco Kid had said, the backbone of the storm was broken, though the wind had veered to the west, where it still blew stiffly.

"If she holds," 'Frisco Kid said, referring to the breeze, "we'll drift to the California coast, somewhere along in, to-morrow. There's nothing to do now but wait."

They said little, oppressed by the loss of their comrades and overcome with exhaustion, preferring to huddle against each other for the sake of warmth and companionship. It was a miserable night, and they shivered constantly from the cold. Nothing dry was to be obtained aboard, food, blankets, everything being soaked with the salt water. Sometimes they dozed; but these intervals were short and harassing, for it seemed as if each of the two boys took turns in waking with such a sudden start as to rouse the other.

At last day broke, and they looked about. Wind and sea had dropped considerably, and there was no question as to the safety of the *Dazzler*. The coast was nearer than they had expected, its cliffs showing dark and forbidding in the gray of dawn. But with the rising of the sun they could see the yellow beaches, flanked by the white surf, and, beyond—it seemed too good to be true—the clustering houses and smoking chimneys of a town.

"It's Santa Cruz!" 'Frisco Kid cried. "And we'll run no risk of being wrecked in the surf!"

"Then you think we'll save the safe?" Joe queried.

"Yes, indeed we will! There isn't much of a sheltered harbor for large vessels, but with this breeze we'll run right up the mouth of the San Lorenzo River. Then there's a little lake like, and boat-houses. Water smooth as glass. Come on. We'll be in in time for breakfast."

Bringing to light some spare coils of rope from the lockers, he put a clove-hitch on the standing part of the sea-anchor hawser, and carried the new running-line aft, making it fast to the stern bitts. Then he cast off from the for'ard bitts. Naturally the *Dazzler* swung off into the trough, completed the evolution, and pointed her nose toward shore. A couple of spare oars from below, and as many water-soaked blankets, sufficed to make a jury-mast and sail. When this was in place Joe cast loose from the wreckage, which was now towing astern, while 'Frisco Kid took the tiller.

"How's that?" said 'Frisco Kid, as he finished making the *Dazzler* fast fore and aft, and stepped upon the stringer-piece of the tiny wharf. "What'll we do next, captain?"

Joe looked up in quick surprise. "Why—I—what's the matter?"

"Well, aren't you captain now? Haven't we reached land? I'm crew from now on, you know. What's your orders?"

Joe caught the spirit of it. "Pipe all hands for breakfast; that is—wait a minute."

Diving below, he possessed himself of the money he had stowed away in his bundle when he came aboard. Then he locked the cabin door, and they went uptown in search of restaurants. Over the breakfast Joe planned the next move, and, when they had done, communicated it to 'Frisco Kid.

In response to his inquiry the cashier told him when the morning train started for San Francisco. He glanced at the clock.

"I've just time to catch it," he said to 'Frisco Kid. "Here is the key to the cabin door. Keep it locked, and don't let anybody come aboard. Here's money. Eat at the restaurants. Dry your blankets and sleep in the cockpit. I'll be back to-morrow. And don't let anybody into that cabin. Good-by."

With a hasty hand-grip, he sped down the street to the depot. The conductor, when he punched his ticket, looked at him with surprise. And well he might, for it was not the custom of his passengers to travel in sea-boots and sou'westers. But Joe did not mind. He did not even notice. He had bought a paper and was absorbed in its contents. Before long his eyes caught an interesting paragraph:

SUPPOSED TO HAVE BEEN LOST

The tug *Sea Queen*, chartered by Bronson & Tate, has returned from a fruitless cruise outside the heads. No news of value could be obtained concerning the pirates who so daringly carried off their safe at San Andreas last Tuesday night. The lighthouse-keeper at the Farralones mentions having sighted the two sloops Wednesday morning, clawing offshore in the teeth of the gale. It is supposed by shipping men that they perished in the storm with their ill-gotten treasure. Rumor has it that, in addition to a large sum in gold, the safe contained papers of even greater importance.

When Joe had read this he felt a great relief. It was evident no one had been killed at San Andreas on the night of the robbery, else there would have been some comment on it in the paper. Nor, if they had had any clue to his own whereabouts, would they have omitted such a striking bit of information.

At the depot in San Francisco the curious on-lookers were surprised to see a boy clad conspicuously in sea-boots and sou'wester hail a cab and dash away in it. But Joe was in a hurry. He knew his father's hours, and was fearful lest he should not catch him before he went to luncheon.

The office-boy scowled at him when he pushed open the door and asked to see Mr. Bronson; nor could the head clerk, when summoned by this strange-looking intruder, recognize him.

"Don't you know me, Mr. Willis?"

Mr. Willis looked a second time. "Why, it's Joe Bronson! Of all things under the sun, where did you drop from? Go right in. Your father's in there."

Mr. Bronson stopped dictating to his stenographer, looked up, and said: "Hello! where have you been?"

"To sea," Joe answered demurely enough, not sure of just what kind of a reception he was to get, and fingering his sou'wester nervously.

"Short trip, eh? How did you make out?"

"Oh, so-so." He had caught the twinkle in his father's eye, and knew that it was all clear sailing. "Not so bad—er—that is, considering."

"Considering?"

"Well, not exactly that; rather, it might have been worse, and, well—I don't know that it could have been better."

"You interest me; sit down." Then, turning to the stenographer, "You may go, Mr. Brown, and—hum—I sha'n't need you any more to-day."

It was all Joe could do to keep from crying, so kindly and naturally had his father received him—making him feel at once as if not the slightest thing uncommon had occurred. It was as if he had just returned from a vacation, or, man-grown, had come back from some business trip.

"Now go ahead, Joe. You were speaking to me a moment ago in conundrums, and have aroused my curiosity to a most uncomfortable degree."

Thereat Joe sat down and told what had happened, all that had happened, from the previous Monday night to that moment. Each little incident he related, every detail, not forgetting his conversations with 'Frisco Kid nor his plans concerning him. His face flushed and he was carried away with the excitement of the narrative, while Mr. Bronson was almost as interested, urging him on whenever he slackened his pace, but otherwise remaining silent.

"So you see," Joe said at last, "it couldn't possibly have turned out any better."

"Ah, well," Mr. Bronson deliberated judiciously, "it may be so, and then again it may not."

"I don't see it." Joe felt sharp disappointment at his father's qualified approval. It seemed to him that the return of the safe merited something stronger.

That Mr. Bronson fully comprehended the way Joe felt about it was clearly in evidence, for he went on: "As to the matter of the safe, all hail to you, Joe. Credit, and plenty of it, is your due. Mr. Tate and I have already spent five hundred dollars in attempting to recover it. So important was it that we have also offered five thousand dollars reward, and this morning were even considering the advisability of increasing the amount. But, my son"—Mr. Bronson stood up, resting a hand affectionately on his boy's shoulder—"there be certain things in this world which are of still greater importance than gold or papers which represent that which gold may buy. How about *yourself?* There's the point. Will you sell the best possibilities of your life right now for a million dollars?"

Joe shook his head.

"As I said, that's the point. A human life the treasure of the world cannot buy; nor can it redeem one which is misspent; nor can it make full and complete and beautiful a life which is dwarfed and warped and ugly. How about yourself? What is to be the effect of all these strange adventures on your life—*your* life, Joe? Are you going to pick yourself up to-morrow and try it over again? Or the next day, or the day after? Do you understand? Why, Joe, do you think for one moment that I could place against the best value of my son's life the paltry value of a safe? And *can* I say, until time has told me, whether this trip of yours could not possibly have been better? Such an experience is as potent for evil as for good. One dollar is exactly like another—there are many in the world; but no Joe is like my Joe, nor can there be any others in the world to take his place. Don't you see, Joe? Don't you understand?"

Mr. Bronson's voice broke slightly, and the next instant Joe was sobbing as though his heart would break. He had never understood this father of his before, and he knew now the pain he must have caused him, to say nothing of his mother and sister. But the four stirring days he had spent had given him a clearer view of the world and humanity, and he had always possessed the power of putting his thoughts into speech; so he spoke of these things and the lessons he had learned, the conclusions he had drawn from his conversations with 'Frisco Kid, from his intercourse with Pete, from the graphic picture he retained of the *Reindeer* and Nelson as they wallowed in the trough beneath him. And Mr. Bronson listened and, in turn, understood.

"But what of 'Frisco Kid, father?" Joe asked when he had finished.

"Hum! there's a great deal of promise in the boy, from what you say of him." Mr. Bronson hid the twinkle in his eye this time. "And, I must confess, he seems perfectly capable of shifting for himself."

"Sir?" Joe could not believe his ears.

"Let us see, then. He is at present entitled to the half of five thousand dollars, the other half of which belongs to you. It was you two who preserved the safe from the bottom of the Pacific, and if you only had waited a little longer, Mr. Tate and I might have increased the reward."

"Oh!" Joe caught a glimmering of the light. "Part of that is easily arranged, father. I simply refuse to take my half. As to the other—that isn't exactly what 'Frisco Kid desires. He wants friends—and—and—though you didn't say so, they are far higher than gold, nor can gold buy them. He wants friends and a chance for an education—not twenty-five hundred dollars."

"Don't you think it would be better that he choose for himself?"

"Ah, no. That's all arranged."

"Arranged?"

"Yes, sir. He's captain on sea, and I'm captain on land. So he's under my charge now."

"Then you have the power of attorney for him in the present negotiations? Good. I'll make a proposition. The twenty-five hundred dollars shall be held in trust by me, on his demand at any time. We'll settle about yours afterward. Then he shall be put on probation for, say, a year—as messenger first, and then in the office. You can either coach him in his studies, or he can attend night-school. And after that, if he comes through his period of probation with flying colors, I'll give him the same opportunities for an education that you possess. It all depends on himself. And now, Mr. Attorney, what have you to say to my offer in the interests of your client?"

"That I close with it at once—and thank you."

Father and son shook hands.

"And what are you going to do now, Joe?"

"I'm going to send a telegram to 'Frisco Kid first, and then hurry home."

"Then wait a minute till I call up San Andreas and tell Mr. Tate the good news, and I'll go with you."

"Mr. Willis," Mr. Bronson said as they left the outer office, "do you remain in charge, and kindly tell the clerks that they are free for the rest of the day.

"And I say," he called back as they entered the elevator, "don't forget the office-boy."

December, 1899

THE KING OF THE GOLDEN WOODS

By Everett McNeil

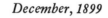

HE home of the King of the Golden Woods was in a snow-white palace of polished marble, crowned by a central dome of burnished gold incrusted with diamonds and rubies, and more beautiful than pen can tell. Around this palace rose a mighty wall of smooth black marble, forty feet thick and one hundred feet high. On top of this wall, at regular intervals, fifty great armed giants kept watch and ward, and each giant had two eyes, one in the center of the forehead and one in the back of the head, as all good sentinels should have. At the four points of the compass four strong gates of bronze guarded the only openings through the wall. Around the wall, for seven leagues in every direction, grew the golden forest of the king, a marvelous wood wherein every tree and shrub was pure gold, from its topmost leaf to its bottommost root. In all the world there was not another forest like to this great wood of gold, and because of it the king was called the King of the Golden Woods.

Through the forest ran four roads to the four gates of the great wall surrounding the king's palace, and at the beginning of each road stood a huge marble block, cut deep with letters which read:

I, the King of the Golden Woods, have a daughter, whom I love, but no son. Therefore, before I die I would see my daughter happily wed to a man fit to be king over her heart and ruler over the Golden Woods. This road leads, through the Golden Woods, to the gate in the great wall surrounding the king's palace; and I, the king, invite all who would do their endeavor to win this priceless guerdon, a king's daughter and a king's throne, to journey hitherward. Let no one in whose heart dwells evil, or vaunting ambition, or cruel hardness, or sordid greediness, or boasting coward-ice, attempt the journey; for I, the king, have beset the road with manifold and deadly perils to all who have evil in their hearts or lives.

For three years had these marble blocks stood at the head of the four roads; yet the daughter of the King of the Golden Woods remained unwed. Not because there had been wanting men to attempt the journey through the woods of gold, for then, as now, men loved gold and beauty and power, and were ready to peril limb and life for their winning; but of all the hundreds who had ventured on the quest, and had bravely entered the golden forest, not one, prince or knight or peasant, had ever returned. Men thought of the horror of this, and the ardor of their hearts grew cold, and none longer cared to venture beneath the somber shadows of the trees of gold, not even to wed a king's daughter and to sit on a king's throne. The grass grew long on the roadways, and the moss began to creep over the white of the marble blocks.

Then came to the north road four brothers, sons of a powerful king whose kingdom was a year's journey from the realm of the King of the Golden Woods, and with the four brothers rode their page,

Yosuff. It had taken one year for the strange proclamation of the King of the Golden Woods to reach the ears of the four brothers; another year had gone ere they had won their father's consent to depart on a quest so distant and so uncertain; and the third year had been passed in making the journey.

Prince Odolph, the eldest of the four brothers, spurred his horse to the side of the huge block of marble, and, leaning forward, read aloud what was written thereon. Then the four brothers looked long and earnestly at the great wood of gold, sparkling in the bright light of the morning. Not a sound, not a movement, came from within its yellow depths, and its shadows hung darkly above the ground.

"I go forward," said Prince Odolph, "without fear, ready to peril all for the winning of so great a prize"; and seating himself firmly in the saddle, he dropped his vizor, gripped his spear-shaft strongly, and rode down the highway leading into the great wood of gold.

"I follow my brother, ready to share his peril, to fight for his safety, and, if it be God's will that he should perish, to continue the quest to the end, fearing death less than defeat," said Prince Ormand, the second of the four brothers, riding close after Prince Odolph.

"I go forward until all of us be dead, or one of us a king. Ride on!" called Prince Armad, the third of the four brothers, touching spurs to his horse, and riding up close to the side of Prince Ormand.

"And I ride forth blithely to win a bride and a throne, or a grave," cried Prince Ized, the youngest of the brothers; and, like a happy school-boy, tossing high his lance into the air and catching it, he dug the spurs into his horse's flanks and galloped after his brothers.

Then said Yosuff the page: "For the love

of the brothers ride I into these weird woods, ready to face whatever comes, and caring not for death, so be it I can die like a man, leaving my honor bright and my sword clean."

No sound came to the ears of the five men as they entered the great woods, save the footfalls of their horses' hoofs and their own deep breathings. Above their heads the golden branches hung silent and motionless. Not a leaf trembled. Around them, like the pillars of a mighty temple, towered the great trunks of gold, and on the ground the grass grew green. Soon the grandeur and the beauty of the scene began to work upon their souls. Their eyes sparkled and their faces flushed. Wealth, boundless wealth, was here—was theirs for the taking! There were no eyes to see, and the gold was everywhere, cumbering the earth with its massive weight.

Suddenly Prince Ized gave a shout, and drawing his sharp sword from its scabbard, cried aloud: "I vow I will have this wondrous branch in spite of all the demons of this marvelous woods!" And as he cried, he swung his sword and cut from a great tree a branch of gold.

At the stroke of the sword a shudder shook the mighty woods, the huge trunks began to sway and to shake until the earth trembled, and the branches lashed the air furiously, as if under the whip of a hurricane; yet there was not a breath of air stirring. Then, with a low, moaning sound, the giant trees began to move bodily through the ground, and swiftly, one by one, to come between Prince Ized and his brothers, until a solid wall of golden trunks surrounded him and held him prisoner.

A great whistling wind blew coldly through the woods, and the trees slowly returned to their places; but Prince Ized had vanished.

The three brothers watched this awesome sight, sitting white and still in their saddles, numb with the terror of it; but Yosuff the page dug his spurs deep into his horse's sides and sprang to the rescue, only to dash vainly against the solid trunks of the intercepting trees.

When the moaning sound grew still, and the great trees again stood motionless, the three brothers continued their journey in silence, riding close together, and shuddering whenever a branch of gold chanced to touch the white plumes of their helmets.

For a league farther they rode thus, and then they came to a mighty river, rolling swiftly between rocky banks, its surface a fierce turmoil of foaming water and whirling cakes of ice. On the bank of the river sat four hideous dwarfs, their bodies having no covering except a fur of coarse red hair. The instant their eyes caught sight of the four men, they jumped to their feet and shouted: "Haste! Haste! The wolves! The wolves!" Then each dwarf ran swiftly to a horseman's side, and begged to be taken up behind and carried across the river, where the wolves could not go.

The men heard the sound of many feet coming from behind, and, turning quickly, saw hundreds of great yellow wolves leaping fiercely toward them.

Prince Odolph and Prince Ormand and Yosuff the page each paused to swing a dwarf upon the horse behind him; but Prince Armad beat the misshapen being from his stirrup's side with the shaft of his long lance, and, all heedless of his piteous cries, dashed away toward the river.

When Yosuff the page saw that the dwarf must perish unless helped, he quickly drew rein. "Come," said he, "I am light and my horse is strong. He can carry three. The wolves shall not eat you"; and he swung the dwarf up in front of himself.

Then a strange thing happened.

Prince Armad, not having been delayed

by the dwarfs, nor his horse cumbered with the weight of one, reached the river first, and dashed into the water. Instantly, like a thing of life, the river leaped upon him, and man and horse vanished in a mighty rush of whirling ice and foam, down the course of the stream.

The three men drew rein, white with wonder and horror; for on the instant of the disappearance of Prince Armad, the swift river sank into the ground, the dwarfs slipped from off the horses' backs and ran into the woods, and the wolves vanished like a thick yellow mist.

"Great must be the prize guarded thus fearfully," said Prince Odolph. "Come, brother, let us go forward and meet the end quickly"; and the two brothers, followed by Yosuff the page, rode swiftly on underneath the trees of gold.

Presently they came to a high hill, and when they had reached the top of the hill, they saw, in a beautiful valley surrounded by the high wall of black marble, the marvelous palace of the King of the Golden Woods. The great dome of burnished gold, with its glittering jewels, the grand palace of white marble, and the mighty surrounding woods of solid gold, all lay beneath their eyes. At this wondrous sight their bosoms swelled. To be lord of all these riches, King of the Golden Woods! What would not man do for splenders such as these?

Long the two brothers looked at the glittering dome of the palace and the surrounding woods of gold; and evil thoughts began to gather in their hearts, and each glanced darkly at the other.

"Brother," said Prince Odolph, roughly, "I am the elder. I will ride to the palace of the king alone. Remain thou here."

"Not so," answered Prince Ormand, shortly. "In this quest all are equal. I go to the king's palace or I die."

"Then die!" cried Prince Odolph, fiercely. "Two cannot win this prize. One of us must perish, and it were better that he should perish here." And the two brothers gripped their lances and charged each at the other. They met with a great crash, and the lances were shivered to the hands, but neither man was unhorsed. Then they drew their swords; but before either could strike a blow, with a roar as of the rushing together of many winds, a great whirling black smoke fell upon the two brothers and bore them swiftly away.

Yosuff the page sat on his horse alone. His heart was heavy, for he had loved the four brothers.

"Now I will go to their father the king," he said; and bowing his head, he rode sadly down the hill.

When he came to the foot of the hill he found an old man lying by the roadside, moaning with the agony of a broken leg. Yosuff dismounted and helped the sufferer upon the back of his horse.

"To the palace," moaned the old man. "There is no help nearer."

"I will then bear you to the palace," answered Yosuff, thinking only of saving the old man's life. And mounting, and holding the old man in his arms so as to ease his pain, he rode to the gate in the great wall around the palace.

The instant he stopped before the gate, the giant sentinel on the top of the wall called with a loud voice, "Ho, the king has come!" and "Ho, the king has come!" repeated all the other giants, all around the wall. The great gate of bronze swung wide open, and there, ready to receive Yosuff the page, was the King of the Golden Woods and all his magnificent court; and back of the king, surrounded by a guard of men-at-arms, stood the four brothers in the midst of a great number of other men who had been unsuccessful.

"I crave thy mercy, O King, for this old

"THE TWO BROTHERS GRIPPED THEIR LANCES AND CHARGED EACH AT THE OTHER."

man, who has received a grievous hurt," said Yosuff, quickly dismounting and bowing low at the feet of the king; "and I beg that he may be given into the hands of thy physicians. As for myself, with thy permission, I will return to the land whence I came, or unhappily hath our enterprise ended for those for whose sake I journeyed hither."

But the king, bending forward, lifted Yosuff to his feet and said: "Arise! Henceforth thou art my son, and the heir to my kingdom; for thou hast proven thyself brave and noblehearted, even as a king should be. But," said the king, pointing to the four brothers and the long row of stately men who stood waiting with bowed heads, "these men, who came hither seeking a great prize, and failed of the winning of it because of the evil in their hearts, shall be thy servants, and learn the worth of true nobility in thy service."

Then the king threw a chain of gold around the neck of the youth, and a purple robe over his shoulders, and led him amid great rejoicings into his palace.

Thus it came about that Yosuff the page, who entered the Golden Woods with a pure and kind heart, and seeking nothing, won all.

JATAKA TALES

Re-told by Ellen C. Babbitt

January, 1912

[INTRODUCTORY NOTE: The Jataka Tales are the very oldest of stories. They were told years and years and years ago in that famous country of the Far East called India. And even to-day the children there hear these stories told and are glad to have them printed in their schoolbooks. They call them "The Jat'-a-kas" or "The Jat-a-ka Tales."

You will be interested to know how these stories have been scattered all over the world. In the long ago when some people moved away from India and made homes for themselves in other countries, they told their children these Tales, and when these little children had grown up, they, too, moved to strange, new countries. They remembered these Jatakas and told them over again to their children.

Perhaps you will find some of the Jataka Tales are like some of the stories Uncle Remus tells! And the fun of these Tales, as ST. NICHOLAS tells them, is that you can read them to yourself.—E. C. B.]

THE MONKEY AND THE CROCODILE

PART I

A MONKEY lived in a great tree on a river bank.

In the river there were many Crocodiles.

A Crocodile watched the Monkeys for a long time, and one day she said to her son: "My son, get one of those Monkeys for me. I want the heart of a Monkey to eat."

"How am I to catch a Monkey?" asked the little Crocodile. "I do not travel on land, and the Monkey does not go into the water."

"Put your wits to work, and you'll find a way," said the mother.

And the little Crocodile thought and thought.

At last he said to himself: "I know what I'll do. I'll get that Monkey that lives in a big tree on the river bank. He wishes to go across the river to the island where the fruit is so ripe."

So the Crocodile swam to the tree where the Monkey lived. But he was a stupid Crocodile.

"Oh, Monkey," he called, "come with me over to the island where the fruit is so ripe."

"How can I go with you?" asked the Monkey. "I do not swim."

"No—but I do. I will take you over on my back," said the Crocodile.

The Monkey was greedy, and wanted the ripe fruit, so he jumped down on the Crocodile's back.

"Off we go!" said the Crocodile.

"This is a fine ride you are giving me!" said the Monkey.

"Do you think so? Well, how do you like this?" asked the Crocodile, diving.

"Oh, don't!" cried the Monkey, as he went under the water. He was afraid to let go, and he did not know what to do under the water.

"'WHY DID YOU TAKE ME UNDER WATER, CROCODILE?' THE MONKEY ASKED."

When the Crocodile came up, the Monkey sputtered and choked. "Why did you take me under water, Crocodile?" he asked.

"I am going to kill you by keeping you under water," answered the Crocodile. "My mother wants Monkey-heart to eat, and I'm going to take yours to her."

"I wish you had told me you wanted my heart," said the Monkey, "then I might have brought it with me."

"How queer!" said the stupid Crocodile. "Do you mean to say that you left your heart back there in the tree?"

"That is what I mean," said the Monkey. "If you want my heart, we must go back to the tree and get it. But we are so near the island where the ripe fruit is, please take me there first."

"No, Monkey," said the Crocodile, "I'll take you straight back to your tree. Never mind the ripe fruit. Get your heart and bring it to me at once. Then we'll see about going to the island."

"Very well," said the Monkey.

But no sooner had he jumped onto the bank of the river than—whisk! whew! up he ran into the tree.

From the topmost branches he called down to the Crocodile in the water below:

"My heart is way up here! If you want it, come for it, come for it!"

PART II

THE MONKEY soon moved away from that tree.

He wanted to get away from the Crocodile, so that he might live in peace.

But the Crocodile found him, far down the river, living in another tree.

In the middle of the river was an island covered with fruit-trees.

Half-way between the bank of the river and the island, a large rock rose out of the water. The Monkey could jump to the rock, and then to the island.

The Crocodile watched the Monkey crossing from the bank of the river to the rock, and then to the island.

He thought to himself, "The Monkey will stay on the island all day, and I'll catch him on his way home at night."

The Monkey had a fine feast, while the Crocodile swam about, watching him all day.

Toward night the Crocodile crawled out of the water and lay on the rock, perfectly still.

When it grew dark among the trees, the Monkey started for home. He ran down to the river bank, and there he stopped.

"What is the matter with the rock?" the Monkey thought to himself. "I never saw it so high before. The Crocodile is lying on it!"

But he went to the edge of the water and called: "Hello, Rock!"

No answer.

Then he called again: "Hello, Rock!"

Three times the Monkey called, and then he said: "Why is it, Friend Rock, that you do not answer me to-night?"

"Oh," said the stupid Crocodile to himself, "the rock answers the Monkey at night. I'll have to answer for the rock this time."

So he answered: "Yes, Monkey! What is it?"

The Monkey laughed, and said: "Oh, it's you, Crocodile, is it?"

"Yes," said the Crocodile. "I am waiting here for you. I am going to eat you."

"You have caught me in a trap this time," said the Monkey. "There is no other way for me to go home. Open your mouth wide so I can jump right into it."

Now the Monkey well knew that when Crocodiles open their mouths wide, they shut their eyes.

While the Crocodile lay on the rock with his mouth wide open and his eyes shut, the Monkey jumped.

But not into his mouth! Oh, no! He landed on the top of the Crocodile's head, and then sprang quickly to the bank. Up he whisked into his tree.

When the Crocodile saw the trick the Monkey had played on him, he said: "Monkey, you have great cunning. You know no fear. I'll let you alone after this."

"Thank you, Crocodile, but I shall be on the watch for you just the same," said the Monkey.

"WHILE THE CROCODILE LAY WITH HIS MOUTH WIDE OPEN AND HIS EYES SHUT, THE MONKEY JUMPED."

HOW THE TURTLE SAVED HIS OWN LIFE

A KING once had a lake made in the courtyard for the young princes to play in. They swam about in it, and sailed their boats and rafts on it. One day the king told them he had asked the men to put some fishes into the lake.

Off the boys ran to see the fishes. Now, along with the fishes, there was a Turtle. The boys were delighted with the fishes, but they had never seen a Turtle, and they were afraid of it, thinking it was a demon. They ran back to their father, crying, "There is a demon on the bank of the lake."

The king ordered his men to catch the demon, and to bring it to the palace. When the Turtle was brought in, the boys cried and ran away.

The king was very fond of his sons, so he

ordered the men who had brought the Turtle to kill it.

"How shall we kill it?" they asked.

"Pound it to powder," said some one. "Bake it in hot coals," said another.

So one plan after another was spoken of. Then an old man who had always been afraid of the water, said: "Throw the thing into the lake where it flows out over the rocks into the river. Then it will surely be killed."

When the Turtle heard what the old man said, he thrust out his head and asked: "Friend, what have I done that you should do such a dreadful thing as that to me? The other plans were bad enough, but to throw me into the lake! Don't speak of such a cruel thing!"

When the king heard what the Turtle said, he told his men to take the Turtle at once and throw it into the lake.

The Turtle laughed to himself as he slid away down the river to his old home. "Good!" he said, "Those people do not know how safe I am in the water!"

"THEN AN OLD MAN SAID: 'THROW THE THING INTO THE LAKE.'"

THE OX WHO WON THE FORFEIT

LONG ago a man owned a very strong Ox. The owner was so proud of his Ox, that he boasted to every man he met about how strong his Ox was.

One day the owner went into a village, and said to the men there: "I will pay a forfeit of a thousand pieces of silver if my strong Ox cannot draw a line of one hundred wagons."

The men laughed, and said: "Very well; bring your Ox, and we will tie a hundred wagons in a line and see your Ox draw them along."

So the man brought his Ox into the village. A crowd gathered to see the sight. The hundred carts were in line, and the strong Ox was yoked to the first wagon.

Then the owner whipped his Ox, and said: "Get up, you wretch! Get along, you rascal!"

But the Ox had never been talked to in that way, and he stood still. Neither the blows nor the hard names could make him move.

At last the poor man paid his forfeit, and went sadly home. There he threw himself on his bed and cried: "Why did that strong Ox act so? Many a time he has moved heavier loads easily. Why did he shame me before all those people?"

At last he got up and went about his work. When he went to feed the Ox that night, the Ox turned to him and said: "Why did you whip me to-day? You never whipped me before. Why did you call me 'wretch' and 'rascal'? You never called me hard names before."

Then the man said: "I will never treat you badly again. I am sorry I whipped you and called you names. I will never do so any more. Forgive me."

"Very well," said the Ox. "To-morrow I will go into the village and draw the one hundred carts for you. You have always been a kind master until to-day. To-morrow you shall gain what you lost."

The next morning the owner fed the Ox well, and hung a garland of flowers about his neck. When they went into the village, the men laughed at the man again.

They said: "Do you come to lose more money?"

"To-day I will pay a forfeit of two thousand pieces of silver if my Ox is not strong enough to pull the one hundred carts," said the owner.

So again the carts were placed in a line, and the Ox was yoked to the first. A crowd came to watch again. The owner said: "Good Ox, show how strong you are! You fine, fine creature!"

He patted him, and at once the Ox pulled with all his strength. The carts moved on until the last cart stood where the first had been.

Then the crowd shouted, and they paid back the forfeit the man had lost saying, "Your Ox is the strongest Ox we ever saw."

And the Ox and the man went home, happy.

"THEN THE OWNER WHIPPED HIS OX, AND SAID: 'GET ALONG, YOU RASCAL!'"

ABOUT FLYING-MACHINES

By Tudor Jenks

April, 1896

ALL signs seem to show that many boys and girls now living will see flying-machines traveling through the air, and some, perhaps, will ride in them.

What remains to be done is difficult rather than impossible. Practical and learned men have lately said that flying will surely come soon; and the men who make this promise are not dreamers nor idle talkers.

Progress in arts and sciences comes, as a rule, by steps; each thinker adds a little until the wished-for result is reached. The art of flying has been more or less seriously studied for several hundred years, and we can now see what remains to be done. The theory has been carefully worked out, and practice must follow.

If you doubt this, it is likely that you have not learned what has been done. To many, Daedalus and Icarus are still the only air navigators, and they flew only in legend. Perhaps some remember that Archytas was believed to have made a dove of wood, propelled by heated air; and a brass fly is also said to have made a short flight—but brief as is this list, it contains all that the ancients have recorded of flying-machines.

But that men have always wished to fly we may know from their giving wings to all superior beings; angelic messengers, fairies, demons, witches receive the power of flight as a matter of course. And, wishing to fly, it was certain that men would study the habits of birds, and would argue as Darius Green did:

What's the use of wings to a bumble-bee
Fur to git a livin' with, more'n to me;
Ain't my business
Important's his'n is?

Certainly it looks easy, when one sees the "swallows skim along the smooth lake's level brim"; and for a long, long time men thought that if they had wings like the dove, of course larger and stronger, they could at least make a beginning. So many tried the experiment. It was not hard to build a pair of wings "of leather or of something or other," or even two pairs; and many kinds were made—so many that the most ingenious of boys with the best sort of tool-box probably could not invent a new variety even if he worked all summer.

Some of these early wing-makers lived in the shadowy days of history. Bladud, a British king, was one; but all that we learn of his flight is that he soared above his city of Trinovante, and then fell upon a temple, thereby ending his wings and himself. Bladud belonged to an unlucky family, being the father of Shakspere's "King Lear." Simon, called "the magician," who lived about the time of the Emperor Nero, lost his life in the same way; another martyr to the science was a monk called Elmer (or Oliver) of Malmesbury, who had foretold the invasion of William the Conqueror, and was therefore taunted by cruel people when he did not know beforehand that he would break his legs on taking flight from a tall tower. This monk is said to have flown one hundred and twenty-five paces. People laughed at him all the more when he said that he failed because he did not fix a tail to his feet; but a recent writer, Chanute, argues that the monk was very likely right in his conclusion.

A hundred years later, and more, a Saracen repeated the attempt, and like poor Oliver, was killed. Then we read of a relative of the poet Dante, who made a successful flight over a lake, and fell in trying to repeat the feat across a square in the city of Perugia—though even upon this second attempt he is said to have "balanced himself a long time in the air," and to have fallen only when his wings broke.

We do not know what wings these men had, but from later facts it seems likely that the stories told of them are true. We know, as you will see, that with stiff wings men can often sail a long distance, and such flights as are reported seem to have been made with fixed wings and from high places.

After men became more skilled in the making of machinery, they tried to make moving wings; but it was found that the moving wings would not raise men from the ground.

Leonardo da Vinci, being a great architect and engineer, as well as painter and sculptor, left note-books proving that he had studied the flight of birds, and had planned flying-machines to be driven by wings or by screw-propellers. But as Leonardo was good at figures, he seems to have abandoned his plans after finding out how much force would be needed.

A French locksmith thought that practice was the great thing; and, fitted with wings, he jumped first from a chair, and afterward from a window, and then from the roof of a small house. In the last experiment he sailed over a cottage roof, but soon after sold his wings to a peddler—and probably saved his own life. Another Frenchman, a marquis, tried to go by the air-route across the River Seine; but he was not drowned, since a washerwoman's boat happened to be where he came down.

From those early days to our own, inventors have kept on building large wings and small wings, driven in every sort of flapping, by legs and by arms, but it is use-less to quote the long list of failures. They proved only this, and boy-inventors will do well to remember it: A man is not strong enough to flap wings big enough to hold him up; and man's muscles move too slowly to flap wings as fast as a small bird can. Whenever men have gone some distance through the air, it has been by sailing, as the larger birds often soar, upon the wind.

All well-instructed inventors of to-day believe that in order to fly with flapping wings man must have some other power than his muscles. Many light motors have been tried. The principal ones are: explosive compounds, steam, electricity, springs and rubber bands. All these and others have been used to make small models, and all have been reasonably successful when the models were small enough.

The subject of flying-models is interesting, but it will be possible here to describe only a few that will serve to show the different kinds.

One of the earliest was made by putting four feathers into a cork so as to make a propeller. Two of these propellers with feathers sloping in opposite ways were set on a stick, one propeller being fixed, the other revolving. A bow of whalebone was attached so that its cord could be twisted around the stick. Upon winding up the

AN EARLY MODEL.

cord, and then letting go, the model would be driven upward.

A drawing will make this clearer. The whalebone-bow is pierced to let a wire through, and works easily on it. The rod is jointed at the bow, and the upper propeller turns from right to left, the lower in the other direction; but the feathers are so sloped that both sets tend to move upward. This model is described because it is not hard to make, and will fly pretty well. To make the upper rod movable, that part may be a hollow stick put on a wire fixed into the lower part.

A simpler model on the same principle is the one known as Pénaud's "Hélicoptère," or, in English, "screw-wing," the invention of a clever young Frenchman who made some of the best models, though he worked only a short time on the subject, and died when he was thirty.

It is the simplest form of the flying-

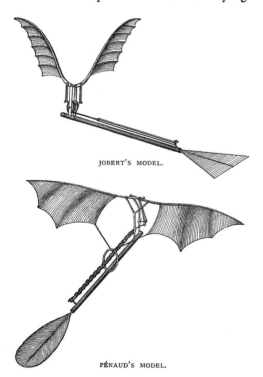

JOBERT'S MODEL.

PÉNAUD'S MODEL.

screw, and is moved by a twisted rubber band. It is wound up by turning the lower wings, or propeller, and when released flies in the same way as the one in the picture. A common Japanese toy sometimes found in toy-shops illustrates this principle. It is an imitation butterfly that will fly as high as the roof of an ordinary house.

These two forms will show how the screw-models work. Those driven by flapping wings may be more briefly described for they do not fly so well and are harder to make. The least complicated ones were made by Jobert and Pénaud. In Jobert's a stretched rubber-band pulls a cord and revolves a pulley. The pulley turns two little cranks that move the wings up and down. Pénaud's model works on a similar plan. In both the wings are stiffened by a rod along the front edge, while the rear edges are flexible; so the wing slides forward on the air as it descends.

A third sort of model shows a new method of flight, and the one that seems likeliest to lead to success in making real flying-machines. This new method uses flat or curved surfaces, sliding quickly upon the air, to support the weight. Scale a card through the air, and it travels upon the air, holding itself up so long as it can keep moving.

These planes, or stiff wings, are called airplanes or aëroplanes. In order to know just how they act, take a piece of writing-paper, about eight inches long, and four inches wide, and cut from it a paper bird like this:

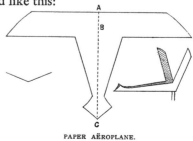

PAPER AËROPLANE.

Then bend it along the line AC into a flat V, putting two pins at B, as near the head as you conveniently can. Now stand on a chair and drop the bird, and it will come down as if it were a hawk after a chick. The weight of the pins pulls it down, the wings resist by pressure against the air, and the paper bird *slides* down instead of falling direct.

If the wings were sloped a little upward at the forward edge, and the paper-bird were pushed forward by a propeller, it would rise on the air. To illustrate how aëroplanes may be caused to rise, here is a model made by the Pénaud already mentioned:

PÉNAUD'S AËROPLANE MODEL.

In this model it will be seen that the larger wings do not move the machine; it is driven by the propeller at the back, just as if it were a tugboat. The wings in front only support the weight of the model during flight. They are pushed against the air, and are held up by the air's resistance, just as a kite is held up by the wind. The kite, however, is held against the moving wind, while the aëroplane is moved against the still air.

The little wings at the rear are set at a greater angle than the large wings; and whenever the front of the model begins to droop, they resist more, and thus bring the head upward again. They do this the more easily because the front wings lose some power whenever they are nearer level.

Many of the little models fly excellently: but when the machines are made big enough to carry men, new difficulties arise. Big machines cannot be driven by twisted rubber bands, or, if they could, the flight would be no safer than if the machines were fired out of cannons, like the projectile in which Jules Verne's heroes made their imaginary *Trip from the Earth to the Moon.* And when any machine fell, it would be smashed to smithereens—together with its passengers. A toy may be allowed to fly into the air, and then fall to the ground; but a flying-machine, to be worth while, must not only rise, but must keep right-side up while on its voyage, and must then descend safely.

What goes up must come down
On your head or on the ground!

Consequently the prudent air-ship maker must in all cases provide, first, enough power to carry his ship aloft and drive it where he chooses, in anything short of a hurricane; second, a method of balancing securely while aloft; third, a method of coming down in safety.

After trying different means of lifting and driving the air-ships—balloons, wings, screw-propellers, and aëroplanes—it has been decided that the planes are the best supports, and that, all things considered, they promise to solve the problem earliest.

And this decision was no piece of guess-work. Careful experiments were made, especially by two Americans— Professor Langley and Mr. Hiram Maxim—both learned men, and both well informed about all that had been done before our own times with all sorts of flying devices, to determine just what form of aëroplanes were best worth trying. Their experiments were made separately.

There was a number from which to choose, for men had tried to fly with planes as with every other apparatus. A model aëroplane was made that flew fairly well, and the design was patented in 1842 by Henson; but he never made a large machine. Du Temple tried a similar plan, but all known engines were too heavy for it—even though this inventor and his brother seem to be the first who made their boiler of light tubes, as Maxim and others have done since. In 1875 an English enthusiast named Moy built a large air-ship driven by screws and held up by planes. It was run around a circular track, being fastened by a rope to a pillar, but did not make speed enough to rise from the ground. Lack of power, which came partly from lack of money, kept Moy from making an air voyage.

Only a word or two more can be spared to these inventors, clever as they were. Each added some useful fact to what was known before him. Thus Wenham in 1866 showed that planes could usefully be put over one another; Brown, in 1873, that planes at the two ends of a rod would balance well; then came Moy, already spoken of, and Tatin, who made a model that flew in a circular track as Moy's machine failed to do. In 1879 Dandrieux, a Frenchman, made a model much like the Japanese toy already spoken of—a paper butterfly driven by twisted rubber. A similar model with undulating wings was made by Brearey, who added an elastic cord extending from the under side of one wing to that of the other. This made the down pressure stronger, and gave better flight.

These machines, and many others, made the task easier for inventors who came afterward, by showing which experiments promised the best results; and their experiences gave Mr. Maxim courage to make his flying-machine on a large scale.

Mr. Langley and Mr. Maxim began as modern men of science do—each made trials of all sorts to find what material and what shape would give best results; and Mr. Maxim built and tried every kind of motor that suited his purpose. He tried engines moved by hot air, oil, steam, or electricity; and at last convinced himself that the steam-engine was the easiest to manage, and gave nearly as much power for its weight as any motor.

While Mr. Langley made less outward show than Mr. Maxim, perhaps it will be found that his study and writing have done as much for the art.

Scientific men thought that if an engine could be made weighing less than forty pounds for each horse-power, flying-machines could lift it and themselves by its aid. Now, by using light tubes to make his boiler (the same plan is adopted in torpedo-boats), Maxim constructed the two lightest engines ever built. Weighing only 640 pounds together, they gave 360 horse-power—much more than is thought necessary for flying. For their weight these engines were nearly five times as powerful as those Mr. Moy had tried, though Moy's were considered a marvel of lightness and power in 1875. The rapid advance in modern science is shown by this improvement in less than twenty years.

The engine being ready, Mr. Maxim tested different fabrics until he had found out the best material for making the aëroplanes—his bird's wings. The tests were made on an ingenious little machine that showed how much each piece of stuff would lift, and how hard it tried to go with the current of air blown against it.

He found that an aëroplane made of a special kind of cloth called "balloon fabric" would, with the same weight and power, carry more than any balloon could lift.

Then Mr. Maxim went to work on a large air-ship to be driven by screws and supported by planes. The body of the machine was a platform car on wheels. The car, forty feet long and eight feet wide, carried the two little engines. Above were the aëroplanes of cloth, stretched by wires upon a framework, the largest being fifty by forty feet, and capable alone of lifting most of the weight. It was meant also to make the machine fall slowly, for it would act as a parachute in falling. At the sides were smaller planes, and in front and behind were planes movable up and down—rudders to steer upward or downward.

The machine ran along its own railroad, a track a third of a mile long, and could be driven by the push of its air-screws as fast as most locomotives.

The inventor soon found that when the car ran at a high speed it tried to rise from the track; so he built guard-rails above to keep his flying-machine down. You see that Mr. Maxim did not intend to go up until he had made sure of keeping his balance and coming safely down.

The air-ship and its appliances were finished in 1893, the engine being so arranged as to use naphtha for fuel, and to condense its own steam into water, so that it could be used over and over.

All these matters required time, labor, and money—to say nothing of the brain-work—and over $50,000 was spent before the air-ship began its trips along the rails.

Then the inventor began his lessons in flying, taking careful notes of the machine's behavior at different rates of speed. It was soon proved that when three quarters of the power was used, three of the car-wheels left the lower track, and at full speed the whole machine ran on the upper track, free from the ground. It was also found that the side-planes would keep the air-ship from rolling over, and that the action of the fore and aft rudders promised to be satisfactory.

When the whole machine was in the best of order, it was run at a speed of thirty-seven miles an hour. The planes lifted all

four wheels and the machine ran upon the *upper* track for some distance. But the lifting-power was too great. An axletree of one of the rear upper wheels was bent—the air-ship was set free and the front wheels broke the guard rail. Steam was shut off and the ship dropped.

The broken rail did some damage; but the ship has since been repaired, and Mr. Maxim is said to be waiting until he can secure a very large and level space in which to proceed with his trials.

Here is Mr. Maxim's opinion upon the result:

> Had it been known twenty years ago that a machine could be made on the aëroplane system which would really lift its own weight, its fuel, and its engineer, we should have plenty of flying-machines in the world to-day. If one half the money, time, and the talent which has been employed by the French balloon corps in their fruitless efforts to construct a navigable balloon should now be employed in the right direction, the whole question of aërial navigation would soon be so perfected that flying-machines would be as common as torpedo-boats, and the whole system of modern warfare would be completely changed.

Such is the present state of the aëroplane flying-machine.

Meanwhile another sort of flight has been attempted, and to some extent successfully, by other inventors. This is the soaring or sailing flight. You may see it in operation almost anywhere if you will keep an eye upon the gulls, hawks, eagles, and other soaring birds. Yet it was long doubted whether any bird could sail in the air with motionless wings. Nowadays the evidence that such flight is not only possible but usual is overwhelming.

Mr. Maxim believes that birds are aided in this soaring by the many minor currents in the air, of which the bird takes full advantage.

A recent writer, Chanute, in his book *Progress in Flying-Machines* (from which book I have learned much that I tell you in this article, and have also secured several diagrams), shrewdly remarks that stories about men flying successfully have come almost entirely from the warm countries—the regions where steady winds make soaring birds a common sight. His book tells nearly all the experiments in flying in which men depended on their own strength.

Among the most striking instances of flying are the experiments made forty years ago by a Frenchman named Le Bris.

Le Bris once held up in the breeze a wing he had taken from an albatross, and, he says, "in spite of me it drew forward into the wind." He wondered if he could make wings that would act in the same way, and about 1855 he built a bird-like boat with outstretched wings that could be moved slightly by rods. Then he placed the machine upon a cart, got into it, and told the driver to drive against the wind. When they started Le Bris kept the front edges of the wings bent downward; but soon the horse began to trot, Le Bris raised the front of the wings, and behold! up went the boat until it was higher than the church steeples, and floating along *against* the wind.

But soon Le Bris heard energetic remarks in the air below him, and found that the driver had been caught in the rope and was then dangling down like the tail to a kite. So Le Bris turned the wings so as to glide downward until the driver was on solid ground, and could run after the runaway horse and cart.

Le Bris tried to return to the upper air, but failed; and he came down unhurt, having only slightly injured the machine.

The air-boat being repaired, Le Bris soon made another start; but this time he had Humpty Dumpty's luck and the machine was smashed to bits. With a second air-ship he once went up forty feet, and he flew the same vessel loaded with ballast even higher. When this second air-ship was smashed Le Bris gave up, for he was a poor man and could not afford another.

These flights were *against* the wind, and proved that surfaces curved in a certain way were drawn forward "into the wind's eye," as sailors express it. This fact was explained in a book written in 1864, and its author, D'Esterno, was laughed at and considered out of his head because he claimed that flight was possible with a machine built to soar rather than fly—that is without power to drive it, and with motionless rather than with flapping wings.

The same belief was urged in *L'Empire de Air* by Mouillard, a book on the flight of birds. Mouillard claimed that, after a start, a bird can rise without motion of the wings provided the wind is strong enough. The author built such wings, and tried them by leaping at a narrow ditch. Up he went, and then glided one hundred and thirty-eight feet before he came down and broke a wing. A second trial was successful also, except that in coming down he sprained his shoulder.

And since then a number of "human birds" have repeated and varied these trials. Although great feats have not yet been done, it looks as if the chief trouble is lack of practice. One of the best known and most skillful fliers is a German named Lilienthal, who, after years of study and trials, made in the summer of 1891 a pair of wings curved like a great bird's. As the result of his studies and experiments, he believes curved surfaces better than flat planes—in which he agrees with Le Bris, Goupil, and Phillips, other students of the subject. All these men believe that the curved shape of birds' wings has much to do with their flying, helping them to go against the wind—a strange effect which the French have named *aspiration.*

Provided, then, with wings and tail, Lilienthal began to practise, at first upon a springboard, and afterward in a hilly region near Berlin. Even after he was able to sail as far as eighty feet, he found that it was best to arrange the wings so that they could be easily thrown off; otherwise, he coolly says, "I might have had a broken neck instead of sprains which always healed in a few weeks."

In 1892 he made larger wings, and learned to sail further than before, rising twenty or thirty feet from the ground upon a favoring wind. Since then Lilienthal

OTTO LILIENTHAL ABOUT TO TAKE FLIGHT.

has attached to his wings a powerful little engine, and he is now making attempts to learn its management. Just what he has done is not known yet; but he has fewer accidents, and improves as time goes on.

Some Americans also are at work with wings. A recent number of the *American Engineer* says that A. M. Herring of New York has been "experimenting with wing-surfaces large enough to carry his own weight for over a year" (!), and has succeeded in sailing *three hundred feet.* The same journal publishes an account of his experiments, and concludes [that] "there is now good reason to believe that soaring for considerable distances is no more difficult than riding on a bicycle . . . The great obstacle is the cost of such apparatus and its

great fragility." The wings alone cost from one hundred and fifty to one hundred and seventy-five dollars while an oil-motor will be perhaps six or seven hundred dollars more; so boys whose allowances are small will not be likely to take up the pastime yet.

Lilienthal, indeed, says that while he is hopeful that men will learn to fly, the task of learning is more difficult than one might suppose; and Mr. Herring, though he has studied the subject seventeen years, considers himself a beginner.

A Vienna manager, learning of Lilienthal's feats, sent an acrobat to take lessons; but at last reports the pupil was said to be "having a hard time of it—developing a dreadful propensity to alight on his nose."

During 1895, a lecturer at Glasgow University, Mr. Pilcher, has made flights with a pair of wings not unlike Lilienthal's; but to guard against being upset by sudden gusts of wind—a constant danger—Mr. Pilcher has bent his wing-tips at the ends. These experiments are still in progress.

There are other experimenters in various parts of the world, but none more successful. Some are studying kites as an aid to flight. Lawrence Hargrave of New South Wales has made a great number of simple and successful models—the latest being driven by compressed air, and flying over three hundred feet. He has lately given his attention to kites; and in November, 1894, made one that carried him up along a string, and brought him safely down. He claims that this kite, which looks like two

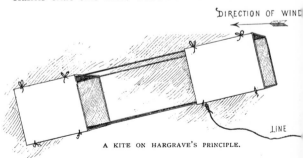

DIRECTION OF WIND

LINE

A KITE ON HARGRAVE'S PRINCIPLE.

boxes, without top or bottom, and fastened to each other by sticks, as shown in the diagram, will carry a man up and bring him down safely, and thus offers an excellent chance to try any new flying apparatus.

Boys can easily make small kites of this sort out of pasteboard boxes and test their merit.

Lately there has been some account of a sail-wheel flying-machine made by a Professor Wellner; but as it is on a novel principle, which has not yet been proved sound, I have not given an account of it. Maxim's ship, although it broke down, is only a new trial of a well-known principle. Some German authorities say that Maxim has not added to our knowledge of how to steer air-ships. But it seems fair to wait a while. After the air-ship really begins to fly, there will be time enough to learn how to steer it.

A bill was brought before the last Congress—not passed—offering $100,000 to the inventor who shall make a successful air-vessel before 1900. But, as a New York paper said, that sum might be a trifle to the inventor of such a machine.

A Boston gentleman much interested in the subject proposes an aëronautical camp-meeting on Cape Cod, and has published an elaborate programme of subjects to be there considered. If we add that a School of Aëronautics has been established in Paris, you will have a very complete idea of where the Art of Flying is to-day.

As was said in the beginning, it is likely that many of you boys and girls will see air-ships in full flight.

And if we should learn to fly—what then?

Let me repeat here what the poet E. C. Stedman told the readers of the *Century* some years ago—for only a poet can do the subject justice:

The air will be the ocean; or, rather, let us say, that ethereal ocean, the atmosphere, at last having been utilized and made available for the commerce, the travel, the swift running to and fro of men, every spot of this globe will be a building-site, every acre a harbor, every open space, plain, hummock, the highest range, the humblest valley, an aërial port.

The change will be gradual. The art of aërial navigation will be slow of perfection. Our primitive vessels and motors will be rude and defective, as Stevenson's locomotive now would seem to us. Heavy freights must long continue to move by water and rail. Aërobats at first will be used for the transmission of the mails and light express packages, and especially for their swift conveyance over sea. Soon the inland companies will have each its own "aërial express." By and by aërobats displaying the insignia and pennons of the great newspapers will leave town at 3 A.M., and whir over the country "as the crow flies," and at their utmost speed, dropping their packages in the towns and villages along the routes in every direction of the compass. Soon the more adventurous and resolute, and finally all classes of travelers, will avail themselves of the great passenger aërobats and enjoy the unsurpassable luxury of flight, experiencing thrills of wonder and ecstasy, and a sense of power, freedom, and safety to which all former delights of travel may well seem tame by comparison.

In every way the resources of social life will be so enlarged that at last it truly may be said, "Existence is itself a joy." Sports and recreations will be strangely multiplied. Rich and poor alike will make of travel an every-day delight, the former in their private aëronons, the latter in large and multiform structures, corresponding in use to the excursion-boats of our rivers and harbors, the "floating palaces" of the people, and far more numerous and splendid. The ends of the earth, its rarest places, will be visited by all. The sportsman can change at pleasure from the woods and waters of the North, the run-ways of the deer, the haunts of the salmon, to the pursuit of the tiger in the jungle or the emu in the Australian bush. An entirely new profession—that of airmanship—will be thoroughly organized, employing a countless army of trained officers and "airmen." The adventurous and well-to-do will have pleasure yachts of the air, and take hazardous and delightful cruises. Their vessels will differ from the cumbrous aërobats intended for freight and emigrant business, will be christened with beautiful and suggestive names—Iris, Aurora, Hebe, Ganymede, Hermes, Ariel, and the like—and will vie with one another in grace, readiness, and speed.

BY PERMISSION, FROM "UEBER LAND UND MEER."

WARFARE IN THE AIR, AS IMAGINED BY A GERMAN ARTIST.

HELEN KELLER

By Florence Howe Hall

September, 1892

MOST children go to three or four schools at the same time, and perhaps that is the reason why they sometimes get just a little bit tired of their lessons.

First come the Eye and Ear schools—and a baby begins to attend these as soon as he is old enough to know anything; nor does he graduate from them while eyesight, hearing, and life remain.

Next comes the Tongue school, and we all know how interesting it is to watch a dear little baby, as he gradually learns to say one word after another, and to pronounce *s*, *th*, and *r*—those sounds which are such dreadful stumbling-blocks to many little folks. About this time, or a little earlier, Baby begins to spend many of his spare moments at the Touch or "Feeling" school; and if he is of an inquiring turn of mind, he may learn many interesting and some very unpleasant facts at this educational establishment. He may learn—if he put his fingers on the stove—that fire burns; also that pins scratch, that knives hurt, and that ice chills. At the schools of Smell and Taste he will learn lessons agreeable and disagreeable. I think that almost all little boys and girls pay an early visit to the pepper or mustard pot, and that the visit leaves sad and very pungent memories behind.

By and by, Baby grows to be quite a big boy or girl, and is sent off to *real* school, as children would say. Here he often finds that he has too many calls upon his thoughts. The Eye-schoolmistress urges him to look out of the window and study the butterflies, the birds, and the flowers; the Ear-schoolmistress perhaps puts it into his head to listen to the recitation of the bigger boys, and learn something in that

way. And all this time the *real*, live schoolmistress is saying, "Johnny, why don't you study your spelling lesson?" or, "Johnny, have you learned that multiplication-table yet?"

For these reasons, Johnny does not always appreciate the really striking beauties of the multiplication-table, nor the joys that lurk even in the most dismally long and hateful spelling-lesson. Johnny feels—and very naturally—that school is a superior sort of prison. When its doors close behind him, they shut out his body from the great world of nature, and he is too young to realize that the glorious gates of knowledge can not open to admit his mind, unless he first prepares it in that narrow school-room, which tires and cramps his active little body.

But suppose that Johnny were entirely cut off from that outer world; suppose that the Eye, and Ear, and Tongue schools had shut their doors upon him, and he sat in utter darkness and silence, with no schoolmistress to help him save the one living in the ends of his fingers, and with no one to answer any of his questions, or to explain to him the meaning of the strange objects which his restless hands felt, but which, alas! he could not understand? In other words, suppose that Johnnie were deaf, dumb, and blind—could neither understand other people, nor make them understand him—would he not hail with delight a schoolmistress who should deliver him from this living death, and would he not love the "real school" which taught him all that he had been longing to know in his dark prison—aye, and much more than he had ever dreamed of?

. . . This month I shall tell you of Helen Keller, blind and deaf and dumb, . . . but otherwise a bright, happy little girl. For five long years she had sat in silent darkness—darkness of the mind as well as of the body. How can we wonder at her delight when a deliverer was found to free her from her prison, at her rapture over the tiresome lessons which meant life—eyes, ears, everything—to her?

Miss Sullivan tells us that after having been two or three months under tuition, Helen would throw her arms around her teacher with a kiss whenever a new word was given her to spell! Because, in Helen's case, spelling a word is the only way of learning it. She must spell out all the letters on her fingers in order to say, or rather *use*, a word. Thus she comes to think—nay, even to dream—in finger language; and her busy hands, as did Laura Bridgman's, move when she sleeps, spelling out the confused dreams that pass through her little brain.

As for arithmetic, Helen found the study so exciting, she was so intensely interested in solving problems on her "type-slate," that it was feared her health would be injured, and, to her great regret, the precious type-slate had for a time to be taken from her, because thinking about all the wonderful things that can be done with figures kept the child awake at night.

Her full name is Helen Adams Keller, and she was born in Tuscumbia, Alabama, June 27, 1880, with all her senses in perfect condition. She was a bright little baby, and could see and hear as well as any of us. She had learned to walk and was learning to talk, when, at nineteen months of age, she was attacked by a severe illness, and when it passed away, it left her blind and deaf. Dumbness is, in almost all cases, the result of deafness—deaf people can not talk, simply because they can not hear; and so our poor little Helen ceased to talk soon after

this terrible illness, because she was unable to hear any sound. The few words that she had learned, faded from her baby brain, and she entered upon a long term of solitary confinement—of the mind—now happily ended forever! She has always been a very intelligent child, and even in these dark days she learned something from the "Touch" schoolmistress, and something more from her kind mother, who allowed little Helen to keep constantly at her side as she went about her household duties. The little girl showed great aptitude for learning about these matters, and she also imitated the motions of people whom she did not see, indeed, but *felt*. All blind children like to touch every one with whom they are brought into contact—it is their only way of *seeing* how their friends look, and what sort of clothes they wear.

Helen also invented a number of signs to express her wants, and some of her thoughts. Since she has learned to talk with her fingers, this natural or sign, language has been gradually laid aside; but when I last saw her, in September, 1888, she still used a number of signs, about which I may tell you by and by. So the "Touch" schoolmistress did all that she could for Helen, and the little girl was, for a time, satisfied with these teachings. But as she grew older, as her brain became more active, she began to long for wider knowledge, and would be almost in despair, when she could not express her ideas in such a way that those about her could understand her meaning. On these occasions, she would be seized with violent paroxysms of anger; but after she had learned to talk with her fingers, she had no more outbursts of rage, and now she seldom loses her temper, for she is a sweet and gentle child, and very affectionate.

But her poor little mind was in prison; she was like a captive bird, and if she had not beaten thus against the doors of her cage her parents would not perhaps have realized that her baby days were over, and that the time had come when she must be set free—when she must be taught the use of language.

So Captain Keller, Helen's father, wrote to Mr. Anagnos, of the Perkins Institution for the Blind, in Boston, to ask whether he could not send a "real" schoolmistress to teach little Helen, and Mr. Anagnos chose for the position a very kind and intelligent young girl who was just graduated from his school. Her name was Annie M. Sullivan. Although she had been almost entirely blind when she had come to study at the Institution, her sight had been mercifully restored to her through the aid of skillful doctors.

But she remembered very well what a sad thing it was to be blind, and felt the greatest sympathy for little Helen. She spent six months in preparing herself for her task, and studied very carefully all that Dr. Howe had written . . . as well as a great many big books on mental development, which you and I would, perhaps, find rather dry reading.

Helen's lessons began in the most agreeable manner, for the first thing she learned about was a handsome doll. Miss Sullivan took the little girl's hand and passed it over the doll. Then she made the letters, d-o-l-l, slowly with the finger alphabet. When she began to make them the second time, Helen dropped the doll, and tried to make the letters herself with one hand, at the same time feeling of Miss Sullivan's fingers with her other hand. Then she tried to spell the word alone, and soon learned to do so correctly, also to spell five other words, *hat*, *mug*, *pin*, *cup*, *ball*. When Miss Sullivan handed her a mug, for instance, Helen would spell m-u-g with her fingers, and it was the same with the other words.

In a little more than a week after this lesson, she understood that all objects have names, and so the first and most difficult step in her education was accomplished in a marvelously short time.

Helen has a baby sister named Mildred, of whom she is very fond. She was delighted when Miss Sullivan put her hand on the baby's head, and spelled b-a-b-y. Now, at last, she had a name for the dear little sister whom she loved so well. Before this time, though of course she had often thought of Mildred, she had known no name nor word by which to call her. How curious Helen's thoughts must have been before the time when Miss Sullivan came to her—thoughts without words.

I do not wonder that she enjoyed her studies, for her teacher taught her in ways so pleasant that her lessons were like so many little plays. Thus she made Helen stand *on* a chair in order to learn the word *on*, and the little girl was put *into* the wardrobe—and so learned the meaning of *into*.

After she had learned a large number of words, Miss Sullivan began to teach her to read as the blind do—that is from raised letters, which they feel with the tips of their fingers. Miss Sullivan took an alphabet sheet, and put Helen's finger on the letter *A*, at the same time making the letter *A* with her own fingers, and so on through the entire alphabet. Helen learned all the printed letters, both capitals and small letters, in one day! Then her teacher put Helen's fingers on the word *cat* in the primer for the blind, at the same time spelling the word in the finger alphabet. The little girl caught the idea instantly, asked for *dog*, and many other words, and was much displeased because her own name, "Helen," was not in the primer! She was so delighted with her book that she would sit for hours feeling of the different words, and "when she touched one with which she was familiar, a peculiarly sweet expression would light up her face."

Mr. Anagnos had some sheets of paper printed with all the words Helen knew. These were cut up into slips, each containing a single word, and the little girl was overjoyed at being able to make sentences for herself. Next she learned to write these same sentences with pencil and paper, on a writing-board such as the blind use—a piece of pasteboard with grooves in it, which is placed under the writing-paper, the letters being written in the grooves, each groove forming a line. At first Miss Sullivan guided her hand, but soon Helen learned to write alone—and she writes a very neat, firm handwriting. The first sentence she wrote was, "Cat does drink milk." When she found that her dear mother could read what she had written she could scarcely restrain her joy and excitement! For now Helen had found two doors leading out of her prison—the finger alphabet, with which she could talk to those around her, and the written alphabet, by means of which she could communicate with friends at a distance.

Would you believe it possible, that Helen could read, and also write, letters? Not letters such as you and I write, but letters written according to what is called the Braille system. This system is simple and ingenious. Each letter of the alphabet is represented by pin-pricks placed in different positions, and the blind can read what has been written, by feeling of the pin-pricks. A little sharp-pointed instrument, like a stiletto, is used for punching the holes, through a piece of brass containing square perforations, each of which is large enough to hold one letter of the alphabet. The paper is fastened firmly into a sort of wooden slate covered with cloth, but can easily be removed when the page is filled.

It seems almost incredible that Helen should have learned in four months to use and spell correctly more than four hundred and fifty words! On the first day of March, 1887, the poor child was almost like a dumb animal: she knew no language—not a single word, nor a single letter. In July, of the same year, she had not only learned to talk fluently with her fingers, but had learned also to read raised type, to write a neat square hand, and to write letters to her friends! Her progress during these first months seems simply marvelous, especially when we remember that she was only six years and eight months old when Miss Sullivan began to teach her. She has gone on acquiring knowledge with the same wonderful rapidity.

After she had been under tuition for one year, she knew the multiplication-tables, and could add, subtract, multiply, and divide numbers, up to 100. At first she had some trouble in understanding that the numbers on her type-slate represented so many apples and oranges in the examples, but in a few days this difficulty was overcome, and she then became much interested in her ciphering, and puzzled her little head so continually with examples that the "big giant, Arithmos," had to be banished from her presence!

Helen's type-slate is like those that the blind use. The types have raised numbers on one end; the slate itself is of metal, covered with square holes, into which Helen sets the types, just as we would write down figures.

She is very fond of writing in her diary, and it is very interesting to trace her progress as shown in this and in her other writings. Here is a short description of rats, which she wrote January 16, 1888, and which, perhaps may amuse some of my young readers:

RATS

JAN. 16th, 1888

Rats are small animals. They are made of flesh and blood and bone. They have four feet and a tail.

They have one head and two ears and two eyes and one nose.

They have one mouth and sharp teeth. They gnaw holes in wood with their teeth. They do walk softly.

Rats killed little, little pigeons. Cats do catch rats and eat them.

Helen never knew that there was such a day as Christmas-day, until Miss Sullivan went to her. Fancy a little girl who never had a Christmas, until she was seven years old! Her teacher tells us that she hailed the glad tidings of the happy Christmas season with the greatest joy, and gave many proofs of the goodness and unselfishness of her little heart. Thus, at a Christmas-tree festival, at which Helen was present, she found one little girl who, through some mistake, had not received any gifts. Helen tried to find the child's presents, but not succeeding in her search, she flew to her own little store of precious things and took from it a mug, which she herself prized very highly. This she gave to the little stranger, "with abundant love."

In the following letter she tells us something of her Christmas experiences, and mentions the very mug, I think, of which I have spoken.

TUSCUMBIA, ALA., Jan. 2, 1888

DEAR SARAH: I am happy to write to you this morning. I hope Mr. Anagnos is coming to see me soon. I will go to Boston in June, and I will buy father gloves, and James nice collar, and Simpson cuffs. I saw Miss Betty and her scholars. They had a pretty Christmas-tree, and there were many pretty presents on it for little children. I had a mug and little bird and candy. I had many lovely things for Christmas. Aunt gave me a trunk for Nancy, and clothes. I went to party with teacher and mother. We did dance and play and eat nuts and candy and cakes and oranges, and I did have fun with little boys and girls. Mrs. Hopkins did send me lovely ring. I do love her and little blind girls.

Men and boys do make carpets in mills. Wool grows on sheep. Men do cut sheep's wool off with large shears, and send it to the mill. Men and women do make wool cloth in mills.

Cotton grows on large stalks in fields. Men and boys and girls and women do pick cotton. We do make thread and cotton dresses of cotton. Cotton has pretty white and red flowers on it. Teacher did tear her dress. Mildred does cry. I will nurse Nancy. Mother will buy me lovely new aprons and dress to take to Boston. I went to Knoxville with father and Aunt. Bessie is weak and little. Mrs. Thompson's chickens killed Leila's chickens. Eva does sleep in my bed. I do love good girls. Good-bye. HELEN KELLER.

The "Nancy" mentioned in this letter is a large rag-doll, of which Helen is very fond. She has a large family of dolls, and enjoys playing with them, and sewing for them, when she is not reading or engaged with her teacher.

Here is an extract from her diary which speaks very tenderly of the finny tribe, and all the troubles which hook and line bring upon them:

MARCH 8, 1888

We had fish for breakfast. Fish live in the deep water. There are many hundreds of fish swimming about in the water. Men catch fish with poles and hooks and lines. They put a little tiny fish on the hook and throw it in the water, and fish does bite the little fish and sharp hook does stick in poor fish's mouth and hurt him much. I am very sad for the poor fish. Fish did not know that very sharp hook was in tiny fish. Men must not kill poor fish. Men do pull fish out and take them home, and cooks do clean them very nice and fry them, and then they are very good to eat for breakfast.

It is slow work, spelling words with one's fingers, and Helen was at first inclined to use only the most important words in a sentence. Thus she would say, "Helen, milk," when she wanted some milk to drink. But Miss Sullivan, who is as firm as she is sweet and gentle, knew that the little girl would never learn to think clearly, and would never make real progress in acquiring knowledge, if allowed to express herself in this babyish way. Miss Sullivan would therefore bring the milk, in order to show Helen that her wish was understood, but would not allow her to drink it, until she had made a complete sentence, her teacher assisting her. When she had said, "Give Helen some milk to drink," she was permitted to drink it. As we have seen, Helen began her lessons with Miss Sullivan in March, 1887, and in one year her progress was so extraordinary that it was thought best to omit her regular lessons, when the month of March came round again.

So Helen took a vacation of several months; but, though her "real" school did not "keep" during all this time, she did not cease to learn, for her "real" schoolmistress is always with the little girl, constantly talking with her, and explaining things to her. Miss Sullivan is, indeed, "eyes to the blind, and ears to the deaf," and a sweeter and gentler pair of eyes it would be hard to find. Through her, Helen learns more and more of this beautiful world and all that is going on in it.

Helen is very cheerful and happy in spite of her sad lot; she does not, of course, fully understand how much she has lost, in losing her sight and hearing, and it is best that she should not do so. Sometimes she longs to see. While riding in the cars, not long ago, she tried to look out of the car window, and said to her companion, "I can't see; I try to see, but I CAN'T!" She told Mr. Anagnos, that she must see a doctor for her eyes. Alas! no doctor lives who is skillful enough to help little Helen's eyes and ears. Her parents and friends have consulted the most skillful oculists and aurists; but the doctors all agree that nothing can be done for her! She herself hopes that, as she grows older, she will be able to see.

While we all must pity her intensely, for her sad deprivations, we should remember that even these afflictions have their bright side, and while they wrap her from the outer world, as in a dark garment, they also shield her from all unkindness, from all wickedness. Every one who comes near little Helen is so moved with pity for her infirmities that all treat her with the utmost gentleness—she does not know what unkindness is, her teacher tells us, and we may fully believe it. Thus, while she can neither see the trees, nor the flowers, nor the bright sunshine, while she can not hear the birds sing, she knows the best side of every human being, and only the best. She lives in a world of love, and goodness, and gentleness. Were we speaking, just now, of pitying little Helen? It may be she does not need our pity—perhaps some of us may need hers!

You will not be surprised, after what I have said, to hear that our little friend is very kind to animals. When driving in a carriage, she will not allow the driver to use a whip because, as she says, "Poor horses will cry."

She was much distressed, one morning,

upon finding that a certain dog named "Pearl," had a block of wood fastened to its collar. It was explained to Helen that this was necessary, in order to keep the dog from running away; but still she was not satisfied, and, at every opportunity during the day, she would seek out Pearl, and carry the block of wood herself, that the dog might rest from its burden.

Helen is very fond of dress, and it makes her very unhappy to find a tear in any of her clothing. She has a little jacket of which she is extremely proud, and which she wished to wear last summer, even when the weather was so warm that she would almost have melted away in it. Her mother said to her one day, "There is a poor little girl who has no cloak to keep her warm. Will you give her yours?"

Helen immediately began to take off the precious jacket, saying, "I must give it to a poor little strange girl."

She is very fond of children younger than herself, and is always ready—as I hope all my readers are—to give up her way for theirs. She loves little babies, and handles them very carefully and tenderly. When she is riding in a horse-car, she always asks whether there are any babies among the passengers; also, how many people there are in the car, what the colors of the horses are, and, most difficult question of all to answer, she demands the names of the conductor and driver! She also wishes to know what is to be seen from the car window—so that, as you may imagine, her teacher does not rest much while going about with Helen. For talking with one's fingers, and understanding what other people say with theirs, is much more fatiguing than talking in the usual way. While "listening," it is necessary to keep one's attention closely fixed on each letter as it is made—for if one misses a single letter, the thread of the whole sentence is often lost, and it must all be repeated.

She asks constantly, when she is traveling, or staying at a hotel, "What do you see? What are people doing?"

She had the pleasure of going all over one of those great steamboats that ply on the Mississippi River, and said, when she had finished the tour of the vessel, "It is like a very large house."

She also made a visit to the Cotton Exchange at Memphis, where she was introduced to many of the gentlemen, and wrote their names on the blackboard. But she did not quite understand why there were maps and blackboards hanging on the wall, and said to her teacher, "Do men go to school?"

In June, 1888, Helen came to New England for a stay of four months, and great was her delight when she made her long anticipated visit to the Perkins Institution for the Blind, at Boston. Here she found many people who could talk with her in her own finger-language. Not only did this give her the greatest pleasure, but also much instruction, for hitherto she had rarely met any one with whom she could talk, save her mother and teacher. And so the doors of her prison grew larger and wider, till our little friend seemed to breathe in more freedom and knowledge, with every breath! You may perhaps think it strange that Helen's father should not be able to talk much to her; but it seems to be more difficult for men to learn to use the finger-language than for women. Their hands are, of course, larger, more clumsy, and less flexible; and perhaps their thoughts do not move quite so nimbly. Mr. Anagnos has learned to talk to Helen, but she finds it rather hard to understand him, since her hand is small and his is large. I saw her "Listening" to him one day, and she "listened" by passing her hand all over his, often straightening out his fingers, because she thought that he did not make the letters correctly! When a woman talks to Helen, she makes the letters in the palm of Helen's hand, and the little girl understands each one instantly. As some of the letters resemble one another very closely, it seems wonderful that Helen can distinguish them so quickly—much more rapidly than I can do, by looking at them. Her little hand closes very slightly over the hand of the person who is speaking to her, as each letter is made—and they are made at a very rapid rate, by those who have practiced the use of the manual alphabet.

Helen is very fond of Mr. Anagnos, and he himself loves the little girl very dearly. He has taught her a few words and phrases of his native language—Greek—as she begged him to do so. Some of these she spelled for me, and spelled them very fast, too. I can not remember all these words; but here are a few, which I wrote down: Good morning, Καλὴ ἡμέρα. Finger-ring, Δακτυλίδιον. I love thee, Σὲ ἀγαπῶ. Good-bye, Χαῖρε. Hair, Τρίχες.

She has also learned several German, French, and Latin words. Indeed, in one of her letters to Mr. Anagnos, she wrote, "I do want to learn much about everything." She is a wonderfully bright child, and her teacher, instead of urging her to study, is often obliged to coax Helen away from some example in arithmetic, or other task, lest the little girl should injure her health by working too hard at her lessons.

The following letter, which was written to her aunt in Tuscumbia, while Helen was visiting at the North, is interesting, because it gives some of the foreign words and phrases which she has learned:

My Dearest Aunt: I am coming home very soon, and I think you and every one will be very glad to see my teacher and me. I am very happy, because I have learned much about many things. I am studying French and German, and Latin and Greek. *Se agapo*, is Greek, and it means, I love thee. *J'ai une bonne petite sœur*, is French, and it means, I have a good little sister. *Nous avons un bon père et une bonne mère* means, We have a good father and a good mother. *Puer* is boy in Latin, and *Mutter* is mother in German. I will teach Mildred many languages when I come home.

Helen A. Keller.

The following account of the noises made by different animals has a sad significance, when we remember that it was written by one who can not hear even the loudest peal of thunder, or the heavy booming of cannon:

July 14, 1888

Some horses are very mild and gentle, and some are wild and very cross. I like to give gentle horse nice, fresh grass to eat, because they will not bite my hand, and I like to pat their soft noses. I think mild horses like to have little girls very kind to them. Horses neigh, and lions roar, and wolves howl, and cows mow, and pigs grunt, and ducks quack, and hens cackle, and roosters crow, and birds sing, and crows caw, and chickens say "peep," and babies cry, and people talk, and laugh, and sing, and groan, and men whistle, and bells ring. Who made many noises?

I wish that space permitted me to tell the readers of *St. Nicholas* more about little Helen—about some of her funny doings and bright sayings. But if I should tell you all the interesting stories that I have heard about her, they would take up nearly the whole magazine.

You will be glad to hear that she is a

healthy, vigorous child, very tall and large for her age, and with a finely developed head. As you will see by her letters, she loves to romp and play with other children, and enjoyed very much playing and studying with the little blind children during her stay at the Kindergarten for the Blind, near Boston. Here she met little Edith Thomas, a child afflicted in the same way as Helen herself; and the two little girls kissed and hugged each other to their hearts' content. Here she learned also to model in clay, to make bead-baskets, and to knit with four needles. She was much pleased with this latter accomplishment, and said that she could now knit some stockings for her father!

She has a wonderfully strong memory, and seldom forgets what she has once learned; and she learns very quickly. But her marvelous progress is not due to her fine memory alone, but also to her great quickness of perception, and to her remarkable powers of thought. To speak a little more clearly, Helen understands with singular rapidity not only what is said to her, but even the feelings and the state of mind of those about her, and she *thinks* more than most children of her age. The "Touch" schoolmistress has done such wonders for her little pupil that you would scarcely believe how many things Helen finds out, as with electric quickness, through her fingers. She knows in a moment whether her companions are sad, or frightened, or impatient—in other words, she has learned so well what movements people make under the influence of different feelings that at times she seems to read our thoughts. Thus, when she was walking one day with her mother, a boy exploded a torpedo which frightened Mrs. Keller. Helen asked at once, "What are you afraid of?" Some of you already know that *sound* (*i.e.*, noise of all sorts) is produced by the vibrations of the air striking against our or-

gans of hearing—that is to say, the ears; and deaf people, even though they can hear absolutely nothing, are still conscious of these vibrations. Thus, they can "feel" loud music, probably because it shakes the floor; and Helen's sense of feeling is so wonderfully acute, that she no doubt learns many things from these vibrations of the air which to us are imperceptible.

The following anecdote illustrates both her quickness of touch and her reasoning powers. The matron of the Perkins Institution for the Blind exhibited one day, to a number of friends, a glass lemon-squeezer of a new pattern. It had never been used, and no one present could guess for what purpose it was intended. Some one handed it to Helen, who spelled "lemonade" on her fingers, and asked for a drinking-glass. When the glass was brought, she placed the squeezer in proper position for use.

The little maid was closely questioned as to how she found out a secret that had baffled all the "seeing" people present. She tapped her forehead twice, and spelled, "*I think.*"

I can not forbear telling you one more anecdote about her, which seems to me a very pathetic one. She is a very good mimic, and loves to imitate the motions and gestures of those about her, and she can do so very cleverly. On a certain Sunday, she went to church with a lady named Mrs. Hopkins, having been cautioned beforehand by her teacher, that she must sit very quiet during the church service. It is very hard to sit perfectly still, however, when you can't hear one word of what the minister is saying, and little Helen presently began to talk to Mrs. Hopkins, and ask what was going on. Mrs. H. told her, and reminded her of Miss Sullivan's injunction about keeping quiet. She immediately obeyed, and turning her head in a listening attitude, she said, "*I listen.*"

The following letter, to her mother, shows how much progress Helen had made in the use of language during her stay at the North:

So. Boston, Mass., Sept. 24th

My Dear Mother: I think you will be very glad to know all about my visit to West Newton. Teacher and I had a lovely time with many kind friends. West Newton is not far from Boston, and we went there in the steam-cars very quickly.

Mrs. Freeman and Carrie, and Ethel and Frank and Helen came to station to meet us in a huge carriage. I was delighted to see my dear little friends, and I hugged and kissed them. Then we rode for a long time to see all the beautiful things in West Newton. Many very handsome houses and large soft green lawns around them, and trees and bright flowers and fountains.

The horse's name was "Prince," and he was gentle and liked to trot very fast. When we went home we saw eight rabbits and two fat puppies, and a nice little white pony, and two wee kittens, and a pretty curly dog named "Don." Pony's name was "Mollie," and I had a nice ride on her back; I was not afraid. I hope my uncle will get me a dear little pony and a little cart very soon.

Clifton did not kiss me, because he does not like to kiss little girls. He is shy. I am very glad that Frank and Clarence, and Robbie and Eddie, and Charles and George were not very shy. I played with many little girls, and we had fun. I rode on Carrie's tricycle, and picked flowers, and ate fruit, and hopped and skipped and danced, and went to ride. Many ladies and gentlemen came to see us. Lucy and Dora and Charles were born in China. I was born in America, and Mr. Anagnos was born in Greece. Mr. Drew says little girls in China can not talk on their fingers, but I think when I go to China I will teach them. Chinese nurse came to see me; her name was Asin. She showed me a tiny atze that very rich ladies in China wear, because their feet never grow large. Amah means a nurse. We came home in horse-cars, because it was Sunday, and steam-cars do not go often on Sunday. Conductors and engineers do get very tired and go home to rest. I saw little Willie Swan in the car, and he gave me a juicy pear. He was six years old. What did I do when I was six years old? Will you please ask my father to come to train to meet teacher and me? I am very sorry that Eva and Bessie are sick. I hope I can have a nice party my birthday, and I do want Carrie and Ethel, and Frank and Helen to come to Alabama to visit me.

With much love and thousand kisses.

From your dear little daughter,
Helen A. Keller.

When I last heard of little Helen, she was in her own happy home, in the sunny South. There we will leave her, with many wishes for her future welfare, and hopes that she may yet be gratified in her great desire: "I do want to learn much about everything."

Miss Sullivan says that it is a pleasure to teach so apt, so gentle and intelligent a pupil; but while Helen is dependent upon others for all the lessons which the Eye and Ear schoolmistresses have failed to teach her, does she not give the world, in return, a very wonderful and beautiful lesson?"

I think that old and young alike may learn much from the daily life of little Helen Keller.

BACHELOR'S BUTTON
By Mary E. Wilkins

April, 1894

In the days of the grandmothers of the roses,
    In the sweet old times of the pinks, 'tis said
The poor little Bachelor lost his button,
His beautiful, black-eyed, blue-rimmed button,
    In dear little Betty's garden-bed.

Tête-à-tête with the grandmother roses
    Stood the little maid Betty, shy and sweet,
When all of a sudden she cried with wonder,
For the Bachelor's button was lying under
    A red rose-bush, at her very feet.

Then straightway Betty must fall to dreaming,
    Through the lavender-scented summer hours:
Could the Bachelor be a soldier or sailor?
But he must have surely a fairy tailor
    To fasten his coat with buttons of flowers.

The little maid Betty stood dreaming, and waiting,
    In the hope that a sweet little ancient beau,
In blue-flower buttons and primrose satin,
With a prince's feather his fine cocked hat in,
    Would come through her garden, a-peering low.

Then Betty planned she would courtesy primly,
    And say like her mother, stately and mild:
"Please, sir, an' please, sir, I've found your button."
But the Bachelor never came for his button,
    And she wondered why, while she was a child.

391

THE LAND OF MAKE-BELIEVE

By Guy Wetmore Carryl

August, 1895

I KNOW of a dear, delightful land,
    Which is not so far away,
That we may not sail to its sunlit strand
    No matter how short the day:
Ah, there the skies are always blue,
    And hearts forget to grieve,
For there's never a dream but must come true
    In the Land of Make-Believe.

There every laddie becomes a knight,
    And a fairy queen each lass;
And lips learn laughter, and eyes grow bright
    As the dewdrops in the grass;
For there's nothing beautiful, brave, and bold
    That one may not achieve,
If he once sets foot on the sands of gold
    Of the Land of Make-Believe.

So spread the sails, and away we go
    Light-winged through the fairy straits;
For the west winds steadily, swiftly blow,
    And the wonderful harbor waits.
On our prow the foam-flecks glance and gleam,
    While we sail from morn till eve,
All bound for the shores of the children's dream
    Of the Land of Make-Believe!

A FATUOUS FLOWER

By Oliver Herford

July, 1897

NCE on a time a Bumblebee
  Addressed a Sunflower. Said he:
  "Dear Sunflower, tell me is it true
  What everybody says of you?"

  Replied the Sunflower: "Tell me, pray,
  How should *I* know what people say?
  Why should I even care? No doubt
  'Tis some ill-natured tale without
  A word of truth; but tell me, Bee,
  What *is* it people say of me?"
  "Oh, no!" the Bee made haste to add;
  " 'Tis really not so very bad.
  I got it from the Ant. She said
  She'd *heard* the Sun had turned your head,
  And that whene'er he walks the skies
  You follow him with all your eyes
  From morn till eve—"
  "Oh, what a shame!"
  Exclaimed the Sunflower, aflame,
  "To say such things of me! They *know*
  The very opposite is so.

"They know full well that it is *he*—
The *Sun*—who always follows me.
I turn away my head until
I fear my stalk will break; and still
He tags along from morn till night,
Starting as soon as it is light,

393

And never takes his eyes off me
Until it is too dark to see!
They really ought to be ashamed.
Soon they'll be saying I was named
For him, when well they know 't was he
Who took the name of Sun from me."

The Sunflower paused, with anger dumb.
The Bee said naught, but murmured, "H'm!"
'Twas very evident that he
Was much impressed—this Bumblebee.
He spread his wings at once and flew
To tell some other bees he knew,
Who, being also much impressed,
Said, "H'm!" and flew to tell the rest.

And now if you should chance to see,
In field or grove, a Bumblebee,
And hear him murmur, "H'm!" then you
Will know what he's alluding to.

THE SLEEPING FLOWERS
By Emily Dickinson

June, 1891

"Whose are the little beds," I asked,
 "Which in the valleys lie?"
Some shook their heads, and others smiled,
 And no one made reply.

Perhaps they did not hear, I said,
 I will inquire again.
"Whose are the beds—the tiny beds
 So thick upon the plain?"

" 'Tis daisy in the shortest;
 A little further one—
Nearest the door, to wake the first—
 Little leontodon.

" 'Tis iris, sir, and aster,
 Anemone and bell;
Batschia in the blanket red,
 And chubby daffodil."

Meanwhile, at many cradles,
 She rocked and gently smiled,
Humming the quaintest lullaby
 That ever soothed a child.

"Hush! Epigea wakens!
 The crocus stirs her hood—
Rhodora's cheek is crimson,
 She's dreaming of the wood."

Then turning from them, reverent,
 "Their bedtime 'tis," she said;
"The bumblebees will wake them
 When April woods are red."

THE ST. NICHOLAS TREASURE-BOX
OF LITERATURE

June, 1881

ALL who live in this favored land know the wealth of its lavish summer and rejoice that its "June may be had of the poorest comer"—June, with its songs, its roses, and its warm, swift breezes—and they will be ready to echo in their hearts every word of Lowell's beautiful verses which the Treasure-box offers you this month.

You will find, as you see more and more of literature, that almost every good writer has his special line or style of writing, and has won fame by excelling in that special line. For instance, of modern authors, we speak of Thackeray, George Eliot, and Dickens as great novelists; of Ruskin and Carlyle as great essayists or critics; of Scott and Hawthorne as romancers; and of Tennyson and Longfellow as poets. But now and then we find a man who, writing in all these ways, proves himself a master in each. Among the foremost of such writers is James Russell Lowell. He is poet, essayist, critic, humorist, all in one. For a long time, he was a professor in Harvard University; but, as many of you know, he is now—to the honor of his country—serving as American minister to England.

Although Lowell has written almost entirely for grown-up readers, there is many a page of his works that would help you to appreciate good literature, and many a description or poem that would charm and delight you. For Lowell, with all his learning and deep thought, keeps himself forever young at heart—as, indeed, do all true poets—and his writings are full of the spirit and joy of youth and of youthful delight in life. This is shown clearly enough in the following short extract describing the sights and sounds of the happy month of June. It is taken from his noble poem, *The Vision of Sir Launfal:*

A JUNE DAY
By James Russell Lowell

AND what is so rare as a day in June?
    Then, if ever, come perfect days;
Then Heaven tries the earth if it be in tune,
    And over it softly her warm ear lays:
Whether we look, or whether we listen,
We hear life murmur, or see it glisten;
Every clod feels a stir of might,
    An instinct within it that reaches and towers,
And, groping blindly above it for light,
    Climbs to a soul in grass and flowers;
The flush of life may well be seen
    Thrilling back over hills and valleys;

The cowslip startles in meadows green,
   The buttercup catches the sun in its chalice,
And there's never a leaf nor a blade too mean
   To be some happy creature's palace;
The little bird sits at his door in the sun,
   Atilt like a blossom among the leaves,
And lets his illumined being o'errun
    With the deluge of summer it receives;
His mate feels the eggs beneath her wings,
And the heart in her dumb breast flutters and sings;
He sings to the wide world, and she to her nest—
In the nice ear of Nature which song is best?
Now is the high tide of the year,
   And whatever of life hath ebbed away
Comes flooding back, with a ripply cheer,
   Into every bare inlet and creek and bay;
Now the heart is so full that a drop overfills it,
We are happy now because God wills it;
No matter how barren the past may have been,
'Tis enough for us now that the leaves are green;
We sit in the warm shade and feel right well
How the sap creeps up and the blossoms swell;
We may shut our eyes, but we can not help knowing
That skies are clear and grass is growing;
The breeze comes whispering in our ear,
That dandelions are blossoming near,
   That maize has sprouted, that streams are flowing,
That the river is bluer than the sky,
That the robin is plastering his house hard by;
And if the breeze kept the good news back,
For other couriers we should not lack;
   We could guess it all by yon heifer's lowing—
And hark! how clear bold chanticleer,
Warmed with the new wine of the year,
   Tells all in his lusty crowing!

THE BLUE AND THE GRAY*
By F. M. Finch

June, 1881

By the flow of the inland river,
　Whence the fleets of iron have fled,
Where the blades of the grave-grass quiver,
　Asleep are the ranks of the dead—
　　Under the sod and the dew,
　　　Waiting the judgment day—
　　Under the one, the Blue;
　　　Under the other, the Gray.

These in the robings of glory,
　Those in the gloom of defeat,
All with the battle-blood gory,
　In the dusk of eternity meet—
　　Under the sod and the dew,
　　　Waiting the judgment day—
　　Under the laurel, the Blue;
　　　Under the willow, the Gray.

From the silence of sorrowful hours
　The desolate mourners go,
Lovingly laden with flowers,
　Alike for the friend and the foe—
　　Under the sod and the dew,
　　　Waiting the judgment day—
　　Under the roses, the Blue;
　　　Under the lilies, the Gray.

So, with an equal splendor,
　The morning sun-rays fall,
With a touch impartially tender,
　On the blossoms blooming for all—
　　Under the sod and the dew,
　　　Waiting the judgment day—
　　Broidered with gold, the Blue;
　　　Mellowed with gold, the Gray.

So, when the summer calleth,
　On forest and field of grain,
With an equal murmur falleth
　The cooling drip of the rain—
　　Under the sod and the dew,
　　　Waiting the judgment day—
　　Wet with the rain, the Blue;
　　　Wet with the rain, the Gray.

Sadly, but not with upbraiding,
　The generous deed was done;
In the storms of the years that are fading,
　No braver battle was won—
　　Under the sod and the dew,
　　　Waiting the judgment day—
　　Under the blossoms, the Blue;
　　　Under the garlands, the Gray.

No more shall the war-cry sever,
　Or the winding rivers be red;
They banish our anger forever
　When they laurel the graves of our dead!
　　Under the sod and the dew,
　　　Waiting the judgment day—
　　Love and tears for the Blue;
　　　Tears and love for the Gray.

*The Union or Northern soldiers wore blue
uniforms; the Confederate soldiers wore gray.

From Our Scrap-Book

- C·T·HILL·

October, 1897

LANTERNS INVENTED BY A KING

KING ALFRED of England, having no means of measuring time, noted the hours by the burning of candles marked with circular lines of different colors, which served as hour-lines. To prevent the wind from blowing out the candles, he had them incased in horn scraped so thin as to be transparent. Glass was then little, if at all, known in England. Thus lanterns may be said to be the invention of a king.

GLASS 3000 YEARS OLD

GLASS was early known. Glass beads were found on the bodies of mummies over three thousand years old.

A STRANGE DERIVATION

THE interrogation-point is said to be formed from the first and last letters of the Latin word *quaestio* (an asking), placed one over the other, thus: ; the exclamation-point, from the Greek word *Io*, signifying joy, placed in the same way: .

THE SUN IN DECEMBER

IT seems hard for us to understand that the distance of the earth from the sun is about 3,000,00 miles less in December than it is June—but it is true.

THE ETERNAL CITY

THOUGH Rome is called "the Eternal City," the name by right belongs to the city of Damascus in Syria, which is the oldest city in the world. As long as man has had written records the city of Damascus has been known.

THE DEATH OF GEORGE WASHINGTON

IT is a curious fact that George Washington drew his last breath in the last hour of the last day of the week, in the last month of the year, in the last century, dying on Saturday night, at twelve o'clock, December 14, 1799.

NEVER BEATEN

THE following three great generals were never defeated: Alexander the Great, who died 300 B.C.; Julius Caesar, who died 44 B.C.; the Duke of Wellington, hero of Waterloo, who died 1852.

THE SEA HORSE

THE sea horse is a small, bony fish with a head much like that of a horse, found on the Atlantic coast, in size from three to six inches long; but a California species is often eight to ten inches long. It looks as though its body were covered with tiny spangles, and it shines like silver. It always swims erect, carrying its head with the neck curved like that of a proud horse. Its two eyes have the power of being independent of each other, gazing two ways at once.

NAPOLEON IN VENICE

In May, 1797, Napoleon Bonaparte rode to the top of the bell-tower or campanile of St. Mark's, Venice, on horseback, that he might signal to his fleet the surrender of the city.

AN ODD TITLE

Luxembourg, the great French soldier, was called "the Upholsterer of Notre Dame" from the number of captured flags he sent to be hung as trophies in that cathedral.

ANIMALS IN PARADISE

According to the Mohammedan creed, ten animals beside man are admitted into Paradise. These ten are: 1, the dog; 2 Balaam's ass; 3, Solomon's ant; 4, Jonah's whale; 5, the ram of Ishmael; 6, the Queen of Sheba's ass; 7, the camel of Salet; 8, the cuckoo of Belkis; 9, the ox of Moses; 10, the animal called Al Borak, which conveyed Mohammed to heaven.

A BEE-LINE

The eyes of bees are made to see great distances. When absent from their hive they go up in the air till they see their home, and then fly toward it in a straight line and with great speed. The shortest line between two places is sometimes called a "bee-line."

TONY'S LETTER

June, 1877

PETER was a funny little boy, who had a dog named Tony. This dog was all covered with long shaggy hair, which hung down over his eyes and his mouth, and made him look very wise. But Tony was not as wise as he looked, and he did not know as much as little Peter thought he knew.

Peter was only three years old. He did not know all the alphabet, but he knew what letters spelled his own name.

Peter was very fond of what he called "writing letters." He would scribble all over a piece of paper, and then fold it up and get his sister Emily to write on it the name of one of the family, or else of one of the neighbors. Then Peter would carry it to that person; and he very often got a written answer, which Emily would read to him. Sometimes these answers had candy in them, which pleased Peter very much.

One day, Peter wrote a long letter to his dog Tony. When he gave it to him, Tony took it in his mouth and carried it to the rug in front of the fire in the sitting-room. There he laid it down, and put his nose to it. Then he laid himself down, with his head on the letter, and shut his eyes. He was sleepy, and he found that the letter was not good to eat.

Peter was very glad to see Tony do this, for he thought he had read the letter and was thinking what he should say when he answered it.

So little Peter said, "Tony shall write me an answer to my letter," and he ran into his grandma's room, to ask for a pencil. She was not there, but on the table there was some paper, and an inkstand with a quill pen in it. His grandma always used a quill pen.

So Peter took a big sheet of paper and the inkstand with the pen in it. Then he saw his grandma's spectacles on the table, and he thought he would take these too, as Tony might write better if he had spectacles on.

Peter waked Tony, who was fast asleep by this time, and made him hold his head up. Peter put the spectacles on Tony, and laid the paper before him. Then he set the inkstand down, close to his right paw.

"Now, Tony," said Peter, "you must write me a letter."

Tony looked at the little boy, but he did not take the pen.

"There, Tony!" said Peter. "There's the ink and the pen. Don't you see them?" And me pushed the inkstand against Tony's paw.

The dog gave the inkstand a tap with his paw, and over it went!

"Oh!" cried Peter. "You naughty dog! Upsetting grandma's inkstand!" And he picked up the inkstand as quickly as he could. Some of the ink had run out on the paper, but none of it had gone on the carpet.

Peter took off Tony's spectacles, and drove him away; and then, with what he called the "tail" of the quill pen (by which he meant the feather end), he spread the ink about on the paper.

Then he took the paper up by a corner, and carried it to his mother.

"Mamma!" said he, "see the letter Tony wrote to me. He upset the inkstand, but none of the letter runned off on the carpet!"

Tony never wrote another letter, and that was the last time that little Peter meddled with his grandma's pen and ink.

AN ALPHABET FROM ENGLAND

By Christina G. Rossetti

November, 1875

A is the Alphabet, A at its head;
A is an Antelope, agile to run.

B is the Baker Boy bringing the bread,
Or black Bear and brown Bear, both begging for bun.

C is a Cornflower come with the corn;
C is a Cat with a comical look.

THE COMICAL CAT.

D is a dinner which Dahlias adorn;
D is a Duchess who dines with a
Duke.

E is an elegant, eloquent Earl;
E is an Egg whence an Eaglet emerges.

THE ELOQUENT EARL.

F is a Falcon, with feathers to furl;
F is a Fountain of full foaming surges.

THE GANDER, THE GOSLING, THE GOOSE.

G is the Gander, the Gosling,
the Goose;
G is a Garnet in girdle of
gold.

H is a Heartsease, harmonious of hues;
H is a huge Hammer, heavy to hold.

I is an Idler who idles on ice;
I am I—who will say I am not I?

J is a Jacinth, a jewel of price;
J is a Jay, full of joy in July.

A HAMMER HEAVY TO HOLD.

K is a King, or a Kaiser still
higher;
K is a Kitten, or quaint Kangaroo.

L is a Lute or a lovely-toned Lyre;
L is a Lily all laden with dew.

A JAY FULL OF JOY IN JULY.

M is a Meadow where Meadow-sweet
blows;
M is a Mountain made dim by a mist.

N is a nut—in a nutshell it grows;
Or a Nest full of Nightingales singing
—oh, list!

O is an Opal, with only one
    spark ;
O is an Olive, with oil on its
    skin.

A PONY, A PET IN THE PARK.

P is a Pony, a pet in a park ;
P is the Point of a Pen or a Pin.

Q is a Quail, quick chirping at morn ;
Q is a Quince quite ripe and near dropping.

A RED-BREASTED ROBIN.

R is a Rose, rosy red on a thorn ;
R is a red-breasted Robin come hopping.

S is a Snow-storm that sweeps o'er the Sea ;
S is the Song that the swift Swallows sing.

T is the Tea-table set out for tea ;
T is a Tiger with terrible spring.

THE UMBRELLA.

U, the Umbrella, went up in a shower ;
Or Unit is useful with ten to unite.

POLICEMAN X EXERCISED.

V is a Violet veined in the flower;
V is a Viper of venomous bite.

W stands for the water-bred Whale;
Stands for the wonderful Wax-work so gay.

X, or X X, or X X X is ale,
Or Policeman X, exercised day after day.

Y is a yellow Yacht, yellow its boat;
Y is the Yucca, the Yam, or the Yew.

Z is a Zebra, zigzagged his coat,
Or Zebu, or Zoöphyte, seen at the Zoo.

"SEEN AT THE ZOO."

JACK-IN-THE-PULPIT

July, 1895

HURRAH for July, my hearers, and for the one dear noisy day that it always brings to young and old of this great republic! Don't you feel sorry for those poor countries that never had any revolution to speak of, and so have no honored old oppressors to forgive, and no rattlety-band way of expressing themselves on a national holiday?

But there were events, I am told, long before there was any Fourth of July, as we know it—and events with youngsters and gunpowder in them. Did you ever hear of the narrow escape of the good ship *Mayflower*—the same that brought your Pilgrim forefathers over from England?

Well, in this explosion-loving part of the year it may interest all good little boys to know that even in the very first ship's company that ever landed in New England there was a youngster who *would* fool with gun and powder, and who actually came near blowing up the *Mayflower!*

My learned correspondent, Mr. Thomas L. Rogers, sends you this stirring and pious account of the boy's dangerous performance. It is copied from the chronicles of Governor Bradford himself.

Through God's mercy we escaped a great danger by the foolishness of a boy who had got gunpowder and made squibs; and there being a fowling-piece in his father's cabin, charged, he shot her off in the cabin; there being a little barrel of gunpowder half full: [and some] scattered in and about the cabin: the fire being within four foot of the bed between the decks, and many flints and iron things about the cabin, and many people about the fire: and yet, by God's mercy, no harm done.

And now for your edification Mr. Rogers has put this incident into clever verse, which he calls

405

A MISCHIEVOUS LITTLE PILGRIM

JOHN BILLINGTON, one of the Pilgrim boys,
  Was as full of mischief as an egg is of meat;
For causing of trouble, for making a noise,
  And for scaring good people, he couldn't be beat.
        He was bad,
        And very sad,
  Is the story told of this Pilgrim lad.

At anchor the staunch old *Mayflower* lay;
  The men, led by Standish, were exploring the shore.
But John was exploring the vessel that day,
  And finding of powder a generous store,
        Just for fun,
        This worthy son
  In one of the cabins fired off a gun.

Of perils by land and dangers by sea.
  The Pilgrims had plenty—that's simply the truth—
But foolish King James, who compelled them to flee,
  Never shocked their poor nerves like this mischievous youth,
        Who for fun
        Made them all run
  To put out the fire from his terrible gun.

NATURAL FIREWORKS

Yes, natural fireworks; and you may be sure they really occurred, for the fact was related by the great Mr. Charles Darwin, an observer who never saw stars that were not there. In his famous book *The Voyage of the* Beagle the dear Little Schoolma'am has found this passage:

As soon as we entered the estuary of the Plata [the Rio de la Plata] the weather was very unsettled. One dark night we were surrounded by numerous seals and penguins, which made such strange noises that the officer on watch reported he could hear the cattle bellowing on shore. On a second night we witnessed a splendid display of natural fireworks: the mast-head and yard-arm-ends shone with St. Elmo's light; and the form of the vane could almost be traced, as if it had been rubbed with phosphorus. The sea was so highly luminous that the tracks of the penguins were marked by fiery wakes, and the darkness of the sky was momentarily illuminated by the most vivid lighting.

And the Deacon kindly adds: "Every boy knows what St. Elmo's light is; and if he doesn't, he can find out by inquiring of the nearest dictionary."

A St. Nicholas Anthology

St. Nicholas League

ANNOUNCEMENT

The St. Nicholas League is an organization of the readers of the St. Nicholas magazine. The League motto is " Live to learn and learn to live."

The League banner is the Stars and Stripes.

The League badge is a beautiful button bearing the League name and emblem.

The St. Nicholas League, it is hoped, will be a very useful association of earnest and enlightened young folks. Every reader of St. Nicholas will be entitled to League membership, whether a subscriber or not; also to membership badge and to all privileges and benefits of the order.

AIMS

The St. Nicholas League stands for intellectual advancement and for higher ideals of life. " To learn more and more of the best that has been thought and done in the world " — to get closer to the heart of nature and acquire a deeper sympathy with her various forms — these are its chief aims, and the League is in favor of any worthy pursuit or pastime that is a means to this end.

Book-study alone is not followed by the best results. Direct friendship with the woods and fields and healthful play are necessary to the proper development of both mind and body.

The St. Nicholas League also stands for intelligent patriotism, and for protection of the oppressed, whether human beings, dumb animals, or birds. These things are the natural result of culture and higher ideals. He who enjoys life and liberty, knowing what they mean, cannot willingly see others deprived of them.

THE GOLD AND SILVER BUTTONS

Six solid gold buttons and six silver buttons will be awarded each month as first and second prizes for the following achievements in the varied competitions offered by the League :

The best two drawings in pen and ink — subject to be announced each month.

The best two poems, not over twenty-four lines each — subject to be announced each month.

The best two school compositions (stories or articles), not over four hundred words each in length, sent with the consent of teacher. Subject to be announced each month.

The best two amateur photographs — not smaller than 3 × 4 nor larger than 5 × 7 — subject to be announced each month.

The best two puzzles (any sort) and

The best and neatest answers to all St. Nicholas puzzles of each issue.

Thus talent, patience, and ingenuity all have an opportunity, and the prize buttons are beautiful tokens of merit and distinction.

CONTENTS

A PRIZE-WINNER?

December, 1899

"I'd like to win a prize," said Sue—
"I'd like to, and I'll do it, too.
I'll write a poem, first," said she,
"And then a tale in prose you'll see,
And then a drawing I will make,
And then a photograph I'll take,
And then a puzzle I will write,
And sent them all by mail to-night,
And puzzle-answers, too; and so
I'll surely win one prize, I know."

The rules she didn't pause to read,
But wrote with diligence and speed
A poem and a story too,
And then, forthwith, a picture drew;
A photograph and puzzle next,
And then, alas! poor Sue was vexed
O'er "answers" harder far (for her)
Than poem, prose, and pictures were.
Still, she got *some*—or thought she had—
And sent them, and her heart was glad
Till, when the prize-list Susie read,
"I haven't got a thing!" she said.

If Susie had but read with care
The rules and all that's printed there
Twice through, at least, from end to end—
On what to send and how to send—
And then resolved, whate'er befell,
To do one thing, and do it well,
And taken time—a day or two—
To think, and then as long to *do*,
It might have been—I cannot say—
Sue *might* have a prize to-day.
    A. B. P.

"HEADING." BY ELISE R. RUSSELL, AGE 13. (SILVER BADGE.)

SOME CHRISTMAS CUSTOMS

By Laura Benét (age 16)

THE quaint old town of Bethlehem, Pennsylvania, was settled by the Moravians, who keep Christmas in a very pretty and unique way. On Christmas Eve, as you enter the church you see that it is a large and rather plain building, decorated inside with evergreens and holly. As you look toward the altar you see a picture of the Holy Night surrounded by greens and tiny Christmas trees, and placed so that the light falls directly upon the beautiful face of the babe in the manger. Then the service begins. It is very pretty and simple. The Moravians on this night always sing some especial hymns, one of which is "Silent Night." The music is unusually fine and the voices of the choir very sweet and thrilling. As the last hymn begins the doors are thrown wide open, and the Moravian Sisters enter bearing little trays of lighted sweet-scented wax tapers. One of these is given to every child in the congregation, who is supposed to keep the light burning even after he leaves the church. The little children of Austria put a lighted candle in their window, lest the Christ Child should stumble as he passes up the street on Christmas Eve. In Germany the children's shoes are put out over night in the hope that Chris Kringle will reward the good ones with sweetmeats and cakes; but the bad ones generally find a bundle of birch rods in their shoes. The people of Norway tie bundles of grain or wheat to every available post, roof, or steeple for the birds. In the morning the birds show their thanks by giving the people a joyous Christmas carol.

"AN OLD FRIEND." BY
MARY CANDACE PANGBORN,
AGE 14. (HONOR MEMBER)

IN DAYS OF OLD

By E. Babette Deutsch (age 10)
(*Silver Badge Winner*)

IN days of old when dolly Belle
  Was just as new as gold
Before she broke her leg and fell,
  In happy days of old—

In days of old when dolly Belle
  Was clad in silk and lace
Before she was knocked near the well
  And cracked her pretty face—

I loved her then, my dolly Belle!
  When she were fair and new.
I love you still, *dear* dolly Belle,
  Spite of your looks, I do!

MY FAIRY-BOOK PRINCE

By Margaret Widdemer (age 16)
(Cash Prize $5.00)

DEAR little prince of Fairyland,
The rose you hold in your outstretched hand
Is not half so sweet as the loving look
You bend from your page of my picture-book
On the calm little princess over the way.
Do you win her, or lose? Do you go or stay?
Ah, you wed, I know! I have but to look
Over the page of my picture-book.

Dear little prince of Fairyland,
Is the red, red rose in your tight-clasped hand
For none but your princess, cold as fair?
Surely she's many a love to spare!
She never would care if you went away!
Could you not step from your page, and stay
With a lone little maid who would love but you?
(And ah, little prince, I would love you true!)

Cold little prince of Fairyland!
Silently, haughtily, still you stand.
"To none but my princess," you seem to say,
"My rose and my love, though there come who may!"
And you'll wed the princess—the book says so;
And I know you lived many a year ago;
Yet—ah, little prince, if you could but look
Loving but me from my picture-book!

QUIET DAYS

By Miriam A. De Ford (age 13)

THE golden haze is reaching to the dreaming, cloudless sky,
And the lazy breezes scarcely stir the red leaves flutt'ring by;
The tall pines raise their beauty from the sunshine-dotted ground,
And the rustling of the tree-tops is the only living sound.

The crimson sky is flecked with gold, a fading field of light;
The breeze is whisp'ring to the grass a lingering long good night;
The pines are silhouetted against the darkened sky,
And sound asleep beneath the moon all nature's wild things lie.

TO A MOUNTAIN

By Clement R. Wood (age 17)
(*Gold Badge*)

MOUNTAIN, as a Titan high,
Looming always in the sky
O'er the vale, incessantly,
Oh, may I thy minstrel be!
In the morning tints of rose
Cause thy ever-capping snows
With a pale-pink light to glow
Ere the valley, far below,
Has received the earliest ray
Of the new-awakened day.
Mountain streamlets, murmuring,
O'er thy rocky ledges spring;
Fluted oak and pine trees hale
In long lines rise o'er the vale.
In the afternoon a beam
Of perfect yellow light doth stream
While the vale's in shadowed rest,
All around thy hoary crest
Making golden castles now
Of the rocks upon thy brow.
Mountain, as a Titan high,
Looming always in the sky,
Clothed in nature's majesty,
Oh, may I thy minstrel be!

AFTER THE CELEBRATION (AS TOLD BY THE FIRE-CRACKER)

By E. Vincent Millay (age 15)
(*Honor Member*)

THE shiny pistol, the little red cap, my torpedo friend and I—
Of our comrades bereft, we are all that is left of the glorious Fourth of July.
We little thought we would come to this; when the morning sun first shone
We could not tell that ere evening fell, we four would be left alone.

The shiny pistol grew warm and moist in a sticky, childish grasp,
And the dull marks made on his side betrayed a smutty finger-clasp.
In the little round box all torn on the grass, this morning the little cap lay,
And the world seemed fair as she nestled there, with her sisters cuddled away.

Torpedo was one of seventeen, snug-tucked in a sawdust bed—
And was it to-day that my comrades lay by my side in their jackets of red?
One by one they were torn away, to leap with a shout through the air,
To fly with a trail of sparks, to lie on the lawn with the others there.

And ah! 'Tis a glorious death to die, in the smoke and the fire-glow—
A hissing call, a blazing fall to the ground where the hot sparks blow.
Oh! How I longed for the grimy hands to carry me off to flight,
But all the day they were borne away—we four are alone to-night.

There on the grass are my comrades strewn, their red coats blackened and torn,
In the quiet I lie and mourn where I am all that is left to mourn.
Oh! That I lay where my comrades lie, as blackened and torn as they.
Exulting I'd go to my death, could I know the smoke and blare of the fray.
But the peaceful light of the setting sun falls calmly down where we lie—
The shiny pistol, the little red cap, my torpedo friend and I.

THE HARVEST

By William R. Benét (age 15)
(*Silver Badge*)

Yon lie the fields all golden with grain,
  (Oh, come, ye Harvesters, reap!)
The dead leaves are falling with autumn's brown stain.
  (Oh, come, ye Harvesters, reap!)
For soon sinks the sun to his bed in the west,
And cawing the crows fly each one to his nest;
The grain soon will wither, so harvest your best.
  (Oh, come, ye Harvesters, reap!)

Swift sweep the scythes o'er the mellowing ears,
  (Reap on, ye Harvesters, reap!)
And soft falls the grain like a fond mother's tears.
  (Reap on, ye Harvesters, reap!)
The sun sinketh down, and the day's work is done,
And slow go the harvesters home one by one.
Night now is at hand, but the harvest's begun.
  (Reap on, ye Harvesters, reap!)

L'Envoi.
Bare lie the fields which of late shone like gold!
  (Farewell, O Harvesters all!)
For the scythes were well handled with arms that were bold.
  (Farewell, O Harvesters all!)
The sunset is lighting the sky with its glow,
A crow's harsh note sounds from the meadow below,
And home from their labors the harvesters go!
  (Farewell, O Harvesters all!)

FRIENDS

By E. Vincent Millay (Honor Member, age 17)
(*Cash Prize*)

THIS bright bit of verse is placed at the head of the League this month because it is a fine example of clever rhyming, as well as of a very ingenious setting for the subject "Friends." Molly and Bob are made to seem very "real" to us just by what they say, in turn; and the contrast between the girl's and the boy's point of view is presented with admirable balance and equal effectiveness. But another striking excellence of the piece lies in the very skilful use of a double rhyme for each couplet—that is, there is a rhyme in the middle of each pair of lines as well as at the close—and these double rhymes are maintained almost throughout the two stanzas, with an ease and grace that a grown-up and practised author could not easily surpass. The contribution is a little gem in the smoothness and perfection of its rhythm, in its deft use of contrast, and in its naturalness of expression from first to last. As its young author has already won both a gold and a silver badge, and, therefore, is an Honor Member of the League, we gladly award a Cash Prize to the clever rhyme.

I. HE

I've sat here all the afternoon, watching her busy fingers send
That needle in and out. How soon, I wonder, will she reach the end?
Embroidery! I can't see how a girl of Molly's common sense
Can spend her time like that. Why, now—just look at that! I may be dense,
But, somehow, I don't see the fun in punching lots of holes down through
A piece of cloth; and, one by one, sewing them up. But Molly'll do
    A dozen of them, right around
    That shapeless bit of stuff she's found.
    A dozen of them! Just like that!
    And thinks it's sense she's working at.
But, then, she's just a girl (although she's quite the best one of the lot!)
And I'll just have to let her sew, whether it's foolishness or not.

II. SHE

He's sat here all the afternoon, talking about an awful game;
One boy will not be out till June, and then he may be always lame.
Foot-ball! I'm sure I can't see why a boy like Bob—so good and kind—
Wishes to see poor fellows lie hurt on the ground. I may be blind,
But, somehow, I don't see the fun. Some one calls, "14-16-9";
You kick the ball, and then you run and try to reach a white chalk-line.
    And Bob would sit right there all day
    And talk like that, and never say
    A single word of sense; or so
    It seems to me. I may not know.
But Bob's a faithful friend to me. So let him talk that game detested,
And I will smile and seem to be most wonderfully interested!

IN JUNE-TIME

By William R. Benet (age 16)

HARK, hark, to the meadow-lark
  As he swells his throat in a burst of song!
By the rippling brook sway the lilies. Look!
  They left their heads in a surpliced throng.
The sun's bright gleam shakes the silver stream
  With ripples of light that dance and play;
The fields are white with the daisies bright;
  The earth rejoices, and all is gay.
      It's June-time, it's June-time,
        The sparkling ripples tell;
      It's June-time, it's June-time,
        So shakes each lily bell.
The sky is smiling blue above; the streams below run clear.
It's June-time, it's June-time, the chosen of the year!
      It's June-time, it's June-time,
        The daisies whispering note.
      It's June-time, it's June-time!
        So swells each robin's throat.
The world is one vast Paradise, and heaven shines more near.
It's June-time, it's June-time, the chosen of the year!

A SONG OF THE WOODS

By Anna Torrey (age 14)
(*Gold Badge*)

DEEP in the forest, where a mighty oak
  Flings grateful shadow o'er a wandering stream,
Where tall ferns nod, and velvet mosses creep,
  I love to lie and dream.

I love to watch the shy, wild wood folk pass,
  To hear the oak leaves murmur in the breeze;
And see the dancing sunlight try to pierce
  Between the shading trees.

I love to hear the brook, with song and laugh,
  Go chattering and gurgling on its way,
By grassy banks where wild flowers scent the air,
  By lichened boulders gray.

And when the twilight comes with soothing touch,
  And whispering breezes healing coolness bring,
I love to linger in the woods at dusk,
  And hear the thrushes sing.

A LOST VALENTINE

By Margaret Widdemer
(*Gold Badge*)

Oʜ, who are you, in silk and gold,
    So gaily riding by?
"A gallant I of faeryland—
An airy land, a merry land—
A true knight I of faeryland
    Upon a dragon-fly."

What seek ye, far from faeryland?
    For fast and fast ye fare.
"I come to seek my valentine—
A ladye fine, a true love mine—
A sweet maid for a valentine,
    With sunlit eyes and hair."

Oh, I have seen your sweet ladye
    In wand'rings wide and far.
But she is held in weary thrall—
In dreary thrall, uncheery thrall;
They hold her fast in cruel thrall
    Where snow and shadows are.

"Oh, I will go and rescue her,
    My faery maiden lone;
And she shall be my valentine,
For whom I pine, this ladye mine—
And she shall be my valentine,
    My true love and my own."

BY FREDERICK LEWIS ALLEN, AGE 9.

A SONG OF THE WOODS

By S. V. Benét (age 13)
(*Silver Badge*)

There's many a forest in the world,
    In many lands leaves fall;
But Sherwood, merry Sherwood,
    Is the fairest wood of all.

They say that on midsummer night,
If mortal eyes could see aright,
    Or mortal ears could hear,
A wanderer on Sherwood's grass
Would see the band of Robin pass,
    Still hunting of the deer.

And sometime to his ears might come
The beating of an elfin drum,
    Where Puck, the tricksy sprite,
Would dance around a fairy ring,
    All on midsummer night.

With others of his gathering,
With all her glittering, courtly train,
'Til dawn begins to glow near by,
And from the kingdom of the sky,
    Through Sherwood's lovely glades;
Queen Guinevere would ride again
    The magic darkness fades.

There's many a forest in the world,
    In many lands leaves fall;
But Sherwood, merry Sherwood,
    Is the fairest wood of all.

THE GIFTS OF THE SEA

By Agnes MacKenzie Miall (age 16)
(*Gold Badge*)

Oʜ, the sea, the azure sea,
Clear and bright of hue;
Calm and stormy, fresh and free,
How it calls to you and me
From its depths of blue.

SIR FRANCIS DRAKE

By Frances MacKenzie (age 13)

In the time of Queen Elizabeth there was a great deal of hatred between England and Spain.

Francis Drake was brought up "to fear God and hate a Spaniard."

When Drake was still a boy, he was apprenticed to the captain of a small trading-vessel, and when the captain died he left Drake his ship, which he used for voyages to South America. Because Drake captured many galleys, and emptied the Spanish treasure-houses of all they were worth, which was a great deal, the Spaniards called him a pirate.

All Drake's work so far had been done on the eastern coast of America, but he was determined to sail on the Pacific, so he went through the Strait of Magellan and up the western coast of America, pillaging the towns as he came to them, until his ship had all she could hold of treasure; then he made his way home by the Cape of Good Hope. He had sailed all the way around the world, a thing no Englishman had ever done before.

So far no open war had been declared between England and Spain, but many a private battle was fought, and the English people wanted war, and they got it.

The great Spanish Armada sailed to England sure of victory, but the English fleet, with Drake and Lord Howard, drove them out of their course, and many were wrecked before they reached Spain.

Drake's last treasure-hunt was fatal. So terrified were Spaniards of him that every town was prepared, or empty of treasure, and deserted, and foul winds made him take shelter behind a deadly tropical island, where many of his crew died, and he himself got the swamp-fever and died; but he had taught the English how to be masters on the sea.

A SEASIDE ADVENTURE

By Josephine R. Carter (age 10)
(*Silver Badge*)

One morning I was playing with a friend in the sand at a little place on Long Island. Not very far away, we saw a life-boat lying on the beach; we thought it would be fun to play in it, so we got in, and were rocking and trying to make it sail (on sand), when a big wave came up and lifted it a little.

We were delighted with this, and rocked it some more. Soon a bigger wave came, and this time it lifted the boat off the sand and carried it out.

When I realized this, I screamed for help. My little friend's mother was sitting on the beach, and when she saw us going, she screamed too.

A life-saver happened to be fussing with a boat near by. He caught the situation at a glance, and, dropping everything, rushed after our boat, which was going quickly out into deep water.

We were terribly frightened when we saw the big waves almost on top of us, and I do not know what would have happened if he had not caught our boat just when he did.

He watched his chance, and when the next wave came, rushed us with it to the shore. In a few moments we were safe and sound on the beach.

I tell you, I was never so glad to get back to the land in my life, and thus end my first "seaside adventure."

GRATITUDE

By Cornelia Otis Skinner (age 11)
(*Silver Badge*)

I THANK thee, gentle breeze that blows,
  For all thy coolness bringing;
I thank thee, happy little bird,
  For all thy cheerful singing.

I thank you, pretty flowers that grow,
  For you carpet all the land;
I thank thee, smooth and sunny beach,
  For thy white and shimmery sand.

But should we thank these things so fair,
  For all their splendid show?
Nay! Bend our knees in gratitude
  To Him that made them so.

GRATITUDE TO THE LEAGUE

By Thérèse H. McDonnell (age 17)
(*Honor Member*)

'TIS time to bid a long farewell,
  To meet the parting of the ways
And only live in retrospect
  The happiness of childhood's days;
But on the page of memory's book
  The brightest picture that I find
Is of the League days, to me dear,
  That ever linger in my mind.

What pleasure did each struggle bring!
  And sweet indeed the victory,
When I had reached ambition's height,
  That brought my Badge of gold to me.
So just a word of gratitude
  As in my heart this toast I give:
"ST. NICHOLAS League—Long may it be
  To live to learn and learn to live!!!"

GRATITUDE

By Ruth Livingston (age 12)
(*Honor Member*)

LIKE amber wine poured with a hand too free
  From the gray cloud cup of the solemn night,
  There now pours down a wondrous golden light,
  Touching the topmost bowers of ev'ry tree,
Transforming them to gold by alchemy,
  Gilding the breast of Sir Lark, the Sun's knight,
  Who poureth out his thanks to Him whose might
  Made all this earth burst out in glory and in light.
Louder the anthem swells upon the breeze,
  And light and song fill all the morning air,
  As liquid sounds rise up from all the trees
And blend with the lark's hymn of thanks, so rare.
  Each flute and pipe and trill, from heavenly seas,
  Falls as the dewdrop, which God's message seems to bear.

A STORY OF THE STARS

By Blanche Olson (age 16)

UNCLE JOE was a large, good-natured man about fifty years of age. He entered his brother's house one cold, winter evening all wet with snow.

As he was taking off his big overcoat, Bob, his youngest nephew, came out from under the table, where he had been playing with the cat, and, with that happy cry Uncle Joe was so used to hearing, asked for a story. "Oh! wait a minute, boy," said Uncle Joe; "can't you give a fellow time to get warmed up a bit?" Bob looked at his uncle a moment; he did not know whether he meant it or not. But he soon found out, however, when Uncle Joe set him on his knee and said: "Well, Bob, as I was a-coming along I was thinking about the stars and my first trip up there. We left here about six o'clock in the evening. Up, up, we went until we could see the city no longer.

"We floated in and out among the clouds a while. It was very bright up there among so many beautiful stars.

"It was midnight before we reached Jupiter."

"Jupiter," repeated Bob. "What's Jupiter?"

"Oh! it's just a big star," said Uncle Joe. "Or I suppose the more correct name is, a planet. As I was saying, we reached Jupiter at midnight. We sailed around it a few times when one of the ropes caught on a smaller star near-by. My, what a time we had to get loose! We swung back and forth all of a half hour before the rope gave way any at all. It finally did give a little, to our surprise and joy. We worked another half hour, then swung off as nicely as if nothing whatever had happened.

"It was now nearly two o'clock. For the last hour the man in the moon had been laughing at us. We waved our hands good-by at him and floated away. We thought we would visit Neptune, but we heard it was very cold there as it is so far away from the sun. So we started home."

By this time Bob was asleep in Uncle Joe's arms. Uncle Joe carried him to his little bed and tucked him in, at the same time saying: "You are a great one to listen to a story."

TO THE STARS

By Frances Hedges (age 17)

SILVERY stars, so sharp and bright,
'Tis you who light us through the night.
At morn your twinkles disappear;
Return again and shine more clear
Still blessing us through all the year.

MYSTERY

By Stephen Vincent Benét (age 15)
(*Gold Badge. Silver Badge won September, 1912*)

THE giant building towered in the night
Like a titanic hand released at last
From under cumbering mountain-ranges vast,
Poised menacingly high, as if to smite
A silent, sudden, deadly blow at Man.
I slunk along its base; then, cowering, ran,
Feeling the while it mattered not how fast,
Since it would strike me from behind at last.

Next morning, as I passed among the hive
Of careless people, to myself I said:
"You do not fear. You've only seen it dead.
I've seen the thing alive!"

MY COUNTRY

By Rachel Lyman Field (age 16)

I HAVE read of merry England
  With its great cathedrals tall,
Of wonderful old castles,
  Of ruins great and small;
Of walls that long ago were built
  By Romans strong and bold,
And many relics of the past,
  Those wondrous days of old.

And I love the other countries,
  Scotland, Germany, and Wales,
With all their long array of knights,
  Their myths, and fairy-tales.
Then there's Spain, and France, and Norway,
  Switzerland, and Denmark, too,
And sunny Italy, where all
  The skies above are blue.

But when I look at the Stars and Stripes,
  Floating against the sky,
And I see the men in blue and gray
  With measured step pass by,
While above them all, the eagle soars,
  High to some mountain dome,
I am sure I love this country best,—
  The country I call home!

REST

By Alice M. MacRae (age 15)
(*Honor Member*)

I STOOD upon the sea-wall
  And gazed across the sea,
Where the fretted waves of Minas
  Beat a mournful melody;
While their rhythmic, restless turmoil
  Stamped itself upon my brain,
Till my soul was filled with longing
  And my heart was full of pain.

I stood upon the sea-beach
  By the waters wild and free.
And I cried: "Oh Waves of Ocean,
  Sing a song of Rest to me!"
But the rolling breakers chanted,
  Dashing on the rocky shore,
"Motion, motion, ceaseless motion
  Is our portion evermore."

I stood in waving meadows
  Where the flowers smiled to me—
Where through white-capped grassy billows
  A brook sang cheerily.
Peace breathed in every winding,
  "Lo! here is Rest," I cried,
"In the murmur of the brooklet
  And the daisies starry-eyed."

"FROM LIFE." BY DOROTHY OCHTMAN, AGE 11.

DAY'S REST-TIME

By E. Vincent Millay (age 16)
(*Honor Member*)

How lovely is the night, how calm and still!
Cool shadows lie upon each field and hill,
From which a fairy wind comes tripping light,
Perching on bush and tree in airy flight.
Across the brook and up the field it blows,
And to my ear there comes, where'er it goes,
A rustling sound as if each blade of grass,
Held back a silken skirt to let it pass.

This is the bedtime of the weary day;
Clouds wrap him warmly in a blanket gray;
From out the dusk where creek and meadow lie,
The frogs chirp out a sleepy lullaby;
A single star, new-kindled in the west,
A flick'ring candle, lights the day to rest.

O lovely night, sink deep into my heart—
Lend me of thy tranquility a part;
Of calmness give to me a kindly loan,
Until I have more calmness of my own.
And, weary day, O let thy candle-light,
And let thy lullaby be mine to-night.

"HEADING." BY LUCIA E. HALSTEAD, AGE 15.
(HONOR MEMBER.)

YOUNG MOTHER HUBBARD

By E. Vincent Millay (age 17)
(*Silver Badge*)

YOUNG Mother Hubbard sent her maid to the cupboard
    To get her French poodle some steak.
But when she got there and the steak was too rare,
    It's a wonder their hearts did not break.

Mother Hubbard cried: "Oh, he will perish, I know!
    He cannot eat that—the poor dear!"
She tore her fair hair with a look of despair,
    On her slipper-toe splashed a big tear.

"My precious! My pet!—Suzette! Quick! Suzette!
    Run, run for the doctor, I pray!
My heart feels so queer!" she cried, "Oh, oh, dear!"
    And gracefully fainted away.

Suzette, the poor maid, had seen, I'm afraid,
    Such swoons as this often before;
But she called up the old family doctor and told him
    "Miladi" had fainted once more.

She then made her way to her mistress, who lay
    On a couch which had chanced to be nigh;
And held to her nose priceless attar of rose,
    And spilt eau-de-cologne in her eye.

Before evening came on, and the doctor had gone,
    Miladi was helped to her feet,
And the poodle was deep in a satisfied sleep—
    But they found not a trace of the meat.

"AN APRIL HEADING." BY RUTH KINKEAD, AGE 12.

AN AUTUMN RIDE

By Frank Stuerm (age 13)

It was an autumn evening, bitingly cold, and we were sitting around the fire in a Swiss farm-house, situated on a foot-hill of a famous mountain-range. We were, in fact, quite out of the tourist section of Switzerland.

All of a sudden we were startled by the sound of a horse's hoofs, and then a sound like that of an American fire horn; and it was a fire horn. As one of the men of the house rushed out, the rider yelled: "*Dorf*" (Village). Immediately, the one able-bodied man in the house got a lantern and hurried toward the village, for the fire rider had signified that a fire was there.

Thus, when a fire occurs in a country section of Switzerland, riders are sent in every direction to call out the men of the township.

If any able-bodied man does not appear at the fire, he must pay a fine; and if he does appear, he enjoys refreshments at the expense of the owner of the building. Accordingly, each man who should and does not go to a fire loses doubly.

The man from the house at which we stopped arrived just as the fire was extinguished, but in time to escape his fine and enjoy a jolly time in the village inn.

THE FOREST

By E. Babette Deutsch (age 10)
(*Silver Badge*)

How romantic is the forest!
What significance is found there!
There where Siegfried forgèd Notung,
There where Red men built their wigwams.
Where in colors gay, the hunters
Shot the deer, and trapped the tiger.
Where in autumn, red and yellow,
Brown and withered, leaves are scattered.
Where in winter grim, and silent,
Bare, and sad, with heads uplifted,
In mute wisdom, stand these old trees.

Then in springtime, little leaflets
In new green appear and blossom.
When hot summer comes how shady
Are these woods, and cool these brooklets!
O, great forest, how I love thee!
Monarch of the realm of beauty!

Where the wild things seek their shelter.
How I love thy singing streamlets,
And thy large, majestic, old trees!
How I love thy wild, bright blossoms!
As a whole thyself! O Forest!

"HEADING." BY JEFFREY C. WEBSTER, AGE 10.

IN THE FOREST

By Hampton Shirer (age 11)

I love to roam in the forest,
And watch the wild birds there,
And see the frisking squirrel,
And chase the fleeing hare.

I look at the little brooklet,
And hear its merry song.
I love to roam in the forest
The whole day long.

FOREST TREES

By E. Vincent Millay (age 14)

MONARCHS of long-forgotten realms, ye stand;
    Majestic, grand;
Unscarred by Time's destructive hand.

Enthroned on dais of velvet
    moss, inset
With the royal purple of
    the violet;
      And crowned with
        mistletoe.

How many ages o'er your
    heads have flown,
      To you is known—
To you, ye forest-founders
    of the past, alone.
No other eyes may scan the
    breadth of years,
      Each with its share of peace, and joy, and tears;
        Of happiness and woe.

Around you all is changed—where now is land
Swift vessels ploughed to foam the seething main;
Kingdoms have risen; and the fire-fiend's hand
Has crushed them to their Mother Earth again;
And through it all ye stand, and still will stand
Till ages yet to come have owned your reign.

"A BIT OF NATURE."
BY MARGARET DOBSON,
AGE 14.

FOREST WINDS

By Elizabeth Taber (age 10)

IN the shade of the stately forest trees,
Amid the flowers and bumble bees,
I like to wander at my ease,
And pick the flowers beneath the trees.
The forest winds are blowing my hair
As I go wandering here and there.

BY SHERWOOD SUNDERLAND DAY, AGE 12.
(SPECIAL SILVER BADGE.)

A CAMP ADVENTURE

By Beatrice N. Blood (age 12)

WE had our camp pitched way out in Colorado, among the cool mountains.

Father, mother and we children. We had been all day out on the small lake. As we were coming home, my sister and I crossed a small stream. It was beautiful! We followed it and it grew more beautiful. We rounded a small curve and came face to face with a bear! We were surprised and frightened, as it was the first bear we had ever seen. He raised on his hind legs and growled. We walked backwards until we were around the curve. Then fled in terror. We were glad enough to see our camp once more.

COUNTING THE COST

By John C. Farrar (age 13)

LYING at home with a broken nose,
Black and blue from head to toes,
Face all skinned, and back all scratched,
Head all bandaged, legs all patched;
Now I've time to count the cost
Of things that I have gained or lost.
Gained? Oh, nothing but lots of scars,
And a very good knowledge of handle-bars.

Down the hill came Bob and I,
As fast as any wheel could fly;
I was on the handle-bars—
Crash! And we were seeing stars.

Well, it cost me quite a bit,
And also Bob; he, too, was hit.
Half a tooth, and doctors' bills,
Lots of bumps, and other ills,
Liniment and plasters, too,
And more, I guess, before we're through.

A CAMP ADVENTURE

By Dorothy Buell (age 12)

IT was on a hot July afternoon, when papa, some of my girl companions and I returned to our camping site on the bank of picturesque Rock River, from a point farther down the stream where we had been bathing.

Several portions of our bank had been caving in, and a large tree had fallen in the water as a result of this. Its roots were firmly fastened in the sod, and the water, which was very swift at this place, formed a foamy whirlpool as it neared the obstacle.

We had intended to land farther up than usual, and as we drew closer to our little port, the current swept us stern foremost down toward the tree. Round and round we whirled like leaves on an autumn day. Then papa lost control of the oars, the boat gave a lurch, and turning on her side, lodged herself firmly between the branches of the fallen oak.

The rest of our party stood on the banks looking at us with horrified faces, while we, frightened beyond speech, clung to our seats helpless with fear. Suddenly the cry "Bring the fishpoles!" arose and in a few seconds a gentleman of the party came back with two long poles.

Carlene, Angela and I caught hold of one pole which drew our end of the boat out of water.

In a half hour, after some hard work, we were gradually pulled from our prison and reached Camp Thunderbolt safe, but greatly excited over our adventure.

THE LAND OF ROMANCE

By E. Vincent Millay (age 14)
(Silver Badge)

"Show me the road to Romance!" I cried, and he raised
    his head;
"I know not the road to Romance, child. 'Tis a warm,
    bright way," he said,
"And I trod it once with one whom I loved—with one
    who is long since dead.
But now—I forget—Ah! The way would be long
    without that other one,"
And he lifted a thin and trembling hand, to shield his
    eyes from the sun.

"Show me the road to Romance!" I cried, but she did
    not stir,
And I heard no sound in the low ceil'ed room save the
    spinning-wheel's busy whirr.
Then came a voice from the down-bent head, from the
    lips that I could not see,
"Oh! Why do you seek for Romance? And why do
    you trouble me?
Little care I for your fancies. They will bring you no
    good," she said,
"Take the wheel that stands in the corner, and get you
    to work, instead."

Then came one with steps so light that I had not
    heard their tread,
"I know where the road to Romance is. I will show it
    you," she said.
She slipped her tiny hand in mine, and smiled up into
    my face,
And lo! A ray of the setting sun shone full upon the
    place,
The little brook danced adown the hill and the grass
    sprang up anew,
And tiny flowers peeped forth as fresh as if newly
    washed with dew.

A little breeze came frolicking by, cooling the heated
  air,
And the road to Romance stretched on before, beck-
  oning, bright and fair.
And I knew that just beyond it, in the hush of the
  dying day,
The mossy walls and ivied towers of the land of Romance lay.
The breath of dying lilies haunted the twilight air,
And the sob of a dreaming violin filled the silence
  everywhere.

LIFE

By Gabrielle Elliot (age 17)
(Honor Member)

YOUTH

LIFE is a song that is caroled in tune,
A roundelay sweet in the gay month of June,
A cup that is filled up with wine to the brim,
A delicate goblet with ruby-crowned rim;
A lilac that fragrantly blooms in the spring;
A bird winging upward, nor ceasing to sing;
A song, and a wine-cup, a bird, and a flower,
A wish to achieve and a yearning for power.

MIDDLE AGE

Life is a burden, a routine of care,
That bows down the figure, and whitens the hair,
A dull, changeless labor that never is done,
'Neath a sky that is laden, with no cheering sun;
Life is a wheel, to which all men are bound,
That grinds men beneath it, each time it goes round;
A reasonless striving, and sighing for wings
To fly from the ceaseless oppression of Things.

OLD AGE

Life is a waiting for what is to come,
A waiting for rest, and the glad going home;
The great preparation for things yet to be,
When all shall be clear, and at last we shall see.
Life is a wonderful, mystical quest
That some take with a sigh, and some with a jest,
But all, like a child who is tired by play,
Stop a moment to rest, and in sleep slip away.

A PATRIOT

By Robert Hillyer (age 13)
(Silver Badge)

A HERO brave, of grandeur and renown,
    Leads forth his force to conquer and begin
    The conquest of the land he sought to win,
    To set a burdened, hopeless people free;
    And what for all his victories finds he?
A laurel crown!

But in the ranks a hero struggles brave,
    And though undaunted is his sturdy heart,
    His life is only an unnoticed part
    Of earth's struggle to keep just and free;
    But what for all his industry finds he?
A lowly grave!

But, though this task seems one long hopeless strife,
    "Uneasy lies the head that wears a crown,"
    So he is fortunate without renown,
    While he, himself, is honest, just, and free.
    So what for all his industry finds he?
Unending life?

A FOREST ADVENTURE

ONE winter my cousin was hunting near Bear Lake. It was a very cold winter, and he and his friends sometimes felt as though they would freeze. One freezing day, while hunting, my cousin was separated from the other members of the party, and soon lost his way in the dense forest.

He shouted and called for help, but without success. He wandered about for a long time, and at last he came upon a little log cabin. He hurried up and was going to knock at the door, but when he touched it, it swung open, and he saw only one bare room. No one lived there. He went inside and found a little mud chimney in the corner. The fireplace was filled with dry leaves, and sticks, that had dropped down the chimney in the summer.

He hunted all through his pockets, and at last found a few matches. He tried to strike them, but they were wet and of no use.

At last, as he became colder and colder, he took his handkerchief and placed it on the leaves and sticks in a way that they could catch fire, and then he put some gunpowder on the handkerchief, and then he shot it until it caught fire and made a good blaze.

After he had warmed his hands (which were numb; he could hardly use them), he looked around for something to eat. At last, after a long search, he found a small lump of bread. It was so hard he could hardly break it, but he was so hungry he was glad to have anything. He was in the hut a good while, before the party found him.

"LIFE"

By E. Vincent Millay (age 15)
(Honor Member)

LIFE is an imitation—we are born,
We live, we die—and do no more, no less
Than all have done before.
To us is given the living only; that at least is ours,
To do with as we please; and let it be
Our constant care to make that living such
That, when we die, it will be deemed more worthy
    Of further imitation.

VACATION SONG

By E. Vincent Millay (age 15)
(Honor Member)

SHINE on me, oh, you gold, gold sun,
    Smile on me, oh, you blue, blue skies,
Sing, birds! and rouse the lazy breeze
    That, in the shadow, sleeping lies,
Calling, "Awaken! Slothful one
    And chase the yellow butterflies."

Laugh! Sober maiden in the brook,
    Shake down your smoothly plaited hair,
Let it fall rippling on the grass
    Daring the wind to leave it there,
Dancing in all its sun-kissed folds—
    Laughing low in the sun-kissed air.

Frown if you will, you staid old trees,
    You cannot silence the birds and me;
You will sing yourself ere we leave you in peace—
    Frown if you will but we shall see.
I'll pelt you with your own green leaves
    Till you echo the strains of our minstrelsy.

Oh, mower! All the world's at play—
    Leave on the grass your sickle bright;
Come, and we'll dance a merry step
    With the birds and the leaves and the gold sunlight,
We'll dance till the shadows leave the hills
    And bring to the fields the quiet night.

VACATION

By Katharine Rutan Neumann (age 13)
(Silver Badge Winner)

THE robins have always vacation,
  Among the cool, green trees,
Or up in the sky they carol,
  Doing whatever they please.

The squirrels have always vacation,
  Running about all day;
As up in the high shady branches
  Of the beautiful trees they play.

The flowers have always vacation,
  For they come up whenever they choose;
And never have to learn lessons,
  And have only themselves to amuse.

But I have never vacation,
  'Cept Summer and Christmas and Spring,
And a day or two at Thanksgiving,
  And I think it's an awful mean thing.

A PATRIOT

By Elizabeth Rogers (age 7)

A PATRIOT, as well you know,
Is one who loves his country so
That he would fight,
From morn to night,
And just to serve his country right.

A JOURNEY TO WONDERLAND

By Ruth Louise Northup (age 16)

THE entrance to this Wonderland, which I visited, is in the Strait of Gibraltar. When, standing on the deck of our little steamer, I saw the many-colored town of Tangier rising out of the sea to greet my amazed eyes, I felt that I had really found my Wonderland.

Slowly the tiny specks, which I had seen in the distance on the bay, changed into little boats, waiting to receive passengers. When the shore was finally reached, I found that my journeys in Wonderland were to be made on the back of a donkey, accompanied by a donkey boy. In this manner I rode through streets so narrow that an umbrella would reach from side to side, past a city well as old as the famous one of Jacob, past Eastern-looking buildings, and, most strange of all, past groups of the inhabitants; wondering, hostile-looking people, and yet with a certain nobility of feature.

A hotel, which was one of the few prosaic places in this Wonderland, now loomed before us.

Next morning, from the balcony of my room, which faced the sea, I could see a procession as wonderful, as varied, and withal as pitiful, as any ever beheld. Long caravans of little donkeys, heavily laden with all sorts of burdens, were constantly passing, with the owner riding in front, peacefully smoking, and away back in the rear, the poor wife, or perhaps wives, of this august personage, staggering along under huge loads.

All of the many strange sights seen that day but confirmed my first impression that this was Wonderland. In the market place especially, numerous, unusual people were seen—a snake charmer, amusing the people; a quaint man whose chief occupation and accomplishment was to open his mouth very wide; Moorish women with modestly-covered faces; strange, barbaric, desert chieftains; old beggars; merchantmen with all their goods spread around them on the ground. All kinds of people in all kinds of clothes, with all kinds of customs, made up scenes certainly like nothing I had ever seen before, and making a Wonderland which I never expect to enter again.

A MYSTERY

By Jean E. Freeman (age 15)
(*Honor Member*)

Two tarts were perched upon a shelf,
　A tempting, juicy pair;
A little lad stood down below,
And when I to that shelf did go,
　They were no longer there.

I glanced about, and where they were
　I really could not see;
Believe me, when I truly say
That to this very latest day,
　'Tis still a mystery.

THE WILD MARCH WIND

By Rachel Lyman Field (age 17)
(*Gold Badge*)

OH! pleasant is the wind of June,
　So balmy, soft, and low
It sings along our garden wall,
　Where the shy, pink roses blow.

The autumn wind is hushed and sad,
　For the flowers are brown and dead
When fields lie bare, and birds have flown,
　And the maple leaves are red.

The winter wind is fierce and bold,
　The snow goes whirling by;
Inside is warmth, but all night long,
　We hear the north wind cry.

But give to me the wild March wind,
　So fearless, strong and free,
He bends the branches, shakes the twigs,
　And laughs aloud in glee!

Men call him cruel, and hate to hear
　His piping loud and long
But the flowers stir, and wake again,
　When they hear the March wind's song

AFTER VACATION

By Bennett Cerf (age 15)
(*Silver Badge*)

SEPTEMBER! Labor Day has come, and with it the end of vacation for the year. One last, fleeting glance at the village and the hotel from the car window, and we are off, bound for home! And as the train draws nearer and nearer to the city, in proportion our excitement grows. A plunge into the tunnel, a jolt, and, "All off!" cries the porter, grinning as we hand him his tip.

Back into the bustle of the large city, the clanging of bells and the tooting of horns. Broadway, with its millions of tiny, yet brilliant, electric lights—we are home! And as we make a dive for the news-stand for an "extra" (which, by the way, is the first evening paper we have seen in ages), our hearts throb; instinctively we throw out our chests. After all, there was something missing in the country, an indefinable something that seemed somewhat to spoil our pleasure. Perhaps it was the air of loneliness and quiet; we were born in the city and brought up in the city—brought up to be one of a great multitude, brought up to dodge autos and the like, to rush and hustle—and we *can't do without it!*

Happily, therefore, we enter our cozy little home, and find to our amazement, that the trunk is already there! Marvel of marvels! Now our happiness is complete! What if Mother's and Sister's dresses are so wrinkled that "they'll have to turn right around and have them pressed all over again"? what if everything smells terribly of camphor? what if the painters are due in a week or two to turn the house topsyturvy? We feel like giving three lusty cheers, and making oodles of resolutions that we're going to work—work hard and well the coming winter!—we're back!

After all, there's no place like home!

TO ONE I LOVED
(My old nurse)

By Nina M. Ryan (age 16)
(Silver Badge)

DEAR wrinkled face and tender, watchful eyes,
    It hurts so not to have you sitting there—
When twilight comes and nursery lamps are lit—
    With outstreched arms, in the old rocking-chair.

There's no one now to sing us fairy songs
    And tell of Sheila and the Holy Well;
No one to chant the strange old Irish words
    That children murmured by the Witches' Fell.

But, Nurse dear, though the little fairy folk
    You loved so well have taken you at last,
Your loyal faith and service still remain,
    As tender memories of a happy past.

BY MARY ELEANOR GEORGE,
AGE 11.

A LEAGUE GOOD-BY

How long ago, a little group, we gathered
  To weave our stories and to build our rhymes!
How tenderly the vagrant muse we tethered
  Through winter eves and drowsy summer-times.

Those days were sweet—the path of inclination
  Lay ribbon fair beneath the lifting sun;
And fast we followed, filled with contemplation
  Of dreams made substance, and of prizes won.

Those days are fled—what echo shall remind us
  Of winter fancy, and of summer rhyme,
When we who say good-by have left behind us
  Our meager drift along the marge of time?

Adieu, adieu, companions of the morning,
  My pathway faces to the sloping sun;
The shadows longer grow—I heed the warning,
  And trim my fires ere nightfall has begun.

ALBERT BIGELOW PAINE,
Editor St. Nicholas League,
Nov., 1899, to Dec., 1908.

Nine years ago last month the first announcement of the *St. Nicholas* League was made in this magazine. That is a long time in a young life. Our oldest members, now, were just little boys and girls then, of not more than eight, and if they sent anything at all to the League it was a crude little drawing or story or poem, or perhaps it was a photograph, accidentally good, because the camera is a happy-go-lucky sort of an artist and sometimes makes a wonderfully good picture for even its youngest friends. And our older members?—they have all gone—one by one and two by two they passed through the little quiet gate that marks the eighteenth milestone along the path of youth, and have closed it from the further side. Most of them are living, busy men and women now—some of them following the work they loved and made their own in the pages of the League; some of them pursuing other and perhaps more congenial employments. But whatever their tasks and wherever they may be, the editor believes there is not one who does not sometimes remember the old League days when the monthly competition with its prize distribution was all important; when the printed list of winners was scanned for the single name which, if found was written as if in letters of gold. It must be so, for the good-by letters that have come all along have told the tale of hope and anxiety and triumph, and they have echoed the sadness of the parting—a sadness that never failed to find answer in the thought of the one who, though always left behind to welcome the new group, never failed to follow affectionately the old familiar names as they vanished from the pages of contribution and from the Honor Roll.

AND now, at last, the League editor himself is to be among those who go. The years have laid so many duties upon him that he is no longer able to give to the League the consideration and the time that it requires and deserves. Certain labors press upon him to be finished, and he must perform them while he has the strength and will, or not at all, for the months fly and the years slip away, and the time of labor is only a little while. He began with the League at its beginning, and in sympathy and spirit he will remain with it, come what may. But the active labor will hereafter be performed by another hand, trained and capable, whose owner will be one in full sympathy with the ambitions and the efforts of youth, with time and talent and energy for the place. To League friends and members old and new the old League editor waves good-by.

"TAIL-PIECE."   BY HENRY THOMAS, AGE 16.

Index of Authors and Artists

Index of Titles and Artwork

Subject Index